Stories of Ourselves

The University of Cambridge International Examinations Anthology of Stories in English

CAMBRIDGE
UNIVERSITY PRESS

CAMBRIDGE UNIVERSITY PRESS

Cambridge, New York, Melbourne, Madrid, Cape Town, Singapore, São Paulo, New Delhi

Cambridge University Press
c/o Cambridge University Press India Pvt. Ltd.
Cambridge House
4381/4, Ansari Road, Daryaganj
New Delhi 110002
India

www.cambridge.org

First published 2008

Reprinted 2009, 2010 (twice), 2011 (twice), 2012 (twice), 2013

Printed at Replika Press Pvt. Ltd.

ISBN 978-0-521-72791-4 paperback

Contents

Introduction

Stories of Ourselves contains selections of stories set for study for CIE's O Level, IGCSE, AS and A Level Literature in English examinations.

As with its companion volume, *Songs of Ourselves* (Foundation Books, 2005), the selection goes beyond being a 'set text', though. As well as preparing the specific set selections, schools have been using *Songs* successfully as background reading for all papers within CIE's English syllabuses, and *Stories* has grown out of requests for a prose equivalent. The aim has been to follow the success of *Songs* by providing centres with a substantial anthology of short stories – including classic, well-known pieces as well as some new and possibly unheard of authors – in one handy volume, with a long 'shelf life'. We hope that teachers will see it as a useful resource in the English classroom, and a good general reader for all levels.

Some well-used anthologies of classic short stories in English have been taught and examined for many years, but are often restricted to stories by British writers. There are also numerous anthologies based on theme or genre: obvious ones such as 'ghost stories' or highly specialised ones such as 'stories of the theatre'; and increasing numbers organised by nationality or gender. These will always remain a source of material for English teachers, but this anthology casts the net much more widely by representing a broad range of different styles, genres, nationalities and author backgrounds, with quality always the rationale for selection. All of the stories were originally written in English: the variety and richness of English as a global language continues to grow, and these stories give witness to its range and power.

Given its use as a classroom text, we have avoided content that is very obscure or problematic; but there has been no intention to limit the choice to stories 'for young people'. An underlying aim of *Stories* is to encourage readers of all ages to challenge some preconceptions they might have about the short story format. There is still sometimes some literary snobbery about a genre such as science fiction, but as J. G. Ballard's 'Billennium' (for example) shows, such a genre can produce superb writing to be ranked alongside more canonical classic fiction. The same is true of 'Ming's Biggest Prey' by Patricia Highsmith, an author primarily known for crime fiction whose prose might be considered on a par with Evelyn Waugh's. By inclusion of these, and others, *Stories of Ourselves* illustrates how good short stories are defined neither by their genre, nor by their 'content'.

One of the best recent short story writers, Raymond Carver, defined a great writer as one who 'has some special way of looking at things and who gives artistic expression to that way of looking'. The short story can be a wonderful vehicle for that kind of talent, and Carver's own story, 'Elephant', included here, is a perfect example of his own description. Carver also stipulated that for a great short story there must be 'no tricks'. In other words, a definition that used to be widespread, that a story needed to have a twist or a special effect, must not be taken as sufficient to explain the success, greatness or impact of all short stories. We hope that as they read the stories in this volume, and compare different stories within it, readers of all ages will start to ponder what exactly might define a great story, and will be enticed to explore other work by the represented writers in their wider reading.

Acknowledgements

Special thanks are due to Noel Cassidy, Nick de Somogyi, and Marica Lopez for their help in the making of this anthology.

Mary Wilmer
Cambridge International Exams 2007

Acknowledgements

'The Lady in the Looking Glass: A Reflection' by Virginia Woolf, reprinted with permission from the Oxford University Press.

'The Custody of the Pumpkin' from THE WORLD OF BLANDINGS by P. G. Wodehouse. Reprinted by permission of The Random House Group Ltd.

'An Englishman's Home' by Evelyn Waugh, reprinted with permission from Penguin Group, UK.

'The Phoenix' from THE CAT'S CRADLE-BOOK by Sylvia Townsend Warner, published by Chatto & Windus. Reprinted by permission of The Random House Group Ltd.

'There Will Come Soft Rains' by Ray Bradbury, reprinted with permission from the Don Congdon Associates.

'The Prison' from THE MAGIC BARREL by Bernard Malamud, published by Chatto & Windus. Reprinted by permission of The Random House Group Ltd.

'The Destructors' from THE COLLECTED SHORT STORIES by Graham Greene, reprinted with permission from David Higham Associates Limited, UK.

'Meteor' from THE SEEDS OF TIME by John Wyndham, reprinted with permission from David Higham Associates Limited.

'The Lemon Orchard' from A WALK IN THE NIGHT AND OTHER STORIES by Alex la Guma reprinted with permission from Harcourt Education Ltd.

'The People Before' by Maurice Shadbolt, reprinted with permission from David Ling Publishing Ltd.

'The Enemy' by V. S. Naipaul, reprinted from 'The Night Watchman's Occurrence Book' from A FLAG ON THE ISLAND, © 1967, copyright renewed 1995 by V. S. Naipaul.

'A Horse and Two Goats' by R. K. Narayan, reprinted with permission from Indian Thought Publications.

'Report on the Threatened City' from THE STORY OF A NON-MARRYING MAN by Doris Lessing, reprinted with permission from Jonathan Clowes Ltd.

'The Village Saint' from THE COLLECTOR OF TREASURES by Bessie Head, reprinted with permission from Harcourt Education Ltd.

'Secrets' from SECRETS AND OTHER STORIES by Bernard MacLaverty, © Bernard MacLaverty. Reproduced by permission of the author c/o Rogers, Coleridge and White Ltd., 20 Powis Mews, London W11 1JN.

'Games at Twilight' from GAMES AT TWILIGHT AND OTHER STORIES by Anita Desai, © 1978 Anita Desai. Reproduced by permission of the author c/o Rogers, Coleridge & White Ltd., 20 Powis Mews, London W11 1JN.

'Journey' from THE DREAM SLEEPERS AND OTHER STORIES by Patricia Grace, reprinted with permission from Penguin Group, New Zealand.

'The Bath' by Janet Frame, © 1983, Janet Frame Literary Trust. Reproduced by permission of The Wylie Agency. All rights reserved.

'Elephant' from WHERE I'M CALLING FROM by Raymond Carver, published by Harvill. Reprinted by permission of The Random House Group Ltd.

'The Third and Final Continent' from INTERPRETER OF MALADIES by Jhumpa Lahiri. Reprinted by permission of HarperCollins Publisher Ltd., © Jhumpa Lahiri, 1999.

'Tyres' from SHIFTS by Adam Thorpe, published by Jonathan Cape. Reprinted by permission of The Random House Group Ltd.

'Real Time' from REAL TIME by Amit Chaudhuri, reprinted with permission from Pan Macmillan. © Amit Chaudhuri, 2002.

'On Her Knees' from THE TURNING by Tim Winton, reprinted with permission from David Higham Associates Limited.

1

The Hollow of the Three Hills

(1830)

Nathaniel Hawthorne

In those strange old times, when fantastic dreams and madmen's reveries were realised among the actual circumstances of life, two persons met together at an appointed hour and place. One was a lady, graceful in form and fair of feature, though pale and troubled, and smitten with an untimely blight in what should have been the fullest bloom of her years; the other was an ancient and meanly dressed woman, of ill-favored aspect, and so withered, shrunken and decrepit, that even the space since she began to decay must have exceeded the ordinary term of human existence. In the spot where they encountered, no mortal could observe them. Three little hills stood near each other, and down in the midst of them sunk a hollow basin, almost mathematically circular, two or three hundred feet in breadth, and of such depth that a stately cedar might but just be visible above the sides. Dwarf pines were numerous upon the hills, and partly fringed the outer verge of the intermediate hollow; within which there was nothing but the brown grass of October, and here and there a tree-trunk, that had fallen long ago, and lay mouldering with no green successor from its roots. One of these masses of decaying wood, formerly a majestic oak, rested close beside a pool of green and sluggish water at the bottom of the basin. Such scenes as this (so gray tradition tells) were once the resort of a Power of Evil and his plighted subjects; and here, at midnight or on the dim verge of evening, they were said to stand round the mantling pool, disturbing its putrid waters in the performance of an impious baptismal rite. The chill beauty of an autumnal sunset was now gilding the three hill-tops, whence a paler tint stole down their sides into the hollow.

'Here is our pleasant meeting come to pass,' said the aged crone, 'according as thou hast desired. Say quickly what thou wouldst have of me, for there is but a short hour that we may tarry here.'

As the old withered woman spoke, a smile glimmered on her countenance, like lamplight on the wall of a sepulchre. The lady trembled, and cast her eyes upward to the verge of the basin, as if meditating to return with her purpose unaccomplished. But it was not so ordained.

'I am stranger in this land, as you know,' said she at length. 'Whence I come it matters not; – but I have left those behind me with whom my fate was intimately bound, and from whom I am cut off forever. There is a weight in my bosom that I cannot away with, and I have come hither to inquire of their welfare.'

'And who is there by this green pool, that can bring thee news from the ends of the Earth?' cried the old woman, peering into the lady's face. 'Not from my lips mayst thou hear these tidings; yet, be thou bold, and the daylight shall not pass away from yonder hill-top, before thy wish be granted.'

'I will do your bidding though I die,' replied the lady desperately.

The old woman seated herself on the trunk of the fallen tree, threw aside the hood that shrouded her gray locks, and beckoned her companion to draw near.

'Kneel down,' she said, 'and lay your forehead on my knees.'

She hesitated a moment, but the anxiety, that had long been kindling, burned fiercely up within her. As she knelt down, the border of her garment was dipped into the pool; she laid her forehead on the old woman's knees, and the latter drew a cloak about the lady's face, so that she was in darkness. Then she heard the muttered words of a prayer, in the midst of which she started, and would have arisen.

'Let me flee, – let me flee and hide myself, that they may not look upon me!' she cried. But, with returning recollection, she hushed herself, and was still as death.

For it seemed as if other voices – familiar in infancy, and unforgotten through many wanderings, and in all the vicissitudes of her heart and fortune – were mingling with the accents of the prayer. At first the words were faint and indistinct, not rendered so by distance, but rather resembling the dim pages of a book, which we strive to read by an imperfect and gradually brightening light. In such a manner, as the prayer proceeded, did those voices strengthen upon the ear; till at length the petition ended, and the conversation of an aged man, and of a woman broken and decayed like himself, became distinctly audible to the lady as she knelt. But those strangers appeared not to stand in the hollow depth between the three hills. Their voices were encompassed and re-echoed by the walls of a chamber, the windows of which were rattling in the breeze; the regular vibration of a clock, the crackling of a fire, and the tinkling of the embers as they fell among the ashes, rendered the scene almost as vivid as if painted to the eye. By a melancholy hearth sat these two old people, the man calmly despondent, the woman querulous and tearful, and their words were all of sorrow. They spoke of a daughter, a wanderer they knew not where, bearing dishonor along with her, and leaving shame and affliction to bring their gray heads to the grave. They alluded also to other and more recent woe, but in the midst of their talk, their voices seemed to melt into the sound of the wind sweeping mournfully among the autumn leaves; and when the lady lifted her eyes, there was she kneeling in the hollow between three hills.

'A weary and lonesome time yonder old couple have of it,' remarked the old woman, smiling in the lady's face.

'And did you also hear them!' exclaimed she, a sense of intolerable humiliation triumphing over her agony and fear.

'Yea; and we have yet more to hear,' replied the old woman. 'Wherefore, cover thy face quickly.'

Again the withered hag poured forth the monotonous words of a prayer that was not meant to be acceptable in Heaven; and soon, in the pauses of her breath, strange murmurings began to thicken, gradually increasing so as to drown and overpower the charm by which they grew. Shrieks pierced through the obscurity of sound, and were succeeded by the singing of sweet female voices, which in their turn gave way to a wild roar of laughter, broken suddenly by groanings and sobs, forming altogether a ghastly confusion of terror and mourning and mirth. Chains were rattling, fierce and stern voices uttered threats, and the scourge resounded at their command. All these noises deepened and became substantial to the listener's ear, till she could distinguish every soft and dreamy accent of the love songs, that died causelessly into funeral hymns. She shuddered at the unprovoked wrath which blazed up like the spontaneous kindling of flame, and she grew faint at the fearful merriment, raging miserably around her. In the midst of this wild scene, where unbound passions jostled each other in a drunken career, there was one solemn voice of a man, and a manly and melodious voice it might once have been. He went to-and-fro continually, and his feet sounded upon the floor. In each member of that frenzied company, whose own burning thoughts had become their exclusive world, he sought an auditor for the story of his individual wrong, and interpreted their laughter and tears as his reward of scorn or pity. He spoke of woman's perfidy, of a wife who had broken her holiest vows, of a home and heart made desolate. Even as he went on, the shout, the laugh, the shriek, the sob, rose up in unison, till they changed into the hollow, fitful, and uneven sound of the wind, as it fought among the pine-trees on those three lonely hills. The lady looked up, and there was the withered woman smiling in her face.

'Couldst thou have thought there were such merry times in a Mad House?' inquired the latter.

'True, true,' said the lady to herself; 'there is mirth within its walls, but misery, misery without.'

'Wouldst thou hear more?' demanded the old woman.

'There is one other voice I would fain listen to again,' replied the lady faintly.

'Then lay down thy head speedily upon my knees, that thou may'st get thee hence before the hour be past.'

The golden skirts of day were yet lingering upon the hills, but deep shades obscured the hollow and the pool, as if sombre night were rising thence to overspread the world. Again that evil woman began to weave her spell. Long did it proceed unanswered, till the knolling of a bell stole in among the intervals of her words, like a clang that had travelled far over valley and rising ground, and was just ready to die in the air. The lady shook upon her companion's knees, as she heard that boding sound. Stronger it grew and sadder, and deepened into the tone of a death-bell, knolling dolefully from some ivy-mantled tower, and bearing tidings of mortality and woe to the cottage, to the hall, and to the solitary wayfarer, that all might weep for the doom appointed in turn to them. Then came a measured tread, passing slowly, slowly on, as of mourners with a coffin, their garments trailing on the ground, so that the ear could measure the length of their melancholy array. Before them went the priest, reading the burial-service, while the leaves of his book were rustling in the breeze. And though no voice but his was heard to speak aloud, still there were revilings and anathemas, whispered but distinct, from women and from men, breathed against the daughter who had wrung the aged hearts of her parents, – the wife who had betrayed the trusting fondness of her husband, – the mother who had sinned against natural affection, and left her child to die. The sweeping sound of the funeral train faded away like a thin vapour, and the wind, that just before had seemed to shake the coffin-pall, moaned sadly round the verge of the Hollow between three Hills. But when the old woman stirred the kneeling lady, she lifted not her head.

'Here has been a sweet hour's sport!' said the withered crone, chuckling to herself.

2

The Fall of the House of Usher

(1839)

Edgar Allan Poe

Son coeur est un luth suspendu;
Sitôt qu'on le touche il résonne.
De Béranger

During the whole of a dull, dark, and soundless day in the autumn of the year, when the clouds hung oppressively low in the heavens, I had been passing alone, on horseback, through a singularly dreary tract of country; and at length found myself, as the shades of the evening drew on, within view of the melancholy House of Usher. I know not how it was – but, with the first glimpse of the building, a sense of insufferable gloom pervaded my spirit. I say insufferable; for the feeling was unrelieved by any of that half-pleasurable, because poetic, sentiment, with which the mind usually receives even the sternest natural images of the desolate or terrible. I looked upon the scene before me – upon the mere house, and the simple landscape features of the domain – upon the bleak walls – upon the vacant eye-like windows – upon a few rank sedges – and upon a few white trunks of decayed trees – with an utter depression of soul which I can compare to no earthly sensation more properly than to the afterdream of the reveller upon opium – the bitter lapse into everyday life – the hideous dropping off of the veil. There was an iciness, a sinking, a sickening of the heart – an unredeemed dreariness of thought which no goading of the imagination could torture into aught of the sublime. What was it – I paused to think – what was it that so unnerved me in the contemplation of the House of Usher? It was a mystery all insoluble; nor could I grapple with the shadowy fancies that crowded upon me as I pondered. I was forced to fall back upon the unsatisfactory conclusion, that while, beyond doubt, there *are* combinations of very simple natural objects which have the power of thus affecting us, still the analysis of this power lies among considerations beyond our depth. It was possible, I reflected, that a mere different arrangement of the particulars of the scene, of the details of the picture, would be sufficient to modify, or perhaps to annihilate its capacity for sorrowful impression; and, acting upon this idea, I reined my horse to the precipitous brink of a black and lurid tarn that lay in unruffled lustre by the dwelling, and gazed down – but with a shudder even more thrilling than before – upon the remodelled and inverted images of the gray sedge, and the ghastly tree-stems, and the vacant and eye-like windows.

Nevertheless, in this mansion of gloom I now proposed to myself a sojourn of some weeks. Its proprietor, Roderick Usher, had been one of my boon companions in boyhood; but many years had elapsed since our last meeting. A letter, however, had lately reached me in a distant part of the country – a letter from him – which, in its wildly importunate nature, had admitted of no other than a personal reply. The MS. gave evidence of nervous agitation. The writer spoke of acute bodily illness – of a mental disorder which oppressed him – and of an earnest desire to see me, as his best, and indeed his only personal friend, with a view of attempting, by the cheerfulness of my society, some alleviation of his malady. It was the manner in which all this, and much more, was said – it was the apparent *heart* that went with his request – which allowed me no room for hesitation; and I accordingly obeyed forthwith what I still considered a very singular summons.

Although, as boys, we had been even intimate associates, yet I really knew little of my friend. His reserve had been always excessive and habitual. I was aware, however, that his very ancient family had been noted, time out of mind, for a peculiar sensibility of temperament, displaying itself, through long ages, in many works of exalted art, and manifested, of late, in repeated deeds of munificent yet unobtrusive charity, as well as in a passionate devotion to the intricacies, perhaps even more than to the orthodox and easily recognisable beauties, of musical science. I had learned, too, the very remarkable fact, that the stem of the Usher race, all time-honoured as it was, had put forth, at no period, any enduring branch; in other words, that the entire family lay in the direct line of descent, and had always, with very trifling and very temporary variation, so lain. It was this deficiency, I considered, while running over in thought the perfect keeping of the character of the premises with the accredited character of the people, and while speculating upon the possible influence which the one, in the long lapse of centuries, might have exercised upon the other – it was this deficiency, perhaps, of collateral issue, and the consequent undeviating transmission, from sire to son, of the patrimony with the name, which had, at length, so identified the two as to merge the original title of the estate in the quaint and equivocal appellation of the 'House of Usher' – an appellation which seemed to include, in the minds of the peasantry who used it, both the family and the family mansion.

I have said that the sole effect of my somewhat childish experiment – that of looking down within the tarn – had been to deepen the first singular impression. There can be no doubt that the consciousness of the rapid increase of my superstition – for why should I not so term it? – served mainly to accelerate the increase itself. Such, I have long known, is the paradoxical law of all sentiments having terror as a basis. And it might have been for this reason only, that, when I again uplifted my eyes to the house itself, from its image in the pool, there grew in my mind a strange fancy – a fancy so ridiculous, indeed, that I but mention it to show the vivid force of the sensations which oppressed me. I had so worked upon my imagination as really to believe that about the whole mansion and domain there hung an atmosphere peculiar to themselves and their immediate vicinity – an atmosphere which had no affinity with the air of heaven, but which had reeked up from the decayed trees, and the gray wall, and the silent tarn – a pestilent and mystic vapour, dull, sluggish, faintly discernible, and leaden-hued.

Shaking off from my spirit what *must* have been a dream, I scanned more narrowly the real aspect of the building. Its principal feature seemed to be that of an excessive antiquity. The discoloration of ages had been great. Minute *fungi* overspread the whole exterior, hanging in a fine tangled web-work from the eaves. Yet all this was apart from any extraordinary dilapidation. No portion of the masonry had fallen; and there appeared to be a wild inconsistency between its still perfect adaptation of parts, and the crumbling condition of the individual stones. In this there was much that reminded me of the specious totality of old wood-work which has rotted for long years in some neglected vault, with no disturbance from the breath of the external air. Beyond this indication of extensive decay, however, the fabric gave little token of instability. Perhaps the eye of a scrutinising observer might have discovered a barely perceptible fissure, which, extending from the roof of the building in front, made its way down the wall in a zigzag direction, until it became lost in the sullen waters of the tarn.

Noticing these things, I rode over a short causeway to the house. A servant in waiting took my horse and I entered the Gothic archway of the hall. A valet, of stealthy step, thence conducted me, in silence, through many dark and intricate passages in my progress to the *studio* of his master. Much that I encountered on the way contributed, I know not how, to heighten the vague sentiments of which I have already spoken. While the objects around me – while the carvings of the ceilings, the sombre tapestries of the walls, the ebon blackness of the floors, and the phantasmagoric armorial trophies which rattled as I strode, were but matters to which, or to such as which, I had been accustomed from my infancy – while I hesitated not to acknowledge how familiar was all this – I still wondered to find how unfamiliar were the fancies which ordinary images were stirring up. On one of the staircases, I met the physician of the family. His countenance, I thought, wore a mingled expression of low cunning and perplexity. He accosted me with trepidation and passed on. The valet now threw open a door and ushered me into the presence of his master.

The room in which I found myself was very large and lofty. The windows were long, narrow, and pointed, and at so vast a distance from the black oaken floor as to be altogether inaccessible from within. Feeble gleams of encrimsoned light made their way through the trellised panes, and served to render sufficiently distinct the more prominent objects around; the eye, however, struggled in vain to reach the remoter angles of the chamber, or the recesses of the vaulted and fretted ceiling. Dark draperies hung upon the walls. The general furniture was profuse, comfortless, antique, and tattered. Many books and musical instruments lay scattered about, but failed to give any vitality to the scene. I felt that I breathed an atmosphere of sorrow. An air of stern, deep, and irredeemable gloom hung over and pervaded all.

Upon my entrance, Usher arose from a sofa on which he had been lying at full length, and greeted me with a vivacious warmth which had much in it, I at first thought, of an overdone cordiality – of the constrained effort of the *ennuyé* man of the world. A glance, however, at his countenance, convinced me of his perfect sincerity. We sat down; and for some moments, while he spoke not, I gazed upon him with a feeling half of pity, half of awe. Surely, man had never before so terribly altered, in so brief a period, as had Roderick Usher! It was with difficulty that I could bring myself to admit the identity of the wan being before me with the companion of my early boyhood. Yet the character of his face had been at all times remarkable. A cadaverousness of complexion; an eye large, liquid, and luminous beyond comparison; lips somewhat thin and very pallid, but of a surpassingly beautiful curve; a nose of a delicate Hebrew model, but with a breadth of nostril unusual in similar formations; a finely moulded chin, speaking, in its want of prominence, of a want of moral energy; hair of a more than web-like softness and tenuity; these features, with an inordinate expansion above the regions of the temple, made up altogether a countenance not easily to be forgotten. And now in the mere exaggeration of the prevailing character of these features, and of the expression they were wont to convey, lay so much of change that I doubted to whom I spoke. The now ghastly pallor of the skin, and the now miraculous lustre of the eye, above all things startled and even awed me. The silken hair, too, had been suffered to grow all unheeded, and as, in its wild gossamer texture, it floated rather than fell about the face, I could not, even with effort, connect its Arabesque expression with any idea of simple humanity.

In the manner of my friend I was at once struck with an incoherence – an inconsistency; and I soon found this to arise from a series of feeble and futile struggles to overcome an habitual trepidancy – an excessive nervous agitation. For something of this nature I had indeed been prepared, no less by his letter, than by reminiscences of certain boyish traits, and by conclusions deduced from his peculiar physical conformation and temperament. His action was alternately vivacious and sullen. His voice varied rapidly from a tremulous indecision (when the animal spirits seemed utterly in abeyance) to that species of energetic concision – that abrupt, weighty, unhurried, and hollow-sounding enunciation – that leaden, self-balanced and perfectly modulated guttural utterance, which may be observed in the lost drunkard, or the irreclaimable eater of opium, during the periods of his most intense excitement.

It was thus that he spoke of the object of my visit, of his earnest desire to see me, and of the solace he expected me to afford him. He entered, at some length, into what he conceived to be the nature of his malady. It was, he said, a constitutional and a family evil, and one for which he despaired to find a remedy—a mere nervous affection, he immediately added, which would undoubtedly soon pass off. It displayed itself in a host of unnatural sensations. Some of these, as he detailed them, interested and bewildered me; although, perhaps, the terms, and the general manner of the narration had their weight. He suffered much from a morbid acuteness of the senses; the most insipid food was alone endurable; he could wear only garments of certain texture; the odours of all flowers were oppressive; his eyes were tortured by even a faint light; and there were but peculiar sounds, and these from stringed instruments, which did not inspire him with horror.

To an anomalous species of terror I found him a bounden slave. 'I shall perish,' said he, 'I *must* perish in this deplorable folly. Thus, thus, and not otherwise, shall I be lost. I dread the events of the future, not in themselves, but in their results. I shudder at the thought of any, even the most trivial, incident, which may operate upon this intolerable agitation of soul. I have, indeed, no abhorrence of danger, except in its absolute effect – in terror. In this unnerved – in this pitiable condition – I feel that the period will sooner or later arrive when I must abandon life and reason together, in some struggle with the grim phantasm, FEAR.'

I learned, moreover, at intervals, and through broken and equivocal hints, another singular feature of his mental condition. He was enchained by certain superstitious impressions in regard to the dwelling which he tenanted, and whence, for many years, he had never ventured forth – in regard to an influence whose supposititious force was conveyed in terms too shadowy here to be re-stated – an influence which some peculiarities in the mere form and substance of his family mansion, had, by dint of long sufferance, he said, obtained over his spirit – an effect which the *physique* of the gray walls and turrets, and of the dim tarn into which they all looked down, had, at length, brought about upon the *morale* of his existence.

He admitted, however, although with hesitation, that much of the peculiar gloom which thus afflicted him could be traced to a more natural and far more palpable origin – to the severe and long-continued illness – indeed to the evidently approaching dissolution – of a tenderly beloved sister – his sole companion for long years – his last and only relative on earth. 'Her decease,' he said, with a bitterness which I can never forget, 'would leave him (him the hopeless and the frail) the last of the ancient race of the Ushers.' While he spoke, the lady Madeline (for so was she called) passed slowly through a remote portion of the apartment, and, without having noticed my presence, disappeared. I regarded her with an utter astonishment not unmingled with dread – and yet I found it impossible to account for such feelings. A sensation of stupor oppressed me, as my eyes followed her retreating steps. When a door, at length, closed upon her, my glance sought instinctively and eagerly the countenance of the brother – but he had buried his face in his hands, and I could only perceive that a far more than ordinary wanness had overspread the emaciated fingers through which trickled many passionate tears.

The disease of the lady Madeline had long baffled the skill of her physicians. A settled apathy, a gradual wasting away of the person, and frequent although transient affections of a partially cataleptical character, were the unusual diagnosis. Hitherto she had steadily borne up against the pressure of her malady, and had not betaken herself finally to bed; but, on the closing in of the evening of my arrival at the house, she succumbed (as her brother told me at night with inexpressible agitation) to the prostrating power of the destroyer; and I learned that the glimpse I had obtained of her person would thus probably be the last I should obtain – that the lady, at least while living, would be seen by me no more.

For several days ensuing, her name was unmentioned by either Usher or myself: and during this period I was busied in earnest endeavours to alleviate the melancholy of my friend. We painted and read together; or I listened, as if in a dream, to the wild improvisations of his speaking guitar. And thus, as a closer and still closer intimacy admitted me more unreservedly into the recesses of his spirit, the more bitterly did I perceive the futility of all attempt at cheering a mind from which darkness, as if an inherent positive quality, poured forth upon all objects of the moral and physical universe, in one unceasing radiation of gloom.

I shall ever bear about me a memory of the many solemn hours I thus spent alone with the master of the House of Usher. Yet I should fail in any attempt to convey an idea of the exact character of the studies, or of the occupations, in which he involved me, or led me the way. An excited and highly distempered ideality threw a sulphureous lustre over all. His long improvised dirges will ring forever in my ears. Among other things, I hold painfully in mind a certain singular perversion and amplification of the wild air of the last waltz of Von Weber. From the paintings over which his elaborate fancy brooded, and which grew, touch by touch, into vaguenesses at which I shuddered the more thrillingly, because I shuddered knowing not why; – from these paintings (vivid as their images now are before me) I would in vain endeavour to educe more than a small portion which should lie within the compass of merely written words. By the utter simplicity, by the nakedness of his designs, he arrested and overawed attention. If ever mortal painted an idea, that mortal was Roderick Usher. For me at least – in the circumstances then surrounding me – there arose out of the pure abstractions which the hypochondriac contrived to throw upon his canvas, an intensity of intolerable awe, no shadow of which felt I ever yet in the contemplation of the certainly glowing yet too concrete reveries of Fuseli.

One of the phantasmagoric conceptions of my friend, partaking not so rigidly of the spirit of abstraction, may be shadowed forth, although feebly, in words. A small picture presented the interior of an immensely long and rectangular vault or tunnel, with low walls, smooth, white, and without interruption or device. Certain accessory points of the design served well to convey the idea that this excavation lay at an exceeding depth below the surface of the earth. No outlet was observed in any portion of its vast extent, and no torch, or other artificial source of light was discernible; yet a flood of intense rays rolled throughout, and bathed the whole in a ghastly and inappropriate splendour.

I have just spoken of that morbid condition of the auditory nerve which rendered all music intolerable to the sufferer, with the exception of certain effects of stringed instruments. It was, perhaps, the narrow limits to which he thus confined himself upon the guitar, which gave birth, in great measure, to the fantastic character of his performances. But the fervid *facility* of his *impromptus* could not be so accounted for. They must have been, and were, in the notes, as well as in the words of his wild fantasias (for he not unfrequently accompanied himself with rhymed verbal improvisations), the result of that intense mental collectedness and concentration to which I have previously alluded as observable only in particular moments of the highest artificial excitement. The words of one of these rhapsodies I have easily remembered. I was, perhaps, the more forcibly impressed with it, as he gave it, because, in the under or mystic current of its meaning, I fancied that I perceived, and for the first time, a full consciousness on the part of Usher, of the tottering of his lofty reason upon her throne. The verses, which were entitled 'The Haunted Palace', ran very nearly, if not accurately, thus:

I

In the greenest of our valleys,
By good angels tenanted,
Once a fair and stately palace –
Radiant palace – reared its head.
In the monarch Thought's dominion –
It stood there!
Never seraph spread a pinion
Over fabric half so fair.

II

Banners yellow, glorious, golden,
On its roof did float and flow;
(This – all this – was in the olden
Time long ago)
And every gentle air that dallied,
In that sweet day,
Along the ramparts plumed and pallid,
A winged odour went away.

III

Wanderers in that happy valley
Through two luminous windows saw
Spirits moving musically
To a lute's well-tunèd law,
Round about a throne, where sitting
(Porphyrogene!)
In state his glory well befitting,
The ruler of the realm was seen.

IV

And all with pearl and ruby glowing
Was the fair palace door,
Through which came flowing, flowing, flowing
And sparkling evermore,
A troop of Echoes whose sweet duty
Was but to sing,
In voices of surpassing beauty,
The wit and wisdom of their king.

V

But evil things, in robes of sorrow,
Assailed the monarch's high estate;
(Ah, let us mourn, for never morrow
Shall dawn upon him, desolate!)

And, round about his home, the glory
That blushed and bloomed
Is but a dim-remembered story
Of the old time entombed.

VI

And travellers now within that valley,
Through the red-litten windows, see
Vast forms that move fantastically
To a discordant melody;
While, like a rapid ghastly river,
Through the pale door,
A hideous throng rush out forever,
And laugh – but smile no more.

I well remember that suggestions arising from this ballad led us into a train of thought wherein there became manifest an opinion of Usher's which I mention not so much on account of its novelty (for other men have thought thus) as on account of the pertinacity with which he maintained it. This opinion, in its general form, was that of the sentience of all vegetable things. But, in his disordered fancy, the idea had assumed a more daring character, and trespassed, under certain conditions, upon the kingdom of inorganisation. I lack words to express the full extent, or the earnest *abandon* of his persuasion. The belief, however, was connected (as I have previously hinted) with the gray stones of the home of his forefathers. The conditions of the sentience had been here, he imagined, fulfilled in the method of collocation of these stones – in the order of their arrangement, as well as in that of the many *fungi* which overspread them, and of the decayed trees which stood around – above all, in the long undisturbed endurance of this arrangement, and in its reduplication in the still waters of the tarn. Its evidence – the evidence of the sentience – was to be seen, he said (and I here started as he spoke), in the gradual yet certain condensation of an atmosphere of their own about the waters and the walls. The result was discoverable, he added, in that silent, yet importunate and terrible influence which for centuries had moulded the destinies of his family, and which made *him* what I now saw him – what he was. Such opinions need no comment, and I will make none.

Our books – the books which, for years, had formed no small portion of the mental existence of the invalid – were, as might be supposed, in strict keeping with this character of phantasm. We pored together over such works as the *Ververt et Chartreuse* of Gresset; the *Belphegor* of Machiavelli; the *Heaven and Hell* of Swedenborg; the *Subterranean Voyage of Nicholas Klimm* by Holberg; the *Chiromancy* of Robert Flud, of Jean D'Indaginé, and of De la Chambre; the *Journey into the Blue Distance* of Tieck; and the *City of the Sun* of Campanella. One favourite volume was a small octavo edition of the *Directorium Inquisitorum*, by the Dominican Eymeric de Gironne; and there were passages in Pomponius Mela, about the old African Satyrs and Ægipans, over which Usher would sit dreaming for hours. His chief delight, however, was found in the perusal of an exceedingly rare and curious book in quarto

Gothic – the manual of a forgotten church – the *Vigiliæ Mortuorum secundum Chorum Ecclesiæ Maguntinæ.*

I could not help thinking of the wild ritual of this work, and of its probable influence upon the hypochondriac, when, one evening, having informed me abruptly that the lady Madeline was no more, he stated his intention of preserving her corpse for a fortnight (previously to its final interment), in one of the numerous vaults within the main walls of the building. The worldly reason, however, assigned for this singular proceeding, was one which I did not feel at liberty to dispute. The brother had been led to his resolution (so he told me) by consideration of the unusual character of the malady of the deceased, of certain obtrusive and eager inquiries on the part of her medical men, and of the remote and exposed situation of the burial-ground of the family. I will not deny that when I called to mind the sinister countenance of the person whom I met upon the staircase, on the day of my arrival at the house, I had no desire to oppose what I regarded as at best but a harmless, and by no means an unnatural, precaution.

At the request of Usher, I personally aided him in the arrangements for the temporary entombment. The body having been encoffined, we two alone bore it to its rest. The vault in which we placed it (and which had been so long unopened that our torches, half smothered in its oppressive atmosphere, gave us little opportunity for investigation) was small, damp, and entirely without means of admission for light; lying, at great depth, immediately beneath that portion of the building in which was my own sleeping apartment. It had been used, apparently, in remote feudal times, for the worst purposes of a donjon-keep, and, in later days, as a place of deposit for powder, or some other highly combustible substance, as a portion of its floor, and the whole interior of a long archway through which we reached it, were carefully sheathed with copper. The door, of massive iron, had been, also, similarly protected. Its immense weight caused an unusually sharp grating sound, as it moved upon its hinges.

Having deposited our mournful burden upon tressels within this region of horror, we partially turned aside the yet unscrewed lid of the coffin, and looked upon the face of the tenant. A striking similitude between the brother and sister now first arrested my attention; and Usher, divining, perhaps, my thoughts, murmured out some few words from which I learned that the deceased and himself had been twins, and that sympathies of a scarcely intelligible nature had always existed between them. Our glances, however, rested not long upon the dead – for we could not regard her unawed. The disease which had thus entombed the lady in the maturity of youth, had left, as usual in all maladies of a strictly cataleptical character, the mockery of a faint blush upon the bosom and the face, and that suspiciously lingering smile upon the lip which is so terrible in death. We replaced and screwed down the lid, and, having secured the door of iron, made our way, with toil, into the scarcely less gloomy apartments of the upper portion of the house.

And now, some days of bitter grief having elapsed, an observable change came over the features of the mental disorder of my friend. His ordinary manner had vanished. His ordinary occupations were neglected or forgotten. He roamed from chamber to chamber with hurried, unequal, and objectless step. The pallor of his countenance had assumed, if possible, a more ghastly hue – but the luminousness of his eye had utterly gone out. The once occasional huskiness of his tone was heard no more; and a tremulous quaver, as if of extreme terror, habitually characterised his utterance. There were times, indeed, when I thought his unceasingly agitated mind was labouring with some oppressive secret, to divulge which he struggled for the necessary courage. At times, again, I was obliged to resolve all into the mere inexplicable vagaries of madness, for I beheld him gazing upon vacancy for long hours, in an attitude of the profoundest attention, as if listening to some imaginary sound. It was no wonder that his condition terrified – that it infected me. I felt creeping upon me, by slow yet certain degrees, the wild influences of his own fantastic yet impressive superstitions.

It was, especially, upon retiring to bed late in the night of the seventh or eighth day after the placing of the lady Madeline within the donjon, that I experienced the full power of such feelings. Sleep came not near my couch – while the hours waned and waned away. I struggled to reason off the nervousness which had dominion over me. I endeavoured to believe that much, if not all of what I felt, was due to the bewildering influence of the gloomy furniture of the room – of the dark and tattered draperies, which, tortured into motion by the breath of a rising tempest, swayed fitfully to and fro upon the walls, and rustled uneasily about the decorations of the bed. But my efforts were fruitless. An irrepressible tremor gradually pervaded my frame; and, at length, there sat upon my very heart an incubus of utterly causeless alarm. Shaking this off with a gasp and a struggle, I uplifted myself upon the pillows, and, peering earnestly within the intense darkness of the chamber, hearkened – I know not why, except that an instinctive spirit prompted me – to certain low and indefinite sounds which came, through the pauses of the storm, at long intervals, I knew not whence. Overpowered by an intense sentiment of horror, unaccountable yet unendurable, I threw on my clothes with haste (for I felt that I should sleep no more during the night), and endeavoured to arouse myself from the pitiable condition into which I had fallen, by pacing rapidly to and fro through the apartment.

I had taken but few turns in this manner, when a light step on an adjoining staircase arrested my attention. I presently recognised it as that of Usher. In an instant afterward he rapped, with a gentle touch, at my door, and entered, bearing a lamp. His countenance was, as usual, cadaverously wan – but, moreover, there was a species of mad hilarity in his eyes – an evidently restrained *hysteria* in his whole demeanour. His air appalled me – but anything was preferable to the solitude which I had so long endured, and I even welcomed his presence as a relief.

'And you have not seen it?' he said abruptly, after having stared about him for some moments in silence – 'you have not then seen it? – but, stay! you shall.' Thus speaking, and having carefully shaded his lamp, he hurried to one of the casements, and threw it freely open to the storm.

The impetuous fury of the entering gust nearly lifted us from our feet. It was, indeed, a tempestuous yet sternly beautiful night, and one wildly singular in its terror and its beauty. A whirlwind had apparently collected its force in our vicinity; for there were frequent and violent alterations in the direction of the wind; and the exceeding density of the clouds (which hung so low as to press upon the turrets of the house) did not prevent our perceiving the life-like velocity with which they flew careering from all points against each other, without passing away into the distance. I say that even their exceeding density did not prevent our perceiving this – yet we had no glimpse of the moon or stars – nor was there any flashing forth of the lightning. But the under surfaces of the huge masses of agitated vapour, as well as all terrestrial objects immediately around us, were glowing in the unnatural light of a faintly luminous and distinctly visible gaseous exhalation which hung about and enshrouded the mansion.

'You must not – you shall not behold this!' said I, shudderingly, to Usher, as I led him, with a gentle violence, from the window to a seat. 'These appearances, which bewilder you, are merely electrical phenomena not uncommon – or it may be that they have their ghastly origin in the rank miasma of the tarn. Let us close this casement; – the air is chilling and dangerous to your frame. Here is one of your favourite romances. I will read, and you shall listen; – and so we will pass away this terrible night together.'

The antique volume which I had taken up was the *Mad Trist* of Sir Launcelot Canning; but I had called it a favourite of Usher's more in sad jest than in earnest; for, in truth, there is little in its uncouth and unimaginative prolixity which could have had interest for the lofty and spiritual ideality of my friend. It was, however, the only book immediately at hand; and I indulged a vague hope that the excitement which now agitated the hypochondriac, might find relief (for the history of mental disorder is full of similar anomalies) even in the extremeness of the folly which I should read. Could I have judged, indeed, by the wild overstrained air of vivacity with which he hearkened, or apparently hearkened, to the words of the tale, I might well have congratulated myself upon the success of my design.

I had arrived at that well-known portion of the story where Ethelred, the hero of the *Trist*, having sought in vain for peaceable admission into the dwelling of the hermit, proceeds to make good an entrance by force. Here, it will be remembered, the words of the narrative run thus:

'And Ethelred, who was by nature of a doughty heart, and who was now mighty withal, on account of the powerfulness of the wine which he had drunken, waited no longer to hold parley with the hermit, who, in sooth, was of an obstinate and maliceful turn, but, feeling the rain upon his shoulders, and fearing the rising of the tempest, uplifted his mace outright, and, with blows, made quickly room in the plankings of the door for his gauntleted hand; and now pulling therewith sturdily, he so cracked, and ripped, and tore all asunder, that the noise of the dry and hollow-sounding wood alarumed and reverberated throughout the forest.'

At the termination of this sentence I started, and for a moment, paused; for it appeared to me (although I at once concluded that my excited fancy had deceived me) – it appeared to me that, from some very remote portion of the mansion, there came, indistinctly, to my ears, what might have been, in its exact similarity of character, the echo (but a stifled and dull one certainly) of the very cracking and ripping sound which Sir Launcelot had so particularly described. It was, beyond doubt, the coincidence alone which had arrested my attention; for, amid the rattling of the sashes of the casements, and the ordinary commingled noises of the still increasing storm, the sound, in itself, had nothing, surely, which should have interested or disturbed me. I continued the story:

'But the good champion Ethelred, now entering within the door, was sore enraged and amazed to perceive no signal of the maliceful hermit; but, in the stead thereof, a dragon of a scaly and prodigious demeanour, and of a fiery tongue, which sate in guard before a palace of gold, with a floor of silver; and upon the wall there hung a shield of shining brass with this legend enwritten –

Who entereth herein, a conqueror hath bin;
Who slayeth the dragon, the shield he shall win;

and Ethelred uplifted his mace, and struck upon the head of the dragon, which fell before him, and gave up his pesty breath, with a shriek so horrid and harsh, and withal so piercing, that Ethelred had fain to close his ears with his hands against the dreadful noise of it, the like whereof was never before heard.'

Here again I paused abruptly, and now with a feeling of wild amazement – for there could be no doubt whatever that, in this instance, I did actually hear (although from what direction it proceeded I found it impossible to say) a low and apparently distant, but harsh, protracted, and most unusual screaming or grating sound – the exact counterpart of what my fancy had already conjured up for the dragon's unnatural shriek as described by the romancer.

Oppressed, as I certainly was, upon the occurrence of the second and most extraordinary coincidence, by a thousand conflicting sensations, in which wonder and extreme terror were predominant, I still retained sufficient presence of mind to avoid exciting, by any observation, the sensitive nervousness of my companion. I was by no means certain that he had noticed the sounds in question; although, assuredly, a strange alteration had, during the last few minutes, taken place in his demeanour. From a position fronting my own, he had gradually brought round his chair, so as to sit with his face to the door of the chamber; and thus I could but partially perceive his features, although I saw that his lips trembled as if he were murmuring inaudibly. His head had dropped upon his breast – yet I knew that he was not asleep, from the wide and rigid opening of the eye as I caught a glance of it in profile. The motion of his body, too, was at variance with this idea – for he rocked from side to side with a gentle yet constant and uniform sway. Having rapidly taken notice of all this, I resumed the narrative of Sir Launcelot, which thus proceeded:

'And now, the champion, having escaped from the terrible fury of the dragon, bethinking himself of the brazen shield, and of the breaking up of the enchantment which was upon it, removed the carcass from out of the way before him, and approached valorously over the silver pavement of the castle to where the shield was upon the wall; which in sooth tarried not for his full coming, but fell down at his feet upon the silver floor, with a mighty great and terrible ringing sound.'

No sooner had these syllables passed my lips, than – as if a shield of brass had indeed, at the moment, fallen heavily upon a floor of silver – I became aware of a distinct, hollow, metallic, and clangorous, yet apparently muffled reverberation. Completely unnerved, I leaped to my feet; but the measured rocking movement of Usher was undisturbed. I rushed to the chair in which he sat. His eyes were bent fixedly before him, and throughout his whole countenance there reigned a stony rigidity. But, as I placed my hand upon his shoulder, there came a strong shudder over his whole person; a sickly smile quivered about his lips; and I saw that he spoke in a low, hurried, and gibbering murmur, as if unconscious of my presence. Bending closely over him, I at length drank in the hideous import of his words.

'Not hear it? – yes, I hear it, and *have* heard it. Long – long – long – many minutes, many hours, many days, have I heard it – yet I dared not – oh, pity me, miserable wretch that I am! – I dared not – I *dared* not speak! *We have put her living in the tomb!* Said I not that my senses were acute? I *now* tell you that I heard her first feeble movements in the hollow coffin. I heard them – many, many days ago – yet I dared not – I *dared not speak!* And now – to-night – Ethelred – ha! ha! – the breaking of the hermit's door, and the death-cry of the dragon, and the clangour of the shield! – say, rather, the rending of her coffin, and the grating of the iron hinges of her prison, and her struggles within the coppered archway of the vault! Oh whither shall I fly? Will she not be here anon? Is she not hurrying to upbraid me for my haste? Have I not heard her footstep on the stair? Do I not distinguish that heavy and horrible beating of her heart? MADMAN!' – here he sprang furiously to his feet, and shrieked out his syllables, as if in the effort he were giving up his soul – 'MADMAN! I TELL YOU THAT SHE NOW STANDS WITHOUT THE DOOR!'

As if in the superhuman energy of his utterance there had been found the potency of a spell – the huge antique panels to which the speaker pointed, threw slowly back, upon the instant, their ponderous and ebony jaws. It was the work of the rushing gust – but then without those doors there DID stand the lofty and enshrouded figure of the lady Madeline of Usher. There was blood upon her white robes, and the evidence of some bitter struggle upon every portion of her emaciated frame. For a moment she remained trembling and reeling to and fro upon the threshold, then, with a low moaning cry, fell heavily inward upon the person of her brother, and in her violent and now final death-agonies, bore him to the floor a corpse, and a victim to the terrors he had anticipated.

From that chamber, and from that mansion, I fled aghast. The storm was still abroad in all its wrath as I found myself crossing the old causeway. Suddenly there shot along the path a wild light, and I turned to see whence a gleam so unusual could have issued; for the vast house and its shadows were alone behind me. The radiance was that of the full, setting, and blood-red moon which now shone vividly through that once barely-discernible fissure of which I have before spoken as extending from the roof of the building, in a zigzag direction, to the base. While I gazed, this fissure rapidly widened – there came a fierce breath of the whirlwind – the entire orb of the satellite burst at once upon my sight – my brain reeled as I saw the mighty walls rushing asunder – there was a long tumultuous shouting sound like the voice of a thousand waters – and the deep and dank tarn at my feet closed sullenly and silently over the fragments of the 'HOUSE OF USHER'.

3

The Signalman

(1866)

Charles Dickens

'Halloa! Below there!

When he heard a voice thus calling to him, he was standing at the door of his box, with a flag in his hand, furled round its short pole. One would have thought, considering the nature of the ground, that he could not have doubted from what quarter the voice came; but instead of looking up to where I stood on the top of the steep cutting nearly over his head, he turned himself about, and looked down the Line. There was something remarkable in his manner of doing so, though I could not have said for my life what. But I know it was remarkable enough to attract my notice, even though his figure was foreshortened and shadowed, down in the deep trench, and mine was high above him, so steeped in the glow of an angry sunset that I had shaded my eyes with my hand before I saw him at all.

'Halloa! Below!'

From looking down the Line, he turned himself about again, and, raising his eyes, saw my figure high above him.

'Is there any path by which I can come down and speak to you?' He looked up at me without replying, and I looked down at him without pressing him too soon with a repetition of my idle question. Just then there came a vague vibration in the earth and air, quickly changing into a violent pulsation, and an oncoming rush that caused me to start back, as though it had force to draw me down. When such vapour as rose to my height from this rapid train had passed me, and was skimming away over the landscape, I looked down again, and saw him refurling the flag he had shown while the train went by.

I repeated my inquiry. After a pause, during which he seemed to regard me with fixed attention, he motioned with his rolled-up flag towards a point on my level, some two or three hundred yards distant. I called down to him, 'All right!' and made for that point. There, by dint of looking closely about me, I found a rough zigzag descending path notched out, which I followed.

The cutting was extremely deep, and unusually precipitate. It was made through a clammy stone, that became oozier and wetter as I went down. For these reasons, I found the way long enough to give me time to recall a singular air of reluctance or compulsion with which he had pointed out the path.

When I came down low enough upon the zigzag descent to see him again, I saw that he was standing between the rails on the way by which the train had lately passed, in an attitude as if he were waiting for me to appear. He had his left hand at his chin, and that left elbow rested on his right hand, crossed over his breast. His attitude was one of such expectation and watchfulness that I stopped a moment, wondering at it.

I resumed my downward way, and stepping out upon the level of the railroad, and drawing nearer to him, saw that he was a dark sallow man, with a dark beard and rather heavy eyebrows. His post was in as solitary and dismal a place as ever I saw. On either side, a dripping-wet wall of jagged stone, excluding all view but a strip of sky; the perspective one way only a crooked prolongation of this great dungeon; the shorter perspective in the other direction terminating in a gloomy red light, and the gloomier entrance to a black tunnel, in whose massive architecture there was a barbarous, depressing, and forbidding air. So little sunlight ever found its way to this spot, that it had an earthy, deadly smell; and so much cold wind rushed through it, that it struck chill to me, as if I had left the natural world.

Before he stirred, I was near enough to him to have touched him. Not even then removing his eyes from mine, he stepped back one step, and lifted his hand.

This was a lonesome post to occupy, I said, and it had riveted my attention when I looked down from up yonder. A visitor was a rarity, I should suppose; not an unwelcome rarity, I hoped? In me, he merely saw a man who had been shut up within narrow limits all his life, and who, being at last set free, had a newly-awakened interest in these great works. To such purpose I spoke to him; but I am far from sure of the terms I used; for, besides that I am not happy in opening any conversation, there was something in the man that daunted me.

He directed a most curious look towards the red light near the tunnel's mouth, and looked all about it, as if something were missing from it, and then looked at me.

That light was part of his charge? Was it not?

He answered in a low voice, 'Don't you know it is?'

The monstrous thought came into my mind, as I perused the fixed eyes and the saturnine face, that this was a spirit, not a man. I have speculated since, whether there may have been infection in his mind.

In my turn I stepped back. But in making the action, I detected in his eyes some latent fear of me. This put the monstrous thought to flight.

'You look at me,' I said, forcing a smile, 'as if you had a dread of me.'

'I was doubtful,' he returned, 'whether I had seen you before.'

'Where?'

He pointed to the red light he had looked at.

'There?' I said.

Intently watchful of me, he replied (but without sound), 'Yes.'

'My good fellow, what should I do there? However, be that as it may, I never was there, you may swear.'

'I think I may,' he rejoined. 'Yes; I am sure I may.'

His manner cleared, like my own. He replied to my remarks with readiness, and in well-chosen words. Had he much to do there? Yes; that was to say, he had enough responsibility to bear; but exactness and watchfulness were what was required of him, and of actual work – manual labour – he had next to none. To change that signal, to trim those lights, and to turn this iron handle now and then, was all he had to do under that head. Regarding those many long and lonely hours of which I seemed to make so much, he could only say that the routine of his life had shaped itself into that form, and he had grown used to it. He had taught himself a language down here – if only to know it by sight, and to have formed his own crude ideas of its pronunciation, could be called learning it. He had also worked at fractions and decimals, and tried a little algebra; but he was, and had been as a boy, a poor hand at figures. Was it necessary for him when on duty always to remain in that channel of damp air, and could he never rise into the sunshine from between those high stone walls? Why, that depended upon times and circumstances. Under some conditions there would be less upon the Line than under others, and the same held good as to certain hours of the day and night. In bright weather, he did choose occasions for getting a little above those lower shadows; but, being at all times liable to be called by his electric bell, and at such times listening for it with redoubled anxiety, the relief was less than I would suppose.

He took me into his box, where there was a fire, a desk for an official book in which he had to make certain entries, a telegraphic instrument with its dial, face, and needles, and the little bell of which he had spoken. On my trusting that he would excuse the remark that he had been well educated, and (I hoped I might say without offence) perhaps educated above that station, he observed that instances of slight incongruity in such wise would rarely be found wanting among large bodies of men; that he had heard it was so in workhouses, in the police force, even in that last desperate resource, the army; and that he knew it was so, more or less, in any great railway staff. He had been, when young (if I could believe it, sitting in that hut – he scarcely could), a student of natural philosophy, and had attended lectures; but he had run wild, misused his opportunities, gone down, and never risen again. He had no complaint to offer about that. He had made his bed, and he lay upon it. It was far too late to make another.

All that I have here condensed he said in a quiet manner, with his grave dark regards divided between me and the fire. He threw in the word 'Sir' from time to time, and especially when he referred to his youth – as though to request me to understand that he claimed to be nothing but what I found him. He was several times interrupted by the little bell, and had to read off messages and send replies. Once he had to stand without the door, and display a flag as a train passed, and make some verbal communication to the driver. In the discharge of his duties, I observed him to be remarkably exact and vigilant, breaking off his discourse at a syllable, and remaining silent until what he had to do was done.

In a word, I should have set this man down as one of the safest of men to be employed in that capacity, but for the circumstance that while he was speaking to me he twice broke off with a fallen colour, turned his face towards the little bell when it did *not* ring, opened the door of the hut (which was kept shut to exclude the unhealthy damp), and looked out towards the red light near the mouth of the tunnel. On both of those occasions he came back to the fire with the inexplicable air upon him which I had remarked, without being able to define, when we were so far asunder.

Said I, when I rose to leave him, 'You almost make me think that I have met with a contented man.'

(I am afraid I must acknowledge that I said it to lead him on.)

'I believe I used to be so,' he rejoined, in the low voice in which he had first spoken; 'but I am troubled, sir, I am troubled.'

He would have recalled the words if he could. He had said them, however, and I took them up quickly.

'With what? What is your trouble?'

'It is very difficult to impart, sir. It is very, very difficult to speak of. If ever you make me another visit, I will try to tell you.'

'But I expressly intend to make you another visit. Say, when shall it be?'

'I go off early in the morning, and I shall be on again at ten tomorrow night, sir.'

'I will come at eleven.'

He thanked me, and went out at the door with me. 'I'll show my white light, sir,' he said, in his peculiar low voice, 'till you have found the way up. When you have found it, don't call out! And when you are at the top, don't call out!'

His manner seemed to make the place strike colder to me, but I said no more than 'Very well.'

'And when you come down tomorrow night, don't call out! Let me ask you a parting question. What made you cry, "Halloa! Below there!" tonight?'

'Heaven knows,' said I, 'I cried something to that effect—'

'Not to that effect, sir. Those were the very words. I know them well.'

'Admit those were the very words. I said them, no doubt, because I saw you below.'

'For no other reason?'

'What other reason could I possibly have?'

'You have no feeling that they were conveyed to you in any supernatural way?'

'No.'

He wished me goodnight, and held up his light. I walked by the side of the down Line of rails (with a very disagreeable sensation of a train coming behind me) until I found the path. It was easier to mount than to descend, and I got back to my inn without any adventure.

Punctual to my appointment, I placed my foot on the first notch of the zigzag next night as the distant clocks were striking eleven. He was waiting for me at the bottom, with his white light on. 'I have not called out,' I said, when we came close together; 'may I speak now?' 'By all means, sir.' 'Goodnight, then, and here's my hand.' 'Goodnight, sir, and here's mine.' With that we walked side by side to his box, entered it, closed the door, and sat down by the fire.

'I have made up my mind, sir,' he began, bending forward as soon as we were seated, and speaking in a tone but a little above a whisper, 'that you shall not have to ask me twice what troubles me. I took you for someone else yesterday evening. That troubles me.'

'That mistake?'

'No. That someone else.'

'Who is it?'

'I don't know.'

'Like me?'

'I don't know. I never saw the face. The left arm is across the face, and the right arm is waved – violently waved. This way.'

I followed his action with my eyes, and it was the action of an arm gesticulating, with the utmost passion and vehemence, 'For God's sake, clear the way!'

'One moonlight night,' said the man, 'I was sitting here, when I heard a voice cry, "Halloa! Below there!" I started up, looked from that door, and saw this someone else standing by the red light near the tunnel, waving as I just now showed you. The voice seemed hoarse with shouting, and it cried, "Look out! Look out!" And then again, "Halloa! Below there! Look out!" I caught up my lamp, turned it on red, and ran towards the figure, calling, "What's wrong? What has happened? Where?" It stood just outside the blackness of the tunnel. I advanced so close upon it that I wondered at its keeping the sleeve across its eyes. I ran right up at it, and had my hand stretched out to pull the sleeve away when it was gone.'

'Into the tunnel?' said I.

'No. I ran on into the tunnel, five hundred yards. I stopped, and held my lamp above my head, and saw the figures of the measured distance, and saw the wet stains stealing down the walls and trickling through the arch. I ran out again faster than I had run in (for I had a mortal abhorrence of the place upon me), and I looked all round the red light with my own red light, and I went up the iron ladder to the gallery atop of it, and I came down again, and ran back here. I telegraphed both ways. "An alarm has been given. Is anything wrong?" The answer came back, both ways, "All well." '

Resisting the slow touch of a frozen finger tracing out my spine, I showed him how that this figure must be a deception of his sense of sight; and how that figures, originating in disease of the delicate nerves that minister to the functions of the eye, were known to have often troubled patients, some of whom had become conscious of the nature of their affliction, and had even proved it by experiments upon themselves. 'As to an imaginary cry,' said I, 'do but listen for a moment to the wind in this unnatural valley while we speak so low, and to the wild harp it makes of the telegraph wires.'

That was all very well, he returned, after we had sat listening for a while, and he ought to know something of the wind and the wires – he who so often passed long winter nights there, alone and watching. But he would beg to remark that he had not finished.

I asked his pardon, and he slowly added these words, touching my arm:

'Within six hours after the Appearance, the memorable accident on this line happened, and within ten hours the dead and wounded were brought along through the tunnel over the spot where the figure had stood.'

A disagreeable shudder crept over me, but I did my best against it. It was not to be denied, I rejoined, that this was a remarkable coincidence, calculated deeply to impress his mind. But it was unquestionable that remarkable coincidences did continually occur, and they must be taken into account in dealing with such a subject. Though to be sure I must admit, I added (for I thought I saw that he was going to bring the objection to bear upon me), men of common sense did not allow much for coincidences in making the ordinary calculations of life.

He again begged to remark that he had not finished.

I again begged his pardon for being betrayed into interruptions.

'This,' he said, again laying his hand upon my arm, and glancing over his shoulder with hollow eyes, 'was just a year ago. Six or seven months passed, and I had recovered from the surprise and shock, when one morning, as the day was breaking, I, standing at the door, looked towards the red light, and saw the spectre again.' He stopped, with a fixed look at me.

'Did it cry out?'

'No. It was silent.'

'Did it wave its arm?'

'No. It leaned against the shaft of the light with both hands before the face. Like this.'

Once more I followed his actions with my eyes. It was an action of mourning. I have seen such an attitude on stone figures on tombs.

'Did you go up to it?'

'I came in and sat down, partly to collect my thoughts, partly because it had turned me faint. When I went to the door again, daylight was above me, and the ghost was gone.'

'But nothing followed? Nothing came of this?'

He touched me on the arm with his forefinger twice or thrice, giving a ghastly nod each time:

'That very day, as a train came out of the tunnel, I noticed, at a carriage window on my side, what looked like a confusion of hands and heads, and something waved. I saw it just in time to signal the driver, Stop! He shut off, and put his brake on, but the train drifted past here a hundred and fifty yards or more. I ran after it, and, as I went along, heard terrible screams and cries. A beautiful young lady had died instantaneously in one of the compartments, and was brought in here, and laid down on this floor between us.'

Involuntarily I pushed my chair back, as I looked from the boards at which he pointed to himself.

'True, sir. True. Precisely as it happened, so I tell it you.' I could think of nothing to say, to any purpose, and my mouth was very dry. The wind and the wires took up the story with a long lamenting wail.

He resumed, 'Now, sir, mark this, and judge how my mind is troubled. The spectre came back a week ago. Ever since, it has been there, now and again, by fits and starts.'

'At the light?'

'At the Danger-light.'

'What does it seem to do?'

He repeated, if possible with increased passion and vehemence, that former gesticulation of 'For God's sake, clear the way!'

Then he went on, 'I have no peace or rest for it. It calls to me, for many minutes together, in an agonised manner, "Below there! Look out! Look out!" It stands waving to me. It rings my little bell—'

I caught at that. 'Did it ring your bell yesterday evening when I was here, and you went to the door?'

'Twice.'

'Why, see,' said I, 'how your imagination misleads you. My eyes were on the bell, and my ears were open to the bell, and if I am a living man, it did *not* ring at those times. No, nor at any other time, except when it was rung in the natural course of physical things by the station communicating with you.'

He shook his head. 'I have never made a mistake as to that yet, sir. I have never confused the spectre's ring with the man's. The ghost's ring is a strange vibration in the bell that it derives from nothing else, and I have not asserted that the bell stirs to the eye. I don't wonder that you failed to hear it. But *I* heard it.'

'And did the spectre seem to be there when you looked out?'

'It *was* there.'

'Both times?'

He repeated firmly: 'Both times.'

'Will you come to the door with me, and look for it now?'

He bit his under lip as though he were somewhat unwilling, but arose. I opened the door, and stood on the step, while he stood in the doorway. There was the Danger-light. There was the dismal mouth of the tunnel. There were the high, wet stone walls of the cutting. There were the stars above them.

'Do you see it?' I asked him, taking particular note of his face. His eyes were prominent and strained, but not very much more so, perhaps, than my own had been when I had directed them earnestly towards the same spot.

'No,' he answered. 'It is not there.'

'Agreed,' said I.

We went in again, shut the door, and resumed our seats. I was thinking how best to improve this advantage, if it might be called one, when he took up the conversation in such a matter-of-course way, so assuming that there could be no serious question of fact between us, that I felt myself placed in the weakest of positions.

'By this time you will fully understand, sir,' he said, 'that what troubles me so dreadfully is the question: What does the spectre mean?'

I was not sure, I told him, that I did fully understand.

'What is its warning against?' he said, ruminating, with his eyes on the fire, and only by times turning them on me. 'What is the danger? Where is the danger? There is danger overhanging somewhere on the Line. Some dreadful calamity will happen. It is not to be doubted this third time, after what has gone before. But surely this is a cruel haunting of *me*. What can I do?'

He pulled out his handkerchief, and wiped the drops from his heated forehead.

'If I telegraph Danger on either side of me, or on both, I can give no reason for it,' he went on, wiping the palms of his hands. 'I should get into trouble and do no good. They would think I was mad. This is the way it would work – Message: "Danger! Take care!" Answer: "What Danger? Where?" Message: "Don't know. But for God's sake, take care!" They would displace me. What else could they do?'

His pain of mind was most pitiable to see. It was the mental torture of a conscientious man, oppressed beyond endurance by an unintelligible responsibility involving life.

'When it first stood under the Danger-light,' he went on, putting his dark hair back from his head, and drawing his hands outward across and across his temples in an extremity of feverish distress, 'why not tell me where that accident was to happen – if it must happen? Why not tell me how it could be averted – if it could have been averted? When on its second coming it hid its face, why not tell me, instead, "She is going to die. Let them keep her at home"? If it came, on those two occasions, only to show me that its warnings were true, and so to prepare me for the third, why not warn me plainly now? And I, Lord help me! A mere poor signalman on this solitary station! Why not go to somebody with credit to be believed, and power to act?'

When I saw him in this state, I saw that for the poor man's sake, as well as for the public safety, what I had to do for the time was to compose his mind. Therefore, setting aside all question of reality or unreality between us, I represented to him that whoever thoroughly discharged his duty must do well, and that at least it was his comfort that he understood his duty, though he did not understand these confounding Appearances. In this effort I succeeded far better than in the attempt to reason him out of his conviction. He became calm; the occupations incidental to his post as the night advanced began to make larger demands on his attention; and I left him at two in the morning. I had offered to stay through the night, but he would not hear of it.

That I more than once looked back at the red light as I ascended the pathway, that I did not like the red light, and that I should have slept but poorly if my bed had been under it, I see no reason to conceal. Nor did I like the two sequences of the accident and the dead girl. I see no reason to conceal that either.

But what ran most in my thoughts was the consideration how ought I to act, having become the recipient of this disclosure? I had proved the man to be intelligent, vigilant, painstaking, and exact; but how long might he remain so, in his state of mind? Though in a subordinate position, still he held a most important trust, and would I (for instance) like to stake my own life on the chances of his continuing to execute it with precision?

Unable to overcome a feeling that there would be something treacherous in my communicating what he had told me to his superiors in the Company, without first being plain with himself and proposing a middle course to him, I ultimately resolved to offer to accompany him (otherwise keeping his secret for the present) to the wisest medical practitioner we could hear of in those parts, and to take his opinion. A change in his time of duty would come round next night, he had apprised me, and he would be off an hour or two after sunrise, and on again soon after sunset. I had appointed to return accordingly.

Next evening was a lovely evening, and I walked out early to enjoy it. The sun was not yet quite down when I traversed the fieldpath near the top of the deep cutting. I would extend my walk for an hour, I said to myself, half an hour on and half an hour back, and it would then be time to go to my signalman's box.

Before pursuing my stroll, I stepped to the brink, and mechanically looked down, from the point from which I had first seen him. I cannot describe the thrill that seized upon me, when, close at the mouth of the tunnel, I saw the appearance of a man, with his left sleeve across his eyes, passionately waving his right arm.

The nameless horror that oppressed me passed in a moment, for in a moment I saw that this appearance of a man was a man indeed, and that there was a little group of other men standing at a short distance, to whom he seemed to be rehearsing the gesture he made. The Danger-light was not yet lighted. Against its shaft a little low hut entirely new to me, had been made of some wooden supports and tarpaulin. It looked no bigger than a bed.

With an irresistible sense that something was wrong – with a flashing self-reproachful fear that fatal mischief had come of my leaving the man there, and causing no one to be sent to overlook or correct what he did – I descended the notched path with all the speed I could make.

'What is the matter?' I asked the men.

'Signalman killed this morning, sir.'

'Not the man belonging to that box?'

'Yes, sir.'

'Not the man I know?'

'You will recognise him, sir, if you knew him,' said the man who spoke for the others, solemnly uncovering his own head, and raising an end of the tarpaulin, 'for his face is quite composed.'

'Oh, how did this happen, how did this happen?' I asked, turning from one to another as the hut closed in again.

'He was cut down by an engine, sir. No man in England knew his work better. But somehow he was not clear of the outer rail. It was just at broad day. He had struck the light, and had the lamp in his hand. As the engine came out of the tunnel, his back was towards her, and she cut him down. That man drove her, and was showing how it happened. Show the gentleman, Tom.'

The man who wore a rough dark dress, stepped back to his former place at the mouth of the tunnel.

'Coming round the curve in the tunnel, sir,' he said, 'I saw him at the end, like as if I saw him down a perspective-glass. There was no time to check speed, and I knew him to be very careful. As he didn't seem to take heed of the whistle, I shut it off when we were running down upon him, and called to him as loud as I could call.'

'What did you say?'

'I said, "Below there! Look out! Look out! For God's sake, clear the way!"'

I started.

'Ah! It was a dreadful time, sir. I never left off calling to him. I put this arm before my eyes not to see, and I waved this arm to the last; but it was no use.'

Without prolonging the narrative to dwell on any one of its curious circumstances more than on any other, I may, in closing it, point out the coincidence that the warning of the engine-driver included, not only the words which the unfortunate signalman had repeated to me as haunting him, but also the words which I myself – not he – had attached, and that only in my own mind, to the gesticulation he had imitated.

4

The Happy Prince

(1888)

Oscar Wilde

High above the city, on a tall column, stood the statue of the Happy Prince. He was gilded all over with thin leaves of fine gold, for eyes he had two bright sapphires, and a large red ruby glowed on his sword-hilt.

He was very much admired indeed. 'He is as beautiful as a weathercock,' remarked one of the Town Councillors who wished to gain a reputation for having artistic tastes; 'only not quite so useful,' he added, fearing lest people should think him unpractical, which he really was not.

'Why can't you be like the Happy Prince?' asked a sensible mother of her little boy who was crying for the moon. 'The Happy Prince never dreams of crying for anything.'

'I am glad there is someone in the world who is quite happy,' muttered a disappointed man as he gazed at the wonderful statue.

'He looks just like an angel,' said the Charity Children as they came out of the cathedral in their bright scarlet cloaks and their clean white pinafores.

'How do you know?' said the Mathematical Master, 'you have never seen one.'

'Ah! but we have, in our dreams,' answered the children; and the Mathematical Master frowned and looked very severe, for he did not approve of children dreaming.

One night there flew over the city a little Swallow. His friends had gone away to Egypt six weeks before, but he had stayed behind, for he was in love with the most beautiful Reed. He had met her early in the spring as he was flying down the river after a big yellow moth, and had been so attracted by her slender waist that he had stopped to talk to her.

'Shall I love you?' said the Swallow, who liked to come to the point at once, and the Reed made him a low bow. So he flew round and round her, touching the water with his wings, and making silver ripples. This was his courtship, and it lasted all through the summer.

'It is a ridiculous attachment,' twittered the other Swallows; 'she has no money, and far too many relations'; and indeed the river was quite full of Reeds. Then, when the autumn came they all flew away.

After they had gone he felt lonely, and began to tire of his lady-love. 'She has no conversation,' he said, 'and I am afraid that she is a coquette, for she is always flirting with the wind.' And certainly, whenever the wind blew, the Reed made the most graceful curtseys. 'I admit that she is domestic,' he continued, 'but I love travelling, and my wife, consequently, should love travelling also.'

'Will you come away with me?' he said finally to her, but the Reed shook her head, she was so attached to her home.

'You have been trifling with me,' he cried. 'I am off to the Pyramids. Good-bye!' and he flew away.

All day long he flew, and at night-time he arrived at the city. 'Where shall I put up?' he said; 'I hope the town has made preparations.'

Then he saw the statue on the tall column.

'I will put up there,' he cried; 'it is a fine position, with plenty of fresh air.' So he alighted just between the feet of the Happy Prince.

'I have a golden bedroom,' he said softly to himself as he looked round, and he prepared to go to sleep; but just as he was putting his head under his wing a large drop of water fell on him. 'What a curious thing!' he cried; 'there is not a single cloud in the sky, the stars are quite clear and bright, and yet it is raining. The climate in the north of Europe is really dreadful. The Reed used to like the rain, but that was merely her selfishness.'

Then another drop fell.

'What is the use of a statue if it cannot keep the rain off?' he said; 'I must look for a good chimney-pot,' and he determined to fly away.

But before he had opened his wings, a third drop fell, and he looked up, and saw – Ah! what did he see?

The eyes of the Happy Prince were filled with tears, and tears were running down his golden cheeks. His face was so beautiful in the moonlight that the little Swallow was filled with pity.

'Who are you?' he said.

'I am the Happy Prince.'

'Why are you weeping then?' asked the Swallow; 'you have quite drenched me.'

'When I was alive and had a human heart,' answered the statue, 'I did not know what tears were, for I lived in the Palace of Sans-Souci, where sorrow is not allowed to enter. In the daytime I played with my companions in the garden, and in the evening I led the dance in the Great Hall. Round the garden ran a very lofty wall, but I never cared to ask what lay beyond it, everything about me was so beautiful. My courtiers called me the Happy Prince, and happy indeed I was, if pleasure be happiness. So I lived, and so I died. And now that I am dead they have set me up here so high that I can see all the ugliness and all the misery of my city, and though my heart is made of lead yet I cannot choose but weep.'

'What! is he not solid gold?' said the Swallow to himself. He was too polite to make any personal remarks out loud.

'Far away,' continued the statue in a low musical voice, 'far away in a little street there is a poor house. One of the windows is open, and through it I can see a woman seated at a table. Her face is thin and worn, and she has coarse, red hands, all pricked by the needle, for she is a seamstress. She is embroidering passion-flowers on a satin gown for the loveliest of the Queen's maids-of-honour to wear at the next Court-ball. In a bed in the corner of the room her little boy is lying ill. He has a fever, and is asking for oranges. His mother has nothing to give him but river water, so he is crying. Swallow, Swallow, little Swallow, will you not bring her the ruby out of my sword-hilt? My feet are fastened to this pedestal and I cannot move.'

'I am waited for in Egypt,' said the Swallow. 'My friends are flying up and down the Nile, and talking to the large lotus-flowers. Soon they will go to sleep in the tomb of the great King. The King is there himself in his painted coffin. He is wrapped in yellow linen, and embalmed with spices. Round his neck is a chain of pale green jade, and his hands are like withered leaves.'

'Swallow, Swallow, little Swallow,' said the Prince, 'will you not stay with me for one night, and be my messenger? The boy is so thirsty, and the mother so sad.'

'I don't think I like boys,' answered the Swallow. 'Last summer, when I was staying on the river, there were two rude boys, the miller's sons, who were always throwing stones at me. They never hit me, of course; we swallows fly far too well for that, and besides, I come of a family famous for its agility; but still, it was a mark of disrespect.'

But the Happy Prince looked so sad that the little Swallow was sorry. 'It is very cold here,' he said; 'but I will stay with you for one night, and be your messenger.'

'Thank you, little Swallow,' said the Prince.

So the Swallow picked out the great ruby from the Prince's sword, and flew away with it in his beak over the roofs of the town.

He passed by the cathedral tower, where the white marble angels were sculptured. He passed by the palace and heard the sound of dancing. A beautiful girl came out on the balcony with her lover. 'How wonderful the stars are,' he said to her, 'and how wonderful is the power of love!'

'I hope my dress will be ready in time for the State-ball,' she answered; 'I have ordered passion-flowers to be embroidered on it; but the seamstresses are so lazy.'

He passed over the river, and saw the lanterns hanging to the masts of the ships. He passed over the Ghetto, and saw the old Jews bargaining with each other, and weighing out money in copper scales. At last he came to the poor house and looked in. The boy was tossing feverishly on his bed, and the mother had fallen asleep, she was so tired. In he hopped, and laid the great ruby on the table beside the woman's thimble. Then he flew gently round the bed, fanning the boy's forehead with his wings. 'How cool I feel!' said the boy, 'I must be getting better': and he sank into a delicious slumber.

Then the Swallow flew back to the Happy Prince, and told him what he had done. 'It is curious,' he remarked, 'but I feel quite warm now, although it is so cold.'

'That is because you have done a good action,' said the Prince. And the little Swallow began to think, and then he fell asleep. Thinking always made him sleepy.

When day broke he flew down to the river and had a bath. 'What a remarkable phenomenon!' said the Professor of Ornithology as he was passing over the bridge. 'A swallow in winter!' And he wrote a long letter about it to the local newspaper. Everyone quoted it, it was full of so many words that they could not understand.

'To-night I go to Egypt,' said the Swallow, and he was in high spirits at the prospect. He visited all the public monuments, and sat a long time on top of the church steeple. Wherever he went the Sparrows chirruped, and said to each other, 'What a distinguished stranger!' so he enjoyed himself very much.

When the moon rose he flew back to the Happy Prince. 'Have you any commissions for Egypt?' he cried; 'I am just starting.'

'Swallow, Swallow, little Swallow,' said the Prince, 'will you not stay with me one night longer?'

'I am waited for in Egypt,' answered the Swallow. 'To-morrow my friends will fly up to the Second Cataract. The river-horse couches there among the bulrushes, and on a great granite house sits the God Memnon. All night long he watches the stars, and when the morning star shines he utters one cry of joy, and then he is silent. At noon the yellow lions come down to the water's edge to drink. They have eyes like green beryls, and their roar is louder than the roar of the cataract.'

'Swallow, Swallow, little Swallow,' said the Prince, 'far away across the city I see a young man in a garret. He is leaning over a desk covered with papers, and in a tumbler by his side there is a bunch of withered violets. His hair is brown and crisp, and his lips are red as a pomegranate, and he has large and dreamy eyes. He is trying to finish a play for the Director of the Theatre, but he is too cold to write any more. There is no fire in the grate, and hunger has made him faint.'

'I will wait with you one night longer,' said the Swallow, who really had a good heart. 'Shall I take him another ruby?'

'Alas! I have no ruby now,' said the Prince; 'my eyes are all that I have left. They are made of rare sapphires, which were brought out of India a thousand years ago. Pluck out one of them and take it to him. He will sell it to the jeweller, and buy firewood, and finish his play.'

'Dear Prince,' said the Swallow, 'I cannot do that'; and he began to weep.

'Swallow, Swallow, little Swallow,' said the Prince, 'do as I command you.'

So the Swallow plucked out the Prince's eye, and flew away to the student's garret. It was easy enough to get in, as there was a hole in the roof. Through this he darted, and came into the room. The young man had his head buried in his hands, so he did not hear the flutter of the bird's wings, and when he looked up he found the beautiful sapphire lying on the withered violets.

'I am beginning to be appreciated,' he cried; 'this is from some great admirer. Now I can finish my play,' and he looked quite happy.

The next day the Swallow flew down to the harbour. He sat on the mast of a large vessel and watched the sailors hauling big chests out of the hold with ropes. 'Heave a-hoy!' they shouted as each chest came up. 'I am going to Egypt!' cried the Swallow, but nobody minded, and when the moon rose he flew back to the Happy Prince.

'I am come to bid you good-bye,' he cried.

'Swallow, Swallow, little Swallow,' said the Prince, 'will you not stay with me one night longer?'

'It is winter,' answered the Swallow, 'and the chill snow will soon be here. In Egypt the sun is warm on the green palm-trees, and the crocodiles lie in the mud and look lazily about them. My companions are building a nest in the Temple of Baalbec, and the pink and white doves are watching them, and cooing to each other. Dear Prince, I must leave you, but I will never forget you, and next spring I will bring you back two beautiful jewels in place of those you have given away. The ruby shall be redder than a red rose, and the sapphire shall be as blue as the great sea.'

'In the square below,' said the Happy Prince, 'there stands a little match-girl. She has let her matches fall in the gutter, and they are all spoiled. Her father will beat her if she does not bring home some money, and she is crying. She has no shoes or stockings, and her little head is bare. Pluck out my other eye, and give it to her, and her father will not beat her.'

'I will stay with you one night longer,' said the Swallow, 'but I cannot pluck out your eye. You would be quite blind then.'

'Swallow, Swallow, little Swallow,' said the Prince, 'do as I command you.'

So he plucked out the Prince's other eye, and darted down with it. He swooped past the match-girl, and slipped the jewel into the palm of her hand. 'What a lovely bit of glass!' cried the little girl; and she ran home, laughing.

Then the Swallow came back to the Prince. 'You are blind now,' he said, 'so I will stay with you always.'

'No, little Swallow,' said the poor prince, 'you must go away to Egypt.'

'I will stay with you always,' said the Swallow, and he slept at the Prince's feet.

All the next day he sat on the Prince's shoulder, and told him stories of what he had seen in strange lands. He told him of the red ibises, who stand in long rows on the banks of the Nile, and catch goldfish in their beaks; of the Sphinx, who is as old as the world itself, and lives in the desert, and knows everything; of the merchants, who walk slowly by the side of their camels and carry amber beads in their hands; of the King of the Mountains of the Moon, who is as black as ebony, and worships a large crystal; of the great green snake that sleeps in a palm-tree, and has twenty priests to feed it with honey-cakes; and of the pygmies who sail over a big lake on large flat leaves, and are always at war with the butterflies.

'Dear little Swallow,' said the Prince, 'you tell me of marvellous things, but more marvellous than anything is the suffering of men and of women. There is no Mystery so great as Misery. Fly over my city, little Swallow, and tell me what you see there.'

So the Swallow flew over the great city, and saw the rich making merry in their beautiful houses, while the beggars were sitting at the gates. He flew into dark lanes, and saw the white faces of starving children looking out listlessly at the black streets. Under the archway of a bridge two little boys were lying in one another's arms to try and keep themselves warm. 'How hungry we are!' they said. 'You must not lie here,' shouted the watchman, and they wandered out into the rain.

Then he flew back and told the Prince what he had seen.

'I am covered with fine gold,' said the Prince, 'you must take it off, leaf by leaf, and give it to my poor; the living always think that gold can make them happy.'

Leaf after leaf of the fine gold the Swallow picked off, till the Happy Prince looked quite dull and grey. Leaf after leaf of the fine gold he brought to the poor, and the children's faces grew rosier, and they laughed and played games in the street. 'We have bread now!' they cried.

Then the snow came, and after the snow came the frost. The streets looked as if they were made of silver, they were so bright and glistening; long icicles like crystal daggers hung down from the eaves of the houses, everybody went about in furs, and the little boys wore scarlet caps and skated on the ice.

The poor little Swallow grew colder and colder, but he would not leave the Prince, he loved him too well. He picked up crumbs outside the baker's door when the baker was not looking, and tried to keep himself warm by flapping his wings.

But at last he knew that he was going to die. He had just enough strength to fly up to the Prince's shoulder once more. 'Good-bye, dear Prince!' he murmured, 'will you let me kiss your hand?'

'I am glad that you are going to Egypt at last, little Swallow,' said the Prince; 'you have stayed too long here; but you must kiss me on the lips, for I love you.'

'It is not to Egypt that I am going,' said the Swallow. 'I am going to the House of Death. Death is the brother of Sleep, is he not?

And he kissed the Happy Prince on the lips, and fell down dead at his feet.

At that moment a curious crack sounded inside the statue, as if something had broken. The fact is that the leaden heart had snapped right in two. It certainly was a dreadfully hard frost.

Early the next morning the Mayor was walking in the square below in company with the Town Councillors. As they passed the column he looked up at the statue: 'Dear me! how shabby the Happy Prince looks!' he said.

'How shabby, indeed!' cried the Town Councillors, who always agreed with the Mayor; and they went up to look at it.

'The ruby has fallen out of his sword, his eyes are gone, and he is golden no longer,' said the Mayor; 'in fact, he is little better than a beggar!'

'Little better than a beggar,' said the Town Councillors.

'And here is actually a dead bird at his feet!' continued the Mayor. 'We must really issue a proclamation that birds are not to be allowed to die here.' And the Town Clerk made a note of the suggestion.

So they pulled down the statue of the Happy Prince. 'As he is no longer beautiful he is no longer useful,' said the Art Professor at the University.

Then they melted the statue in a furnace, and the Mayor held a meeting of the Corporation to decide what was to be done with the metal. 'We must have another statue, of course,' he said, 'and it shall be a statue of myself.'

'Of myself,' said each of the Town Councillors, and they quarrelled. When I last heard of them they were quarrelling still.

'What a strange thing!' said the overseer of the workmen at the foundry. 'This broken lead heart will not melt in the furnace. We must throw it away.' So they threw it on a dust-heap where the dead Swallow was also lying.

'Bring me the two most precious things in the city,' said God to one of His Angels; and the Angel brought Him the leaden heart and the dead bird.

'You have rightly chosen,' said God, 'for in my garden of Paradise this little bird shall sing for evermore, and in my city of gold the Happy Prince shall praise me.'

5

The Yellow Wall Paper

(1892)

Charlotte Perkins Gilman

It is very seldom that mere ordinary people like John and myself secure ancestral halls for the summer.

A colonial mansion, a hereditary estate, I would say a haunted house, and reach the height of romantic felicity – but that would be asking too much of fate!

Still I will proudly declare that there is something queer about it.

Else, why should it be let so cheaply? And why have stood so long untenanted?

John laughs at me, of course, but one expects that in marriage.

John is practical in the extreme. He has no patience with faith, an intense horror of superstition, and he scoffs openly at any talk of things not to be felt and seen and put down in figures.

John is a physician, and *perhaps* – (I would not say it to a living soul, of course, but this is dead paper and a great relief to my mind) – *perhaps* that is one reason I do not get well faster.

You see, he does not believe I am sick!

And what can one do?

If a physician of high standing, and one's own husband, assures friends and relatives that there is really nothing the matter with one but temporary nervous depression – a slight hysterical tendency – what is one to do?

My brother is also a physician, and also of high standing, and he says the same thing.

So I take phosphates or phosphites – whichever it is – and tonics, and journeys, and air, and exercise, and am absolutely forbidden to 'work' until I am well again.

Personally I believe that congenial work, with excitement and change, would do me good.

But what is one to do?

I did write for a while in spite of them; but it *does* exhaust me a good deal – having to be so sly about it, or else meet with heavy opposition.

I sometimes fancy that in my condition if I had less opposition and more society and stimulus – but John says the very worst thing I can do is to think about my condition, and I confess it always makes me feel bad.

So I will let it alone and talk about the house.

The most beautiful place! It is quite alone, standing well back from the road, quite three miles from the village. It makes me think of English places that you read about, for there are hedges, and walls, and gates that lock, and lots of separate little houses for the gardeners and people.

There is a *delicious* garden! I never saw such a garden – large and shady, full of box-bordered paths, and lined with long grape-covered arbours and seats under them.

There were greenhouses, too, but they are all broken now.

There was some legal trouble, I believe, something about the heirs and co-heirs; anyhow, the place has been empty for years.

That spoils my ghostliness, I am afraid; but I don't care – there is something strange about the house – I can feel it.

I even said so to John one moonlight evening, but he said what I felt was a *draught*, and shut the window.

I get unreasonably angry with John sometimes. I'm sure I never used to be so sensitive. I think it is due to this nervous condition.

But John says if I feel so I shall neglect proper self-control; so I take pains to control myself – before him, at least, and that makes me very tired.

I don't like our room a bit. I wanted one downstairs that opened on the piazza and had roses all over the window, and such pretty, old-fashioned chintz hangings! But John would not hear of it.

He said there was only one window and not room for two beds, and no near room for him if he took another.

He is very careful and loving, and hardly lets me stir without special direction.

I have a schedule prescription for each hour in the day; he takes all care from me, and so I feel basely ungrateful not to value it more.

He said we came here solely on my account, that I was to have perfect rest and all the air I could get. 'Your exercise depends on your strength, my dear,' said he, 'and your food somewhat on your appetite; but air you can absorb all the time.' So we took the nursery, at the top of the house.

It is a big, airy room, the whole floor nearly, with windows that look all ways, and air and sunshine galore. It was nursery first and then playground and gymnasium, I should judge; for the windows are barred for little children, and there are rings and things in the walls.

The paint and paper look as if a boys' school had used it. It is stripped off – the paper – in great patches all around the head of my bed, about as far as I can reach, and in a great place on the other side of the room low down. I never saw a worse paper in my life.

One of those sprawling flamboyant patterns committing every artistic sin.

It is dull enough to confuse the eye in following, pronounced enough to constantly irritate, and provoke study, and when you follow the lame, uncertain curves for a little distance they suddenly commit suicide – plunge off at outrageous angles, destroy themselves in unheard – of contradictions.

The colour is repellent, almost revolting; a smouldering, unclean yellow, strangely faded by the slow-turning sunlight.

It is a dull yet lurid orange in some places, a sickly sulphur tint in others.

No wonder the children hated it! I should hate it myself if I had to live in this room long.

There comes John, and I must put this away – he hates to have me write a word.

We have been here two weeks, and I haven't felt like writing before, since that first day.

I am sitting by the window now, up in this atrocious nursery, and there is nothing to hinder my writing as much as I please, save lack of strength.

John is away all day, and even some nights when his cases are serious.

I am glad my case is not serious!

But these nervous troubles are dreadfully depressing.

John does not know how much I really suffer. He knows there is no *reason* to suffer, and that satisfies him.

Of course it is only nervousness. It does weigh on me so not to do my duty in any way!

I meant to be such a help to John, such a real rest and comfort, and here I am a comparative burden already!

Nobody would believe what an effort it is to do what little I am able – to dress and entertain, and order things.

It is fortunate Mary is so good with the baby. Such a dear baby! And yet I *cannot* be with him, it makes me so nervous.

I suppose John never was nervous in his life. He laughs at me so about this wall paper!

At first he meant to repaper the room, but afterwards, he said that I was letting it get the better of me, and that nothing was worse for a nervous patient than to give way to such fancies.

He said that after the wall paper was changed it would be the heavy bedstead, and then the barred windows, and then that gate at the head of the stairs, and so on.

'You know the place is doing you good,' he said, 'and really, dear, I don't care to renovate the house just for a three months' rental.'

'Then do let us go downstairs,' I said, 'there are such pretty rooms there.'

Then he took me in his arms and called me a blessed little goose, and said he would go down cellar if I wished, and would have it whitewashed into the bargain.

But he is right enough about the beds and windows and things.

It is as airy and comfortable a room as any one need wish, and of course, I would not be so silly as to make him uncomfortable just for a whim.

I'm really getting quite fond of the big room, all but that horrid paper.

Out of one window I can see the garden, those mysterious deep-shaded arbours, the riotous old-fashioned flowers, and bushes and gnarly trees.

Out of another I get a lovely view of the bay and a little private wharf belonging to the estate. There is a beautiful shaded lane that runs down there from the house. I always fancy I see people walking in these numerous paths and arbours, but John has cautioned me not to give way to fancy in the least. He says that with my imaginative power and habit of story-making a nervous weakness like mine is sure to lead to all manner of excited fancies, and that I ought to use my will and good sense to check the tendency. So I try.

I think sometimes that if I were only well enough to write a little it would relieve the press of ideas and rest me.

But I find I get pretty tired when I try.

It is so discouraging not to have any advice and companionship about my work. When I get really well John says we will ask Cousin Henry and Julia down for a long visit; but he says he would as soon put fireworks in my pillow-case as to let me have those stimulating people about now.

I wish I could get well faster.

But I must not think about that. This paper looks to me as if it *knew* what a vicious influence it had!

There is a recurrent spot where the pattern lolls like a broken neck and two bulbous eyes stare at you upside-down.

I got positively angry with the impertinence of it and the everlastingness. Up and down and sideways they crawl, and those absurd, unblinking eyes are everywhere. There is one place where two breadths didn't match, and the eyes go all up and down the line, one a little higher than the other.

I never saw so much expression in an inanimate thing before, and we all know how much expression they have!

I used to lie awake as a child and get more entertainment and terror out of blank walls and plain furniture than most children could find in a toy store.

I remember what a kindly wink the knobs of our big old bureau used to have, and there was one chair that always seemed like a strong friend.

I used to feel that if any of the other things looked too fierce I could always hop into that chair and be safe.

The furniture in this room is no worse than inharmonious, however, for we had to bring it all from downstairs. I suppose when this was used as a playroom they had to take the nursery things out, and no wonder! I never saw such ravages as the children have made here.

The wall paper, as I said before, is torn off in spots, and it sticketh closer than a brother – they must have had perseverance as well as hatred.

Then the floor is scratched and gouged and splintered, the plaster itself is dug out here and there, and this great heavy bed, which is all we found in the room, looks as if it had been through the wars.

But I don't mind it a bit – only the paper.

There comes John's sister. Such a dear girl as she is, and so careful of me! I must not let her find me writing.

She is a perfect, an enthusiastic housekeeper, and hopes for no better profession. I verily believe she thinks it is the writing which made me sick!

But I can write when she is out, and see her a long way off from these windows.

There is one that commands the road, a lovely, shaded, winding road, and one that just looks off over the country. A lovely country, too, full of great elms and velvet meadows.

This wall paper has a kind of sub-pattern in a different shade, a particularly irritating one, for you can only see it in certain lights, and not clearly then.

But in the places where it isn't faded, and where the sun is just so, I can see a strange, provoking, formless sort of figure, that seems to sulk about that silly and conspicuous front design.

There's Sister on the stairs!

Well, the Fourth of July is over! The people are all gone and I am tired out. John thought it might do me good to see a little company, so we just had Mother and Nellie and the children down for a week.

Of course I didn't do a thing. Jennie sees to everything now.

But it tired me all the same.

John says if I don't pick up faster he shall send me to Weir Mitchell in the fall.

But I don't want to go there at all. I had a friend who was in his hands once, and she says he is just like John and my brother, only more so!

Besides, it is such an undertaking to go so far.

I don't feel as if it was worth while to turn my hand over for anything, and I'm getting dreadfully fretful and querulous.

I cry at nothing, and cry most of the time.

Of course I don't when John is here, or anybody else, but when I am alone.

And I am alone a good deal just now, John is kept in town very often by serious cases, and Jennie is good and lets me alone when I want her to.

So I walk a little in the garden or down that lovely lane, sit on the porch under the roses, and lie down up here a good deal.

I'm getting really fond of the room in spite of the wall paper. Perhaps *because* of the wall paper.

It dwells in my mind so!

I lie here on this great immovable bed – it is nailed down, I believe – and follow that pattern about by the hour. It is as good as gymnastics, I assure you. I start, we'll say, at the bottom, down in the corner over there where it has not been touched, and I determine for the thousandth time that I *will* follow that pointless pattern to some sort of a conclusion.

I know a little of the principles of design, and I know this thing was not arranged on any laws of radiation, or alternation, or repetition, or symmetry, or anything else that I ever heard of.

It is repeated, of course, by the breadths, but not otherwise.

Looked at in one way, each breadth stands alone, the bloated curves and flourishes – a kind of 'debased Romanesque' with *delirium tremens* – go waddling up and down in isolated columns of fatuity.

But, on the other hand, they connect diagonally, and the sprawling outlines run off in great slanting waves of optic horror, like a lot of wallowing seaweeds in full chase.

The whole thing goes horizontally, too, at least it seems so, and I exhaust myself in trying to distinguish the order of its going in that direction.

They have used a horizontal breadth for a frieze, and that adds wonderfully to the confusion.

There is one end of the room where it is almost intact, and there, when the cross-lights fade and the low sun shines directly upon it, I can almost fancy radiation, after all – the interminable grotesques seem to form around a common centre and rush off in headlong plunges of equal distraction.

It makes me tired to follow it. I will take a nap, I guess.

I don't know why I should write this. I don't want to.

I don't feel able.

And I know John would think it absurd. But I *must* say what I feel and think in some way – it is such a relief!

But the effort is getting to be greater than the relief.

Half the time now I am awfully lazy, and lie down ever so much. John says I mustn't lose my strength, and has me take cod-liver oil and lots of tonics and things, to say nothing of ale and wine and rare meat.

Dear John! He loves me very dearly, and hates to have me sick. I tried to have a real earnest reasonable talk with him the other day, and tell him how I wished he would let me go and make a visit to Cousin Henry and Julia.

But he said I wasn't able to go, nor able to stand it after I got there; and I did not make out a very good case for myself, for I was crying before I had finished.

It is getting to be a great effort for me to think straight. Just this nervous weakness, I suppose.

And dear John gathered me up in his arms, and just carried me upstairs and laid me on the bed, and sat by me and read to me till he tired my head.

He said I was his darling and his comfort and all he had, and that I must take care of myself for his sake, and keep well.

He says no one but myself can help me out of it, that I must use my will and self-control and not let my silly fancies run away with me.

There's one comfort, the baby is well and happy, and does not have to occupy this nursery with the horrid wall paper.

If we had not used it that blessed child would have! What a fortunate escape! Why, I wouldn't have a child of mine, an impressionable little thing, live in such a room for worlds.

I never thought of it before, but it is lucky that John kept me here, after all. I can stand it so much easier than a baby, you see.

Of course I never mention it to them any more – I am too wise – but I keep watch of it all the same.

There are things in that paper that nobody knows but me, or ever will.

Behind that outside pattern the dim shapes get clearer every day.

It is always the same shape, only very numerous.

And it is like a woman stooping down and creeping about behind that pattern. I don't like it a bit. I wonder – I begin to think – I wish John would take me away from here!

It is so hard to talk with John about my case, because he is so wise, and because he loves me so.

But I tried it last night.

It was moonlight. The moon shines in all around, just as the sun does.

I hate to see it sometimes, it creeps so slowly, and always comes in by one window or another.

John was asleep and I hated to waken him, so I kept still and watched the moonlight on that undulating wall paper till I felt creepy.

The faint figure behind seemed to shake the pattern, just as if she wanted to get out.

I got up softly and went to feel and see if the paper *did* move, and when I came back John was awake.

'What is it, little girl?' he said. 'Don't go walking about like that – you'll get cold.'

I thought it was a good time to talk, so I told him that I really was not gaining here, and that I wished he would take me away.

'Why, darling!' said he, 'our lease will be up in three weeks, and I can't see how to leave before.

'The repairs are not done at home, and I cannot possibly leave town just now. Of course if you were in any danger I could and would, but you really are better, dear, whether you can see it or not. I am a doctor, dear, and I know. You are gaining flesh and colour, your appetite is better. I feel really much easier about you.'

'I don't weigh a bit more,' said I, 'nor as much; and my appetite may be better in the evening, when you are here, but it is worse in the morning, when you are away.'

'Bless her little heart!' said he with a big hug; 'she shall be as sick as she pleases. But now let's improve the shining hours by going to sleep, and talk about it in the morning.'

'And you won't go away?' I asked gloomily.

'Why, how can I, dear? It is only three weeks more and then we will take a nice little trip of a few days while Jennie is getting the house ready. Really, dear, you are better!'

'Better in body, perhaps—' I began, and stopped short, for he sat up straight and looked at me with such a stern, reproachful look that I could not say another word.

'My darling,' said he, 'I beg of you, for my sake and for our child's sake, as well as for your own, that you will never for one instant let that idea enter your mind! There is nothing so dangerous, so fascinating, to a temperament like yours. It is a false and foolish fancy. Can you not trust me as a physician when I tell you so?'

So of course I said no more on that score, and we went to sleep before long. He thought I was asleep first, but I wasn't – I lay there for hours trying to decide whether that front pattern and the back pattern really did move together or separately.

On a pattern like this, by daylight, there is a lack of sequence, a defiance of law, that is a constant irritant to a normal mind.

The colour is hideous enough, and unreliable enough, and infuriating enough, but the pattern is torturing.

You think you have mastered it, but just as you get well under way in following, it turns a back somersault, and there you are. It slaps you in the face, knocks you down, and tramples upon you. It is like a bad dream.

The outside pattern is a florid arabesque, reminding one of a fungus. If you can imagine a toadstool in joints, an interminable string of toadstools, budding and sprouting in endless convolutions – why, that is something like it.

That is, sometimes!

There is one marked peculiarity about this paper, a thing nobody seems to notice but myself, and that is that it changes as the light changes.

When the sun shoots in through the east window – I always watch for that first long, straight ray – it changes so quickly that I never can quite believe it.

That is why I watch it always.

By moonlight – the moon shines in all night when there is a moon – I wouldn't know it was the same paper.

At night in any kind of light, in twilight, candlelight, lamplight, and worst of all by moonlight, it becomes bars! The outside pattern, I mean, and the woman behind it is as plain as can be.

I didn't realise for a long time what the thing was that showed behind – that dim sub-pattern – but now I am quite sure it is a woman.

By daylight she is subdued, quiet. I fancy it is the pattern that keeps her so still. It is so puzzling. It keeps me quiet by the hour.

I lie down ever so much now. John says it is good for me, and to sleep all I can.

Indeed, he started the habit by making me lie down for an hour after each meal.

It is a very bad habit, I am convinced, for, you see, I don't sleep.

And that cultivates deceit, for I don't tell them I'm awake – oh, no!

The fact is, I am getting a little afraid of John.

He seems very queer sometimes, and even Jennie has an inexplicable look.

It strikes me occasionally, just as a scientific hypothesis, that perhaps it is the paper!

I have watched John when he did not know I was looking, and come into the room suddenly on the most innocent excuses, and I've caught him several times *looking at the paper!* And Jennie too. I caught Jennie with her hand on it once.

She didn't know I was in the room, and when I asked her in a quiet, a very quiet voice, with the most restrained manner possible, what she was doing with the paper she turned around as if she had been caught stealing, and looked quite angry – asked me why I should frighten her so!

Then she said that the paper stained everything it touched, and that she had found yellow smooches on all my clothes and John's, and she wished we would be more careful!

Did not that sound innocent? But I know she was studying that pattern, and I am determined that nobody shall find it out but myself!

*

Life is very much more exciting now than it used to be. You see I have something more to expect, to look forward to, to watch. I really do eat better, and am more quiet than I was.

John is so pleased to see me improve! He laughed a little the other day, and said I seemed to be flourishing in spite of my wall paper.

I turned it off with a laugh. I had no intention of telling him that it was *because* of the wall paper – he would make fun of me. He might even want to take me away.

I don't want to leave now until I have found it out. There is a week more, and I think that will be enough.

I'm feeling ever so much better! I don't sleep much at night, for it is so interesting to watch developments; but I sleep a good deal in the daytime.

In the daytime it is tiresome and perplexing.

There are always new shoots on the fungus, and new shades of yellow all over it. I cannot keep count of them, though I have tried conscientiously.

It is the strangest yellow, that wall paper! It makes me think of all the yellow things I ever saw – not beautiful ones like buttercups, but old foul, bad yellow things.

But there is something else about that paper – the smell! I noticed it the moment we came into the room, but with so much air and sun it was not bad. Now we have had a week of fog and rain, and whether the windows are open or not the smell is here.

It creeps all over the house.

I find it hovering in the dining-room, skulking in the parlour, hiding in the hall, lying in wait for me on the stairs.

It gets into my hair.

Even when I go to ride, if I turn my head suddenly and surprise it – there is that smell!

Such a peculiar odour, too! I have spent hours in trying to analyse it, to find what it smelled like.

It is not bad – at first, and very gentle, but quite the subtlest, most enduring odour I ever met.

In this damp weather it is awful. I wake up in the night and find it hanging over me.

It used to disturb me at first. I thought seriously of burning the house – to reach the smell.

But now I am used to it. The only thing I can think of that it is like is the *colour* of the paper – a yellow smell!

There is a very funny mark on this wall, low down, near the mopboard. A streak that runs around the room. It goes behind every piece of furniture, except the bed, a long, straight, even *smooch*, as if it had been rubbed over and over.

I wonder how it was done and who did it, and what they did it for. Round and round and round – round and round and round – it makes me dizzy!

I really have discovered something at last.

Through watching so much at night, when it changes so, I have finally found out.

The front pattern *does* move – and no wonder! The woman behind shakes it!

Sometimes I think there are a great many women behind, and sometimes only one, and she crawls around fast, and her crawling shakes it all over.

Then in the very bright spots she keeps still, and in the very shady spots she just takes hold of the bars and shakes them hard.

And she is all the time trying to climb through. But nobody could climb through that pattern – it strangles so; I think that is why it has so many heads.

They get through, and then the pattern strangles them off and turns them upside-down, and makes their eyes white!

If those heads were covered or taken off it would not be half so bad.

I think that woman gets out in the daytime!

And I'll tell you why – privately – I've seen her!

I can see her out of every one of my windows!

It is the same woman, I know, for she is always creeping, and most women do not creep by daylight.

I see her in that long shaded lane, creeping up and down. I see her in those dark grape arbours, creeping all around the garden.

I see her on that long road under the trees, creeping along, and when a carriage comes she hides under the blackberry vines.

I don't blame her a bit. It must be very humiliating to be caught creeping by daylight!

I always lock the door when I creep by daylight. I can't do it at night, for I know John would suspect something at once.

And John is so queer, now, that I don't want to irritate him. I wish he would take another room! Besides, I don't want anybody to get that woman out at night but myself.

I often wonder if I could see her out of all the windows at once.

But, turn as fast as I can, I can only see out of one at one time.

And though I always see her she *may* be able to creep faster than I can turn!

I have watched her sometimes away off in the open country, creeping as fast as a cloud shadow in a high wind.

If only that top pattern could be gotten off from the under one! I mean to try it, little by little.

I have found out another funny thing, but I sha'n't tell it this time! It does not do to trust people too much.

There are only two more days to get this paper off, and I believe John is beginning to notice. I don't like the look in his eyes.

And I heard him ask Jennie a lot of professional questions about me. She had a very good report to give.

She said I slept a good deal in the daytime.

John knows I don't sleep very well at night, for all I'm so quiet!

He asked me all sorts of questions, too, and pretended to be very loving and kind.

As if I couldn't see through him!

Still, I don't wonder he acts so, sleeping under this paper for three months.

It only interests me, but I feel sure John and Jennie are secretly affected by it.

Hurrah! This is the last day, but it is enough. John is to stay in town over night, and won't be out until this evening.

Jennie wanted to sleep with me – the sly thing! but I told her I should undoubtedly rest better for a night all alone.

That was clever, for really I wasn't alone a bit! As soon as it was moonlight, and that poor thing began to crawl and shake the pattern, I got up and ran to help her.

I pulled and she shook, I shook and she pulled, and before morning we had peeled off yards of that paper.

A strip about as high as my head and half around the room.

And then when the sun came and that awful pattern began to laugh at me I declared I would finish it today!

We go away tomorrow, and they are moving all my furniture down again to leave things as they were before.

Jennie looked at the wall in amazement, but I told her merrily that I did it out of pure spite at the vicious thing.

She laughed and said she wouldn't mind doing it herself, but I must not get tired.

How she betrayed herself that time!

But I am here, and no person touches this paper but me – not *alive!*

She tried to get me out of the room – it was too patent! But I said it was so quiet and empty and clean now that I believed I would lie down again and sleep all I could; and not to wake me even for dinner – I would call when I woke.

So now she is gone, and the servants are gone, and the things are gone, and there is nothing left but that great bedstead nailed down, with the canvas mattress we found on it.

We shall sleep downstairs tonight, and take the boat home tomorrow.

I quite enjoy the room, now it is bare again.

How those children did tear about here!

This bedstead is fairly gnawed!

But I must get to work.

I have locked the door and thrown the key down into the front path.

I don't want to go out, and I don't want to have anybody come in, till John comes.

I want to astonish him.

I've got a rope up here that even Jennie did not find. If that woman does get out, and tries to get away, I can tie her!

But I forgot I could not reach far without anything to stand on!

This bed will *not* move!

I tried to lift and push it until I was lame, and then I got so angry I bit off a little piece at one corner – but it hurt my teeth.

Then I peeled off all the paper I could reach standing on the floor. It sticks horribly and the pattern just enjoys it! All those strangled heads and bulbous eyes and waddling fungus growths just shriek with derision!

I am getting angry enough to do something desperate. To jump out of the window would be admirable exercise, but the bars are too strong even to try.

Besides, I wouldn't do it. Of course not. I know well enough that a step like that is improper and might be misconstrued.

I don't like to *look* out of the windows even – there are so many of those creeping women, and they creep so fast.

I wonder if they all come out of that wallpaper, as I did?

But I am securely fastened now by my well-hidden rope – you don't get *me* out in the road there!

I suppose I shall have to get back behind the pattern when it comes night, and that is hard!

It is so pleasant to be out in this great room and creep around as I please!

I don't want to go outside. I won't, even if Jennie asks me to.

For outside you have to creep on the ground, and everything is green instead of yellow.

But here I can creep smoothly on the floor, and my shoulder just fits in that long smooch around the wall, so I cannot lose my way.

Why, there's John at the door!

It is no use, young man, you can't open it!

How he does call and pound!

Now he's crying for an axe.

It would be a shame to break down that beautiful door!

'John, dear!' said I in the gentlest voice, 'the key is down by the front steps, under a plantain leaf!'

That silenced him for a few moments.

Then he said – very quietly indeed, 'Open the door, my darling!'

'I can't,' said I. 'The key is down by the front door, under a plaintain leaf!'

And then I said it again, several times, very gently and slowly, and said it so often that he had to go and see, and he got it, of course, and came in. He stopped short by the door.

'What is the matter?' he cried. 'For God's sake, what are you doing?'

I kept on creeping just the same, but I looked at him over my shoulder.

'I've got out at last,' said I, 'in spite of you and Jennie! And I've pulled off most of the paper, so you can't put me back!'

Now why should that man have fainted? But he did, and right across my path by the wall, so that I had to creep over him every time!

6

The Son's Veto

(1894)

Thomas Hardy

I

To the eyes of a man viewing it from behind, the nut-brown hair was a wonder and a mystery. Under the black beaver hat surmounted by its tuft of black feathers, the long locks, braided and twisted and coiled like the rushes of a basket, composed a rare, if somewhat barbaric, example of ingenious art. One could understand such weavings and coilings being wrought to last intact for a year, or even a calendar month; but that they should be all demolished regularly at bedtime, after a single day of permanence, seemed a reckless waste of successful fabrication.

And she had done it all herself, poor thing. She had no maid, and it was almost the only accomplishment she could boast of. Hence the unstinted pains.

She was a young invalid lady – not so very much of an invalid – sitting in a wheeled chair, which had been pulled up in the front part of a green enclosure, close to a bandstand where a concert was going on, during a warm June afternoon. It had place in one of the minor parks or private gardens that are to be found in the suburbs of London, and was the effort of a local association to raise money for some charity. There are worlds within worlds in the great city, and though nobody outside the immediate district had ever heard of the charity, or the band, or the garden, the enclosure was filled with an interested audience sufficiently informed on all these.

As the strains proceeded many of the listeners observed the chaired lady, whose back hair, by reason of her prominent position, so challenged inspection. Her face was not easily discernible, but the aforesaid cunning tress-weavings, the white ear and poll, and the curve of a cheek which was neither flaccid nor sallow, were signals that led to the expectation of good beauty in front. Such expectations are not infrequently disappointed as soon as the disclosure comes; and in the present case, when the lady, by a turn of the head, at length revealed herself, she was not so handsome as the people behind her had supposed, and even hoped – they did not know why.

For one thing (alas! the commonness of this complaint), she was less young than they had fancied her to be. Yet attractive her face unquestionably was, and not at all sickly.

The revelation of its details came each time she turned to talk to a boy of twelve or thirteen who stood beside her, and the shape of whose hat and jacket implied that he belonged to a well-known public school. The immediate bystanders could hear that he called her 'Mother'.

When the end of the recital was reached, and the audience withdrew, many chose to find their way out by passing at her elbow. Almost all turned their heads to take a full and near look at the interesting woman, who remained stationary in the chair till the way should be clear enough for her to be wheeled out without obstruction. As if she expected their glances, and did not mind gratifying their curiosity, she met the eyes of several of her observers by lifting her own, showing these to be soft, brown, and affectionate orbs, a little plaintive in their regard.

She was conducted out of the gardens, and passed along the pavement till she disappeared from view, the schoolboy walking beside her. To inquiries made by some persons who watched her away, the answer came that she was the second wife of the incumbent of a neighbouring parish, and that she was lame. She was generally believed to be a woman with a story – an innocent one, but a story of some sort or other.

In conversing with her on their way home the boy who walked at her elbow said that he hoped his father had not missed them.

'He have been so comfortable these last few hours that I am sure he cannot have missed us,' she replied.

'*Has*, dear mother – not *have*!' exclaimed the public-school boy, with an impatient fastidiousness that was almost harsh. 'Surely you know that by this time!'

His mother hastily adopted the correction, and did not resent his making it, or retaliate, as she might well have done, by bidding him to wipe that crumby mouth of his, whose condition had been caused by surreptitious attempts to eat a piece of cake without taking it out of the pocket wherein it lay concealed. After this the pretty woman and the boy went onward in silence.

That question of grammar bore upon her history, and she fell into reverie, of a somewhat sad kind to all appearance. It might have been assumed that she was wondering if she had done wisely in shaping her life as she had shaped it, to bring out such a result as this.

In a remote nook in North Wessex, forty miles from London, near the thriving county-town of Aldbrickham, there stood a pretty village with its church and parsonage, which she knew well enough, but her son had never seen. It was her native village, Gaymead, and the first event bearing upon her present situation had occurred at that place when she was only a girl of nineteen.

How well she remembered it, that first act in her little tragi-comedy, the death of her reverend husband's first wife. It happened on a spring evening, and she who now and for many years had filled that first wife's place was then parlour-maid in the parson's house.

When everything had been done that could be done, and the death was announced, she had gone out in the dusk to visit her parents, who were living in the same village, to tell them the sad news. As she opened the white swing-gate and looked towards the trees which rose westward, shutting out the pale light of the evening sky, she discerned, without much surprise, the figure of a man standing in the hedge, though she roguishly exclaimed as a matter of form, ‘O, Sam, how you frightened me!’

He was a young gardener of her acquaintance. She told him the particulars of the late event, and they stood silent, these two young people, in that elevated, calmly philosophic mind which is engendered when a tragedy has happened close at hand, and has not happened to the philosophers themselves. But it had its bearing upon their relations.

‘And will you stay on now at the Vicarage, just the same?’ asked he.

She had hardly thought of that. ‘O yes – I suppose!’ she said. ‘Everything will be just as usual, I imagine?’

He walked beside her towards her mother’s. Presently his arm stole round her waist. She gently removed it; but he placed it there again, and she yielded the point. ‘You see, dear Sophy, you don’t know that you’ll stay on; you may want a home, and I shall be ready to offer one some day, though I may not be ready just yet.’

‘Why, Sam, how can you be so fast! I’ve never even said I liked ’ee; and it is all your own doing, coming after me!’

‘Still, it is nonsense to say I am not to have a try at you like the rest.’ He stooped to kiss her a farewell, for they had reached her mother’s door.

‘No, Sam; you shan’t!’ she cried, putting her hand over his mouth. ‘You ought to be more serious on such a night as this.’ And she bade him adieu without allowing him to kiss her or to come indoors.

The vicar just left a widower was at this time a man about forty years of age, of good family, and childless. He had led a secluded existence in this college living, partly because there were no resident landowners; and his loss now intensified his habit of withdrawal from outward observation. He was seen still less than heretofore, kept himself still less in time with the rhythm and racket of the movements called progress in the world without. For many months after his wife’s decease the economy of his household remained as before; the cook, the housemaid, the parlour-maid, and the man out-of-doors performed their duties or left them undone, just as nature prompted them – the vicar knew not which. It was then represented to him that his servants seemed to have nothing to do in his small family of one. He was struck with the truth of this representation, and decided to cut down his establishment. But he was forestalled by Sophy, the parlour-maid, who said one evening that she wished to leave him.

‘And why?’ said the parson.

‘Sam Hobson has asked me to marry him, sir.’

‘Well – do you want to marry?’

‘Not much. But it would be a home for me. And we have heard that one of us will have to leave.’

A day or two after she said: ‘I don’t want to leave just yet, sir, if you don’t wish it. Sam and I have quarrelled.’

He looked up at her. He had hardly ever observed her before, though he had been frequently conscious of her soft presence in the room. What a kitten-like, flexuous, tender creature she was! She was the only one of the servants with whom he came into immediate and continuous relation. What should he do if Sophy were gone?

Sophy did not go, but one of the others did, and things went on quietly again.

When Mr Twycott, the vicar, was ill, Sophy brought up his meals to him, and she had no sooner left the room one day than he heard a noise on the stairs. She had slipped down with the tray, and so twisted her foot that she could not stand. The village surgeon was called in; the vicar got better, but Sophy was incapacitated for a long time; and she was informed that she must never again walk much or engage in any occupation which required her to stand long on her feet. As soon as she was comparatively well she spoke to him alone. Since she was forbidden to walk and bustle about, and, indeed, could not do so, it became her duty to leave. She could very well work at something sitting down, and she had an aunt a seamstress.

The parson had been very greatly moved by what she had suffered on his account, and he exclaimed, 'No, Sophy; lame or not lame, I cannot let you go. You must never leave me again!'

He came close to her, and, though she could never exactly tell how it happened, she became conscious of his lips upon her cheek. He then asked her to marry him. Sophy did not exactly love him, but she had a respect for him which almost amounted to veneration. Even if she had wished to get away from him she hardly dared refuse a personage so reverend and august in her eyes, and she assented forthwith to be his wife.

Thus it happened that one fine morning, when the doors of the church were naturally open for ventilation, and the singing birds fluttered in and alighted on the tie-beams of the roof, there was a marriage-service at the communion-rails, which hardly a soul knew of. The parson and a neighbouring curate had entered at one door, and Sophy at another, followed by two necessary persons, whereupon in a short time there emerged a newly-made husband and wife.

Mr Twycott knew perfectly well that he had committed social suicide by this step, despite Sophy's spotless character, and he had taken his measures accordingly. An exchange of livings had been arranged with an acquaintance who was incumbent of a church in the south of London, and as soon as possible the couple removed thither, abandoning their pretty country home, with trees and shrubs and glebe, for a narrow, dusty house in a long, straight street, and their fine peal of bells for the wretchedest one-tongued clangour that ever tortured mortal ears. It was all on her account. They were, however, away from every one who had known her former position; and also under less observation from without than they would have had to put up with in any country parish.

Sophy the woman was as charming a partner as a man could possess, though Sophy the lady had her deficiencies. She showed a natural aptitude for little domestic refinements, so far as related to things and manners; but in what is called culture she was less intuitive. She had now been married more than fourteen years, and her husband had taken much trouble with her education; but she still held confused ideas on the use of 'was' and 'were', which did not beget a respect for her among the few acquaintances she made. Her great grief in this relation was that her only child, on whose education no expense had been and would be spared, was now old enough to perceive these deficiencies in his mother, and not only to see them but to feel irritated at their existence.

Thus she lived on in the city, and wasted hours in braiding her beautiful hair, till her once apple cheeks waned to pink of the very faintest. Her foot had never regained its natural strength after the accident, and she was mostly obliged to avoid walking altogether. Her husband had grown to like London for its freedom and its domestic privacy; but he was twenty years his Sophy's senior, and had latterly been seized with a serious illness. On this day, however, he had seemed to be well enough to justify her accompanying her son Randolph to the concert.

II

The next time we get a glimpse of her is when she appears in the mournful attire of a widow.

Mr Twycott had never rallied, and now lay in a well-packed cemetery to the south of the great city, where, if all the dead it contained had stood erect and alive, not one would have known him or recognised his name. The boy had dutifully followed him to the grave, and was now again at school.

Throughout these changes Sophy had been treated like the child she was in nature though not in years. She was left with no control over anything that had been her husband's beyond her modest personal income. In his anxiety lest her inexperience should be overreached he had safeguarded with trustees all he possibly could. The completion of the boy's course at the public school, to be followed in due time by Oxford and ordination, had been all previsioned and arranged, and she really had nothing to occupy her in the world but to eat and drink, and make a business of indolence, and go on weaving and coiling the nut-brown hair, merely keeping a home open for the son whenever he came to her during vacations.

Foreseeing his probable decease long years before her, her husband in his lifetime had purchased for her use a semi-detached villa in the same long, straight road whereon the church and parsonage faced, which was to be hers as long as she chose to live in it. Here she now resided, looking out upon the fragment of lawn in front, and through the railings at the ever-flowing traffic; or, bending forward over the window-sill on the first floor, stretching her eyes far up and down the vista of sooty trees, hazy air, and drab house-façades, along which echoed the noises common to a suburban main thoroughfare.

Somehow, her boy, with his aristocratic school-knowledge, his grammars, and his aversions, was losing those wide infantine sympathies, extending as far as to the sun and moon themselves, with which he, like other children, had been born, and which his mother, a child of nature herself, had loved in him; he was reducing their compass to a population of a few thousand wealthy and titled people, the mere veneer of a thousand million or so of others who did not interest him at all. He drifted further and further away from her. Sophy's *milieu* being a suburb of minor tradesmen and under-clerks, and her almost only companions the two servants of her own house, it was not surprising that after her husband's death she soon lost the little artificial tastes she had acquired from him, and became – in her son's eyes – a mother whose mistakes and origin it was his painful lot as a gentleman to blush for. As yet he was far from being man enough – if he ever would be – to rate these sins of hers at their true infinitesimal value beside the yearning fondness that welled up and remained penned in her heart till it should be more fully accepted by him, or by some other person or thing. If he had lived at home with her he would have had all of it; but he seemed to require so very little in present circumstances, and it remained stored.

Her life became insupportably dreary; she could not take walks, and had no interest in going for drives, or, indeed, in travelling anywhere. Nearly two years passed without an event, and still she looked on that suburban road, thinking of the village in which she had been born, and whither she would have gone back – O how gladly! – even to work in the fields.

Taking no exercise she often could not sleep, and would rise in the night or early morning to look out upon the then vacant thoroughfare, where the lamps stood like sentinels waiting for some procession to go by. An approximation to such a procession was indeed made early every morning about one o'clock, when the country vehicles passed up with loads of vegetables for Covent Garden market. She often saw them creeping along at this silent and dusky hour – waggon after waggon, bearing green bastions of cabbages nodding to their fall, yet never falling, walls of baskets enclosing masses of beans and peas, pyramids of snow-white turnips, swaying howdahs of mixed produce – creeping along behind aged night-horses, who seemed ever patiently wondering between their hollow coughs why they had always to work at that still hour when all other sentient creatures were privileged to rest. Wrapped in a cloak it was soothing to watch and sympathise with them when depression and nervousness hindered sleep, and to see how the fresh green-stuff brightened to life as it came opposite the lamp, and how the sweating animals steamed and shone with their miles of travel.

They had an interest, almost a charm, for Sophy, these semi-rural people and vehicles moving in an urban atmosphere, leading a life quite distinct from that of the daytime toilers on the same road. One morning a man who accompanied a waggon-load of potatoes gazed rather hard at the house-fronts as he passed, and with a curious emotion she thought his form was familiar to her. She looked out for him again. His being an old-fashioned conveyance, with a yellow front, it was easily recognisable, and on the third night after she saw it a second time. The man alongside was, as she had fancied, Sam Hobson, formerly gardener at Gaymead, who would at one time have married her.

She had occasionally thought of him, and wondered if life in a cottage with him would not have been a happier lot than the life she had accepted. She had not thought of him passionately, but her now dismal situation lent an interest to his resurrection – a tender interest which it is impossible to exaggerate. She went back to bed, and began thinking. When did these market-gardeners, who travelled up to town so regularly at one or two in the morning, come back? She dimly recollected seeing their empty waggons, hardly noticeable amid the ordinary day-traffic, passing down at some hour before noon.

It was only April, but that morning, after breakfast, she had the window opened, and sat looking out, the feeble sun shining full upon her. She affected to sew, but her eyes never left the street. Between ten and eleven the desired waggon, now unladen, reappeared on its return journey. But Sam was not looking round him then, and drove on in a reverie.

'Sam!' cried she.

Turning with a start, his face lighted up. He called to him a little boy to hold the horse, alighted, and came and stood under the window.

'I can't come down easily, Sam, or I would!' she said. 'Did you know I lived here?'

'Well, Mrs Twycott, I knew you lived along here somewhere. I have often looked out for 'ee.'

He briefly explained his own presence on the scene. He had long since given up his gardening in the village near Aldbrickham, and was now manager at a market-gardener's on the south side of London, it being part of his duty to go up to Covent Garden with waggon-loads of produce two or three times a week. In answer to her curious inquiry, he admitted that he had come to this particular district because he had seen in the Aldbrickham paper, a year or two before, the announcement of the death in South London of the aforetime vicar of Gaymead, which had revived an interest in her dwelling-place that he could not extinguish, leading him to hover about the locality till his present post had been secured.

They spoke of their native village in dear old North Wessex, the spots in which they had played together as children. She tried to feel that she was a dignified personage now, that she must not be too confidential with Sam. But she could not keep it up, and the tears hanging in her eyes were indicated in her voice.

'You are not happy, Mrs Twycott, I'm afraid?' he said.

'O, of course not! I lost my husband only the year before last.'

'Ah! I meant in another way. You'd like to be home again?'

'This is my home – for life. The house belongs to me. But I understand—' She let it out then. 'Yes, Sam. I long for home – *our* home! I *should* like to be there, and never leave it, and die there.' But she remembered herself. 'That's only a momentary feeling. I have a son, you know, a dear boy. He's at school now.'

'Somewhere handy, I suppose? I see there's lots on 'em along this road.'

'O no! Not in one of these wretched holes! At a public school – one of the most distinguished in England.'

'Chok' it all! of course! I forget, ma'am, that you've been a lady for so many years.'

'No, I am not a lady,' she said sadly. 'I never shall be. But he's a gentleman, and that – makes it – O how difficult for me!'

III

The acquaintance thus oddly reopened proceeded apace. She often looked out to get a few words with him by night or by day. Her sorrow was that she could not accompany her one old friend on foot a little way, and talk more freely than she could do while he paused before the house. One night, at the beginning of June, when she was again on the watch after an absence of some days from the window, he entered the gate and said softly, 'Now, wouldn't some air do you good? I've only half a load this morning. Why not ride up to Covent Garden with me? There's a nice seat on the cabbages, where I've spread a sack. You can be home again in a cab before anybody is up.'

She refused at first, and then, trembling with excitement, hastily finished her dressing, and wrapped herself up in cloak and veil, afterwards sidling downstairs by the aid of the handrail, in a way she could adopt on an emergency. When she had opened the door she found Sam on the step, and he lifted her bodily on his strong arm across the little forecourt into his vehicle. Not a soul was visible or audible in the infinite length of the straight, flat highway, with its ever-waiting lamps converging to points in each direction. The air was fresh as country air at this hour, and the stars shone, except to the north-eastward, where there was a whitish light – the dawn. Sam carefully placed her in the seat and drove on.

They talked as they had talked in old days, Sam pulling himself up now and then, when he thought himself too familiar. More than once she said with misgiving that she wondered if she ought to have indulged in the freak. 'But I am so lonely in my house,' she added, 'and this makes me so happy!'

'You must come again, dear Mrs Twycott. There is no time o' day for taking the air like this.'

It grew lighter and lighter. The sparrows became busy in the streets, and the city waxed denser around them. When they approached the river it was day, and on the bridge they beheld the full blaze of morning sunlight in the direction of St Paul's, the river glistening towards it, and not a craft stirring.

Near Covent Garden he put her into a cab, and they parted, looking into each other's faces like the very old friends they were. She reached home without adventure, limped to the door, and let herself in with her latch-key unseen.

The air and Sam's presence had revived her: her cheeks were quite pink – almost beautiful. She had something to live for in addition to her son. A woman of pure instincts, she knew there had been nothing really wrong in the journey, but supposed it conventionally to be very wrong indeed.

Soon, however, she gave way to the temptation of going with him again, and on this occasion their conversation was distinctly tender, and Sam said he never should forget her, notwithstanding that she had served him rather badly at one time. After much hesitation he told her of a plan it was in his power to carry out, and one he should like to take in hand, since he did not care for London work: it was to set up as a master greengrocer down at Aldbrickham, the county-town of their native place. He knew of an opening – a shop kept by aged people who wished to retire.

'And why don't you do it, then, Sam?' she asked with a slight heartsinking.

'Because I'm not sure if – you'd join me. I know you wouldn't – couldn't! Such a lady as ye've been so long, you couldn't be a wife to a man like me.'

'I hardly suppose I could!' she assented, also frightened at the idea.

'If you could,' he said eagerly, 'you'd on'y have to sit in the back parlour and look through the glass partition when I was away sometimes – just to keep an eye on things. The lameness wouldn't hinder that . . . I'd keep you as genteel as ever I could, dear Sophy – if I might think of it!' he pleaded.

'Sam, I'll be frank,' she said, putting her hand on his. 'If it were only myself I would do it, and gladly, though everything I possess would be lost to me by marrying again.'

'I don't mind that! It's more independent.'

'That's good of you, dear, dear Sam. But there's something else. I have a son . . . I almost fancy when I am miserable sometimes that he is not really mine, but one I hold in trust for my late husband. He seems to belong so little to me personally, so entirely to his dead father. He is so much educated and I so little that I do not feel dignified enough to be his mother . . . Well, he would have to be told.'

'Yes. Unquestionably.' Sam saw her thought and her fear. 'Still, you can do as you like, Sophy – Mrs Twycott,' he added. 'It is not you who are the child, but he.'

'Ah, you don't know! Sam, if I could, I would marry you, some day. But you must wait a while, and let me think.'

It was enough for him, and he was blithe at their parting. Not so she. To tell Randolph seemed impossible. She could wait till he had gone up to Oxford, when what she did would affect his life but little. But would he ever tolerate the idea? And if not, could she defy him?

She had not told him a word when the yearly cricket-match came on at Lord's between the public schools, though Sam had already gone back to Aldbrickham. Mrs Twycott felt stronger than usual: she went to the match with Randolph, and was able to leave her chair and walk about occasionally. The bright idea occurred to her that she could casually broach the subject while moving round among the spectators, when the boy's spirits were high with interest in the game, and he would weigh domestic matters as feathers in the scale beside the day's victory. They promenaded under the lurid July sun, this pair, so wide apart, yet so near, and Sophy saw the large proportion of boys like her own, in their broad white collars and dwarf hats, and all around the rows of great coaches under which was jumbled the *débris* of luxurious luncheons: bones, pie-crusts, champagne-bottles, glasses, plates, napkins, and the family silver; while on the coaches sat the proud fathers and mothers; but never a poor mother like her. If Randolph had not appertained to these, had not centred all his interests in them, had not cared exclusively for the class they belonged to, how happy would things have been! A great huzza at some small performance with the bat burst from the multitude of relatives, and Randolph jumped wildly into the air to see what had happened. Sophy fetched up the sentence that had been already shaped; but she could not get it out. The occasion was, perhaps, an inopportune one. The contrast between her story and the display of fashion to which Randolph had grown to regard himself as akin would be fatal. She awaited a better time.

It was on an evening when they were alone in their plain suburban residence, where life was not blue but brown, that she ultimately broke silence, qualifying her announcement of a probable second marriage by assuring him that it would not take place for a long time to come, when he would be living quite independently of her.

The boy thought the idea a very reasonable one, and asked if she had chosen anybody. She hesitated; and he seemed to have a misgiving. He hoped his stepfather would be a gentleman, he said.

'Not what you call a gentleman,' she answered timidly. 'He'll be much as I was before I knew your father'; and by degrees she acquainted him with the whole. The youth's face remained fixed for a moment; then he flushed, leant on the table, and burst into passionate tears.

His mother went up to him, kissed all of his face that she could get at, and patted his back as if he were still the baby he once had been, crying herself the while. When he had somewhat recovered from his paroxysm he went hastily to his own room and fastened the door.

Parleyings were attempted through the keyhole, outside which she waited and listened. It was long before he would reply, and when he did it was to say sternly at her from within: 'I am ashamed of you! It will ruin me! A miserable boor! a churl! a clown! It will degrade me in the eyes of all the gentlemen of England!'

'Say no more – perhaps I am wrong! I will struggle against it!' she cried miserably.

Before Randolph left her that summer a letter arrived from Sam to inform her that he had been unexpectedly fortunate in obtaining the shop. He was in possession; it was the largest in the town, combining fruit with vegetables, and he thought it would form a home worthy even of her some day. Might he not run up to town to see her?

She met him by stealth, and said he must still wait for her final answer. The autumn dragged on, and when Randolph was home at Christmas for the holidays she broached the matter again. But the young gentleman was inexorable.

It was dropped for months; renewed again; abandoned under his repugnance; again attempted; and thus the gentle creature reasoned and pleaded till four or five long years had passed. Then the faithful Sam revived his suit with some peremptoriness. Sophy's son, now an undergraduate, was down from Oxford one Easter, when she again opened the subject. As soon as he was ordained, she argued, he would have a home of his own, wherein she, with her bad grammar and her ignorance, would be an encumbrance to him. Better obliterate her as much as possible.

He showed a more manly anger now, but would not agree. She on her side was more persistent, and he had doubts whether she could be trusted in his absence. But by indignation and contempt for her taste he completely maintained his ascendency; and finally taking her before a little cross and altar that he had erected in his bedroom for his private devotions, there bade her kneel, and swear that she would not wed Samuel Hobson without his consent. 'I owe this to my father!' he said.

The poor woman swore, thinking he would soften as soon as he was ordained and in full swing of clerical work. But he did not. His education had by this time sufficiently ousted his humanity to keep him quite firm; though his mother might have led an idyllic life with her faithful fruiterer and greengrocer, and nobody have been anything the worse in the world.

Her lameness became more confirmed as time went on, and she seldom or never left the house in the long southern thoroughfare, where she seemed to be pining her heart away. 'Why mayn't I say to Sam that I'll marry him? Why mayn't I?' she would murmur plaintively to herself when nobody was near.

Some four years after this date a middle-aged man was standing at the door of the largest fruiterer's shop in Aldbrickham. He was the proprietor, but to-day, instead of his usual business attire, he wore a neat suit of black; and his window was partly shuttered. From the railway-station a funeral procession was seen approaching: it passed his door and went out of the town towards the village of Gaymead. The man, whose eyes were wet, held his hat in his hand as the vehicles moved by; while from the mourning-coach a young smooth-shaven priest in a high waistcoat looked black as a cloud at the shopkeeper standing there.

7

The Open Boat

A Tale Intended to be after the Fact: Being the Experience of Four Men from the Sunk Steamer *Commodore*

(1898)

Stephen Crane

I

None of them knew the color of the sky. Their eyes glanced level, and were fastened upon the waves that swept toward them. These waves were of the hue of slate, save for the tops, which were of foaming white, and all of the men knew the colors of the sea. The horizon narrowed and widened, and dipped and rose, and at all times its edge was jagged with waves that seemed thrust up in points like rocks.

Many a man ought to have a bathtub larger than the boat which here rode upon the sea. These waves were most wrongfully and barbarously abrupt and tall, and each froth-top was a problem in small-boat navigation.

The cook squatted in the bottom, and looked with both eyes at the six inches of gunwale which separated him from the ocean. His sleeves were rolled over his fat forearms, and the two flaps of his unbuttoned vest dangled as he bent to bail out the boat. Often he said, 'Gawd! that was a narrow clip.' As he remarked it he invariably gazed eastward over the broken sea.

The oiler, steering with one of the two oars in the boat, sometimes raised himself suddenly to keep clear of water that swirled in over the stern. It was a thin little oar, and it seemed often ready to snap.

The correspondent, pulling at the other oar, watched the waves and wondered why he was there.

The injured captain, lying in the bow, was at this time buried in that profound dejection and indifference which comes, temporarily at least, to even the bravest and most enduring when, willy-nilly, the firm fails, the army loses, the ship goes down. The mind of the master of a vessel is rooted deep in the timbers of her, though he commands for a day or a decade; and this captain had on him the stern impression of a scene in the grays of dawn of seven turned faces, and later a stump of a topmast with a white ball on it, that slashed to and fro at the waves, went low and lower, and down. Thereafter there was something strange in his voice. Although steady, it was deep with mourning, and of a quality beyond oration or tears.

'Keep 'er a little more south, Billie,' said he.

'A little more south, sir,' said the oiler in the stern.

A seat in this boat was not unlike a seat upon a bucking broncho, and by the same token a broncho is not much smaller. The craft pranced and reared and plunged like an animal. As each wave came, and she rose for it, she seemed like a horse making at a fence outrageously high. The manner of her scramble over these walls of water is a mystic thing, and, moreover, at the top of them were ordinarily these problems in white water, the foam racing down from the summit of each wave requiring a new leap, and a leap from the air. Then, after scornfully bumping a crest, she would slide and race and splash down a long incline, and arrive bobbing and nodding in front of the next menace.

A singular disadvantage of the sea lies in the fact that after successfully surmounting one wave you discover that there is another behind it just as important and just as nervously anxious to do something effective in the way of swamping boats. In a ten-foot dinghy one can get an idea of the resources of the sea in the line of waves that is not probable to the average experience, which is never at sea in a dinghy. As each slaty wall of water approached, it shut all else from the view of the men in the boat, and it was not difficult to imagine that this particular wave was the final outburst of the ocean, the last effort of the grim water. There was a terrible grace in the move of the waves, and they came in silence, save for the snarling of the crests.

In the wan light the faces of the men must have been gray. Their eyes must have glinted in strange ways as they gazed steadily astern. Viewed from a balcony, the whole thing would doubtless have been weirdly picturesque. But the men in the boat had no time to see it, and if they had had leisure, there were other things to occupy their minds. The sun swung steadily up the sky, and they knew it was broad day because the color of the sea changed from slate to emerald-green streaked with amber lights, and the foam was like tumbling snow. The process of the breaking day was unknown to them. They were aware only of this effect upon the color of the waves that rolled toward them.

In disjointed sentences the cook and the correspondent argued as to the difference between a lifesaving station and a house of refuge. The cook had said: 'There's a house of refuge just north of the Mosquito Inlet Light, and as soon as they see us they'll come off in their boat and pick us up.'

'As soon as who see us?' said the correspondent.

'The crew,' said the cook.

'Houses of refuge don't have crews,' said the correspondent. 'As I understand them, they are only places where clothes and grub are stored for the benefit of shipwrecked people. They don't carry crews.'

'Oh, yes, they do,' said the cook.

'No, they don't,' said the correspondent.

'Well, we're not there yet, anyhow,' said the oiler, in the stern.

'Well,' said the cook, 'perhaps it's not a house of refuge that I'm thinking of as being near Mosquito Inlet Light; perhaps it's a lifesaving station.'

'We're not there yet,' said the oiler in the stern.

II

As the boat bounced from the top of each wave the wind tore through the hair of the hatless men, and as the craft plopped her stern down again the spray slashed past them. The crest of each of these waves was a hill, from the top of which the men surveyed for a moment a broad tumultuous expanse, shining and wind-riven. It was probably splendid, it was probably glorious, this play of the free sea, wild with lights of emerald and white and amber.

'Bully good thing it's an onshore wind,' said the cook. 'If not, where would we be? Wouldn't have a show.'

'That's right,' said the correspondent.

The busy oiler nodded his assent.

Then the captain, in the bow, chuckled in a way that expressed humor, contempt, tragedy, all in one. 'Do you think we've got much of a show now, boys?' said he.

Whereupon the three were silent, save for a trifle of hemming and hawing. To express any particular optimism at this time they felt to be childish and stupid, but they all doubtless possessed this sense of the situation in their minds. A young man thinks doggedly at such times. On the other hand, the ethics of their condition was decidedly against any open suggestion of hopelessness. So they were silent.

'Oh, well,' said the captain, soothing his children, 'we'll get ashore all right.'

But there was that in his tone which made them think; so the oiler quoth, 'Yes! if this wind holds.'

The cook was bailing. 'Yes! if we don't catch hell in the surf.'

Canton-flannel gulls flew near and far. Sometimes they sat down on the sea, near patches of brown seaweed that rolled over the waves with a movement like carpets on a line in a gale. The birds sat comfortably in groups, and they were envied by some in the dinghy, for the wrath of the sea was no more to them than it was to a covey of prairie chickens a thousand miles inland. Often they came very close and stared at the men with black bead-like eyes. At these times they were uncanny and sinister in their unblinking scrutiny, and the men hooted angrily at them, telling them to be gone. One came, and evidently decided to alight on the top of the captain's head. The bird flew parallel to the boat and did not circle, but made short sidelong jumps in the air in chicken fashion. His black eyes were wistfully fixed upon the captain's head. 'Ugly brute,' said the oiler to the bird, 'You look as if you were made with a jackknife.' The cook and the correspondent swore darkly at the creature. The captain naturally wished to knock it away with the end of the heavy painter, but he did not dare do it, because anything resembling an emphatic gesture would have capsized this freighted boat; and so, with his open hand, the captain gently and carefully waved the gull away. After it had been discouraged from the pursuit the captain breathed easier on account of his hair, and others breathed easier because the bird struck their minds at this time as being somehow gruesome and ominous.

In the meantime the oiler and the correspondent rowed. And also they rowed. They sat together in the same seat, and each rowed an oar. Then the oiler took both oars; then the correspondent took both oars; then the oiler; then the correspondent. They rowed and they rowed. The very ticklish part of the business was when the time came for the reclining one in the stern to take his turn at the oars. By the very last star of truth, it is easier to steal eggs from under a hen than it was to change seats in the dinghy. First the man in the stern slid his hand along the thwart and moved with care, as if he were of Sèvres. Then the man in the rowing-seat slid his hand along the other thwart. It was all done with the most extraordinary care. As the two sidled past each other, the whole party kept watchful eyes on the coming wave, and the captain cried: 'Look out, now! Steady, there!'

The brown mats of seaweed that appeared from time to time were like islands, bits of earth. They were traveling, apparently, neither one way nor the other. They were, to all intents, stationary. They informed the men in the boat that it was making progress slowly toward the land.

The captain, rearing cautiously in the bow after the dinghy soared on a great swell, said that he had seen the lighthouse at Mosquito Inlet. Presently the cook remarked that he had seen it. The correspondent was at the oars then, and for some reason he too wished to look at the lighthouse; but his back was toward the far shore, and the waves were important, and for some time he could not seize an opportunity to turn his head. But at last there came a wave more gentle than the others, and when at the crest of it he swiftly scoured the western horizon.

'See it?' said the captain.

'No,' said the correspondent, slowly; 'I didn't see anything.'

'Look again,' said the captain. He pointed. 'It's exactly in that direction.'

At the top of another wave the correspondent did as he was bid, and this time his eyes chanced on a small, still thing on the edge of the swaying horizon. It was precisely like the point of a pin. It took an anxious eye to find a lighthouse so tiny.

'Think we'll make it, Captain?'

'If this wind holds and the boat don't swamp, we can't do much else,' said the captain.

The little boat, lifted by each towering sea and splashed viciously by the crests, made progress that in the absence of seaweed was not apparent to those in her. She seemed just a wee thing wallowing, miraculously top up, at the mercy of five oceans. Occasionally a great spread of water, like white flames, swarmed into her.

'Bail her, cook,' said the captain, serenely.

'All right, Captain,' said the cheerful cook.

III

It would be difficult to describe the subtle brotherhood of men that was here established on the seas. No one said that it was so. No one mentioned it. But it dwelt in the boat, and each man felt it warm him. They were a captain, an oiler, a cook, and a correspondent, and they were friends – friends in a more curiously ironbound degree than may be common. The hurt captain, lying against the water jar in the bow, spoke always in a low voice and calmly; but he could never command a more ready and swiftly obedient crew than the motley three of the dinghy. It was more than a mere recognition of what was best for the common safety. There was surely in it a quality that was personal and heartfelt. And after this devotion to the commander of the boat, there was this comradeship, that the correspondent, for instance, who had been taught to be cynical of men, knew even at the time was the best experience of his life. But no one said that it was so. No one mentioned it.

'I wish we had a sail,' remarked the captain. 'We might try my overcoat on the end of an oar, and give you two boys a chance to rest.' So the cook and the correspondent held the mast and spread wide the overcoat; the oiler steered; and the little boat made good way with her new rig. Sometimes the oiler had to scull sharply to keep a sea from breaking into the boat, but otherwise sailing was a success.

Meanwhile the lighthouse had been growing slowly larger. It had now almost assumed color, and appeared like a little gray shadow on the sky. The man at the oars could not be prevented from turning his head rather often to try for a glimpse of this little gray shadow.

At last, from the top of each wave, the men in the tossing boat could see land. Even as the lighthouse was an upright shadow on the sky, this land seemed but a long black shadow on the sea. It certainly was thinner than paper. 'We must be about opposite New Smyrna,' said the cook, who had coasted this shore often in schooners. 'Captain, by the way, I believe they abandoned that lifesaving station there about a year ago.'

'Did they?' said the captain.

The wind slowly died away. The cook and the correspondent were not now obliged to slave in order to hold high the oar. But the waves continued their old impetuous swooping at the dinghy, and the little craft, no longer under way, struggled woundily over them. The oiler or the correspondent took the oars again.

Shipwrecks are *apropos* of nothing. If men could only train for them and have them occur when the men had reached pink condition, there would be less drowning at sea. Of the four in the dinghy none had slept any time worth mentioning for two days and two nights previous to embarking in the dinghy, and in the excitement of clambering about the deck of a foundering ship they had also forgotten to eat heartily.

For these reasons, and for others, neither the oiler nor the correspondent was fond of rowing at this time. The correspondent wondered ingenuously how in the name of all that was sane could there be people who thought it amusing to row a boat. It was not an amusement; it was a diabolical punishment, and even a genius of mental aberrations could never conclude that it was anything but a horror to the muscles and a crime against the back. He mentioned to the boat in general how the amusement of rowing struck him, and the weary-faced oiler smiled in full sympathy. Previously to the foundering, by the way, the oiler had worked a double watch in the engine room of the ship.

'Take her easy now, boys,' said the captain. 'Don't spend yourselves. If we have to run a surf you'll need all your strength, because we'll sure have to swim for it. Take your time.'

Slowly the land arose from the sea. From a black line it became a line of black and a line of white – trees and sand. Finally the captain said that he could make out a house on the shore. 'That's the house of refuge, sure,' said the cook. 'They'll see us before long, and come out after us.'

The distant lighthouse reared high. 'The keeper ought to be able to make us out now, if he's looking through a glass,' said the captain. 'He'll notify the lifesaving people.'

'None of those other boats could have got ashore to give word of this wreck,' said the oiler, in a low voice, 'else the lifeboat would be out hunting us.'

Slowly and beautifully the land loomed out of the sea. The wind came again. It had veered from the northeast to the southeast. Finally a new sound struck the ears of the men in the boat. It was the low thunder of the surf on the shore. 'We'll never be able to make the lighthouse now,' said the captain. 'Swing her head a little more north, Billie.'

'A little more north, sir,' said the oiler.

Whereupon the little boat turned her nose once more down the wind, and all but the oarsman watched the shore grow. Under the influence of this expansion doubt and direful apprehension were leaving the minds of the men. The management of the boat was still most absorbing, but it could not prevent a quiet cheerfulness. In an hour, perhaps, they would be ashore.

Their backbones had become thoroughly used to balancing in the boat, and they now rode this wild colt of a dinghy like circus men. The correspondent thought that he had been drenched to the skin, but happening to feel in the top pocket of his coat, he found therein eight cigars. Four of them were soaked with seawater; four were perfectly scatheless. After a search, somebody produced three dry matches; and thereupon the four waifs rode impudently in their little boat and, with an assurance of an impending rescue shining in their eyes, puffed at the big cigars, and judged well and ill of all men. Everybody took a drink of water.

IV

'Cook,' remarked the captain, 'there don't seem to be any signs of life about your house of refuge.'

'No,' replied the cook. 'Funny they don't see us!'

A broad stretch of lowly coast lay before the eyes of the men. It was of low dunes topped with dark vegetation. The roar of the surf was plain, and sometimes they could see the white lip of a wave as it spun up the beach. A tiny house was blocked out black upon the sky. Southward, the slim lighthouse lifted its little gray length.

Tide, wind, and waves were swinging the dinghy northward. 'Funny they don't see us,' said the men.

The surf's roar was here dulled, but its tone was nevertheless thunderous and mighty. As the boat swam over the great rollers the men sat listening to this roar. 'We'll swamp sure,' said everybody.

It is fair to say here that there was not a lifesaving station within twenty miles in either direction; but the men did not know this fact, and in consequence they made dark and opprobrious remarks concerning the eyesight of the nation's lifesavers. Four scowling men sat in the dinghy and surpassed records in the invention of epithets.

'Funny they don't see us.'

The light-heartedness of a former time had completely faded. To their sharpened minds it was easy to conjure pictures of all kinds of incompetency and blindness and, indeed, cowardice. There was the shore of the populous land, and it was bitter and bitter to them that from it came no sign.

'Well,' said the captain, ultimately, 'I suppose we'll have to make a try for ourselves. If we stay out here too long, we'll none of us have strength left to swim after the boat swamps.'

And so the oiler, who was at the oars, turned the boat straight for the shore. There was a sudden tightening of muscles. There was some thinking.

'If we don't all get ashore,' said the captain – 'if we don't all get ashore, I suppose you fellows know where to send news of my finish?'

They then briefly exchanged some addresses and admonitions. As for the reflections of the men, there was a great deal of rage in them. Perchance they might be formulated thus: 'If I am going to be drowned – if I am going to be drowned – if I am going to be drowned, why, in the name of the seven mad gods who rule the sea, was I allowed to come thus far and contemplate sand and trees? Was I brought here merely to have my nose dragged away as I was about to nibble the sacred cheese of life? It is preposterous. If this old ninny-woman, Fate, cannot do better than this, she should be deprived of the management of men's fortunes. She is an old hen who knows not her intention. If she has decided to drown me, why did she not do it in the beginning and save me all this trouble? The whole affair is absurd . . . But no; she cannot mean to drown me. She dare not drown me. She cannot drown me. Not after all this work.' Afterward the man might have had an impulse to shake his fist at the clouds. 'Just you drown me, now, and then hear what I call you!'

The billows that came at this time were more formidable. They seemed always just about to break and roll over the little boat in a turmoil of foam. There was a preparatory and long growl in the speech of them. No mind unused to the sea would have concluded that the dinghy could ascend these sheer heights in time. The shore was still afar. The oiler was a wily surf-man. 'Boys,' he said swiftly, 'she won't live three minutes more, and we're too far out to swim. Shall I take her to sea again, Captain?'

'Yes; go ahead!' said the captain.

This oiler, by a series of quick miracles and fast and steady oarsmanship, turned the boat in the middle of the surf and took her safely to sea again.

There was a considerable silence as the boat bumped over the furrowed sea to deeper water. Then somebody in gloom spoke: 'Well, anyhow, they must have seen us from the shore by now.'

The gulls went in slanting flight up the wind toward the gray, desolate east. A squall, marked by dingy clouds and clouds brick-red, like smoke from a burning building, appeared from the southeast.

'What do you think of those lifesaving people? Ain't they peaches?'

'Funny they haven't seen us.'

'Maybe they think we're out here for sport! Maybe they think we're fishin'. Maybe they think we're damned fools.'

It was a long afternoon. A changed tide tried to force them southward, but wind and wave said northward. Far ahead, where coastline, sea, and sky formed their mighty angle, there were little dots which seemed to indicate a city on the shore.

'St Augustine?'

The captain shook his head. 'Too near Mosquito Inlet.'

And the oiler rowed, and then the correspondent rowed; then the oiler rowed. It was a weary business. The human back can become the seat of more aches and pains than are registered in books for the composite anatomy of a regiment. It is a limited area, but it can become the theater of innumerable muscular conflicts, tangles, wrenches, knots, and other comforts.

'Did you ever like to row, Billie?' asked the correspondent.

'No,' said the oiler; 'hang it!'

When one exchanged the rowing-seat for a place in the bottom of the boat, he suffered a bodily depression that caused him to be careless of everything save an obligation to wiggle one finger. There was cold seawater swashing to and fro in the boat, and he lay in it. His head, pillowed on a thwart, was within an inch of the swirl of a wave-crest, and sometimes a particularly obstreperous sea came inboard and drenched him once more. But these matters did not annoy him. It is almost certain that if the boat had capsized he would have tumbled comfortably out upon the ocean as if he felt sure that it was a great soft mattress.

'Look! There's a man on the shore!'

'Where?'

'There! See 'im? See 'im?'

'Yes, sure! He's walking along.'

'Now he's stopped. Look! He's facing us!'

'He's waving at us!'

'So he is! By thunder!'

'Ah, now we're all right! Now we're all right! There'll be a boat out here for us in half an hour.'

'He's going on. He's running. He's going up to that house there.'

The remote beach seemed lower than the sea, and it required a searching glance to discern the little black figure. The captain saw a floating stick, and they rowed to it. A bath towel was by some weird chance in the boat, and, tying this on the stick, the captain waved it. The oarsman did not dare turn his head, so he was obliged to ask questions.

'What's he doing now?'

'He's standing still again. He's looking, I think . . . There he goes again – toward the house . . . Now he's stopped again.'

'Is he waving at us?'

'No, not now; he was, though.'

'Look! There comes another man!'

'He's running.'

'Look at him go, would you!'

'Why, he's on a bicycle. Now he's met the other man. They're both waving at us. Look!'

'There comes something up the beach.'

'What the devil is that thing?'

'Why, it looks like a boat.'

'Why, certainly, it's a boat.'

'No; it's on wheels.'

'Yes, so it is. Well, that must be the lifeboat. They drag them along shore on a wagon.'

'That's the lifeboat, sure.'

'No, by God, it's – it's an omnibus.'

'I tell you it's a lifeboat.'

'It is not! It's an omnibus. I can see it plain. See? One of these big hotel omnibuses.'

'By thunder, you're right. It's an omnibus, sure as fate. What do you suppose they are doing with an omnibus? Maybe they are going around collecting the life-crew, hey?'

'That's it, likely. Look! There's a fellow waving a little black flag. He's standing on the steps of the omnibus. There come those other two fellows.

Now they're all talking together. Look at the fellow with the flag. Maybe he ain't waving it!'

'That ain't a flag, is it? That's his coat. Why, certainly, that's his coat.'

'So it is; it's his coat. He's taken it off and is waving it around his head. But would you look at him swing it!'

'Oh, say, there isn't any lifesaving station there. That's just a winter-resort hotel omnibus that has brought over some of the boarders to see us drown.'

'What's that idiot with the coat mean? What's he signaling, anyhow?'

'It looks as if he were trying to tell us to go north. There must be a lifesaving station up there.'

'No; he thinks we're fishing. Just giving us a merry hand. See? Ah, there, Willie!'

'Well, I wish I could make something out of those signals. What do you suppose he means?'

'He don't mean anything; he's just playing.'

'Well, if he'd just signal us to try the surf again, or to go to sea and wait, or go north, or go south, or go to hell, there would be some reason in it. But look at him! He just stands there and keeps his coat revolving like a wheel. The ass!'

'There come more people.'

'Now there's quite a mob. Look! Isn't that a boat?'

'Where? Oh, I see where you mean. No, that's no boat.'

'That fellow is still waving his coat.'

'He must think we like to see him do that. Why don't he quit it? It don't mean anything.'

'I don't know. I think he is trying to make us go north. It must be that there's a lifesaving station there somewhere.'

'Say, he ain't tired yet. Look at 'im wave!'

'Wonder how long he can keep that up. He's been revolving his coat ever since he caught sight of us. He's an idiot. Why aren't they getting men to bring a boat out? A fishing boat – one of those big yawls – could come out here all right. Why don't he do something?'

'Oh, it's all right now.'

'They'll have a boat out here for us in less than no time, now that they've seen us.'

A faint yellow tone came into the sky over the low land. The shadows on the sea slowly deepened. The wind bore coldness with it, and the men began to shiver.

'Holy smoke!' said one, allowing his voice to express his impious mood, 'if we keep on monkeying out here! If we've got to flounder out here all right!'

'Oh, we'll never have to stay here all night! Don't you worry. They've seen us now, and it won't be long before they'll come chasing out after us.'

The shore grew dusky. The man waving a coat blended gradually into this gloom, and it swallowed in the same manner the omnibus and the group of people. The spray, when it dashed uproariously over the side, made the voyagers shrink and swear like men who were being branded.

'I'd like to catch the chump who waved the coat. I feel like socking him one, just for luck.'

'Why? What did he do?'

'Oh, nothing, but then he seemed so damned cheerful.'

In the meantime the oiler rowed, and then the correspondent rowed, and then the oiler rowed. Gray-faced and bowed forward, they mechanically, turn by turn, plied the leaden oars. The form of the lighthouse had vanished from the southern horizon, but finally a pale star appeared, just lifting from the sea. The streaked saffron in the west passed before the all-merging darkness, and the sea to the east was black. The land had vanished, and was expressed only by the low and drear thunder of the surf.

'If I am going to be drowned – if I am going to be drowned – if I am going to be drowned, why, in the name of the seven mad gods who rule the sea, was I allowed to come thus far and contemplate sand and trees? Was I brought here merely to have my nose dragged away as I was about to nibble the sacred cheese of life?'

The patient captain, drooped over the water jar, was sometimes obliged to speak to the oarsman.

'Keep her head up! Keep her head up!'

'Keep her head up, sir.' The voices were weary and low.

This was surely a quiet evening. All save the oarsman lay heavily and listlessly in the boat's bottom. As for him, his eyes were just capable of noting the tall black waves that swept forward in a most sinister silence, save for an occasional subdued growl of a crest.

The cook's head was on a thwart, and he looked without interest at the water under his nose. He was deep in other scenes. Finally he spoke. 'Billie,' he murmured, dreamfully, 'what kind of pie do you like best?'

V

'Pie!' said the oiler and the correspondent, agitatedly. 'Don't talk about those things, blast you!'

'Well,' said the cook, 'I was just thinking about ham sandwiches, and—'

A night on the sea in an open boat is a long night. As darkness settled finally, the shine of the light, lifting from the sea in the south, changed to full gold. On the northern horizon a new light appeared, a small bluish gleam on the edge of the waters. These two lights were the furniture of the world. Otherwise there was nothing but waves.

Two men huddled in the stern, and distances were so magnificent in the dinghy that the rower was enabled to keep his feet partly warm by thrusting them under his companions. Their legs indeed extended far under the rowing seat until they touched the feet of the captain forward. Sometimes, despite the efforts of the tired oarsman, a wave came piling into the boat, an icy wave of the night, and the chilling water soaked them anew. They would twist their bodies for a moment and groan, and sleep the dead sleep once more, while the water in the boat gurgled about them as the craft rocked.

The plan of the oiler and the correspondent was for one to row until he lost the ability, and then arouse the other from his sea-water couch in the bottom of the boat.

The oiler plied the oars until his head drooped forward and the overpowering sleep blinded him; and he rowed yet afterward. Then he touched a man in the bottom of the boat, and called his name. 'Will you spell me for a little while?' he said meekly.

'Sure, Billie,' said the correspondent, awaking and dragging himself to a sitting position. They exchanged places carefully, and the oiler, cuddling down in the seawater at the cook's side, seemed to go to sleep instantly.

The particular violence of the sea had ceased. The waves came without snarling. The obligation of the man at the oars was to keep the boat headed so that the tilt of the rollers would not capsize her, and to preserve her from filling when the crests rushed past. The black waves were silent and hard to be seen in the darkness. Often one was almost upon the boat before the oarsman was aware.

In a low voice the correspondent addressed the captain. He was not sure that the captain was awake, although this iron man seemed to be always awake. 'Captain, shall I keep her making for that light north, sir?'

The same steady voice answered him. 'Yes. Keep it about two points off the port bow.'

The cook had tied a lifebelt around himself in order to get even the warmth which this clumsy cork contrivance could donate, and he seemed almost stove-like when a rower, whose teeth invariably chattered wildly as soon as he ceased his labor, dropped down to sleep.

The correspondent, as he rowed, looked down at the two men sleeping underfoot. The cook's arm was around the oiler's shoulders, and, with their fragmentary clothing and haggard faces, they were the babes of the sea – a grotesque rendering of the old babes in the wood.

Later he must have grown stupid at his work, for suddenly there was a growling of water, and a crest came with a roar and a swash into the boat, and it was a wonder that it did not set the cook afloat in his lifebelt. The cook continued to sleep, but the oiler sat up, blinking his eyes and shaking with the new cold.

'Oh, I'm awful sorry, Billie,' said the correspondent, contritely.

'That's all right, old boy,' said the oiler, and lay down again and was asleep.

Presently it seemed that even the captain dozed, and the correspondent thought that he was the one man afloat on all the oceans. The wind had a voice as it came over the waves, and it was sadder than the end.

There was a long, loud swishing astern of the boat, and a gleaming trail of phosphorescence, like blue flame, was furrowed on the black waters. It might have been made by a monstrous knife.

Then there came a stillness, while the correspondent breathed with open mouth and looked at the sea.

Suddenly there was another swish and another long flash of bluish light, and this time it was alongside the boat, and might almost have been reached with an oar. The correspondent saw an enormous fin speed like a shadow through the water, hurling the crystalline spray and leaving the long glowing trail.

The correspondent looked over his shoulder at the captain. His face was hidden, and he seemed to be asleep. He looked at the babes of the sea. They certainly were asleep. So, being bereft of sympathy, he leaned a little way to one side and swore softly into the sea.

But the thing did not then leave the vicinity of the boat. Ahead or astern, on one side or the other, at intervals long or short, fled the long sparkling streak, and there was to be heard the *whirroo* of the dark fin. The speed and power of the thing was greatly to be admired. It cut the water like a gigantic and keen projectile.

The presence of this biding thing did not affect the man with the same horror that it would if he had been a picnicker. He simply looked at the sea dully and swore in an undertone.

Nevertheless, it is true that he did not wish to be alone with the thing. He wished one of his companions to awake by chance and keep him company with it. But the captain hung motionless over the water jar, and the oiler and the cook in the bottom of the boat were plunged in slumber.

VI

'If I am going to be drowned – if I am going to be drowned – if I am going to be drowned, why, in the name of the seven mad gods who rule the sea, was I allowed to come thus far and contemplate sand and trees?'

During this dismal night, it may be remarked that a man would conclude that it was really the intention of the seven mad gods to drown him, despite the abominable injustice of it. For it was certainly an abominable injustice to drown a man who had worked so hard, so hard. The man felt it would be a crime most unnatural. Other people had drowned at sea since galleys swarmed with painted sails, but still—

When it occurs to a man that nature does not regard him as important, and that she feels she would not maim the universe by disposing of him, he at first wishes to throw bricks at the temple, and he hates deeply the fact that there are no bricks and no temples. Any visible expression of nature would surely be pelleted with his jeers.

Then, if there be no tangible thing to hoot, he feels, perhaps, the desire to confront a personification and indulge in pleas, bowed to one knee, and with hands supplicant, saying, 'Yes, but I love myself.'

A high cold star on a winter's night is the word he feels that she says to him. Thereafter he knows the pathos of his situation.

The men in the dinghy had not discussed these matters, but each had, no doubt, reflected upon them in silence and according to his mind. There was seldom any expression upon their faces save the general one of complete weariness. Speech was devoted to the business of the boat.

To chime the notes of his emotion, a verse mysteriously entered the correspondent's head. He had even forgotten that he had forgotten this verse, but it suddenly was in his mind.

> A soldier of the Legion lay dying in Algiers;
> There was lack of woman's nursing, there was dearth of woman's tears;
> But a comrade stood beside him, and he took that comrade's hand,
> And he said, 'I never more shall see my own, my native land.'

In his childhood the correspondent had been made acquainted with the fact that a soldier of the Legion lay dying in Algiers, but he had never regarded the fact as important. Myriads of his schoolfellows had informed him of the soldier's plight, but the dinning had naturally ended by making him perfectly indifferent. He had never considered it his affair that a soldier of the Legion lay dying in Algiers, nor had it appeared to him as a matter for sorrow. It was less to him than the breaking of a pencil's point.

Now, however, it quaintly came to him as a human, living thing. It was no longer merely a picture of a few throes in the breast of a poet, meanwhile drinking tea and warming his feet at the grate; it was an actuality – stern, mournful, and fine.

The correspondent plainly saw the soldier. He lay on the sand with his feet out straight and still. While his pale left hand was upon his chest in an attempt to thwart the going of his life, the blood came between his fingers. In the far Algerian distance, a city of low square forms was set against a sky that was faint with the last sunset hues. The correspondent, plying the oars and dreaming of the slow and slower movements of the lips of the soldier, was moved by a profound and perfectly impersonal apprehension. He was sorry for the soldier of the Legion who lay dying in Algiers.

The thing which had followed the boat and waited had evidently grown bored at the delay. There was no longer to be heard the slash of the cutwater, and there was no longer the flame of the long trail. The light in the north still glimmered, but it was apparently no nearer to the boat. Sometimes the boom of the surf rang in the correspondent's ears, and he turned the craft seaward then and rowed harder. Southward, someone had evidently built a watch fire on the beach. It was too low and too far to be seen, but it made a shimmering, roseate reflection upon the bluff in back of it, and this could be discerned from the boat. The wind came stronger, and sometimes a wave suddenly raged out like a mountain cat, and there was to be seen the sheen and sparkle of a broken crest.

The captain, in the bow, moved on his water jar and sat erect. 'Pretty long night,' he observed to the correspondent. He looked at the shore. 'Those lifesaving people take their time.'

'Did you see that shark playing around?'

'Yes, I saw him. He was a big fellow, all right.'

'Wish I had known you were awake.'

Later the correspondent spoke into the bottom of the boat. 'Billie!' There was a slow and gradual disentanglement. 'Billie, will you spell me?'

'Sure,' said the oiler.

As soon as the correspondent touched the cold, comfortable seawater in the bottom of the boat and had huddled close to the cook's lifebelt he was deep in sleep, despite the fact that his teeth played all the popular airs. This sleep was so good to him that it was but a moment before he heard a voice call his name in a tone that demonstrated the last stages of exhaustion. 'Will you spell me?'

'Sure, Billie.'

The light in the north had mysteriously vanished, but the correspondent took his course from the wide-awake captain.

Later in the night they took the boat farther out to sea, and the captain directed the cook to take one oar at the stern and keep the boat facing the seas. He was to call out if he should hear the thunder of the surf. This plan enabled the oiler and the correspondent to get respite together. 'We'll give those boys a chance to get into shape again,' said the captain. They curled down and, after a few preliminary chatterings and trembles, slept once more the dead sleep. Neither knew they had bequeathed to the cook the company of another shark, or perhaps the same shark.

As the boat caroused on the waves, spray occasionally bumped over the side and gave them a fresh soaking, but this had no power to break their repose. The ominous slash of the wind and the water affected them as it would have affected mummies.

'Boys,' said the cook, with the notes of every reluctance in his voice, 'she's drifted in pretty close. I guess one of you had better take her to sea again.' The correspondent, aroused, heard the crash of the toppled crests.

As he was rowing, the captain gave him some whiskey-and-water, and this steadied the chills out of him. 'If I ever get ashore and anybody shows me even a photograph of an oar—'

At last there was a short conversation.

'Billie! . . . Billie, will you spell me?'

'Sure,' said the oiler.

VII

When the correspondent again opened his eyes, the sea and the sky were each of the gray hue of the dawning. Later, carmine and gold was painted upon the waters. The morning appeared finally, in its splendor, with a sky of pure blue, and the sunlight flamed on the tips of the waves.

On the distant dunes were set many little black cottages, and a tall white windmill reared above them. No man, nor dog, nor bicycle appeared on the beach. The cottages might have formed a deserted village.

The voyagers scanned the shore. A conference was held in the boat. 'Well,' said the captain, 'if no help is coming, we might better try a run through the surf right away. If we stay out here much longer we will be too weak to do anything for ourselves at all.' The others silently acquiesced in this reasoning. The boat was headed for the beach. The correspondent wondered if none ever ascended the tall wind-tower, and if then they never looked seaward. This tower was a giant, standing with its back to the plight of the ants. It represented in a degree, to the correspondent, the serenity of nature amid the struggles of the individual – nature in the wind, and nature in the vision of men. She did not seem cruel to him then, nor beneficent, nor treacherous, nor wise. But she was indifferent, flatly indifferent. It is, perhaps, plausible that a man in this situation, impressed with the unconcern of the universe, should see the innumerable flaws of his life, and have them taste wickedly in his mind, and wish for another chance. A distinction between right and wrong seems absurdly clear to him, then, in this new ignorance of the grave-edge, and he understands that if he were given another opportunity he would mend his conduct and his words, and be better and brighter during an introduction or at a tea.

'Now, boys,' said the captain, 'she is going to swamp sure. All we can do is to work her in as far as possible, and then when she swamps, pile out and scramble for the beach. Keep cool now, and don't jump until she swamps sure.'

The oiler took the oars. Over his shoulders he scanned the surf. 'Captain,' he said, 'I think I'd better bring her about and keep her head-on to the seas and back her in.'

'All right, Billie,' said the captain, 'Back her in.' The oiler swung the boat then, and, seated in the stern, the cook and the correspondent were obliged to look over their shoulders to contemplate the lonely and indifferent shore.

The monstrous inshore rollers heaved the boat high until the men were again enabled to see the white sheets of water scudding up the slanted beach. 'We won't get in very close,' said the captain. Each time a man could wrest his attention from the rollers, he turned his glance toward the shore, and in the expression of the eyes during this contemplation there was a singular quality. The correspondent, observing the others, knew that they were not afraid, but the full meaning of their glances was shrouded.

As for himself, he was too tired to grapple fundamentally with the fact. He tried to coerce his mind into thinking of it, but the mind was dominated at this time by the muscles, and the muscles said they did not care. It merely occurred to him that if he should drown it would be a shame.

There were no hurried words, no pallor, no plain agitation. The men simply looked at the shore. 'Now, remember to get well clear of the boat when you jump,' said the captain.

Seaward the crest of a roller suddenly fell with a thunderous crash, and the long white comber came roaring down upon the boat.

'Steady now,' said the captain. The men were silent. They turned their eyes from the shore to the comber and waited. The boat slid up the incline, leaped at the furious top, bounced over it, and swung down the long back of the wave. Some water had been shipped, and the cook bailed it out.

But the next crest crashed also. The tumbling, boiling flood of white water caught the boat and whirled it almost perpendicular. Water swarmed in from all sides. The correspondent had his hands on the gunwale at this time, and when the water entered at that place he swiftly withdrew his fingers, as if he objected to wetting them.

The little boat, drunken with this weight of water, reeled and snuggled deeper into the sea.

'Bail her out, cook! Bail her out!' said the captain.

'All right, Captain,' said the cook.

'Now, boys, the next one will do for us sure,' said the oiler. 'Mind to jump clear of the boat.'

The third wave moved forward, huge, furious, implacable. It fairly swallowed the dinghy, and almost simultaneously the men tumbled into the sea. A piece of lifebelt had lain in the bottom of the boat, and as the correspondent went overboard he held this to his chest with his left hand.

The January water was icy, and he reflected immediately that it was colder than he had expected to find it off the coast of Florida. This appeared to his dazed mind as a fact important enough to be noted at the time. The coldness of the water was sad; it was tragic. This fact was somehow mixed and confused with his opinion of his own situation, so that it seemed almost a proper reason for tears. The water was cold.

When he came to the surface he was conscious of little but the noisy water. Afterward he saw his companions in the sea. The oiler was ahead in the race. He was swimming strongly and rapidly. Off to the correspondent's left, the cook's great white and corked back bulged out of the water; and in the rear the captain was hanging with his one good hand to the keel of the overturned dinghy.

There is a certain immovable quality to a shore, and the correspondent wondered at it amid the confusion of the sea.

It seemed also very attractive; but the correspondent knew that it was a long journey, and he paddled leisurely. The piece of life preserver lay under him, and sometimes he whirled down the incline of a wave as if he were on a hand-sled.

But finally he arrived at a place in the sea where travel was beset with difficulty. He did not pause swimming to inquire what manner of current had caught him, but there his progress ceased. The shore was set before him like a bit of scenery on a stage, and he looked at it and understood with his eyes each detail of it.

As the cook passed, much farther to the left, the captain was calling to him, 'Turn over on your back, cook! Turn over on your back and use the oar.'

'All right, sir.' The cook turned on his back, and, paddling with an oar, went ahead as if he were a canoe.

Presently the boat also passed to the left of the correspondent, with the captain clinging with one hand to the keel. He would have appeared like a man raising himself to look over a board fence if it were not for the extraordinary gymnastics of the boat. The correspondent marveled that the captain could still hold to it.

They passed on nearer to shore – the oiler, the cook, the captain – and following them went the water jar, bouncing gaily over the seas.

The correspondent remained in the grip of this strange new enemy – a current. The shore, with its white slope of sand and its green bluff topped with little silent cottages, was spread like a picture before him. It was very near to him then, but he was impressed as one who, in a gallery, looks at a scene from Brittany or Algiers.

He thought: 'I am going to drown? Can it be possible? Can it be possible? Can it be possible?' Perhaps an individual must consider his own death to be the final phenomenon of nature.

But later a wave perhaps whirled him out of this small deadly current, for he found suddenly that he could again make progress toward the shore. Later still he was aware that the captain, clinging with one hand to the keel of the dinghy, had his face turned away from the shore and toward him, and was calling his name. 'Come to the boat! Come to the boat!'

In his struggle to reach the captain and the boat, he reflected that when one gets properly wearied drowning must really be a comfortable arrangement – a cessation of hostilities accompanied by a large degree of relief; and he was glad of it, for the main thing in his mind for some moments had been horror of the temporary agony. He did not wish to be hurt.

Presently he saw a man running along the shore. He was undressing with most remarkable speed. Coat, trousers, shirt, everything flew magically off him.

'Come to the boat!' called the captain.

'All right, Captain.' As the correspondent paddled, he saw the captain let himself down to bottom and leave the boat. Then the correspondent performed his one little marvel of the voyage. A large wave caught him and flung him with ease and supreme speed completely over the boat and far beyond it. It struck him even then as an event in gymnastics and a true miracle of the sea. An overturned boat in the surf is not a plaything to a swimming man.

The correspondent arrived in water that reached only to his waist, but his condition did not enable him to stand for more than a moment. Each wave knocked him into a heap, and the undertow pulled at him.

Then he saw the man who had been running and undressing, and undressing and running, come bounding into the water. He dragged ashore the cook, and then waded toward the captain; but the captain waved him away and sent him to the correspondent. He was naked – naked as a tree in winter; but a halo was about his head, and he shone like a saint. He gave a strong pull, and a long drag, and a bully heave at the correspondent's hand. The correspondent, schooled in the minor formulae, said, 'Thanks, old man.' But suddenly the man cried, 'What's that?' He pointed a swift finger. The correspondent said, 'Go.'

In the shallows, face downward, lay the oiler. His forehead touched sand that was periodically, between each wave, clear of the sea.

The correspondent did not know all that transpired afterward. When he achieved safe ground he fell, striking the sand with each particular part of his body. It was as if he had dropped from a roof, but the thud was grateful to him.

It seems that instantly the beach was populated with men with blankets, clothes, and flasks, and women with coffeepots and all the remedies sacred to their minds. The welcome of the land to the men from the sea was warm and generous; but a still and dripping shape was carried slowly up the beach, and the land's welcome for it could only be the different and sinister hospitality of the grave.

When it came night, the white waves paced to and fro in the moonlight, and the wind brought the sound of the great sea's voice to the men on the shore, and they felt that they could then be interpreters.

8

The Moving Finger

(1899)

Edith Wharton

I

This news of Mrs Grancy's death came to me with the shock of an immense blunder – one of fate's most irretrievable acts of vandalism. It was as though all sorts of renovating forces had been checked by the clogging of that one wheel. Not that Mrs Grancy contributed any perceptible momentum to the social machine: her unique distinction was that of filling to perfection her special place in the world. So many people are like badly-composed statues, over-lapping their niches at one point and leaving them vacant at another. Mrs Grancy's niche was her husband's life; and if it be argued that the space was not large enough for its vacancy to leave a very big gap, I can only say that, at the last resort, such dimensions must be determined by finer instruments than any ready-made standard of utility. Ralph Grancy's was in short a kind of disembodied usefulness: one of those constructive influences that, instead of crystallising into definite forms, remain as it were a medium for the development of clear thinking and fine feeling. He faithfully irrigated his own dusty patch of life, and the fruitful moisture stole far beyond his boundaries. If, to carry on the metaphor, Grancy's life was a sedulously-cultivated enclosure, his wife was the flower he had planted in its midst – the embowering tree, rather, which gave him rest and shade at its foot and the wind of dreams in its upper branches.

We had all – his small but devoted band of followers – known a moment when it seemed likely that Grancy would fail us. We had watched him pitted against one stupid obstacle after another – ill-health, poverty, misunderstanding and, worst of all for a man of his texture, his first wife's soft insidious egotism. We had seen him sinking under the leaden embrace of her affection like a swimmer in a drowning clutch; but just as we despaired he had always come to the surface again, blinded, panting, but striking out fiercely for the shore. When at last her death released him it became a question as to how much of the man she had carried with her. Left alone, he revealed numb withered patches, like a tree from which a parasite has been stripped. But gradually he began to put out new leaves; and when he met the lady who was to become his second wife – his one *real* wife, as his friends reckoned – the whole man burst into flower.

The second Mrs Grancy was past thirty when he married her, and it was clear that she had harvested that crop of middle joy which is rooted in young despair. But if she had lost the surface of eighteen she had kept its inner light; if her cheek lacked the gloss of immaturity her eyes were young with the stored youth of half a life-time. Grancy had first known her somewhere in the East – I believe she was the sister of one of our consuls out there – and when he brought her home to New York she came among us as a stranger. The idea of Grancy's remarriage had been a shock to us all. After one such calcining most men would have kept out of the fire; but we agreed that he was predestined to sentimental blunders, and we awaited with resignation the embodiment of his latest mistake. Then Mrs Grancy came – and we understood. She was the most beautiful and the most complete of explanations. We shuffled our defeated omniscience out of sight and gave it hasty burial under a prodigality of welcome. For the first time in years we had Grancy off our minds. 'He'll do something great now!' the least sanguine of us prophesied; and our sentimentalist emended: 'He *has* done it – in marrying her!'

It was Claydon, the portrait-painter, who risked this hyperbole; and who soon afterward, at the happy husband's request, prepared to defend it in a portrait of Mrs Grancy. We were all – even Claydon – ready to concede that Mrs Grancy's unwontedness was in some degree a matter of environment. Her graces were complementary and it needed the mate's call to reveal the flash of color beneath her neutral-tinted wings. But if she needed Grancy to interpret her, how much greater was the service she rendered him! Claydon professionally described her as the right frame for him; but if she defined she also enlarged, if she threw the whole into perspective she also cleared new ground, opened fresh vistas, reclaimed whole areas of activity that had run to waste under the harsh husbandry of privation. This interaction of sympathies was not without its visible expression. Claydon was not alone in maintaining that Grancy's presence – or indeed the mere mention of his name – had a perceptible effect on his wife's appearance. It was as though a light were shifted, a curtain drawn back, as though, to borrow another of Claydon's metaphors, Love the indefatigable artist were perpetually seeking a happier 'pose' for his model. In this interpretative light Mrs Grancy acquired the charm which makes some women's faces like a book of which the last page is never turned. There was always something new to read in her eyes. What Claydon read there – or at least such scattered hints of the ritual as reached him through the sanctuary doors – his portrait in due course declared to us. When the picture was exhibited it was at once acclaimed as his masterpiece; but the people who knew Mrs Grancy smiled and said it was flattered. Claydon, however, had not set out to paint *their* Mrs Grancy – or ours even – but Ralph's; and Ralph knew his own at a glance. At the first confrontation he saw that Claydon had understood. As for Mrs Grancy, when the finished picture was shown to her she turned to the painter and said simply: 'Ah, you've done me facing the east!'

The picture, then, for all its value, seemed a mere incident in the unfolding of their double destiny, a foot-note to the illuminated text of their lives. It was not till afterward that it acquired the significance of last words spoken on a threshold never to be recrossed. Grancy, a year after his marriage, had given up his town house and carried his bliss an hour's journey away, to a little place among the hills. His various duties and interests brought him frequently to New York but we necessarily saw him less often than when his house had served as the rallying-point of kindred enthusiasms. It seemed a pity that such an influence should be withdrawn, but we all felt that his long arrears of happiness should be paid in whatever coin he chose. The distance from which the fortunate couple radiated warmth on us was not too great for friendship to traverse; and our conception of a glorified leisure took the form of Sundays spent in the Grancys' library, with its sedative rural outlook and the portrait of Mrs Grancy illuminating its studious walls. The picture was at its best in that setting; and we used to accuse Claydon of visiting Mrs Grancy in order to see her portrait. He met this by declaring that the portrait *was* Mrs Grancy; and there were moments when the statement seemed unanswerable. One of us, indeed – I think it must have been the novelist – said that Claydon had been saved from falling in love with Mrs Grancy only by falling in love with his picture of her; and it was noticeable that he, to whom his finished work was no more than the shed husk of future effort, showed a perennial tenderness for this one achievement. We smiled afterward to think how often, when Mrs Grancy was in the room, her presence reflecting itself in our talk like a gleam of sky in a hurrying current, Claydon, averted from the real woman, would sit as it were listening to the picture. His attitude, at the time, seemed only a part of the unusualness of those picturesque afternoons, when the most familiar combinations of life underwent a magical change. Some human happiness is a landlocked lake; but the Grancys' was an open sea, stretching a buoyant and illimitable surface to the voyaging interests of life. There was room and to spare on those waters for all our separate ventures; and always, beyond the sunset, a mirage of the fortunate isles toward which our prows were bent.

II

It was in Rome that, three years later, I heard of her death. The notice said 'suddenly'; I was glad of that. I was glad too – basely perhaps – to be away from Grancy at a time when silence must have seemed obtuse and speech derisive.

I was still in Rome when, a few months afterward, he suddenly arrived there. He had been appointed secretary of legation at Constantinople and was on the way to his post. He had taken the place, he said frankly, 'to get away'. Our relations with the Porte held out a prospect of hard work, and that, he explained, was what he needed. He could never be satisfied to sit down among the ruins. I saw that, like most of us in moments of extreme moral tension, he was playing a part, behaving as he thought it became a man to behave in the eye of disaster. The instinctive posture of grief is a shuffling compromise between defiance and prostration; and pride feels the need of striking a worthier attitude in face of such a foe. Grancy, by nature musing and retrospective, had chosen the rôle of the man of action, who answers blow for blow and opposes a mailed front to the thrusts of destiny; and the completeness of the equipment testified to his inner weakness. We talked only of what we were not thinking of, and parted, after a few days, with a sense of relief that proved the inadequacy of friendship to perform, in such cases, the office assigned to it by tradition.

Soon afterward my own work called me home, but Grancy remained several years in Europe. International diplomacy kept its promise of giving him work to do, and during the year in which he acted as *chargé d'affaires* he acquitted himself, under trying conditions, with conspicuous zeal and discretion. A political redistribution of matter removed him from office just as he had proved his usefulness to the government; and the following summer I heard that he had come home and was down at his place in the country.

On my return to town I wrote him and his reply came by the next post. He answered as it were in his natural voice, urging me to spend the following Sunday with him, and suggesting that I should bring down any of the old set who could be persuaded to join me. I thought this a good sign, and yet – shall I own it? – I was vaguely disappointed. Perhaps we are apt to feel that our friends' sorrows should be kept like those historic monuments from which the encroaching ivy is periodically removed.

That very evening at the club I ran across Claydon. I told him of Grancy's invitation and proposed that we should go down together; but he pleaded an engagement. I was sorry, for I had always felt that he and I stood nearer Ralph than the others, and if the old Sundays were to be renewed I should have preferred that we two should spend the first alone with him. I said as much to Claydon and offered to fit my time to his; but he met this by a general refusal.

'I don't want to go to Grancy's,' he said bluntly. I waited a moment, but he appended no qualifying clause.

'You've seen him since he came back?' I finally ventured. Claydon nodded.

'And is he so awfully bad?'

'Bad? No: he's all right.'

'All right? How can he be, unless he's changed beyond all recognition?'

'Oh, you'll recognise *him*,' said Claydon, with a puzzling deflection of emphasis.

His ambiguity was beginning to exasperate me, and I felt myself shut out from some knowledge to which I had as good a right as he.

'You've been down there already, I suppose?'

'Yes; I've been down there.'

'And you've done with each other – the partnership is dissolved?'

'Done with each other? I wish to God we had!' He rose nervously and tossed aside the review from which my approach had diverted him. 'Look here,' he said, standing before me, 'Ralph's the best fellow going and there's nothing under heaven I wouldn't do for him – short of going down there again.' And with that he walked out of the room.

Claydon was incalculable enough for me to read a dozen different meanings into his words; but none of my interpretations satisfied me. I determined, at any rate, to seek no farther for a companion; and the next Sunday I travelled down to Grancy's alone. He met me at the station and I saw at once that he had changed since our last meeting. Then he had been in fighting array, but now if he and grief still housed together it was no longer as enemies. Physically the transformation was as marked but less reassuring.

If the spirit triumphed the body showed its scars. At five-and-forty he was gray and stooping, with the tired gait of an old man. His serenity, however, was not the resignation of age. I saw that he did not mean to drop out of the game. Almost immediately he began to speak of our old interests; not with an effort, as at our former meeting, but simply and naturally, in the tone of a man whose life has flowed back into its normal channels. I remembered, with a touch of self-reproach, how I had distrusted his reconstructive powers; but my admiration for his reserved force was now tinged by the sense that, after all, such happiness as his ought to have been paid with his last coin. The feeling grew as we neared the house and I found how inextricably his wife was interwoven with my remembrance of the place: how the whole scene was but an extension of that vivid presence.

Within doors nothing was changed, and my hand would have dropped without surprise into her welcoming clasp. It was luncheon-time, and Grancy led me at once to the dining-room, where the walls, the furniture, the very plate and porcelain, seemed a mirror in which a moment since her face had been reflected. I wondered whether Grancy, under the recovered tranquillity of his smile, concealed the same sense of her nearness, saw perpetually between himself and the actual her bright unappeasable ghost. He spoke of her once or twice, in an easy incidental way, and her name seemed to hang in the air after he had uttered it, like a chord that continues to vibrate. If he felt her presence it was evidently as an enveloping medium, the moral atmosphere in which he breathed. I had never before known how completely the dead may survive.

After luncheon we went for a long walk through the autumnal fields and woods, and dusk was falling when we re-entered the house. Grancy led the way to the library, where, at this hour, his wife had always welcomed us back to a bright fire and a cup of tea. The room faced the west, and held a clear light of its own after the rest of the house had grown dark. I remembered how young she had looked in this pale gold light, which irradiated her eyes and hair, or silhouetted her girlish outline as she passed before the windows. Of all the rooms the library was most peculiarly hers; and here I felt that her nearness might take visible shape. Then, all in a moment, as Grancy opened the door, the feeling vanished and a kind of resistance met me on the threshold. I looked about me. Was the room changed? Had some desecrating hand effaced the traces of her presence? No; here too the setting was undisturbed. My feet sank into the same deep-piled Daghestan; the book-shelves took the firelight on the same rows of rich subdued bindings; her arm-chair stood in its old place near the tea-table; and from the opposite wall her face confronted me.

Her face – but *was* it hers? I moved nearer and stood looking up at the portrait. Grancy's glance had followed mine and I heard him move to my side.

'You see a change in it?' he said.

'What does it mean?' I asked.

'It means – that five years have passed.'

'Over *her*?'

'Why not? – Look at me!' He pointed to his gray hair and furrowed temples. 'What do you think kept *her* so young? It was happiness! But now—' he looked up at her with infinite tenderness. 'I like her better so,' he said. 'It's what she would have wished.'

'Have wished?'

'That we should grow old together. Do you think she would have wanted to be left behind?'

I stood speechless, my gaze travelling from his worn grief-beaten features to the painted face above. It was not furrowed like his; but a veil of years seemed to have descended on it. The bright hair had lost its elasticity, the cheek its clearness, the brow its light: the whole woman had waned.

Grancy laid his hand on my arm. 'You don't like it?' he said sadly.

'Like it? I – I've lost her!' I burst out.

'And I've found her,' he answered.

'In *that*?' I cried with a reproachful gesture.

'Yes; in that.' He swung round on me almost defiantly. 'The other had become a sham, a lie! This is the way she would have looked – does look, I mean. Claydon ought to know, oughtn't he?'

I turned suddenly. 'Did Claydon do this for you?'

Grancy nodded.

'Since your return?'

'Yes. I sent for him after I'd been back a week—.' He turned away and gave a thrust to the smouldering fire. I followed, glad to leave the picture behind me. Grancy threw himself into a chair near the hearth, so that the light fell on his sensitive variable face. He leaned his head back, shading his eyes with his hand, and began to speak.

III

'You fellows knew enough of my early history to guess what my second marriage meant to me. I say guess, because no one could understand – really. I've always had a feminine streak in me, I suppose: the need of a pair of eyes that should see with me, of a pulse that should keep time with mine. Life is a big thing, of course; a magnificent spectacle; but I got so tired of looking at it alone! Still, it's always good to live, and I had plenty of happiness – of the evolved kind. What I'd never had a taste of was the simple inconscient sort that one breathes in like the air.

'Well – I met her. It was like finding the climate in which I was meant to live. You know what she was – how indefinitely she multiplied one's points of contact with life, how she lit up the caverns and bridged the abysses! Well, I swear to you (though I suppose the sense of all that was latent in me) that what I used to think of on my way home at the end of the day, was simply that when I opened this door she'd be sitting over there, with the lamp-light falling in a particular way on one little curl in her neck . . . When Claydon painted her he caught just the look she used to lift to mine when I came in – I've wondered, sometimes, at his knowing how she looked when she and I were alone. – How I rejoiced in that picture! I used to say to her, "You're my prisoner now – I shall never lose you. If you grew tired of me and left me you'd leave your real self there on the wall!" It was always one of our jokes that she was going to grow tired of me—

'Three years of it – and then she died. It was so sudden that there was no change, no diminution. It was as if she had suddenly become fixed, immovable, like her own portrait: as if Time had ceased at its happiest hour, just as Claydon had thrown down his brush one day and said, "I can't do better than that."

'I went away, as you know, and stayed over there five years. I worked as hard as I knew how, and after the first black months a little light stole in on me. From thinking that she would have been interested in what I was doing I came to feel that she *was* interested – that she was there and that she knew. I'm not talking any psychical jargon – I'm simply trying to express the sense I had that an influence so full, so abounding as hers couldn't pass like a spring shower. We had so lived into each other's hearts and minds that the consciousness of what she would have thought and felt illuminated all I did. At first she used to come back shyly, tentatively, as though not sure of finding me; then she stayed longer and longer, till at last she became again the very air I breathed . . . There were bad moments, of course, when her nearness mocked me with the loss of the real woman; but gradually the distinction between the two was effaced and the mere thought of her grew warm as flesh and blood.

'Then I came home. I landed in the morning and came straight down here. The thought of seeing her portrait possessed me and my heart beat like a lover's as I opened the library door. It was in the afternoon and the room was full of light. It fell on her picture – the picture of a young and radiant woman. She smiled at me coldly across the distance that divided us. I had the feeling that she didn't even recognise me. And then I caught sight of myself in the mirror over there – a gray-haired broken man whom she had never known!

'For a week we two lived together – the strange woman and the strange man. I used to sit night after night and question her smiling face; but no answer ever came. What did she know of me, after all? We were irrevocably separated by the five years of life that lay between us. At times, as I sat here, I almost grew to hate her; for her presence had driven away my gentle ghost, the real wife who had wept, aged, struggled with me during those awful years . . . It was the worst loneliness I've ever known. Then, gradually, I began to notice a look of sadness in the picture's eyes; a look that seemed to say: "Don't you see that *I* am lonely too?" And all at once it came over me how she would have hated to be left behind! I remembered her comparing life to a heavy book that could not be read with ease unless two people held it together; and I thought how impatiently her hand would have turned the pages that divided us! – So the idea came to me: "It's the picture that stands between us; the picture that is dead, and not my wife. To sit in this room is to keep watch beside a corpse." As this feeling grew on me the portrait became like a beautiful mausoleum in which she had been buried alive: I could hear her beating against the painted walls and crying to me faintly for help . . .

'One day I found I couldn't stand it any longer and I sent for Claydon. He came down and I told him what I'd been through and what I wanted him to do. At first he refused point-blank to touch the picture. The next morning I went off for a long tramp, and when I came home I found him sitting here alone. He looked at me sharply for a moment and then he said: "I've changed my mind; I'll do it." I arranged one of the north rooms as a studio and he shut himself up there for a day; then he sent for me. The picture stood there as you see it now – it was as though she'd met me on the threshold and taken me in her arms! I tried to thank him, to tell him what it meant to me, but he cut me short.

' "There's an up train at five, isn't there?" he asked. "I'm booked for a dinner to-night. I shall just have time to make a bolt for the station and you can send my traps after me." I haven't seen him since.

'I can guess what it cost him to lay hands on his masterpiece; but, after all, to him it was only a picture lost, to me it was my wife regained!'

IV

After that, for ten years or more, I watched the strange spectacle of a life of hopeful and productive effort based on the structure of a dream. There could be no doubt to those who saw Grancy during this period that he drew his strength and courage from the sense of his wife's mystic participation in his task. When I went back to see him a few months later I found the portrait had been removed from the library and placed in a small study up-stairs, to which he had transferred his desk and a few books. He told me he always sat there when he was alone, keeping the library for his Sunday visitors. Those who missed the portrait of course made no comment on its absence, and the few who were in his secret respected it. Gradually all his old friends had gathered about him and our Sunday afternoons regained something of their former character; but Claydon never reappeared among us.

As I look back now I see that Grancy must have been failing from the time of his return home. His invincible spirit belied and disguised the signs of weakness that afterward asserted themselves in my remembrance of him. He seemed to have an inexhaustible fund of life to draw on, and more than one of us was a pensioner on his superfluity.

Nevertheless, when I came back one summer from my European holiday and heard that he had been at the point of death, I understood at once that we had believed him well only because he wished us to.

I hastened down to the country and found him midway in a slow convalescence. I felt then that he was lost to us and he read my thought at a glance.

'Ah,' he said, 'I'm an old man now and no mistake. I suppose we shall have to go half-speed after this; but we shan't need towing just yet!'

The plural pronoun struck me, and involuntarily I looked up at Mrs Grancy's portrait. Line by line I saw my fear reflected in it. It was the face of a woman *who knows that her husband is dying*. My heart stood still at the thought of what Claydon had done.

Grancy had followed my glance. 'Yes, it's changed her,' he said quietly. 'For months, you know, it was touch and go with me – we had a long fight of it, and it was worse for her than for me.' After a pause he added: 'Claydon has been very kind; he's so busy nowadays that I seldom see him, but when I sent for him the other day he came down at once.'

I was silent and we spoke no more of Grancy's illness; but when I took leave it seemed like shutting him in alone with his death-warrant.

The next time I went down to see him he looked much better. It was a Sunday and he received me in the library, so that I did not see the portrait again. He continued to improve and toward spring we began to feel that, as he had said, he might yet travel a long way without being towed.

One evening, on returning to town after a visit which had confirmed my sense of reassurance, I found Claydon dining alone at the club. He asked me to join him and over the coffee our talk turned to his work.

'If you're not too busy,' I said at length, 'you ought to make time to go down to Grancy's again.'

He looked up quickly. 'Why?' he asked.

'Because he's quite well again,' I returned with a touch of cruelty. 'His wife's prognostications were mistaken.'

Claydon stared at me a moment. 'Oh, *she* knows,' he affirmed with a smile that chilled me.

'You mean to leave the portrait as it is then?' I persisted.

He shrugged his shoulders. 'He hasn't sent for me yet!'

A waiter came up with the cigars and Claydon rose and joined another group.

It was just a fortnight later that Grancy's housekeeper telegraphed for me. She met me at the station with the news that he had been 'taken bad' and that the doctors were with him. I had to wait for some time in the deserted library before the medical men appeared. They had the baffled manner of empirics who have been superseded by the great Healer; and I lingered only long enough to hear that Grancy was not suffering and that my presence could do him no harm.

I found him seated in his arm-chair in the little study. He held out his hand with a smile.

'You see she was right after all,' he said.

'She?' I repeated, perplexed for the moment.

'My wife.' He indicated the picture. 'Of course I knew she had no hope from the first. I saw that' – he lowered his voice – 'after Claydon had been here. But I wouldn't believe it at first!'

I caught his hands in mine. 'For God's sake don't believe it now!' I adjured him.

He shook his head gently. 'It's too late,' he said. 'I might have known that she knew.'

'But, Grancy, listen to me,' I began; and then I stopped. What could I say that would convince him? There was no common ground of argument on which we could meet; and after all it would be easier for him to die feeling that she *had* known. Strangely enough, I saw that Claydon had missed his mark.

V

Grancy's will named me as one of his executors; and my associate, having other duties on his hands, begged me to assume the task of carrying out our friend's wishes. This placed me under the necessity of informing Claydon that the portrait of Mrs Grancy had been bequeathed to him; and he replied by the next post that he would send for the picture at once. I was staying in the deserted house when the portrait was taken away; and as the door closed on it I felt that Grancy's presence had vanished too. Was it his turn to follow her now, and could one ghost haunt another?

After that, for a year or two, I heard nothing more of the picture, and though I met Claydon from time to time we had little to say to each other. I had no definable grievance against the man and I tried to remember that he had done a fine thing in sacrificing his best picture to a friend; but my resentment had all the tenacity of unreason.

One day, however, a lady whose portrait he had just finished begged me to go with her to see it. To refuse was impossible, and I went with the less reluctance that I knew I was not the only friend she had invited. The others were all grouped around the easel when I entered, and after contributing my share to the chorus of approval I turned away and began to stroll about the studio. Claydon was something of a collector and his things were generally worth looking at. The studio was a long tapestried room with a curtained archway at one end. The curtains were looped back, showing a smaller apartment, with books and flowers and a few fine bits of bronze and porcelain. The tea-table standing in this inner room proclaimed that it was open to inspection, and I wandered in. A *bleu poudré* vase first attracted me; then I turned to examine a slender bronze Ganymede, and in so doing found myself face to face with Mrs Grancy's portrait. I stared up at her blankly and she smiled back at me in all the recovered radiance of youth. The artist had effaced every trace of his later touches and the original picture had reappeared. It throned alone on the panelled wall, asserting a brilliant supremacy over its carefully-chosen surroundings. I felt in an instant that the whole room was tributary to it: that Claydon had heaped his treasures at the feet of the woman he loved. Yes – it was the woman he had loved and not the picture; and my instinctive resentment was explained.

Suddenly I felt a hand on my shoulder.

'Ah, how could you?' I cried, turning on him.

'How could I?' he retorted. 'How could I *not*? Doesn't she belong to me now?'

I moved away impatiently.

'Wait a moment,' he said with a detaining gesture. 'The others have gone and I want to say a word to you. – Oh, I know what you've thought of me – I can guess! You think I killed Grancy, I suppose?'

I was startled by his sudden vehemence, 'I think you tried to do a cruel thing,' I said.

'Ah – what a little way you others see into life!' he murmured. 'Sit down a moment – here, where we can look at her – and I'll tell you.'

He threw himself on the ottoman beside me and sat gazing up at the picture, with his hands clasped about his knee.

'Pygmalion,' he began slowly, 'turned his statue into a real woman; *I* turned my real woman into a picture. Small compensation, you think – but you don't know how much of a woman belongs to you after you've painted her! – Well, I made the best of it, at any rate – I gave her the best I had in me; and she gave me in return what such a woman gives by merely being. And after all she rewarded me enough by making me paint as I shall never paint again! There was one side of her, though, that was mine alone, and that was her beauty; for no one else understood it. To Grancy even it was the mere expression of herself – what language is to thought. Even when he saw the picture he didn't guess my secret – he was so sure she was all his! As though a man should think he owned the moon because it was reflected in the pool at his door—

'Well – when he came home and sent for me to change the picture it was like asking me to commit murder. He wanted me to make an old woman of her – of her who had been so divinely, unchangeably young! As if any man who really loved a woman would ask her to sacrifice her youth and beauty for his sake! At first I told him I couldn't do it – but afterward, when he left me alone with the picture, something queer happened. I suppose it was because I was always so confoundedly fond of Grancy that it went against me to refuse what he asked. Anyhow, as I sat looking up at her, she seemed to say, "I'm not yours but his, and I want you to make me what he wishes." And so I did it. I could have cut my hand off when the work was done – I daresay he told you I never would go back and look at it. He thought I was too busy – he never understood . . .

'Well – and then last year he sent for me again – you remember. It was after his illness, and he told me he'd grown twenty years older and that he wanted her to grow older too – he didn't want her to be left behind. The doctors all thought he was going to get well at that time, and he thought so too; and so did I when I first looked at him. But when I turned to the picture – ah, now I don't ask you to believe me; but I swear it was *her* face that told me he was dying, and that she wanted him to know it! She had a message for him and she made me deliver it.'

He rose abruptly and walked toward the portrait; then he sat down beside me again.

'Cruel? Yes, it seemed so to me at first; and this time, if I resisted, it was for *his* sake and not for mine. But all the while I felt her eyes drawing me, and gradually she made me understand. If she'd been there in the flesh (she seemed to say) wouldn't she have seen before any of us that he was dying? Wouldn't he have read the news first in her face? And wouldn't it be horrible if now he should discover it instead in strange eyes? – Well – that was what she wanted of me and I did it – I kept them together to the last!' He looked up at the picture again. 'But now she belongs to me,' he repeated . . .

9

The Door in the Wall

(1911)

H. G. Wells

I

One confidential evening, not three months ago, Lionel Wallace told me this story of the Door in the Wall. And at the time I thought that so far as he was concerned it was a true story.

He told it me with such direct simplicity of conviction that I could not do otherwise than believe in him. But in the morning, in my own flat, I woke to a different atmosphere; and as I lay in bed and recalled the things he had told me, stripped of the glamour of his earnest slow voice, denuded of the focused, shaded table light, the shadowy atmosphere that wrapped about him and me, and the pleasant bright things, the dessert and glasses and napery of the dinner we had shared, making them for the time a bright little world quite cut off from everyday realities, I saw it all as frankly incredible. 'He was mystifying!' I said, and then: 'How well he did it! . . . It isn't quite the thing I should have expected of him, of all people, to do well.'

Afterwards as I sat up in bed and sipped my morning tea, I found myself trying to account for the flavour of reality that perplexed me in his impossible reminiscences, by supposing they did in some way suggest, present, convey – I hardly know which word to use – experiences it was otherwise impossible to tell.

Well, I don't resort to that explanation now. I have got over my intervening doubts. I believe now, as I believed at the moment of telling, that Wallace did to the very best of his ability strip the truth of his secret for me. But whether he himself saw, or only thought he saw, whether he himself was the possessor of an inestimable privilege or the victim of a fantastic dream, I cannot pretend to guess. Even the facts of his death, which ended my doubts for ever, throw no light on that.

That much the reader must judge for himself.

I forget now what chance comment or criticism of mine moved so reticent a man to confide in me. He was, I think, defending himself against an imputation of slackness and unreliability I had made in relation to a great public movement, in which he had disappointed me. But he plunged suddenly. 'I have,' he said, 'a preoccupation –'

'I know,' he went on, after a pause, 'I have been negligent. The fact is – it isn't a case of ghosts or apparitions – but – it's an odd thing to tell of, Redmond – I am haunted. I am haunted by something – that rather takes the light out of things, that fills me with longings . . .'

He paused, checked by that English shyness that so often overcomes us when we speak of moving or grave or beautiful things. 'You were at Saint Athelstan's all through,' he said, and for a moment that seemed to me quite irrelevant. 'Well' – and he paused. Then very haltingly at first, but afterwards more easily, he began to tell of the thing that was hidden in his life, the haunting memory of a beauty and happiness that filled his heart with insatiable longings, that made all the interests and spectacle of worldly life seem dull and tedious and vain to him.

Now that I have the clue to it, the thing seems written visibly in his face. I have a photograph in which that look of detachment has been caught and intensified. It reminds me of what a woman once said of him – a woman who had loved him greatly. 'Suddenly,' she said, 'the interest goes out of him. He forgets you. He doesn't care a rap for you – under his very nose . . .'

Yet the interest was not always out of him, and when he was holding his attention to a thing Wallace could contrive to be an extremely successful man. His career, indeed, is set with successes. He left me behind him long ago; he soared up over my head, and cut a figure in the world that I couldn't cut – anyhow. He was still a year short of forty, and they say now that he would have been in office and very probably in the new Cabinet if he had lived. At school he always beat me without effort – as it were by nature. We were at school together at Saint Athelstan's College in West Kensington for almost all our school-time. He came into the school as my co-equal, but he left far above me, in a blaze of scholarships and brilliant performance. Yet I think I made a fair average running. And it was at school I heard first of the 'Door in the Wall' – that I was to hear of a second time only a month before his death.

To him at least the Door in the Wall was a real door, leading through a real wall to immortal realities. Of that I am now quite assured.

And it came into his life quite early, when he was a little fellow between five and six. I remember how, as he sat making his confession to me with a slow gravity, he reasoned and reckoned the date of it. 'There was,' he said, 'a crimson Virginia creeper in it – all one bright uniform crimson, in a clear amber sunshine against a white wall. That came into the impression somehow, though I don't clearly remember how, and there were horse-chestnut leaves upon the clean pavement outside the green door. They were blotched yellow and green, you know, not brown nor dirty, so that they must have been new fallen. I take it that means October. I look out for horse-chestnut leaves every year and I ought to know.

'If I'm right in that, I was about five years and four months old.'

He was, he said, rather a precocious little boy – he learned to talk at an abnormally early age, and he was so sane and 'old-fashioned', as people say, that he was permitted an amount of initiative that most children scarcely attain by seven or eight. His mother died when he was two, and he was under the less vigilant and authoritative care of a nursery governess. His father was a stern, preoccupied lawyer, who gave him little attention and expected great things of him. For all his brightness he found life grey and dull, I think. And one day he wandered.

He could not recall the particular neglect that enabled him to get away, nor the course he took among the West Kensington roads. All that had faded among the incurable blurs of memory. But the white wall and the green door stood out quite distinctly.

As his memory of that childish experience ran, he did at the very first sight of that door experience a peculiar emotion, an attraction, a desire to get to the door and open it and walk in. And at the same time he had the clearest conviction that either it was unwise or it was wrong of him – he could not tell which – to yield to this attraction. He insisted upon it as a curious thing that he knew from the very beginning – unless memory has played him the queerest trick – that the door was unfastened, and that he could go in as he chose.

I seem to see the figure of that little boy, drawn and repelled. And it was very clear in his mind, too, though why it should be so was never explained, that his father would be very angry if he went in through that door.

Wallace described all these moments of hesitation to me with the utmost particularity. He went right past the door, and then, with his hands in his pockets and making an infantile attempt to whistle, strolled right along beyond the end of the wall. There he recalls a number of mean dirty shops, and particularly that of a plumber and decorator with a dusty disorder of earthenware pipes, sheet lead, ball taps, pattern books of wallpaper, and tins of enamel. He stood pretending to examine these things, and *coveting*, passionately desiring, the green door.

Then, he said, he had a gust of emotion. He made a run for it, lest hesitation should grip him again, he went plumb with outstretched hand through the green door and let it slam behind him. And so, in a trice, he came into the garden that has haunted all his life.

It was very difficult for Wallace to give me his full sense of that garden into which he came.

There was something in the very air of it that exhilarated, that gave one a sense of lightness and good happening and well-being, there was something in the sight of it that made all its colour clean and perfect and subtly luminous. In the instant of coming into it one was exquisitely glad – as only in rare moments, and when one is young and joyful one can be glad in this world. And everything was beautiful there . . .

Wallace mused before he went on telling me. 'You see,' he said, with the doubtful inflection of a man who pauses at incredible things, 'there were two great panthers there . . . Yes, spotted panthers. And I was not afraid. There was a long wide path with marble-edged flower borders on either side, and these two huge velvety beasts were playing there with a ball. One looked up and came towards me, a little curious as it seemed. It came right up to me, rubbed its soft round ear very gently against the small hand I held out, and purred. It was, I tell you, an enchanted garden. I know. And the size? Oh! it stretched far and wide, this way and that. I believe there were hills far away. Heaven knows where West Kensington had suddenly got to. And somehow it was just like coming home.

'You know, in the very moment the door swung to behind me, I forgot the road with its fallen chestnut leaves, its cabs and tradesmen's carts, I forgot the sort of gravitational pull back to the discipline and obedience of home, I forgot all hesitations and fear, forgot discretion, forgot all the intimate realities of this life. I became in a moment a very glad and wonder-happy little boy – in another world. It was a world with a different quality, a warmer, more penetrating, and mellower light, with a faint clear gladness in its air, and wisps of sun-touched cloud in the blueness of its sky. And before me ran this long wide path, invitingly, with weedless beds on either side, rich with untended flowers, and these two great panthers. I put my little hands fearlessly on their soft fur, and caressed their round ears and the sensitive corners under their ears, and played with them, and it was as though they welcomed me home. There was a keen sense of homecoming in my mind, and when presently a tall, fair girl appeared in the pathway and came to meet me, smiling, and said, 'Well?' to me, and lifted me and kissed me and put me down and led me by the hand, there was no amazement, but only an impression of delightful rightness, of being reminded of happy things that had in some strange way been overlooked. There were broad red steps, I remember, that came into view between spikes of delphinium, and up these we went to a great avenue between very old and shady dark trees. All down this avenue, you know, between the red chapped stems, were marble seats of honour and statuary, and very tame and friendly white doves.

'Along this cool avenue my girl-friend led me, looking down – I recall the pleasant lines, the finely-modelled chin of her sweet kind face – asking me questions in a soft, agreeable voice, and telling me things, pleasant things, I know, though what they were I was never able to recall . . . Presently a Capuchin monkey, very clean, with a fur of ruddy brown and kindly hazel eyes, came down a tree to us and ran beside me, looking up at me and grinning, and presently leaped to my shoulder. So we two went on our way in great happiness.'

He paused.

'Go on,' I said.

'I remember little things. We passed an old man musing among laurels, I remember, and a place gay with parakeets, and came through a broad shaded colonnade to a spacious cool palace, full of pleasant fountains, full of beautiful things, full of the quality and promise of heart's desire. And there were many things and many people, some that still seem to stand out clearly and some that are vaguer; but all these people were beautiful and kind. In some way – I don't know how – it was conveyed to me that they all were kind to me, glad to have me there, and filling me with gladness by their gestures, by the touch of their hands, by the welcome and love in their eyes. Yes –'

He mused for a while. 'Playmates I found there. That was much to me, because I was a lonely little boy. They played delightful games in a grass-covered court where there was a sundial set about with flowers. And as one played one loved . . .

'But – it's odd – there's a gap in my memory. I don't remember the games we played. I never remembered. Afterwards, as a child, I spent long hours trying, even with tears, to recall the form of that happiness. I wanted to play it all over again – in my nursery – by myself. No! All I remember is the happiness and two dear playfellows who were most with me . . . Then presently came a sombre dark woman, with a grave, pale face and dreamy eyes, a sombre women, wearing a soft long robe of pale purple, who carried a book, and beckoned and took me aside with her into a gallery above a hall – though my playmates were loth to have me go, and ceased their game and stood watching as I was carried away. "Come back to us!" they cried. "Come back to us soon!" I looked up at her face, but she heeded them not at all. Her face was very gentle and grave. She took me to a seat in the gallery, and I stood beside her, ready to look at her book as she opened it upon her knee. The pages fell open. She pointed, and I looked, marvelling, for in the living pages of that book I saw myself, it was a story about myself, and in it were all the things that had happened to me since ever I was born . . .

'It was wonderful to me, because the pages of that book were not pictures, you understand, but realities.'

Wallace paused gravely – looked at me doubtfully.

'Go on,' I said. 'I understand.'

'They were realities – yes, they must have been; people moved and things came and went in them; my dear mother, whom I had near forgotten; then my father, stern and upright, the servants, the nursery, all the familiar things of home. Then the front door and the busy streets, with traffic to and fro. I looked and marvelled, and looked half doubtfully again into the woman's face and turned the pages over, skipping this and that, to see more of this book and more, and so at last I came to myself hovering and hesitating outside the green door in the long white wall, and felt again the conflict and the fear.

' "And next?" I cried, and would have turned on, but the cool hand of the grave woman delayed me.

' "Next?" I insisted, and struggled gently with her hand, pulling up her fingers with all my childish strength, and as she yielded and the page came over she bent down upon me like a shadow and kissed my brow.

'But the page did not show the enchanted garden, nor the panthers, nor the girl who had led me by the hand, nor the playfellows who had been so loth to let me go. It showed a long grey street in West Kensington, in that chill hour of afternoon before the lamps are lit; and I was there, a wretched little figure, weeping aloud, for all that I could do to restrain myself, and I was weeping because I could not return to my dear playfellows who had called after me, "Come back to us! Come back to us soon!" I was there. This was no page in a book, but harsh reality; that enchanted place and the restraining hand of the grave mother at whose knee I stood had gone – whither had they gone?'

He halted again, and remained for a time staring into the fire.

'Oh! the woefulness of that return!' he murmured.

'Well?' I said, after a minute or so.

'Poor little wretch I was! – brought back to this grey world again! As I realised the fullness of what had happened to me, I gave way to quite ungovernable grief. And the shame and humiliation of that public weeping and my disgraceful home-coming remain with me still. I see again the benevolent-looking old gentleman in gold spectacles who stopped and spoke to me – prodding me first with his umbrella. "Poor little chap," said he; "and are you lost then?" – and me a London boy of five and more! And he must needs bring in a kindly young policeman and make a crowd of me, and so march me home. Sobbing, conspicuous, and frightened, I came back from the enchanted garden to the steps of my father's house.

'That is as well as I can remember my vision of that garden – the garden that haunts me still. Of course, I can convey nothing of that indescribable quality of translucent unreality, that difference from the common things of experience that hung about it all; but that – that is what happened. If it was a dream, I am sure it was a daytime and altogether extraordinary dream . . . H'm! – naturally there followed a terrible questioning, by my aunt, my father, the nurse, the governess – everyone . . .

'I tried to tell them, and my father gave me my first thrashing for telling lies. When afterwards I tried to tell my aunt, she punished me again for my wicked persistence. Then, as I said, everyone was forbidden to listen to me, to hear a word about it. Even my fairy-tale books were taken away from me for a time – because I was too "imaginative". Eh! Yes, they did that! My father belonged to the old school . . . And my story was driven back upon myself. I whispered it to my pillow – my pillow that was often damp and salt to my whispering lips with childish tears. And I added always to my official and less fervent prayers this one heartfelt request: "Please God I may dream of the garden. O! take me back to my garden." Take me back to my garden! I dreamt often of the garden. I may have added to it, I may have changed it; I do not know . . . All this, you understand, is an attempt to reconstruct from fragmentary memories a very early experience. Between that and the other consecutive memories of my boyhood there is a gulf. A time came when it seemed impossible I should ever speak of that wonder glimpse again.'

I asked an obvious question.

'No,' he said. 'I don't remember that I ever attempted to find my way back to the garden in those early years. This seems odd to me now, but I think that very probably a closer watch was kept on my movements after this misadventure to prevent my going astray. No, it wasn't till you knew me that I tried for the garden again. And I believe there was a period – incredible as it seems now – when I forgot the garden altogether – when I was about eight or nine it may have been. Do you remember me as a kid at Saint Athelstan's?'

'Rather!'

'I didn't show any signs, did I, in those days of having a secret dream?'

II

He looked up with a sudden smile.

'Did you ever play North-West Passage with me? . . . No, of course you didn't come my way!

'It was the sort of game,' he went on, 'that every imaginative child plays all day. The idea was the discovery of a North-West Passage to school. The way to school was plain enough; the game consisted of finding some way that wasn't plain, starting off ten minutes early in some almost hopeless direction, and working my way round through unaccustomed streets to my goal. And one day I got entangled among some rather low-class streets on the other side of Campden Hill, and I began to think that for once the game would be against me and that I should get to school late. I tried rather desperately a street that seemed a cul-de-sac, and found a passage at the end. I hurried through that with renewed hope. "I shall do it yet," I said, and passed a row of frowsy little shops that were inexplicably familiar to me, and behold! there was my long white wall and the green door that led to the enchanted garden!

'The thing whacked upon me suddenly. Then, after all, that garden, that wonderful garden, wasn't a dream!'

He paused.

'I suppose my second experience with the green door marks the world of difference there is between the busy life of a schoolboy and the infinite leisure of a child. Anyhow, this second time I didn't for a moment think of going in straight away. You see – For one thing, my mind was full of the idea of getting to school in time – set on not breaking my record for punctuality. I must surely have felt *some* little desire at least to try the door – yes. I must have felt that . . . But I seem to remember the attraction of the door mainly as another obstacle to my overmastering determination to get to school. I was immensely interested by this discovery I had made, of course – I went on with my mind full of it – but I went on. It didn't check me. I ran past, tugging out my watch, found I had ten minutes still to spare, and then I was going downhill into familiar surroundings. I got to school, breathless, it is true, and wet with perspiration, but in time. I can remember hanging up my coat and hat . . . Went right by it and left it behind me. Odd, eh?'

He looked at me thoughtfully. 'Of course I didn't know then that it wouldn't always be there. Schoolboys have limited imaginations. I suppose I thought it was an awfully jolly thing to have it there, to know my way back to it; but there was the school tugging at me. I expect I was a good deal distraught and inattentive that morning, recalling what I could of the beautiful strange people I should presently see again. Oddly enough I had no doubt in my mind that they would be glad to see me . . . Yes, I must have thought of the garden that morning just as a jolly sort of place to which one might resort in the interludes of a strenuous scholastic career.

'I didn't go that day at all. The next day was a half-holiday, and that may have weighed with me. Perhaps, too, my state of inattention brought down impositions upon me, and docked the margin of time necessary for the *détour*. I don't know. What I do know is that in the meantime the enchanted garden was so much upon my mind that I could not keep it to myself.

'I told – what was his name? – a ferrety-looking youngster we used to call Squiff.'

'Young Hopkins,' said I.

'Hopkins it was. I did not like telling him. I had a feeling that in some way it was against the rules to tell him, but I did. He was walking part of the way home with me; he was talkative, and if we had not talked about the enchanted garden we should have talked of something else, and it was intolerable to me to think about any other subject. So I blabbed.

'Well, he told my secret. The next day in the play interval I found myself surrounded by half a dozen bigger boys, half teasing, and wholly curious to hear more of the enchanted garden. There was that big Fawcett – you remember him? – and Carnaby and Morley Reynolds. You weren't there by any chance? No, I think I should have remembered if you were . . .

'A boy is a creature of odd feelings. I was, I really believe, in spite of my secret self-disgust, a little flattered to have the attention of these big fellows. I remember particularly a moment of pleasure caused by the praise of Crawshaw – you remember Crawshaw major, the son of Crawshaw the composer? – who said it was the best lie he had ever heard. But at the same time there was a really painful undertow of shame at telling what I felt was indeed a sacred secret. That beast Fawcett made a joke about the girl in green—'

Wallace's voice sank with the keen memory of that shame. 'I pretended not to hear,' he said. 'Well, then Carnaby suddenly called me a young liar, and disputed with me when I said the thing was true. I said I knew where to find the green door, could lead them all there in ten minutes. Carnaby became outrageously virtuous, and said I'd have to – and bear out my words or suffer. Did you ever have Carnaby twist your arm? Then perhaps you'll understand how it went with me. I swore my story was true. There was nobody in the school then to save a chap from Carnaby, though Crawshaw put in a word or so. Carnaby had got his game. I grew excited and red-eared, and a little frightened. I behaved altogether like a silly little chap, and the outcome of it all was that instead of starting alone for my enchanted garden, I led the way presently – cheeks flushed, ears hot, eyes smarting, and my soul one burning misery and shame – for a party of six mocking, curious, and threatening schoolfellows.

'We never found the white wall and the green door . . .'

'You mean—'

'I mean I couldn't find it. I would have found it if I could.

'And afterwards when I could go alone I couldn't find it. I never found it. I seem now to have been always looking for it through my schoolboy days, but I never came upon it – never.'

'Did the fellows – make it disagreeable?'

'Beastly . . . Carnaby held a council over me for wanton lying. I remember how I sneaked home and upstairs to hide the marks of my blubbering. But when I cried myself to sleep at last it wasn't for Carnaby, but for the garden, for the beautiful afternoon I had hoped for, for the sweet friendly woman and the waiting playfellows, and the game I had hoped to learn again, that beautiful forgotten game . . .

'I believed firmly that if I had not told – I had bad times after that – crying at night and wool-gathering by day. For two terms I slacked and had bad reports. Do you remember? Of course you would! It was *you* – your beating me in mathematics that brought me back to the grind again.'

III

For a time my friend stared silently into the red heart of the fire. Then he said: 'I never saw it again until I was seventeen.

'It leaped upon me for the third time – as I was driving to Paddington on my way to Oxford and a scholarship. I had just one momentary glimpse. I was leaning over the apron of my hansom smoking a cigarette, and no doubt thinking myself no end of a man of the world, and suddenly there was the door, the wall, the dear sense of unforgettable and still attainable things.

'We clattered by – I too taken by surprise to stop my cab until we were well past and round a corner. Then I had a queer moment, a double and divergent movement of my will: I tapped the little door in the roof of the cab, and brought my arm down to pull out my watch. "Yes, sir!" said the cabman smartly. "Er – well – it's nothing," I cried. "*My* mistake! We haven't much time! Go on!" And he went on . . .

'I got my scholarship. And the night after I was told of that I sat over my fire in my little upper room, my study, in my father's house, with his praise – his rare praise – and his sound counsels ringing in my ears, and I smoked my favourite pipe – the formidable bulldog of adolescence – and thought of that door in the long white wall. "If I had stopped," I thought, "I should have missed my scholarship. I should have missed Oxford – muddled all the fine career before me! I begin to see things better!" I fell to musing deeply, but I did not doubt then this career of mine was a thing that merited sacrifice.

'Those dear friends and that clear atmosphere seemed very sweet to me, very fine but remote. My grip was fixing now upon the world. I saw another door opening – the door of my career.'

He stared again into the fire. Its red light picked out a stubborn strength in his face for just one flickering moment, and then it vanished again.

'Well,' he said and sighed, 'I have served that career. I have done – much work, much hard work. But I have dreamt of the enchanted garden a thousand dreams, and seen its door, or at least glimpsed its door, four times since then. Yes – four times. For a while this world was so bright and interesting, seemed so full of meaning and opportunity, that the half-effaced charm of the garden was by comparison gentle and remote. Who wants to pat panthers on the way to dinner with pretty women and distinguished men? I came down to London from Oxford, a man of bold promise that I have done something to redeem. Something – and yet there have been disappointments . . .

'Twice I have been in love – I will not dwell on that – but once, as I went to some one who, I knew, doubted whether I dared to come, I took a short cut at a venture through an unfrequented road near Earl's Court, and so happened on a white wall and a familiar green door. "Odd!" said I to myself, "but I thought this place was on Campden Hill. It's the place I never could find somehow – like counting Stonehenge – the place of that queer daydream of mine." And I went by it intent upon my purpose. It had no appeal to me that afternoon.

'I had just a moment's impulse to try the door, three steps aside were needed at the most – though I was sure enough in my heart that it would open to me – and then I thought that doing so might delay me on the way to that appointment in which my honour was involved. Afterwards I was sorry for my punctuality – I might at least have peeped in and waved a hand to those panthers, but I knew enough by this time not to seek again belatedly that which is not found by seeking. Yes, that time made me very sorry . . .

'Years of hard work after that, and never a sight of the door. It's only recently it has come back to me. With it there has come a sense as though some thin tarnish had spread itself over my world. I began to think of it as a sorrowful and bitter thing that I should never see that door again. Perhaps I was suffering a little from overwork – perhaps it was what I've heard spoken of as the feeling of forty. I don't know. But certainly the keen brightness that makes effort easy has gone out of things recently, and that just at a time – with all these new political developments – when I ought to be working. Odd, isn't it? But I do begin to find life toilsome, its rewards, as I come near them, cheap. I began a little while ago to want the garden quite badly. Yes – and I've seen it three times.'

'The garden?'

'No – the door! And I haven't gone in!'

He leaned over the table to me, with an enormous sorrow in his voice as he spoke. 'Thrice I have had my chance – thrice! If ever that door offers itself to me again, I swore, I will go in, out of this dust and heat, out of this dry glitter of vanity, out of these toilsome futilities. I will go and never return. This time I will stay . . . I swore it, and when the time came – I *didn't* go.

'Three times in one year I have passed that door and failed to enter. Three times in the last year.

'The first time was on the night of the snatch division on the Tenants' Redemption Bill, on which the Government was saved by a majority of three. You remember? No one on our side – perhaps very few on the opposite side – expected the end that night. Then the debate collapsed like egg-shells. I and Hotchkiss were dining with his cousin at Brentford; we were both unpaired, and we were called up by telephone, and set off at once in his cousin's motor. We got in barely in time, and on the way we passed my wall and door – livid in the moonlight, blotched with hot yellow as the glare of our lamps lit it, but unmistakable. "My God!" cried I. "What?" said Hotchkiss. "Nothing!" I answered, and the moment passed.

' "I've made a great sacrifice," I told the whip as I got in. "They all have," ' he said, and hurried by.

'I do not see how I could have done otherwise then. And the next occasion was as I rushed to my father's bedside to bid that stern old man farewell. Then, too, the claims of life were imperative. But the third time was different; it happened a week ago. It fills me with hot remorse to recall it. I was with Gurker and Ralphs – it's no secret now, you know, that I've had my talk with Gurker. We had been dining at Frobisher's, and the talk had become intimate between us. The question of my place in the reconstructed Ministry lay always just over the boundary of the discussion. Yes – yes. That's all settled. It needn't be talked about yet, but there's no reason to keep a secret from you . . . Yes – thanks! thanks! But let me tell you my story.

'Then, on that night things were very much in the air. My position was a very delicate one. I was keenly anxious to get some definite word from Gurker, but was hampered by Ralphs' presence. I was using the best power of my brain to keep that light and careless talk not too obviously directed to the point that concerned me. I had to. Ralphs' behaviour since has more than justified my caution . . . Ralphs, I knew, would leave us beyond the Kensington High Street, and then I could surprise Gurker by a sudden frankness. One has sometimes to resort to these little devices . . . And then it was that in the margin of my field of vision I became aware once more of the white wall, the green door before us down the road.

'We passed it talking. I passed it. I can still see the shadow of Gurker's marked profile, his opera hat tilted forward over his prominent nose, the many folds of his neck wrap going before my shadow and Ralphs' as we sauntered past.

'I passed within twenty inches of the door. "If I say goodnight to them, and go in," I asked myself, "what will happen?" And I was all a-tingle for that word with Gurker.

'I could not answer that question in the tangle of my other problems. "They will think me mad," I thought. "And suppose I vanish now? – Amazing disappearance of a prominent politician!" That weighed with me. A thousand inconceivable petty worldlinesses weighed with me in that crisis.'

Then he turned on me with a sorrowful smile, and, speaking slowly, 'Here I am!' he said.

'Here I am!' he repeated, 'and my chance has gone from me. Three times in one year the door has been offered me – that door that goes into peace, into delight, into a beauty beyond dreaming, a kindness no man on earth can know. And I have rejected it, Redmond, and it has gone—'

'How do you know?'

'I know, I know. I am left now to work it out, to stick to the tasks that held me so strongly when my moments came. You say I have success – this vulgar, tawdry, irksome, envied thing. I have it.' He had a walnut in his big hand. 'If that was my success,' he said, and crushed it, and held it out for me to see.

'Let me tell you something, Redmond. This loss is destroying me. For two months, for ten weeks nearly now, I have done no work at all, except the most necessary and urgent duties. My soul if full of inappeasable regrets. At nights – when it is less likely I shall be recognised – I go out. I wander. Yes. I wonder what people would think of that if they knew. A Cabinet Minister, the responsible head of that most vital of all departments, wandering alone – grieving – sometimes near audibly lamenting – for a door, for a garden!'

IV

I can see now his rather pallid face, and the unfamiliar sombre fire that had come into his eyes. I see him very vividly tonight. I sit recalling his words, his tones, and last evening's *Westminster Gazette* still lies on my sofa, containing the notice of his death. At lunch today the club was busy with his death. We talked of nothing else.

They found his body very early yesterday morning in a deep excavation near East Kensington Station. It is one of two shafts that have been made in connection with an extension of the railway southward. It is protected from the intrusion of the public by a hoarding upon the high road, in which a small doorway has been cut for the convenience of some of the workmen who live in that direction. The doorway was left unfastened through a misunderstanding between two gangers, and through it he made his way.

My mind is darkened with questions and riddles.

It would seem he walked all the way from the House that night – he has frequently walked home during the past Session – and so it is I figure his dark form coming along the late and empty streets, wrapped up, intent. And then did the pale electric lights near the station cheat the rough planking into a semblance of white? Did that fatal unfastened door awaken some memory?

Was there, after all, ever any green door in the wall at all?

I do not know. I have told his story as he told it to me. There are times when I believe that Wallace was no more than the victim of the coincidence between a rare but not unprecedented type of hallucination and a careless trap, but that indeed is not my profoundest belief. You may think me superstitious, if you will, and foolish; but, indeed, I am more than half convinced that he had, in truth, an abnormal gift, and a sense, something – I know not what – that in the guise of a wall and door offered him an outlet, a secret and peculiar passage of escape into another and altogether more beautiful world. At any rate, you will say, it betrayed him in the end. But did it betray him? There you touch the inmost mystery of these dreamers, these men of vision and the imagination. We see our world fair and common, the hoarding and the pit. By our daylight standard he walked out of security into darkness, danger, and death.

But did he see like that?

10

Sredni Vashtar

(1912)

Saki (Hector Hugh Munro)

Conradin was ten years old, and the doctor had pronounced his professional opinion that the boy would not live another five years. The doctor was silky and effete, and counted for little, but his opinion was endorsed by Mrs De Ropp, who counted for nearly everything. Mrs De Ropp was Conradin's cousin and guardian, and in his eyes she represented those three-fifths of the world that are necessary and disagreeable and real; the other two-fifths, in perpetual antagonism to the foregoing, were summed up in himself and his imagination. One of these days Conradin supposed he would succumb to the mastering pressure of wearisome necessary things – such as illnesses and coddling restrictions and drawn-out dullness. Without his imagination, which was rampant under the spur of loneliness, he would have succumbed long ago.

Mrs De Ropp would never, in her honestest moments, have confessed to herself that she disliked Conradin, though she might have been dimly aware that thwarting him 'for his good' was a duty which she did not find particularly irksome. Conradin hated her with a desperate sincerity which he was perfectly able to mask. Such few pleasures as he could contrive for himself gained an added relish from the likelihood that they would be displeasing to his guardian, and from the realm of his imagination she was locked out – an unclean thing, which should find no entrance.

In the dull, cheerless garden, overlooked by so many windows that were ready to open with a message not to do this or that, or a reminder that medicines were due, he found little attraction. The few fruit-trees that it contained were set jealously apart from his plucking, as though they were rare specimens of their kind blooming in an arid waste; it would probably have been difficult to find a market-gardener who would have offered ten shillings for their entire yearly produce. In a forgotten corner, however, almost hidden behind a dismal shrubbery, was a disused tool-shed of respectable proportions, and within its walls Conradin found a haven, something that took on the varying aspects of a playroom and a cathedral. He had peopled it with a legion of familiar phantoms, evoked partly from fragments of history and partly from his own brain, but it also boasted two inmates of flesh and blood. In one corner lived a ragged-plumaged Houdan hen, on which the boy lavished an affection that had scarcely another outlet. Further back in the gloom stood a large hutch, divided into two compartments, one of which was fronted with close iron bars. This was the abode of a large polecat-ferret, which a friendly butcher-boy had once smuggled, cage and all, into its present quarters, in exchange for a long-secreted hoard of small silver. Conradin was dreadfully afraid of the lithe, sharp-fanged beast, but it was his most treasured possession. Its very presence in the tool-shed was a secret and fearful joy, to be kept scrupulously from the knowledge of the Woman, as he privately dubbed his cousin. And one day, out of Heaven knows what material, he spun the beast a wonderful name, and from that moment it grew into a god and a religion. The Woman indulged in religion once a week at a church near by and took Conradin with her, but to him the church service was an alien rite in the House of Rimmon. Every Thursday, in the dim and musty silence of the tool-shed he worshipped with mystic and elaborate ceremonial before the wooden hutch where dwelt Sredni Vashtar, the great ferret. Red flowers in their season and scarlet berries in the winter-time were offered at his shrine, for he was a god who laid some special stress on the fierce impatient side of things, as opposed to the Woman's religion which, as far as Conradin could observe, went to great lengths in the contrary direction. And on great festivals powdered nutmeg was strewn in front of his hutch, an important feature of the offering being that the nutmeg had to be stolen. These festivals were of irregular occurrence, and were chiefly appointed to celebrate some passing event. On one occasion, when Mrs De Ropp suffered from acute toothache for three days, Conradin kept up the festival during the entire three days, and almost succeeded in persuading himself that Sredni Vashtar was personally responsible for the toothache. If the malady had lasted for another day the supply of nutmeg would have given out.

The Houdan hen was never drawn into the cult of Sredni Vashtar. Conradin had long ago settled that she was an Anabaptist. He did not pretend to have the remotest knowledge as to what an Anabaptist was, but he privately hoped that it was dashing and not very respectable. Mrs De Ropp was the ground plan on which he based and detested all respectability.

After a while Conradin's absorption in the tool-shed began to attract the notice of his guardian. 'It is not good for him to be pottering down there in all weathers,' she promptly decided, and at breakfast one morning she announced that the Houdan hen had been sold and taken away overnight. With her short-sighted eyes she peered at Conradin, waiting for an outbreak of rage and sorrow, which she was ready to rebuke with a flow of excellent precepts and reasoning. But Conradin said nothing: there was nothing to be said. Something perhaps in his white set face gave her a momentary qualm, for at tea that afternoon there was toast on the table, a delicacy which she usually banned on the ground that it was bad for him; also because the making of it 'gave trouble', a deadly offence in the middle-class feminine eye.

'I thought you liked toast,' she exclaimed, with an injured air, observing that he did not touch it.

'Sometimes,' said Conradin.

In the shed that evening there was an innovation in the worship of the hutch god. Conradin had been wont to chant his praises, tonight he asked a boon.

'Do one thing for me, Sredni Vashtar.'

The thing was not specified. As Sredni Vashtar was a god he must be supposed to know. And choking back a sob as he looked at that other empty corner, Conradin went back to the world he so hated.

And every night, in the welcome darkness of his bedroom, and every evening in the dusk of the tool-shed, Conradin's bitter litany went up: 'Do one thing for me, Sredni Vashtar.'

Mrs De Ropp noticed that the visits to the shed did not cease, and one day she made a further journey of inspection.

'What are you keeping in that locked hutch?' she asked. 'I believe it's guinea-pigs. I'll have them all cleared away.'

Conradin shut his lips tight, but the Woman ransacked his bedroom till she found the carefully hidden key, and forthwith marched down to the shed to complete her discovery. It was a cold afternoon, and Conradin had been bidden to keep to the house. From the furthest window of the dining-room the door of the shed could just be seen beyond the corner of the shrubbery, and there Conradin stationed himself. He saw the Woman enter, and then he imagined her opening the door of the sacred hutch and peering down with her short-sighted eyes into the thick straw bed where his god lay hidden. Perhaps she would prod at the straw in her clumsy impatience. And Conradin fervently breathed his prayer for the last time. But he knew as he prayed that he did not believe. He knew that the Woman would come out presently with that pursed smile he loathed so well on her face, and that in an hour or two the gardener would carry away his wonderful god, a god no longer, but a simple brown ferret in a hutch. And he knew that the Woman would triumph always as she triumphed now, and that he would grow ever more sickly under her pestering and domineering and superior wisdom, till one day nothing would matter much more with him, and the doctor would be proved right. And in the sting and misery of his defeat, he began to chant loudly and defiantly the hymn of his threatened idol:

> Sredni Vashtar went forth,
> His thoughts were red thoughts and his teeth were white.
> His enemies called for peace, but he brought them death.
> Sredni Vashtar the Beautiful.

And then of a sudden he stopped his chanting and drew closer to the window-pane. The door of the shed still stood ajar as it had been left, and the minutes were slipping by. They were long minutes, but they slipped by nevertheless. He watched the starlings running and flying in little parties across the lawn; he counted them over and over again, with one eye always on that swinging door. A sour-faced maid came in to lay the table for tea, and still Conradin stood and waited and watched. Hope had crept by inches into his heart, and now a look of triumph began to blaze in his eyes that had only known the wistful patience of defeat. Under his breath, with a furtive exultation, he began once again the pæan of victory and devastation. And presently his eyes were rewarded: out through that doorway came a long, low, yellow-and-brown beast, with eyes a-blink at the waning daylight, and dark wet stains around the fur of jaws and throat. Conradin dropped on his knees. The great polecat-ferret made its way down to a small brook at the foot of the garden, drank for a moment, then crossed a little plank bridge and was lost to sight in the bushes. Such was the passing of Sredni Vashtar.

'Tea is ready,' said the sour-faced maid; 'where is the mistress?'

'She went down to the shed some time ago,' said Conradin.

And while the maid went to summon her mistress to tea, Conradin fished a toasting-fork out of the sideboard drawer and proceeded to toast himself a piece of bread. And during the toasting of it and the buttering of it with much butter and the slow enjoyment of eating it, Conradin listened to the noises and silences which fell in quick spasms beyond the dining-room door. The loud foolish screaming of the maid, the answering chorus of wondering ejaculations from the kitchen region, the scuttering footsteps and hurried embassies for outside help, and then, after a lull, the scared sobbings and the shuffling tread of those who bore a heavy burden into the house.

'Whoever will break it to the poor child? I couldn't for the life of me!' exclaimed a shrill voice. And while they debated the matter among themselves, Conradin made himself another piece of toast.

11

How It Happened

(1918)

Arthur Conan Doyle

I can remember some things upon that evening most distinctly, and others are like some vague, broken dreams. That is what makes it so difficult to tell a connected story. I have no idea now what it was that had taken me to London and brought me back so late. It just merges into all my other visits to London. But from the time that I got out at the little country station everything is extraordinarily clear. I can live it again – every instant of it.

I remember so well walking down the platform and looking at the illuminated clock at the end which told me that it was half-past eleven. I remember also my wondering whether I could get home before midnight. Then I remember the big motor, with its glaring headlights and litter of polished brass, waiting for me outside. It was my new thirty-horse-power Robur, which had only been delivered that day. I remember also asking Perkins, my chauffeur, how she had gone, and his saying that he thought she was excellent.

'I'll try her myself,' said I, and I climbed into the driver's seat.

'The gears are not the same,' said he, 'Perhaps, sir, I had better drive.'

'No; I should like to try her,' said I.

And so we started on the five-mile drive for home.

My old car had the gears as they used always to be in notches on a bar. In this car you passed the gear-lever through a gate to get on the higher ones. It was not difficult to master, and soon I thought that I understood it. It was foolish, no doubt, to begin to learn a new system in the dark, but one often does foolish things, and one has not always to pay the full price for them. I got along very well until I came to Claystall Hill. It is one of the worst hills in England, a mile and a half long and one in six in places, with three fairly sharp curves. My park gate stands at the very foot of it upon the main London road.

We were just over the brow of this hill, where the grade is steepest, when the trouble began. I had been on the top speed, and wanted to get her on the free; but she stuck between gears, and I had to get her back on the top again. By this time she was going at a great rate, so I clapped on both brakes, and one after the other they gave way. I didn't mind so much when I felt my foot-brake snap, but when I put all my weight on my side-brake, and the lever clanged to its full limit without a catch, it brought a cold sweat out of me. By this time we were fairly tearing down the slope. The lights were brilliant, and I brought her round the first curve all right. Then we did the second one, though it was a close shave for the ditch. There was a mile of straight then with the third curve beneath it, and after that the gate of the park. If I could shoot into that harbour all would be well, for the slope up to the house would bring her to a stand.

Perkins behaved splendidly. I should like that to be known. He was perfectly cool and alert. I had thought at the very beginning of taking the bank, and he read my intention.

'I wouldn't do it, sir,' said he. 'At this pace it must go over and we should have it on the top of us.'

Of course he was right. He got to the electric switch and had it off, so we were in the free; but we were still running at a fearful pace. He laid his hands on the wheel.

'I'll keep her steady,' said, 'if you care to jump and chance it. We can never get round that curve. Better jump, sir.'

'No,' said I; 'I'll stick it out. You can jump if you like.'

'I'll stick it with you, sir,' said he.

If it had been the old car I should have jammed the gear-lever into the reverse, and seen what would happen. I expect she would have stripped her gears or smashed up somehow, but it would have been a chance. As it was, I was helpless. Perkins tried to climb across, but you couldn't do it going at that pace. The wheels were whirring like a high wind and the big body creaking and groaning with the strain. But the lights were brilliant, and one could steer to an inch. I remember thinking what an awful and yet majestic sight we should appear to anyone who met us. It was a narrow road, and we were just a great, roaring, golden death to anyone who came in our path.

We got round the corner with one wheel three feet high upon the bank. I thought we were surely over, but after staggering for a moment she righted and darted onwards. That was the third corner and the last one. There was only the park gate now. It was facing us, but, as luck would have it, not facing us directly. It was about twenty yards to the left up the main road into which we ran. Perhaps I could have done it, but I expect that the steering-gear had been jarred when we ran on the bank. The wheel did not turn easily. We shot out of the lane. I saw the open gate on the left. I whirled round my wheel with all the strength of my wrist. Perkins and I threw our bodies across, and then the next instant, going at fifty miles an hour, my right wheel struck full on the right-hand pillar of my own gate. I heard the crash. I was conscious of flying through the air, and then – and then—!

When I became aware of my own existence once more I was among some brushwood in the shadow of the oaks upon the lodge side of the drive. A man was standing beside me. I imagined at first that it was Perkins, but when I looked again I saw that it was Stanley, a man whom I had known at college some years before, and for whom I had a really genuine affection. There was always something peculiarly sympathetic to me in

Stanley's personality; and I was proud to think that I had some similar influence upon him. At the present moment I was surprised to see him, but I was like a man in a dream, giddy and shaken and quite prepared to take things as I found them without questioning them.

'What a smash!' I said. 'Good Lord, what an awful smash!'

He nodded his head, and even in the gloom I could see that he was smiling the gentle, wistful smile which I connected with him.

I was quite unable to move. Indeed, I had not any desire to try to move. But my senses were exceedingly alert. I saw the wreck of the motor lit up by the moving lanterns. I saw the little group of people and heard the hushed voices. There were the lodge-keeper and his wife, and one or two more. They were taking no notice of me, but were very busy round the car. Then suddenly I heard a cry of pain.

'The weight is on him. Lift it easy,' cried a voice.

'It's only my leg!' said another one, which I recognised as Perkins'. 'Where's master?' he cried.

'Here I am,' I answered, but they did not seem to hear me. They were all bending over something which lay in front of the car.

Stanley laid his hand upon my shoulder, and his touch was inexpressibly soothing, I felt light and happy, in spite of all.

'No pain, of course?' said he.

'None,' said I.

'There never is,' said he.

And then suddenly a wave of amazement passed over me. Stanley! Stanley! Why, Stanley had surely died of enteric at Bloemfontein in the Boer War!

'Stanley!' I cried, and the words seemed to choke my throat – 'Stanley, you are dead.'

He looked at me with the same old gentle, wistful smile.

'So are you,' he answered.

12

Her First Ball

(1921)

Katherine Mansfield

Exactly when the ball began Leila would have found it hard to say. Perhaps her first real partner was the cab. It did not matter that she shared the cab with the Sheridan girls and their brother. She sat back in her own little corner of it, and the bolster on which her hand rested felt like the sleeve of an unknown young man's dress suit: and away they bowled, past waltzing lamp-posts and houses and fences and trees.

'Have you really never been to a ball before, Leila? But, my child, how too weird—' cried the Sheridan girls.

'Our nearest neighbour was fifteen miles,' said Leila softly, gently opening and shutting her fan.

Oh dear, how hard it was to be indifferent like the others! She tried not to smile too much; she tried not to care. But every single thing was so new and exciting . . . Meg's tuberoses, Jose's long loop of amber, Laura's little dark head, pushing above her white fur like a flower through snow. She would remember for ever. It even gave her a pang to see her cousin Laurie throw away the wisps of tissue paper he pulled from the fastenings of his new gloves. She would like to have kept those wisps as a keepsake, as a remembrance. Laurie leaned forward and put his hand on Laura's knee.

'Look here, darling' he said. 'The third and the ninth as usual. Twig?'

Oh, how marvellous to have a brother! In her excitement Leila felt that if there had been time, if it hadn't been impossible, she couldn't have helped crying because she was an only child and no brother had ever said 'Twig?' to her; no sister would ever say, as Meg said to Jose that moment, 'I've never known your hair go up more successfully than it has tonight!'

But, of course, there was not time. They were at the drill hall already; there were cabs in front of them and cabs behind. The road was bright on either side with moving fan-like lights, and on the pavement gay couples seemed to float through the air; little satin shoes chased each other like birds.

'Hold on to me, Leila; you'll get lost,' said Laura.

'Come on, girls, let's make a dash for it,' said Laurie.

Leila put two fingers on Laura's pink velvet cloak, and they were somehow lifted past the big golden lantern, carried along the passage, and pushed into the little room marked 'Ladies'. Here the crowd was so great there was hardly space to take off their things; the noise was deafening. Two benches on either side were stacked high with wraps. Two old women in white aprons ran up and down tossing fresh armfuls. And everybody was pressing forward trying to get at the little dressing-table and mirror at the far end.

A great quivering jet of gas lighted the ladies' room. It couldn't wait; it was dancing already. When the door opened again and there came a burst of tuning from the drill hall, it leaped almost to the ceiling.

Dark girls, fair girls were patting their hair, tying ribbons again, tucking handkerchiefs down the fronts of their bodies, smoothing marble-white gloves. And because they were all laughing it seemed to Leila that they were all lovely.

'Aren't there any invisible hairpins?' cried a voice. 'How most extraordinary! I can't see a single invisible hairpin.'

'Powder my back, there's a darling,' cried someone else.

'But I must have a needle and cotton. I've torn simply miles and miles of the frill,' wailed a third.

Then, 'Pass them along, pass them along!' The straw basket of programmes was tossed from arm to arm. Darling little pink-and-silver programmes, with pink pencils and fluffy tassels. Leila's fingers shook as she took one out of the basket. She wanted to ask someone, 'Am I meant to have one too?' but she had just time to read: 'Waltz 3. *Two, Two in a Canoe*. Polka 4. *Making the Feathers Fly*', when Meg cried, 'Ready, Leila?' and they pressed their way through the crush in the passage towards the big double doors of the drill hall.

Dancing had not begun yet, but the band had stopped tuning, and the noise was so great it seemed that when it did begin to play it would never be heard. Leila, pressing close to Meg, looking over Meg's shoulder, felt that even the little quivering coloured flags strung across the ceiling were talking. She quite forgot to be shy; she forgot how in the middle of dressing she had sat down on the bed with one shoe off and one shoe on and begged her mother to ring up her cousins and say she couldn't go after all. And the rush of longing she had had to be sitting on the veranda of their forsaken up-country home, listening to the baby owls crying 'More pork' in the moonlight, was changed to a rush of joy so sweet that it was hard to bear alone. She clutched her fan, and, gazing at the gleaming, golden floor, the azaleas, the lanterns, the stage at one end with its red carpet and gilt chairs and the band in a corner, she thought breathlessly, 'How heavenly; how simply heavenly!'

All the girls stood grouped together at one side of the doors, the men at the other, and the chaperones in dark dresses, smiling rather foolishly, walked with little careful steps over the polished floor towards the stage.

'This is my little country cousin Leila. Be nice to her. Find her partners; she's under my wing,' said Meg, going up to one girl after another.

Strange faces smiled at Leila – sweetly, vaguely. Strange voices answered, 'Of course, my dear.' But Leila felt the girls didn't really see her. They were looking towards the men. Why didn't the men begin? What were they waiting for? There they stood, smoothing their gloves, patting their glossy hair and smiling among themselves. Then, quite suddenly, as if they had only just made up their minds that that was what they had to do, the men came gliding over the parquet. There was a joyful flutter among the girls. A tall, fair man flew up to Meg, seized her programme, scribbled something; Meg passed him on to Leila. 'May I have the pleasure?' He ducked and smiled. There came a dark man wearing an eyeglass, then cousin Laurie with a friend, and Laura with a little freckled fellow whose tie was crooked. Then quite an old man – fat, with a big bald patch on his head – took her programme and murmured, 'Let me see, let me see!' And he was a long time comparing his programme, which looked black with names, with hers. It seemed to give him so much trouble that Leila was ashamed. 'Oh, please don't bother,' she said eagerly. But instead of replying the fat man wrote something, glanced at her again. 'Do I remember this bright little face?' he said softly. 'Is it known to me of yore?' At that moment the band began playing; the fat man disappeared. He was tossed away on a great wave of music that came flying over the gleaming floor, breaking the groups up into couples, scattering them, sending them spinning . . .

Leila had learned to dance at boarding school. Every Saturday afternoon the boarders were hurried off to a little corrugated iron mission hall where Miss Eccles (of London) held her 'select' classes. But the difference between that dusty-smelling hall – with calico texts on the walls, the poor, terrified little woman in a brown velvet toque with rabbit's ears thumping the cold piano, Miss Eccles poking the girls' feet with her long white wand – and this, was so tremendous that Leila was sure if her partner didn't come and she had to listen to that marvellous music and to watch the others sliding, gliding over the golden floor, she would die at least, or faint, or lift her arms and fly out of one of those dark windows that showed the stars.

'Ours, I think –' Someone bowed, smiled, and offered her his arm; she hadn't to die after all. Someone's hand pressed her waist, and she floated away like a flower that is tossed into a pool.

'Quite a good floor, isn't it?' drawled a faint voice close to her ear.

'I think it's most beautifully slippery,' said Leila.

'Pardon!' The faint voice sounded surprised, Leila said it again. And there was a tiny pause before the voice echoed, 'Oh, quite!' and she was swung round again.

He steered so beautifully. That was the great difference between dancing with girls and men, Leila decided. Girls banged into each other and stamped on each other's feet; the girl who was gentleman always clutched you so.

The azaleas were separate flowers no longer; they were pink and white flags streaming by.

'Were you at the Bells' last week?' the voice came again. It sounded tired. Leila wondered whether she ought to ask him if he would like to stop.

'No, this is my first dance,' said she.

Her partner gave a little gasping laugh. 'Oh, I say,' he protested.

'Yes, it is really the first dance I've ever been to.' Leila was most fervent. it was such a relief to be able to tell somebody. 'You see, I've lived in the country all my life up till now . . .'

At that moment the music stopped and they went to sit on two chairs against the wall. Leila tucked her pink satin feet under and fanned herself, while she blissfully watched the other couples passing and disappearing through the swing doors.

'Enjoying yourself, Leila?' asked Jose, nodding her golden head.

Laura passed and gave her the faintest little wink; it made Leila wonder for a moment whether she was quite grown up after all. Certainly her partner did not say very much. He coughed, tucked his handkerchief away, pulled down his waistcoat, took a minute thread off his sleeve. But it didn't matter. Almost immediately the band started and her second partner seemed to spring from the ceiling.

'Floor's not bad,' said the new voice. Did one always begin with the floor? And then, 'Were you at the Neaves' on Tuesday?' And again Leila explained. Perhaps it was a little strange that her partners were not more interested. For it was thrilling. Her first ball! She was only at the beginning of everything. It seemed to her that she had never known what the night was like before. Up till now it had been dark, silent, beautiful very often – oh yes – but mournful somehow. Solemn. And now it would never be like that again – it had opened dazzling bright.

'Care for an ice?' said her partner. And they went through the swing doors, down the passage, to the supper-room. Her cheeks burned, she was fearfully thirsty. How sweet the ices looked on little glass plates and how cold the frosted spoon was, iced too! And when they came back to the hall there was the fat man waiting for her by the door. It gave her quite a shock again to see how old he was; he ought to have been on the stage with the fathers and mothers. And when Leila compared him with her other partners he looked shabby. His waistcoat was creased, there was a button off his glove, his coat looked as if it was dusty with French chalk.

'Come along, little lady,' said the fat man. He scarcely troubled to clasp her, and they moved away so gently, it was more like walking than dancing. But he said not a word about the floor. 'Your first dance, isn't it?' he murmured.

'How *did* you know?'

'Ah,' said the fat man, 'that's what it is to be old!' He wheezed faintly as he steered her past an awkward couple. 'You see, I've been doing this kind of thing for the last thirty years.'

'Thirty years?' cried Leila. Twelve years before she was born!

'It hardly bears thinking about, does it?' said the fat man gloomily. Leila looked at his bald head, and she felt quite sorry for him.

'I think it's marvellous to be still going on,' she said kindly.

'Kind little lady,' said the fat man, and he pressed her a little closer and hummed a bar of the waltz. 'Of course,' he said, 'you can't hope to last anything like as long as that. No-o,' said the fat man, 'long before that you'll be sitting up there on the stage, looking on, in your nice black velvet. And these pretty arms will have turned into little short fat ones, and you'll beat time with such a different kind of fan – a black ebony one.' The fat man seemed to shudder. 'And you'll smile away like the poor old dears up there, and point to your daughter, and tell the elderly lady next to you how some dreadful man tried to kiss her at the club ball. And your heart will ache, ache' – the fat man squeezed her closer still, as if he really was sorry for that poor heart – 'because no one wants to kiss you now. And you'll say how unpleasant these polished floors are to walk on, how dangerous they, are. Eh, Mademoiselle Twinkletoes?' said the fat man softly.

Leila gave a light little laugh, but she did not feel like laughing. Was it – could it all be true? It sounded terribly true. Was this first ball only the beginning of her last ball, after all? At that the music seemed to change; it sounded sad, sad; it rose upon a great sigh. Oh, how quickly things changed! Why didn't happiness last for ever? For ever wasn't a bit too long.

'I want to stop,' she said in a breathless voice. The fat man led her to the door.

'No,' she said, 'I won't go outside. I won't sit down. I'll just stand here, thank you.' She leaned against the wall, tapping with her foot, pulling up her gloves and trying to smile. But deep inside her a little girl threw her pinafore over her head and sobbed. Why had he spoiled it all?

'I say, you know,' said the fat man, 'you mustn't take me seriously, little lady.'

'As if I should!' said Leila, tossing her small dark head and sucking her underlip . . .

Again the couples paraded. The swing doors opened and shut. Now new music was given out by the bandmaster. But Leila didn't want to dance any more. She wanted to be home, or sitting on the veranda listening to those baby owls. When she looked through the dark windows at the stars they had long beams like wings . . .

But presently a soft, melting, ravishing tune began, and a young man with curly hair bowed before her. She would have to dance, out of politeness, until she could find Meg. Very stiffly she walked into the middle; very haughtily she put her hand on his sleeve. But in one minute, in one turn, her feet glided, glided. The lights, the azaleas, the dresses, the pink faces, the velvet chairs, all became one beautiful flying wheel. And when her next partner bumped her into the fat man and he said, 'Par*don*,' she smiled at him more radiantly than ever. She didn't even recognise him again.

13

The Lady in the Looking-Glass: A Reflection

(1929)

Virginia Woolf

People should not leave looking-glasses hanging in their rooms any more than they should leave open cheque books or letters confessing some hideous crime. One could not help looking, that summer afternoon, in the long glass that hung outside in the hall. Chance had so arranged it. From the depths of the sofa in the drawing-room one could see reflected in the Italian glass not only the marble-topped table opposite, but a stretch of the garden beyond. One could see a long grass path leading between banks of tall flowers until, slicing off an angle, the gold rim cut it off.

The house was empty, and one felt, since one was the only person in the drawing-room, like one of those naturalists who, covered with grass and leaves, lie watching the shyest animals – badgers, otters, kingfishers – moving about freely, themselves unseen. The room that afternoon was full of such shy creatures, lights and shadows, curtains blowing, petals falling – things that never happen, so it seems, if someone is looking. The quiet old country room with its rugs and stone chimney pieces, its sunken book-cases and red and gold lacquer cabinets, was full of such nocturnal creatures. They came pirouetting across the floor, stepping delicately with high-lifted feet and spread tails and pecking allusive beaks as if they had been cranes or flocks of elegant flamingoes whose pink was faded, or peacocks whose trains were veined with silver. And there were obscure flushes and darkenings too, as if a cuttlefish had suddenly suffused the air with purple; and the room had its passions and rages and envies and sorrows coming over it and clouding it, like a human being. Nothing stayed the same for two seconds together.

But, outside, the looking-glass reflected the hall table, the sunflowers, the garden path so accurately and so fixedly that they seemed held there in their reality unescapably. It was a strange contrast – all changing here, all stillness there. One could not help looking from one to the other. Meanwhile, since all the doors and windows were open in the heat, there was a perpetual sighing and ceasing sound, the voice of the transient and the perishing, it seemed, coming and going like human breath, while in the looking-glass things had ceased to breathe and lay still in the trance of immortality.

Half an hour ago the mistress of the house, Isabella Tyson, had gone down the grass path in her thin summer dress, carrying a basket, and had vanished, sliced off by the gilt rim of the looking-glass. She had gone presumably into the lower garden to pick flowers; or as it seemed more natural to suppose, to pick something light and fantastic and leafy and trailing, traveller's joy, or one of those elegant sprays of convolvulus that twine round ugly walls and burst here and there into white and violet blossoms. She suggested the fantastic and the tremulous convolvulus rather than the upright aster, the starched zinnia, or her own burning roses alight like lamps on the straight posts of their rose trees. The comparison showed how very little, after all these years, one knew about her; for it is impossible that any woman of flesh and blood of fifty-five or sixty should be really a wreath or a tendril. Such comparisons are worse than idle and superficial – they are cruel even, for they come like the convolvulus itself trembling between one's eyes and the truth. There must be truth; there must be a wall. Yet it was strange that after knowing her all these years one could not say what the truth about Isabella was; one still made up phrases like this about convolvulus and traveller's joy. As for facts, it was a fact that she was a spinster; that she was rich; that she had bought this house and collected with her own hands – often in the most obscure corners of the world and at great risk from poisonous stings and Oriental diseases – the rugs, the chairs, the cabinets which now lived their nocturnal life before one's eyes. Sometimes it seemed as if they knew more about her than we, who sat on them, wrote at them, and trod on them so carefully, were allowed to know. In each of these cabinets were many little drawers, and each almost certainly held letters, tied with bows of ribbon, sprinkled with sticks of lavender or rose leaves. For it was another fact – if facts were what one wanted – that Isabella had known many people, had had many friends; and thus if one had the audacity to open a drawer and read her letters, one would find the traces of many agitations, of appointments to meet, of upbraidings for not having met, long letters of intimacy and affection, violent letters of jealousy and reproach, terrible final words of parting – for all those interviews and assignations had led to nothing – that is, she had never married, and yet, judging from the mask-like indifference of her face, she had gone through twenty times more of passion and experience than those whose loves are trumpeted forth for all the world to hear. Under the stress of thinking about Isabella, her room became more shadowy and symbolic; the corners seemed darker, the legs of chairs and tables more spindly and hieroglyphic.

Suddenly these reflections were ended violently and yet without a sound. A large black form loomed into the looking-glass; blotted out everything, strewed the table with a packet of marble tablets veined with pink and grey, and was gone. But the picture was entirely altered. For the moment it was unrecognisable and irrational and entirely out of focus. One could not relate these tablets to any human purpose. And then by degrees some logical process set to work on them and began ordering and arranging them and bringing them into the fold of common experience. One realised at last that they were merely letters. The man had brought the post.

There they lay on the marble-topped table, all dripping with light and colour at first and crude and unabsorbed. And then it was strange to see how they were drawn in and arranged and composed and made part of the picture and granted that stillness and immortality which the looking-glass conferred. They lay there invested with a new reality and significance and with a greater heaviness, too, as if it would have needed a chisel to dislodge them from the table. And, whether it was fancy or not, they seemed to have become not merely a handful of casual letters but to be tablets graven with eternal truth – if one could read them, one would know everything there was to be known about Isabella, yes, and about life, too. The pages inside those marble-looking envelopes must be cut deep and scored thick with meaning. Isabella would come in, and take them, one by one, very slowly, and open them, and read them carefully word by word, and then with a profound sigh of comprehension, as if she had seen to the bottom of everything, she would tear the envelopes to little bits and tie the letters together and lock the cabinet drawer in her determination to conceal what she did not wish to be known.

The thought served as a challenge. Isabella did not wish to be known – but she should no longer escape. It was absurd, it was monstrous. If she concealed so much and knew so much one must prize her open with the first tool that came to hand – the imagination. One must fix one's mind upon her at that very moment. One must fasten her down there. One must refuse to be put off any longer with sayings and doings such as the moment brought forth – with dinners and visits and polite conversations. One must put oneself in her shoes. If one took the phrase literally, it was easy to see the shoes in which she stood, down in the lower garden, at this moment. They were very narrow and long and fashionable – they were made of the softest and most flexible leather. Like everything she wore, they were exquisite. And she would be standing under the high hedge in the lower part of the garden, raising the scissors that were tied to her waist to cut some dead flower, some overgrown branch. The sun would beat down on her face, into her eyes; but no, at the critical moment a veil of cloud covered the sun, making the expression of her eyes doubtful – was it mocking or tender, brilliant or dull? One could only see the indeterminate outline of her rather faded, fine face looking at the sky. She was thinking, perhaps, that she must order a new net for the strawberries; that she must send flowers to Johnson's widow; that it was time she drove over to see the Hippesleys in their new house. Those were the things she talked about at dinner certainly. But one was tired of the things that she talked about at dinner. It was her profounder state of being that one wanted to catch and turn to words, the state that is to the mind what breathing is to the body, what one calls happiness or unhappiness. At the mention of those words it became obvious, surely, that she must be happy. She was rich; she was distinguished; she had many friends; she travelled – she bought rugs in Turkey and blue pots in Persia. Avenues of pleasure radiated this way and that from where she stood with her scissors raised to cut the trembling branches while the lacy clouds veiled her face.

Here with a quick movement of her scissors she snipped the spray of traveller's joy and it fell to the ground. As it fell, surely some light came in too, surely one could penetrate a little farther into her being. Her mind then was filled with tenderness and regret . . . To cut an overgrown branch saddened her because it had once lived, and life was dear to her. Yes, and at the same time the fall of the branch would suggest to her how she must die herself and all the futility and evanescence of things. And then again quickly catching this thought up, with her instant good sense, she thought life had treated her well; even if fall she must, it was to lie on the earth and moulder sweetly into the roots of violets. So she stood thinking. Without making any thought precise – for she was one of those reticent people whose minds hold their thoughts enmeshed in clouds of silence – she was filled with thoughts. Her mind was like her room, in which lights advanced and retreated, came pirouetting and stepping delicately, spread their tails, pecked their way; and then her whole being was suffused, like the room again, with a cloud of some profound knowledge, some unspoken regret, and then she was full of locked drawers, stuffed with letters, like her cabinets. To talk of 'prizing her open' as if she were an oyster, to use any but the finest and subtlest and most pliable tools upon her was impious and absurd. One must imagine – here was she in the looking-glass. It made one start.

She was so far off at first that one could not see her clearly. She came lingering and pausing, here straightening a rose, there lifting a pink to smell it, but she never stopped; and all the time she became larger and larger in the looking-glass, more and more completely the person into whose mind one had been trying to penetrate. One verified her by degrees – fitted the qualities one had discovered into this visible body. There were her grey-green dress, and her long shoes, her basket, and something sparkling at her throat. She came so gradually that she did not seem to derange the pattern in the glass, but only to bring in some new element which gently moved and altered the other objects as if asking them, courteously, to make room for her. And the letters and the table and the grass walk and the sunflowers which had been waiting in the looking-glass separated and opened out so that she might be received among them. At last there she was, in the hall. She stopped dead. She stood by the table. She stood perfectly still. At once the looking-glass began to pour over her a light that seemed to fix her; that seemed like some acid to bite off the unessential and superficial and to leave only the truth. It was an enthralling spectacle. Everything dropped from her – clouds, dress, basket, diamond – all that one had called the creeper and convolvulus. Here was the hard wall beneath. Here was the woman herself. She stood naked in that pitiless light. And there was nothing. Isabella was perfectly empty. She had no thoughts. She had no friends. She cared for nobody. As for her letters, they were all bills. Look, as she stood there, old and angular, veined and lined, with her high nose and her wrinkled neck, she did not even trouble to open them.

People should not leave looking-glasses hanging in their rooms.

14

The Fly in the Ointment

(1932)

V. S. Pritchett

It was the dead hour of a November afternoon. Under the ceiling of level mud-coloured cloud, the latest office buildings of the city stood out alarmingly like new tombstones, among the mass of older buildings. And along the streets the few cars and the few people appeared and disappeared slowly as if they were not following the roadway or the pavement but some inner, personal route. Along the road to the main station, at intervals of two hundred yards or so, unemployed men and one or two beggars were dribbling slowly past the desert of public buildings to the next patch of shop fronts.

Presently a taxi stopped outside one of the underground stations and a man of thirty-five paid his fare and made off down one of the small streets.

Better not arrive in a taxi, he was thinking. The old man will wonder where I got the money.

He was going to see his father. It was his father's last day at his factory, the last day of thirty years' work and life among these streets, building a business out of nothing, and then, after a few years of prosperity, letting it go to pieces in a chafer of rumour, idleness, quarrels, accusations and, at last, bankruptcy.

Suddenly all the money quarrels of the family, which nagged in the young man's mind, had been dissolved. His dread of being involved in them vanished. He was overcome by the sadness of his father's situation. Thirty years of your life come to an end. I must see him. I must help him. All the same, knowing his father, he had paid off the taxi and walked the last quarter of a mile.

It was a shock to see the name of the firm, newly painted too, on the sign outside the factory and on the brass of the office entrance, newly polished. He pressed the bell at the office window inside and it was a long time before he heard footsteps cross the empty room and saw a shadow cloud the frosted glass of the window.

'It's Harold, Father,' the young man said. The door was opened.

'Hullo, old chap. This is very nice of you, Harold,' said the old man shyly, stepping back from the door to let his son in, and lowering his pleased, blue eyes for a second's modesty.

'Naturally I had to come,' said the son, shyly also. And then the father, filled out with assurance again and taking his son's arm, walked him across the floor of the empty workroom.

'Hardly recognise it, do you? When were you here last?' said the father.

This had been the machine-room, before the machines had gone. Through another door was what had been the showroom, where the son remembered seeing his father, then a dark-haired man, talking in a voice he had never heard before, a quick, bland voice, to his customers. Now there were only dust-lines left by the shelves on the white brick walls, and the marks of the showroom cupboards on the floor. The place looked large and light. There was no throb of machines, no hum of voices, no sound at all, now, but the echo of their steps on the empty floors. Already, though only a month bankrupt, the firm was becoming a ghost.

The two men walked towards the glass door of the office. They were both short. The father was well-dressed in an excellent navy-blue suit. He was a vigorous, broad man with a pleased impish smile. The sunburn shone through the clipped white hair of his head and he had the simple, trim, open-air look of a snow-man. The son beside him was round-shouldered and shabby, a keen but anxious fellow in need of a hair-cut and going bald.

'Come in, Professor,' said the father. This was an old family joke. He despised his son, who was, in fact, not a professor but a poorly paid lecturer at a provincial university.

'Come in,' said the father, repeating himself, not with the impatience he used to have, but with the habit of age. 'Come inside, into my office. If you can call it an office now,' he apologised. 'This used to be my room, do you remember, it used to be my office. Take a chair. We've still got a chair. The desk's gone, yes, that's gone, it was sold, fetched a good price – what was I saying?' he turned a bewildered look to his son. 'The chair. I was saying they have to leave you a table and a chair. I was just going to have a cup of tea, old boy, but – pardon me,' he apologised again, 'I've only one cup. Things have been sold for the liquidators and they've cleaned out nearly everything. I found this cup and teapot upstairs in the foreman's room. Of course, he's gone, all the hands have gone, and when I looked around just now to lock up before taking the keys to the agent when I hand over today, I saw this cup. Well, there it is. I've made it. Have a cup?'

'No, thanks,' said the son, listening patiently to his father. 'I have had my tea.'

'You've had your tea? Go on. Why not have another?'

'No, really, thanks,' said the son. 'You drink it.'

'Well,' said the father, pouring out the tea and lifting the cup to his soft rosy face and blinking his eyes as he drank, 'I feel badly about this. This is terrible. I feel really awful drinking this tea and you standing there watching me, but you say you've had yours – well, how are things with you? How are you? And how is Alice? Is she better? And the children? You know I've been thinking about you – you look worried. Haven't lost sixpence and found a shilling have you, because I wouldn't mind doing that?'

'I'm all right,' the son said, smiling to hide his irritation. 'I'm not worried about anything. I'm just worried about you. This' – he nodded with embarrassment to the dismantled showroom, the office from which even the calendars and wastepaper-basket had gone – 'this' – what was the most tactful and sympathetic word to use? – 'this is bad luck,' he said.

'Bad luck?' said the old man sternly.

'I mean,' stammered his son, 'I heard about the creditors' meeting. I knew it was your last day – I thought I'd come along, I . . . to see how you were.'

'Very sweet of you, old boy,' said the old man with zest. 'Very sweet. We've cleared everything up. They got most of the machines out today. I'm just locking up and handing over. Locking up is quite a business. There are so many keys. It's tiring, really. How many keys do you think there are to a place like this? You wouldn't believe it, if I told you.'

'It must have been worrying,' the son said.

'Worrying? You keep on using that word. I'm not worrying. Things are fine,' said the old man, smiling aggressively. 'I feel they're fine. I *know* they're fine.'

'Well, you always were an optimist,' smiled his son.

'Listen to me a moment. I want you to get this idea,' said his father, his warm voice going dead and rancorous and his nostrils fidgeting. His eyes went hard, too. A different man was speaking, and even a different face; the son noticed for the first time that like all big-faced men his father had two faces. There was the outer face like a soft warm and careless daub of innocent sealing-wax and inside it, as if thumbed there by a seal, was a much smaller one, babyish, shrewd, scared and hard. Now this little inner face had gone greenish and pale and dozens of little veins were broken on the nose and cheeks. The small, drained, purplish lips of this little face were speaking. The son leaned back instinctively to get just another inch away from this little face.

'Listen to this,' the father said and leaned forward on the table as his son leaned back, holding his right fist up as if he had a hammer in his hand and was auctioning his life. 'I am sixty-five. I don't know how long I shall live, but let me make this clear: if I were not an optimist I wouldn't be here. I wouldn't stay another minute.' He paused, fixing his son's half-averted eyes to let the full meaning of his words bite home. 'I've worked hard,' the father went on. 'For thirty years I built up this business from nothing. You wouldn't know it, you were a child, but many's the time coming down from the North I've slept in this office to be on the job early the next morning.' He looked decided and experienced like a man of forty, but now he softened to sixty again. The ring in the hard voice began to soften into a faint whine and his thick nose sniffed. 'I don't say I've always done right,' he said. 'You can't live your life from A to Z like that. And now I haven't a penny in the world. Not a cent. It's not easy at my time of life to begin again. What do you think I've got to live for? There's nothing holding me back. My boy, if I wasn't an optimist I'd go right out. I'd finish it.' Suddenly the father smiled and the little face was drowned in a warm flood of triumphant smiles from the bigger face. He rested his hands on his waistcoat and that seemed to be smiling too, his easy coat smiling, his legs smiling and even winks of light on the shining shoes. Then he frowned.

'Your hair's going thin,' he said. 'You oughtn't to be losing your hair at your age. I don't want you to think I'm criticising you, you're old enough to live your own life, but your hair you know – you ought to do something about it. If you used oil every day and rubbed it in with both hands, the thumbs and forefingers is what you want to use, it would be better. I'm often thinking about you and I don't want you to think I'm lecturing you, because I'm not, so don't get the idea this is a lecture, but I was thinking, what you want, what we all want, I say this for myself as well as you, what we all want is ideas – big ideas. We go worrying along but you just want bigger and better ideas. You ought to think big. Take your case. You're a lecturer. I wouldn't be satisfied with lecturing to a small batch of people in a university town. I'd lecture the world. You know, you're always doing yourself injustice. We all do. Think big.'

'Well,' said his son, still smiling, but sharply. He was very angry. 'One's enough in the family. You've thought big till you bust.'

He didn't mean to say this, because he hadn't really the courage, but his pride was touched.

'I mean,' said the son, hurriedly covering it up in a panic, 'I'm not like you . . . I . . .'

'What did you say?' said the old man. 'Don't say that.' It was the smaller of the two faces speaking in a panic. 'Don't say that. Don't use that expression. That's not a right idea. Don't you get a wrong idea about me. We paid sixpence in the pound,' said the old man proudly.

The son began again, but his father stopped him.

'Do you know,' said the bigger of his two faces, getting bigger as it spoke, 'some of the oldest houses in the city are in Queer Street, some of the biggest firms in the country? I came up this morning with Mr Higgins, you remember Higgins? They're in liquidation. They are. Oh yes. And Moore, he's lost everything. He's got his chauffeur, but it's his wife's money. Did you see Beltman in the trade papers? Quarter of a million deficit. And how long are Prestons going to last?'

The big face smiled and overflowed on the smaller one. The whole train, the old man said, was practically packed with bankrupts every morning. Thousands had gone. Thousands? Tens of thousands. Some of the biggest men in the City were broke.

A small man himself, he was proud to be bankrupt with the big ones; it made him feel rich.

'You've got to realise, old boy,' he said gravely, 'the world's changing. You've got to move with the times.'

The son was silent. The November sun put a few strains of light through the frosted window and the shadow of its bars and panes was weakly placed on the wall behind his father's head. Some of the light caught the tanned scalp that showed between the white hair. So short the hair was that the father's ears protruded and, framed against that reflection of the window bars, the father suddenly took (to his son's fancy) the likeness of a convict in his cell and the son, startled, found himself asking: Were they telling the truth when they said the old man was a crook and that his balance sheets were cooked? What about that man they had to shut up at the meeting, the little man from Birmingham, in a mackintosh . . . ?

'There's a fly in this room,' said the old man suddenly, looking up in the air and getting to his feet. 'I'm sorry to interrupt what you were saying, but I can hear a fly. I must get it out.'

'A fly?' said his son, listening.

'Yes, can't you hear it? It's peculiar how you can hear everything now the machines have stopped. It took me quite a time to get used to the silence. Can you see it, old chap? I can't stand flies, you never know where they've been. Excuse me one moment.'

The old man pulled a duster out of a drawer.

'Forgive this interruption. I can't sit in a room with a fly in it,' he said apologetically. They both stood up and listened. Certainly in the office was the small dying fizz of a fly, deceived beyond its strength by the autumn sun.

'Open the door, will you, old boy,' said the old man with embarrassment. 'I hate them.'

The son opened the door and the fly flew into the light. The old man struck at it but it sailed away higher.

'There it is,' he said, getting up on the chair. He struck again and the son struck too as the fly came down. The old man got on top of his table. An expression of disgust and fear was curled on his smaller face; and an expression of apology and weakness.

'Excuse me,' he said again, looking up at the ceiling.

'If we leave the door open or open the window it will go,' said the son.

'It may seem a fad to you,' said the old man shyly. 'I don't like flies. Ah, here it comes.'

They missed it. They stood helplessly gaping up at the ceiling where the fly was buzzing in small circles round the cord of the electric light.

'I don't like them,' the old man said.

The table creaked under his weight. The fly went on to the ceiling and stayed there. Unavailingly the old man snapped the duster at it.

'Be careful,' said the son. 'Don't lose your balance.'

The old man looked down. Suddenly he looked tired and old, his body began to sag and a look of weakness came on to his face.

'Give me a hand, old boy,' the old man said in a shaky voice. He put a heavy hand on his son's shoulder and the son felt the great helpless weight of his father's body.

'Lean on me.'

Very heavily and slowly the old man got cautiously down from the table to the chair. 'Just a moment, old boy,' said the old man. Then, after getting his breath, he got down from the chair to the floor.

'You all right?' his son asked.

'Yes, yes,' said the old man out of breath. 'It was only that fly. Do you know, you're actually more bald at the back than I thought. There's a patch there as big as my hand. I saw it just then. It gave me quite a shock. You really must do something about it. How are your teeth? Do you have any trouble with your teeth? That may have something to do with it. Hasn't Alice told you how bald you are?'

'You've been doing too much. You're worried,' said the son, soft with repentance and sympathy. 'Sit down. You've had a bad time.'

'No, nothing,' said the old man shyly, breathing rather hard. 'A bit. Everyone's been very nice. They came in and shook hands. The staff came in. They all came in just to shake hands. They said, "We wish you good luck." '

The old man turned his head away. He actually wiped a tear from his eye. A glow of sympathy transported the younger man. He felt as though a sun had risen.

'You know –' the father said uneasily, flitting a glance at the fly on the ceiling as if he wanted the fly as well as his son to listen to what he was going to say – 'you know,' he said, 'the world's all wrong. I've made my mistakes. I was thinking about it before you came. You know where I went wrong? You know where I made my mistake?'

The son's heart started to a panic of embarrassment. For heaven's sake, he wanted to shout, don't! Don't stir up the whole business. Don't humiliate yourself before me. Don't start telling the truth. Don't oblige me to say we know all about it, that we have known for years the mess you've been in, that we've seen through the plausible stories you've spread, that we've known the people you've swindled.

'Money's been my trouble,' said the old man. 'I thought I needed money. That's one thing it's taught me. I've done with money. Absolutely done and finished with it. I never want to see another penny as long as I live. I don't want to see or hear of it. If you came in now and offered me a thousand pounds I should laugh at you. We deceive ourselves. We don't want the stuff. All I want now is just to go to a nice little cottage by the sea,' the old man said. 'I feel I need air, sun, life.'

The son was appalled.

'You want money even for that,' the son said irritably. 'You want quite a lot of money to do that.'

'Don't say I want money,' the old man said vehemently. 'Don't say it. When I walk out of this place tonight I'm going to walk into freedom. I am not going to think of money. You never know where it will come from. You may see something. You may meet a man. You never know. Did the children of Israel worry about money? No, they just went out and collected the manna. That's what I want to do.'

The son was about to speak. The father stopped him.

'Money,' the father said, 'isn't necessary at all.'

Now, like the harvest moon in full glow, the father's face shone up at his son.

'What I came round about was this,' said the son awkwardly and dryly. 'I'm not rich. None of us is. In fact, with things as they are we're all pretty shaky and we can't do anything. I wish I could, but I can't. But' – after the assured beginning he began to stammer and to crinkle his eyes timidly – 'but the idea of your being – you know, well short of some immediate necessity, I mean – well, if it is ever a question of – well, to be frank, *cash*, I'd raise it somehow.'

He coloured. He hated to admit his own poverty, he hated to offer charity to his father. He hated to sit there knowing the things he knew about him. He was ashamed to think how he, how they all dreaded having the gregarious, optimistic, extravagant, uncontrollable, disingenuous old man on their hands. The son hated to feel he was being in some peculiar way which he could not understand, mean, cowardly and dishonest.

The father's sailing eyes came down and looked at his son's nervous, frowning face and slowly the dreaming look went from the father's face. Slowly the harvest moon came down from its rosy voyage. The little face suddenly became dominant within the outer folds of skin like a fox looking out of a hole of clay. He leaned forward brusquely on the table and somehow a silver-topped pencil was in his hand preparing to note something briskly on a writing-pad.

'Raise it?' said the old man sharply. 'Why didn't you tell me before you could raise money? How can you raise it? Where? By when?'

15

The Custody of the Pumpkin

(1935)

P. G. Wodehouse

The morning sunshine descended like an amber shower-bath on Blandings Castle, lighting up with a heartening glow its ivied walls, its rolling parks, its gardens, outhouses, and messuages, and such of its inhabitants as chanced at the moment to be taking the air. It fell on green lawns and wide terraces, on noble trees and bright flower-beds. It fell on the baggy trousers-seat of Angus McAllister, head-gardener to the ninth Earl of Emsworth, as he bent with dour Scottish determination to pluck a slug from its reverie beneath the leaf of a lettuce. It fell on the white flannels of the Hon. Freddie Threepwood, Lord Emsworth's second son, hurrying across the water-meadows. It also fell on Lord Emsworth himself and on Beach, his faithful butler. They were standing on the turret above the west wing, the former with his eye to a powerful telescope, the latter holding the hat which he had been sent to fetch.

'Beach,' said Lord Emsworth.

'M'lord?'

'I've been swindled. This dashed thing doesn't work.'

'Your lordship cannot see clearly?'

'I can't see at all, dash it. It's all black.'

The butler was an observant man.

'Perhaps if I were to remove the cap at the extremity of the instrument, m'lord, more satisfactory results might be obtained.'

'Eh? Cap? Is there a cap? So there is. Take it off, Beach.'

'Very good, m'lord.'

'Ah!' There was satisfaction in Lord Emsworth's voice. He twiddled and adjusted, and the satisfaction deepened. 'Yes, that's better. That's capital. Beach, I can see a cow.'

'Indeed, m'lord?'

'Down in the water-meadows. Remarkable. Might be two yards away. All right, Beach. Shan't want you any longer.'

'Your hat, m'lord?'

'Put it on my head.'

'Very good, m'lord.'

The butler, this kindly act performed, withdrew. Lord Emsworth continued gazing at the cow.

The ninth Earl of Emsworth was a fluffy-minded and amiable old gentleman with a fondness for new toys. Although the main interest of his life was his garden, he was always ready to try a side line, and the latest of these side lines was this telescope of his. Ordered from London in a burst of enthusiasm consequent upon the reading of an article on astronomy in a monthly magazine, it had been placed in position on the previous evening. What was now in progress was its trial trip.

Presently, the cow's audience-appeal began to wane. It was a fine cow, as cows go, but, like so many cows, it lacked sustained dramatic interest. Surfeited after a while by the spectacle of it chewing the cud and staring glassily at nothing, Lord Emsworth decided to swivel the apparatus round in the hope of picking up something a trifle more sensational. And he was just about to do so, when into the range of his vision there came the Hon. Freddie. White and shining, he tripped along over the turf like a Theocritan shepherd hastening to keep an appointment with a nymph, and a sudden frown marred the serenity of Lord Emsworth's brow. He generally frowned when he saw Freddie, for with the passage of the years that youth had become more and more of a problem to an anxious father.

Unlike the male codfish, which, suddenly finding itself the parent of three million five hundred thousand little codfish, cheerfully resolves to love them all, the British aristocracy is apt to look with a somewhat jaundiced eye on its younger sons. And Freddie Threepwood was one of those younger sons who rather invite the jaundiced eye. It seemed to the head of the family that there was no way of coping with the boy. If he was allowed to live in London, he piled up debts and got into mischief; and when you jerked him back into the purer surroundings of Blandings Castle, he just mooned about the place, moping broodingly. Hamlet's society at Elsinore must have had much the same effect on his stepfather as did that of Freddie Threepwood at Blandings on Lord Emsworth. And it is probable that what induced the latter to keep a telescopic eye on him at this moment was the fact that his demeanour was so mysteriously jaunty, his bearing so intriguingly free from its customary crushed misery. Some inner voice whispered to Lord Emsworth that this smiling, prancing youth was up to no good and would bear watching.

The inner voice was absolutely correct. Within thirty seconds its case had been proved up to the hilt. Scarcely had his lordship had time to wish, as he invariably wished on seeing his offspring, that Freddie had been something entirely different in manners, morals, and appearance, and had been the son of somebody else living a considerable distance away, when out of a small spinney near the end of the meadow there bounded a girl. And Freddie, after a cautious glance over his shoulder, immediately proceeded to fold this female in a warm embrace.

Lord Emsworth had seen enough. He tottered away from the telescope, a shattered man. One of his favourite dreams was of some nice, eligible girl, belonging to a good family, and possessing a bit of money of her own, coming along some day and taking

Freddie off his hands; but that inner voice, more confident now than ever, told him that this was not she. Freddie would not sneak off in this furtive fashion to meet eligible girls, nor could he imagine any eligible girl, in her right senses, rushing into Freddie's arms in that enthusiastic way. No, there was only one explanation. In the cloistral seclusion of Blandings, far from the Metropolis with all its conveniences for that sort of thing, Freddie had managed to get himself entangled. Seething with anguish and fury, Lord Emsworth hurried down the stairs and out on to the terrace. Here he prowled like an elderly leopard waiting for feeding-time, until in due season there was a flicker of white among the trees that flanked the drive and a cheerful whistling announced the culprit's approach.

It was with a sour and hostile eye that Lord Emsworth watched his son draw near. He adjusted his pince-nez, and with their assistance was able to perceive that a fatuous smile of self-satisfaction illumined the young man's face, giving him the appearance of a beaming sheep. In the young man's buttonhole there shone a nosegay of simple meadow flowers, which, as he walked, he patted from time to time with a loving hand.

'Frederick!' bellowed his lordship.

The villain of the piece halted abruptly. Sunk in a roseate trance, he had not observed his father. But such was the sunniness of his mood that even this encounter could not damp him. He gambolled happily up.

'Hullo, guv'nor!' he carolled. He searched in his mind for a pleasant topic of conversation – always a matter of some little difficulty on these occasions. 'Lovely day, what?'

His lordship was not to be diverted into a discussion of the weather.

He drew a step nearer, looking like the man who smothered the young princes in the Tower.

'Frederick,' he demanded, 'who was that girl?'

The Hon. Freddie started convulsively. He appeared to be swallowing with difficulty something large and jagged.

'Girl?' he quavered. 'Girl? Girl, guv'nor?'

'That girl I saw you kissing ten minutes ago down in the water-meadows.'

'Oh!' said the Hon. Freddie. He paused. 'Oh, ah!' He paused again.

'Oh, ah, yes! I've been meaning to tell you about that, guv'nor.'

'You have, have you?'

'All perfectly correct, you know. Oh, yes, indeed! All most absolutely correct-o! Nothing fishy, I mean to say, or anything like that. She's my fiancée.'

A sharp howl escaped Lord Emsworth, as if one of the bees humming in the lavender-beds had taken time off to sting him in the neck.

'Who is she?' he boomed. 'Who is this woman?'

'Her name's Donaldson.'

'Who is she?'

'Aggie Donaldson. Aggie's short for Niagara. Her people spent their honeymoon at the Falls, she tells me. She's American and all that. Rummy names they give kids in America,' proceeded Freddie, with hollow chattiness. 'I mean to say! Niagara! I ask you!'

'Who is she?'

'She's most awfully bright, you know. Full of beans. You'll love her.'

'Who is she?'

'And can play the saxophone.'

'Who,' demanded Lord Emsworth for the sixth time, 'is she? And where did you meet her?'

Freddie coughed. The information, he perceived, could no longer be withheld, and he was keenly alive to the fact that it scarcely fell into the class of tidings of great joy.

'Well, as a matter of fact, guv'nor, she's a sort of cousin of Angus McAllister's. She's come over to England for a visit, don't you know, and is staying with the old boy. That's how I happened to run across her.'

Lord Emsworth's eyes bulged and he gargled faintly. He had had many unpleasant visions of his son's future, but they had never included one of him walking down the aisle with a sort of cousin of his head-gardener.

'Oh!' he said. 'Oh, indeed?'

'That's the strength of it, guv'nor.'

Lord Emsworth threw his arms up, as if calling on Heaven to witness a good man's persecution, and shot off along the terrace at a rapid trot. Having ranged the grounds for some minutes, he ran his quarry to earth at the entrance to the yew alley.

The head-gardener turned at the sound of his footsteps, He was a sturdy man of medium height, with eyebrows that would have fitted a bigger forehead. These, added to a red and wiry beard, gave him a formidable and uncompromising expression. Honesty Angus McAllister's face had in full measure, and also intelligence; but it was a bit short on sweetness and light.

'McAllister,' said his lordship, plunging without preamble into the matter of his discourse. 'That girl. You must send her away.'

A look of bewilderment clouded such of Mr McAllister's features as were not concealed behind his beard and eyebrows.

'Gurrul?'

'That girl who is staying with you. She must go!'

'Gae where?'

Lord Emsworth was not in the mood to be finicky about details.

'Anywhere,' he said. 'I won't have her here a day longer.'

'Why?' inquired Mr McAllister, who liked to thresh these things out.

'Never mind why. You must send her away immediately.'

Mr McAllister mentioned an insuperable objection.

'She's payin' me twa poon' a week,' he said simply.

Lord Emsworth did not grind his teeth, for he was not given to that form of displaying emotion; but he leaped some ten inches into the air and dropped his pince-nez. And, though normally a fair-minded and reasonable man, well aware that modern earls must think twice before pulling the feudal stuff on their employees, he took on the forthright truculence of a large landowner of the early Norman period ticking off a serf.

'Listen, McAllister! Listen to me! Either you send that girl away today or you can go yourself. I mean it!'

A curious expression came into Angus McAllister's face – always excepting the occupied territories. It was the look of a man who has not forgotten Bannockburn, a man conscious of belonging to the country of William Wallace and Robert the Bruce. He made Scotch noises at the back of his throat.

'Y'r lorrudsheep will accept ma notis,' he said, with formal dignity.

'I'll pay you a month's wages in lieu of notice and you will leave this afternoon,' retorted Lord Emsworth with spirit.

'Mphm!' said Mr McAllister.

Lord Emsworth left the battlefield with a feeling of pure exhilaration, still in the grip of the animal fury of conflict. No twinge of remorse did he feel at the thought that Angus McAllister had served him faithfully for ten years. Nor did it cross his mind that he might miss McAllister.

But that night, as he sat smoking his after-dinner cigarette, Reason, so violently expelled, came stealing timidly back to her throne, and a cold hand seemed suddenly placed upon his heart.

With Angus McAllister gone, how would the pumpkin fare?

The importance of this pumpkin in the Earl of Emsworth's life requires, perhaps, a word of explanation. Every ancient family in England has some little gap in its scroll of honour, and that of Lord Emsworth was no exception. For generations back his ancestors had been doing notable deeds; they had sent out from Blandings Castle statesmen and warriors, governors and leaders of the people: but they had not – in the opinion of the present holder of the title – achieved a full hand. However splendid the family record might appear at first sight, the fact remained that no Earl of Emsworth had ever won a first prize for pumpkins at the Shrewsbury Show. For roses, yes. For tulips, true. For spring onions, granted. But not for pumpkins; and Lord Emsworth felt it deeply.

For many a summer past he had been striving indefatigably to remove this blot on the family escutcheon, only to see his hopes go tumbling down. But this year at last victory had seemed in sight, for there had been vouchsafed to Blandings a competitor of such amazing parts that his lordship, who had watched it grow practically from a pip, could not envisage failure. Surely, he told himself as he gazed on its golden roundness, even Sir Gregory Parsloe-Parsloe, of Matchingham Hall, winner for three successive years, would never be able to produce anything to challenge this superb vegetable.

And it was this supreme pumpkin whose welfare he feared he had jeopardised by dismissing Angus McAllister. For Angus was its official trainer. He understood the pumpkin. Indeed, in his reserved Scottish way, he even seemed to love it. With Angus gone, what would the harvest be?

Such were the meditations of Lord Emsworth as he reviewed the position of affairs. And though, as the days went by, he tried to tell himself that Angus McAllister was not the only man in the world who understood pumpkins, and that he had every confidence, the most complete and unswerving confidence, in Robert Barker, recently Angus's second-in-command, now promoted to the post of head-gardener and custodian of the Blandings Hope, he knew that this was but shallow bravado. When you are a pumpkin owner with a big winner in your stable, you judge men by hard standards, and every day it became plainer that Robert Barker was only a makeshift. Within a week Lord Emsworth was pining for Angus McAllister.

It might be purely imagination, but to his excited fancy the pumpkin seemed to be pining for Angus too. It appeared to be drooping and losing weight. Lord Emsworth could not rid himself of the horrible idea that it was shrinking. And on the tenth night after McAllister's departure he dreamed a strange dream. He had gone with King George to show his Gracious Majesty the pumpkin, promising him the treat of a lifetime; and, when they arrived, there in the corner of the frame was a shrivelled thing the size of a pea. He woke, sweating, with his Sovereign's disappointed screams ringing in his ears; and Pride gave its last quiver and collapsed. To reinstate Angus would be a surrender, but it must be done.

'Beach,' he said that morning at breakfast, 'do you happen to – er – to have McAllister's address?'

'Yes, your lordship,' replied the butler. 'He is in London, residing at number eleven Buxton Crescent.'

'Buxton Crescent? Never heard of it.'

'It is, I fancy, your lordship, a boarding-house or some such establishment off the Cromwell Road. McAllister was accustomed to make it his headquarters whenever he visited the Metropolis on account of its handiness for Kensington Gardens. He liked,' said Beach with respectful reproach, for Angus had been a friend of his for nine years, 'to be near the flowers, your lordship.'

Two telegrams, passing through it in the course of the next twelve hours, caused some gossip at the post office of the little town of Market Blandings.

The first ran:

MCALLISTER,
11 BUXTON CRESCENT
CROMWELL ROAD
LONDON

RETURN IMMEDIATELY – EMSWORTH

The second:

LORD EMSWORTH
BLANDINGS CASTLE
SHROPSHIRE

I WILL NOT – MCALLISTER

Lord Emsworth had one of those minds capable of accommodating but one thought at a time – if that; and the possibility that Angus McAllister might decline to return had not occurred to him. It was difficult to adjust himself to this new problem, but he managed it at last. Before nightfall he had made up his mind. Robert Barker, that broken reed, could remain in charge for another day or so, and meanwhile he would go up to London and engage a real head-gardener, the finest head-gardener that money could buy.

*

It was the opinion of Dr Johnson that there is in London all that life can afford. A man, he held, who is tired of London is tired of life itself. Lord Emsworth, had he been aware of this statement, would have contested it warmly. He hated London. He loathed its crowds, its smells, its noises; its omnibuses, its taxis, and its hard pavements. And, in addition to all its other defects, the miserable town did not seem able to produce a single decent head-gardener. He went from agency to agency, interviewing candidates, and not one of them came within a mile of meeting his requirements. He disliked their faces, he distrusted their references. It was a harsh thing to say of any man, but he was dashed if the best of them was even as good as Robert Barker.

It was, therefore, in a black and soured mood that his lordship, having lunched frugally at the Senior Conservative Club on the third day of his visit, stood on the steps in the sunshine, wondering how on earth he was to get through the afternoon. He had spent the morning rejecting head-gardeners, and the next batch was not due until the morrow. And what – besides rejecting head-gardeners – was there for a man of reasonable tastes to do with his time in this hopeless town?

And then there came into his mind a remark which Beach the butler had made at the breakfast-table about flowers in Kensington Gardens. He could go to Kensington Gardens and look at the flowers.

He was about to hail a taxicab from the rank down the street when there suddenly emerged from the Hotel Magnificent over the way a young man. This young man proceeded to cross the road, and, as he drew near, it seemed to Lord Emsworth that there was about his appearance something oddly familiar. He stared for a long instant before he could believe his eyes, then with a wordless cry bounded down the steps just as the other started to mount them.

'Oh, hullo, guv'nor!' ejaculated the Hon. Freddie, plainly startled.

'What – what are you doing here?' demanded Lord Emsworth.

He spoke with heat, and justly so. London, as the result of several spirited escapades which still rankled in the mind of a father who had had to foot the bills, was forbidden ground to Freddie.

The young man was plainly not at his ease. He had the air of one who is being pushed towards dangerous machinery in which he is loath to become entangled. He shuffled his feet for a moment, then raised his left shoe and rubbed the back of his right calf with it.

'The fact is, guv'nor—'

'You know you are forbidden to come to London.'

'Absolutely, guv'nor, but the fact is—'

'And why anybody but an imbecile should want to come to London when he could be at Blandings—'

'I know, guv'nor, but the fact is –' Here Freddie, having replaced his wandering foot on the pavement, raised the other, and rubbed the back of his left calf. 'I wanted to see you,' he said. 'Yes. Particularly wanted to see you.'

This was not strictly accurate. The last thing in the world which the Hon. Freddie wanted was to see his parent. He had come to the Senior Conservative Club to leave a carefully written note. Having delivered which, it had been his intention to bolt like a rabbit. This unforeseen meeting had upset his plans.

'To see me?' said Lord Emsworth. 'Why?'

'Got – er – something to tell you. Bit of news.'

'I trust it is of sufficient importance to justify your coming to London against my express wishes.'

'Oh, yes. Oh, yes, yes-yes. Oh, rather. It's dashed important. Yes – not to put too fine a point upon it – most dashed important. I say, guv'nor, are you in fairly good form to stand a bit of a shock?'

A ghastly thought rushed into Lord Emsworth's mind. Freddie's mysterious arrival – his strange manner – his odd hesitation and uneasiness – could it mean –? He clutched the young man's arm feverishly.

'Frederick! Speak! Tell me! Have the cats got at it?'

It was a fixed idea of Lord Emsworth, which no argument would have induced him to abandon, that cats had the power to work some dreadful mischief on his pumpkin and were continually lying in wait for the opportunity of doing so; and his behaviour on the occasion when one of the fast sporting set from the stables, wandering into the kitchen garden and finding him gazing at the Blandings Hope, had rubbed itself sociably against his leg, lingered long in that animal's memory.

Freddie stared.

'Cats? Why? Where? Which? What cats?'

'Frederick! Is anything wrong with the pumpkin?'

In a crass and materialistic world there must inevitably be a scattered few here and there in whom pumpkins touch no chord. The Hon. Freddie Threepwood was one of these. He was accustomed to speak in mockery of all pumpkins, and had even gone so far as to allude to the Hope of Blandings as 'Percy'. His father's anxiety, therefore, merely caused him to giggle.

'Not that I know of,' he said.

'Then what do you mean?' thundered Lord Emsworth, stung by the giggle. 'What do you mean, sir, by coming here and alarming me – scaring me out of my wits, by Gad! – with your nonsense about giving me shocks?'

The Hon. Freddie looked carefully at his fermenting parent. His fingers, sliding into his pocket, closed on the note which nestled there. He drew it forth.

'Look here, guv'nor,' he said nervously. 'I think the best thing would be for you to read this. Meant to leave it for you with the hall-porter. It's – well, you just cast your eye over it. Goodbye, guv'nor. Got to see a man.'

And, thrusting the note into his father's hand, the Hon. Freddie turned and was gone. Lord Emsworth, perplexed and annoyed, watched him skim up the road and leap into a cab. He seethed impotently. Practically any behaviour on the part of his son Frederick had the power to irritate him, but it was when he was vague and mysterious and incoherent that the young man irritated him most.

He looked at the letter in his hand, turned it over, felt it. Then – for it had suddenly occurred to him that if he wished to ascertain its contents he had better read it – he tore open the envelope.

The note was brief, but full of good reading matter.

DEAR GUV'NOR,

Awfully sorry and all that, but couldn't hold out any longer. I've popped up to London in the two-seater and Aggie and I were spliced this morning. There looked like being a bit of a hitch at one time, but Aggie's guv'nor, who has come over from America, managed to wangle it all right by getting a special licence or something of that order. A most capable Johnny. He's coming to see you. He wants to have a good long talk with you about the whole binge. Lush him up hospitably and all that, would you mind, because he's a really sound egg, and you'll like him.

Well, cheerio: Your affectionate son,

FREDDIE

P.S. – You won't mind if I freeze on to the two-seater for the nonce, what? It may come in useful for the honeymoon.

The Senior Conservative Club is a solid and massive building, but, as Lord Emsworth raised his eyes dumbly from the perusal of this letter, it seemed to him that it was performing a kind of whirling dance. The whole of the immediate neighbourhood, indeed, appeared to be shimmying in the middle of a thick mist. He was profoundly stirred. It is not too much to say that he was shaken to the core of his being. No father enjoys being flouted and defied by his own son; nor is it reasonable to expect a man to take a cheery view of life who is faced with the prospect of supporting for the remainder of his years a younger son, a younger son's wife, and possibly younger grandchildren.

For an appreciable space of time he stood in the middle of the pavement, rooted to the spot. Passers-by bumped into him or grumblingly made detours to avoid a collision. Dogs sniffed at his ankles. Seedy-looking individuals tried to arrest his attention in order to speak of their financial affairs. Lord Emsworth heeded none of them. He remained where he was, gaping like a fish, until suddenly his faculties seemed to return to him.

An imperative need for flowers and green trees swept upon Lord Emsworth. The noise of the traffic and the heat of the sun on the stone pavement were afflicting him like a nightmare. He signalled energetically to a passing cab.

'Kensington Gardens,' he said, and sank back on the cushioned seat.

Something dimly resembling peace crept into his lordship's soul as he paid off his cab and entered the cool shade of the gardens. Even from the road he had caught a glimpse of stimulating reds and yellows; and as he ambled up the asphalt path and plunged round the corner the flower-beds burst upon his sight in all their consoling glory.

'Ah!' breathed Lord Emsworth rapturously, and came to a halt before a glowing carpet of tulips. A man of official aspect, wearing a peaked cap and a uniform, stopped as he heard the exclamation and looked at him with approval and even affection.

'Nice weather we're 'avin',' he observed.

Lord Emsworth did not reply. He had not heard. There is that about a well-set-out bed of flowers which acts on men who love their gardens like a drug, and he was in a sort of trance. Already he had completely forgotten where he was, and seemed to himself to be back in his paradise of Blandings. He drew a step nearer to the flower-bed, pointing like a setter.

The official-looking man's approval deepened. This man with the peaked cap was the park-keeper, who held the rights of the high, the low, and the middle justice over that section of the gardens. He, too, loved these flower-beds, and he seemed to see in Lord Emsworth a kindred soul. The general public was too apt to pass by, engrossed in its own affairs, and this often wounded the park-keeper. In Lord Emsworth he thought that he recognised one of the right sort.

'Nice—' he began.

He broke off with a sharp cry. If he had not seen it with his own eyes, he would not have believed it. But, alas, there was no possibility of a mistake. With a ghastly shock he realised that he had been deceived in this attractive stranger. Decently, if untidily, dressed; clean; respectable to the outward eye; the stranger was in reality a dangerous criminal, the blackest type of evil-doer on the park-keeper's index. He was a Kensington Gardens flower-picker.

For, even as he uttered the word 'Nice', the man had stepped lightly over the low railing, had shambled across the strip of turf, and before you could say 'weather' was busy on his dark work. In the brief instant in which the park-keeper's vocal cords refused to obey him, he was two tulips ahead of the game and reaching out to scoop in a third.

'Hi!!!' roared the park-keeper, suddenly finding speech. ''I there!!!'

Lord Emsworth turned with a start.

'Bless my soul!' he murmured reproachfully.

He was in full possession of his senses now, such as they were, and understood the enormity of his conduct. He shuffled back on to the asphalt, contrite.

'My dear fellow—' he began remorsefully.

The park-keeper began to speak rapidly and at length. From time to time Lord Emsworth moved his lips and made deprecating gestures, but he could not stem the flood. Louder and more rhetorical grew the park-keeper and denser and more interested the rapidly assembling crowd of spectators. And then through the stream of words another voice spoke.

'Wot's all this?'

The Force had materialised in the shape of a large, solid constable.

The park-keeper seemed to understand that he had been superseded. He still spoke, but no longer like a father rebuking an erring son. His attitude now was more that of an elder brother appealing for justice against a delinquent junior. In a moving passage he stated his case.

''E Says,' observed the constable judicially, speaking slowly and in capitals, as if addressing an untutored foreigner, ''E Says You Was Pickin' The Flowers.'

'I saw 'im. I was standin' as close as I am to you.'

''E Saw You,' interpreted the constable. ''E Was Standing At Your Side.'

Lord Emsworth was feeling weak and bewildered. Without a thought of annoying or doing harm to anybody, he seemed to have unchained the fearful passions of a French

Revolution; and there came over him a sense of how unjust it was that this sort of thing should be happening to him, of all people – a man already staggering beneath the troubles of a Job.

'I'll 'ave to ask you for your name and address,' said the constable, more briskly. A stubby pencil popped for an instant into his stern mouth and hovered, well and truly moistened, over the virgin page of his notebook – that dreadful notebook before which taxi-drivers shrink and hardened bus-conductors quail.

'I – I – why, my dear fellow – I mean, officer – I am the Earl of Emsworth.'

Much has been written of the psychology of crowds, designed to show how extraordinary and inexplicable it is, but most of such writing is exaggeration. A crowd generally behaves in a perfectly natural and intelligible fashion. When, for instance, it sees a man in a badly fitting tweed suit and a hat he ought to be ashamed of getting put through it for pinching flowers in the Park, and the man says he is an earl, it laughs. This crowd laughed.

'Ho?' The constable did not stoop to join in the merriment of the rabble, but his lip twitched sardonically. 'Have you a card, your lordship?'

Nobody intimate with Lord Emsworth would have asked such a foolish question. His card-case was the thing he always lost second when visiting London – immediately after losing his umbrella.

'I – er – I'm afraid—'

'R!' said the constable. And the crowd uttered another happy, hyena-like laugh, so intensely galling that his lordship raised his bowed head and found enough spirit to cast an indignant glance. And, as he did so, the hunted look faded from his eyes.

'McAllister!' he cried.

Two new arrivals had just joined the throng, and, being of rugged and knobbly physique, had already shoved themselves through to the ringside seats. One was a tall, handsome, smooth-faced gentleman of authoritative appearance, who, if he had not worn rimless glasses, would have looked like a Roman emperor. The other was a shorter, sturdier man with a bristly red beard.

'McAllister!' moaned his lordship piteously. 'McAllister, my dear fellow, do please tell this man who I am.'

After what had passed between himself and his late employer, a lesser man than Angus McAllister might have seen in Lord Emsworth's predicament merely a judgement. A man of little magnanimity would have felt that here was where he got a bit of his own back.

Not so this splendid Glaswegian.

'Aye,' he said. 'Yon's Lorrud Emsworruth.'

'Who are you?' inquired the constable searchingly.

'I used to be head-gardener at the cassel.'

'Exactly,' bleated Lord Emsworth. 'Precisely. My head-gardener.'

The constable was shaken. Lord Emsworth might not look like an earl, but there was no getting away from the fact that Angus McAllister was supremely head-gardeneresque. A staunch admirer of the aristocracy, the constable perceived that zeal had caused him to make a bit of a bloomer.

In this crisis, however, he comported himself with masterly tact. He scowled blackly upon the interested throng.

'Pass along there, please. Pass along,' he commanded austerely. Ought to know better than block up a public thoroughfare like this. Pass along!'

He moved off, shepherding the crowd before him. The Roman emperor with the rimless glasses advanced upon Lord Emsworth, extending a large hand.

'Pleased to meet you at last,' he said. 'My name is Donaldson, Lord Emsworth.'

For a moment the name conveyed nothing to his lordship. Then its significance hit him, and he drew himself up with hauteur.

'You'll excuse us, Angus,' said Mr Donaldson. 'High time you and I had a little chat, Lord Emsworth.'

Lord Emsworth was about to speak, when he caught the other's eye. It was a strong, keen, level grey eye, with a curious forcefulness about it that made him feel strangely inferior. There is every reason to suppose that Mr Donaldson had subscribed for years to those personality courses advertised in the magazines which guarantee to impart to the pupil who takes ten correspondence lessons the ability to look the boss in the eye and make him wilt. Mr Donaldson looked Lord Emsworth in the eye, and Lord Emsworth wilted.

'How do you do?' he said weakly.

'Now listen, Lord Emsworth,' proceeded Mr Donaldson. 'No sense in having hard feelings between members of a family. I take it you've heard by this that your boy and my girl have gone ahead and fixed it up? Personally, I'm delighted. That boy is a fine young fellow.'

Lord Emsworth blinked.

'You are speaking of my son Frederick?' he said incredulously.

'Of your son Frederick. Now, at the moment, no doubt, you are feeling a trifle sore. I don't blame you. You have every right to be sorer than a gumboil. But you must remember – young blood, eh? It will, I am convinced, be a lasting grief to that splendid young man—'

'You are still speaking of my son Frederick?'

'Of Frederick, yes. It will, I say, be a lasting grief to him if he feels he has incurred your resentment. You must forgive him, Lord Emsworth. He must have your support.'

'I suppose he'll have to have it, dash it!' said his lordship unhappily. 'Can't let the boy starve.'

Mr Donaldson's hand swept round in a wide, grand gesture.

'Don't you worry about that, I'll look after that end of it. I am not a rich man—'

'Ah!' said Lord Emsworth rather bleakly. There had been something about the largeness of the other's manner which had led him to entertain hopes.

'I doubt,' continued Mr Donaldson frankly, for he was a man who believed in frankness in these matters, 'if, all told, I have as much as ten million dollars in the world.'

Lord Emsworth swayed like a sapling in the breeze.

'Ten million? Ten million? Did you say you had ten million dollars?'

'Between nine and ten, I suppose. Not more. You must remember,' said Mr Donaldson, with a touch of apology, 'that conditions have changed very much in America of late. We have been through a tough time, a mighty tough time. Many of my friends have been harder hit than I have. But things are coming back. Yes, sir, they're coming right back. I am a firm believer in President Roosevelt and the New Deal. Under the New Deal, the American dog is beginning to eat more biscuits. That, I should have mentioned, is my line. I am Donaldson's Dog-Biscuits.'

'Donaldson's Dog-Biscuits? Indeed? Really! Fancy that!'

'You have heard of Donaldson's Dog-Biscuits?' asked their proprietor eagerly.

'Never,' said Lord Emsworth cordially.

'Oh! Well, that's who I am. And, as I say, the business is beginning to pick up nicely after the slump. All over the country our salesmen are reporting that the American dog is once more becoming biscuit-conscious. And so I am in a position, with your approval, to offer Frederick a steady and possibly a lucrative job. I propose, always with your consent, of course, to send him over to Long Island City to start learning the business. I have no doubt that he will in time prove a lost valuable asset to the firm.'

Lord Emsworth could conceive of no way in which Freddie could be of value to a dog-biscuit firm, except possibly as a taster; but he refrained from damping the other's enthusiasm by saying so. In any case, the thought of the young man actually earning his living, and doing so three thousand miles from Blandings Castle, would probably have held him dumb.

'He seems full of keenness. But, in my opinion, to be able to give of his best and push the Donaldson biscuit as it should be pushed, he must feel that he has your moral support, Lord Emsworth – his father's moral support.'

'Yes, yes, yes,' said Lord Emsworth heartily. A feeling of positive adoration for Mr Donaldson was thrilling him. The getting rid of Freddie, which he himself had been unable to achieve in twenty-six years, this godlike dog-biscuit manufacturer had accomplished in less than a week. What a man! felt Lord Emsworth. 'Oh, yes, yes, yes!' he said. 'Yes, indeed. Most decidedly.'

'They sail on Wednesday.'

'Capital!'

'Early in the morning.'

'Splendid!'

'I may give them a friendly message from you? A forgiving, fatherly message?'

'Certainly, certainly, certainly. Inform Frederick that he has my best wishes.'

'I will.'

'Mention that I shall watch his future progress with considerable interest.'

'Exactly.'

'Say that I hope he will work hard and make a name for himself.'

'Just so.'

'And,' concluded Lord Emsworth, speaking with a paternal earnestness well in keeping with this solemn moment, 'tell him – er – not to hurry home.'

He pressed Mr Donaldson's hand with feelings too deep for further speech. Then he galloped swiftly to where Angus McAllister stood brooding over the tulip bed.

'McAllister!'

The head-gardener's beard waggled grimly. He looked at his late employer with cold eyes. It is never difficult to distinguish between a Scotsman with a grievance and a ray of sunshine, and Lord Emsworth, gazing upon the dour man, was able to see at a glance into which category Angus McAllister fell. His tongue seemed to cleave to his palate, but he forced himself to speak.

'McAllister . . . I wish . . . I wonder . . .'

'Weel?'

'I wonder . . . I wish . . . What I want to say,' faltered Lord Emsworth humbly, 'is, have you accepted another situation yet?'

'I am conseederin' twa.'

'Come back to me!' pleaded his lordship, his voice breaking. 'Robert Barker is worse than useless. Come back to me!'

Angus McAllister gazed woodenly at the tulips.

'A' weel—' he said at length.

'You will?' cried Lord Emsworth joyfully. 'Splendid! Capital! Excellent!'

'A' didna say I wud.'

'I thought you said "I will",' said his lordship, dashed.

'I didna say "A' weel"; I said "A' weel",' said Mr McAllister stiffly. 'Meanin' mebbe I might, mebbe not.'

Lord Emsworth laid a trembling hand upon his shoulder.

'McAllister, I will raise your salary.'

The beard twitched.

'Dash it, I'll double it.'

The eyebrows flickered.

'McAllister . . . Angus . . .' said Lord Emsworth in a low voice. 'Come back! The pumpkin needs you.'

In an age of rush and hurry like that of today, an age in which there are innumerable calls on the time of everyone, it is possible that here and there throughout the ranks of those who have read this chronicle there may be one or two who for various reasons found themselves unable to attend the last Agricultural Show at Shrewsbury. For these a few words must be added.

Sir Gregory Parsloe-Parsloe, of Matchingham Hall, was there, of course, but it would not have escaped the notice of a close observer that his mien lacked something of the haughty arrogance which had characterised it in other years. From time to time, as he paced the tent devoted to the exhibition of vegetables, he might have been seen to bite his lip, and his eye had something of that brooding look which Napoleon's must have worn at Waterloo.

But there was the right stuff in Sir Gregory. He was a gentleman and a sportsman. In the Parsloe tradition there was nothing small or mean. Halfway down the tent he stopped, and with a quick, manly gesture thrust out his hand.

'Congratulate you, Emsworth,' he said huskily.

Lord Emsworth looked up with a start. He had been deep in his thoughts.

'Eh? Oh, thanks. Thanks, my dear fellow, thanks, thanks. Thank you very much.' He hesitated. 'Er – can't both win, eh?'

Sir Gregory puzzled it out and saw that he was right.

'No,' he said. 'No. See what you mean. Can't both win. No getting round that.'

He nodded and walked on, with who knows what vultures gnawing at his broad bosom. And Lord Emsworth – with Angus McAllister, who had been a silent, beard-waggling witness of the scene, at his side – turned once more to stare reverently at that which lay on the strawy bottom of one of the largest packing-cases ever seen in Shrewsbury town.

A card had been attached to the exterior of the packing-case. It bore the simple legend:

PUMPKINS. FIRST PRIZE

16

An Englishman's Home

(1938)

Evelyn Waugh

I

Mr Beverley Metcalfe tapped the barometer in the back hall and noted with satisfaction that it had fallen several points during the night. He was by nature a sun-loving man, but he believed it was one of the marks of a true countryman to be eternally in need of rain. He had made a study and noted the points of true countrymen. Had he been of literary habit and of an earlier generation, his observations might have formed a little book of aphorisms. The true countryman wore a dark suit on Sundays unlike the flannelled tripper from the cities; he loved a bargain and would go to any expense to do his marketing by private treaty instead of through the normal channels of retail trade; while ostensibly sceptical and conservative he was readily fascinated by mechanical gadgets; he was genial but inhospitable, willing to gossip for hours across a fence with any passing stranger, but reluctant to allow his closest friends into his house . . . These and a hundred other characteristics Mr Metcalfe noted for emulation.

'That's what we need – rain,' he said to himself, and opening the garden door stepped into the balmy morning air. There was no threat in the cloudless heavens. His gardener passed, pushing the water-barrow.

'Good morning, Boggett. The glass has dropped, I'm glad to say.'

'Ur.'

'Means rain.'

'Noa.'

'Down quite low.'

'Ah.'

'Pity to spend a lot of time watering.'

'Them'll burn up else.'

'Not if it rains.'

'Am't agoin to rain. Don't never rain around heres except you can see clear down-over.'

'See clear down-over?'

'Ur. Can always see Pilbury Steeple when rains a-coming.'

Mr Metcalfe accepted this statement gravely. 'These old fellows know a thing or two that the scientists don't,' he would often remark, simulating an air of patronage which was far from sincere. Boggett, the gardener, was not particularly old and he knew very little; the seeds he planted seldom grew; he wrought stark havoc whenever he was allowed to use the pruning-knife; his ambition in horticulture went no further than the fattening of the largest possible pumpkin; but Mr Metcalfe regarded him with the simple reverence of peasant for priest. For Mr Metcalfe was but lately initiated into the cult of the countryside, and any features of it still claimed his devotion – its agricultural processes, its social structure, its vocabulary, its recreations; the aspect of it, glittering now under the cool May sunshine, fruit trees in flower, chestnut in full leaf, the ash budding; the sound and smell of it – Mr Westmacott calling his cows at dawn, the scent of wet earth and Boggett splashing clumsily among the wall-flowers; the heart of it – or what Mr Metcalfe took to be its heart – pulsing all round him; his own heart beating time, for was he not part of it, a true countryman, a landowner?

He was, it is true, a landowner in rather a small way, but, as he stood on his terrace and surveyed the untroubled valley below him, he congratulated himself that he had not been led away by the house-agents into the multitudinous cares of a wider territory. He owned seven acres, more or less, and it seemed to him exactly the right amount; they comprised the policies of the house and a paddock; sixty further acres of farmland had also been available, and for a day or two he had toyed with the rather inebriating idea of acquiring them. He could well have afforded it, of course, but to his habit of mind there was something perverse and downright wrong in an investment which showed a bare two per cent yield on his capital. He wanted a home, not a 'seat', and he reflected on the irony of that word; he thought of Lord Brakehurst, with whose property he sometimes liked to say that his own 'marched' – there was indeed a hundred yards of ha-ha between his paddock and one of Lord Brakehurst's pastures. What could be less sedentary than Lord Brakehurst's life, every day of which was agitated by the cares of his great possessions? No, seven acres, judiciously chosen, was the ideal property, and Mr Metcalfe *had* chosen judiciously. The house-agent had spoken no more than the truth when he described Much Malcock as one of the most unspoilt Cotswold villages. It was exactly such a place as Mr Metcalfe had dreamed of in the long years in the cotton trade in Alexandria. Mr Metcalfe's own residence, known for generations by the singular name of Grumps, had been rechristened by a previous owner as Much Malcock Hall. It bore the new name pretty well. It was 'a dignified Georgian house of mellowed Cotswold stone; four recep., six principal bed and dressing rooms, replete with period features'. The villagers, Mr Metcalfe observed with regret, could not be induced to speak of it as 'the Hall'. Boggett always said that he worked 'up to Grumps', but the name was not of Mr Metcalfe's choosing and it looked well on his notepaper. It suggested a primacy in the village that was not undisputed.

Lord Brakehurst, of course, was in a class apart; he was Lord Lieutenant of the County with property in fifty parishes. Lady Brakehurst had not in fact called on Mrs Metcalfe, living as she did in a world where card-leaving had lost its importance, but, of the calling class, there were two other households in Much Malcock, and a border-line case – besides the vicar, who had a plebeian accent and an inclination to preach against bankers.

The rival gentry were Lady Peabury and Colonel Hodge, both, to the villagers, newcomers, but residents of some twenty years priority to Mr Metcalfe.

Lady Peabury lived at Much Malcock House, whose chimneys, soon to be hidden in the full foliage of summer, could still be seen among its budding limes on the opposite slope of the valley. Four acres of meadowland lay between her property and Mr Metcalfe's, where Westmacott's plump herd enriched the landscape and counter-balanced the slightly suburban splendour of her flower gardens. She was a widow and, like Mr Metcalfe, had come to Much Malcock from abroad. She was rich and kind and rather greedy, a diligent reader of fiction, mistress of many Cairn terriers and of five steady old maidservants who never broke the Crown Derby.

Colonel Hodge lived at the Manor, a fine gabled house in the village street, whose gardens, too, backed on to Westmacott's meadow. He was impecunious but active in the affairs of the British Legion and the Boy Scouts; he accepted Mr Metcalfe's invitation to dinner, but spoke of him, in his family circle, as 'the cotton wallah'.

These neighbours were of unequivocal position; the Hornbeams at the Old Mill were a childless, middle-aged couple who devoted themselves to craftsmanship. Mr Hornbeam senior was a genuine, commercial potter in Staffordshire; he supported them reluctantly and rather exiguously, but this backing of unearned quarterly cheques placed them definitely in the upper strata of local society. Mrs Hornbeam attended church and Mr Hornbeam was quite knowledgeable about vegetables. In fact, had they preferred a tennis court to their herb garden, and had Mr Hornbeam possessed an evening-suit, they might easily have mixed with their neighbours on terms of ostensible equality. At the time of the Peace Ballot, Mrs Hornbeam had canvassed every cottage in bicycling distance, but she eschewed the Women's Institute, and in Lady Peabury's opinion failed to pull her weight in the village. Mr Metcalfe thought Mr Hornbeam Bohemian, and Mr Hornbeam thought Mr Metcalfe Philistine. Colonel Hodge had fallen out with them some time back, on a question relating to his Airedale, and cut them year in, year out, three or four times a day.

Under their stone-tiled roofs the villagers derived substantial comfort from all these aliens. Foreign visitors impressed by the charges of London restaurants and the splendour of the more accessible ducal palaces often express wonder at the wealth of England. A half has not been told them. It is in remote hamlets like Much Malcock that the great reservoirs of national wealth seep back to the soil. The villagers had their Memorial Hall and their club. In the rafters of their church the death-watch beetle had been expensively exterminated for them; their scouts had a bell tent and silver bugles; the district nurse drove her own car; at Christmas their children were surfeited with trees and parties and the cottagers loaded with hampers; if one of them was indisposed port and soup and grapes and tickets for the seaside arrived in profusion; at evening their menfolk returned from work laden with perquisites, and all the year round they feasted on forced vegetables. The Vicar found it impossible to interest them in the Left Book Club.

'God gave all men all earth to love,' Mr Metcalfe quoted, dimly remembering the lines from a calendar which had hung in his office in Alexandria, 'but since our hearts are small, Ordained for each one spot should prove, Beloved over all.'

He pottered round to the engine-house where his chauffeur was brooding over batteries. He popped his head into another outbuilding and saw that no harm had befallen the lawnmower during the night. He paused in the kitchen garden to nip the blossom off some newly planted black-currant which must not be allowed to fruit that summer. Then, his round finished, he pottered in to breakfast.

His wife was already there.

'I've done my round,' he said.

'Yes, dear.'

'Everything coming along very nicely.'

'Yes, dear.'

'You can't see Pilbury Steeple, though.'

'Good gracious, Beverley, why should you want to do that?'

'It's a sign of rain when you can.'

'What a lot of nonsense. You've been listening to Boggett again.'

She rose and left him with his papers. She had to see the cook. Servants seem to take up so much time in England; she thought wistfully of the white-gowned Berber boys who had pattered about the cool, tiled floors of her house in Alexandria.

Mr Metcalfe finished his breakfast and retired to his study with pipe and papers. The *Gazette* came out that morning. A true countryman always reads his 'local rag' first, so Mr Metcalfe patiently toiled through the columns of Women's Institute doings and the reports of a Council meeting on the subject of sewage, before he allowed himself to open *The Times*.

Serene opening of a day of wrath!

II

Towards eleven o'clock Mr Metcalfe put aside the crossword. In the lobby by the garden-door he kept a variety of garden implements specially designed for the use of the elderly. Selecting from among them one which had newly arrived, he sauntered out into the sunshine and addressed himself to the plantains on the lawn. The tool had a handsomely bound leather grip, a spliced cane handle and a head of stainless steel; it worked admirably, and with a minimum of effort Mr Metcalfe had soon scarred a large area with neat little pits.

He paused and called towards the house, 'Sophie, Sophie, come and see what I've done.'

His wife's head emerged from an upper window. 'Very pretty, dear,' she said.

Encouraged, he set to work again. Boggett passed.

'Useful little tool this, Boggett.'

'Ur.'

'Think we ought to sow some seed in the bare patches?'

'Noa.'

'You think the grass will grow over them?'

'Noa. Plantains'll come up again.'

'You don't think I've killed the roots?'

'Noa. Makes the roots powerful strong topping 'em off same as you've done.'

'Well, what ought I to do?'

'Bain't nothing you can do with plantains. They do always come up again.'

Boggett passed. Mr Metcalfe looked at his gadget with sudden distaste, propped it petulantly against the sundial, and with his hands in his pockets stared out across the valley. Even at this distance Lady Peabury's aubrietias struck a discordant note. His eyes dropped and he noticed, casually at first, then with growing curiosity, two unfamiliar figures among Westmacott's cows. They were young men in dark, urban clothes, and they were very busy about something. They had papers in their hands which they constantly consulted; they paced up and down the field as though measuring it; they squatted on their haunches as though roughly taking a level; they pointed into the air, to the ground, and to the horizon.

'Boggett,' said Mr Metcalfe sharply, 'come here a minute.'

'Urr.'

'Do you see two men in Mr Westmacott's field?'

'Noa.'

'You don't?'

''Er bain't Mr Westmacott's field. 'E've a sold of 'er.'

'Sold it! Good heavens! Who to?'

'Couldn't rightly say who 'e've a sold 'er to. Gentleman from London staying at the Brakehurst. Paid a tidy price for 'er too I've a heard said.'

'What on earth for?'

'Couldn't rightly say, but I reckon it be to build hisself a house.'

Build. It was a word so hideous that no one in Much Malcock dared use it above a whisper. 'Housing scheme', 'Development', 'Clearance', 'Council houses', 'Planning' – these obscene words had been expunged from the polite vocabulary of the district, only to be used now and then, with the licence allowed to anthropologists, of the fierce tribes beyond the parish boundary. And now the horror was in their midst, the mark of Plague in the court of the Decameron.

After the first moment of shock, Mr Metcalfe rallied for action, hesitated for a moment whether or no to plunge down the hill and challenge the enemy on his own ground, and decided against it; this was the moment to act with circumspection. He must consult Lady Peabury.

It was three-quarters of a mile to the house; the lane ran past the gate which gave access to Westmacott's field; a crazily-hung elm gate and deep cow-trodden mud, soon in Mr Metcalfe's imagination, to give place to golden privet and red gravel. Mr Metcalfe could see the heads of the intruders bobbing beyond the hedge; they bore urban, purposeful black hats. He drove on, miserably.

Lady Peabury was in the morning-room reading a novel; early training gave a guilty spice to this recreation, for she had been brought up to believe that to read a novel before luncheon was one of the gravest sins it was possible for a gentlewoman to commit. She slipped the book under a cushion and rose to greet Mr Metcalfe.

'I was just getting ready to go out,' she explained.

Mr Metcalfe had no time for politenesses.

'Lady Peabury,' he began at once, 'I have very terrible news.'

'Oh dear! Is poor Mr Cruttwell having trouble with the Wolf Cub account again?'

'No; at least, he is; there's another fourpence gone astray; on the credit side this time, which makes it more worrying. But that isn't what I came about. It is something that threatens our whole lives. They are going to build in Westmacott's field.' Briefly, but with emotion, he told Lady Peabury what he had seen.

She listened gravely. When he had finished there was silence in the morning-room; six little clocks ticked among the chintzes and the potted azaleas. At last Lady Peabury spoke:

'Westmacott has behaved very badly,' she said.

'I suppose you can't blame him.'

'I do blame him, Mr Metcalfe, very severely. I can't understand it at all. He always seemed a very decent man . . . I was thinking of making Mrs Westmacott secretary of the Women's Institute. He had no right to do a thing like that without consulting us. Why, I look right on to that field from my bedroom windows. I could never understand why you didn't buy the field yourself.'

It was let for £3 18s.; they had asked £170 for it; there was tithe and property tax on top of that. Lady Peabury knew this.

'Any of us could have bought it at the time of sale,' said Mr Metcalfe rather sharply.

'It always went with your house.'

In another minute, Mr Metcalfe felt, she would be telling him that *he* had behaved very badly; that *he* had always seemed a very decent man.

She was, in fact, thinking on just those lines at the moment. 'I daresay it's not too late even now for you to make an offer,' she said.

'We are all equally threatened,' said Mr Metcalfe. 'I think we ought to act together. Hodge won't be any too pleased when he hears the news.'

Colonel Hodge had heard, and he was none too pleased. He was waiting at the Hall when Mr Metcalfe got back.

'Do you know what that scoundrel Westmacott has done?'

'Yes,' said Mr Metcalfe rather wearily, 'I know.' The interview with Lady Peabury had not gone off quite as he had hoped. She had shown no enthusiasm for common action.

'Sold his field to a lot of jerry builders.'

'Yes, I know.'

'Funny, I always thought it was *your* field.'

'No,' said Mr Metcalfe, 'never.'

'It always used to go with this house.'

'Yes, I know, but I didn't happen to want it.'

'Well, it's put us all in a pretty nasty fix, I must say. D'you suppose they'd sell it back to you now?'

'I don't know that I want to buy it. Why, they'll probably want a building-land price – seventy or eighty pounds an acre.'

'More, I daresay. But, good heavens man, you wouldn't let that stop you. Think how it would depreciate your property having a whole town of bungalows right under your windows.'

'Come, come, Hodge. We've no reason to suppose that it will be bungalows.'

'Well, villas then. You surely aren't sticking up for the fellows?'

'Certainly not. We shall all suffer very much from any development there. My belief is that it can be stopped by law; there's the Society for the Protection of Rural England. We could interest them in it. The County Council could be approached. We could write letters to the papers and petition the Office of Works. The great thing is that we must all stand together over this.'

'Fat lot of change we shall get out of that. Think of the building that's gone on over at Metbury.'

Mr Metcalfe thought, and shuddered.

'I should say that this was one of the times when money talked loudest. Have you tried Lady Peabury?'

For the first time in their acquaintance Mr Metcalfe detected a distinctly coarse strain in Colonel Hodge. 'I have discussed it with her. She is naturally very much concerned.'

'That field has always been known as Lower Grumps,' said the Colonel, reverting to his former and doubly offensive line of thought. 'It's not really her chicken.'

'It is all our chickens,' said Mr Metcalfe, getting confused with the metaphor.

'Well, I don't know what you expect me to do about it,' said Colonel Hodge. 'You know how I'm placed. It all comes of that parson preaching Bolshevism Sunday after Sunday.'

'We ought to get together and discuss it.'

'Oh, we'll discuss it all right. I don't suppose we shall discuss anything else for the next three months.'

No one in Much Malcock took the crisis harder than the Hornbeams. News of it reached them at midday by means of the village charwoman, who dropped in twice a week to despoil their larder. She told them with some pride, innocently assuming that all city gentlemen – as she continued to regard Mr Hornbeam, in spite of his home-spuns and his beard – would welcome an addition to their numbers.

Nervous gloom descended on the Old Mill. There was no explosion of wrath as there had been at the Manor; no moral condemnation as at the House; no call to action as had come from the Hall. Hopeless sorrow reigned unrelieved. Mrs Hornbeam's pottery went to pieces. Mr Hornbeam sat listless at the loom. It was their working hour; they sat at opposite ends of the raftered granary. Often, on other afternoons, they sang to one another catches and refrains of folk music as their busy fingers muddled with the clay and the shuttles. To-day they sat in silence each, according to a Japanese mystical practice, attempting to drive the new peril into the World of Unbeing. It had worked well enough with Colonel Hodge and the Airedale, with the Abyssinian War, and with Mr Hornbeam senior's yearly visit, but by sunset the new peril remained obstinately concrete.

Mrs Hornbeam set their simple meal of milk, raisins, and raw turnip; Mr Hornbeam turned away from his elm platter. 'There is no place for the Artist in the Modern World,' he said. 'We ask nothing of their brutish civilisation except to be left alone, to be given one little corner of land, an inch or two of sky where we can live at peace and occupy ourselves with making seemly and beautiful things. You wouldn't think it was too much to ask. We give them the entire globe for their machines. But it is not enough. They have to hunt us out and harry us. They know that as long as there is one spot of loveliness and decency left it is a standing reproach to them.'

It was growing dark; Mrs Hornbeam struck a flint and lit the rush lights. She wandered to the harp and plucked a few poignant notes. 'Perhaps Mr Metcalfe will stop it,' she said.

'That we should be dependent for the essentials of life upon a vulgarian like that . . .'

It was in this mood that he received an invitation from Mr Metcalfe to confer with his neighbours at Much Malcock House on the following afternoon.

The choice of meeting place had been a delicate one, for Lady Peabury was loth to abdicate her position of general leadership or to appear as leader in this particular matter; on the other hand, it touched her too closely for her to be able to ignore it. Accordingly the invitations were issued by Mr Metcalfe, who thereby accepted responsibility for the agenda, while the presence of the meeting in her morning-room gave something of the atmosphere of a Cabinet meeting at the Palace.

Opinion had hardened during the day and there was general agreement with Colonel Hodge's judgement: 'Metcalfe has got us into this hole by not buying the field in the first place; it's up to him to get us out of it.' Though nothing as uncompromising as this was said in front of Mr Metcalfe, he could feel it in the air. He was the last to arrive. Lady Peabury's welcome to her guests had been lukewarm. 'It is very kind of you to come. I really cannot think that it is necessary, but Mr Metcalfe particularly wished it. I suppose he intends telling us what he is going to do.' To Mr Metcalfe she said, 'We are full of curiosity.'

'Sorry to be late. I've had a day of it, I can tell you. Been to all the local offices, got on to all the Societies, and I may as well tell you at once, there's nothing doing from that end. We are not even scheduled as a rural area.'

'No,' said Colonel Hodge, 'I saw to that. Halves the potential value of one's property.'

'*Schedules*,' moaned Mr Hornbeam, 'that is what we have become. We must be *scheduled* to lead a free life.'

'. . . And so,' persisted Mr Metcalfe, in his board-room manner, 'we are left to find the solution ourselves. Now this young man has no particular reason, I imagine, for preferring this district above any other in the country. The building has not yet begun; he has no commitments. I cannot help feeling that if he were tactfully approached and offered a reasonable profit on the transaction, he might be induced to re-sell.'

'I am sure,' said Lady Peabury, 'we shall all owe a deep debt of gratitude to Mr Metcalfe.'

'Very public spirited of you,' said Colonel Hodge.

'Profits, the cancer of the age . . .'

'I am perfectly willing,' said Mr Metcalfe, 'to bear my share of the burden . . .' At the word 'share' his hearers stiffened perceptibly. 'My suggestion is that we make a common fund proportionate to our present land holdings. By a rough calculation I work that out as being in the ratio of one to Mr Hornbeam, two to Colonel Hodge, two to myself, and five to our hostess here. The figures could be adjusted,' he added as he noted that his suggestion was falling a little flat.

'You can count me out,' said Colonel Hodge. 'Couldn't possibly run to it.'

'And me,' said Mr Hornbeam.

Lady Peabury was left in, with a difficult hand to stake. Delicacy forbade recognition of the vital fact that Mr Metcalfe was very much the richer – delicacy tempered with pride. The field must be saved, but there seemed no system of joint purchase by which she could honourably fail to bear the largest part. Duty called, clearly and unmistakably, to Mr Metcalfe alone. She held her cards and passed the bidding. 'Surely,' she said, 'as a business man you must see a great many objections to joint ownership. Do you propose to partition the field, or are we all to share the rent, the tithe and the tax? It would be highly inconvenient. I doubt if it is even legal.'

'Certainly, certainly. I merely wished to assure you of my readiness to co-operate. The field, as such, is of no interest to me, I can assure you. I would willingly stand down.'

There was a threat, almost a lack of politeness in his tone. Colonel Hodge scented danger.

'Wouldn't it be best,' he said, 'to find out first if this fellow is willing to re-sell? Then you can decide which of you keep it.'

'I am sure we shall be very interested to hear the results of Mr Metcalfe's negotiations,' said Lady Peabury.

She should not have said that. She would gladly have recalled the words the moment after they were uttered. She had vaguely wanted to say something disagreeable, to punish Mr Metcalfe for the discomfort in which she found herself. She had not meant to antagonise him, and this she had unmistakably done.

Mr Metcalfe left the House abruptly, almost precipitately, and all that evening he chafed. For fifteen years Mr Metcalfe had been president of the British Chamber of Commerce. He had been greatly respected by the whole business community. No one could put anything across him, and he would not touch anything that was not above-board. Egyptian and Levantine merchants who tried to interest Metcalfe in shady business went away with a flea in the ear. It was no good trying to squeeze Metcalfe. That was his reputation in the Union Club, and here, at home, in his own village, an old woman had tried to catch him napping. There was a sudden change. He was no longer the public-spirited countryman; he was cards-on-the-table-brass-tacks-and-twenty-shillings-in-the-pound-treat-him-fair-or-mind-your-step Metcalfe, Metcalfe with his back up, fighting Metcalfe once again, Metcalfe who would cut off his nose any day to spite his face, sink any ship for a ha'p'orth of tar that was not legally due, Metcalfe the lion of the Rotarians.

'She should not have said that,' said Colonel Hodge, reporting the incident to his wife over their horrible dinner. 'Metcalfe won't do anything now.'

'Why don't *you* go and talk to the man who's bought the field?' said Mrs Hodge.

'I might . . . I think I will . . . Tell you what, I'll go now.'

He went.

He found the man without difficulty, since there was no other visitor staying at the Brakehurst Arms. An enquiry from the landlord elicited his name – Mr Hargood-Hood. He was sitting alone in the parlour, sipping whisky and soda and working at *The Times*' crossword.

The Colonel said, 'Evening. My name is Hodge.'

'Yes?'

'I daresay you know who I am.'

'I'm very sorry, I'm afraid . . .'

'I own the Manor. My garden backs on to Westmacott's field – the one you've bought.'

'Oh,' said Mr Hargood-Hood, 'was he called Westmacott? I didn't know. I leave all these things to my lawyer. I simply told him to find me a suitable, secluded site for my work. He told me last week he had found one here. It seems very suitable. But he didn't tell me anyone's name.'

'You didn't pick this village for any particular reason?'

'No, no. But I think it perfectly charming,' he added politely.

There was a pause.

'I wanted to talk to you,' said Colonel Hodge superfluously. 'Have a drink.'

'Thank you.'

Another pause.

'I'm afraid you won't find it a very healthy site,' said the Colonel. 'Down in the hollow there.'

'I never mind things like that. All I need is seclusion.'

'Ah, a writer no doubt.'

'No.'

'A painter?'

'No, no. I suppose you would call me a scientist.'

'I see. And you would be using your house for weekends?'

'No, no, quite the reverse. I and my staff will be working here all the week. And it's not exactly a house I'm building, although of course there will be living quarters attached. Perhaps, since we are going to be such close neighbours, you would like to see the plans . . .'

'. . . You never saw such a thing,' said Colonel Hodge next morning to Mr Metcalfe. 'An experimental industrial laboratory he called it. Two great chimneys – have to have those, he said, by law, because of poison fumes, a water tower to get high pressures, six bungalows for his staff . . . ghastly. The odd thing was he seemed quite a decent sort of fellow. Said it hadn't occurred to him anyone would find it objectionable. Thought we should all be interested. When I brought up the subject of re-selling – tactful, you know – he just said he left all that to his lawyer . . .'

III

Much Malcock Hall.

Dear Lady Peabury,

In pursuance of our conversation of three days ago, I beg to inform you that I have been in communication with Mr Hargood-Hood, the purchaser of the field which separates our two properties, and his legal representative. As Col. Hodge has already informed you, Mr Hargood-Hood proposes to erect an experimental industrial laboratory fatal to the amenities of the village. As you are doubtless aware, work has not yet been commenced, and Mr Hargood-Hood is willing to re-sell the property if duly compensated. The price proposed is to include re-purchase of the field, legal fees and compensation for the architect's work. The young blackguard has us in a cleft stick. He wants £500. It is excessive, but I am prepared to pay half of this if you will pay the other half. Should you not accede to this generous offer I shall take steps to safeguard my own interests at whatever cost to the neighbourhood.

Yours sincerely,
Beverley Metcalfe.

P.S. – I mean I shall sell the Hall and develop the property as building lots.

Much Malcock House.

Lady Peabury begs to inform Mr Metcalfe that she has received his note of this morning, the tone of which I am unable to account for. She further begs to inform you that she has no wish to increase my already extensive responsibilities in the district. She cannot accept the principle of equal obligation with Mr Metcalfe as he has far less land to look after, and the field in question should rightly form part of your property. She does not think that the scheme for developing his garden as a housing estate is likely to be a success if Mr Hargood-Hood's laboratory is as unsightly as is represented, which I rather doubt.

'All right,' said Mr Metcalfe. 'That's that and be damned to her.'

IV

It was ten days later. The lovely valley, so soon to be defiled, lay resplendent in the sunset. Another year, thought Mr Metcalfe, and this fresh green foliage would be choked with soot, withered with fumes; these mellow roofs and chimneys which for two hundred years or more had enriched the landscape below the terrace, would be hidden by functional monstrosities in steel and glass and concrete. In the doomed field Mr Westmacott, almost for the last time, was calling his cattle; next week building was to begin and they must seek other pastures. So, in a manner of speaking, must Mr Metcalfe. Already his desk was littered with house-agents' notices. All for £500, he told himself. There would be redecorations; the cost and loss of moving. The speculative builders to whom he had viciously appealed showed no interest in the site. He was going to lose much more than £500 on the move. But so, he grimly assured himself, was

Lady Peabury. She would learn that no one could put a fast one over on Beverley Metcalfe.

And she, on the opposing slope, surveyed the scene with corresponding melancholy. The great shadows of the cedars lay across the lawn; they had scarcely altered during her long tenancy, but the box hedge had been of her planting; it was she who had planned the lily pond and glorified it with lead flamingoes; she had reared the irregular heap of stones under the west wall and stocked it with Alpines; the flowering shrubs were hers; she could not take them with her where she was going. Where? She was too old now to begin another garden, to make other friends. She would move, like so many of her contemporaries, from hotel to hotel, at home and abroad, cruise a little, settle for prolonged rather unwelcome visits, on her relatives. All this for £250, for £12 10s. a year, for less than she gave to charity. It was not the money; it was Principle. She would not compromise with Wrong; with that ill-bred fellow on the hill opposite.

Despite the splendour of the evening an unhappy spirit obsessed Much Malcock. The Hornbeams moped and drooped; Colonel Hodge fretted. He paced the threadbare carpet of his smoking-room. 'It's enough to make a fellow turn Bolshie, like that parson,' he said. 'What does Metcalfe care? He's rich. He can move anywhere. What does Lady Peabury care? It's the small man, trying to make ends meet, who suffers.'

Even Mr Hargood-Hood seemed affected by the general gloom. His lawyer was visiting him at the Brakehurst. All day they had been in intermittent, rather anxious consultation. 'I think I might go and talk to that Colonel again,' he said, and set off up the village street, under the deepening shadows, for the Manor House. And from this dramatic, last-minute move for conciliation sprang the great Hodge Plan for appeasement and peace-in-our-time.

V

'. . . the Scouts are badly in need of a new hut,' said Colonel Hodge.

'No use coming to me,' said Mr Metcalfe. 'I'm leaving the neighbourhood.'

'I was thinking,' said Colonel Hodge, 'that Westmacott's field would be just the place for it . . .'

And so it was arranged. Mr Hornbeam gave a pound, Colonel Hodge a guinea, Lady Peabury £250. A jumble sale, a white-elephant-tea, a raffle, a pageant, and a house-to-house collection, produced a further 30s. Mr Metcalfe found the rest. It cost him, all told, a little over £500. He gave with a good heart. There was no question now of jockeying him into a raw deal. In the rôle of public benefactor he gave with positive relish, and when Lady Peabury suggested that the field should be reserved for a camping site and the building of the hut postponed, it was Mr Metcalfe who pressed on with the building and secured the old stone tiles from the roof of a dismantled barn. In the circumstances, Lady Peabury could not protest when the building was named the Metcalfe-Peabury Hall. Mr Metcalfe found the title invigorating and was soon in negotiation with the brewery for a change of name at the Brakehurst Arms. It is true that Boggett still speaks of it as 'the Brakehurst', but the new name is plainly lettered for all to read: The Metcalfe Arms.

*

And so Mr Hargood-Hood passed out of the history of Much Malcock. He and his lawyer drove away to their home beyond the hills. The lawyer was Mr Hargood-Hood's brother.

'We cut that pretty fine, Jock. I thought, for once, we were going to be left with the baby.'

They drove to Mr Hargood-Hood's home, a double quadrangle of mellow brick that was famous far beyond the county.

On the days when the gardens were open to the public, record crowds came to admire the topiary work, yews and boxes of prodigious size and fantastic shape which gave perpetual employment to three gardeners. Mr Hargood-Hood's ancestors had built the house and planted the gardens in a happier time, before the days of property tax and imported grain. A sterner age demanded more strenuous efforts for their preservation.

'Well, that has settled Schedule A for another year and left something over for cleaning the fish-ponds. But it was an anxious month. I shouldn't care to go through it again. We must be more careful next time, Jock. How about moving east?'

Together the two brothers unfolded the inch ordnance map of Norfolk, spread it on the table of the Great Hall and began their preliminary, expert search for a likely, unspoilt, well-loved village.

17

The Phoenix

(1940)

Sylvia Townsend Warner

Lord Strawberry, a nobleman, collected birds. He had the finest aviary in Europe, so large that eagles did not find it uncomfortable, so well laid out that both humming-birds and snow-buntings had a climate that suited them perfectly. But for many years the finest set of apartments remained empty, with just a label saying: 'PHOENIX. *Habitat: Arabia.*'

Many authorities on bird life had assured Lord Strawberry that the phoenix is a fabulous bird, or that the breed was long extinct. Lord Strawberry was unconvinced: his family had always believed in phoenixes. At intervals he received from his agents (together with statements of their expenses) birds which they declared were the phoenix but which turned out to be orioles, macaws, turkey buzzards dyed orange, etc., or stuffed cross-breeds, ingeniously assembled from various plumages. Finally Lord Strawberry went himself to Arabia, where, after some months, he found a phoenix, won its confidence, caught it, and brought it home in perfect condition.

It was a remarkably fine phoenix, with a charming character – affable to the other birds in the aviary and much attached to Lord Strawberry. On its arrival in England it made a great stir among ornithologists, journalists, poets, and milliners, and was constantly visited. But it was not puffed up by these attentions, and when it was no longer in the news, and the visits fell off, it showed no pique or rancour. It ate well, and seemed perfectly contented.

It costs a great deal of money to keep up an aviary. When Lord Strawberry died he died penniless. The aviary came on the market. In normal times the rarer birds, and certainly the phoenix, would have been bid for by the trustees of Europe's great zoological societies, or by private persons in the USA; but as it happened Lord Strawberry died just after a world war, when both money and bird-seed were hard to come by (indeed the cost of bird-seed was one of the things which had ruined Lord Strawberry). The London *Times* urged in a leader that the phoenix be bought for the Zoo, saying that a nation of birdlovers had a moral right to own such a rarity; and a fund called the Strawberry Phoenix Fund, was opened. Students, naturalists, and schoolchildren contributed according to their means: but their means were small, and there were no large donations. So Lord Strawberry's executors (who had the death duties to consider) closed with the higher offer of Mr Tancred Poldero, owner and proprietor of Poldero's Wizard Wonderworld.

For quite a while Mr Poldero considered his phoenix a bargain. It was a civil and obliging bird, and adapted itself readily to its new surroundings. It did not cost much to feed, it did not mind children; and though it had no tricks, Mr Poldero supposed it would soon pick up some. The publicity of the Strawberry Phoenix Fund was now most helpful. Almost every contributor now saved up another half-crown in order to see the phoenix. Others, who had not contributed to the fund, even paid double to look at it on the five-shilling days.

But then business slackened. The phoenix was as handsome as ever, and as amiable; but, as Mr Poldero said, it hadn't got Allure. Even at popular prices the phoenix was not really popular. It was too quiet, too classical. So people went instead to watch the antics of the baboons, or to admire the crocodile who had eaten the woman.

One day Mr Poldero said to his manager, Mr Ramkin:

'How long since any fool paid to look at the phoenix?'

'Matter of three weeks,' replied Mr Ramkin.

'Eating his head off,' said Mr Poldero. 'Let alone the insurance. Seven shillings a week it costs me to insure that bird, and I might as well insure the Archbishop of Canterbury.'

'The public don't like him. He's too quiet for them, that's the trouble. Won't mate nor nothing. And I've tried him with no end of pretty pollies, ospreys, and Cochin-Chinas, and the Lord knows what. But he won't look at them.'

'Wonder if we could swap him for a livelier one,' said Mr Poldero.

'Impossible. There's only one of him at a time.'

'Go on!'

'I mean it. Haven't you ever read what it says on the label?'

They went to the phoenix' cage. It flapped its wings politely, but they paid no attention. They read:

'PANSY. *Phoenix phoenixissima formosissima arabiana.* This rare and fabulous bird is UNIQUE. The World's Old Bachelor. Has no mate and doesn't want one. When old, sets fire to itself and emerges miraculously reborn. Specially imported from the East.'

'I've got an idea.' said Mr Poldero. 'How old do you suppose that bird is?'

'Looks in its prime to me,' said Mr Ramkin.

'Suppose,' continued Mr Poldero, 'we could somehow get him alight? We'd advertise it beforehand, of course, work up interest. Then we'd have a new bird, and a bird with some romance about it, a bird with a life-story. We could sell a bird like that.'

Mr Ramkin nodded.

'I've read about it in a book,' he said. 'You've got to give them scented woods and whatnot, and they build a nest and sit down on it and catch fire spontaneous. But they won't do it till they're old. That's the snag.'

'Leave that to me,' said Mr Poldero. 'You get those scented woods, and I'll do the ageing.'

It was not easy to age the phoenix. Its allowance of food was halved, and halved again, but though it grew thinner its eyes were undimmed and its plumage glossy as ever. The heating was turned off; but it puffed out its feathers against the cold, and seemed none the worse. Other birds were put into its cage, birds of a peevish and quarrelsome nature. They pecked and chivvied it; but the phoenix was so civil and amiable that after a day or two they lost their animosity. Then Mr Poldero tried alley cats. These could not be won by good manners, but the phoenix darted above their heads and flapped its golden wings in their faces, and daunted them.

Mr Poldero turned to a book on Arabia, and read that the climate was dry. 'Aha!' said he. The phoenix was moved to a small cage that had a sprinkler in the ceiling. Every night the sprinkler was turned on. The phoenix began to cough. Mr Poldero had another good idea. Daily he stationed himself in front of the cage to jeer at the bird and abuse it.

When spring was come, Mr Poldero felt justified in beginning a publicity campaign about the ageing phoenix. The old public favourite, he said, was nearing its end. Meanwhile he tested the bird's reactions every few days by putting a little dirty straw into the cage, to see if it were interested in nesting yet. One day the phoenix began turning over the straw. Mr Poldero signed a contract for the film rights. At last the hour seemed ripe. It was a fine Saturday evening in May. For some weeks the public interest in the ageing phoenix had been working up, and the admission charge had risen to five shillings. The enclosure was thronged. The lights and the cameras were trained on the cage, and a loud-speaker proclaimed to the audience the rarity of what was about to take place.

'The phoenix,' said the loud-speaker, 'is the aristocrat of bird-life. Only the rarest and most expensive specimens of oriental woods, drenched in exotic perfumes, will tempt him to construct his strange love-nest.'

Now a neat assortment of twigs and shavings, strongly scented, was shoved into the cage.

'The phoenix,' the loud-speaker continued, 'is as capricious as Cleopatra, as luxurious as the du Barry, as heady as a strain of wild gypsy music. All the fantastic pomp and passion of the ancient East, its languorous magic, its subtle cruelties—'

'Lawks!' cried a woman in the crowd. 'He's at it!'

A quiver stirred the dulled plumage. The phoenix turned its head from side to side. It descended, staggering, from its perch. Then wearily it began to pull about the twigs and shavings.

The cameras clicked, the lights blazed full on the cage. Rushing to the loudspeaker Mr Poldero exclaimed:

'Ladies and gentlemen, this is the thrilling moment the world has breathlessly awaited. The legend of centuries is materialising before our modern eyes. The phoenix . . .'

The phoenix settled on its pyre and appeared to fall asleep.

The film director said:

'Well, if it doesn't evaluate more than this, mark it instructional.'

At that moment the phoenix and the pyre burst into flames. The flames streamed upwards, leaped out on every side. In a minute or two everything was burned to ashes, and some thousand people, including Mr Poldero, perished in the blaze.

18

There Will Come Soft Rains

(1950)

Ray Bradbury

In the living room the voice-clock sang, *Tick-tock, seven o'clock, time to get up, time to get up, seven o'clock!* as if it were afraid that nobody would. The morning house lay empty. The clock ticked on, repeating and repeating its sounds into the emptiness. *Seven-nine, breakfast time, seven-nine!*

In the kitchen the breakfast stove gave a hissing sigh and ejected from its warm interior eight pieces of perfectly browned toast, eight eggs sunnyside up, sixteen slices of bacon, two coffees, and two cool glasses of milk.

'Today is August 4, 2026,' said a second voice from the kitchen ceiling, 'in the city of Allendale, California.' It repeated the date three times for memory's sake. 'Today is Mr Featherstone's birthday. Today is the anniversary of Tilita's marriage. Insurance is payable, as are the water, gas, and light bills.'

Somewhere in the walls, relays clicked, memory tapes glided under electric eyes.

Eight-one, tick-tock, eight-one o'clock, off to school, off to work, run, run, eight-one! But no doors slammed, no carpets took the soft tread of rubber heels. It was raining outside. The weather box on the front door sang quietly: 'Rain, rain, go away; rubbers, raincoats for today . . .' And the rain tapped on the empty house, echoing.

Outside, the garage chimed and lifted its door to reveal the waiting car. After a long wait the door swung down again.

At eight-thirty the eggs were shriveled and the toast was like stone. An aluminum wedge scraped them into the sink, where hot water whirled them down a metal throat which digested and flushed them away to the distant sea. The dirty dishes were dropped into a hot washer and emerged twinkling dry.

Nine-fifteen, sang the clock, *time to clean.*

Out of warrens in the wall, tiny robot mice darted. The rooms were acrawl with the small cleaning animals, all rubber and metal. They thudded against chairs, whirling their mustached runners, kneading the rug nap, sucking gently at hidden dust. Then, like mysterious invaders, they popped into their burrows. Their pink electric eyes faded. The house was clean.

Ten o'clock. The sun came out from behind the rain. The house stood alone in a city of rubble and ashes. This was the one house left standing. At night the ruined city gave off a radioactive glow which could be seen for miles.

Ten-fifteen. The garden sprinklers whirled up in golden founts, filling the soft morning air with scatterings of brightness. The water pelted windowpanes running down the charred west side where the house had been burned evenly free of its white paint. The entire west face of the house was black, save for five places. Here the silhouette in paint of a man mowing a lawn. Here, as in a photograph, a woman bent to pick flowers. Still farther over, their images burned on wood in one titanic instant, a small boy, hands flung into the air; higher up, the image of a thrown ball, and opposite him a girl, hands raised to catch a ball which never came down.

The five spots of paint – the man, the woman, the children, the ball – remained. The rest was a thin charcoaled layer.

The gentle sprinkler rain filled the garden with falling light.

Until this day, how well the house had kept its peace. How carefully it had inquired, 'Who goes there? What's the password?' and, getting no answer from lonely foxes and whining cats, it had shut up its windows and drawn shades in an old-maidenly preoccupation with self-protection which bordered on a mechanical paranoia.

It quivered at each sound, the house did. If a sparrow brushed a window, the shade snapped up. The bird, startled, flew off! No, not even a bird must touch the house!

The house was an altar with ten thousand attendants, big, small, servicing, attending, in choirs. But the gods had gone away, and the ritual of the religion continued senselessly, uselessly.

Twelve noon.

A dog whined, shivering, on the front porch.

The front door recognised the dog voice and opened. The dog, once huge and fleshy, but now gone to bone and covered with sores, moved in and through the house, tracking mud. Behind it whirred angry mice, angry at having to pick up mud, angry at inconvenience.

For not a leaf fragment blew under the door but what the wall panels flipped open and the copper scrap rats flashed swiftly out. The offending dust, hair, or paper, seized in miniature steel jaws, was raced back to the burrows. There, down tubes which fed into the cellar, it was dropped into the sighing vent of an incinerator which sat like evil Baal in a dark corner.

The dog ran upstairs, hysterically yelping to each door, at last realising, as the house realised, that only silence was here.

If sniffed the air and scratched the kitchen door. Behind the door, the stove was making pancakes which filled the house with a rich baked odor and the scent of maple syrup.

The dog frothed at the mouth, lying at the door, sniffing, its eyes turned to fire. It ran wildly in circles, biting at its tail, spun in a frenzy, and died. It lay in the parlor for an hour.

Two o'clock, sang a voice.

Delicately sensing decay at last, the regiments of mice hummed out as softly as blown gray leaves in an electrical wind.

Two-fifteen.

The dog was gone.

In the cellar, the incinerator glowed suddenly and a whirl of sparks leaped up the chimney.

Two thirty-five.

Bridge tables sprouted from patio walls. Playing cards fluttered onto pads in a shower of pips. Martinis manifested on an oaken bench with egg-salad sandwiches. Music played.

But the tables were silent and the cards untouched.

At four o'clock the tables folded like great butterflies back through the paneled walls.

Four-thirty.

The nursery walls glowed.

Animals took shape: yellow giraffes, blue lions, pink antelopes, lilac panthers cavorting in crystal substance. The walls were glass. They looked out upon color and fantasy. Hidden films clocked through well-oiled sprockets, and the walls lived. The nursery floor was woven to resemble a crisp, cereal meadow. Over this ran aluminum roaches and iron crickets, and in the hot still air butterflies of delicate red tissue wavered among the sharp aroma of animal spoors! There was the sound like a great matted yellow hive of bees within a dark bellows, the lazy bumble of a purring lion. And there was the patter of okapi feet and the murmur of a fresh jungle rain, like other hoofs, falling upon the summer-starched grass. Now the walls dissolved into distances of parched weed, mile on mile, and warm endless sky. The animals drew away into thorn brakes and water holes.

It was the children's hour.

Five o'clock. The bath filled with clear hot water.

Six, seven, eight o'clock. The dinner dishes manipulated like magic tricks, and in the study a *click*. In the metal stand opposite the hearth where a fire now blazed up warmly, a cigar popped out, half an inch of soft gray ash on it, smoking, waiting.

Nine o'clock. The beds warmed their hidden circuits, for nights were cool here.

Nine-five. A voice spoke from the study ceiling:

'Mrs McClellan, which poem would you like this evening?'

The house was silent.

The voice said at last, 'Since you express no preference, I shall select a poem at random.' Quiet music rose to back the voice. 'Sara Teasdale. As I recall, your favorite . . .

'There will come soft rains and the smell of the ground,
And swallows circling with their shimmering sound;

And frogs in the pools singing at night,
And wild plum-trees in tremulous white;

Robins will wear their feathery fire
Whistling their whims on a low fence-wire;

And not one will know of the war, not one
Will care at last when it is done.

Not one would mind, either bird nor tree
If mankind perished utterly;

And Spring herself, when she woke at dawn,
Would scarcely know that we were gone.'

The fire burned on the stone hearth and the cigar fell away into a mound of quiet ash on its tray. The empty chairs faced each other between the silent walls, and the music played.

At ten o'clock the house began to die.

The wind blew. A falling tree bough crashed through the kitchen window. Cleaning solvent, bottled, shattered over the stove. The room was ablaze in an instant!

'Fire!' screamed a voice. The house lights flashed, water pumps shot water from the ceilings. But the solvent spread on the linoleum, licking, eating under the kitchen door, while the voices took it up in chorus: 'Fire, fire, fire!'

The house tried to save itself. Doors sprang tightly shut, but the windows were broken by the heat and the wind blew and sucked upon the fire.

The house gave ground as the fire in ten billion angry sparks moved with flaming ease from room to room and then up the stairs. While scurrying water rats squeaked from the walls, pistoled their water, and ran for more. And the wall sprays let down showers of mechanical rain.

But too late. Somewhere, sighing, a pump shrugged to a stop. The quenching rain ceased. The reserve water supply which had filled baths and washed dishes for many quiet days was gone.

The fire crackled up the stairs. It fed upon Picassos and Matisses in the upper halls, like delicacies, baking off the oily flesh, tenderly crisping the canvases into black shavings.

Now the fire lay in beds, stood in windows, changed the colors of drapes!

And then, reinforcements.

From attic trapdoors, blind robot faces peered down with faucet mouths gushing green chemical.

The fire backed off, as even an elephant must at the sight of a dead snake. Now there were twenty snakes whipping over the floor, killing the fire with a clear cold venom of green froth.

But the fire was clever. It had sent flame outside the house, up through the attic to the pumps there. An explosion! The attic brain which directed the pumps was shattered into bronze shrapnel on the beams

The fire rushed back into every closet and felt of the clothes hung there.

The house shuddered, oak bone on bone, its bared skeleton cringing from the heat, its wire, its nerves revealed as if a surgeon had torn the skin off to let the red veins and capillaries quiver in the scalded air. Help, help! Fire! Run, run! Heat snapped mirrors like the first brittle winter ice. And the voices wailed Fire, fire. run, run, like a tragic nursery rhyme, a dozen voices, high, low, like children dying in a forest, alone, alone. And the voices fading as the wires popped their sheathings like hot chestnuts. One, two, three, four, five voices died.

In the nursery the jungle burned. Blue lions roared, purple giraffes bounded off. The panthers ran in circles, changing color, and ten million animals, running before the fire, vanished off toward a distant steaming river . . .

Ten more voices died. In the last instant under the fire avalanche, other choruses, oblivious, could be heard announcing the time, playing music, cutting the lawn by remote-control mower, or setting an umbrella frantically out and in the slamming and opening front door, a thousand things happening, like a clock shop when each clock strikes the hour insanely before or after the other, a scene of maniac confusion, yet unity; singing, screaming, a few last cleaning mice darting bravely out to carry the horrid ashes away! And one voice, with sublime disregard for the situation, read poetry aloud in the fiery study, until all the film spools burned, until all the wires withered and the circuits cracked.

The fire burst the house and let it slam flat down, puffing out skirts of spark and smoke.

In the kitchen, an instant before the rain of fire and timber, the stove could be seen making breakfasts at a psychopathic rate, ten dozen eggs, six loaves of toast, twenty dozen bacon strips, which, eaten by fire, started the stove working again, hysterically hissing!

The crash. The attic smashing into kitchen and parlor. The parlor into cellar, cellar into sub-cellar. Deep freeze, armchair, film tapes, circuits, beds, and all like skeletons thrown in a cluttered mound deep under.

Smoke and silence. A great quantity of smoke.

Dawn showed faintly in the east. Among the ruins, one wall stood alone. Within the wall, a last voice said, over and over again and again, even as the sun rose to shine upon the heaped rubble and steam:

'Today is August 5, 2026, today is August 5, 2026, today is . . .'

19

The Prison

(1950)

Bernard Malamud

Though he tried not to think of it, at twenty-nine Tommy Castelli's life was a screaming bore. It wasn't just Rosa or the store they tended for profits counted in pennies, or the unendurably slow hours and endless drivel that went with selling candy, cigarettes, and soda water; it was this sick-in-the-stomach feeling of being trapped in old mistakes, even some he had made before Rosa changed Tony into Tommy. He had been as Tony a kid of many dreams and schemes, especially getting out of this tenement-crowded, kid-squawking neighborhood, with its lousy poverty, but everything had fouled up against him before he could. When he was sixteen he quit the vocational school where they were making him into a shoemaker, and began to hang out with the gray-hatted, thick-soled-shoe boys, who had the spare time and the mazuma and showed it in fat wonderful rolls down in the cellar clubs to all who would look, and everybody did, popeyed. They were the ones who had bought the silver caffe espresso urn and later the television, and they arranged the pizza parties and had the girls down; but it was getting in with them and their cars, leading to the holdup of a liquor store, that had started all the present trouble. Lucky for him the coal-and-ice man who was their landlord knew the leader in the district, and they arranged something so nobody bothered him after that. Then before he knew what was going on – he had been frightened sick by the whole mess – there was his father cooking up a deal with Rosa Agnello's old man that Tony would marry her and the father-in-law would, out of his savings, open a candy store for him to make an honest living. He wouldn't spit on a candy store, and Rosa was too plain and lank a chick for his personal taste, so he beat it off to Texas and bummed around in too much space, and when he came back everybody said it was for Rosa and the candy store, and it was all arranged again and he, without saying no, was in it.

That was how he had landed on Prince Street in the Village, working from eight in the morning to almost midnight every day, except for an hour off each afternoon when he went upstairs to sleep, and on Tuesdays, when the store was closed and he slept some more and went at night alone to the movies. He was too tired always for schemes now, but once he tried to make a little cash on the side by secretly taking in punchboards some syndicate was distributing in the neighborhood, on which he collected a nice cut and in this way saved fifty-five bucks that Rosa didn't know about; but then the syndicate was written up by a newspaper, and the punchboards all disappeared. Another time, when Rosa was at her mother's house, he took a chance and let them put in a slot machine that could guarantee a nice piece of change if he kept it long enough. He knew of course he couldn't hide it from her, so when she came and screamed when she saw it, he was ready and patient, for once not yelling back when she yelled, and he explained it was not the same as gambling because anybody who played it got a roll of mints every time he put in a nickel. Also the machine would supply them a few extra dollars cash they could use to buy television so he could see the fights without going to a bar; but Rosa wouldn't let up screaming, and later her father came in shouting that he was a criminal and chopped the machine apart with a plumber's hammer. The next day the cops raided for slot machines and gave out summonses wherever they found them, and though Tommy's place was practically the only candy store in the neighborhood that didn't have one, he felt bad about the machine for a long time.

Mornings had been his best time of day because Rosa stayed upstairs cleaning, and since few people came into the store till noon, he could sit around alone, a toothpick in his teeth, looking over the *News and Mirror* on the fountain counter, or maybe gab with one of the old cellar-club guys who had happened to come by for a pack of butts, about a horse that was running that day or how the numbers were paying lately; or just sit there, drinking coffee and thinking how far away he could get on the fifty-five he had stashed away in the cellar. Generally the mornings were this way, but after the slot machine, usually the whole day stank and he along with it. Time rotted in him, and all he could think of the whole morning, was going to sleep in the afternoon, and he would wake up with the sour remembrance of the long night in the store ahead of him, while everybody else was doing as he damn pleased. He cursed the candy store and Rosa, and cursed, from its beginning, his unhappy life.

It was on one of these bad mornings that a ten-year-old girl from around the block came in and asked for two rolls of colored tissue paper, one red and one yellow. He wanted to tell her to go to hell and stop bothering, but instead went with bad grace to the rear, where Rosa, whose bright idea it was to keep the stuff, had put it. He went from force of habit, for the girl had been coming in every Monday since the summer for the same thing, because her rock-faced mother, who looked as if she arranged her own widowhood, took care of some small kids after school and gave them the paper to cut out dolls and such things. The girl, whose name he didn't know, resembled her mother, except her features were not quite so sharp and she had very light skin with dark eyes; but she was a plain kid and would be more so at twenty. He had noticed, when he went to get the paper, that she always hung back as if afraid to go where it was dark, though he kept the comics there and most of the other kids had to be slapped away from them; and that when he brought her the tissue paper her skin seemed to grow whiter and her eyes shone. She always handed him two hot dimes and went out without glancing back.

It happened that Rosa, who trusted nobody, had just hung a mirror on the back wall, and as Tommy opened the drawer to get the girl her paper this Monday morning that he felt so bad, he looked up and saw in the glass something that made it seem as if he were dreaming. The girl had disappeared, but he saw a white hand reach into the candy case for a chocolate bar and for another, then she came forth from behind the counter and stood there, innocently waiting for him. He felt at first like grabbing her by the neck and socking till she threw up, but he had been caught, as he sometimes was, by this thought of how his Uncle Dom, years ago before he went away, used to take with him Tony alone of all the kids, when he went crabbing to Sheepshead Bay. Once they went at night and threw the baited wire traps into the water and after a while pulled them up and they had this green lobster in one, and just then this fat-faced cop came along and said they had to throw it back unless it was nine inches. Dom said it was nine inches, but the cop said not to be a wise guy so Dom measured it and it was ten, and they laughed about that lobster all night. Then he remembered how he had felt after Dom was gone, and tears filled his eyes. He found himself thinking about the way his life had turned out, and then about this girl, moved that she was so young and a thief. He felt he ought to do something for her, warn her to cut it out before she got trapped and fouled up her life before it got started. His urge to do this was strong, but when he went forward she looked up frightened because he had taken so long. The fear in her eyes bothered him and he didn't say anything. She thrust out the dimes, grabbed at the tissue rolls and ran out of the store.

He had to sit down. He kept trying to make the desire to speak to her go away, but it came back stronger than ever. He asked himself what difference does it make if she swipes candy – so she swipes it; and the role of reformer was strange and distasteful to him, yet he could not convince himself that what he felt he must do was unimportant. But he worried he would not know what to say to her. Always he had trouble speaking right, stumbled over words, especially in new situations. He was afraid he would sound like a jerk and she would not take him seriously. He had to tell her in a sure way so that even if it scared her, she would understand he had done it to set her straight. He mentioned her to no one but often thought about her, always looking around whenever he went outside to raise the awning or wash the window, to see if any of the girls playing in the street was her, but they never were. The following Monday, an hour after opening the store he had smoked a full pack of butts. He thought he had found what he wanted to say but was afraid for some reason she wouldn't come in, or if she did, this time she would be afraid to take the candy. He wasn't sure he wanted that to happen until he had said what he had to say. But at about eleven, while he was reading the *News*, she appeared, asking for the tissue paper, her eyes shining so he had to look away. He knew she meant to steal. Going to the rear he slowly opened the drawer, keeping his head lowered as he sneaked a look into the glass and saw her slide behind the counter. His heart beat hard and his feet felt nailed to the floor. He tried to remember what he had intended to do, but his mind was like a dark, empty room so he let her, in the end, slip away and stood tongue-tied, the dimes burning his palm.

Afterwards, he told himself that he hadn't spoken to her because it was while she still had the candy on her, and she would have been scared worse than he wanted. When he went upstairs, instead of sleeping, he sat at the kitchen window, looking out into the back yard. He blamed himself for being too soft, too chicken, but then he thought, no there was a better way to do it. He would do it indirectly, slip her a hint he knew, and he was pretty sure that would stop her. Sometime after, he would explain her why it was good she had stopped. So next time he cleaned out this candy platter she helped herself from, thinking she might get wise he was on to her, but she seemed not to, only hesitated with her hand before she took two candy bars from the next plate and dropped them into the black patent leather purse she always had with her. The time after that he cleaned out the whole top shelf, and still she was not suspicious, and reached down to the next and took something different. One Monday he put some loose change, nickels and dimes, on the candy plate, but she left them there, only taking the candy, which bothered him a little. Rosa asked him what he was mooning about so much and why was he eating chocolate lately. He didn't answer her, and she began to look suspiciously at the women who came in, not excluding the little girls; and he would have been glad to rap her in the teeth, but it didn't matter as long as she didn't know what he had on his mind. At the same time he figured he would have to do something sure soon, or it would get harder for the girl to stop her stealing. He had to be strong about it. Then he thought of a plan that satisfied him. He would leave two bars on the plate and put in the wrapper of one a note she could read when she was alone. He tried out on paper many messages to her, and the one that seemed best he cleanly printed on a strip of cardboard and slipped it under the wrapper of one chocolate bar. It said, 'Don't do this any more or you will suffer your whole life.' He puzzled whether to sign it A Friend or Your Friend and finally chose Your Friend.

This was Friday, and he could not hold his impatience for Monday. But on Monday she did not appear. He waited for a long time, until Rosa came down, then he had to go up and the girl still hadn't come. He was greatly disappointed because she had never failed to come before. He lay on the bed, his shoes on, staring at the ceiling. He felt hurt, the sucker she had played him for and was now finished with because she probably had another on her hook. The more he thought about it the worse he felt. He worked up a splitting headache that kept him from sleeping, then he suddenly slept and woke without it. But he had awaked depressed, saddened. He thought about Dom getting out of jail and going away God knows where. He wondered whether he would ever meet up with him somewhere, if he took the fifty-five bucks and left. Then he remembered Dom was a pretty old guy now, and he might not know him if they did meet. He thought about life. You never really got what you wanted. No matter how hard you tried you made mistakes and couldn't get past them. You could never see the sky outside or the ocean because you were in a prison, except nobody called it a prison, and if you did they didn't know what you were talking about, or they said they didn't. A pall settled on him. He lay motionless, without thought or sympathy for himself or anybody.

But when he finally went downstairs, ironically amused that Rosa had allowed him so long a time off without bitching, there were people in the store and he could hear her screeching. Shoving his way through the crowd he saw in one sickening look that she had caught the girl with the candy bars and was shaking her so hard the kid's head bounced back and forth like a balloon on a stick. With a curse he tore her away from the girl, whose sickly face showed the depth of her fright.

'Whatsamatter,' he shouted at Rosa, 'you want her blood?'

'She's a thief,' cried Rosa.

'Shut your face.'

To stop her yowling he slapped her across her mouth, but it was a harder crack than he had intended. Rosa fell back with a gasp. She did not cry but looked around dazedly at everybody, and tried to smile, and everybody there could see her teeth were flecked with blood.

'Go home,' Tommy ordered the girl, but then there was a movement near the door and her mother came into the store.

'What happened?' she said.

'She stole my candy,' Rosa cried.

'I let her take it,' said Tommy.

Rosa stared at him as if she had been hit again, then with mouth distorted began to sob.

'One was for you, Mother,' said the girl.

Her mother socked her hard across the face. 'You little thief, this time you'll get your hands burned good.'

She pawed at the girl, grabbed her arm and yanked it. The girl, like a grotesque dancer, half ran, half fell forward, but at the door she managed to turn her white face and thrust out at him her red tongue.

20

The Destructors

(1954)

Graham Greene

I

It was on the eve of August Bank Holiday that the latest recruit became the leader of the Wormsley Common gang. No one was surprised except Mike, but Mike at the age of nine was surprised by everything. 'If you don't shut your mouth,' somebody once said to him, 'you'll get a frog down it.' After that Mike had kept his teeth tightly clamped except when the surprise was too great.

The new recruit had been with the gang since the beginning of the summer holidays, and there were possibilities about his brooding silence that all recognised. He never wasted a word even to tell his name until that was required of him by the rules. When he said 'Trevor' it was a statement of fact, not as it would have been with the others a statement of shame or defiance. Nor did anyone laugh except Mike, who finding himself without support and meeting the dark gaze of the new-comer opened his mouth and was quiet again. There was every reason why T., as he was afterwards referred to, should have been an object of mockery – there was his name (and they substituted the initial because otherwise they had no excuse not to laugh at it), the fact that his father, a former architect and present clerk, had 'come down in the world' and that his mother considered herself better than the neighbours. What but an odd quality of danger, of the unpredictable, established him in the gang without any ignoble ceremony of initiation?

The gang met every morning in an impromptu car-park, the site of the last bomb of the first blitz. The leader, who was known as Blackie, claimed to have heard it fall, and no one was precise enough in his dates to point out that he would have been one year old and fast asleep on the down platform of Wormsley Common Underground Station. On one side of the car-park leant the first occupied house, number 3, of the shattered Northwood Terrace – literally leant, for it had suffered from the blast of the bomb and the side walls were supported on wooden struts. A smaller bomb and some incendiaries had fallen beyond, so that the house stuck up like a jagged tooth and carried on the further wall relics of its neighbour, a dado, the remains of a fireplace. T., whose words were almost confined to voting 'Yes' or 'No' to the plan of operations proposed each day by Blackie, once startled the whole gang by saying broodingly, 'Wren built that house, father says.'

'Who's Wren?'

'The man who built St Paul's.'

'Who cares?' Blackie said. 'It's only Old Misery's.'

Old Misery – whose real name was Thomas – had once been a builder and decorator. He lived alone in the crippled house, doing for himself: once a week you could see him coming back across the common with bread and vegetables, and once as the boys played in the car-park he put his head over the smashed wall of his garden and looked at them.

'Been to the loo,' one of the boys said, for it was common knowledge that since the bombs fell something had gone wrong with the pipes of the house and Old Misery was too mean to spend money on the property. He could do the redecorating himself at cost price, but he had never learnt plumbing. The loo was a wooden shed at the bottom of the narrow garden with a star-shaped hole in the door: it had escaped the blast which had smashed the house next door and sucked out the window-frames of number 3.

The next time the gang became aware of Mr Thomas was more surprising. Blackie, Mike, and a thin yellow boy, who for some reason was called by his surname Summers, met him on the common coming back from the market. Mr Thomas stopped them. He said glumly, 'You belong to the lot that play in the car-park?'

Mike was about to answer when Blackie stopped him. As the leader he had responsibilities. 'Suppose we are?' he said ambiguously.

'I got some chocolates,' Mr Thomas said. 'Don't like 'em myself. Here you are. Not enough to go round, I don't suppose. There never is,' he added with sombre conviction. He handed over three packets of Smarties.

The gang were puzzled and perturbed by this action and tried to explain it away. 'Bet someone dropped them and he picked 'em up,' somebody suggested.

'Pinched 'em and then got in a bleeding funk,' another thought aloud.

'It's a bribe,' Summers said. 'He wants us to stop bouncing balls on his wall.'

'We'll show him we don't take bribes,' Blackie said, and they sacrificed the whole morning to the game of bouncing that only Mike was young enough to enjoy. There was no sign from Mr Thomas.

Next day T. astonished them all. He was late at the rendezvous, and the voting for that day's exploit took place without him. At Blackie's suggestion the gang was to disperse in pairs, take buses at random, and see how many free rides could be snatched from unwary conductors (the operation was to be carried out in pairs to avoid cheating). They were drawing lots for their companions when T. arrived.

'Where you been, T.?' Blackie asked. 'You can't vote now. You know the rules.'

'I've been *there*,' T. said. He looked at the ground, as though he had thoughts to hide.

'Where?'

'At Old Misery's.' Mike's mouth opened and then hurriedly closed again with a click. He had remembered the frog.

'At Old Misery's?' Blackie said. There was nothing in the rules against it, but he had a sensation that T. was treading on dangerous ground. He asked hopefully, 'Did you break in?'

'No. I rang the bell.'

'And what did you say?'

'I said I wanted to see his house.'

'What did he do?'

'He showed it me.'

'Pinch anything?'

'No.'

'What did you do it for then?'

The gang had gathered round: it was as though an impromptu court were about to form and to try some case of deviation. T. said, 'It's a beautiful house,' and still watching the ground, meeting no one's eyes, he licked his lips first one way, then the other.

'What do you mean, a beautiful house?' Blackie asked with scorn.

'It's got a staircase two hundred years old like a corkscrew. Nothing holds it up.'

'What do you mean, nothing holds it up. Does it float?'

'It's to do with opposite forces, Old Misery said.'

'What else?'

'There's panelling.'

'Like in the Blue Boar?'

'Two hundred years old.'

'Is Old Misery two hundred years old?'

Mike laughed suddenly and then was quiet again. The meeting was in a serious mood. For the first time since T. had strolled into the car-park on the first day of the holidays his position was in danger. It only needed a single use of his real name and the gang would be at his heels.

'What did you do it for?' Blackie asked. He was just, he had no jealousy, he was anxious to retain T. in the gang if he could. It was the word 'beautiful' that worried him – that belonged to a class world that you could still see parodied at the Wormsley Common Empire by a man wearing a top hat and a monocle, with a haw-haw accent. He was tempted to say, 'My dear Trevor, old chap,' and unleash his hell hounds. 'If you'd broken in,' he said sadly – that indeed would have been an exploit worthy of the gang.

'This was better,' T. said, 'I found out things.' He continued to stare at his feet, not meeting anybody's eye, as though he were absorbed in some dream he was unwilling – or ashamed – to share.

'What things?'

'Old Misery's going to be away all tomorrow and Bank Holiday.'

Blackie said with relief, 'You mean we could break in?'

'And pinch things?' somebody asked.

Blackie said, 'Nobody's going to pinch things. Breaking in – that's good enough, isn't it? We don't want any court stuff.'

'I don't want to pinch anything,' T. said. 'I've got a better idea.'

'What is it?'

T. raised eyes, as grey and disturbed as the drab August day. 'We'll pull it down,' he said. 'We'll destroy it.'

Blackie gave a single hoot of laughter and then, like Mike, fell quiet, daunted by the serious implacable gaze. 'What'd the police be doing all the time?' he said.

'They'd never know. We'd do it from inside. I've found a way in.' He said with a sort of intensity, 'We'd be like worms, don't you see, in an apple. When we came out again there'd be nothing there, no staircase, no panels, nothing but just walls, and then we'd make the walls fall down – somehow.'

'We'd go to jug,' Blackie said.

'Who's to prove? And anyway we wouldn't have pinched anything.' He added without the smallest flicker of glee, 'There wouldn't be anything to pinch after we'd finished.'

'I've never heard of going to prison for breaking things,' Summers said.

'There wouldn't be time,' Blackie said. 'I've seen housebreakers at work.'

'There are twelve of us,' T. said. 'We'd organise.'

'None of us know how—'

'I know,' T. said. He looked across at Blackie. 'Have you got a better plan?'

'Today,' Mike said tactlessly, 'we're pinching free rides—'

'Free rides,' T. said. 'You can stand down, Blackie, if you'd rather . . .'

'The gang's got to vote.'

'Put it up then.'

Blackie said uneasily, 'It's proposed that tomorrow, and Monday we destroy Old Misery's house.'

'Here, here,' said a fat boy called Joe.

'Who's in favour?'

T. said, 'It's carried.'

'How do we start?' Summers asked.

'He'll tell you,' Blackie said. It was the end of his leadership. He went away to the back of the car-park and began to kick a stone, dribbling it this way and that. There was only one old Morris in the park, for few cars were left there except lorries: without an attendant there was no safety. He took a flying kick at the car and scraped a little paint off the rear mudguard. Beyond, paying no more attention to him than to a stranger, the gang had gathered round T.; Blackie was dimly aware of the fickleness of favour. He thought of going home, of never returning, of letting them all discover the hollowness of T.'s leadership, but suppose after all what T. proposed was possible – nothing like it had ever been done before. The fame of the Wormsley Common car-park gang would surely reach around London. There would be headlines in the papers. Even the grown-up gangs who ran the betting at the all-in wrestling and the barrow-boys would hear with respect of how Old Misery's house had been destroyed. Driven by the pure, simple, and altruistic ambition of fame for the gang, Blackie came back to where T. stood in the shadow of Misery's wall.

T. was giving his orders with decision: it was as though this plan had been with him all his life, pondered through the seasons, now in his fifteenth year crystallised with the pain of puberty. 'You,' he said to Mike, 'bring some big nails, the biggest you can find, and a hammer. Anyone else who can better bring a hammer and a screwdriver. We'll need plenty of them. Chisels too. We can't have too many chisels. Can anybody bring a saw?'

'I can,' Mike said.

'Not a child's saw,' T. said. 'A real saw.'

Blackie realised he had raised his hand like any ordinary member of the gang.

'Right, you bring one, Blackie. But now there's a difficulty. We want a hacksaw.'

'What's a hacksaw?' someone asked.

'You can get 'em at Woolworth's,' Summers said.

The fat boy called Joe said gloomily, 'I knew it would end in a collection.'

'I'll get one myself,' T. said. 'I don't want your money. But I can't buy a sledge-hammer.'

Blackie said, 'They are working on number fifteen. I know where they'll leave their stuff for Bank Holiday.'

'Then that's all,' T. said. 'We meet here at nine sharp.'

'I've got to go to church,' Mike said.

'Come over the wall and whistle. We'll let you in.'

II

On Sunday morning all were punctual except Blackie, even Mike. Mike had had a stroke of luck. His mother felt ill, his father was tired after Saturday night, and he was told to go to church alone with many warnings of what would happen if he strayed. Blackie had had difficulty in smuggling out the saw, and then in finding the sledge-hammer at the back of number 15. He approached the house from a lane at the rear of the garden, for fear of the policeman's beat along the main road. The tired evergreens kept off a stormy sun: another wet Bank Holiday was being prepared over the Atlantic, beginning in swirls of dust under the trees. Blackie climbed the wall into Misery's garden.

There was no sign of anybody anywhere. The loo stood like a tomb in a neglected graveyard. The curtains were drawn. The house slept. Blackie lumbered nearer with the saw and the sledge-hammer. Perhaps after all nobody had turned up: the plan had been a wild invention: they had woken wiser. But when he came close to the back door he could hear a confusion of sound, hardly louder than a hive in swarm: a clickety-clack, a bang bang bang, a scraping, a creaking, a sudden painful crack. He thought, It's true, and whistled.

They opened the back door to him and he came in. He had at once the impression of organisation, very different from the old happy-go-lucky ways under his leadership. For a while he wandered up and down stairs looking for T. Nobody addressed him: he had a sense of great urgency, and already he could begin to see the plan. The interior of the house was being carefully demolished without touching the outer walls. Summers with hammer and chisel was ripping out the skirting-boards in the ground floor dining-room: he had already smashed the panels of the door. In the same room Joe was heaving up the parquet blocks, exposing the soft wood floor-boards over the cellar. Coils of wire came out of the damaged skirting and Mike sat happily on the floor, clipping the wires.

On the curved stairs two of the gang were working hard with an inadequate child's saw on the banisters – when they saw Blackie's big saw they signalled for it wordlessly. When he next saw them a quarter of the banisters had been dropped into the hall. He found T. at last in the bathroom – he sat moodily in the least cared-for room in the house, listening to the sounds coming up from below.

'You've really done it,' Blackie said with awe. 'What's going to happen?'

'We've only just begun,' T, said. He looked at the sledge-hammer and gave his instructions, 'You stay here and break the bath and the wash-basin. Don't bother about the pipes. They come later.'

Mike appeared at the door. 'I've finished the wire, T.,' he said.

'Good. You've just got to go wandering round now. The kitchen's in the basement. Smash all the china and glass and bottles you can lay hold of. Don't turn on the taps – we don't want a flood – yet. Then go into all the rooms and turn out drawers. If they are locked get one of the others to break them open. Tear up any papers you find and smash all the ornaments. Better take a carving-knife with you from the kitchen. The bedroom's opposite here. Open the pillows and tear up the sheets. That's enough for the moment. And you, Blackie, when you've finished in here crack the plaster in the passage up with your sledge-hammer.'

'What are you going to do?' Blackie asked.

'I'm looking for something special,' T. said.

It was nearly lunch-time before Blackie had finished and went in search of T. Chaos had advanced. The kitchen was a shambles of broken glass and china. The dining-room was stripped of parquet, the skirting was up, the door had been taken off its hinges, and the destroyers had moved up a floor. Streaks of light came in through the closed shutters where they worked with the seriousness of creators – and destruction after all is a form of creation. A kind of imagination had seen this house as it had now become.

Mike said, 'I've got to go home for dinner.'

'Who else?' T. asked, but all the others on one excuse or another had brought provisions with them.

They squatted in the ruins of the room and swapped unwanted sandwiches. Half an hour for lunch and they were at work again. By the time Mike returned, they were on the top floor, and by six the superficial damage was completed. The doors were all off, all the skirtings raised, the furniture pillaged and ripped and smashed – no one could have slept in the house except on a bed of broken plaster. T. gave his orders – eight o'clock next morning – and to escape notice they climbed singly over the garden wall, into the car-park, Only Blackie and T. were left; the light had nearly gone, and when they touched a switch, nothing worked – Mike had done his job thoroughly.

'Did you find anything special?' Blackie asked.

T. nodded. 'Come over here,' he said, 'and look.' Out of both pockets he drew bundles of pound notes. 'Old Misery's savings,' he said. 'Mike ripped out the mattress, but he missed them.'

'What are you going to do? Share them?'

'We aren't thieves,' T, said. 'Nobody's going to steal anything from this house. I kept these for you and me – a celebration.' He knelt down on the floor and counted them out – there were seventy in all. 'We'll burn them,' he said, 'one by one,' and taking it in turns they held a note upwards and lit the top corner, so that the flame burnt slowly towards their fingers. The grey ash floated above them and fell on their heads like age. 'I'd like to see Old Misery's face when we are through,' T. said.

'You hate him a lot?' Blackie asked.

'Of course I don't hate him,' T. said, 'There'd be no fun if I hated him.' The last burning note illuminated his brooding face. 'All this hate and love,' he said, 'it's soft, it's hooey. There's only things, Blackie,' and he looked round the room crowded with the unfamiliar shadows of half things, broken things, former things, 'I'll race you home, Blackie,' he said.

III

Next morning the serious destruction started. Two were missing – Mike and another boy, whose parents were off to Southend and Brighton in spite of the slow warm drops that had begun to fall and the rumble of thunder in the estuary like the first guns of the old blitz. 'We've got to hurry,' T. said.

Summers was restive. 'Haven't we done enough?' he said. 'I've been given a bob for slot machines. This is like work.'

'We've hardly started,' T. said. 'Why, there's all the floors left, and the stairs. We haven't taken out a single window. You voted like the others. We are going to *destroy* this house. There won't be anything left when we've finished.'

They began again on the first floor picking up the top floor-boards next the outer wall, leaving the joists exposed. Then they sawed through the joists and retreated into the hall, as what was left of the floor heeled and sank. They had learnt with practice, and the second floor collapsed more easily. By the evening an odd exhilaration seized them as they looked down the great hollow of the house. They ran risks and made mistakes: when they thought of the windows it was too late to reach them. 'Cor,' Joe said, and dropped a penny down into the dry rubble-filled well. It cracked and span among the broken glass.

'Why did we start this?' Summers asked with astonishment; T. was already on the ground, digging at the rubble, clearing a space along the outer wall. 'Turn on the taps,' he said. 'It's too dark for anyone to see now, and in the morning it won't matter.' The water overtook them on the stairs and fell through the floorless rooms.

It was then they heard Mike's whistle at the back. 'Something's wrong,' Blackie said. They could hear his urgent breathing as they unlocked the door.

'The bogies?' Summers asked.

'Old Misery,' Mike said. 'He's on his way.' He put his head between his knees and retched. 'Ran all the way,' he said with pride.

'But why?' T. said. 'He told me . . .' He protested with the jury of the child he had never been, 'It isn't fair.'

'He was down at Southend,' Mike said, 'and he was on the train coming back. Said it was too cold and wet.' He paused and gazed at the water. 'My, you've had a storm here. Is the roof leaking?'

'How long will he be?'

'Five minutes, I gave Ma the slip and ran.'

'We better clear,' Summers said. 'We've done enough, anyway.'

'Oh, no, we haven't. Anybody could do this—' 'This' was the shattered hollowed house with nothing left but the walls. Yet walls could be preserved. Façades were valuable. They could build inside again more beautifully than before. This could again be a home. He said angrily, 'We've got to finish. Don't move. Let me think.'

'There's no time,' a boy said.

'There's got to be a way,' T. said. 'We couldn't have got thus far . . .'

'We've done a lot,' Blackie said.

'No. No, we haven't. Somebody watch the front.'

'We can't do any more.'

'He may come in at the back.'

'Watch the back too.' T. began to plead. 'Just give me a minute and I'll fix it. I swear I'll fix it.' But his authority had gone with his ambiguity. He was only one of the gang. 'Please,' he said.

'Please,' Summers mimicked him, and then suddenly struck home with the fatal name. 'Run along home, Trevor.'

T. stood with his back to the rubble like a boxer knocked groggy against the ropes. He had no words as his dreams shook and slid. Then Blackie acted before the gang had time to laugh, pushing Summers backward. 'I'll watch the front, T.,' he said, and cautiously he opened the shutters of the hall. The grey wet common stretched ahead, and the lamps gleamed in the puddles. 'Someone's coming, T. No, it's not him. What's your plan, T.?'

'Tell Mike to go out to the loo and hide close beside it. When he hears me whistle he's got to count ten and start to shout.'

'Shout what?'

'Oh, "Help," anything.'

'You hear, Mike,' Blackie said. He was the leader again. He took a quick look between the shutters. 'He's coming, T.'

'Quick, Mike. The loo. Stay here, Blackie, all of you till I yell.'

'Where are you going, T.?'

'Don't worry. I'll see to this. I said I would, didn't I?'

Old Misery came limping off the common. He had mud on his shoes and he stopped to scrape them on the pavement's edge. He didn't want to soil his house, which stood jagged and dark between the bomb-sites, saved so narrowly, as he believed, from destruction. Even the fan-light had been left unbroken by the bomb's blast. Somewhere somebody whistled. Old Misery looked sharply round. He didn't trust whistles. A child was shouting: it seemed to come from his own garden. Then a boy ran into the road from the car-park. 'Mr Thomas,' he called, 'Mr Thomas.'

'What is it?'

'I'm terribly sorry, Mr Thomas, One of us got taken short, and we thought you wouldn't mind, and now he can't get out.'

'What do you mean, boy?'

'He's got stuck in your loo,'

'He'd no business – Haven't I seen you before?'

'You showed me your house.'

'So I did. So I did. That doesn't give you the right to—'

'Do hurry, Mr Thomas. He'll suffocate.'

'Nonsense. He can't suffocate. Wait till I put my bag in.'

'I'll carry your bag.'

'Oh, no, you don't. I carry my own.'

'This way, Mr Thomas.'

'I can't get in the garden that way. I've got to go through the house.'

'But you *can* get in the garden this way, Mr Thomas. We often do.'

'You often do?' He followed the boy with a scandalised fascination. 'When? What right . . .'

'Do you see . . . ? The wall's low.'

'I'm not going to climb walls into my own garden. It's absurd.'

'This is how we do it. One foot here, one foot there, and over.' The boy's face peered down, an arm shot out, and Mr Thomas found his bag taken and deposited on the other side of the wall.

'Give me back my bag,' Mr Thomas said. From the loo a boy yelled and yelled. 'I'll call the police.'

'Your bag's all right, Mr Thomas. Look. One foot there. On your right. Now just above. To your left.' Mr Thomas climbed over his own garden wall. 'Here's your bag, Mr Thomas.'

'I'll have the wall built up,' Mr Thomas said. 'I'll not have you boys coming over here, using my loo.' He stumbled on the path, but the boy caught his elbow and supported him. 'Thank you, thank you, my boy,' he murmured automatically. Somebody shouted again through the dark. 'I'm coming, I'm coming,' Mr Thomas called. He said to the boy beside him, 'I'm not unreasonable. Been a boy myself. As long as things are done regular. I don't mind you playing round the place Saturday mornings. Sometimes I like company. Only it's got to be regular. One of you asks leave and I say Yes. Sometimes I'll say No. Won't feel like it. And you come in at the front door and out at the back. No garden walls.'

'Do get him out, Mr Thomas.'

'He won't come to any harm in my loo,' Mr Thomas said, stumbling slowly down the garden. 'Oh, my rheumatics,' he said. 'Always get 'em on Bank Holiday. I've got to go careful. There's loose stones here. Give me your hand. Do you know what my horoscope said yesterday? "Abstain from any dealings in first half of week. Danger of serious crash." That might be on this path,' Mr Thomas said. 'They speak in parables and double meanings.' He paused at the door of the loo. 'What's the matter in there?' he called. There was no reply.

'Perhaps he's fainted,' the boy said.

'Not in my loo. Here, you, come out,' Mr Thomas said, and giving a great jerk at the door he nearly fell on his back when it swung easily open. A hand first supported him and then pushed him hard. His head hit the opposite wall and he sat heavily down. His bag hit his feet. A hand whipped the key out of the lock and the door slammed. 'Let me out,' he called, and heard the key turn in the lock. 'A serious crash,' he thought, and felt dithery and confused and old.

A voice spoke to him softly through the star-shaped hole in the door. 'Don't worry, Mr Thomas,' it said, 'we won't hurt you, not if you stay quiet.'

Mr Thomas put his head between his hands and pondered. He had noticed that there was only one lorry in the car-park, and he felt certain that the driver would not come for it before the morning. Nobody could hear him from the road in front, and the lane at the back was seldom used. Anyone who passed there would be hurrying home and would not pause for what they would certainly take to be drunken cries. And if he did call 'Help,' who, on a lonely Bank Holiday evening, would have the courage to investigate? Mr Thomas sat on the loo and pondered with the wisdom of age.

After a while it seemed to him that there were sounds in the silence – they were faint and came from the direction of his house. He stood up and peered through the ventilation-hole – between the cracks in one of the shutters he saw a light, not the light of a lamp, but the wavering light that a candle might give. Then he thought he heard the sound of hammering and scraping and chipping. He thought of burglars – perhaps they had employed the boy as a scout, but why should burglars engage in what sounded more and more like a stealthy form of carpentry? Mr Thomas let out an experimental yell, but nobody answered. The noise could not even have reached his enemies.

IV

Mike had gone home to bed, but the rest stayed. The question of leadership no longer concerned the gang. With nails, chisels, screwdrivers, anything that was sharp and penetrating they moved around the inner walls worrying at the mortar between the bricks. They started too high, and it was Blackie who hit on the damp course and realised the work could be halved if they weakened the joints immediately above. It was a long, tiring, unamusing job, but at last it was finished. The gutted house stood there balanced on a few inches of mortar between the damp course and the bricks.

There remained the most dangerous task of all, out in the open at the edge of the bomb-site. Summers was sent to watch the road for passers-by, and Mr Thomas, sitting on the loo, heard clearly now the sound of sawing. It no longer came from his house, and that a little reassured him. He felt less concerned. Perhaps the other noises too had no significance.

A voice spoke to him through the hole. 'Mr Thomas.'

'Let me out,' Mr Thomas said sternly.

'Here's a blanket,' the voice said, and a long grey sausage was worked through the hole and fell in swathes over Mr Thomas's head.

'There's nothing personal,' the voice said. 'We want you to be comfortable tonight.'

'Tonight,' Mr Thomas repeated incredulously.

'Catch,' the voice said. 'Penny buns – we've buttered them, and sausage-rolls. We don't want you to starve, Mr Thomas.'

Mr Thomas pleaded desperately. 'A joke's a joke, boy. Let me out and I won't say a thing. I've got rheumatics. I got to sleep comfortable.'

'You wouldn't be comfortable, not in your house, you wouldn't. Not now.'

'What do you mean, boy?' but the footsteps receded. There was only the silence of night: no sound of sawing. Mr Thomas tried one more yell, but he was daunted and rebuked by the silence – a long way off an owl hooted and made away again on its muffled flight through the soundless world.

At seven next morning the driver came to fetch his lorry. He climbed into the seat and tried to start the engine. He was vaguely aware of a voice shouting, but it didn't concern him. At last the engine responded and he backed the lorry until it touched the great wooden shore that supported Mr Thomas's house. That way he could drive right out and down the street without reversing. The lorry moved forward, was momentarily checked as though something were pulling it from behind, and then went on to the sound of a long rumbling crash. The driver was astonished to see bricks bouncing ahead of him, while stones hit the roof of his cab. He put on his brakes. When he climbed out the whole landscape had suddenly altered. There was no house beside the car-park, only a hill of rubble. He went round and examined the back of his car for damage, and found a rope tied there that was still twisted at the other end round part of a wooden strut.

The driver again became aware of somebody shouting. It came from the wooden erection which was the nearest thing to a house in that desolation of broken brick. The driver climbed the smashed wall and unlocked the door. Mr Thomas came out of the loo. He was wearing a grey blanket to which flakes of pastry adhered. He gave a sobbing cry. 'My house,' he said. 'Where's my house?'

'Search me,' the driver said. His eye lit on the remains of a bath and what had once been a dresser and he began to laugh. There wasn't anything left anywhere.

'How dare you laugh,' Mr Thomas said. 'It was my house. My house.'

'I'm sorry,' the driver said, making heroic efforts, but when he remembered the sudden check to his lorry, the crash of bricks falling, he became convulsed again. One moment the house had stood there with such dignity between the bomb-sites like a man in a top hat, and then, bang, crash, there wasn't anything left – not anything. He said, 'I'm sorry. I can't help it, Mr Thomas. There's nothing personal, but you got to admit it's funny.'

21

Meteor

(1956)

John Wyndham

The house shook, the windows rattled, a framed photograph slipped off the mantel-shelf and fell into the hearth. The sound of a crash somewhere outside arrived just in time to drown the noise of the breaking glass. Graham Toffts put his drink down carefully, and wiped the spilt sherry from his fingers.

'That sort of thing takes you back a bit,' he observed. 'First instalment of the new one, would you think?'

Sally shook her head, spinning the fair hair out a little so that it glistened in the shaded light.

'I shouldn't think so. Not like the old kind, anyway – they used to come with a sort of double-bang as a rule,' she said

She crossed to the window and pulled back the curtain. Outside there was complete darkness and a sprinkle of rain on the panes.

'Could have been an experimental one gone astray?' she suggested.

Footsteps sounded in the hall. The door opened, and her father's head looked in.

'Did you hear that?' he asked, unnecessarily. 'A small meteor, I fancy. I thought I saw a dim flash in the field beyond the orchard.' He withdrew. Sally made after him. Graham, following more leisurely, found her firmly grasping her father's arm.

'No!' she was saying, decisively. 'I'm not going to have my dinner kept waiting and spoiled. Whatever it is, it will keep.'

Mr Fontain looked at her, and then at Graham.

'Bossy; much too bossy. Always was. Can't think what you want to marry her for,' he said.

After dinner they went out to search with electric lamps. There was not much trouble in locating the scene of the impact. A small crater, some eight feet across, had appeared almost in the middle of the field. They regarded it without learning much, while Sally's terrier, Mitty, sniffed over the newly turned earth. Whatever had caused it had presumably buried itself in the middle.

'A small meteorite, without a doubt,' said Mr Fontain. 'We'll set a gang on digging it out tomorrow.'

Extract from Onns's Journal:

As an introduction to the notes which I intend to keep, I can scarcely do better than give the gist of the address given to us on the day preceding our departure from Forta* by His Excellency Cottafts. In contrast to our public farewell, this meeting was deliberately made as informal as a gathering of several thousands can be.

His Excellency emphasised almost in his opening words that though we had leaders for the purposes of administration, there was, otherwise, no least amongst us.

'There is not one of you men and women† who is not a volunteer,' looking slowly round his huge audience. 'Since you are individuals, the proportions of the emotions which led you to volunteer may differ quite widely, but, however personal, or however altruistic your impulses may have been, there is a common denominator for all – and that is the determination that our race shall survive.

'Tomorrow the Globes will go out.

'Tomorrow, God willing, the skill and science of Forta will break through the threats of Nature.

'Civilisation is, from its beginning, the ability to co-ordinate and direct natural forces – and once that direction has been started, it must be constantly maintained. There have been other dominant species on Forta before ours: they were not civilised, they did not direct nature: they dwindled and died as conditions changed. But we, so far, have been able to *meet* conditions as they have changed, and we flourish.

'We flourish, moreover, in such numbers as undirected Nature could never have sustained. In the past we have surmounted problem after problem to make this possible, but now we find ourselves faced with the gravest problem yet. Forta, our world, is becoming senile, but we are not. We are like spirits that are still young, trapped in a failing body . . .

'For centuries we have kept going, adapted, substituted, patched, but now the trap is closing faster, and there is little left to prop it open with. So it is now, while we are still healthy and strong, that we must escape and find ourselves a new home.

'I do not doubt that great-grandchildren of the present generation's great-grand-children will be born on Forta, but life will be harder for them: they will have to spend much more labour simply to keep alive. That is why the Globes must go now, while we have strength and wealth to spare.

'And for you who go in them – what? Even guesses are vain. The Globes will set out for the four corners of the heavens, and where they land they may find anything – or nothing. All our arts and skills will set you on your courses. But, once you have left, we can do no more than pray that you, our seed, will find fruitful soil.'

---

* Onns gives no clues to Forta's position, nor as to whether it is a planet, a moon, or an asteroid.

† The terms 'men' and 'women' are not used biologically, but in the sense of the dominant species referring to its own members.

He paused, lengthily. Then he went on:

'Your charge you know, or you would not have offered yourselves. Nevertheless, it is one which you will not be able to learn too well, nor teach too often. In the hands of each and every one of you lies a civilisation. Every man and woman of you is at once the receptacle and the potential fountain of all that Forta signifies. You have the history, the culture, the civilisation of a planet. Use it. Use it well. Give it to others where it will help. Be willing to learn from others, and improve it if you can. Do not try to preserve it intact; a culture must grow to live. For those who cling too fondly to the past there is likely to be no future. Remember that it is possible that there is no intelligence elsewhere in the universe, which means that some of you will hold a trust not only for our race, but for all conscious life that may evolve.

'Go forth, then. Go in wisdom, kindliness, peace, and truth.

'And our prayers will go out with you into the mysteries of space . . .'

. . . I have looked again through the telescope at our new home. Our group is, I think, lucky. It is a planet which is neither too young nor too old. Conditions were better than before, with less cloud over its surface. It shines like a blue pearl. Much of the part I saw was covered with water – more than two-thirds of it, they tell me, is under water. It will be good to be in a place where irrigation and water supply are not one of the main problems of life. Nevertheless, one hopes that we shall be fortunate enough to make our landing on dry ground or there may be very great difficulties . . .

I looked, too, at some of the places to which other Globes are bound, some small, some large, some new, with clouded surfaces that are a mystery. One at least is old, and in not much better case than our own poor Forta – though the astronomers say that it has the ability to support life for several millions of years. But I am glad that our group is going to the blue, shining world: it seems to beckon us, and I am filled with a hope which helps to quieten my fears of the journey.

Not that fears trouble me so much now; I have learnt some fatalism in the past year. I shall go into the Globe, and the anaesthetic gas will lull me to sleep without my being aware of it. When I wake again it will be on our shimmering new world . . . If I do not wake, something will have gone wrong, but I shall never know that . . .

Very simple, really – if one has faith . . .

This evening I went down to look at the Globes; to see them objectively for the last time. Tomorrow, in all the bustle and preparation there will be no time for reflection – and it will be better so.

What a staggering, amazing – one had almost said impossible – work they are! The building of them has entailed labour beyond computation. They look more likely to crush the ground and sink into Forta herself than to fly off into space. The most massive things ever built! I find it almost impossible to believe that we can have built thirty of these metal mountains, yet there they stand, ready for tomorrow . . .

And some of them will be lost . . .

Oh, God, if ours may survive, let us never forget. Let us show ourselves worthy of this supreme effort . . .

It can well be that these are the last words I shall ever write. If not, it will be in a new world and under a strange sky that I continue . . .

'You shouldn't have touched it,' said the Police Inspector, shaking his head. 'It ought to have been left where it was until the proper authorities had inspected it.'

'And who,' inquired Mr Fontain coldly, 'are the proper authorities for the inspection of meteors?'

'That's beside the point. You couldn't be sure it was a meteor, and these days a lot of other things besides meteors can fall out of the sky. Even now you've got it up you can't be sure.'

'It doesn't look like anything else.'

'All the same, it should have been left to us. It might be some device still on the Secret List.'

'The Police, of course, knowing all about things on the Secret List?'

Sally considered it time to break in.

'Well, we shall know what to do next time we have a meteor, shan't we? Suppose we all go and have a look at it? It's in the outhouse now, looking quite unsecret.'

She led the way round to the yard, still talking to stave off a row between the Inspector and her father.

'It only went a surprisingly short way down, so the men were soon able to get it out. And it turned out to be not nearly as hot as we'd expected, either, so they could handle it quite easily.'

'You'd not say "quite easily" if you'd heard the language they used about the weight of it,' observed her father.

'It's in here,' Sally said, leading the party of four into a musty, single-storey shed.

The meteor was not an impressive sight. It lay in the middle of the bare board floor; just a rugged, pitted, metallic-looking sphere something over two feet in diameter.

'The only kind of weapon that it suggests to me is a cannon-ball,' said Mr Fontain.

'It's the principle,' retorted the Inspector. 'We have standing orders that any mysterious falling object is to remain untouched until it has been examined by a War Office expert. We have already informed them, and it must not be moved again until their man has had a look at it.'

Graham who had hitherto taken no part, stepped forward and put his hand on it.

'Almost cold now,' he reported. 'What's it made of?' he added curiously.

Mr Fontain shrugged.

'I imagine it's just an ordinary chunk of meteoric iron. The only odd thing about it to me is that it didn't come down with more of a bump. If it were any kind of secret weapon, it would certainly be an exceedingly dull one.'

'All the same, I shall have to give orders that it is not to be moved until the W.O. man has seen it,' said the Inspector.

They started to move back into the yard, but on the threshold he paused.

'What's that sizzling sound?' he inquired.

'Sizzling?' repeated Sally.

'Kind of hissing noise. Listen!'

They stood still, the Inspector with his head a little on one side. Undeniably there was a faint, persistent sound on a note just within the range of audibility. It was difficult to place. By common impulse they turned back to regard the ball uneasily. Graham hesitated, and then stepped inside again. He leaned over the ball, his right ear turned down to it.

'Yes,' he said. 'It is.'

Then his eyes closed, and he swayed. Sally ran forward and caught him as he sagged. The others helped her to drag him out. In the fresh air he revived almost immediately.

'That's funny. What happened?' he asked.

'You're sure the sound is coming from that thing?' asked the Inspector.

'Oh, yes. Not a doubt about it.'

'You didn't smell anything queer?'

Graham raised his eyebrows: 'Oh, gas, you mean. No, I don't think so.'

'H'm,' said the Inspector. He turned a mildly triumphant eye on the older man. 'Is it usual for meteors to sizzle?' he inquired.

'Er – I really don't know. I shouldn't think so,' Mr Fontain admitted.

'I see. Well, in the circumstances I suggest that we all withdraw – preferably to a well-shielded spot on the other side of the house, just in case – while we wait for the expert,' announced the Inspector.

Extract from Onns's Journal:

I am bewildered. I have just woken. But has it happened – or have we failed to start? I cannot tell. Was it an hour, a day, a year, or a century ago that we entered the Globe? No, it cannot have been an hour ago; I am sure of that by the tiredness of my limbs, and the way my body aches. We were warned about that:

'You will know nothing,' they said, 'nothing until it is all over. Then you will feel physically weary because your bodies will have been subjected to great strains. That should pass quite soon, but we shall give you some capsules of concentrated food and stimulants to help you overcome the effects more quickly.'

I have taken one capsule, and I begin to feel the benefit of it already, but it is still hard to believe that it is over.

It seems such a short time ago that we climbed the long passage into the interior of the Globe and dispersed as we had been instructed. Each of us found his or her elastic compartment, and crawled into it. I released the valve to inflate the space between the inner and outer walls of my compartment. As the lining distended I felt myself lifted on a mattress of air. The top bulged down, the sides closed in, and so, insulated from shock in all directions, I waited.

Waited for what? I still cannot say. One moment, it seems, I lay there fresh and strong: the next, I was tired and aching.

Only that, to indicate that one life has ended and a new one is about to begin. My compartment has deflated. The pumps have been exchanging the gas for fresh air. That must mean that we are now on that beautiful, shining blue planet, with Forta only a speck in our new heavens.

I feel different for knowing that. All my life hitherto has been spent on a dying planet where our greatest enemy was lethal discouragement. But now I feel rejuvenated. There will be work, hope, and life here: a world to build, and a future to build it for . . .

I can hear the drills at work, cutting a way out for us. What, I wonder, shall we find? We must watch ourselves closely. It may be easier for us to keep faith if we face hardships than if we find ourselves among plenty. But, whatever this world is like, faith *must* be kept. We hold a million years of history, a million years of knowledge, that *must* be preserved.

Yet we must also, as His Excellency said, be ready to adapt ourselves. Who can tell what forms of life may already exist here? One could scarcely expect to find real consciousness on a planet so young, but there may be the first stirrings of intelligence here. We must watch for them, seek them out, cultivate them. They may be quite different from us, but we must remember that it is their world, and help them where we can. We must keep in mind that it would be a wicked thing to frustrate even an alien form of life, on its own planet. If we find any such beings, our task must be to teach, to learn, to co-operate with them, and perhaps one day we may achieve a civilisation even greater than Forta's own . . .

'And just what,' inquired the Inspector, 'do you think you're doing with that, Sergeant Brown?'

The police-sergeant held the limp, furry body dangling by its tail.

'It's a cat, sir.'

'That's what I meant.'

'Well, I thought the W.O. gentleman might want to examine it, sir.'

'What makes you think the War Office is interested in dead cats, Sergeant?'

The sergeant explained. He had decided to risk a trip into the outhouse to note developments, if any. Bearing in mind the Inspector's suggestion of gas, he had tied a rope round his waist so that he could be dragged back if he were overcome, and crawled in, keeping as low as possible. The precautions had proved unnecessary, however. The hissing or sizzling had ceased, and the gas had evidently dispersed. He had been able to approach the ball without feeling any effects whatever. Nevertheless, when he had come so close to it that his ear was almost against it he had noticed a faint buzzing.

'Buzzing?' repeated the Inspector. 'You mean sizzling.'

'No, sir, buzzing.' He paused, searching for a simile. 'The nearest thing, to my mind, would be a circular saw, but as you might hear it from a very long way off.'

Deducing from this that the thing, whatever it was, was still active, the sergeant had ordered his constables away to cover on the far side of an earth bank. He himself had looked into the shed from time to time during the next hour and a half, but observed no change.

He had noticed the cat prowl into the yard just as they were settling down to a snack of sandwiches. It had gone nosing round the shed door, but he had not bothered about it. Half an hour later, when he had finished his meal and cigarette, he had gone across to take another look. He had discovered the cat lying close to the 'meteor'. When he brought it out, he had found it was dead.

'Gassed?' asked the Inspector.

The sergeant shook his head. 'No, sir. That's what's funny about it.'

He laid the cat's body on top of a convenient wall, and turned the head to expose the under side of the jaw. A small circle of the black fur had been burnt away, and in the centre of the burn was a minute hole.

'H'm,' said the Inspector. He touched the wound, and then sniffed at his forefinger. 'Fur's burnt, all right, but no smell of explosive fumes,' he said.

'That's not all, sir.'

The sergeant turned the head over to reveal an exactly similar blemish on the crown. He took a thin, straight wire from his pocket, and probed into the hole beneath the jaw. It emerged from the other hole at the top of the head.

'Can you make anything of that, sir?' he asked.

The Inspector frowned. A weapon of minute bore, at point-blank range might have made one of the wounds. But the two appeared to be entrance and exit holes of the same missile. But a bullet did not come out leaving a neat hole like that, nor did it singe the hair about its exit. To all appearances, two of these microscopic bullets must have been fired in exactly the same line from above and below the head – which made no kind of sense.

'Have you any theories?' he asked the sergeant.

'Beats me, sir,' the other told him.

'What's happened to the thing now? Is it still buzzing?' the Inspector inquired.

'No, sir. There wasn't a sound from it when I went in and found the cat.'

'H'm,' said the Inspector. 'Isn't it about time that W.O. man showed up?'

Extract from Onns's Journal:

This is a terrible place! As though we were condemned to some fantastic hell. Can this be our beautiful blue planet that beckoned us so bravely? We cannot understand, we are utterly bewildered, our minds reel with the horror of this place. We, the flower of civilisation, now cower before the hideous monstrosities that face us. How can we ever hope to bring order into such a world as this?

We are hiding now in a dark cavern while Iss, our leader, consults to decide our best course. None of us envies him his responsibility. What provisions can a man make against not only the unknown, but the incredible? Nine hundred and sixty-four of us depend on him. There were a thousand: this is the way it happened.

I heard the drill stop, then there was a clanking as it was dismantled and drawn from the long shaft it had bored. Soon after that came the call for assembly. We crawled out of our compartments, collected our personal belongings, and met in the centre hall. Sunss, our leader then, himself called the roll. Everyone answered except four poor fellows who had not stood the strain of the journey. Then Sunss made a brief speech.

He reminded us that what had been done was irrevocable. No one yet knew what awaited us outside the Globe. If it should somehow happen that our party was divided, each group must elect its leader and act independently until contact with the rest was re-established.

'We need long courage, not brief bravery,' he said. 'Not heroics. We have to think of ourselves always as the seed of the future; and every grain of that seed is precious.'

He hammered home the responsibility to all of us.

'We do not know, and we shall never know, how the other globes may have fared. So, not knowing, we must act as though we alone had survived, and as if all that Forta has ever stood for is in our hands alone.'

It was he who led the way down the newly-bored passage, and he who first set foot in the new land. I followed with the rest, filled with such a conflict of feelings as I have never known before.

And this world into which we have emerged: how can I describe it in all its alien qualities?

To begin with; it was gloomy and shadowed – and yet it was not night-time. Such light as there was came from a vast, grey panel hanging in the dusky sky. From where we stood it appeared trapezoid, but I suspect that was a trick of perspective, and that it was in fact a square, bisected twice, by two dark bars, into four smaller squares. In the murk over our heads it was possible to make out dimly-faint darker lines intersecting at strange angles. I could not guess at their significance.

The ground we stood on was like nothing I had known. It was a vast level plain, but ridged, and covered with small, loose boulders. The ridges were somewhat like strata that had been laid side by side instead of one on another. They lay all one way, disappearing into gloomy distance before and behind. Close beside us was a crevasse, as wide as my own height, also running either way, in a perfectly straight line. Some considerable distance beyond it was another, similar crevasse running exactly parallel to it, and beyond that a third, and an indication of a fourth.

The man beside me was nervous. He muttered something about a geometrical world lit by a square sun.

'Rubbish!' I told him shortly.

'Then how do you explain it?' he asked.

'I do not rush into swift, facile explanations,' I told him. 'I observe, and then, when I have gathered enough data, I deduce.'

'What do you deduce from a square sun?' he asked, but I ignored him.

Soon we were all assembled outside the Globe, and waiting for Sunss to give directions. He was just about to speak when we were interrupted by a strange sound – a kind of regular soft padding, sometimes with a rasping scratch accompanying it. There was something ominous about it, and for a moment we were all frozen with apprehension – then, before we could move, the most fearsome monster emerged from behind our Globe.

Every historic travellers' tale pales beside the reality of the thing we faced. Never would I have believed that such a creature could exist had I not seen it for myself. The first we saw of it was an enormous face, thrusting round the side of the Globe, hanging in the air far above us. It was a sight to make the bravest shudder.

It was black, too, so that in the darkness it was difficult to be certain of its outline; but it widened across the top, and above the head itself one seemed to catch a glimpse of two towering pointed ears. It looked down on us out of two vast, glowing eyes set somewhat aslant.

It paused for a moment, the great eyes blinked, and then it came closer. The legs which then came into view were like massive pillars, yet they moved with a dexterity and control that was amazing in anything so vast. Both legs and feet were covered with close set fibres that looked like strands of shining black metal. It bent its legs, lowering its head to look at us, and the fearful stench of its breath blew over us. The face was still more alarming at close quarters. It opened a cavern of a mouth; an enormous pink tongue flicked out and back. Above the mouth huge, pointed spines stood out sideways, trembling. The eyes which were fixed on us were cold, cruel, non-intelligent.

Until then we had been transfixed, but now panic took some of us. Those nearest to it fell back hurriedly, and at that one of the monstrous feet moved like lightning. A huge black paw with suddenly out-thrust claws smacked down. When it drew back, twenty of our men and women were no more than smears on the ground.

We were paralysed, all of us except Sunss. He, forgetting his instructions about personal safety, ran towards the creature. The great paw rose, hovered, and struck again. Eleven more fell at that second murderous blow.

Then I noticed Sunss again. He was standing right between the paws. His fire-rod was in his hands, and he was looking up at the monstrous head above him. As I watched, he lifted the weapon, and aimed. It seemed such folly against that huge thing, heroic folly. But Sunss was wiser than I. Suddenly the head jerked, a tremor shook the limbs, and without a sound the monster dropped where it stood.

And Sunss was under it. A very brave man . . .

Then Iss took charge.

He decided that we must find a place of safety as soon as possible in case there were other such monsters lurking near. Once we had found that, we could start to remove our instruments and equipment from the Globe, and consider our next step. He decided to lead us forward down the broad way between two of the crevasses.

After travelling a considerable distance we reached the foot of a towering and completely perpendicular cliff with curiously regular rectangular formations on its face. At the base of it we found this cavern which seems to run a great distance both inwards and to both sides, and with a height that is oddly regular. Perhaps the man who spoke about a geometrical world was not so stupid as he seemed . . .

Anyway, here we have a refuge from monsters such as that which Sunss killed. It is too narrow for those huge paws to reach, and even the fearful claws could only rake a little way inside.

Later. A terrible thing has happened! Iss and a party of twenty went exploring the cavern to see if they could find another way out other than on to the plain where our Globe lay.

Yes – lay! Past tense. That is our calamity.

After he had gone off, the rest of us waited, keeping watch. For some time nothing happened. Evidently and mercifully the monster had been alone. It lay in a great black mound where it had fallen, close to the Globe. Then a curious thing took place. More light suddenly poured over the plain. An enormous hooked object descended upon the slain monster, and dragged it away out of sight. Then there was a thunderous noise which shook everything about us, and the light dimmed again.

I do not pretend to explain these things: none of us can understand them. I simply do my best to keep a faithful record.

Another, much longer, period passed without any event. We were beginning to worry about what might have happened to Iss and his party for they had been a long time away, when almost the worst thing that could happen to us occurred without warning.

Again the plain became lighter. The ground beneath us set up a reverberating rumble and shook so violently to a series of shocks that we were hard put to keep on our feet. Peering out of the cavern I saw a sight that even now I can scarcely credit. Forms beside which our previous monster was insignificant: living, moving creatures reared up to three or four times the height of our vast Globe. I know this will not be believed – but it is the truth. Little wonder that the whole plain groaned and rumbled under the burden of four such. They bent over our Globe, they put their forelegs to it, and lifted it – yes, actually lifted that stupendous mass of metal from the ground. Then the shaking all about us became worse as they took its weight and tramped away on colossal feet.

The sight of that was too much for some of us. A hundred men ran out from our cavern, cursing, weeping, and brandishing their fire-rods. But it was too late, and the range was too great for them to do anything effective, besides, how could we hope to affect colossi such as these?

Now our Globe, with all its precious contents is lost. Our inheritance is gone. We have nothing now; nothing, but our own few trifling possessions, with which to start building our new world . . .

It is bitter, bitter to have worked so hard and come so far, for this . . .

Nor was that the only calamity. Only a little later two of Iss's companions came back with a dreadful tale.

Behind our cavern they had discovered a warren of broad tunnels, foul with the smell of unknown creatures and their droppings. They had made their way down them with difficulty. Several times they had been beset by different varieties of six-legged creatures, and sometimes eight-legged ones, all of horrible appearance. Many of these were a great deal larger than themselves, armed with fearful jaws and claws, and filled with a vicious ferocity which made them attack on sight. Terrifying though they looked, it soon became clear, however, that they were only really dangerous when they made unexpected attacks for they were non-sentient and the fire-rods made short work of them once they had been seen.

After a number of such encounters Iss had succeeded in reaching open country beyond the tunnels without the loss of a man. It had been when they were on the way back to fetch us that catastrophe had overtaken them. They had been attacked by fierce grey creatures about half the size of our first monster, which they guessed to be the builders of the tunnels. It was a terrible fight in which almost all the party perished before the monsters were overcome. Iss himself had fallen, and of all his men only these two had been left in a fit condition to make the journey back to the rest of us.

This new, ghastly tragedy is starting to sap our spirits, and our courage . . .

We have chosen Muin as our new leader. He has decided that we must go forward, through the tunnels. The plain behind us is quite barren, our Globe is gone, if we stay here we shall starve; so we must try to get through to the open country beyond, trusting that Iss's sacrifice has not been in vain, and that there are no more grey monsters to attack us . . .

God grant that beyond the tunnels this nightmare world gives place to sanity . . .

Is it so much that we ask – simply to live, to work, to build, in peace . . . ?

Graham looked in to see Sally and her father a couple of days later.

'Thought you might like an interim report on your "meteor",' he said to Mr Fontain.

'What was it, actually?' asked the older man.

'Oh, I don't say they've got that far. They've established that it was no meteor; but just what it really was still has them absolutely guessing. I'd got pretty curious by the time they decided to take it away, and after I'd talked big and waved my wartime status at them a bit, they consented to stretch a point and take me along, too. So you'd better grade this as confidential.

'When we went over the thing carefully at the research place it appeared to be simply a solid ball of some metal on which there's been no report issued as yet. But in one place there was a hole, quite smooth, about half an inch in diameter, which went straight in, roughly to the middle. Well, they scratched their heads about the best way to tackle it, and decided in the end to cut it in half and see what. So they rigged up an automatic sawing device in a pit and set it going, and we all retreated to a reasonable distance, just in case. Now they're all a bit more puzzled than they were before.'

'Why, what happened?' Sally asked.

'Well, nothing actually *happened.* When the saw ran free we switched off and went back, and there *was* the ball lying in neat halves. But they weren't solid halves as we had expected. There was a solid metal rind about six inches thick, but then there was an inch or so of soft, fine dust, which has insulating qualities that seem to be interesting them quite a bit. Then inside a thinner metal wall was an odd formation of cells; more like a section of honeycomb than anything, only made of some flexible, rubbery material, and every one empty. Next a belt about two inches wide, divided into metal compartments this time, all considerably larger than the cells in the outer part, and crammed with all sorts of things – packs of minute tubes, things that look like tiny seeds, different sorts of powders that have spilled about when the thing came apart, and which nobody's got around to examining properly yet, and finally a four-inch space in the middle separated into layers by dozens of paper-thin fins, and absolutely empty otherwise.

'So there is the secret weapon – and if you can make anything of that lot, I'm sure they'll be pleased to hear about it. Even the dust layer disappointed them by not being explosive. Now they're asking one another what the hell such a thing could be remotely expected to do.'

'That's disappointing. It seemed so like a meteor – until it started sizzling,' said Mr Fontain.

'One of them has suggested that in a way it may be. A sort of artificial meteor,' Graham said. 'That's a bit too fancy for the rest, though. They feel that if something could be sent across space at all, surely it would be something more intelligible.'

'It would be exciting if it were,' Sally said. 'I mean, it would be such a much more hopeful thing than just another secret weapon – a sort of sign that perhaps one day we shall be able to do it ourselves . . .

'Just think how wonderful it might be if we really could do that! Think of all the people who are sick to death of secret weapons, and wars, and cruelties setting out one day in a huge ship for a clean, new planet where we could start again. We'd be able to leave behind all the things that make this poor old world get boggier and boggier. All we'd want is a place where people could live, and work, and build, and be happy. If we could only start again somewhere else, what a lovely, lovely world we might—' She stopped suddenly at the sound of a frenzied yapping outside. She jumped up as it changed to a long-drawn howl.

'That's Mitty!' she said. 'What on earth—?'

The two men followed her out of the house.

'Mitty! Mitty!' she called, but there was no sign of the dog, nor sound from it now.

They made round to the left, where the sound had seemed to come from. Sally was the first to see the white patch lying in the grass beside the outhouse wall. She ran towards it, calling; but the patch did not move.

'Oh, poor Mitty!' she said. 'I believe she's dead!'

She went down on her knees beside the dog's limp body.

'She *is*!' she said. 'I wonder what—' She broke off abruptly, and stood up. 'Oh, something stung me! Oh, it *hurts*!' She clutched at her leg, tears of anguish suddenly coming into her eyes.

'What on earth—?' began her father, looking down at the dog. 'What are all those things – ants?'

Graham bent down to look.

'No, they're not ants. I don't know what they are.'

He picked one of the little creatures up and put it on the palm of his hand to look at it more closely.

'Never seen anything like that before,' he said.

Mr Fontain beside him, peered at it, too.

It was a queer-looking little thing, under a quarter of an inch long. Its body seemed to be an almost perfect hemisphere with the flat side below and the round top surface coloured pink, and as shiny as a ladybird's wing-cases. It was insect-like, except that it stood on only four short legs. There was no clearly defined head; just two eyes set in the edge of the shiny dome. As they watched, it reared up on two of its legs, showing a pale, flat underside, with a mouth set just below the eyes. In its forelegs it seemed to be holding a bit of grass or thin wire.

Graham felt a sudden, searing pain in his hand.

'Hell's bells!' he said, shaking it off. 'The little brute certainly can sting. I don't know what they are, but they're nasty things to have around. Got a spray handy?'

'There's one in the scullery,' Mr Fontain told him. He turned his attention to his daughter. 'Better?' he inquired.

'Hurts like hell,' Sally said, between her teeth.

'Just hang on a minute till we've dealt with this, then we'll have a look at it,' he told her.

Graham hurried back with the spray in his hand. He cast around and discovered several hundreds of the little pink objects crawling towards the wall of the outhouse. He pumped a cloud of insecticide over them and watched while they slowed, waved feeble legs, and then lay still. He sprayed the locality a little more, to make sure.

'That ought to fix 'em,' he said. 'Nasty, vicious little brutes. Never seen anything quite like them – I wonder what on earth they were?'

22

Billennium

(1961)

J. G. Ballard

All day long, and often into the early hours of the morning, the tramp of feet sounded up and down the stairs outside Ward's cubicle. Built into a narrow alcove in a bend of the staircase between the fourth and fifth floors, its plywood walls flexed and creaked with every footstep like the timbers of a rotting windmill. Over a hundred people lived in the top three floors of the old rooming house, and sometimes Ward would lie awake on his narrow bunk until 2 or 3 a.m., mechanically counting the last residents returning from the all-night movies in the stadium half a mile away. Through the window he could hear giant fragments of the amplified dialogue booming among the rooftops. The stadium was never empty. During the day the huge four-sided screen was raised on its davit and athletics meetings or football matches ran continuously. For the people in the houses abutting the stadium the noise must have been unbearable.

Ward, at least, had a certain degree of privacy. Two months earlier, before he came to live on the staircase, he had shared a room with seven others on the ground floor of a house in 755th Street, and the ceaseless press of people jostling past the window had reduced him to a state of exhaustion. The street was always full, an endless clamour of voices and shuffling feet. By 6.30, when he woke, hurrying to take his place in the bathroom queue, the crowds already jammed it from sidewalk to sidewalk, the din punctuated every half minute by the roar of the elevated trains running over the shops on the opposite side of the road. As soon as he saw the advertisement describing the staircase cubicle he had left (like everyone else, he spent most of his spare time scanning the classifieds in the newspapers, moving his lodgings an average of once every two months) despite the higher rental. A cubicle on a staircase would almost certainly be on its own.

However, this had its drawbacks. Most evenings his friends from the library would call in, eager to rest their elbows after the bruising crush of the public reading room. The cubicle was slightly more than four and a half square metres in floor area, half a square metre over the statutory maximum for a single person, the carpenters having taken advantage, illegally, of a recess beside a nearby chimney breast. Consequently

Ward had been able to fit a small straight-backed chair into the interval between the bed and the door, so that only one person at a time needed to sit on the bed – in most single cubicles host and guest had to sit side by side on the bed, conversing over their shoulders and changing places periodically to avoid neck-strain.

'You were lucky to find this place,' Rossiter, the most regular visitor, never tired of telling him. He reclined back on the bed, gesturing at the cubicle. 'It's enormous, the perspectives really zoom. I'd be surprised if you haven't got at least five metres here, perhaps six.'

Ward shook his head categorically. Rossiter was his closest friend, but the quest for living space had forged powerful reflexes. 'Just over four and a half, I've measured it carefully. There's no doubt about it.'

Rossiter lifted one eyebrow. 'I'm amazed. It must be the ceiling then.'

Manipulating the ceiling was a favourite trick of unscrupulous landlords – most assessments of area were made upon the ceiling, out of convenience, and by tilting back the plywood partitions the rated area of a cubicle could be either increased, for the benefit of a prospective tenant (many married couples were thus bamboozled into taking a single cubicle), or decreased temporarily on the visits of the housing inspectors. Ceilings were criss-crossed with pencil marks staking out the rival claims of tenants on opposite sides of a party wall. Someone timid of his rights could be literally squeezed out of existence – in fact, the advertisement 'quiet clientele' was usually a tacit invitation to this sort of piracy.

'The wall does tilt a little,' Ward admitted. 'Actually, it's about four degrees out – I used a plumb-line. But there's still plenty of room on the stairs for people to get by.'

Rossiter grinned. 'Of course, John. I'm just envious, that's all. My room is driving me crazy.' Like everyone, he used the term 'room' to describe his tiny cubicle, a hangover from the days fifty years earlier when people had indeed lived one to a room, sometimes, unbelievably, one to an apartment or house. The microfilms in the architecture catalogues at the library showed scenes of museums, concert halls and other public buildings in what appeared to be everyday settings, often virtually empty, two or three people wandering down an enormous gallery or staircase. Traffic moved freely along the centre of streets, and in the quieter districts sections of sidewalk would be deserted for fifty yards or more.

Now, of course, the older buildings had been torn down and replaced by housing batteries, or converted into apartment blocks. The great banqueting room in the former City Hall had been split horizontally into four decks, each of these cut up into hundreds of cubicles.

As for the streets, traffic had long since ceased to move about them. Apart from a few hours before dawn when only the sidewalks were crowded, every thoroughfare was always packed with a shuffling mob of pedestrians, perforce ignoring the countless 'Keep Left' signs suspended over their heads, wrestling past each other on their way to home and office, their clothes dusty and shapeless. Often 'locks' would occur when a huge crowd at a street junction became immovably jammed. Sometimes these locks would last for days. Two years earlier Ward had been caught in one outside the stadium, for over forty-eight hours was trapped in a gigantic pedestrian jam containing over 20,000 people, fed by the crowds leaving the stadium on one side and those approaching it on the other. An entire square mile of the local neighbourhood had been paralysed, and he vividly remembered the nightmare of swaying helplessly on his feet as the jam shifted and heaved, terrified of losing his balance and being trampled underfoot. When the police had finally sealed off the stadium and dispersed the jam he had gone back to his cubicle and slept for a week, his body blue with bruises.

'I hear they may reduce the allocation to three and a half metres.' Rossiter remarked.

Ward paused to allow a party of tenants from the sixth floor to pass down the staircase, holding the door to prevent it jumping off its latch. 'So they're always saying,' he commented. 'I can remember that rumour ten years ago.'

'It's no rumour,' Rossiter warned him. 'It may well be necessary soon. Thirty million people are packed into this city now, a million increase in just one year. There's been some pretty serious talk at the Housing Department.'

Ward shook his head. 'A drastic revaluation like that is almost impossible to carry out. Every single partition would have to be dismantled and nailed up again, the administrative job alone is so vast it's difficult to visualise. Millions of cubicles to be redesigned and certified, licences to be issued, plus the complete resettlement of every tenant. Most of the buildings put up since the last revaluation are designed around a four-metre modulus – you can't simply take half a metre off the end of each cubicle and then say that makes so many new cubicles. They may be only six inches wide.' He laughed. 'Besides, how can you live in just three and a half metres?'

Rossiter smiled. 'That's the ultimate argument, isn't it? They used it twenty-five years ago at the last revaluation, when the minimum was cut from five to four. It couldn't be done they all said, no one could stand living in only four square metres, it was enough room for a bed and suitcase, but you couldn't open the door to get in.' Rossiter chuckled softly. 'They are all wrong. It was merely decided that from then on all doors would open outwards. Four square metres was here to stay.'

Ward looked at his watch. It was 7.30. 'Time to eat. Let's see if we can get into the food-bar across the road.'

Grumbling at the prospect, Rossiter pulled himself off the bed. They left the cubicle and made their way down the staircase. This was crammed with luggage and packing cases so that only a narrow interval remained around the banister. On the floors below the congestion was worse. Corridors were wide enough to be chopped up into single cubicles, and the air was stale and dead, cardboard walls hung with damp laundry and makeshift larders. Each of the five rooms on the floors contained a dozen tenants, their voices reverberating through the partitions.

People were sitting on the steps above the second floor, using the staircase as an informal lounge, although this was against the fire regulations, women talking to the men queueing in their shirt-sleeves outside the washroom, children diving around them. By the time they reached the entrance Ward and Rossiter were having to force their way through the tenants packed together on every landing, loitering around the notice boards or pushing in from the street below.

Taking a breath at the top of the steps, Ward pointed to the food-bar on the other side of the road. It was only thirty yards away, but the throng moving down the street swept past like a river at full tide, crossing them from right to left. The first picture show at the stadium started at 9 o'clock, and people were setting off already to make sure of getting in.

'Can't we go somewhere else?' Rossiter asked, screwing his face up at the prospect of the food-bar. Not only was it packed and would take them half an hour to be served, but the food was flat and unappetising. The journey from the library four blocks away had given him an appetite.

Ward shrugged. 'There's a place on the corner, but I doubt if we can make it.' This was two hundred yards upstream; they would be fighting the crowd all the way.

'Maybe you're right.' Rossiter put his hand on Ward's shoulder. 'You know, John, your trouble is that you never go anywhere, you're too disengaged, you just don't realise how bad everything is getting.'

Ward nodded. Rossiter was right. In the morning, when he set off for the library, the pedestrian traffic was moving with him towards the down-town offices; in the evening, when he came back, it was flowing in the opposite direction. By and large he never altered his routine. Brought up from the age of ten in a municipal hostel, he had gradually lost touch with his father and mother, who lived on the east side of the city and had been unable, or unwilling, to make the journey to see him. Having surrendered his initiative to the dynamics of the city he was reluctant to try to win it back merely for a better cup of coffee. Fortunately his job at the library brought him into contact with a wide range of young people of similar interests. Sooner or later he would marry, find a double cubicle near the library and settle down. If they had enough children (three was the required minimum) they might even one day own a small room of their own.

They stepped out into the pedestrian stream, carried along by it for ten or twenty yards, then quickened their pace and side-stepped through the crowd, slowly tacking across to the other side of the road. There they found the shelter of the shopfronts, slowly worked their way back to the food-bar, shoulders braced against the countless minor collisions.

'What are the latest population estimates?' Ward asked as they circled a cigarette kiosk, stepping forward whenever a gap presented itself.

Rossiter smiled. 'Sorry, John, I'd like to tell you but you might start a stampede. Besides, you wouldn't believe me.'

Rossiter worked in the Insurance Department at the City Hall, had informal access to the census statistics. For the last ten years these had been classified information, partly because they were felt to be inaccurate, but chiefly because it was feared they might set off a mass attack of claustrophobia. Minor outbreaks had taken place already, and the official line was that the world population had reached a plateau, levelling off at 20,000 million. No one believed this for a moment, and Ward assumed that the 3 per cent annual increase maintained since the 1960s was continuing.

How long it could continue was impossible to estimate. Despite the gloomiest prophecies of the Neo-Malthusians, world agriculture had managed to keep pace with the population growth, although intensive cultivation meant that 95 per cent of the population was permanently trapped in vast urban conurbations. The outward growth of cities had at last been checked; in fact, all over the world former suburban areas were being reclaimed for agriculture and population additions were confined within the existing urban ghettos. The countryside, as such, no longer existed. Every single square foot of ground sprouted a crop of one type or other. The one-time fields and meadows of the world were now, in effect, factory floors, as highly mechanised and closed to the public as any industrial area. Economic and ideological rivalries had long since faded before one overriding quest – the internal colonisation of the city.

Reaching the food-bar, they pushed themselves into the entrance and joined the scrum of customers pressing six deep against the counter.

'What is really wrong with the population problem,' Ward confided to Rossiter, 'is that no one has ever tried to tackle it. Fifty years ago short-sighted nationalism and industrial expansion put a premium on a rising population curve, and even now the hidden incentive is to have a large family so that you can gain a little privacy. Single people are penalised simply because there are more of them and they don't fit neatly into double or triple cubicles. But it's the large family with its compact, space-saving logistic that is the real villain.'

Rossiter nodded, edging nearer the counter, ready to shout his order. 'Too true. We all look forward to getting married just so that we can have our six square metres.'

Directly in front of them, two girls turned around and smiled. 'Six square metres,' one of them, a dark-haired girl with a pretty oval face, repeated. 'You sound like the sort of young man I ought to get to know. Going into the real estate business, Henry?'

Rossiter grinned and squeezed her arm. 'Hello, Judith. I'm thinking about it actively. Like to join me in a private venture?'

The girl leaned against him as they reached the counter. 'Well, I might. It would have to be legal, though.'

The other girl, Helen Waring, an assistant at the library, pulled Ward's sleeve. 'Have you heard the latest, John? Judith and I have been kicked out of our room. We're on the street right at this minute.'

'What?' Rossiter cried. They collected their soups and coffee and edged back to the rear of the bar. 'What on earth happened?'

Helen explained: 'You know that little broom cupboard outside our cubicle? Judith and I have been using it as a sort of study hole, going in there to read. It's quiet and restful, if you can get used to not breathing. Well, the old girl found out and kicked up a big fuss, said we were breaking the law and so on. In short, out.' Helen paused. 'Now we've heard she's going to let it as a single.'

Rossiter pounded the counter ledge. 'A broom cupboard? Someone's going to live there? But she'll never get a licence.'

Judith shook her head. 'She's got it already. Her brother works in the Housing Department.'

Ward laughed into his soup. 'But how can she let it? No one will live in a broom cupboard.'

Judith stared at him sombrely. 'You really believe that, John?'

Ward dropped his spoon. 'No. I suppose you're right. People will live anywhere. God, I don't know who I feel more sorry for – you two, or the poor devil who'll be living in that cupboard. What are you going to do?'

'A couple in a place two blocks west are sub-letting half their cubicle to us. They've hung a sheet down the middle and Helen and I'll take turns sleeping on a camp bed. I'm not joking, our room's about two feet wide. I said to Helen that we ought to split up again and sublet one half at twice our rent.'

They had a good laugh over all this. Then Ward said good night to the others and went back to his rooming house.

There he found himself with similar problems.

The manager leaned against the flimsy door, damp cigar butt revolving around his mouth, an expression of morose boredom on his unshaven face.

'You got four point seven two metres,' he told Ward, who was standing out on the staircase, unable to get into his room. Other tenants pressed by on to the landing, where two women in curlers and dressing gowns were arguing with each other, tugging angrily at the wall of trunks and cases. Occasionally the manager glanced at them irritably. 'Four seven two. I worked it out twice.' He said this as if it ended all possibility of argument.

'Ceiling or floor?' Ward asked.

'Ceiling, whaddya think? How can I measure the floor with all this junk?' He kicked at a crate of books protruding from under the bed.

Ward let this pass. 'There's quite a tilt on the wall,' he pointed out. 'As much as three or four degrees.'

The manager nodded vaguely. 'You're definitely over the four. Way over.' He turned to Ward, who had moved down several steps to allow a man and woman to get past. 'I can rent this as a double.'

'What, only four and a half?' Ward said incredulously. 'How?'

The man who had just passed him leaned over the manager's shoulder and sniffed at the room, taking in every detail in a one-second glance. 'You renting a double here, Louie?'

The manager waved him away and then beckoned Ward into the room, closing the door after him.

'It's a nominal five,' he told Ward. 'New regulation, just came out. Anything over four five is a double now.' He eyed Ward shrewdly. 'Well, whaddya want? It's a good room, there's a lot of space here, feels more like a triple. You got access to the staircase, window slit—' He broke off as Ward slumped down on the bed and started to laugh. 'Whatsa matter? Look, if you want a big room like this you gotta pay for it. I want an extra half rental or you get out.'

Ward wiped his eyes, then stood up wearily and reached for the shelves. 'Relax, I'm on my way. I'm going to live in a broom cupboard. "Access to the staircase" – that's really rich. Tell me, Louie, is there life on Uranus?'

Temporarily, he and Rossiter teamed up to rent a double cubicle in a semi-derelict house a hundred yards from the library. The neighbourhood was seedy and faded, the rooming houses crammed with tenants. Most of them were owned by absentee landlords or by the city corporation, and the managers employed were of the lowest type, mere rent-collectors who cared nothing about the way their tenants divided up the living space, and never ventured beyond the first floors. Bottles and empty cans littered the corridors, and the washrooms looked like sumps. Many of the tenants were old and infirm, sitting about listlessly in their narrow cubicles, wheedling at each other back to back through the thin partitions.

Their double cubicle was on the third floor, at the end of a corridor that ringed the building. Its architecture was impossible to follow, rooms letting off at all angles, and luckily the corridor was a cul-de-sac. The mounds of cases ended four feet from the end wall and a partition divided off the cubicle, just wide enough for two beds. A high window overlooked the area ways of the buildings opposite.

Possessions loaded on to the shelf above his head, Ward lay back on his bed and moodily surveyed the roof of the library through the afternoon haze.

'It's not bad here,' Rossiter told him, unpacking his case. 'I know there's no real privacy and we'll drive each other insane within a week, but at least we haven't got six other people breathing into our ears two feet away.'

The nearest cubicle, a single, was built into the banks of cases half a dozen steps along the corridor, but the occupant, a man of seventy, was deaf and bed-ridden.

'It's not bad,' Ward echoed reluctantly. 'Now tell me what the latest growth figures are. They might console me.'

Rossiter paused, lowering his voice. 'Four per cent. *Eight hundred million extra people in one year* – just less than half the earth's total population in 1950.'

Ward whistled slowly. 'So they will revalue. What to? Three and a half?'

'Three. From the first of next year.'

'Three square metres!' Ward sat up and looked around him. 'It's unbelievable! The world's going insane, Rossiter. For God's sake, when are they going to do something about it? Do you realise there soon won't be room enough to sit down, let alone lie down?'

Exasperated, he punched the wall beside him, on the second blow knocked in one of the small wooden panels that had been lightly papered over.

'Hey!' Rossiter yelled. 'You're breaking the place down.' He dived across the bed to retrieve the panel, which hung downwards supported by a strip of paper. Ward slipped his hand into the dark interval, carefully drew the panel back on to the bed.

'Who's on the other side?' Rossiter whispered. 'Did they hear?'

Ward peered through the interval, eyes searching the dim light. Suddenly he dropped the panel and seized Rossiter's shoulder, pulled him down on to the bed.

'Henry! Look!'

Directly in front of them, faintly illuminated by a grimy skylight, was a medium-sized room some fifteen feet square, empty except for the dust silted up against the skirting boards. The floor was bare, a few strips of frayed linoleum running across it, the walls covered with a drab floral design. Here and there patches of the paper peeled off and segments of the picture rail had rotted away, but otherwise the room was in habitable condition.

Breathing slowly, Ward closed the open door of the cubicle with his foot, then turned to Rossiter.

'Henry, do you realise what we've found? Do you realise it, man?'

'Shut up. For Pete's sake keep your voice down.' Rossiter examined the room carefully. 'It's fantastic. I'm trying to see whether anyone's used it recently.'

'Of course they haven't,' Ward pointed out. 'It's obvious. There's no door into the room. We're looking through it now. They must have panelled over this door years ago and forgotten about it. Look at that filth everywhere.'

Rossiter was staring into the room, his mind staggered by its vastness.

'You're right,' he murmured. 'Now, when do we move in?'

Panel by panel, they prised away the lower half of the door and nailed it on to a wooden frame, so that the dummy section could be replaced instantly.

Then, picking an afternoon when the house was half empty and the manager asleep in his basement office, they made their first foray into the room, Ward going in alone while Rossiter kept guard in the cubicle.

For an hour they exchanged places, wandering silently around the dusty room, stretching their arms out to feel its unconfined emptiness, grasping at the sensation of absolute spatial freedom. Although smaller than many of the sub-divided rooms in which they had lived, this room seemed infinitely larger, its walls huge cliffs that soared upward to the skylight.

Finally, two or three days later, they moved in.

For the first week Rossiter slept alone in the room, Ward in the cubicle outside, both there together during the day. Gradually they smuggled in a few items of furniture: two armchairs, a table, a lamp fed from the socket in the cubicle. The furniture was heavy and Victorian; the cheapest available, its size emphasised the emptiness of the room. Pride of place was taken by an enormous mahogany wardrobe, fitted with carved angels and castellated mirrors, which they were forced to dismantle and carry into the house in their suitcases. Towering over them, it reminded Ward of the microfilms of Gothic cathedrals, with their massive organ lofts crossing vast naves.

After three weeks they both slept in the room, finding the cubicle unbearably cramped. An imitation Japanese screen divided the room adequately and did nothing to diminish its size. Sitting there in the evenings, surrounded by his books and albums, Ward steadily forgot the city outside. Luckily he reached the library by a back alley and avoided the crowded streets. Rossiter and himself began to seem the only real inhabitants of the world, everyone else a meaningless by-product of their own existence, a random replication of identity which had run out of control.

It was Rossiter who suggested that they ask the two girls to share the room with them.

'They've been kicked out again and may have to split up,' he told Ward, obviously worried that Judith might fall into bad company. 'There's always a rent freeze after a revaluation but all the landlords know about it so they're not re-letting. It's damned difficult to find anywhere.'

Ward nodded, relaxing back around the circular redwood table. He played with the tassel of the arsenic-green lamp shade, for a moment felt like a Victorian man of letters, leading a spacious, leisurely life among overstuffed furnishings.

'I'm all for it,' he agreed, indicating the empty corners. 'There's plenty of room here. But we'll have to make sure they don't gossip about it.'

After due precautions, they let the two girls into the secret, enjoying their astonishment at finding this private universe.

'We'll put a partition across the middle,' Rossiter explained, 'then take it down each morning. You'll be able to move in within a couple of days. How do you feel?'

'Wonderful!' They goggled at the wardrobe, squinting at the endless reflections in the mirrors.

There was no difficulty getting them in and out of the house. The turnover of tenants was continuous and bills were placed in the mail rack. No one cared who the girls were or noticed their regular calls at the cubicle.

However, half an hour after they arrived neither of them had unpacked her suitcase.

'What's up, Judith?' Ward asked, edging past the girls' beds into the narrow interval between the table and wardrobe.

Judith hesitated, looking from Ward to Rossiter, who sat on the bed, finishing off the plywood partition. 'John, it's just that . . .'

Helen Waring, more matter-of-fact, took over, her fingers straightening the bed-spread. 'What Judith's trying to say is that our position here is a little embarrassing. The partition is—'

Rossiter stood up. 'For heaven's sake, don't worry, Helen,' he assured her, speaking in the loud whisper they had all involuntarily cultivated. 'No funny business, you can trust us. This partition is as solid as a rock.'

The two girls nodded. 'It's not that,' Helen explained, 'but it isn't up all the time. We thought that if an older person were here, say Judith's aunt – she wouldn't take up much room and be no trouble, she's really awfully sweet – we wouldn't need to bother about the partition – except at night,' she added quickly.

Ward glanced at Rossiter, who shrugged and began to scan the floor.

'Well, it's an idea,' Rossiter said. 'John and I know how you feel. Why not?'

'Sure,' Ward agreed. He pointed to the space between the girls' beds and the table. 'One more won't make any difference.'

The girls broke into whoops. Judith went over to Rossiter and kissed him on the cheek. 'Sorry to be a nuisance, Henry.' She smiled at him. 'That's a wonderful partition you've made. You couldn't do another one for Auntie – just a little one? She's very sweet but she is getting on.'

'Of course,' Rossiter said. 'I understand. I've got plenty of wood left over.'

Ward looked at his watch. 'It's seven-thirty, Judith. You'd better get in touch with your aunt. She may not be able to make it tonight.'

Judith buttoned her coat. 'Oh she will,' she assured Ward. 'I'll be back in a jiffy.'

The aunt arrived within five minutes, three heavy suitcases soundly packed.

'It's amazing,' Ward remarked to Rossiter three months later. 'The size of this room still staggers me. It almost gets larger every day.'

Rossiter agreed readily, averting his eyes from one of the girls changing behind the central partition. This they now left in place as dismantling it daily had become tiresome.

Besides, the aunt's subsidiary partition was attached to it and she resented the continuous upsets. Ensuring she followed the entrance and exit drills through the camouflaged door and cubicle was difficult enough.

Despite this, detection seemed unlikely. The room had obviously been built as an afterthought into the central well of the house and any noise was masked by the luggage stacked in the surrounding corridor. Directly below was a small dormitory occupied by several elderly women, and Judith's aunt, who visited them socially, swore that no sounds came through the heavy ceiling. Above, the fanlight let out through a dormer window, its lights indistinguishable from the hundred other bulbs in the windows of the house. Rossiter finished off the new partition he was building and held it upright, fitting it into the slots nailed to the wall between his bed and Ward's. They had agreed that this would provide a little extra privacy.

'No doubt I'll have to do one for Judith and Helen,' he confided to Ward.

Ward adjusted his pillow. They had smuggled the two armchairs back to the furniture shop as they took up too much space. The bed, anyway, was more comfortable. He had never become completely used to the soft upholstery.

'Not a bad idea. What about some shelving around the wall? I've got nowhere to put anything.'

The shelving tidied the room considerably, freeing large areas of the floor. Divided by their partitions, the five beds were in line along the rear wall, facing the mahogany wardrobe. In between was an open space of three or four feet, a further six feet on either side of the wardrobe.

The sight of so much spare space fascinated Ward. When Rossiter mentioned that Helen's mother was ill and badly needed personal care he immediately knew where her cubicle could be placed – at the foot of his bed, between the wardrobe and the side wall.

Helen was overjoyed. 'It's awfully good of you, John,' she told him, 'but would you mind if Mother slept beside me? There's enough space to fit an extra bed in.'

So Rossiter dismantled the partitions and moved them closer together, six beds now in line along the wall. This gave each of them an interval two and a half feet wide, just enough room to squeeze down the side of their beds. Lying back on the extreme right, the shelves two feet above his head, Ward could barely see the wardrobe, but the space in front of him, a clear six feet to the wall ahead, was uninterrupted.

Then Helen's father arrived.

Knocking on the door of the cubicle, Ward smiled at Judith's aunt as she let him in. He helped her swing out the made-up bed which guarded the entrance, than rapped on the wooden panel. A moment later Helen's father, a small, grey-haired man in an undershirt, braces tied to his trousers with string, pulled back the panel.

Ward nodded to him and stepped over the luggage piled around the floor at the foot of the beds. Helen was in her mother's cubicle, helping the old woman to drink her evening broth. Rossiter, perspiring heavily, was on his knees by the mahogany wardrobe, wrenching apart the frame of the central mirror with a jemmy. Pieces of the wardrobe lay on his bed and across the floor.

'We'll have to start taking these out tomorrow,' Rossiter told him. Ward waited for Helen's father to shuffle past and enter his cubicle. He had rigged up a small cardboard door, and locked it behind him with a crude hook of bent wire.

Rossiter watched him, frowning irritably. 'Some people are happy. This wardrobe's a hell of a job. How did we ever decide to buy it?'

Ward sat down on his bed. The partition pressed against his knees and he could hardly move. He looked up when Rossiter was engaged and saw that the dividing line he had marked in pencil was hidden by the encroaching partition. Leaning against the wall, he tried to ease it back again, but Rossiter had apparently nailed the lower edge to the floor.

There was a sharp tap on the outside cubicle door – Judith returning from her office. Ward started to get up and then sat back. 'Mr Waring,' he called softly. It was the old man's duty night.

Waring shuffled to the door of his cubicle and unlocked it fussily, clucking to himself.

'Up and down, up and down,' he muttered. He stumbled over Rossiter's tool-bag and swore loudly, then added meaningly over his shoulder: 'If you ask me there's too many people in here. Down below they've only got six to our seven, and it's the same size room.'

Ward nodded vaguely and stretched back on his narrow bed, trying not to bang his head on the shelving. Waring was not the first to hint that he move out. Judith's aunt had made a similar suggestion two days earlier. Since he had left his job at the library (the small rental he charged the others paid for the little food he needed) he spent most of his time in the room, seeing rather more of the old man than he wanted to, but he had learned to tolerate him.

Settling himself, he noticed that the right-hand spire of the wardrobe, all he had been able to see of it for the past two months, was now dismantled.

It had been a beautiful piece of furniture, in a way symbolising this whole private world, and the salesman at the store told him there were few like it left. For a moment Ward felt a sudden pang of regret, as he had done as a child when his father, in a moment of exasperation, had taken something away from him and he had known he would never see it again.

Then he pulled himself together. It was a beautiful wardrobe, without doubt, but when it was gone it would make the room seem even larger.

23

The Lemon Orchard

(1962)

Alex la Guma

The men came down between two long, regular rows of trees. The winter had not passed completely and there was a chill in the air; and the moon was hidden behind long, high parallels of cloud which hung like suspended streamers of dirty cotton wool in the sky. All of the men but one wore thick clothes against the coolness of the night. The night and earth was cold and damp, and the shoes of the men sank into the soil and left exact, ridged foot prints, but they could not be seen in the dark.

One of the men walked ahead holding a small cycle lantern that worked from a battery, leading the way down the avenue of trees while the others came behind in the dark. The night close around was quiet now that the crickets had stopped their small noises, but far out others that did not feel the presence of the men continued the monotonous creek-creek-creek. Somewhere, even further, a dog started barking in short high yaps, and then stopped abruptly. The men were walking through an orchard of lemons and the sharp, bitter-sweet citrus smell hung gently on the night air.

'Do not go so fast,' the man who brought up the rear of the party called to the man with the lantern. 'It's as dark as a kaffir's soul here at the back.'

He called softly, as if the darkness demanded silence. He was a big man and wore khaki trousers and laced-up riding boots, and an old shooting jacket with leather patches on the right breast and the elbows.

The shotgun was loaded. In the dark this man's face was invisible except for a blur of shadowed hollows and lighter crags. Although he walked in the rear he was the leader of the party. The lantern-bearer slowed down for the rest to catch up with him.

'It's cold, too, Oom,' another man said.

'Cold?' the man with the shotgun asked, speaking with sarcasm. 'Are you colder than this verdomte hotnot, here?' And he gestured in the dark with the muzzle of the gun at the man who stumbled along in their midst and who was the only one not warmly dressed.

This man wore trousers and a raincoat which they had allowed him to pull on over his pyjamas when they had taken him from his lodgings, and he shivered now with chill, clenching his teeth to prevent them from chattering. He had not been given time to tie his shoes and the metal-covered ends of the laces clicked as he moved.

'Are you cold, hotnot?' the man with the light jeered.

The coloured man did not reply. He was afraid, but his fear was mixed with a stubbornness which forbade him to answer them.

'He is not cold,' the fifth man in the party said. 'He is shivering with fear. Is it not so, hotnot?'

The coloured man said nothing, but stared ahead of himself into the half-light made by the small lantern. He could see the silhouette of the man who carried the light, but he did not want to look at the two who flanked him, the one who had complained of the cold, and the one who had spoken of his fear. They each carried a sjambok and every now and then one of them slapped a corduroyed leg with his.

'He is dumb also,' the one who had spoken last chuckled.

'No, Andries. Wait a minute,' the leader who carried the shotgun said, and they all stopped between the row of trees. The man with the lantern turned and put the light on the rest of the party.

'What is it?' he asked.

'Wag'n oomblikkie. Wait a moment,' the leader said, speaking with forced casualness. 'He is not dumb. He is a slim hotnot; one of those educated bushmen. Listen, hotnot,' he addressed the coloured man, speaking angrily now. 'When a baas speaks to you, you answer him. Do you hear?' The coloured man's wrists were tied behind him with a riem and the leader brought the muzzle of the shotgun down, pressing it hard into the small of the man's back above where the wrists met. 'Do you hear, hotnot? Answer me or I will shoot a hole through your spine.'

The bound man felt the hard round metal of the gun muzzle through the loose raincoat and clenched his teeth. He was cold and tried to prevent himself from shivering in case it should be mistaken for cowardice. He heard the small metallic noise as the man with the gun thumbed back the hammer of the shotgun. In spite of the cold little drops of sweat began to form on his upper lip under the overnight stubble.

'For God's sake, don't shoot him,' the man with the light said, laughing a little nervously. 'We don't want to be involved in any murder.'

'What are you saying, man?' the leader asked. Now with the beam of the battery-lamp on his face the shadows in it were washed away to reveal the mass of tiny wrinkled and deep creases which covered the red-clay complexion of his face like the myriad lines which indicate rivers, streams, roads and railways on a map. They wound around the ridges of his chin and climbed the sharp range of his nose and the peaks of his chin and cheekbones, and his eyes were hard and blue like two frozen lakes.

'This is mos a slim hotnot,' he said again. 'A teacher in a school for which we pay. He lives off our sweat, and he had the audacity to be cheeky and uncivilised towards a minister of our church and no hotnot will be cheeky to a white man while I live.'

'Ja, man,' the lantern-bearer agreed. 'But we are going to deal with him. There is no necessity to shoot him. We don't want that kind of trouble.'

'I will shoot whatever hotnot or kaffir I desire, and see me get into trouble over it. I demand respect from these donders. Let them answer when they're spoken to.'

He jabbed the muzzle suddenly into the coloured man's back so that he stumbled struggling to keep his balance. 'Do you hear, jong? Did I not speak to you?' The man who had jeered about the prisoner's fear stepped up then, and hit him in the face, striking him on a cheekbone with the clenched fist which still held the sjambok. He was angry over the delay and wanted the man to submit so that they could proceed. 'Listen you hotnot bastard,' he said loudly. 'Why don't you answer?'

The man stumbled, caught himself and stood in the rambling shadow of one of the lemon trees. The lantern-light swung on him and he looked away from the centre of the beam. He was afraid the leader would shoot him in anger and he had no wish to die. He straightened up and looked away from them.

'Well?' demanded the man who had struck him.

'Yes, baas,' the bound man said, speaking with a mixture of dignity and contempt which was missed by those who surrounded him.

'Yes there,' the man with the light said. 'You could save yourself trouble. Next time you will remember. Now let us get on.' The lantern swung forward again and he walked ahead. The leader shoved their prisoner on with the muzzle of the shotgun, and he stumbled after the bobbing lantern with the other men on each side of him.

'The amazing thing about it is that this bliksem should have taken the principal, and the meester of the church before the magistrate and demand payment for the hiding they gave him for being cheeky to them,' the leader said to all in general. 'This verdomte hotnot. I have never heard of such a thing in all my born days.'

'Well, we will give him a better hiding,' the man, Andries said. 'This time we will teach him a lesson, Oom. He won't demand damages from anybody when we're done with him.'

'And afterwards he won't be seen around here again. He will pack his things and go and live in the city where they're not so particular about the dignity of the volk. Do you hear, hotnot?' This time they were not concerned about receiving a reply but the leader went on, saying, 'We don't want any educated hottentots in our town.'

'Neither black Englishmen,' added one of the others.

The dog started barking again at the farm house which was invisible on the dark hillside at the other end of the little valley. 'It's that Jagter,' the man with the lantern said. 'I wonder what bothers him. He is a good watchdog. I offered Meneer Marais five pounds for that dog, but he won't sell. I would like to have a dog like that. I would take great care of such a dog.'

The blackness of the night crouched over the orchard and the leaves rustled with a harsh whispering that was inconsistent with the pleasant scent of the lemons. The chill in the air had increased, and far-off the creek-creek-creek of the crickets blended into solid strips of high-pitched sound. Then the moon came from behind the banks of cloud and its white light touched the leaves with wet silver, and the perfume of lemons seemed to grow stronger, as if the juice was being crushed from them.

They walked a little way further in the moonlight and the man with the lantern said, 'This is as good a place as any, Oom.'

They had come into a wide gap in the orchard, a small amphitheatre surrounded by fragrant growth, and they all stopped within it. The moonlight clung for a while to the leaves and the angled branches, so that along their tips and edges the moisture gleamed with the quivering shine of scattered quicksilver.

24

The People Before

(1963)

Maurice Shadbolt

I

My father took on that farm not long after he came back from the first war. It was pretty well the last farm up the river. Behind our farm, and up the river, there was all kind of wild country. Scrub and jagged black humps on the hills, bush in gullies where fire hadn't reached; hills and more hills, deep valleys with caves and twisting rivers, and mountains white with winter in the distance. We had the last piece of really flat land on the river. It wasn't the first farm my father'd taken on – and it certainly wasn't to be the last – but it was the most remote. He always said that was why he'd got the place for a song. This puzzled me as a child. For I'd heard, of course, of having to sing for your supper. I wondered what words, to what tune, he was obliged to sing for the farm; and where, and why? Had he travelled up the river, singing a strange song, charming his way into possession of the land? It always perplexed me.

And it perplexed me because there wasn't much room for singing in my father's life. I can't remember ever having heard him sing. There was room for plodding his paddocks in all weathers, milking cows and sending cream down river to the dairy factory, and cursing the bloody Government; there was room in his life for all these things and more, but not for singing.

In time, of course, I understood that he only meant he'd bought the place cheaply. Cheaply meant for a song. I couldn't, even then, quite make the connexion. It remained for a long while one of those adult mysteries. And it was no use puzzling over it, no use asking my father for a more coherent explanation.

'Don't be difficult,' he'd say. 'Don't ask so many damn questions. Life's difficult enough, boy, without all your damn questions.'

He didn't mean to be unkind; it was just his way. His life was committed to winning order from wilderness. Questions were a disorderly intrusion, like gorse or weed springing up on good pasture. The best way was to hack them down, grub out the roots, before they could spread. And in the same way as he checked incipient anarchy on his land he hoped, perhaps, to check it in his son.

By that time I was old enough to understand a good many of the things that were to be understood. One of them, for example, was that we weren't the first people on that particular stretch of land. Thirty or forty years before, when white men first came into our part of the country, it was mostly forest. Those first people fired the forest, right back into the hills, and ran sheep. The sheep grazed not only the flat, but the hills which rose sharply behind our farm; the hills which, in our time, had become stubbly with manuka and fern. The flatland had been pretty much scrub too, the day my father first saw it; and the original people had been gone twenty years – they'd given up, or been ruined by the land; we never quite knew the story. The farmhouse stood derelict among the returning wilderness.

Well, my father saw right away that the land – the flat land – was a reasonable proposition for a dairy farm. There was a new launch service down to the nearest dairy factory, in the township ten miles away; only in the event of flood, or a launch breakdown, would he have to dispose of his cream by carrying it on a sledge across country, three miles, to the nearest road.

So he moved in, cleared the scrub, sowed new grass, and brought in cows. Strictly speaking, the hills at the back of the farm were his too, but he had no use for them. They made good shelter from the westerlies. Otherwise he never gave the hills a thought, since he had all the land he could safely manage; he roamed across them after wild pig, and that was about all. There were bones up there, scattered skeletons of lost sheep, in and about the scrub and burnt stumps.

Everything went well; he had the place almost paid off by the time of the depression. 'I never looked back, those years,' he said long afterwards. It was characteristic of him not to look back. He was not interested in who had the farm before him. He had never troubled to inquire. So far as he was concerned, history only began the day he first set foot on the land. It was his, by sweat and legal title: that was all that mattered. That was all that could matter.

He had two boys; I was the elder son. 'You and Jim will take this place over one day,' he often told me. 'You'll run it when I get tired.'

But he didn't look like getting tired. He wasn't a big man, but he was wiry and thin with a lean face and cool blue eyes; he was one of those people who can't keep still. When neighbours called he couldn't ever keep comfortable in a chair, just sitting and sipping tea, but had to start walking them round the farm – or at least the male neighbours – pointing out things here and there. Usually work he'd done, improvements he'd made: the new milking-shed, the new water-pump on the river. He didn't strut or boast, though; he just pointed them out quietly, these jobs well done. He wanted others to share his satisfaction. There was talk of electricity coming through to the farm, the telephone; a road up the river was scheduled. It would all put the value of the property up. The risk he'd taken on the remote and abandoned land seemed justified in every way.

He didn't ever look like getting tired. It was as if he'd been wound up years before, like something clockwork, and set going: first fighting in the war, then fighting with the land; now most of the fighting was done, he sometimes found it quite an effort to keep busy. He never took a holiday. There was talk of taking a holiday, one winter when the cows dried off; talk of us all going down to the sea, and leaving a neighbour to look after the place. But I don't think he could have trusted anyone to look after his land, not even for a week or two in winter when the cows were dried off. Perhaps, when Jim and I were grown, it would be different. But not until? He always found some reason for us not to get away. Like our schooling.

'I don't want to interfere with their schooling,' he said once. 'They only get it once in their lives. And they might as well get it while they can. I didn't get much. And, by God, I regret it now. I don't know much, and I might have got along all right, but I might have got along a damn sight better if I'd had more schooling. And I'm not going to interfere with theirs by carting them off for a holiday in the middle of the year.'

Yet even then I wondered if he meant a word of it, if he really wasn't just saying that for something to say. He was wrangling at the time with my mother, who held opinions on a dwindling number of subjects. She never surrendered any of these opinions, exactly; she just kept them more and more to herself until, presumably, they lapsed quietly and died. As she herself, much later, was to lapse quietly from life, without much complaint.

For if he'd really been concerned about our schooling, he might have been more concerned about the way we fell asleep in afternoon classes. Not that we were the only ones. Others started getting pretty ragged in the afternoons too. A lot of us had been up helping our fathers since early in the morning. Jim and I were up at half-past four most mornings to help with the milking and working the separators. My father increased his herd year after year, right up to the depression. After school we rode home just in time for the evening milking. And by the time we finished it was getting dark; in winter it was dark by the time we were half-way through the herd.

I sometimes worried about Jim looking worn in the evenings, and I often chased him off inside before milking was finished. I thought Jim needed looking after; he wasn't anywhere near as big as me. I'd hear him scamper off to the house, and then I'd set about stripping the cows he had left. Father sometimes complained.

'You'll make that brother of yours a softy,' he said. 'The boy's got to learn what work means.'

'Jim's all right,' I answered. 'He's not a softy. He's just not very big. That's all.'

He detested softies, even the accomplices of softies. My mother, in a way, was such an accomplice. She'd never been keen about first me, then Jim, helping with work on the farm. But my father said he couldn't afford to hire a man to help with the herd. And he certainly couldn't manage by himself, without Jim and me.

'Besides,' he said, 'my Dad and me used to milk two hundred cows' – sometimes, when he became heated, the number rose to three hundred – 'when I was eight years old. And thin as a rake too, I was. Eight years old and thin as a rake. It didn't do me no harm. You boys don't know what work is, let me tell you.'

So there all argument finished. My mother kept one more opinion to herself.

And I suppose that, when I chased Jim off inside, I was only taking my mother's side in the argument – and was only another accomplice of softies. Anyway, it would give me a good feeling afterwards – despite anything my father would have to say –

when we tramped back to the house, through the night smelling of frost or rain, to find Jim sitting up at the table beside my mother while she ladled out soup under the warm yellow lamplight. He looked as if he belonged there, beside her; and she always looked, at those times, a little triumphant. Her look seemed to say that one child of hers, at least, was going to be saved from the muck of the cowshed. And I suppose that was the beginning of how Jim became his mother's boy.

I remained my father's. I wouldn't have exchanged him for another father. I liked seeing him with people, a man among men. This happened on winter Saturdays when we rode to the township for the football. We usually left Jim behind to look after my mother. We tethered our horses near the football field and went off to join the crowd. Football was one of the few things which interested my father outside the farm. He'd been a fine rugby forward in his day and people respected what he had to say about the game. He could out-argue most people; probably out-fight them too, if it ever came to that. He often talked about the fights he'd had when young. For he'd done a bit of boxing too, only he couldn't spare the time from his father's farm to train properly. He knocked me down once, with his bare fists, in the cowshed; and I was careful never to let it happen again. I just kept my head down for days afterwards, so that he wouldn't see the bruises on my face or the swelling round my eye.

At the football he barracked with the best of them in the thick of the crowd. Sometimes he called out when the rest of the crowd was silent and tense; he could be very sarcastic about poor players, softies who were afraid to tackle properly.

After the game he often called in, on the way home, to have a few beers with friends in the township's sly-grog shop – we didn't have a proper pub in the township – while I looked after the horses outside. Usually he'd find time, while he gossiped with friends, to bring me out a glass of lemonade. At times it could be very cold out there, holding the horses while the winter wind swept round, but it would be nice to know that I was remembered. When he finished we rode home together for a late milking. He would grow talkative, as we cantered towards dark, and even give me the impression he was glad of my company. He told me about the time he was young, what the world looked like when he was my age. His father was a sharemilker, travelling from place to place; that is, he owned no land of his own and did other people's work.

'So I made up my mind, boy,' he told me as we rode along together, 'I made up my mind I'd never be like that. I'd bend my head to no man. And you know what the secret of that is, boy? Land. Land of your own. You're independent, boy. You can say no to the world. That's if you got your own little kingdom. I reckon it was what kept me alive, down there on the beach at Gallipoli, knowing I'd have some land I could call my own.' This final declaration seemed to dismay him for some reason or other, perhaps because he feared he'd given too much of himself away. So he added half-apologetically, 'I had to think of something, you know, while all that shooting was going on. They say it's best to fix your mind on something if you don't want to be afraid. That's what I fixed my mind on, anyhow. Maybe it did keep me alive.'

In late winter or spring we sometimes arrived back, on Saturdays, to see the last trembling light of sunset fade from the hills and land. We'd canter along a straight stretch, coast up a rise, rein in the horses, and there it was – his green kingdom, his tight tamed acres beneath the hills and beside the river, a thick spread of fenced grass from the dark fringe of hillscrub down to the ragged willows above the water. And at the centre was his castle, the farmhouse, with the sheds scattered round, and the pine trees.

Reining in on that rise, I knew, gave him a good feeling. It would also be the time when he remembered all the jobs he'd neglected, all the work he should have done instead of going to the football. His conscience would keep him busy all day Sunday.

At times he wondered – it was a conversation out loud with himself – why he didn't sell up and buy another place. There were, after all, more comfortable farms, in more convenient locations nearer towns or cities. 'I've built this place up from nothing,' he said, 'I've made it pay, and pay well. I've made this land worth something. I could sell out for a packet. Why don't I?'

He never really – in my presence anyway – offered himself a convincing explanation. Why didn't he? He'd hardly have said he loved the land: love, in any case, would have been an extravagance. Part of whatever it was, I suppose, was the knowledge that he'd built where someone else had failed; part was that he'd given too much of himself there, to be really free anywhere else. It wouldn't be the same, walking on to another successful farm, a going concern, everything in order. No, this place – this land from the river back up to the hills – was his. In a sense it had only ever been his. That was why he felt so secure.

If Sunday was often the day when he worked hardest, it was also the best day for Jim and me, our free day. After morning milking, and breakfast, we did more or less what we liked. In summer we swam down under the river-willows; we also had a canoe tied there and sometimes we paddled up-river, under great limestone bluffs shaggy with toi toi, into country which grew wilder and wilder. There were huge bearded caves in the bush above the water which we explored from time to time. There were also big eels to be fished from the pools of the river.

As he grew older Jim turned more into himself, and became still quieter. You could never guess exactly what he was thinking. It wasn't that he didn't enjoy life; he just had his own way of enjoying it. He didn't like being with his father, as I did; I don't even know that he always enjoyed being with me. He just tagged along with me: we were, after all, brothers. When I was old enough, my father presented me with a .22 rifle; Jim never showed great enthusiasm for shooting. He came along with me, all right, but he never seemed interested in the rabbits or wild goat I shot, or just missed. He wandered around the hills, way behind me, entertaining himself and collecting things. He gathered leaves, and tried to identify the plants from which the leaves came. He also collected stones, those of some interesting shape or texture; he had a big collection of stones. He tramped along, in his slow, quiet way, poking into everything, adding to his collections. He wasn't too slow and quiet at school, though; he was faster than most of us with an answer. He borrowed books from the teacher, and took them home. So in time he became even smarter with his answers. I grew to accept his difference from most people. It didn't disturb me particularly: on the farm he was still quiet, small Jim. He was never too busy with his books to come along with me on Sundays.

*

There was a night when Jim was going through some new stones he'd gathered. Usually, in the house, my father didn't take much notice of Jim, his reading or his hobbies. He'd fought a losing battle for Jim, through the years, and now accepted his defeat. Jim still helped us with the herd, night and morning, but in the house he was ignored. But this night my father went across to the table and picked up a couple of the new stones. They were greenish, both the same triangular shape.

'Where'd you get these?' he asked.

Jim thought for a moment; he seemed pleased by the interest taken in him. 'One was back in the hills,' he said. 'The other was in a cave up the river. I just picked them up.'

'You mean you didn't find them together?'

'No,' Jim said.

'Funny,' my father said. 'They look like greenstone. I seen some greenstone once. A joker found it, picked it up in the bush. Jade, it is; same thing. This joker sold it in the city for a packet. Maori stuff. Some people'll buy anything.'

We all crossed to the table and looked down at the greenish stone. Jim's eyes were bright with excitment.

'You mean these used to belong to the Maoris?' he said. 'These stones?'

'Must have,' my father said. 'Greenstone doesn't come natural round here. You look it up in your books and you'll see. Comes from way down south, near the mountains and glaciers. Had to come up here all the way by canoe. They used to fight about greenstone once.' He paused and looked at the stones again. 'Yes,' he added. 'I reckon that's greenstone, all right. You never know, might be some money in that stuff.'

Money was a very important subject in our house at that time. It was in a lot of households, since that time was the depression. In the cities they were marching in the streets and breaking shop windows. Here on the farm it wasn't anywhere near so dramatic. The grass looked much the same as it had always looked; so did the hills and river. All that had happened, really, was that the farm had lost its value. Prices had fallen; my father sometimes wondered if it was worth while sending cream to the factory. Some of the people on poorer land, down the river, had walked off their properties. Everything was tighter. We had to do without new clothes, and there wasn't much variety in our eating. We ran a bigger garden, and my father went out more frequently shooting wild pig for meat. He had nothing but contempt for the noisy people in the city, the idlers and wasters who preferred to go shouting in the streets rather than fetch a square meal for their families, as he did with his rifle. He thought they, in some way, were to blame for the failure of things. Even so, he became gripped by the idea that he might have failed himself, somehow; he tried to talk himself out of this idea – in my presence – but without much success. Now he had the land solid beneath his feet, owned it entirely, it wasn't much help at all. If it wasn't for our garden and the wild pig we might starve. The land didn't bring him any money; he might even have to leave it. He had failed, perhaps much as the land's former owners had failed; why? He might have answered the question for himself satisfactorily, while he grubbed away at the scrub encroaching on our pasture; but I doubt it.

'Yes,' he said. 'Might be some money in that stuff.'

But Jim didn't seem to hear, or understand. His eyes were still bright. 'That means there must have been Maoris here in the old days,' he said.

'I suppose there must have,' my father agreed. He didn't seem much interested. Maoris were Maoris. There weren't many around our part of the river; they were mostly down towards the coast. (Shortly after this, Jim did some research and told me the reason why. It turned out that the land about our part of the river had been confiscated from them after the Maori wars.) 'They were most places, weren't they?' he added.

'Yes,' Jim said. 'But I mean they must have been here. On our place.'

'Well, yes. They could of been. Like I said, they were most places.'

It didn't seem to register as particularly important. He picked up the greenstone again. 'We ought to find out about this,' he continued. 'There might be a bit of money in it.'

Later Jim took the stones to school and had them identified as Maori adzes. My father said once again that perhaps there was money in them. But the thing was, where to find a buyer? It mightn't be as easy as it used to be. So somehow it was all forgotten. Jim kept the adzes.

Jim and I did try to find again that cave in which he had picked up an adze. We found a lot of caves, but none of them seemed the right one. Anyway we didn't pick up another adze. We did wander down one long dripping cave, striking matches, and in the dark I tripped on something. I struck another match and saw some brownish-looking bones. 'A sheep,' I said. 'It must have come in here and got lost.'

Jim was silent; I wondered why. Then I saw he wasn't looking at the bones, but at a human skull propped on a ledge of the cave. It just sat there sightless, shadows dancing in its sockets.

We got out of that cave quickly. We didn't even talk about it when we reached home. On the whole I preferred going out with my .22 after rabbits.

II

It was near the end of the depression. But we didn't know that then, of course. It might have been just the beginning, for all we knew. My father didn't have as much interest in finishing jobs as he used to have. He tired easily. He'd given his best to the land, and yet his best still wasn't good enough. There wasn't much sense in anything and his dash was done. He kept going out of habit.

I'd been pulled out of school to help with the farm. Jim still more or less went to school. I say more or less because he went irregularly. This was because of sickness. Once he was away in hospital two months. And of course it cost money; my father said we were to blame, we who allowed Jim to become soft and sickly. But the doctor thought otherwise; he thought Jim had been worked hard enough already. And when Jim returned to the farm he no longer helped with the herd. And this was why I had to leave school: if he couldn't have both of us working with him part-time, my father wanted one full-time. Jim was entirely surrendered at last, to the house and books, to school and my mother. I didn't mind working on the farm all day, with my father; it was, after all, what I'd always wanted. All the same, I would have been happier if he had been: his doubts about himself, more and more frequently expressed, disturbed me. It wasn't like my father at all. He was convinced now he'd done the wrong thing, somewhere. He went back through the years, levering each year up like a stone, to see what lay beneath; he never seemed to find anything. It was worst of all in winter, when the land looked bleak, the hills were grey with low cloud, and the rain swirled out of the sky. All life vanished from his face and I knew he detested everything: the land which had promised him independence was now only a muddy snare; he was bogged here, between hills and river, and couldn't escape. He had no pride left in him for the place. If he could have got a price for the farm he would have gone. But there was no longer any question of a price. He could walk off if he liked. Only the bush would claim it back.

It was my mother who told us there were people coming. She had taken the telephone message while we were out of the house, and Jim was at the school.

'Who are they?' my father said.

'I couldn't understand very well. It was a bad connexion. I think they said they were the people who were here before.'

'The people who were here before? What the hell do they want here?' His eyes became suspicious under his frown.

'I think they said they just wanted to have a look around.'

'What the hell do they want here?' my father repeated, baffled. 'Nothing for them to see. This farm's not like it was when they were here. Everything's different. I've made a lot of changes. They wouldn't know the place. What do they want to come back for?'

'Well,' my mother sighed, 'I'm sure I don't know.'

'Perhaps they want to buy it,' he said abruptly; the words seemed simultaneous with his thought, and he stiffened with astonishment. 'By God, yes. They might want to buy the place back again. I hadn't thought of that. Wouldn't that be a joke? I'd sell, all right – for just about as much as I paid for the place. I tell you, I'd let it go for a song, for a bloody song. They're welcome.'

'But where would we go?' she said, alarmed.

'Somewhere,' he said. 'Somewhere new. Anywhere.'

'But there's nowhere,' she protested. 'Nowhere any better. You know that.'

'And there's nowhere any worse,' he answered. 'I'd start again somewhere. Make a better go of things.'

'You're too old to start again,' my mother observed softly.

There was a silence. And in the silence I knew that what my mother said was true. We all knew it was true.

'So we just stay here,' he said. 'And rot. Is that it?' But he really wished to change the subject. 'When are these people coming?'

'Tomorrow, I think. They're staying the night down in the township. Then they're coming up by launch.'

'They didn't say why they were interested in the place?'

'No. And they certainly didn't say they wanted to buy it. You might as well get that straight now. They said they just wanted a look around.'

'I don't get it. I just don't get it. If I walked off this place I wouldn't ever want to see it again.'

'Perhaps they're different,' my mother said. 'Perhaps they've got happy memories of this place.'

'Perhaps they have. God knows.'

It was early summer, with warm lengthening days. That sunny Saturday morning I loitered about the house with Jim, waiting for the people to arrive. Eventually, as the sun climbed higher in the sky, I grew impatient and went across the paddocks to help my father. We were working together when we heard the sound of the launch coming up the river.

'That's them,' he said briefly. He dropped his slasher for a moment, and spat on his hands. Then he took up the slasher again and chopped into a new patch of unruly gorse.

I was perplexed. 'Well,' I said, 'aren't you going down to meet them?'

'I'll see them soon enough. Don't worry.' He seemed to be conducting an argument with himself as he hacked into the gorse. 'I'm in no hurry. No, I'm in no hurry to see them.'

I just kept silent beside him.

'Who are they, anyway?' he went on. 'What do they want to come traipsing round my property for? They've got a bloody cheek.'

The sound of the launch grew. It was probably travelling round the last bend in the river now, past the swamp of raupo, and banks prickly with flax and toi toi. They were almost at the farm. Still chopping jerkily, my father tried to conceal his unease.

'What do they want?' he asked for the last time. 'By God, if they've come to gloat, they've got another thing coming. I've made something decent out of this place, and I don't care who knows it.'

He had tried everything in his mind and it was no use: he was empty of explanation. Now we could see the launch white on the gleaming river. It was coasting up to the bank. We could also see people clustered on board.

'Looks like a few of them,' I observed. If I could have done so without upsetting my father, I would have run down to meet the launch, eager with curiosity. But I kept my distance until he finished arguing with himself.

'Well,' he said, as if he'd never suggested otherwise, 'we'd better go down to meet them, now they're here.' He dug his slasher into the earth and began to stalk off down to the river. I followed him. His quick strides soon took him well ahead of me; I had to run to keep up.

Then we had our surprise. My father's step faltered; I blundered up alongside him. We saw the people climbing off the launch. And we saw who they were, at last. My father stopped perfectly still and silent. They were Maoris. We were still a hundred yards or more away, but there was no mistaking their clothing and colour. They were Maoris, all right.

'There's something wrong somewhere,' he said at last. 'It doesn't make sense. No Maori ever owned this place. I'd have known. Who the hell do they think they are, coming here?'

I couldn't answer him. He strode on down to the river. There were young men, and two old women with black head-scarves. And last of all there was something the young men carried. As we drew nearer we saw it was an old man in a rough litter. The whole party of them fussed over making the old man comfortable. The old women, particularly; they had tattoos on their chins and wore sharktooth necklaces. They straightened the old man's blankets and fixed the pillow behind his head. He had a sunken, withered face and he didn't look so much sick, as tired. His eyes were only half-open as everyone fussed around. It looked as if it were a great effort to keep them that much open. His hair was mostly grey, and his dry flesh sagged in thin folds about his ancient neck. I reckoned that he must have been near enough to a hundred years old. The young men talked quickly among themselves as they saw my father approaching. One came forward, apparently as spokesman. He looked about the oldest of them, perhaps thirty. He had a fat, shiny face.

'Here,' said my father. 'What's all this about?' I knew his opinion of Maoris: they were lazy, drank too much, and caused trouble. They just rode on the backs of the men on the land, like the loafers in the cities. He always said we were lucky there were so few in our district. 'What do you people think you're doing here?' he demanded.

'We rang up yesterday,' the spokesman said. 'We told your missus we might be coming today.'

'I don't know about that. She said someone else was coming. The people who were here before.'

'Well,' said the young man, smiling. 'We were the people before.'

'I don't get you. You trying to tell me you owned this place?'

'That's right. We owned all the land round this end of the river. Our tribe.'

'That must have been a hell of a long time ago.'

'Yes,' agreed the stranger. 'A long time.' He was pleasantly spoken and patient. His round face, which I could imagine looking jolly, was very solemn just then.

I looked around and saw my mother and Jim coming slowly down from the house.

'I still don't get it,' my father said. 'What do you want?'

'We just want to go across your land, if that's all right. Look, we better introduce ourselves. My name is Tom Taikaka. And this—'

My father was lost in a confusion of introductions. But he still didn't shake anyone's hand. He just stood his ground, aloof and faintly hostile. Finally there was the old man. He looked as though he had gone to sleep again.

'You see he's old,' Tom explained. 'And has not so long to live. He is the last great man of our tribe, the oldest. He wishes to see again where he was born. The land over which his father was chief. He wishes to see this before his spirit departs for Rerengawairua.'

By this time my mother and Jim had joined us. They were as confused as we were.

'You mean you've come just to—' my father began.

'We've come a long way,' Tom said. 'Nearly a hundred miles, from up the coast. That's where we live now.'

'All this way. Just so—'

'Yes,' Tom said. 'That's right.'

'Well,' said my father. 'What do you know? What do you know about that?' Baffled, he looked at me, at my mother, and even finally at Jim. None of us had anything to say.

'I hope we're not troubling you,' Tom said politely. 'We don't want to be any trouble. We just want to go across your land, if that's all right. We got our own tucker and everything.'

We saw this was true. The two old women had large flax kits of food.

'No liquor?' my father said suspiciously. 'I don't want any drinking round my place.'

'No,' Tom replied. His face was still patient. 'No liquor. We don't plan on any drinking.'

The other young men shyly agreed in the background. It was not, they seemed to say, an occasion for drinking.

'Well,' said my father stiffly, 'I suppose it's all right. Where are you going to take him?' He nodded towards the old sleeping man.

'Just across your land. And up to the old *pa*.'

'I didn't know there used to be any *pa* round here.'

'Well,' said Tom. 'It used to be up there.' He pointed out the largest hill behind our farm, one that stood well apart and above the others. We called it Craggy Hill, because of limestone outcrops. Its flanks and summit were patchy with tall scrub. We seldom went near it, except perhaps when out shooting; then we circled its steep slopes rather than climbed it. 'You'd see the terraces,' Tom said, 'if it wasn't for the scrub. It's all hidden now.'

Now my father looked strangely at Tom. 'Hey,' he said, 'You sure you aren't having me on? How come you know that hill straight off? You ever been here before?'

'No,' Tom said. His face shone as he sweated with the effort of trying to explain everything. 'I never been here before. I never been in this part of the country before.'

'Then how do you know that's the hill, eh?'

'Because,' Tom said simply, 'the old men told me. They described it so well I could find the place blindfold. All the stories of our tribe are connected with that hill. That's where we lived, up there, for hundreds of years.'

'Well, I'll be damned. What do you know about that?' My father blinked, and looked up at the hill again. 'Just up there, eh? And for hundreds of years.'

'That's right.'

'And I never knew. Well, I'll be damned.'

'There's lots of stories about that hill,' Tom said. 'And a lot of battles fought round here. Over your place.'

'Right over my land?'

'That's right. Up and down here, along the river.'

My father was so astonished he forgot to be aloof. He was trying to fit everything into his mind at once – the hill where they'd lived hundreds of years, the battles fought across his land – and it was too much.

'The war canoes would come up here,' Tom went on. 'I reckon they'd drag them up somewhere here' – he indicated the grassy bank on which we were standing – 'in the night, and go on up to attack the *pa* before sunrise. That's if we hadn't sprung a trap for them down here. There'd be a lot of blood soaked into this soil.' He kicked at the earth beneath our feet. 'We had to fight a long while to keep this land here, a lot of battles. Until there was a day when it was no use fighting any more. That was when we left.'

We knew, without him having to say it, what he meant. He meant the day when the European took the land. So we all stood quietly for a moment. Then my mother spoke.

'You'd better come up to the house,' she said. 'I'll make you all a cup of tea.'

A cup of tea was her solution to most problems.

We went up to the house slowly. The young men followed behind, carrying the litter. They put the old man in the shade of a tree, outside the house. Since it seemed the best thing to do, we all sat around him; there wouldn't have been room for everyone in our small kitchen anyway. We waited for my mother to bring out the tea.

Then the old man woke. He seemed to shiver, his eyes opened wide, and he said something in Maori. 'He wonders where he is,' Tom explained. He turned back to the old man and spoke in Maori.

He gestured, he pointed. Then the old man knew. We all saw it the moment the old man knew. It was as if we were all willing him towards that moment of knowledge. He quivered and tried to lift himself weakly; the old women rushed forward to help him. His eyes had a faint glitter as he looked up to the place we called Craggy Hill. He did not see us, the house, or anything else. Some more Maori words escaped him in a long, sighing rush. '*Te Wahiokoahoki*,' he said.

'It is the name,' Tom said, repeating it. 'The name of the place.'

The old man lay back against the women, but his eyes were still bright and trembling. They seemed to have a life independent of his wrinkled flesh. Then the lids came down, and they were gone again. We could all relax.

'*Te Wahiokoahoki*,' Tom said. 'It means the place of happy return. It got the name when we returned there after our victories against other tribes.'

My father nodded. 'Well, I'll be damned,' he said. 'That place there. And I never knew.' He appeared quite affable now.

My mother brought out tea. The hot cups passed from hand to hand, steaming and sweet.

'But not so happy now, eh?' Tom said. 'Not for us.'

'No. I don't suppose so.'

Tom nodded towards the old man. 'I reckon he was just about the last child born up there. Before we had to leave. Soon there'll be nobody left who lived there. That's why they wanted young men to come back. So we'd remember too.'

Jim went into the house and soon returned. I saw he carried the greenstone adzes he'd found. He approached Tom shyly.

'I think these are really yours,' he said, the words an effort.

Tom turned the adzes over in his hand. Jim had polished them until they were a vivid green. 'Where'd you get these, eh?' he asked.

Jim explained how and where'd he found them. 'I think they're really yours,' he repeated.

There was a brief silence. Jim stood with his eyes downcast, his treasure surrendered. My father watched anxiously; he plainly thought Jim a fool.

'You see,' Jim added apologetically, 'I didn't think they really belonged to anyone. That's why I kept them.'

'Well,' Tom said, embarrassed. 'That's real nice of you. Real nice of you, son. But you better keep them, eh? They're yours now. You find, you keep. We got no claims here any more. This is your father's land now.'

Then it was my father who seemed embarrassed. 'Leave me out of this,' he said sharply. 'You two settle it between you. It's none of my business.'

'I think you better keep them all the same,' Tom said to Jim.

Jim was glad to keep the greenstone, yet a little hurt by rejection of his gift. He received the adzes back silently.

'I tell you what,' Tom went on cheerfully, 'you ever find another one, you send it to me, eh? Like a present. But you keep those two.'

'All right,' Jim answered, clutching the adzes. He seemed much happier. 'I promise if I find any more, I'll send them to you.'

'Fair enough,' Tom smiled, his face jolly. Yet I could see that he too really wanted the greenstone.

After a while they got up to leave. They made the old man comfortable again and lifted him. 'We'll see you again tomorrow,' Tom said. 'The launch will be back to pick us up.'

'Tomorrow?' my father said. It hadn't occurred to him that they might be staying overnight on his land.

'We'll make ourselves a bit of a camp up there tonight,' Tom said, pointing to Craggy Hill. 'We ought to be comfortable up there. Like home, eh?' The jest fell mildly from his lips.

'Well, I suppose that's all right.' My father didn't know quite what to say. 'Nothing you want?'

'No,' Tom said. 'We got all we want, thanks. We'll be all right. We got ourselves. That's the important thing, eh?'

We watched them move away, the women followed by the young men with the litter. Tom went last, Jim trotting along beside him. They seemed, since the business of the greenstone, to have made friends quickly. Tom appeared to be telling Jim a story.

I thought for a moment that my father might call Jim back. But he didn't. He let him go.

The old women now, I noticed, carried green foliage. They beat it about them as they walked across our paddocks and up towards Craggy Hill; they were chanting or singing, and their wailing sound came back to us. Their figures grew smaller with distance. Soon they were clear of the paddocks and beginning to climb.

My father thumbed back his hat and rubbed a handkerchief across his brow. 'Well, I'll be damned,' he said.

*

We sat together on the porch that evening, as we often did in summer after milking and our meal. Yet that evening was very different from any other. The sun had set, and in the dusk we saw faint smoke rising from their campfire on Craggy Hill, the place of happy return. Sometimes I thought I heard the wailing sound of the women again, but I couldn't quite be sure.

What were they doing up there, what did they hope to find? We both wondered and puzzled, yet didn't speak to each other.

Jim had returned long before, with stories. It seemed he had learned, one way and another, just about all there was to be learned about the tribe that had once lived on Craggy Hill. At the dinner table he told the stories breathlessly. My father affected to be not much interested; and so, my father's son, did I. Yet we listened, all the same.

'Then there was the first musket,' Jim said. 'The first musket in this part of the country. Someone bought it from a trader down south and carried it back to the *pa*. Another tribe, one of their old enemies, came seeking *utu* – *utu* means revenge – for something that had been done to them the year before. And when they started climbing up the hill they were knocked off, one by one, with the musket. They'd never seen anything like it before. So the chief of the tribe on Craggy Hill made a sign of peace and called up his enemies. It wasn't a fair fight, he said, only one tribe with a musket. So he'd let his enemies have the musket for a while. They would have turns with the musket, each tribe. He taught the other tribe how to fire and point the musket. Then they separated and started the battle again. And the next man to be killed by the musket was the chief's eldest son. That was the old man's uncle – the old man who was here today.'

'Well, I don't know', said my father. 'Sounds bloody queer to me. That's no way to fight a battle.'

'That's the way they fought,' Jim maintained.

So we left Jim, still telling stories to my mother, and went out on the porch.

The evening thickened. Soon the smoke of the campfire was lost. The hills grew dark against the pale sky. And at last my father, looking up at the largest hill of all, spoke softly.

'I suppose a man's a fool,' he said. 'I should never have let that land go. Shouldn't ever have let it go back to scrub. I could have run a few sheep up there. But I just let it go. Perhaps I'll burn it off one day, run a few sheep. Sheep might pay better too, the way things are now.'

But it wasn't somehow, quite what I expected him to say. I suppose he was trying to make sense of things in his own fashion.

III

They came down off Craggy Hill the next day. The launch had been waiting for them in the river some time.

When we saw the cluster of tiny figures, moving at a fair pace down the hills, we sensed there was something wrong. Then, as they drew nearer, approaching us across the paddocks, we saw what was wrong. There was no litter, no old man. They all walked freely, separately. They were no longer burdened.

Astonished, my father strode up to Tom. 'Where is he?' he demanded.

'We left him back up there,' Tom said. He smiled sadly and I had a queer feeling that I knew exactly what he would say.

'Left him up there?'

'He died last night, or this morning. When we went to wake him he was cold. So we left him up there. That's where he wanted to be.'

'You can't do that,' my father protested. 'You can't just leave a dead man like that. Leave him anywhere. And, besides, it's my land you're leaving him on.'

'Yes,' Tom said. 'Your land.'

'Don't you understand? You can't just leave dead people around. Not like that.'

'But we didn't just leave him around. We didn't just leave him anywhere. We made him all safe and comfortable. He's all right. You needn't worry.'

'Christ, man,' my father said. 'Don't you see?'

But he might have been asking a blind man to see. Tom just smiled patiently and said not to worry. Also he said they'd better be catching the launch. They had a long way to go home, a tiring journey ahead.

And as he walked off, my father still arguing beside him, the old women clashed their dry greenery, wailing, and their shark-tooth necklaces danced under their heaving throats.

In a little while the launch went noisily off down the river. My father stood on the bank, still yelling after them. When he returned to the house, his voice was hoarse.

He had a police party out, a health officer too. They scoured the hills, and most of the caves they could find. They discovered no trace of a burial, nor did they find anything in the caves. At one stage someone foolishly suggested we might have imagined it all. So my father produced the launchman and people from the township as witnesses to the fact that an old Maori, dying, had actually been brought to our farm.

That convinced them. But it didn't take them anywhere near finding the body. They traced the remnants of the tribe, living up the coast, and found that indeed an old man of the tribe was missing. No one denied that there had been a visit to our farm. But they maintained that they knew nothing about a body. The old man, they said, had just wandered off into the bush; they hadn't found him again.

He might, they added, even still be alive. Just to be on the safe side, in case there was any truth in their story, the police put the old man on the missing persons register, for all the good that might have done.

But we knew. We knew every night we looked up at the hills that he was there, somewhere.

So he was still alive, in a way. Certainly it was a long time before he let us alone.

And by then my father had lost all taste for the farm. It seemed the land itself had heaped some final indignity upon him, made a fool of him. He never talked again, anyway, about running sheep on the hills.

When butter prices rose and land values improved, a year or two afterwards, he had no hesitation in selling out. We shifted into another part of the country entirely, for a year or two, and then into another. Finally we found ourselves milking a small herd for town supply, not far from the city. We're still on that farm, though there's talk of the place being purchased soon for a city sub-division. We think we might sell, but we'll face the issue when it arises.

Now and then Jim comes to see us, smart in a city suit, a lecturer at the university. My father always found it difficult to talk to Jim, and very often now he goes off to bed and leaves us to it. One thing I must say about Jim: he has no objection to helping with the milking. He insists that he enjoys it; perhaps he does. It's all flatland round our present farm, with one farm much like another, green grass and square farmhouses and pine shelter belts, and it's not exactly the place to sit out on a summer evening and watch shadows gathering on the hills. Because there aren't hills within sight; or shadows either, for that matter. It's all very tame and quiet, apart from cars speeding on the highway.

I get on reasonably well with Jim. We read much the same books, have much the same opinions on a great many subjects. The city hasn't made a great deal of difference to him. We're both married, with young families. We also have something else in common: we were both in the war, fighting in the desert. One evening after milking, when we stood smoking and yarning in the cool, I remembered something and decided I might put a question to Jim.

'You know,' I began, 'they say it's best, when you're under fire in the war, to fix your mind on something remote. So you won't be afraid. I remember Dad telling me that. I used to try. But it never seemed any good. I couldn't think of anything. I was still as scared as hell.'

'I was too. Who wasn't?'

'But, I mean, did you ever think of anything?'

'Funny thing,' he said. 'Now I come to think of it, I did. I thought of the old place – you know, the old place by the river. Where,' he added, and his face puckered into a grin, 'where they buried that old Maori. And where I found those greenstones. I've still got it at home, you know, up on the mantelpiece. I seem to remember trying to give it away once, to those Maoris. Now I'm glad I didn't. It's my only souvenir from there, the only thing that makes that place still live for me.' He paused. 'Well, anyway, that's what I thought about. That old place of ours.'

I had a sharp pain. I felt the dismay of a long-distance runner who, coasting confidently to victory, imagining himself well ahead of the field, finds himself overtaken and the tape snapped at the very moment he leans forward to breast it. For one black moment it seemed I had been robbed of something which was rightfully mine.

I don't think I'll ever forgive him.

25

The Enemy

(1967)

V. S. Naipaul

I had always considered this woman, my mother, as the enemy. She was sure to misunderstand anything I did, and the time came when I thought she not only misunderstood me, but quite definitely disapproved of me. I was an only child, but for her I was one too many.

She hated my father, and even after he died she continued to hate him.

She would say, 'Go ahead and do what you doing. You is your father child, you hear, not mine.'

The real split between my mother and me happened not in Miguel Street, but in the country.

My mother had decided to leave my father, and she wanted to take me to her mother.

I refused to go.

My father was ill, and in bed. Besides, he had promised that if I stayed with him I was to have a whole box of crayons.

I chose the crayons and my father.

We were living at the time in Cunupia, where my father was a driver on the sugar estates. He wasn't a slave-driver, but a driver of free people, but my father used to behave as though the people were slaves. He rode about the estates on a big clumsy brown horse, cracking his whip at the labourers and people said – I really don't believe this – that he used to kick the labourers.

I don't believe it because my father had lived all his life in Cunupia and he knew that you really couldn't push the Cunupia people around. They are not tough people, but they think nothing of killing, and they are prepared to wait years for the chance to kill someone they don't like. In fact, Cunupia and Tableland are the two parts of Trinidad where murders occur often enough to ensure quick promotion for the policemen stationed there.

At first we lived in the barracks, but then my father wanted to move to a little wooden house not far away.

My mother said, 'You playing hero. Go and live in your house by yourself, you hear.'

She was afraid, of course, but my father insisted. So we moved to the house, and then trouble really started.

A man came to the house one day about midday and said to my mother, 'Where your husband?'

My mother said, 'I don't know.'

The man was cleaning his teeth with a twig from a hibiscus plant. He spat and said, 'It don't matter. I have time. I could wait.'

My mother said, 'You ain't doing nothing like that. I know what you thinking, but I have my sister coming here right now.'

The man laughed and said, 'I not doing anything. I just want to know when he coming home.'

I began to cry in terror.

The man laughed.

My mother said, 'Shut up this minute or I give you something really to cry about.'

I went to another room and walked about saying, 'Rama! Rama! Sita Rama!' This was what my father had told me to say when I was in danger of any sort.

I looked out of the window. It was bright daylight, and hot, and there was nobody else in all the wide world of bush and trees.

And then I saw my aunt walking up the road.

She came and she said, 'Anything wrong with you here? I was at home just sitting quite quiet, and I suddenly feel that something was going wrong. I feel I had to come to see.'

The man said, 'Yes, I know the feeling.'

My mother, who was being very brave all the time, began to cry.

But all this was only to frighten us, and we were certainly frightened. My father always afterwards took his gun with him, and my mother kept a sharpened cutlass by her hand.

Then, at night, there used to be voices, sometimes from the road, sometimes from the bushes behind the house. The voices came from people who had lost their way and wanted lights, people who had come to tell my father that his sister had died suddenly in Debe, people who had come just to tell my father that there was a big fire at the sugar-mill. Sometimes there would be two or three of these voices, speaking from different directions, and we would sit awake in the dark house, just waiting, waiting for the voices to fall silent. And when they did fall silent it was even more terrible.

My father used to say, 'They still outside. They want you to go out and look.'

And at four or five o'clock when the morning light was coming up we would hear the tramp of feet in the bush, feet going away.

As soon as darkness fell we would lock ourselves up in the house, and wait. For days there would sometimes be nothing at all, and then we would hear them again.

My father brought home a dog one day. We called it Tarzan. He was more of a playful dog than a watch-dog, a big hairy brown dog, and I would ride on its back.

When evening came I said, 'Tarzan coming in with us?'

He wasn't. He remained whining outside the door, scratching it with his paws.

Tarzan didn't last long.

One morning we found him hacked to pieces and flung on the top step.

We hadn't heard any noise the night before.

My mother began to quarrel with my father, but my father was behaving as though he didn't really care what happened to him or to any of us.

My mother used to say, 'You playing brave. But bravery ain't going to give any of us life, you hear. Let us leave this place.'

My father began hanging up words of hope on the walls of the house, things from the Gita and the Bible, and sometimes things he had just made up.

He also lost his temper more often with my mother, and the time came when as soon as she entered a room he would scream and pelt things at her.

So she went back to her mother and I remained with my father.

During those days my father spent a lot of his time in bed, and so I had to lie down with him. For the first time I really talked to my father. He taught me three things.

The first was this.

'Boy,' my father asked. 'Who is your father?'

I said, 'You is my father.'

'Wrong.'

'How that wrong?'

My father said, 'You want to know who your father really is? God is your father.'

'And what you is, then?'

'Me, what I is? I is – let me see, well, I is just a second sort of father, not your real father.'

This teaching was later to get me into trouble, particularly with my mother.

The second thing my father taught me was the law of gravity.

We were sitting on the edge of the bed, and he dropped the box of matches.

He asked, 'Now, boy, tell me why the matches drop.'

I said, 'But they bound to drop. What you want them to do? Go sideways?'

My father said, 'I will tell why they drop. They drop because of the laws of gravity.'

And he showed me a trick. He half filled a bucket with water and spun the bucket fast over his shoulder.

He said, 'Look, the water wouldn't fall.'

But it did. He got a soaking and the floor was wet.

He said, 'It don't matter. I just put too much water, that's all. Look again.'

The second time it worked.

The third thing my father taught me was the blending of colours. This was just a few days before he died. He was very ill, and he used to spend a lot of time shivering and mumbling; and even when he fell asleep I used to hear him groaning.

I remained with him on the bed most of the time.

He said to me one day, 'You got the coloured pencils?'

I took them from under the pillow.

He said, 'You want to see some magic?'

I said, 'What, you know magic really?'

He took the yellow pencil and filled in a yellow square.

He asked, 'Boy, what colour this is?'

I said, 'Yellow.'

He said, 'Just pass me the blue pencil now, and shut your eyes tight tight.'

When I opened my eyes he said, 'Boy, what colour this square is now?'

I said, 'You sure you ain't cheating?'

He laughed and showed me how blue and yellow make green.

I said. 'You mean if I take a leaf and wash it and wash it and wash it really good, it go be yellow or blue when I finish with it?'

He said, 'No. You see, is God who blend those colours. God, your father.'

I spent a lot of my time trying to make up tricks. The only one I could do was to put two match-heads together, light them, and make them stick. But my father knew that. But at last I found a trick that I was sure my father didn't know. He never got to know about it because he died on the night I was to show it him.

It had been a day of great heat, and in the afternoon the sky had grown low and heavy and black. It felt almost chilly in the house, and my father was sitting wrapped up in the rocking chair. The rain began to fall drop by heavy drop, beating like a hundred fists on the roof. It grew dark and I lit the oil lamp, sticking a pin in the wick, to keep away bad spirits from the house.

My father suddenly stopped rocking and whispered, 'Boy, they here tonight. Listen. Listen.'

We were both silent and I listened carefully, but my ears could catch nothing but the wind and the rain.

A window banged itself open. The wind whooshed in with heavy raindrops.

'God!' my father screamed.

I went to the window. It was a pitch black night, and the world was a wild and lonely place, with only the wind and the rain on the leaves. I had to fight to pull the window in, and before I could close it, I saw the sky light up with a crack of lightning.

I shut the window and waited for the thunder.

It sounded like a steamroller on the roof.

My father said, 'Boy, don't frighten. Say what I tell you to say.'

I went and sat at the foot of the rocking chair and I began to say, 'Rama! Rama! Sita Rama!'

My father joined in. He was shivering with cold and fright.

Suddenly he shouted, 'Boy, they here. They here. I hear them talking under the house. They could do what they like in all this noise and nobody could hear them.'

I said, 'Don't fraid, I have this cutlass here, and you have your gun.'

But my father wasn't listening.

He said, 'But it dark, man. It so dark. It so dark.'

I got up and went to the table for the oil lamp to bring it nearer. But just then there was an explosion of thunder so low it might have been just above the roof. It rolled and rumbled for a long long time. Then another window blew open and the oil lamp was blown out. The wind and the rain tore into the dark room.

My father screamed out once more, 'Oh God, it dark.'

I was lost in the black world. I screamed until the thunder died away and the rain had become a drizzle. I forgot all about the trick I had prepared for my father: the soap I had rubbed into the palms of my hands until it had dried and disappeared.

Everybody agreed on one thing. My mother and I had to leave the country. Port-of-Spain was the safest place. There was too a lot of laughter against my father, and it appeared that for the rest of my life I would have to bear the cross of a father who died from fright. But in a month or so I had forgotten my father, and I had begun to look upon myself as the boy who had no father. It seemed natural.

In fact, when we moved to Port-of-Spain and I saw what the normal relationship between father and son was – it was nothing more than the relationship between the beater and the beaten – when I saw this I was grateful.

My mother made a great thing at first about keeping me in my place and knocking out all the nonsense my father had taught me. I don't know why she didn't try harder, but the fact is that she soon lost interest in me, and she let me run about the street, only rushing down to beat me from time to time.

Occasionally, though, she would take the old firm line.

One day she kept me home. She said, 'No school for you today. I just sick of tying your shoe-laces for you. Today you go have to learn that!'

I didn't think she was being fair. After all, in the country none of us wore shoes and I wasn't used to them.

That day she beat me and beat me and made me tie knot after knot and in the end I still couldn't tie my shoe-laces. For years afterwards it was a great shame to me that I couldn't do a simple thing like that, just as how I couldn't peel an orange. But about the shoes I made up a little trick. I never made my mother buy shoes the correct size. I pretended that those shoes hurt, and I made her get me shoes a size or two bigger. Once the attendant had tied the laces up for me, I never undid them, and merely slipped my feet in and out of the shoes. To keep them on my feet, I stuck paper in the toes.

To hear my mother talk, you would think I was a freak. Nearly every little boy she knew was better and more intelligent. There was one boy she knew who helped his mother paint her house. There was another boy who could mend his own shoes. There was still another boy who at the age of thirteen was earning a good twenty dollars a month, while I was just idling and living off her blood.

Still, there were surprising glimpses of kindness.

There was the time, for instance, when I was cleaning some tumblers for her one Saturday morning. I dropped a tumbler and it broke. Before I could do anything about it my mother saw what had happened.

She said, 'How you break it?'

I said, 'It just slip off. It smooth smooth.'

She said, 'Is a lot of nonsense drinking from glass. They break up so easy.'

And that was all. I got worried about my mother's health.

She was never worried about mine.

She thought that there was no illness in the world a stiff dose of hot Epsom Salts couldn't cure. That was a penance I had to endure once a month. It completely ruined my weekend. And if there was something she couldn't understand, she sent me to the Health Officer in Tragarete Road. That was an awful place. You waited and waited and waited before you went in to see the doctor.

Before you had time to say, 'Doctor, I have a pain—' he would be writing out a prescription for you. And again you had to wait for the medicine. All the Health Office medicines were the same. Water and pink sediment half an inch thick.

Hat used to say of the Health Office, 'The Government taking up faith healing.'

My mother considered the Health Office a good place for me to go to. I would go there at eight in the morning and return any time after two in the afternoon. It kept me out of mischief, and it cost only twenty-four cents a year.

But you mustn't get the impression that I was a saint all the time. I wasn't. I used to have odd fits where I just couldn't take an order from anybody, particularly my mother. I used to feel that I would dishonour myself for life if I took anybody's orders. And life is a funny thing, really. I sometimes got these fits just when my mother was anxious to be nice to me.

The day after Hat rescued me from drowning at Docksite I wrote an essay for my schoolmaster on the subject, 'A Day at the Seaside'. I don't think any schoolmaster ever got an essay like that. I talked about how I was nearly drowned and how calmly I was facing death, with my mind absolutely calm, thinking, 'Well, boy, this is the end.' The teacher was so pleased he gave me ten marks out of twelve.

He said, 'I think you are a genius.'

When I went home I told my mother, 'That essay I write today, I get ten out of twelve for it.'

My mother said, 'How you so bold-face to lie brave brave so in front of my face? You want me give you a slap to turn your face?'

In the end I convinced her.

She melted at once. She sat down in the hammock and said. 'Come and sit down by me, son.'

Just then the crazy fit came on me.

I got very angry for no reason at all and I said, 'No, I not going to sit by you.'

She laughed and coaxed.

And the angrier she made me.

Slowly the friendliness died away. It had become a struggle between two wills. I was prepared to drown rather than dishonour myself by obeying.

'I ask you to come and sit down here.'

'I not sitting down.'

'Take off your belt.'

I took it off and gave it to her. She belted me soundly, and my nose bled, but still I didn't sit in the hammock.

At times like these I used to cry, without meaning it, 'If my father was alive you wouldn't be behaving like this.'

So she remained the enemy. She was someone from whom I was going to escape as soon as I grew big enough. That was, in fact, the main lure of adulthood.

Progress was sweeping through Port-of-Spain in those days. The Americans were pouring money into Trinidad and there was a lot of talk from the British about colonial development and welfare.

One of the visible signs of this progress was the disappearance of the latrines. I hated the latrines, and I used to wonder about the sort of men who came with their lorries at night and carted away the filth; and there was always the horrible fear of falling into a pit.

One of the first men to have decent lavatories built was Hat, and we made a great thing of knocking down his old latrine. All the boys and men went to give a hand. I was too small to give a hand, but I went to watch. The walls were knocked down one by one and in the end there was only one remaining.

Hat said, 'Boys, let we try to knock this one down in one big piece.'

And they did.

The wall swayed and began to fall.

I must have gone mad in that split second, for I did a Superman act and tried to prevent the wall falling.

I just remember people shouting, 'O God! Look out!'

I was travelling in a bus, one of the green buses of Sam's Super Service, from Port-of-Spain to Petit Valley. The bus was full of old women in bright bandanas carrying big baskets of eddoes, yams, bananas, with here and there some chickens. Suddenly the old women all began chattering, and the chickens began squawking. My head felt as though it would split, but when I tried to shout at the old women I found I couldn't open my mouth. I tried again, but all I heard, more distinctly now, was the constant chattering.

Water was pouring down my face.

I was flat out under a tap and there were faces above me looking down.

Somebody shouted, 'He recover. Is all right.'

Hat said, 'How you feeling?'

I said, trying to laugh, 'I feeling all right.'

Mrs Bhakcu said, 'You have any pains?'

I shook my head.

But, suddenly, my whole body began to ache. I tried to move my hand and it hurt.

I said, 'I think I break my hand.'

But I could stand, and they made me walk into the house.

My mother came and I could see her eyes glassy and wet with tears.

Somebody, I cannot remember who, said, 'Boy, you had your mother really worried.'

I looked at her tears, and I felt I was going to cry too. I had discovered that she could be worried and anxious for me.

I wished I were a Hindu god at that moment, with two hundred arms, so that all two hundred could be broken, just to enjoy that moment, and to see again my mother's tears.

26

Five-Twenty

(1968)

Patrick White

Most evenings, weather permitting, the Natwicks sat on the front veranda to watch the traffic. During the day the stream flowed, but towards five it began to thicken, it sometimes jammed solid like: the semi-trailers and refrigeration units, the decent old-style sedans, the mini-cars, the bombs, the Holdens and the Holdens. She didn't know most of the names. Royal did, he was a man, though never ever mechanical himself. She liked him to tell her about the vehicles, or listen to him take part in conversation with anyone who stopped at the fence. He could hold his own, on account of he was more educated, and an invalid has time to think.

They used to sit side by side on the tiled veranda, him in his wheelchair she had got him after the artheritis took over, her in the old cane. The old cane chair wasn't hardly presentable any more; she had torn her winter cardy on a nail and laddered several pair of stockings. You hadn't the heart to get rid of it, though. They brought it with them from Sarsaparilla after they sold the business. And now they could sit in comfort to watch the traffic, the big steel insects of nowadays, which put the wind up her at times.

Royal said, 'I reckon we're a shingle short to'uv ended up on the Parramatta Road.'

'You said we'd still see life,' she reminded, 'even if we lost the use of our legs.'

'But look at the traffic! Worse every year. And air. Rot a man's lungs quicker than the cigarettes. You should'uv headed me off. You who's supposed to be practical!'

'I thought it was what you wanted,' she said, keeping it soft; she had never been one to crow.

'Anyway, I already lost the use of me legs.'

As if she was to blame for that too. She was so shocked the chair sort of jumped. It made her blood run cold to hear the metal feet screak against the little draught-board tiles.

'Well, I 'aven't!' she protested. 'I got me legs, and will be able to get from 'ere to anywhere and bring 'ome the shopping. While I got me strength.'

She tried never to upset him by any show of emotion, but now she was so upset herself.

They watched the traffic in the evenings, as the orange light was stacked up in thick slabs, and the neon signs were coming on.

'See that bloke down there in the parti-coloured Holden?'

'Which?' she asked.

'The one level with our own gate.'

'The pink and brown?' She couldn't take all that interest tonight, only you must never stop humouring a sick man.

'Yairs. Pink. Fancy a man in a pink car!'

'Dusty pink is fashionable.' She knew that for sure.

'But a man!'

'Perhaps his wife chose it. Perhaps he's got a domineering wife.'

Royal laughed low. 'Looks the sort of coot who might like to be domineered, and if that's what he wants, it's none of our business, is it?'

She laughed to keep him company. They were such mates, everybody said. And it was true. She didn't know what she would do if Royal passed on first.

That evening the traffic had jammed. Some of the drivers began tooting. Some of them stuck their heads out, and yarned to one another. But the man in the pink-and-brown Holden just sat. He didn't look to either side.

Come to think of it, she had noticed him pass before. Yes. Though he wasn't in no way a noticeable man. Yes. She looked at her watch.

'Five-twenty,' she said. 'I seen that man in the pink-and-brown before. He's pretty regular. Looks like a business executive.'

Royal cleared his throat and spat. It didn't make the edge of the veranda. Better not to notice it, because he'd only create if she did. She'd get out the watering-can after she had pushed him inside.

'Business executives!' she heard. 'They're afraid people are gunner think they're poor class without they *execute*. In our day nobody was ashamed to *do*. Isn't that about right, eh?' She didn't answer because she knew she wasn't meant to. 'Funny sort of head that cove's got. Like it was half squashed. Silly-lookun bloody head!'

'Could have been born with it,' she suggested. 'Can't help what you're born with. Like your religion.'

There was the evening the Chev got crushed, only a young fellow too. Ahhh, it had stuck in her throat, thinking of the wife and kiddies. She ran in, and out again as quick as she could, with a couple of blankets, and the rug that was a present from Hazel. She had grabbed a pillow off their own bed.

She only faintly heard Royal shouting from the wheel-chair.

She arranged the blankets and the pillow on the pavement, under the orange sky. The young fellow was looking pretty sick, kept on turning his head as though he recognised and wanted to tell her something. Then the photographer from the *Mirror* took his picture, said she ought to be in it to add a touch of human interest, but she wouldn't. A priest came, the *Mirror* took his picture, administering what Mrs Dolan said they call Extreme Unkshun. Well, you couldn't poke fun at a person's religion any more than the shape of their head, and Mrs Dolan was a decent neighbour, the whole family, and clean.

When she got back to the veranda, Royal, a big man, had slipped down in his wheelchair.

He said, or gasped, 'Wotcher wanter do that for, Ella? How are we gunner get the blood off?'

She hadn't thought about the blood, when of course she was all smeared with it, and the blankets, and Hazel's good Onkaparinka. Anyway, it was her who would get the blood off.

'You soak it in milk or something,' she said. 'I'll ask. Don't you worry.'

Then she did something. She bent down and kissed Royal on the forehead in front of the whole Parramatta Road. She regretted it at once, because he looked that powerless in his invalid chair, and his forehead felt cold and sweaty.

But you can't undo things that are done.

It was a blessing they could sit on the front veranda. Royal suffered a lot by now. He had his long-standing hernia, which they couldn't have operated on, on account of he was afraid of his heart. And then the artheritis.

'Arthritis.'

'All right,' she accepted the correction. 'Arth-er-itis.'

It was all very well for men, they could manage more of the hard words.

'What have we got for tea?' he asked.

'Well,' she said, fanning out her hands on the points of her elbows, and smiling, 'it's a surprise.'

She looked at her watch. It was five-twenty.

'It's a coupler nice little bits of fillet Mr Ballard let me have.'

'Wotcher mean let you have? Didn't you pay for them?'

She had to laugh. 'Anything I have I pay for!'

'Well? Think we're in the fillet-eating class?'

'It's only a treat, Royal,' she said. 'I got a chump chop for myself. I like a nice chop.'

He stopped complaining, and she was relieved.

'There's that gentleman,' she said, 'in the Holden.'

They watched him pass, as sober as their own habits.

Royal – he had been his mother's little king. Most of his mates called him 'Roy'. Perhaps only her and Mrs Natwick had stuck to the christened name, they felt it suited.

She often wondered how Royal had ever fancied her: such a big man, with glossy hair, black, and a nose like on someone historical. She would never have said it, but she was proud of Royal's nose. She was proud of the photo he had of the old family home in Kent, the thatch so lovely, and Grannie Natwick sitting in her apron on a rush-bottom chair in front, looking certainly not all that different from Mum, with the aunts gathered round in leggermutton sleeves, all big nosey women like Royal.

She had heard Mum telling Royal's mother, 'Ella's a plain little thing, but what's better than cheerful and willing?' She had always been on the mousey side, she supposed, which didn't mean she couldn't chatter with the right person. She heard Mum telling Mrs Natwick, 'My Ella can wash and bake against any comers. Clever with her needle too.' She had never entered any of the competitions, like they told her she ought to, it would have made her nervous.

It was all the stranger that Royal had ever fancied her.

Once as they sat on the veranda watching the evening traffic, she said, 'Remember how you used to ride out in the old days from "Bugilbar" to Cootramundra?'

'Cootamundra.'

'Yes,' she said. 'Cootramundra.' (That's why they'd called the house 'Coota' when they moved to the Parramatta Road.)

She had been so dazzled on one occasion by his parti-coloured forehead and his black hair, after he had got down from the saddle, after he had taken off his hat, she had run and fetched a duster, and dusted Royal Natwick's boots. The pair of new elastic-sides was white with dust from the long ride. It only occurred to her as she polished she might be doing something shameful, but when she looked up, it seemed as though Royal Natwick saw nothing peculiar in Ella McWhirter dusting his boots. He might even have expected it. She was so glad she could have cried.

Old Mr Natwick had come out from Kent when a youth, and after working at several uncongenial jobs, and studying at night, had been taken on as book-keeper at 'Bugilbar'. He was much valued in the end by the owners, and always made use of. The father would have liked his son to follow in his footsteps, and taught him how to keep the books, but Royal wasn't going to hang around any family of purse-proud squatters, telling them the things they wanted to hear. He had ideas of his own for becoming rich and important.

So when he married Ella McWhirter, which nobody could ever understand, not even Ella herself, perhaps only Royal, who never bothered to explain (why should he?) they moved to Juggerawa, and took over the general store. It was in a bad way, and soon was in a worse, because Royal's ideas were above those of his customers.

Fulbrook was the next stage. He found employment as book-keeper on a grazing property outside. She felt so humiliated on account of his humiliation. It didn't matter about herself because she always expected less. She took a job in Fulbrook from the start, at the 'Dixie Cafe' in High Street. She worked there several years as waitress, helping out with the scrubbing for the sake of the extra money. She had never hated anything, but got to hate the flies trampling in the sugar and on the necks of the tomato sauce bottles.

At weekends her husband usually came in, and when she wasn't needed in the shop, they lay on the bed in her upstairs room, listening to the corrugated iron and the warping whitewashed weatherboard. She would have loved to do something for him, but in his distress he complained about 'wet kisses'. It surprised her. She had always been afraid he might find her a bit too dry in her show of affection.

Those years at the 'Dixie Cafe' certainly dried her up. She got those freckly patches and seams in her skin in spite of the lotions used as directed. Not that it matters so much in anyone born plain. Perhaps her plainness helped her save. There was never a day when she didn't study her savings-book, it became her favourite recreation.

Royal, on the other hand, wasn't the type that dried up, being fleshier, and dark. He even put on weight out at the grazing property, where they soon thought the world of him. When the young ladies were short of a man for tennis the book-keeper was often invited, and to a ball once at the homestead. He was earning good money, and he too saved a bit, though his instincts weren't as mean as hers. For instance, he fancied a choice cigar. In his youth Royal was a natty dresser.

Sometimes the young ladies, if they decided to inspect the latest at Ryan's Emporium, or Mr Philup, if he felt like grogging up with the locals, would drive him in, and as he got out they would look funny at the book-keeper's wife they had heard about, they must have, serving out the plates of frizzled steak and limp chips. Royal always waited to see his employers drive off before coming in.

In spite of the savings, this might have gone on much longer than it did if old Mr Natwick hadn't died. It appeared he had been a very prudent man. He left them a nice little legacy. The evening of the news, Royal was driven in by Mr Philup and they had a few at the Imperial. Afterwards the book-keeper was dropped off, because he proposed to spend the night with his wife and catch the early train to attend his father's funeral.

They lay in the hot little room and discussed the future. She had never felt so hectic. Royal got the idea he would like to develop a grocery business in one of the posh outer suburbs of Sydney. 'Interest the monied residents in some of the luxury lines. Appeal to the imagination as well as the stomach.'

She was impressed, of course, but not as much as she should have been. She wasn't sure, but perhaps she was short on imagination. Certainly their prospects had made her downright feverish, but for no distinct, sufficient reason.

'And have a baby.' She heard her own unnatural voice.

'Eh?'

'We could start a baby.' Her voice grew word by word drier.

'There's no reason why we couldn't have a baby. Or two.' He laughed. 'But starting a new life isn't the time to start a baby.' He dug her in the ribs. 'And you the practical one!'

She agreed it would be foolish, and presently Royal fell asleep.

What could she do for him? As he lay there breathing she would have loved to stroke his nose she could see faintly in the light from the window. Again unpractical, she would have liked to kiss it. Or bite it suddenly off.

She was so disgusted with herself she got creaking off the bed and walked flat across the boards to the washstand and swallowed a couple of Aspros to put her solidly to sleep.

All their life together she had to try in some way to make amends to Royal, not only for her foolishness, but for some of the thoughts that got into her head. Because she hadn't the imagination, the thoughts couldn't have been her own. They must have been put into her.

It was easier of course in later life, after he had cracked up, what with his hernia, and heart, and the artheritis taking over. Fortunately she was given the strength to help him into the wheel-chair, and later still, to lift, or drag him up on the pillows and over, to rub the bed-sores, and stick the pan under him. But even during the years at

Sarsaparilla she could make amends in many little ways, though with him still in his prime, naturally he mustn't know of them. So all her acts were mostly for her own self-gratification.

The store at Sarsaparilla, if it didn't exactly flourish, gave them a decent living. She had her problems, though. Some of the locals just couldn't accept that Royal was a superior man. Perhaps she had been partly to blame, she hardly dared admit it, for showing one or two 'friends' the photo of the family home in Kent. She couldn't resist telling the story of one of the aunts, Miss Ethel Natwick, who followed her brother to New South Wales. Ethel was persuaded to accept a situation at Government House, but didn't like it and went back, in spite of the Governor's lady insisting she valued Ethel as a close personal friend. When people began to laugh at Royal on account of his auntie and the family home, as you couldn't help finding out in a place like Sarsaparilla, it was her, she knew, it was her to blame. It hurt her deeply.

Of course Royal could be difficult. Said stockbrokers had no palate and less imagination. Royal said no Australian grocer could make a go of it if it wasn't for flour, granulated sugar, and tomato sauce. Some of the customers turned nasty in retaliation. This was where she could help, and did, because Royal was out on delivery more often than not. It embarrassed her only when some of them took it for granted she was on their side. As if he wasn't her husband. Once or twice she had gone out crying afterwards, amongst the wormy wattles and hens' droppings. Anyone across the gully could have heard her blowing her nose behind the store, but she didn't care. Poor Royal.

There was that Mr Ogburn said, 'A selfish, swollen-headed slob who'll chew you up and swallow you down.' She wouldn't let herself hear any more of what he had to say. Mr Ogburn had a hare-lip, badly sewn, opening and closing. There was nothing frightened her so much as even a well-disguised hare-lip. She got the palpitations after the scene with Mr Ogburn.

Not that there was anything wrong with her.

She only hadn't had the baby. It was her secret grief on black evenings as she walked slowly looking for the eggs a flighty hen might have hid in the bracken.

Dr Bamforth said, looking at the nib of his fountain pen, 'You know, don't you, it's sometimes the man?'

She didn't even want to hear, let alone think about it. In any case she wouldn't tell Royal, because a man's pride could be so easily hurt.

After they had sold out at Sarsaparilla and come to live at what they called 'Coota' on the Parramatta Road, it was both easier and more difficult, because if they were not exactly elderly they were getting on. Royal used to potter about in the beginning, while taking care, on account of the hernia and his heart. There was the business of the lawn-mowing, not that you could call it lawn, but it was what she had. She loved her garden. In front certainly there was only the two square of rather sooty grass which she would keep in order with the push-mower. The lawn seemed to get on Royal's nerves until the artheritis took hold of him. He had never liked mowing. He would lean against the veranda post, and shout, 'Don't know why we don't do what they've done down the street. Root the stuff out. Put down a green concrete lawn.'

'That would be copying,' she answered back.

She hoped it didn't sound stubborn. As she pushed the mower she bent her head, and smiled, waiting for him to cool off. The scent of grass and a few clippings flew up through the traffic fumes reminding you of summer.

While Royal shuffled along the veranda and leaned against another post. 'Or pebbles. You can buy clean, river pebbles. A few plastic shrubs, and there's the answer.'

He only gave up when his trouble forced him into the chair. You couldn't drive yourself up and down a veranda shouting at someone from a wheel-chair without the passers-by thinking you was a nut. So he quietened.

He watched her, though. From under the peak of his cap. Because she felt he might still resent her mowing the lawn, she would try to reassure him as she pushed. 'What's wrong, *eh*? While I still have me health, me *strength* – I was always what they call *wiry* – why shouldn't I cut the *grass*?'

She would come and sit beside him, to keep him company in watching the traffic, and invent games to amuse her invalid husband.

'Isn't that the feller we expect?' she might ask. 'The one that passes at five-twenty,' looking at her watch, 'in the old pink-and-brown Holden?'

They enjoyed their snort of amusement all the better because no one else knew the reason for it.

Once when the traffic was particularly dense, and that sort of chemical smell from one of the factories was thickening in the evening air, Royal drew her attention. 'Looks like he's got something on his mind.'

Could have too. Or it might have been the traffic block. The way he held his hands curved listlessly around the inactive wheel reminded her of possums and monkeys she had seen in cages. She shifted a bit. Her squeaky old chair. She felt uneasy for ever having found the man, not a joke, but half of one.

Royal's chair moved so smoothly on its rubber-tyred wheels it was easy to push him, specially after her practice with the mower. There were ramps where necessary now, to cover steps, and she would sometimes wheel him out to the back, where she grew hollyhock and sunflower against the palings, and a vegetable or two on raised beds.

Royal would sit not looking at the garden from under the peak of his cap.

She never attempted to take him down the shady side, between them and Dolans, because the path was narrow from plants spilling over, and the shade might have lowered his spirits.

She loved her garden.

The shady side was where she kept her staghorn ferns, and fishbones, and the pots of maidenhair. The water lay sparkling on the maidenhair even in the middle of the day. In the blaze of summer the light at either end of the tunnel was like you were looking through a sheet of yellow cellophane, but as the days shortened, the light deepened to a cold, tingling green, which might have made a person nervous who didn't know the tunnel by heart.

Take Mrs Dolan the evening she came in to ask for the loan of a cupful of sugar. 'You gave me a shock, Mrs Natwick. What ever are you up to?'

'Looking at the plants,' Mrs Natwick answered, whether Mrs Dolan would think it peculiar or not.

It was the season of cinerarias, which she always planted on that side, it was sheltered and cold-green. The wind couldn't bash the big spires and umbrellas of blue and purple. Visiting cats were the only danger, messing and pouncing. She disliked cats for the smell they left, but didn't have the heart to disturb their elastic forms curled at the cineraria roots, exposing their colourless pads, and sometimes pink, swollen teats. Blushing only slightly for it, she would stand and examine the details of the sleeping cats.

If Royal called she could hear his voice through the window. 'Where'uv you got to, Ella?'

After he was forced to take to his bed, his voice began to sort of dry up like his body. There were times when it sounded less like a voice than a breath of drowsiness or pain.

'Ella?' he was calling. 'I dropped the paper. Where are yer all this time? You know I can't pick up the paper.'

She knew. Guilt sent her scuttling to him, deliberately composing her eyes and mouth so as to arrive looking cheerful.

'I was in the garden,' she confessed, 'looking at the cinerarias.'

'The what?' It was a name Royal could never learn.

The room was smelling of sickness and the bottles standing on odd plates.

'It fell,' he complained.

She packed up the paper as quick as she could.

'Want to go la-la first?' she asked, because by now he depended on her to raise him and stick the pan under.

But she couldn't distract him from her shortcomings; he was shaking the paper at her. 'Haven't you lived with me long enough to know how to treat a newspaper?'

He hit it with his set hand, and certainly the paper looked a mess, like an old white battered brolly.

'Mucked up! You gotter keep the pages *aligned.* A paper's not readable otherwise. Of course you wouldn't understand because you don't read it, without it's to see who's died.' He began to cough.

'Like me to bring you some Bovril?' she asked him as tenderly as she knew.

'Bovril's the morning,' he coughed.

She knew that, but wanted to do something for him.

After she had rearranged the paper she walked out so carefully it made her go lopsided, out to the front veranda. Nothing would halt the traffic, not sickness, not death even.

She sat with her arms folded, realising at last how they were aching.

'He hasn't been,' she had to call after looking at her watch.

'Who?' she heard the voice rustling back.

'The gentleman in the pink Holden.'

She listened to the silence, wondering whether she had done right.

When Royal called back, 'Could'uv had a blow-out.' Then he laughed. 'Could'uv stopped to get grogged up.' She heard the frail rustling of the paper. 'Or taken an axe to somebody like they do nowadays.'

She closed her eyes, whether for Royal, or what she remembered of the man sitting in the Holden.

Although it was cold she continued watching after dark. Might have caught a chill, when she couldn't afford to. She only went inside to make the bread-and-milk Royal fancied of an evening.

She watched most attentively, always at the time, but he didn't pass, and didn't pass.

'Who?'

'The gentleman in the Holden.'

'Gone on holiday.' Royal sighed, and she knew it was the point where a normal person would have turned over, so she went to turn him.

One morning she said on going in, 'Fancy, I had a dream, it was about that man! He was standing on the side path alongside the cinerarias. I know it was him because of his funny-shaped head.'

'What happened in the dream?' Royal hadn't opened his eyes yet; she hadn't helped him in with his teeth.

'I dunno,' she said, 'it was just a dream.'

That wasn't strictly truthful, because the Holden gentleman had looked at her, she had seen his eyes. Nothing was spoken, though.

'It was a sort of red and purple dream. That was the cinerarias,' she said.

'I don't dream. You don't when you don't sleep. Pills aren't sleep.'

She was horrified at her reverberating dream. 'Would you like a nice soft-boiled egg?'

'Eggs all have a taste.'

'But you gotter eat *something*!'

On another morning she told him – she could have bitten off her tongue – she *was* stupid, *stupid*, 'I had a dream.'

'What sort of dream?'

'Oh,' she said, 'a silly one, Not worth telling. I dreamed I dropped an egg on the side path, and it turned into two. Not two. A double-yolker.'

She never realised Royal was so much like Mrs Natwick. It was as she raised him on his pillows. Or he had got like that in his sickness. Old men and old women were not unlike.

'Wasn't that a silly one?' she coaxed.

Every evening she sat on the front veranda and watched the traffic as though Royal had been beside her. Looked at her watch. And turned her face away from the steady-flowing stream. The way she bunched her small chest she could have had a sour breath mounting in her throat. Sometimes she had, it was nervousness.

When she went inside she announced, 'He didn t pass.'

Royal said – he had taken to speaking from behind his eyelids, 'Something muster happened to 'im. He didn't go on holiday. He went and died.'

'Oh, no! He wasn't of an age!'

At once she saw how stupid she was, and went out to get the bread-and-milk.

She would sit at the bedside, almost crouching against the edge of the mattress, because she wanted Royal to feel she was close, and he seemed to realise, though he mostly kept his eyelids down.

Then one evening she came running, she felt silly, her calves felt silly, her voice, 'He's come! At five-twenty! In a new cream Holden!'

Royal said without opening his eyes, 'See? I said 'e'd gone on holiday.'

More than ever she saw the look of Mrs Natwick.

Now every evening Royal asked, 'Has he been, Ella?'

Trying not to make it sound irritable or superior, she would answer, 'Not yet. It's only five.'

Every evening she sat watching, and sometimes would turn proud, arching her back, as she looked down from the veranda. The man was so small and ordinary.

She went in on one occasion, into the more than electric light, lowering her eyelids against the dazzle. 'You know, Royal, you could feel prouder of men when they rode horses. As they looked down at yer from under the brim of their hats. Remember that hat you used to wear? Riding in to Cootramundra?'

Royal died quietly that same year before the cinerarias had folded, while the cold westerlies were still blowing; the back page of the *Herald* was full of those who had been carried off. She was left with his hand, already set, in her own. They hadn't spoken, except about whether she had put out the garbage.

Everybody was very kind. She wouldn't have liked to admit it was enjoyable being a widow. She sat around for longer than she had ever sat, and let the dust gather. In the beginning acquaintances and neighbours brought her little presents of food: a billy-can of giblet soup, moulded veal with hard-boiled egg making a pattern in the jelly, cakes so dainty you couldn't taste them. But when she was no longer a novelty they left off coming. She didn't care any more than she cared about the dust. Sometimes she would catch sight of her face in the glass, and was surprised to see herself looking so calm and white.

Of course she was calm. The feeling part of her had been removed. What remained was a slack, discardable eiderdown. Must have been the pills Doctor gave.

Well-meaning people would call to her over the front fence, 'Don't you feel lonely, Mrs Natwick?' They spoke with a restrained horror, as though she had been suffering from an incurable disease.

But she called back proud and slow, 'I'm under sedation.'

'Arrr!' They nodded thoughtfully. 'What's 'e given yer?'

She shook her head. 'Pills,' she called back. 'They say they're the ones the actress died of.'

The people walked on, impressed.

As the evenings grew longer and heavier she sat later on the front veranda watching the traffic of the Parramatta Road, its flow becoming syrupy and almost benign: big bulbous sedate buses, chrysalis cars still without a life of their own, clinging in line to the back of their host-articulator, trucks loaded for distances, empty loose-sounding jolly lorries. Sometimes women, looking out from the cabins of trucks from beside their men, shared her lack of curiosity. The light was so fluid nobody lasted long enough. You would never have thought boys could kick a person to death, seeing their long soft hair floating behind their sports models.

Every evening she watched the cream Holden pass. And looked at her watch. It was like Royal was sitting beside her. Once she heard herself, 'Thought he was gunner look round tonight, in our direction.' How could a person feel lonely?

She was, though. She came face to face with it walking through the wreckage of her garden in the long slow steamy late summer. The Holden didn't pass of course of a Saturday or Sunday. Something, something had tricked her, not the pills, before the pills. She couldn't blame anybody, probably only herself. Everything depended on yourself. Take the garden. It was a shambles. She would have liked to protest, but began to cough from running her head against some powdery mildew. She could only blunder at first, like a cow, or runty starved heifer, on breaking into a garden. She had lost her old wiriness. She shambled, snapping dead stems, uprooting. Along the bleached palings there was a fretwork of hollyhock, the brown fur of rotting sunflower. She rushed at a praying mantis, a big pale one, and deliberately broke its back, and was sorry afterwards for what was done so easy and thoughtless.

As she stood panting in her black, finally yawning, she saw all she had to repair. The thought of the seasons piling up ahead made her feel tired but necessary, and she went in to bathe her face. Royal's denture in a tumbler on top of the medicine cabinet, she ought to move, or give to the Sallies. In the meantime she changed the water. She never forgot it. The teeth looked amazingly alive.

All that autumn, winter, she was continually amazed, at the dust she had let gather in the house, at old photographs, books, clothes. There was a feather she couldn't remember wearing, a scarlet feather, she *can't* have worn, and gloves with little fussy ruffles at the wrists, silver piping, like a snail had laid its trail round the edges. There was, she knew, funny things she had bought at times, and never worn, but she couldn't remember the gloves or the feather. And books. She had collected a few, though never a reader herself. Old people liked to give old books, and you took them so as not to hurt anybody's feelings. *Hubert's Crusade*, for instance. Lovely golden curls. Could have been Royal's father's book. Everybody was a child once. And almost everybody had one. At least if she had had a child she would have known it wasn't a white turnip, more of a praying mantis, which snaps too easy.

In the same box she had put away a coloured picture *Cities of the Plain*, she couldn't remember seeing it before. The people escaping from the burning cities had committed some sin or other nobody ever thought, let alone talked, about. As they hurried between rocks, through what must have been the 'desert places', their faces looked long and wooden. All they had recently experienced could have shocked the expression out of them. She was fascinated by what made her shiver. And the couples with their arms still around one another. Well, if you were damned, better hang on to your sin. She didn't blame them.

She put the box away. Its inlay as well as its contents made it something secret and precious.

The autumn was still and golden, the winter vicious only in fits. It was what you could call a good winter. The cold floods of air and more concentrated streams of dark-green light poured along the shady side of the house where her cinerarias had massed. She had never seen such cinerarias: some of the spired ones reached almost as high as her chin, the solid heads of others waited in the tunnel of dark light to club you with their colours, of purple and drenching blue, and what they called 'wine'. She couldn't believe wine would have made her drunker.

Just as she would sit every evening watching the traffic, evening was the time she liked best to visit the cinerarias, when the icy cold seemed to make the flowers burn their deepest, purest. So it was again evening when her two objects converged: for some blissfully confident reason she hadn't bothered to ask herself whether she had seen the car pass, till here was this figure coming towards her along the tunnel. She knew at once who it was, although she had never seen him on his feet; she had never seen him full-face, but knew from the funny shape of his head as Royal had been the first to notice. He was not at all an impressive man, not much taller than herself, but broad. His footsteps on the brickwork sounded purposeful.

'Will you let me use your phone, please, madam?' he asked in a prepared voice. 'I'm having trouble with the Holden.'

This was the situation she had always been expecting: somebody asking to use the phone as a way to afterwards murdering you. Now that it might be about to happen she couldn't care.

She said yes. She thought her voice sounded muzzy. Perhaps he would think she was drunk.

She went on looking at him, at his eyes. His nose, like the shape of his head, wasn't up to much, but his eyes, his eyes, she dared to think, were filled with kindness.

'Cold, eh? but clean cold!' He laughed friendly, shuffling on the brick paving because she was keeping him waiting.

Only then she noticed his mouth. He had a hare-lip, there was no mistaking, although it was well sewn. She felt so calm in the circumstances. She would have even liked to touch it.

But said, 'Why, yes – the telephone,' she said, 'it's this way,' she said, 'it's just off the kitchen – because that's where you spend most of your life. Or in bed,' she ended.

She wished she hadn't added that. For the first time since they had been together she felt upset, thinking he might suspect her of wrong intentions.

But he laughed and said, 'That's correct! You got something there!' It sounded manly rather than educated.

She realised he was still waiting, and took him to the telephone.

While he was phoning she didn't listen. She never listened when other people were talking on the phone. The sight of her own kitchen surprised her. While his familiar voice went on. It was the voice she had held conversations with.

But he was ugly, real ugly, *deformed.* If it wasn't for the voice, the eyes. She couldn't remember the eyes, but seemed to know about them.

Then she heard him laying the coins beside the phone, extra loud, to show.

He came back into the kitchen smiling and looking. She could smell him now, and he had the smell of a clean man.

She became embarrassed at herself, and took him quickly out.

'Fair bit of garden you got.' He stood with his calves curved through his trousers. A cocky little chap, but nice.

'Oh,' she said, 'this', she said, angrily almost, 'is nothing. You oughter see it. There's sunflower and hollyhock all along the palings. I'm famous for me hollyhocks!' She had never boasted in her life. 'But not now – it isn't the season. And I let it go. Mr Natwick passed on. You should'uv seen the cassia this autumn. Now it's only sticks, of course. And hibiscus. There's cream, gold, cerise, scarlet – double and single.'

She was dressing in them for him, revolving on high heels and changing frilly skirts.

He said, 'Gardening's not in my line,' turning his head to hide something, perhaps he was ashamed of his hare-lip.

'No,' she agreed. 'Not everybody's a gardener.'

'But I like a garden.'

'My husband didn't even like it. He didn't have to tell me,' she added.

As they moved across the wintry grass, past the empty clothes-line, the man looked at his watch, and said, 'I was reckoning on visiting somebody in hospital tonight. Looks like I shan't make it if the N.R.M.A. takes as long as usual.'

'Do they?' she said, clearing her throat. 'It isn't somebody close, I hope? The sick person?'

Yes he said they was close.

'Nothing serious?' she almost bellowed.

He said it was serious.

Oh she nearly burst out laughing at the bandaged figure they were sitting beside particularly at the bandaged face. She would have laughed at a brain tumour.

'I'm sorry,' she said. 'I understand. Mr Natwick was for many years an invalid.'

Those teeth in the tumbler on top of the medicine cabinet. Looking at her. Teeth can look, worse than eyes. But she couldn't help it, she meant everything she said, and thought.

At this moment they were pressing inside the dark-green tunnel, her sleeve rubbing his, as the crimson-to-purple light was dying.

'These are the cinerarias,' she said.

'The what?' He didn't know, any more than Royal.

As she was about to explain she got switched to another language. Her throat became a long palpitating funnel through which the words she expected to use were poured out in a stream of almost formless agonised sound.

'What is it?' he asked, touching her.

If it had happened to herself she would have felt frightened, it occurred to her, but he didn't seem to be.

'What is it?' he kept repeating in his familiar voice, touching, even holding her.

And for answer, in the new language, she was holding him. They were holding each other, his hard body against her eiderdowny one. As the silence closed round them again, inside the tunnel of light, his face, to which she was very close, seemed to be unlocking, the wound of his mouth, which should have been more horrible, struggling to open. She could see he had recognised her.

She kissed above his mouth. She kissed as though she might never succeed in healing all the wounds they had ever suffered.

How long they stood together she wasn't interested in knowing. Outside them the river of traffic continued to flow between its brick and concrete banks. Even if it overflowed it couldn't have drowned them.

When the man said in his gentlest voice, 'Better go out in front. The N.R.M.A. might have come.'

'Yes,' she agreed. 'The N.R.M.A.'

So they shuffled, still holding each other, along the narrow path. She imagined how long and wooden their faces must look. She wouldn't look at him now, though, just as she wouldn't look back at the still faintly smouldering joys they had experienced together in the past.

When they came out, apart, and into the night, there was the N.R.M.A., his pointed ruby of a light burning on top of the cabin.

'When will you come?' she asked.

'Tomorrow.'

'Tomorrow. You'll stay to tea.'

He couldn't stay.

'I'll make you a *pot* of tea?'

But he didn't drink it.

'Coffee, then?'

He said, 'I like a nice cup of coffee.'

Going down the path he didn't look back, or opening the gate. She would not let herself think of reasons or possibilities, she would not think, but stood planted in the path, swayed slightly by the motion of the night.

Mrs Dolan said, 'You bring the saucepan to the boil. You got that?'

'Yeeehs.' Mrs Natwick had never been a dab at coffee.

'Then you throw in some cold water. That's what sends the gravel to the bottom.' This morning Mrs Dolan had to laugh at her own jokes.

'That's the part that frightens me,' Mrs Natwick admitted.

'Well, you just do it, and see,' said Mrs Dolan; she was too busy.

After she had bought the coffee Mrs Natwick stayed in the city to muck around. If she had stayed at home her nerves might have wound themselves tighter, waiting for evening to come. Though mucking around only irritated in the end. She had never been an idle woman. So she stopped at the cosmetics as though she didn't have to decide, this was her purpose, and said to the young lady lounging behind one of the counters, 'I'm thinking of investing in a lipstick, dear. Can you please advise me?'

As a concession to the girl she tried to make it a laughing matter, but the young person was bored, she didn't bat a silver eyelid. 'Elderly ladies,' she said, 'go for the brighter stuff.'

Mrs Natwick ('my little Ella') had never felt so meek. Mum must be turning in her grave.

'This is a favourite.' With a flick of her long fingers the girl exposed the weapon. It looked too slippery-pointed, crimson-purple, out of its golden sheath.

Mrs Natwick's knees were shaking. 'Isn't it a bit noticeable?' she asked, again trying to make it a joke.

But the white-haired girl gave a serious laugh. 'What's wrong with noticeable?'

As Mrs Natwick tried it out on the back of her hand the way she had seen others do, the girl was jogging from foot to foot behind the counter. She was humming between her teeth, behind her white-smeared lips, probably thinking about a lover. Mrs Natwick blushed. What if she couldn't learn to get the tip of her lipstick back inside its sheath?

She might have gone quickly away without another word if the young lady hadn't been so professional and bored. Still humming, she brought out a little pack of rouge.

'Never saw myself with mauve cheeks!' It was at least dry, and easy to handle.

'It's what they wear.'

Mrs Natwick didn't dare refuse. She watched the long fingers with their silver nails doing up the parcel. The fingers looked as though they might resent touching anything but cosmetics; a lover was probably beneath contempt.

The girl gave her the change, and she went away without counting it.

She wasn't quiet, though, not a bit, booming and clanging in front of the toilet mirror. She tried to make a thin line, but her mouth exploded into a purple flower. She dabbed the dry-feeling pad on either cheek, and thick, mauve-scented shadows fell. She could hear and feel her heart behaving like a squeezed, rubber ball as she stood looking. Then she got at the lipstick again, still unsheathed. Her mouth was becoming enormous, so thick with grease she could hardly close her own lips underneath. A visible dew was gathering round the purple shadows on her cheeks.

She began to retch like, but dry, and rub, over the basin, scrubbing with the nailbrush. More than likely some would stay behind in the pores and be seen. Though you didn't have to see, to see.

There were Royal's teeth in the tumbler on top of the medicine cabinet. Ought to hide the teeth. What if somebody wanted to use the toilet? She must move the teeth. But didn't. In the present circumstances she couldn't have raised her arms that high.

Around five she made the coffee, throwing in the cold water at the end with a gesture copied from Mrs Dolan. If the gravel hadn't sunk to the bottom he wouldn't notice the first time, provided the coffee was hot. She could warm up the made coffee in a jiffy.

As she sat on the veranda waiting, the cane chair shifted and squealed under her. If it hadn't been for her weight it might have run away across the tiles, like one of those old planchette boards, writing the answers to questions.

There was an accident this evening down at the intersection. A head-on collision. Bodies were carried out of the crumpled cars, and she remembered a past occasion when she had run with blankets, and Hazel's Onkaparinka, and a pillow from their own bed. She had been so grateful to the victim. She could not give him enough, or receive enough of the warm blood. She had come back, she remembered, sprinkled.

This evening she had to save herself up. Kept on looking at her watch. The old cane chair squealing, ready to write the answers if she let it. Was he hurt? Was he killed, then? Was he – what?

Mrs Dolan it was, sticking her head over the palings. 'Don't like the accidents, Mrs Natwick. It's the blood. The blood turns me up.'

Mrs Natwick averted her face. Though unmoved by present blood. If only the squealing chair would stop trying to buck her off.

'Did your friend enjoy the coffee?' Mrs Dolan shouted; nothing nasty in her: Mrs Dolan was sincere.

'Hasn't been yet,' Mrs Natwick mumbled from glancing at her watch. 'Got held up.'

'It's the traffic. The traffic at this time of evenun.'

'Always on the dot before.'

'Working back. Or made a mistake over the day.'

Could you make a mistake? Mrs Natwick contemplated. Tomorrow had always meant tomorrow.

'Or he could'uv,' Mrs Dolan shouted, but didn't say it. 'I better go inside,' she said instead. 'They'll be wonderun where I am.'

Down at the intersection the bodies were lying wrapped in someone else's blankets, looking like the grey parcels of mice cats sometimes vomit up.

It was long past five-twenty, not all that long really, but drawing in. The sky was heaped with cold fire. Her city was burning.

She got up finally, and the chair escaped with a last squeal, writing its answer on the tiles.

No, it wasn't lust, not if the Royal God Almighty with bared teeth should strike her down. Or yes, though, it was. She was lusting after the expression of eyes she could hardly remember for seeing so briefly.

In the effort to see, she drove her memory wildly, while her body stumbled around and around the paths of the burning city there was now no point in escaping. You would shrivel up in time along with the polyanthers and out-of-season hibiscus. All the randy mouths would be stopped sooner or later with black.

The cinerarias seemed to have grown so luxuriant she had to force her way past them, down the narrow brick path. When she heard the latch click, and saw him coming towards her.

'Why,' she screamed laughing though it sounded angry, she *was*, 'I'd given you up, you know! It's long after five-twenty!'

As she pushed fiercely towards him, past the cinerarias, snapping one or two of those which were most heavily loaded, she realised he couldn't have known that she set her watch, her life, by his constant behaviour. He wouldn't have dawdled so.

'What is it?' she called at last, in exasperation at the distance which continued separating them.

He was far too slow, treading the slippery moss of her too shaded path. While she floundered on. She couldn't reach the expression of his eyes.

He said, and she could hardly recognise the faded voice, 'There's something – I been feeling off colour most of the day.' His mis-shapen head was certainly lolling as he advanced.

'Tell me!' She heard her voice commanding, like that of a man, or a mother, when she had practised to be a lover; she could still smell the smell of rouge. 'Won't you tell me – *dearest*?' It was thin and unconvincing now. (As a girl she had once got a letter from her cousin Kath Salter, who she hardly knew: *Dearest Ella . . .*)

Oh dear. She had reached him. And was given all strength – that of the lover she had aimed at being.

Straddling the path, unequally matched – he couldn't compete against her strength – she spoke with an acquired, a deafening softness, as the inclining cinerarias snapped.

'You will tell me what is wrong – dear, dear.' She breathed with trumpets.

He hung his head. 'It's all right. It's the pain – here – in my arm – no, the shoulder.'

'Ohhhhh!' She ground her face into his shoulder forgetting it wasn't *her* pain.

Then she remembered, and looked into his eyes and said, 'We'll save you. You'll see.'

It was she who needed saving. She knew she was trying to enter by his eyes. To drown in them rather than be left.

Because, in spite of her will to hold him, he was slipping from her, down amongst the cinerarias, which were snapping off one by one around them.

A cat shot out. At one time she had been so poor in spirit she had wished she was a cat.

'It's all right,' either voice was saying.

Lying amongst the smashed plants, he was smiling at her dreadfully, not his mouth, she no longer bothered about that lip, but with his eyes.

'More air!' she cried. 'What you need is air!' hacking at one or two cinerarias which remained erect.

Their sap was stifling, their bristling columns callous.

'Oh! Oh!' she panted. 'Oh God! Dear love!' comforting with hands and hair and words.

Words.

While all he could say was, 'It's all right.'

Or not that at last. He folded his lips into a white seam. His eyes were swimming out of reach.

'Eh? Dear – dearest – darl – darlig – darling love – *love* – LOVE?' All the new words still stiff in her mouth, that she had heard so far only from the mouths of actors.

The words were too strong she could see. She was losing him. The traffic was hanging together only by charred silences.

She flung herself and covered his body, trying to force kisses – no, breath, into his mouth, she had heard about it.

She had seen turkeys, feathers sawing against each other's feathers, rising afterwards like new noisy silk.

She knelt up, and the wing-tips of her hair still dabbled limply in his cheeks. 'Eh? Ohh luff!' She could hardly breathe it.

She hadn't had time to ask his name, before she must have killed him by loving too deep, and too adulterously.

27

A Horse and Two Goats

(1970)

R. K. Narayan

Of the seven hundred thousand villages dotting the map of India, in which the majority of India's five hundred million live, flourish, and die, Kritam was probably the tiniest, indicated on the district survey map by a microscopic dot, the map being meant more for the revenue official out to collect tax than for the guidance of the motorist, who in any case could not hope to reach it since it sprawled far from the highway at the end of a rough track furrowed up by the iron-hooped wheels of bullock carts. But its size did not prevent its giving itself the grandiose name Kritam, which meant in Tamil 'coronet' or 'crown' on the brow of this subcontinent. The village consisted of less than thirty houses, only one of them built with brick and cement. Painted a brilliant yellow and blue all over with gorgeous carvings of gods and gargoyles on its balustrade, it was known as the Big House. The other houses, distributed in four streets, were generally of bamboo thatch, straw, mud, and other unspecified material. Muni's was the last house in the fourth street, beyond which stretched the fields. In his prosperous days Muni had owned a flock of forty sheep and goats and sallied forth every morning driving the flock to the highway a couple of miles away. There he would sit on the pedestal of a clay statue of a horse while his cattle grazed around. He carried a crook at the end of a bamboo pole and snapped foliage from the avenue trees to feed his flock; he also gathered faggots and dry sticks, bundled them, and carried them home for fuel at sunset.

His wife lit the domestic fire at dawn, boiled water in a mud pot, threw into it a handful of millet flour, added salt, and gave him his first nourishment for the day. When he started out, she would put in his hand a packed lunch, once again the same millet cooked into a little ball, which he could swallow with a raw onion at midday. She was old, but he was older and needed all the attention she could give him in order to be kept alive.

His fortunes had declined gradually, unnoticed. From a flock of forty which he drove into a pen at night, his stock had now come down to two goats which were not worth the rent of a half rupee a month the Big House charged for the use of the pen in their back yard. And so the two goats were tethered to the trunk of a drumstick tree which grew in front of his hut and from which occasionally Muni could shake down drumsticks. This morning he got six. He carried them in with a sense of triumph. Although no one could say precisely who owned the tree, it was his because he lived in its shadow.

She said, 'If you were content with the drumstick leaves alone, I could boil and salt some for you.'

'Oh, I am tired of eating those leaves. I have a craving to chew the drumstick out of sauce, I tell you.'

'You have only four teeth in your jaw, but your craving is for big things. All right, get the stuff for the sauce, and I will prepare it for you. After all, next year you may not be alive to ask for anything. But first get me all the stuff, including a measure of rice or millet, and I will satisfy your unholy craving. Our store is empty today. Dhal, chili, curry leaves, mustard, coriander, gingelley oil, and one large potato. Go out and get all this.' He repeated the list after her in order not to miss any item and walked off to the shop in the third street.

He sat on an upturned packing case below the platform of the shop. The shopman paid no attention to him. Muni kept clearing his throat, coughing, and sneezing until the shopman could not stand it any more and demanded, 'What ails you? You will fly off that seat into the gutter if you sneeze so hard, young man.' Muni laughed inordinately, in order to please the shopman, at being called 'young man'. The shopman softened and said, 'You have enough of the imp inside to keep a second wife busy, but for the fact the old lady is still alive.' Muni laughed appropriately again at this joke. It completely won the shopman over; he liked his sense of humour to be appreciated. Muni engaged his attention in local gossip for a few minutes, which always ended with a reference to the postman's wife who had eloped to the city some months before.

The shopman felt most pleased to hear the worst of the postman, who had cheated him. Being an itinerant postman, he returned home to Kritam only once in ten days and every time managed to slip away again without passing the shop in the third street. By thus humouring the shopman, Muni could always ask for one or two items of food, promising repayment later. Some days the shopman was in a good mood and gave in, and sometimes he would lose his temper suddenly and bark at Muni for daring to ask for credit. This was such a day, and Muni could not progress beyond two items listed as essential components. The shopman was also displaying a remarkable memory for old facts and figures and took out an oblong ledger to support his observations. Muni felt impelled to rise and flee. But his self-respect kept him in his seat and made him listen to the worst things about himself. The shopman concluded, 'If you could find five rupees and a quarter, you would pay off an ancient debt and then could apply for admission to swarga. How much have you got now?'

'I will pay you everything on the first of the next month.'

'As always, and whom do you expect to rob by then?'

Muni felt caught and mumbled, 'My daughter has sent word that she will be sending me money.'

'Have you a daughter?' sneered the shopman. 'And she is sending you money! For what purpose, may I know?'

'Birthday, fiftieth birthday,' said Muni quietly.

'Birthday! How old are you?'

Muni repeated weakly, not being sure of it himself, 'Fifty.' He always calculated his age from the time of the great famine when he stood as high as the parapet around the village well, but who could calculate such things accurately nowadays with so many famines occurring? The shopman felt encouraged when other customers stood around to watch and comment. Muni thought helplessly, My poverty is exposed to everybody. But what can I do?

'More likely you are seventy,' said the shopman. 'You also forget that you mentioned a birthday five weeks ago when you wanted castor oil for your holy bath.'

'Bath! Who can dream of a bath when you have to scratch the tank-bed for a bowl of water? We would all be parched and dead but for the Big House, where they let us take a pot of water from their well.' After saying this Muni unobtrusively rose and moved off.

He told his wife, 'That scoundrel would not give me anything. So go out and sell the drumsticks for what they are worth.'

He flung himself down in a corner to recoup from the fatigue of his visit to the shop. His wife said, 'You are getting no sauce today, nor anything else. I can't find anything to give you to eat. Fast till the evening, it'll do you good. Take the goats and be gone now,' she cried and added, 'Don't come back before the sun is down.' He knew that if he obeyed her she would somehow conjure up some food for him in the evening. Only he must be careful not to argue and irritate her. Her temper was undependable in the morning but improved by evening time. She was sure to go out and work – grind corn in the Big House, sweep or scrub somewhere, and earn enough to buy foodstuff and keep a dinner ready for him in the evening.

Unleashing the goats from the drumstick tree, Muni started out, driving them ahead and uttering weird cries from time to time in order to urge them on. He passed through the village with his head bowed in thought. He did not want to look at anyone or be accosted. A couple of cronies lounging in the temple corridor hailed him, but he ignored their call. They had known him in the days of affluence when he lorded over a flock of fleecy sheep, not the miserable gawky goats that he had today. Of course he also used to have a few goats for those who fancied them, but real wealth lay in sheep; they bred fast and people came and bought the fleece in the shearing season; and then that famous butcher from the town came over on the weekly market days bringing him betel leaves, tobacco, and often enough some bhang, which they smoked in a hut in the coconut grove, undisturbed by wives and well-wishers. After a smoke one felt light and elated and inclined to forgive everyone including that brother-in-law of his who had once tried to set fire to his home. But all this seemed like the memoirs of a previous birth. Some pestilence afflicted his cattle (he could of course guess who had laid his animals under a curse) and even the friendly butcher would not touch one at half the price . . . and now here he was left with the two scraggy creatures. He wished someone would rid him of their company too. The shopman had said that he was seventy. At seventy, one only waited to be summoned by God. When he was dead what would his wife do? They had lived in each other's company since they were children. He was told on their day of wedding that he was ten years old and she was eight. During the wedding ceremony they had had to recite their respective ages and names. He had thrashed her only a few times in their career, and later she had the upper hand. Progeny, none. Perhaps a large progeny would have brought him the blessing of the gods. Fertility brought merit. People with fourteen sons were always so prosperous and at peace with the world and themselves. He recollected the thrill he had felt when he mentioned a daughter to that shopman; although it was not believed, what if he did not have a daughter? – his cousin in the next village had many daughters, and any one of them was as good as his; he was fond of them all and would buy them sweets if he could afford it. Still, everyone in the village whispered behind their backs that Muni and his wife were a barren couple. He avoided looking at anyone; they all professed to be so high up, and everyone else in the village had more money than he. 'I am the poorest fellow in our caste and no wonder that they spurn me, but I won't look at them either,' and so he passed on with his eyes downcast along the edge of the street, and people left him also very much alone, commenting only to the extent, 'Ah, there he goes with his two great goats; if he slits their throats, he may have more peace of mind.' 'What has he to worry about anyway? They live on nothing and have nobody to worry about.' Thus people commented when he passed through the village. Only on the outskirts did he lift his head and look up. He urged and bullied the goats until they meandered along to the foot of the horse statue on the edge of the village. He sat on its pedestal for the rest of the day. The advantage of this was that he could watch the highway and see the lorries and buses pass through to the hills, and it gave him a sense of belonging to a larger world. The pedestal of the statue was broad enough for him to move around as the sun travelled up and westward; or he could also crouch under the belly of the horse, for shade.

The horse was nearly life-size, moulded out of clay, baked, burnt, and brightly coloured, and reared its head proudly, prancing its forelegs in the air and flourishing its tail in a loop; beside the horse stood a warrior with scythe-like mustachios, bulging eyes, and aquiline nose. The old image-makers believed in indicating a man of strength by bulging out his eyes and sharpening his moustache tips, and also had decorated the man's chest with beads which looked today like blobs of mud through the ravages of sun and wind and rain (when it came), but Muni would insist that he had known the beads to sparkle like the nine gems at one time in his life. The horse itself was said to have been as white as a dhobi-washed sheet, and had had on its back a cover of pure brocade of red and black lace, matching the multi-coloured sash around the waist of the warrior. But none in the village remembered the splendour as no one noticed its existence. Even Muni, who spent all his waking hours at its foot, never bothered to look up. It was untouched by the young vandals of the village who gashed tree trunks with knives and tried to topple off milestones and inscribed lewd designs on all the walls. This statue had been closer to the population of the village at one time, when this spot bordered the village; but when the highway was laid through (or perhaps when the tank and wells dried up completely here) the village moved a couple of miles inland.

Muni sat at the foot of the statue, watching his two goats graze in the arid soil among the cactus and lantana bushes. He looked at the sun; it had tilted westward no doubt, but it was not the time yet to go back home; if he went too early his wife would have no food for him. Also he must give her time to cool off her temper and feel sympathetic, and then she would scrounge and manage to get some food. He watched the mountain road for a time signal. When the green bus appeared around the bend he could leave, and his wife would feel pleased that he had let the goats feed long enough.

He noticed now a new sort of vehicle coming down at full speed. It looked both like a motor car and a bus. He used to be intrigued by the novelty of such spectacles, but of late work was going on at the source of the river on the mountain and an assortment of people and traffic went past him, and he took it all casually and described to his wife, later in the day, not everything as he once did, but only some things, only if he noticed anything special. Today, while he observed the yellow vehicle coming down, he was wondering how to describe it later when it sputtered and stopped in front of him. A red-faced foreigner who had been driving it got down and went round it, stooping, looking, and poking under the vehicle; then he straightened himself up, looked at the dashboard, stared in Muni's direction, and approached him. 'Excuse me, is there a gas station nearby, or do I have to wait until another car comes—' He suddenly looked up at the clay horse and cried, 'Marvellous!' without completing his sentence. Muni felt he should get up and run away, and cursed his age. He could not readily put his limbs into action; some years ago he could outrun a cheetah, as happened once when he went to the forest to cut fuel and it was then that two of his sheep were mauled – a sign that bad times were coming. Though he tried, he could not easily extricate himself from his seat, and then there was also the problem of the goats. He could not leave them behind.

The red-faced man wore khaki clothes – evidently a policeman or a soldier. Muni said to himself, 'He will chase or shoot if I start running. Sometimes dogs chase only those who run – O Shiva protect me. I don't know why this man should be after me.' Meanwhile the foreigner cried, 'Marvellous!' again, nodding his head. He paced around the statue with his eyes fixed on it. Muni sat frozen for a while, and then fidgeted and tried to edge away. Now the other man suddenly pressed his palms together in a salute, smiled, and said, 'Namaste! How do you do?'

At which Muni spoke the only English expressions he had learnt, 'Yes, no.' Having exhausted his English vocabulary, he started in Tamil: 'My name is Muni. These two goats are mine, and no one can gainsay it – though our village is full of slanderers these days who will not hesitate to say that what belongs to a man doesn't belong to him.' He rolled his eyes and shuddered at the thought of evil-minded men and women peopling his village.

The foreigner faithfully looked in the direction indicated by Muni's fingers, gazed for a while at the two goats and the rocks, and with a puzzled expression took out his silver cigarette-case and lit a cigarette. Suddenly remembering the courtesies of the season, he asked, 'Do you smoke?' Muni answered, 'Yes, no.' Whereupon the red faced man took a cigarette and gave it to Muni, who received it with surprise, having had no offer of a smoke from anyone for years now. Those days when he smoked bhang were gone with his sheep and the large-hearted butcher. Nowadays he was not able to find even matches, let alone bhang. (His wife went across and borrowed a fire at dawn from a neighbour.) He had always wanted to smoke a cigarette; only once had the shopman given him one on credit, and he remembered how good it had tasted. The other flicked the lighter open and offered a light to Muni. Muni felt so confused about how to act that he blew on it and put it out. The other, puzzled but undaunted, flourished his lighter, presented it again, and lit Muni's cigarette. Muni drew a deep puff and started coughing; it was racking, no doubt, but extremely pleasant. When his cough subsided he wiped his eyes and took stock of the situation, understanding that the other man was not an inquisitor of any kind. Yet, in order to make sure, he remained wary. No need to run away from a man who gave him such a potent smoke. His head was reeling from the effect of one of those strong American cigarettes made with roasted tobacco. The man said, 'I come from New York,' took out a wallet from his hip pocket, and presented his card.

Muni shrank away from the card. Perhaps he was trying to present a warrant and arrest him. Beware of khaki, one part of his mind warned. Take all the cigarettes or bhang or whatever is offered, but don't get caught. Beware of khaki. He wished he weren't seventy as the shopman had said. At seventy one didn't run, but surrendered to whatever came. He could only ward off trouble by talk. So he went on, all in the chaste Tamil for which Kritam was famous. (Even the worst detractors could not deny that the famous poetess Avvaiyar was born in this area, although no one could say whether it was in Kritam or Kuppam, the adjoining village.) Out of this heritage the Tamil language gushed through Muni in an unimpeded flow. He said, 'Before God, sir, Bhagwan, who sees everything, I tell you, sir, that we know nothing of the case. If the murder was committed, whoever did it will not escape. Bhagwan is all-seeing. Don't ask me about it. I know nothing.' A body had been found mutilated and thrown under a tamarind tree at the border between Kritam and Kuppam a few weeks before, giving rise to much gossip and speculation. Muni added an explanation, 'Anything is possible there. People over there will stop at nothing.' The foreigner nodded his head and listened courteously though he understood nothing.

'I am sure you know when this horse was made,' said the red man and smiled ingratiatingly.

Muni reacted to the relaxed atmosphere by smiling himself, and pleaded, 'Please go away, sir, I know nothing. I promise we will hold him for you if we see any bad character around, and we will bury him up to his neck in a coconut pit if he tries to escape; but our village has always had a clean record. Must definitely be the other village.'

Now the red man implored, 'Please, please, I will speak slowly, please try to understand me. Can't you understand even a simple word of English? Everyone in this country seems to know English. I have got along with English everywhere in this country, but you don't speak it. Have you any religious or spiritual scruples for avoiding the English speech?'

Muni made some indistinct sounds in his throat and shook his head. Encouraged, the other went on to explain at length, uttering each syllable with care and deliberation. Presently he sidled over and took a seat beside the old man, explaining, 'You see, last August, we probably had the hottest summer in history, and I was working in shirt sleeves in my office on the fortieth floor of the Empire State Building. You must have heard of the power failure, and there I was stuck for four hours, no elevator, no air conditioning. All the way in the train I kept thinking, and the minute I reached home in Connecticut, I told my wife Ruth, "We will visit India this winter, it's time to look at other civilisations." Next day she called the travel agent first thing and told him to fix it, and so here I am. Ruth came with me but is staying back at Srinagar, and I am the one doing the rounds and joining her later.'

Muni looked reflective at the end of this long peroration and said, rather feebly, 'Yes, no,' as a concession to the other's language, and went on in Tamil, 'When I was this high,' he indicated a foot high, 'I heard my uncle say . . .'

No one can tell what he was planning to say as the other interrupted him at this stage to ask, 'Boy, what is the secret of your teeth? How old are you?'

The old man forgot what he had started to say and remarked, 'Sometimes we too lose our cattle. Jackals or cheetahs may carry them off, but sometimes it is just theft from over in the next village, and then we will know who has done it. Our priest at the temple can see in the camphor flame the face of the thief, and when he is caught . . .' He gestured with his hands a perfect mincing of meat.

The American watched his hands intently and said, 'I know what you mean. Chop something? Maybe I am holding you up and you want to chop wood? Where is your axe? Hand it to me and show me what to chop. I do enjoy it, you know, just a hobby. We get a lot of driftwood along the backwater near my house, and on Sundays I do nothing but chop wood for the fireplace. I really feel different when I watch the fire in the fireplace, although it may take all the sections of the Sunday *New York Times* to get a fire started,' and he smiled at this reference.

Muni felt totally confused but decided the best thing would be to make an attempt to get away from this place. He tried to edge out, saying, 'Must go home,' and turned to go. The other seized his shoulder and said desperately, 'Is there no one, absolutely no one here, to translate for me?' He looked up and down the road, which was deserted in this hot afternoon; a sudden gust of wind churned up the dust and dead leaves on the roadside into a ghostly column and propelled it towards the mountain road. The stranger almost pinioned Muni's back to the statue and asked, 'Isn't this statue yours? Why don't you sell it to me?'

The old man now understood the reference to the horse, thought for a second, and said in his own language, 'I was an urchin this high when I heard my grandfather explain this horse and warrior, and my grandfather himself was this high when he heard his grandfather, whose grandfather . . .'

The other man interrupted him with, 'I don't want to seem to have stopped here for nothing. I will offer you a good price for this,' he said, indicating the horse. He had concluded without the least doubt that Muni owned this mud horse. Perhaps he guessed by the way he sat at its pedestal, like other souvenir-sellers in this country presiding over their wares.

Muni followed the man's eyes and pointing fingers and dimly understood the subject matter and, feeling relieved that the theme of the mutilated body had been abandoned at least for the time being, said again, enthusiastically, 'I was this high when my grandfather told me about this horse and the warrior, and my grandfather was this high when he himself . . .' and he was getting into a deeper bog of reminiscence each time he tried to indicate the antiquity of the statue.

The Tamil that Muni spoke was stimulating even as pure sound, and the foreigner listened with fascination. 'I wish I had my tape-recorder here,' he said, assuming the pleasantest expression. 'Your language sounds wonderful. I get a kick out of every word you utter, here' – he indicated his ears – 'but you don't have to waste your breath in sales talk. I appreciate the article. You don't have to explain its points.'

'I never went to a school, in those days only Brahmin went to schools, but we had to go out and work in the fields morning till night, from sowing to harvest time . . . and when Pongal came and we had cut the harvest, my father allowed me to go out and play with others at the tank, and so I don't know the Parangi language you speak, even little fellows in your country probably speak the Parangi language, but here only learned men and officers know it. We had a postman in our village who could speak to you boldly in your language, but his wife ran away with someone and he does not speak to anyone at all nowadays. Who would if a wife did what she did? Women must be watched; otherwise they will sell themselves and the home,' and he laughed at his own quip.

The foreigner laughed heartily, took out another cigarette, and offered it to Muni, who now smoked with ease, deciding to stay on if the fellow was going to be so good as to keep up his cigarette supply. The American now stood up on the pedestal in the attitude of a demonstrative lecturer and said, running his finger along some of the carved decorations around the horse's neck, speaking slowly and uttering his words syllable by syllable, 'I could give a sales talk for this better than anyone else . . . This is a marvellous combination of yellow and indigo, though faded now . . . How do you people of this country achieve these flaming colours?'

Muni, now assured that the subject was still the horse and not the dead body, said, 'This is our guardian, it means death to our adversaries. At the end of Kali Yuga, this world and all other worlds will be destroyed, and the Redeemer will come in the shape of a horse called Kalki; this horse will come to life and gallop and trample down all bad men.' As he spoke of bad men the figures of his shopman and his brother-in-law assumed concrete forms in his mind, and he revelled for a moment in the predicament of the fellow under the horse's hoof: served him right for trying to set fire to his home . . .

While he was brooding on this pleasant vision, the foreigner utilised the pause to say, 'I assure you that this will have the best home in the USA. I'll push away the bookcase, you know I love books and am a member of five book clubs, and the choice and bonus volumes really mount up to a pile in our living-room, as high as this horse itself. But they'll have to go. Ruth may disapprove, but I will convince her. The TV may have to be shifted too. We can't have everything in the living-room. Ruth will probably say what about when we have a party? I'm going to keep him right in the middle of the room. I don't see how that can interfere with the party – we'll stand around him and have our drinks.'

Muni continued his description of the end of the world. 'Our pundit discoursed at the temple once how the oceans are going to close over the earth in a huge wave and swallow us – this horse will grow bigger than the biggest wave and carry on its back only the good people and kick into the floods the evil ones – plenty of them about,' he said reflectively. 'Do you know when it is going to happen?' he asked.

The foreigner now understood by the tone of the other that a question was being asked and said, 'How am I transporting it? I can push the seat back and make room in the rear. That van can take in an elephant' – waving precisely at the back of the seat.

Muni was still hovering on visions of avatars and said again, 'I never missed our pundit's discourses at the temple in those days during every bright half of the month, although he'd go on all night, and he told us that Vishnu is the highest god. Whenever evil men trouble us, he comes down to save us. He has come many times. The first time he incarnated as a great fish, and lifted the scriptures on his back when the floods and sea-waves . . .'

'I am not a millionaire, but a modest businessman. My trade is coffee.'

Amidst all this wilderness of obscure sound Muni caught the word 'coffee' and said, 'If you want to drink "kapi", drive further up, in the next town, they have Friday market, and there they open "kapi-otels" – so I learn from passers-by. Don't think I wander about. I go nowhere and look for nothing.' His thoughts went back to the avatars. 'The first avatar was in the shape of a little fish in a bowl of water, but every hour it grew bigger and bigger and became in the end a huge whale which the seas could not contain, and on the back of the whale the holy books were supported, saved, and carried.' Having launched on the first avatar it was inevitable that he should go on to the next, a wild boar on whose tusk the earth was lifted when a vicious conqueror of the earth carried it off and hid it at the bottom of the sea. After describing this avatar Muni concluded, 'God will always save us whenever we are troubled by evil beings. When we were young we staged at full moon the story of the avatars. That's how I know the stories; we played them all night until the sun rose, and sometimes the European collector would come to watch, bringing his own chair. I had a good voice and so they always taught me songs and gave me the women's rôles. I was always Goddess Laxmi, and they dressed me in a brocade sari, loaned from the Big House . . .'

The foreigner said, 'I repeat I am not a millionaire. Ours is a modest business; after all, we can't afford to buy more than sixty minutes' TV time in a month, which works out to two minutes a day, that's all, although in the course of time we'll maybe sponsor a one-hour show regularly if our sales graph continues to go up . . .'

Muni was intoxicated by the memory of his theatrical days and was about to explain how he had painted his face and worn a wig and diamond earrings when the visitor, feeling that he had spent too much time already, said, 'Tell me, will you accept a hundred rupees or not for the horse? I'd love to take the whiskered soldier also but I've no space for him this year. I'll have to cancel my air ticket and take a boat home, I suppose. Ruth can go by air if she likes, but I will go with the horse and keep him in my cabin all the way if necessary,' and he smiled at the picture of himself voyaging across the seas hugging this horse. He added, 'I will have to pad it with straw so that it doesn't break . . .'

'When we played *Ramayana*, they dressed me as Sita,' added Muni. 'A teacher came and taught us the songs for the drama and we gave him fifty rupees. He incarnated himself as Rama, and he alone could destroy Ravana, the demon with ten heads who shook all the worlds; do you know the story of Ramayana?'

'I have my station-wagon as you see. I can push the seat back and take the horse in if you will just lend me a hand with it.'

'Do you know *Mahabharata*? Krishna was the eighth avatar of Vishnu, incarnated to help the Five Brothers regain their kingdom. When Krishna was a baby he danced on the thousand-hooded giant serpent and trampled it to death; and then he suckled the breasts of the demoness and left them flat as a disc though when she came to him her bosoms were large, like mounds of earth on the banks of a dug-up canal.' He indicated two mounds with his hands. The stranger was completely mystified by the gesture. For the first time he said, 'I really wonder what you are saying because your answer is crucial. We have come to the point when we should be ready to talk business.'

'When the tenth avatar comes, do you know where you and I will be?' asked the old man.

'Lend me a hand and I can lift off the horse from its pedestal after picking out the cement at the joints. We can do anything if we have a basis of understanding.'

At this stage the mutual mystification was complete, and there was no need even to carry on a guessing game at the meaning of words. The old man chattered away in a spirit of balancing off the credits and debits of conversational exchange, and said in order to be on the credit side, 'O honourable one, I hope God has blessed you with numerous progeny. I say this because you seem to be a good man, willing to stay beside an old man and talk to him, while all day I have none to talk to except when somebody stops by to ask for a piece of tobacco. But I seldom have it, tobacco is not what it used to be at one time, and I have given up chewing. I cannot afford it nowadays.' Noting the other's interest in his speech, Muni felt encouraged to ask, 'How many children have you?' with appropriate gestures with his hands. Realising that a question was being asked, the red man replied, 'I said a hundred,' which encouraged Muni to go into details, 'How many of your children are boys and how many girls? Where are they? Is your daughter married? Is it difficult to find a son-in-law in your country also?'

In answer to these questions the red man dashed his hand into his pocket and brought forth his wallet in order to take immediate advantage of the bearish trend in the market. He flourished a hundred-rupee currency note and asked, 'Well, this is what I meant.'

The old man now realised that some financial element was entering their talk. He peered closely at the currency note, the like of which he had never seen in his life; he knew the five and ten by their colours although always in other people's hands, while his own earning at any time was in coppers and nickels. What was this man flourishing the note for? Perhaps asking for change. He laughed to himself at the notion of anyone coming to him for changing a thousand- or ten-thousand-rupee note. He said with a grin, 'Ask our village headman, who is also a moneylender; he can change even a lakh of rupees in gold sovereigns if you prefer it that way; he thinks nobody knows, but dig the floor of his puja room and your head will reel at the sight of the hoard. The man disguises himself in rags just to mislead the public. Talk to the headman yourself because he goes mad at the sight of me. Someone took away his pumpkins with the creeper and he, for some reason, thinks it was me and my goats . . . that's why I never let my goats be seen anywhere near the farms.' His eyes travelled to his goats nosing about, attempting to wrest nutrition from minute greenery peeping out of rock and dry earth.

The foreigner followed his look and decided that it would be a sound policy to show an interest in the old man's pets. He went up casually to them and stroked their backs with every show of courteous attention. Now the truth dawned on the old man. His dream of a lifetime was about to be realised. He understood that the red man was actually making an offer for the goats. He had reared them up in the hope of selling them some day and, with the capital, opening a small shop on this very spot. Sitting here, watching the hills, he had often dreamt how he would put up a thatched roof here, spread a gunny sack out on the ground, and display on it fried nuts, coloured sweets, and green coconut for the thirsty and famished wayfarers on the highway, which was sometimes very busy. The animals were not prize ones for a cattle show, but he had spent his occasional savings to provide them some fancy diet now and then, and they did not look too bad. While he was reflecting thus, the red man shook his hand and left on his palm one hundred rupees in tens now. 'It is all for you or you may share it if you have the partner.'

The old man pointed at the station-wagon and asked, 'Are you carrying them off in that?'

'Yes, of course,' said the other, understanding the transportation part of it.

The old man said, 'This will be their first ride in a motor car. Carry them off after I get out of sight, otherwise they will never follow you, but only me even if I am travelling on the path to Yama Loka.' He laughed at his own joke, brought his palms together in a salute, turned round and went off, and was soon out of sight beyond a clump of thicket.

The red man looked at the goats grazing peacefully. Perched on the pedestal of the horse, as the westerly sun touched the ancient faded colours of the statue with a fresh splendour, he ruminated, 'He must be gone to fetch some help, I suppose!' and settled down to wait. When a truck came downhill, he stopped it and got the help of a couple of men to detach the horse from its pedestal and place it in his station-wagon. He gave them five rupees each, and for a further payment they siphoned off gas from the truck and helped him to start his engine.

Muni hurried homeward with the cash securely tucked away at his waist in his dhoti. He shut the street door and stole up softly to his wife as she squatted before the lit oven wondering if by a miracle food would drop from the sky. Muni displayed his fortune for the day. She snatched the notes from him, counted them by the glow of the fire, and cried, 'One hundred rupees! How did you come by it? Have you been stealing?'

'I have sold our goats to a red-faced man. He was absolutely crazy to have them, gave me all this money and carried them off in his motor car!'

Hardly had these words left his lips when they heard bleating outside. She opened the door and saw the two goats at her door. 'Here they are!' she said. 'What's the meaning of all this?'

He muttered a great curse and seized one of the goats by its ears and shouted, 'Where is that man? Don't you know you are his? Why did you come back?' The goat only wriggled in his grip. He asked the same question of the other too. The goat shook itself off. His wife glared at him and declared, 'If you have thieved, the police will come tonight and break your bones. Don't involve me. I will go away to my parents . . .'

28

Report on the Threatened City

(1972)

Doris Lessing

PRIORITY FLASH ONE

All coordinates all plans all prints cancelled. As of now condition unforeseen by us obtaining this city. Clear all programmes all planners all forecasters for new setting on this information.

PRIORITY

Base to note well that transmisson this channel will probably be interrupted by material originating locally. Our fuel is low and this channel therefore only one now operative.

Summary of Background to Mission

Since our planet discovered that this city was due for destruction or severe damage, all calculations and plans of our department have been based on one necessity: how to reach the city to warn its inhabitants of what is to come. Observing their behaviour, both through Astroviewers and from our unmanned machines launched at intervals this past year, their time, our Commissioners for External Affairs decided these people could have no idea at all of what threatened, that their technology, while so advanced in some ways, had a vast gap in it, a gap that could be defined, in fact, precisely by that area of ignorance – not knowing what was to befall them. This gap seemed impossible. Much time was spent by our technicians trying to determine what form of brain these creatures could have that made this contradiction possible – as already stated, a technology so advanced in one area and blank in another. Our technicians had to shelve the problem, since their theories became increasingly improbable and since no species known to us anywhere corresponds even at a long remove with what we believed this one to be. It became, perhaps, the most intriguing of our unsolved problems, challenging and defeating one department after another.

Summary of Objective this Mission

Meanwhile, putting all speculations on one side, attractive though they were, all our resources have been used, at top speed and pressure, to develop a spacecraft that could, in fact, land a team on this planet, since it was our intention, having given the warning, offered the information available to us, but (we thought) not to them, which made the warning necessary, to offer them more; our assistance. We meant to help clear the area, transport the population elsewhere, cushion the shock to the area and then, having done what, after all, we have done for other planets, our particular mental structure being suited to this kind of forecasting and assistance, return to base, taking some suitable specimens of them with us, in order to train them in a way that would overcome the gap in their minds and, therefore, their science. The first part we achieved: that is, we managed, in the time set for it, to develop a spacecraft that could make the journey here, carrying the required number of personnel. It strained our own technology and postponed certain cherished plans of our own. But our craft landed here, on the western shore of the land mass, as planned, and without any trouble, seven days ago.

The Nature of the Problem

You will have wondered why there have been no transmissions before this. There have been two reasons. One: we realised at once that there would be heavier demands on our fuel than we had anticipated and that we would have to conserve it. Two: we were waiting to understand what it was we had to tell you. We did not understand the problem. For it was almost at once clear to us that all our thinking about 'the gap in their mental structure' was off the point. We have never understood the nature of the problem. So improbable is it that we delayed communicating until we were sure. The trouble with this species is not that it is unable to forecast its immediate future; it is that it doesn't seem to care. Yet that is altogether too simple a stating of its condition. If it were so simple – that it knew that within five years its city was to be destroyed, or partly destroyed, and that it was indifferent – we should have to say: This species lacks the first quality necessary to any animal species; it lacks the will to live. Finding out what the mechanism is has caused the delay. Which I now propose partially to remedy by going into an account of what befell us, step by step. This will entail a detailed description of a species and a condition absolutely without precedent in our experience of the inhabited planets.

An Impossible Fact

But, first, there is a fact that you will find hard to believe. We did not find this out at once, but when we did, it was a moment of focus in our investigation, enabling us to see our problem clearly. *This city experienced a disaster, on a fairly large scale, about 65 years ago, their time.*

A thought immediately suggests itself: our experts did not know about this past disaster, only about the one to come. Our thinking is as defective in its way as theirs is. We had decided that they had a gap, that this gap made it impossible for them to see into the immediate future. Having decided this, we never once considered another possibility, the truth – that they had no gap, that they knew about the threatened danger and did not care. Or behaved as if they did not. Since we were unable to conceive of this latter possibility, we did not direct our thoughts and our instruments back in time –

their time. We took it absolutely for granted, an assumption so strong that it prevented our effective functioning as much as these creatures' assumptions prevent them from acting – we believed (since we are so built ourselves) that it would be impossible for a disaster to have occurred already, because if we had experienced such a thing, we would have learned from the event and taken steps accordingly. Because of a series of assumptions, then, and an inability to move outside our own mental set, we missed a fact that might have been a clue to their most extraordinary characteristic – the fact that such a very short time ago they experienced a disaster of the sort that threatens again, and soon.

The Landing

Our unmanned craft have been landing on their planet for centuries and have taken various shapes, been of varying substances. These landings were at long intervals until one year ago. These intervals were because, except for its unique destructiveness and belligerence, this species is not the most remarkable or interesting of those made available to our study by our Technological Revolution in its Space Phase. But 12 times recently, each during a period when their planet was at full light potential, we have landed craft, and each time close to the place in question. This was easy, because the terrain is semi-desert and lightly populated. We chose material for the craft that would manifest as their substance light – which is why we always used maximum their planet light as landing times. These craft were visible, if at all, as strong moonlight. The craft we were using on this present mission, the 13th in this series, is of higher concentration, since it is manned.

We landed as planned. The sky was clear, the light of their moon strong. We knew at once that we were visible, because a herd of their young was near, some 50 or 60 of them, engaged in a mating ritual that involved fire, food and strong sound, and as we descended, they dispersed. Tapping their mind streams established that they believed our machine was extra-terrestrial but that they were indifferent – no, that is not an exact description, but remember, we are trying to describe a mind state that none of us could have believed was possible. It was not that they were indifferent to us but that indifference was generalised throughout their processes, felt by us as a block or a barrier. After the young creatures had gone, we surveyed the terrain and discovered that we were on high land rising to mountains, inland from the water mass on the edge of which stands the city. A group of older specimens arrived. We know now that they live nearby and are all some variety or other of agriculturalist. They stood quite close, watching the craft. An examination of their minds showed a different type of block. Even at that early stage, we were able to establish a difference in texture between their thought streams and those of the young, which we later understood amounted to this: the older ones felt a responsibility or a power to act, as members of society, while the young ones were excluded or had decided to exclude themselves. As this area of the planet turned into the sunlight, it was clear to us that our craft ceased to be visible, for two of these older creatures came so close we were afraid they would actually enter the concentration. But they showed an awareness of our presence by other symptoms – headache and nausea. They were angry because of this damage being done to them

– which they could have alleviated by moving farther off; but at the same time, they were feeling pride. This reaction highlighted the differences between them and the young – the pride was because of what they thought we represented; for, unlike the young, they believed we were some kind of weapon, either of their own land mass or of a hostile one, but from their own planet.

War-Making Patterns

Everyone in the System knows that this species is in the process of self-destruction, or part destruction. This is endemic. The largest and most powerful groupings – based on geographical positions – are totally governed by their war-making functions. Rather, each grouping *is* a war-making function, since its economies, its individual lives, its movements, are all subservient to the need to prepare for or wage war. This complete domination of a land area by its war-making machinery is not always visible to the inhabitants of that area, as this species is able, while making war or preparing for it, to think of itself as peace-loving – yes, indeed, this is germane to our theme, the essence of it.

Rational Action Impossible

Here we approach the nature of the block, or patterning of their minds – we state it now, though we did not begin to understand it until later. *It is that they are able to hold in their minds at the same time several contradictory beliefs without noticing it.* Which is why rational action is so hard for them. Now, the war-making function of each geographical area is not controlled by its inhabitants but is controlled by itself. Each is engaged in inventing, bringing to perfection – and keeping secret from its own inhabitants as well as from the 'enemy' – highly evolved war weapons of all sorts, ranging from devices for the manipulation of men's minds to spacecraft.

Subservient Populations

For instance, recent landings on their moon, much publicised by the geographical groupings that made them and followed breathlessly by the inhabitants of the whole planet, were by no means the first achieved by the said groupings. No, the first 'moon landings' were made in secret, in service of one grouping's dominance in war over another, and the slavish populations knew nothing about them. A great many of the devices and machines used by the war departments are continuously under test in all parts of the earth and are always being glimpsed or even seen fully by inhabitants who report them to the authorities. But some of these devices are similar (in appearance, at least) to machines of extra-terrestrial origin. Citizens reporting 'flying saucers' – to use one of their descriptive phrases – may as well have seen the latest of their own grouping's machines on test as one of our observation craft or observation craft from the Jupiter family. Such a citizen will find that after reaching a certain level in the hierarchies of officialdom, silence will blanket him and his observations – he will in various ways be repulsed, ridiculed or even threatened. As usually happens, a council of highly placed officials was recently ordered to take evidence and report on the by now innumerable sightings of 'unidentified flying objects', but this council finished its deliberations with public words that left the situation exactly as it was before. The official report nowhere stated that there was a minority report by some of its own number. This is the level of behaviour in their public representatives that is tolerated by them. Large numbers, everywhere on the planet, see craft like ours, or like other planets' craft or war machines from their own or other geographical areas. But such is the atmosphere created by the war departments that dominate everything that these individuals are regarded as mentally inadequate or deluded. Until one of them has actually seen a machine or a spacecraft, he tends to believe that anyone who claims he has is deranged. Knowing this, when he does see something, he often does not say so. But so many individuals now have seen things for themselves that there are everywhere all kinds of dissident or sullen subgroupings. These are of all ages and they cut across the largest and most widespread subculture of them all, that of the young of the species who have grown up in a society of total war-preparedness, who are naturally reluctant to face a future that can only mean early death or maiming and who react in the way mentioned earlier, with a disinclination to take part in the administration of their various societies. The older ones seem much more able to delude themselves, to use words like peace when engaged in warlike behaviour, to identify with their geographical areas. The young ones are clear-minded, more easily see the planet as a single organism, but are also more passive and hopeless. We put forward the suggestion that the greater, or at least more purposive, energy of the older ones may be because of their comparative narrowness and identification with smaller ideas.

We are now able to explain why the young we met on the night we landed moved away. Some had already had the experience of insisting to the authorities that they had seen strange machines and objects of various kinds and of being discouraged or threatened. They would be prepared to publicise what they had seen in their own news sheets or to spread it by word of mouth; but, unlike their elders, most of them seem unable to understand the extent to which they are subjugated to the needs of war, they would never put themselves in a position where their authorities could capture or question them. But the older ones of the area who had seen our previous 12 craft, which had all landed there, had evolved a different attitude. Some had reported what they had seen and had been discouraged. One or two, persisting, had been described as mad and had been threatened with incarceration. But, on the whole, they had taken the attitude of the authorities as a directive to mind their own business. Discussing it among themselves, they had agreed to keep watch on their own account, not saying too much about what they saw. In this group are two spies, who report to the war departments on what is seen and on the reactions of their fellow agriculturalists.

First Attempt at a Warning

Now we come to our first attempt to communicate a warning. Since the 20 or so elders were already on the spot and were unafraid, staying on the site where they believed we might redescend – they did not know it was only the strength of the sun's light that made us invisible – we decided to use them and again made contact with their thought streams, this time in an attempt to project our message. But there was a barrier, or at least something we could not understand, and it was time-consuming for us. We were already aware that we might run short of power.

Incapacity for Fear

Now, of course, we know we made a wrong assessment, for, expecting that the news of the expected disaster would jam their thought machinery in panic, we fed it in very carefully and slowly, taking an entire day and night. When we hit the block, or resistance, we put it down to fear. We were mistaken. This is perhaps the time to state a psychological law we consider basic to them: this is a species immune from fear – but this will be elaborated later, if the power holds. At the end of the day and night, still meeting the same resistance, we allowed ourselves another period of a day and a night to repeat the message, hoping that the fear – as we then saw it – would be overcome. At the end of the second period of transmitting, there was no change in their mental structure. I repeat, none. We know now what was far from our understanding then, that we were telling them something they already knew. As we were not prepared at that time to entertain that hypothesis, we decided that this particular group of individuals was for some reason unsuitable for our purposes and that we must try an altogether different type, and preferably of a different age group. We had tried mature individuals. We had already suspected what we since have confirmed, that in this species the older they get, the less open they are to new thought material. Now, it so happens that the place where our craft descended is in an area much used for the before-mentioned mating rituals. Several times in the two day-and-night periods of our attempt with the older group, youngsters had arrived in various types of metal machines from the city – and had quite soon gone away, sensing our presence, if they did not see us. They all arrived in daylight. But on the third day, as the sunlight went, four young ones arrived in a metal conveyance, got out of it and sat fairly close to us on a small rocky rise.

Second Attempt at a Warning

They looked like healthy, strong specimens, and we began to transmit our information, but in greater concentration than we had used with the older individuals. But in spite of the increased power these four absorbed what we fed into them and reacted in exactly the same way as their elders. We did not understand this and, taking the chance of setting them into a panic flight, concentrated our entire message (which had taken two entire days and nights with the mature group) into the space of time between the sunlight's going and its return. Their minds did not reject what we said nor jam up in fear. They were voicing to one another in a mechanical way, what we were feeding into them. It sounded like this, over and over again – with variations:

'They say we have only five years.'

'That's bad.'

'Yeah, it's going to be real bad.'

'When it comes, it's going to be the worst yet.'

'Half the city might be killed.'

'They say it might be as bad as that.'

'Any time in the next five years, they say.'

It was like pouring a liquid into a container that has a hole in it. The group of older ones had sat around for two days and nights repeating that the city was due for destruction, as if they were saying that they could expect a headache, and now these four were doing the same. At one point they stopped the monotone exchanges and one, a young female, accompanying herself on a stringed musical instrument, began what they call a song; that is, the vocalisations cease to be an exchange between two or more individuals, but an individual, or a group, very much enlarging the range of tones uses in ordinary exchange, makes a statement. The information we fed into these four emerged in these words, from the young female:

We know the earth we live upon
Is due to fall.
We know the ground we walk upon
Must shake.
We know, and so . . .
We eat and drink and love,
Keep high,
Keep love,
For we must die.

Phase I Abandoned

And they continued with their mating rituals. We then discontinued the emission of thought material, if for no other reason than that we had already used up a fourth of our power supply with no result. This, then, was the end of Phase I, which was the attempt to transfer the warning material into the brains of selected members of the species for automatic telepathic transmission to others. We set about Phase II, which was to take possession of the minds of suitable individuals in a planned campaign to use them as mouthpieces for the warnings. We decided to abandon the first phase in the belief that the material was running straight through their mental apparatus like water through sieves because it was so foreign to the existing mental furniture of their minds that they were not able to recognise what we were saying. In other words, we still had no idea that the reason they did not react was that the idea was a commonplace.

Phase II Attempted

Three of us therefore accompanied the four youngsters in their machine when they returned to the city, because we thought that in their company we would most quickly find suitable individuals to take over – we had decided the young men were more likely to be useful than the mature. The way they handled this machine was a shock to us. It was suicidal. Their methods of transport are lethal. In the time it took to reach the suburbs of the city – between the lightening of the dark and the sun's appearance – there were four near collisions with other, equally recklessly driven vehicles. Yet the four youngsters showed no fear and reacted with the mechanism called laughter; that is, with repeated violent contractions of the lungs, causing noisy emissions of air. This journey, their recklessness, their indifference to death or pain, made us conclude that this group of four, like the group of 20 older ones, was perhaps atypical. We were playing with the idea that there are large numbers of defective animals in this species and that we had been unlucky in our choices. The machine was stopped to refuel and the four got out and walked about. Three more youngsters were sitting on a bench huddled against one another, in a stupor. Like all the young, they wore a wide variety of clothing, and had long head fur. They had several musical instruments. Our four attempted to rouse them and partly succeeded: the responses of the three were slow and, it seemed to us, even more clumsy and inadequate. They either did not understand what was being said or could not communicate what they understood. We then saw that they were in the power of some kind of drug. They had quantities of it, and the four wished also to put themselves in its power. It was a drug that sharpens sensitivity while it inhibits ordinary response: the three were more sensitive to our presence than the four had been – they had not been aware of our presence in the vehicle at all. The three, once roused from their semi-consciousness, seemed to see, or at least feel, us and directed towards us muttered sounds of approval or welcome. They seemed to associate us with the sun's appearance over the roof of the refuelling station. The four, having persuaded the three to give them some of the drug, went to their vehicle. We decided to stay with the three, believing that their sensitivity to our presence was a good sign. Testing their thought streams, we found them quite free and loose, without the resistances and tensions of the others we had tested. We then took possession of their minds – this was the only moment of real danger during the whole mission. Your envoys might very well have been lost then, dissolving into a confusion and violence that we find hard to describe. For one thing, at that time we did not know how to differentiate between the effects of the drug and the effects of their senses. We now do know and will attempt a short description. The drug causes the mechanisms dealing with functions such as walking, talking, eating, and so on, to become slowed or dislocated. Meanwhile, the receptors for sound, scent, sight, touch, are open and sensitised. But, for us, to enter their minds is in any case an assault, because of the phenomenon they call beauty, which is a description of their sense intake in an ordinary condition. For us, this is like entering an explosion of colour; for it is this that is the most startling difference between our mode of perceiving and theirs: the physical structure of their level appears in vibrations of brilliant colour. To enter an undrugged mind is hard enough for one of us; to keep one's balance is difficult. As it was, it might easily have happened that we were swept away in contemplation of vivid colour.

Necessity to Condense Report, Power Failing

Although the temptation to dwell on this is great, we must condense this report if we wish to keep any use of this channel: the pressure of local material is getting very strong. In brief, then, the three youngsters, reeling with pleasure because of this dimension of brilliance which we of course all know about through deduction but which I assure you, we have never even approached in imagination, shouting and singing that the city was doomed, stood on the side of the road until one of the plentiful machines stopped for us. We were conveyed rapidly into the city. There were two individuals in the vehicle, both young, and neither reacted in any way to the warnings we were giving them through the minds or, rather, voices of our hosts. At the end of the rapid movement, we arrived in the city, which is large, populous and built around a wide indentation of the shore of the water mass. It is all extremely vivid, colourful, powerfully affecting the judgment, and it heightened the assault on our balance. We made a tentative decision that it is impracticable for our species to make use of this method: of actually possessing selected minds for the purpose of passing on information. It is too violent a transformation for us. However, since we were there, and succeeding in not being swept away into a highly tinted confusion of pleasure, we agreed to stay where we were, and the three we were possessing left the vehicle and walked out into the streets, shouting out the facts as we thought them: that there was little doubt that at some moment between now and five years from now, there would be a strong vibration of the planet at this point and that the greater part of the city might be destroyed, with severe loss of life. It was early in the day, but many of them were about. We were waiting for some sort of reaction to what we were saying, interest at the very least; queries; some sort of response to which we could respond ourselves with advice or offers of help. But of the very many we met in that brief progress through the streets, *no one took any notice at all*, except for a glance or a short indifferent state.

Capture by the Authorities

Soon there was a screeching and a wailing, which we at first took to be the reaction of these creatures to what we were saying, some sort of warning, perhaps, to the inhabitants, or statements that measures towards self-preservation must be taken; but it was another vehicle, of a military sort, and the three (we) were taken up from the streets and to a prison because of the disturbance we were making. This is how we understood it afterwards. At the time, we thought that the authorities had gathered us in to question us as to the revelations we had to make. In the hands of the guards, in the street and the military vehicle and the prison, we kept up a continuous shouting and crying-out of the facts and did not stop until a doctor injected our three hosts with some other drug, which caused them instantly to become unconscious. It was when we heard the doctor talking to the guards that we first heard the fact of the previous catastrophe. This was such a shock to us that we could not then take in its implications. But we decided at once to leave our hosts, who, being in any case unconscious, would not be any use to us for some time, even if this method of conveying warnings had turned out to be efficacious – and it obviously was not – and make different plans. The doctor was also saying that he had to treat large numbers of people, particularly the young ones, for 'paranoia'. This was what our three hosts were judged to be suffering from. Apparently, it is a condition when people show fear of forthcoming danger and try to warn others about it, and then show anger when stopped by authority. This diagnosis, together with the fact that the doctor and the authorities knew of the coming danger and of the past catastrophe – in other words, that they consider it an illness or a faulty mental condition to be aware of what threatens and to try to take steps to avoid or soften it – was something so extraordinary that we did not then have time to evaluate it in depth, nor have we had time since to do so, because – . . . AND FINALLY, TO END THIS NEWS FLASH, A REAL HEART WARMER. FIVE ORDINARY PEOPLE, NOT RICH FOLKS, NO, BUT PEOPLE LIKE YOU AND ME, HAVE GIVEN UP A MONTH'S PAY TO SEND LITTLE JANICE WANAMAKER, THE CHILD WITH THE HOLE IN THE HEART, TO THE WORLD-FAMED HEART CENTRE IN FLORIDA. LITTLE JANICE, WHO IS TWO YEARS OLD, COULD HAVE EXPECTED A LONGLIFE OF INVALIDISM; BUT

NOW THE FAIRY WAND OF LOVE HAS CHANGED ALL THAT AND SHE WILL BE FLYING TOMORROW MORNING TO HAVE HER OPERATION, ALL THANKS TO THE FIVE GOOD NEIGHBOURS OF ARTESIA STREET – . . . The expected interruptions of this wavelength; but, as we have no way of knowing at which point the interruption began, to recapitulate, we left the doctor and the guards in discussion of the past catastrophe, in which 200 miles of ground were ripped open, hundreds of people were killed and the whole city was shaken down in fragments. This was succeeded by a raging fire.

Humour as a Mechanism

The doctor was recalling *humorously* (note previous remarks about laughter, a possible device for release of tension to ward off or relieve fear and, therefore, possibly one of the mechanisms to keep these animals passive in the face of possible extinction) that for some years after the previous catastrophe, this entire geographical grouping referred to the great fire, rather than to the earth vibration. This circumlocution is still quite common. In other words, a fire being a smaller, more manageable phenomenon, they preferred, and sometimes still prefer, to use that word, instead of the word for the uncontrollable shaking of the earth itself. A pitiable device, showing helplessness and even fear. But we emphasise here again that everywhere else in the System, fear is a mechanism to protect or to warn, and in these creatures, the function is faulty. As for helplessness, this is tragic anywhere, even among these murderous brutes, but there is no apparent need for them to be helpless, since they have every means to evacuate the city altogether and so – . . . THE NEW SUBURB PLANNED TO THE WEST. THIS WILL HOUSE 100,000 PEOPLE AND WILL BE OPEN IN THE AUTUMN OF NEXT YEAR FULLY EQUIPPED WITH SHOPS, CINEMAS, A CHURCH, SCHOOLS AND A NEW MOTORWAY. THE RAPID EXPANSION OF OUR BEAUTIFUL CITY, WITH ITS UNIQUE CLIMATE, ITS SETTING, ITS SHORE LINE, CONTINUES. THIS NEW SUBURB WILL DO SOMETHING TO COMBAT THE OVERCROWDING AND –

The Jettisoning of Phases I, II and III

In view of the failure of Phases I and II, we decided to abandon Phase III, which was planned to be a combination of I and II – inhabiting suitable hosts to use them as loudspeakers and, at the same time, putting material into available thought streams for retransmission. Before making further attempts to communicate, we needed more information. To summarise the results of Phase II, when we inhabited the three drugged young, we understood we must be careful to assume the shapes of older animals, and those of a technically trained kind, as it was clear from our experience in the prison that the authorities disliked the young of their species. We did not yet know whether they were capable of listening to the older ones, who are shaped in the image of their society

Inability to Assess Truth

While at that stage we were still very confused about what we were finding, we had at least grasped this: that this species, on being told something, has no means of judging whether or not it is true. We on our planet assume, because it is our mental structure and that of all the species we have examined, that if a new fact is made evident by material progress, or by a new and hitherto unexpected juxtaposition of ideas, then it is accepted as a fact, a truth – until an evolutionary development bypasses it. Not so with this species. It is not able to accept information, new material, unless it is from a source it is not suspicious about. This is a handicap to its development that it is not possible to exaggerate. We choose this moment to suggest, though of necessity briefly, that in future visits to this planet, with information of use to this species (if it survives), infinite care must be taken to prepare plenipotentiaries who resemble in every respect the most orthodox and harmless members of the society. For it is as if the mechanism fear has been misplaced from where it would be useful – preventing or softening calamity – to an area of their minds that makes them suspicious of anything but the familiar. As a small example, in the prison, because the three young animals were drugged and partly incoherent, and because (as it has become clear to us) the older animals who run the society despise those who are not similar to the norms they have established, it would not have mattered what they said. If they had said (or shouted or sung) that they had actually observed visitors from another planet (they had, in fact, sensed us, felt us) as structures of finer substance manifesting as light – if they had stated they had seen three roughly man-sized creatures shaped in light – no notice at all would have been taken of them. But if an individual from that section of their society which is especially trained for that class of work (it is an infinitely subdivided society) had said that he had observed *with his instruments* (they have become so dependent on machinery that they have lost confidence in their own powers of observation) three rapidly vibrating light structures, he would at least have been credited with good faith. Similarly, great care has to be taken with verbal formulation. An unfamiliar fact described in one set of words may be acceptable. Present it in a pattern of words outside what they are used to and they may react with all the signs of panic – horror, scorn, fear.

Adaptation to their Norm for their Dominant Animals

We incarnated as two males of mature age. We dressed ourselves with the attention to detail they find reassuring. An item of clothing cut differently from what is usual for older animals will arouse disapproval or suspicion. Sober tones of colour are acceptable; bright tones, except in small patches, are not. We assure you that if we had dressed even slightly outside their norm, we could have done nothing at all. It is the dominant males who have to restrict their choice of clothing. Women's garb is infinitely variable, but always changing, suddenly and dramatically, from one norm or pattern to another. The young can wear what they please as long as they are not part of the machinery of government. The cutting and arranging of their head fur is also important. Women and the young enjoy latitude in this, too, but we had to see that our head fur was cut short and kept flattened. We also assumed a gait indicating soberness and control, and facial expressions that we had noted they found reassuring. For instance, they have a way of stretching the lips sideways and exposing the teeth in a sort of facial arrangement they call a smile that indicates that they are not hostile, will not attack, that their intentions are to keep the peace.

Thus disguised, we walked about the city engaged in observation, on the whole astounded that so little notice was taken of us. For while we were fair copies, we were not perfect, and a close scrutiny would have shown us up. But one of their characteristics is that they, in fact, notice very little about one another; it is a remarkably unnoticing species. Without arousing suspicion, we discovered that everybody we talked to knew that a disturbance of the earth was expected in the next five years, that while they 'knew' this, they did not really believe it, or seemed not to, since their plans to live as if nothing whatsoever was going to happen were unaltered and that a laboratory or institute existed to study the past upheaval and make plans for the forthcoming one – . . . AT THE BASEBALL GAME THIS AFTERNOON, A PORTION OF THE SCAFFOLDING GAVE WAY AND 60 PEOPLE WERE KILLED. THERE HAVE BEEN MESSAGES OF SYMPATHY FROM THE PRESIDENT, HER MAJESTY THE QUEEN OF GREAT BRITAIN AND THE POPE. THE MANAGER OF THE SPORTS STADIUM WAS IN TEARS AS HE SAID: 'THIS IS THE MOST TERRIBLE THING THAT I HAVE EVER SEEN. I KEEP SEEING THOSE DEAD FACES BEFORE MY EYES.' THE CAUSE OF THE ACCIDENT IS THAT THE BUILDING OF THE STANDS AND THEIR MAINTENANCE, AND THE PROVISION OF CRUSH BARRIERS, ARE SUBJECT TO MAXIMUM PROFIT BEING EARNED BY THE OWNERS. THE FUND SET UP AS THE CORPSES WERE CARRIED FROM THE STADIUM HAD ALREADY REACHED $200,000, AND MORE KEEPS POURING –

The Institute

We entered the Institute for Prognosis and Prevention of Earth Disturbance as visitors from Geographical Area 2 – one allied at this time with this area and, therefore, welcome to observe its work.

A short description of this organisation may be of use. There are 50 of their most highly skilled technicians in it, all at work on some of the most advanced (as advanced as ours in this field) equipment for the diagnosis of vibrations, tremors, quakes. The very existence of this institute is because of the knowledge that the city cannot survive another five years – or is unlikely to do so. All these technicians live in the city, spend their free time in it – and the institute itself is in the danger area. They are all likely to be present when the event occurs. Yet they are all cheerful, unconcerned and – it is easy to think – of extreme bravery. But after a short time in their company, discussing their devices for predicting the upheaval, it is difficult to resist the conclusion that like the youngsters in the machine for transportation, who steer it in such a way that they are bound to kill or maim themselves or others, they are in some way set not to believe what they say – that they are in danger and will most certainly be killed or maimed together with the rest of the population – . . . THE FIRE BROKE OUT AT DAWN, WHEN FEW PEOPLE WERE IN THE STREETS, AND WAS SO POWERFUL THAT IT REACHED THE FOURTH STOREY FROM THE BASEMENT IN MINUTES. THE SCORES OF PEOPLE IN THE BUILDING WERE DRIVEN UPWARD BY THE FIRE, A FEW MANAGING TO NEGIOTATE THE FIRE ESCAPES, WHICH WERE MOSTLY ENGULFED IN FLAMES. AN UNKNOWN MAN IN THE STREET PENETRATED THE BUILDING, IN SPITE OF THE SMOKE AND THE FLAMES, AND RESCUED TWO SMALL CHILDREN LEFT CRYING ON THE SECOND FLOOR. ANOTHER TWO MINUTES AND IT WOULD HAVE BEEN TOO LATE. HE INSTANTLY PLUNGED BACK INTO THE INFERNO AND BROUGHT OUT AN OLD WOMAN ON HIS BACK. IN SPITE OF PROTESTS FROM THE BY NOW LARGE CROWD, HE INSISTED ON RE-ENTERING THE FLAMING BUILDING AND WAS LAST SEEN AT A SECOND-FLOOR WINDOW FROM WHICH HE THREW DOWN A BABY TO THE PEOPLE BELOW. THE BABY WILL SURVIVE, BUT THE UNKNOWN HERO FELL BACK INTO THE FLAMES AND –

A Basic Mechanism

We believe we have established one of their mechanisms for maintaining themselves in impotence and indecision. It is precisely this: that they do continuously discuss and analyse. For instance, the technicians of this institute are always issuing warnings to the city's officials and to the populace. Their prognoses, one after another, come true – that minor vibrations are likely to occur in this or that area – yet warnings continue to be issued, discussion goes on. So accustomed have they become to this state of affairs that we found it was not possible to discuss active means for prevention with them. They would have become suspicious that we were some sort of trouble-makers. In short, they do not find frightening discussion about the timing, the nature, the power of probable earth convulsions, but they are hostile to suggestions about the possible transfer of population or rebuilding of the city elsewhere. We have said that this is an infinitely subdivided society: it is the institute's task to warn, to forecast, not its responsibility to suggest solutions. But this mechanism – the rôle of talk – is merely part of a much deeper one. We now suspect that a great many of the activities that they themselves see as methods of furthering change, saving life, improving society, are in fact methods of preventing change. It is almost as if they were afflicted with a powerful lassitude, a lack of vital energy, which must resist change, because it is so easily exhausted. Their infinite number of varieties of oral, verbal activity are expenditures of vital energy. They are soothed and relieved by stating a problem, but, having done this, seldom have the energy left to act on their verbal formulations. We have even concluded that they feel that by stating a problem, it becomes in some way nearer solution – . . . PROTESTS THAT THE THREE SKYSCRAPERS ON THE THIRD STREET ARE TO BE PULLED DOWN IN ORDER TO BUILD THREE MUCH HIGHER BUILDINGS, INSTEAD OF PUTTING THE MONEY INTO PROVIDING LOW-RATE ACCOMMODATION FOR THE CITY'S POOR, OF WHICH RECENT SURVEYS REVEAL THERE ARE 1,000,000 OR MORE, NEARLY A QUARTER OF THE TOTAL POPULATION, AND ALL IN ACCOMMODATIONS SO INADEQUATE THAT – . . . for instance debates, discussions, verbal contests of all sorts, public and private, continue all the time. All their activities, public and private, are defined in talk, public or private. It is possible that they are so constituted that, for them, an event has not occurred at all unless it has been discussed, presented in words – . . . 35 CONVENTIONS IN THE MONTH OF MAY ALONE, TOTALLING 75,000 DELEGATES FROM EVERY PART OF THE CONTINENT, WHILE AT THE SAME TIME THE TOURIST FIGURES FOR MAY TOPPED THOSE FOR ANY PREVIOUS MAY. THIS YEAR IS ALREADY A RECORD FOR CONVENTIONS AND TOURISM GENERALLY, PROVING THAT THE ATTRACTIONS OF OUR CITY, ITS SITUATION, ITS CLIMATE, ITS AMENITIES, ITS REPUTATION FOR HOSPITALITY, EVER INCREASE IN EVERY PART OF THE CIVILISED GLOBE. IT IS ESSENTIAL TO STEP UP THE BUILDING OF NEW HOTELS, MOTELS AND RESTAURANTS AND TO – . . . the one thing they do not seem able to contemplate is the solution that has seemed to us obvious ever since we observed their probable future and decided to devote so much of our own planet's resources to trying to help our sister planet – to evacuate the city altogether. This is incredible, we know. Of course, you will find it so.

Indifference to Loss of Life

We can only report what we find – that at no point have the inhabitants of this city even considered the possibility of abandoning it and moving to an area that is not absolutely certain to be destroyed. Their attitude towards life is that it is unimportant. They are indifferent to their own suffering, assume that their species must continuously lose numbers and strength and health by natural disasters, famine, constant war. That this attitude goes side by side with infinite care and devotion to individuals or to small groups seems to us to indicate – . . . THE DONATED SUM IS TO BE USED TO BUILD A MEMORIAL, TO BE ERECTED IN THE SQUARE. IT WILL BE IN THE SHAPE OF A COLUMN, WITH THE HEAD OF WILLIAM UNDERSCRIBE, THE DECEASED, IN RELIEF ON ONE SIDE.

LAID TO REST
UPON THE BREAST
OF NATURE
GONE BUT NOT FORGOTTEN

WILL BE CARVED ON THE OTHER. JOAN UNDERSCRIBE, WHO LOST HER HUSBAND FIVE YEARS AGO, HAS WORKED SEVEN DAYS A WEEK FROM SIX IN THE MORNING UNTIL TEN AT NIGHT AT THE AVENUE MOTEL TO EARN THE SUM NECESSARY FOR THIS SIMPLE BUT MOVING MEMORIAL. SHE HAD JEOPARDISED HER HEALTH, SHE CLAIMS. THE FIVE YEARS OF UNREMITTING TOIL HAVE TAKEN THEIR TOLL. BUT SHE HAS NO REGRETS. HE WAS THE BEST HUSBAND A WOMAN EVER HAD, SHE TOLD OUR REPORTER – . . . on the point of deciding there was nothing we could do against such total indifference to their condition; but since they are at least prepared to talk about situations, we devised a plan – . . . THE BIGGEST ENTERTAINMENT EVER, COMBINING THE WORLD'S TOP CIRCUSES, ICE SHOWS, NON-STOP POP CONCERTS FOR THE ENTIRE WEEK, DAY AND NIGHT, NOT TO MENTION THREE OPERAS FROM THE WORLD'S GREATEST, THE BRITISH NATIONAL THEATRE COMPANY IN THAT PERENNIAL ATTRACTION, THE INTERNATIONAL CULTURAL STAR ACE, 'THE THREE SISTERS', WHICH WILL BE ATTENDED BY OUR OWN FIRST LADY AND HER CHARMING DAUGHTERS AND A GLITTERING ARRAY OF STARS, INCLUDING BOB HOPE – . . . 'calling a conference' is to gather a large number of individuals in one place, in order to exchange verbal formulations. This is probably their main anxiety-calming mechanism, they certainly resort to it on every occasion, whether under that name, called by governments, administrative bodies, authorities of all kinds, or under other names, for very often this procedure is social. For instance, a conference can be called a party and be for pleasure, but discussion on a theme or themes will be, in fact, the chief activity. The essential factor is that many of the creatures assemble in one place, to exchange word patterns with others, afterwards telling others not present what had occurred – . . . THE CITY'S CONSERVATION YEAR IS OVER AND MUST BE COUNTED A REMARKABLE SUCCESS. IT BURNED AN AWARENESS OF WHAT WE CAN EXPECT SO DEEPLY INTO ALL OUR MINDS AND HEARTS THAT INTEREST IS NOW NOT LIKELY TO FADE. A CONFERENCE TO – . . . opinions.

Their Education

The ability to define these, and to differentiate them from those of other people, forms a large part of their education. When two of these creatures meet for the first time, they will set about finding out what opinions the other holds and will tolerate each other accordingly. Non-stimulating, easily tolerated opinions can also be called 'received ideas'. This means that an idea or a fact has been stamped with approval by some form of authority. The phrase is used like this: 'That is a received idea.' 'Those are all received ideas.' This does not necessarily mean that the idea or fact has been acted on or that behaviour has been changed. Essentially, a received idea is one that has become familiar, whether effective or not, and no longer arouses hostility or fear. The mark of an educated individual is this: that he has spent years absorbing received ideas and is able readily to repeat them. People who have absorbed opinions counter to the current standard of ideas are distrusted and may be called opinionated. This description is earned most easily by women and young people.

By that time, we were well known to everyone in the institute as Herbert Bond, 35 years old, male, and John Hunter, 40 years old, male. We had learned enough to avoid the direct 'Why don't you take such and such steps?' since we had learnt that this approach caused some sort of block or fault in their functioning, but approached like this: 'Let us discuss the factors militating against the taking of such and such a step'; for instance, making sure that new buildings were not erected close to the areas where tremors or vibrations must occur.

This formulation was initially successful, evoking the maximum amount of animated talk without arousing hostility. But, very shortly, a strong emotion was aroused by phrases and words of which we list a few here: profit motive, conflicting commercial interests, vested interests, capitalism, socialism, democracy – there are many such emotive words. We were not able to determine, or not in a way that our economic experts would recognise as satisfactory, the significance of these phrases, since the emotions became too violent to allow the conference to continue. The animals would certainly have begun to attack one another physically. In other words, the range of opinion (see above) was too wide to be accommodated. Opinion, that is, on matters to do with disposal and planning of population. Opinion concerning earth disturbance was virtually unanimous.

Barbaric Method of Town Planning Unique in Our System, but See Histories of Planets 2 and 4

It appears that their population disposal, their city planning, is not determined by the needs of the people who live in an area but is the result of a balance come to by many conflicting bodies and individuals whose reason for participating in such schemes is self-interest. For instance: before the violence engendered by this subject closed the conference, we had gathered that the reason a particularly large and expensive group of buildings was built directly in the line of maximum earth disturbance was that that part of the city commands high 'rents' – that is, people are prepared to pay more to live and work in that area than elsewhere. Nor can the willingness of the builders and planners to erect buildings in the maximum danger area to be put down to callousness, since in many cases the individuals concerned themselves live and work there – . . . THE EMERGENCY UNIT AT THE HOSPITAL IN WHICH A TEAM OF TEN DOCTORS AND NURSES WORKS AROUND THE CLOCK TO SAVE LIVES THAT WOULD HAVE BEEN LOST AS RECENTLY AS FIVE YEARS AGO – AND ARE STILL LOST IN HOSPITALS NOT EQUIPPED WITH EMERGENCY UNITS. THE PATIENTS ARE USUALLY THE VICTIMS OF CAR ACCIDENTS OR STREET FIGHTS AND ARRIVE AT THE UNIT IN A STATE OR SEVERE SHOCK, SINCE AS SHORT A DELAY AS FIVE MINUTES CAN MAKE THE DIFFERENCE BETWEEN LIFE AND DEATH, TREATMENT IS STARTED AS THE PATIENT IS LIFTED OUT OF THE AMBULANCE – . . . as a good deal of the anger was directed against their own young, we left the institute and returned to the centre of the city, where we again made contact with the young.

The Institute Found Not Useful

The young ones working at the institute in menial and assistive positions were all of a different subculture, patterned on the older animals in clothing and behaviour. The young animals we met in the city were in herds, or smaller groups, and not easily contacted by Herbert Bond and John Hunter, who, being older and dressed in the uniform of the dominant males, were suspected of being spies of some sort. We therefore reincarnated ourselves as two youngsters, male and female, having decided to spend a fourth of what was left of our supply of power in trying to persuade them to agree on one issue and to act on it. For, like their elders, they discuss and talk and sing endlessly, enjoying pleasurable sensations of satisfaction and agreement with others, making these an end in themselves. We suggested that in view of what was going to happen to the city, they, the young ones, might try to persuade all those of their age to leave and live elsewhere, to make for themselves some sort of encampment, if to build a new city was beyond their resources, at any rate a place in which refugees would be welcomed and cared for.

Failure with the Young

All that happened was that a number of new songs were sung, all of a melancholy nature, all on the theme of unavoidable tragedy. Our encounter with these young ones was taking place on the beach and at the time of the fading of the sunlight. This is a time that has a powerfully saddening effect on all the animals. But it was not until afterwards that we understood we should have chosen any time of the day but that one. There were large numbers of young, many with musical instruments. Half a dozen of them converted the occasion into a conference (see above) by addressing the mass not as their elders do, through talking, but through singing – the heightened and emotional sound. The emotion was of a different kind from that at the conference at the institute. That had been violent and aggressive and nearly resulted in physical attack. This was heavy, sad, passive. Having failed to get them to discuss, either by talking or by singing, a mass exodus from the city, we then attempted discussing how to prevent individuals from massing in the most threatened areas (we were in one at the time) and how, when the shock occurred, to prevent mass deaths and injuries and how to treat the injured, and so forth.

Despair of the Young

All these attempts failed. We might have taken a clue from the drugged condition of the three whose minds we at first occupied and from the indifference to death of the four in the metal conveyance. We have concluded that the young are in a state of disabling despair. While more clear-minded, in some ways, than their elders – that is, more able to voice and maintain criticism of wrongs and faults – they are not able to believe in their own effectiveness. Again and again, on the beach, as the air darkened, versions of this exchange took place:

'But you say you believe it must happen, and within five years.'

'So they say.'

'But you don't think it will?'

'If it happens, it happens.'

'But it isn't *if* – it will happen.'

'They are all corrupt, what can we do? They want to kill us all.'

'Who are corrupt?'

'The old ones. They run everything.'

'But why don't you challenge them?'

'You can't challenge them. They are too strong. We have to evade. We must be fluid. We must be like water.'

'But you are still here, where it is going to happen.'

'So they say.'

A song swept the whole gathering. It was now quite dark. There were many thousands massed near the water.

> It will happen soon,
> So they say,
> We will not live to fight
> Another day
> They are blind.
> They have blown our mind.
> We shall not live to fight,
> We live to die.

Mass Suicides

And hundreds of them committed suicide – by swimming out into the water in the dark, while those who stood on higher ledges by the water threw themselves in – . . . A DONATION OF $500,000 TO BUILD A BIRD SANCTUARY IN THE PARK. THIS WILL HAVE SPECIMENS OF EVERY KNOWN SPECIES IN THE WORLD. IT IS HOPED THAT SPECIES THREATENED WITH EXTINCTION DUE TO MAN'S CRUELTY AND UNCONCERN WILL FIND THIS SANCTUARY A USEFUL BANK FROM WHICH THEY CAN REPLENISH AND STRENGTHEN VARIETIES UNDER THREAT – . . . very low stock of power. We decided to make one last attempt, to concentrate our material in a single place. We decided to leave the herds of young and return to the older animals, since these were in authority. Not to the institute, since we had proved their emotional instability. It was essential to choose a set of words that would not cause emotion – a received idea.

Now, the idea that the behaviour of an individual or a group can be very different from its, or their, self-description is already part of their mental furniture and is enshrined in many time-worn word sets. For instance, 'Don't judge by what he says but by what he does.'

We decided to reinforce this soothing received idea with another of their anxiety reducing devices. We have already noted that a conference is such a device. A variety of this is to put ideas into heightened or emotional sound, as was done by the young on the beach. We decided that neither of these was suitable for our last attempt. We considered and discarded a third that we have not yet mentioned. This is when disturbing or unpalatable ideas are put into ritual form and acted out in public to small groups or relayed by a technical device, 'television', which enables visual images to be transmitted simultaneously to millions of people. A sequence of events that may fall outside their formal code of morality, or be on its border line, will be acted out, causing violent approval or disapproval – it is a form of catharsis. After a time, these sequences of acted-out events become familiar and are constantly performed. This way of trying out, of acclimatising unfamiliar ideas, goes on all the time, side by side with ritual acting-out of situations that are familiar and banal – thus making them appear more interesting. This is a way of making a life situation that an individual may find intolerably tedious and repetitive more stimulating and enable him to suffer it without rebelling. These dramas, of both the first and the second kind, can be of any degree of sophistication. But we decided on a fourth mechanism or method: a verbal game. One of their games is when sets of words are discussed by one, two or more individuals, and these are most often transmitted through the above-mentioned device.

We had reassumed our identities as Herbert Bond and John Hunter, since we were again contacting authority, and approached a television centre with forged credentials from a geographical area called Britain, recently a powerful and combative subspecies, which enjoys a sort of prestige because of past aggressiveness and military prowess.

Laughter, Functions of, See Above

We proposed a game of words, on the theme 'Don't judge by words but by actions'. The debate took place last night. To begin with, there was a good deal of laughter, a sign that should have warned us. This was not antagonistic, 'laughing at', which is found disagreeable but which, in fact, is much safer a reaction than 'laughing with', which is laughter of agreement, of feeling flattered. This second type is evoked by ideas that are minority ideas, when the minority consider they are in advance of the mass. The aggressive and hostile laughter is a safer reaction because it reassures onlookers that a balance is being kept, whereas the sympathetic laughter arouses feelings of anxiety in those watching, if the ideas put forward are challenging to norms accepted by them. Our thesis was simple and as already outlined: that this society is indifferent to death and to suffering. Fear is not experienced, or not in a way that is useful for protecting society or the individual. No one sees these facts, because all the sets of words that describe behaviour are in contrast to the facts. The official sets of words are all to do with protection of oneself and others, caution about the future, pity and compassion for others. Throughout all this – that is, while we developed our thesis – we were greeted by laughter.

These games have audiences invited to the places where they are played, so that the makers of the ritual can judge the probable reaction of the individuals outside, all over the city, in front of their television. The laughter was loud and prolonged. Opposing Herbert Bond and John Hunter, professors of words from Britain, were two professors of words from the local university. They have rules of debate, the essence of which is that each statement must have the same weight of importance as the preceding. The opposing professors' statements, of equal length to ours, stated the opposite view and were light and humorous in tone. Our turn coming again, we proved our point by stating the facts about this city's behaviour in the face of a certain disaster – but we did not get very far. As soon as we switched from the theoretical, the general, to the particular, the laughter died away and violent hostility was shown. There is a custom that if people watching a ritual dislike it, they send hostile messages to the relay point. What Herbert Bond and John Hunter said caused so much violent emotion that the technical equipment for listening to these messages broke down. While the two local professors maintained the calmness of manner expected during these games, they were nervous and, the ritual over, they said they thought they would lose their employment. They were hostile to us, as being responsible. They complained that, as 'foreigners', we did not realise that these rituals must be kept light in tone and general in theme.

When we two got to the door of the building, there was a mob outside, mostly of older animals, very hostile. The managers of the ritual game pulled us back and took us up to the top of the building and set guards on us, as apparently the mob was angered to the point of wishing to kill us – again, the focus of their anger was that we were foreign. We complied, since there was no point in creating further disorder and – . . . BRING YOUR DECEASED TO US, WHO ARE FRIENDS OF YOUR FAMILY . . . CARED FOR AS YOU CARED WHEN MOTHER, FATHER, HUSBAND, WIFE, BROTHER OR LITTLE SISTER WAS STILL WITH YOU, THE SLEEPING ONE WILL BE BORNE TO THE LAST HOME, LAID GENTLY TO REST IN A PLOT WHERE FLOWERS AND BIRDS WILL ALWAYS PLAY AND WHERE YOU CAN VISIT AND MUSE . . . IN YOUR LEISURE HOURS, YOU WILL ALWAYS HAVE A HAVEN WHERE YOUR THOUGHTS CAN DWELL IN LOVING HAPPINESS IN YOUR DEPARTED FRIENDS, WHO – . . . We are running very short of power. There is nothing more we can do. This mission must be regarded as a failure. We have been able to achieve nothing. We have also failed to understand what is the cause of their defectiveness. There is no species like this one on any other planet known to us.

As the guards on our place of detention relaxed their vigilance, we simply dematerialised and returned to the craft. They will think we escaped or perhaps were the subjects of kidnapping by the still-hostile crowd that we could see from the top of the building where – . . . SHOCKING AND DISGUSTING PROGRAMME THAT OFFENDED IN A WAY NO OTHER PROGRAMME HAS IN THIS COMMENTATOR'S MEMORY. IT IS NOT WHAT WAS SAID BY OUR TWO VISITORS, IT WAS THE WAY IT WAS SAID. AFTER ALL, WE ALL HAVE TO LIVE WITH 'THE FACTS' THAT THEY SO NAIVELY SEEM TO IMAGINE ARE A REVELATION TO US. FOR SHEER BAD TASTE, CRUDITY OF TONE, UGLINESS OF MANNER AND INSENSITIVITY TO THE DEEPER FEELINGS OF THE VIEWERS, NOTHING CAN BE COMPARED WITH PROFESSORS BOND AND HUNTER LAST NIGHT.

Departure from the Planet

We are now reassembled as our original six and will shortly be returning. We have a tentative conclusion. It is this: that a society that is doomed to catastrophe, and that is unable to prepare for it, can expect that few people will survive except those already keyed to chaos and disaster. The civil, the ordered, the conforming, the well-tempered, can expect to fall victim at first exposure. But the vagabonds, criminals, mad, extremely poor, will have the means to survive. We conclude, therefore, that when, within the next five years, the eruption occurs, no one will be left but those types the present managers of society consider undesirable, for the present society is too inflexible to adapt – as we have already said, we have no idea why this should be so, what is wrong with them. But perhaps concealed in this city are groups of individuals we did not contact, who saw no reason to contact us, who not only foresee the future even but who are taking steps to –

THE WEST COAST EXAMINER

> Sam Baker, a farmer from Long Ridge, said he saw a 'shining round thing' take off one hundred yards away from his fence yesterday evening as the sun went down. Says Sam: 'It rose into the air at such a rate it was almost impossible to follow it with my eyes. Then it disappeared.' Others from the same area claim to have seen 'unusual sights' during the past few days. The official explanation is that the unusually vivid sunsets of the past month have caused strong reflections and mirages off rocks and stretches of sand.

Military Sector III to HQ (Top Confidential)

The UFO that landed some time in the night of the 14th, and was viewed as it landed, remained stationary for the entire period of seven days. No one was seen to leave the UFO. This is exactly in line with the previous 12 landings in the same spot. This was the 13th UFO of this series. But this was rather larger and more powerful than the previous 12. The difference registered by Sonoscope 15 was considerable. This UFO, like the previous 12, was only just visible to ordinary vision. Our observer, farmer Jansen H. Blackson, recruited by us after the first landing a year ago, volunteered that this one was much more easily seen. 'You had to stare hard to see the others, but I saw this one coming down, also lifting off, but it went up so fast I lost it at once.' The suggestion from M 8 is that all 13 are observation craft from the Chinese. The view of this section is that they are from our Naval Department 15, and it is our contention that as they have no right to access to this terrain, which is under the aegis of War Department 4, we should blast them to hell and gone next time they try it on.

Air Force 14 to Centre

The alightings continue – Number 13 last week. This was also unmanned. Confirm belief Russian origin. Must report also two further landings to the south of the city, both in the same place and separated by an interval of three weeks. These two craft identical with the series of 55 alighting to north of city last year. The two southern landings coincided with the disappearance of 11 people, five the first time, six the second. This makes 450 people gone without trace during the past two years. We suggest it is no longer possible to dismiss the fact that the landings of these craft always mean the disappearance of two to ten people with the word 'coincidence'. We must face the possibility that all or some are manned, but by individuals so dissimilar in structure to ourselves that we cannot see them. We would point out that Sonoscope 4 is only just able to bring these types of craft within vision and that, therefore, the levels of density that might indicate the presence of 'people' might escape the machine. We further suggest that the facetiousness of the phrase 'little green men' might mask an attitude of mind that is inimical to a sober evaluation or assessment of this possibility.

Confirm at earliest if we are to continue policy of minimising these disappearances. We can still find no common denominator in the *type* of person taken off. The only thing they all have in common is that they were, for a variety of reasons, somewhere in the areas in which these craft choose to descend.

THE WEST COAST EXAMINER

> Our observer at filling station Lost Pine reports that groups of people are driving south out of the city to the area where the latest UFOs are known to descend and take off. Last night they numbered over 50,000.

Air Force 14 to Centre

In spite of Total Policy 19, rumours are out. We consider it advisable to cordon off the area, although this might precipitate extreme panic situation. But we see no alternative. The cult called Be Ready for the Day is already thousands strong and sweeping the city and environs. Suggest an announcement that the area is contaminated with a chance leak of radio-activity.

29

The Rain Horse

(1974)

Ted Hughes

As the young man came over the hill the first thin blowing of rain met him. He turned his coat-collar up and stood on top of the shelving rabbit-riddled hedgebank, looking down into the valley.

He had come too far. What had set out as a walk along pleasantly remembered tarmac lanes had turned dreamily by gate and path and hedge-gap into a cross ploughland trek, his shoes ruined, the dark mud of the lower fields inching up the trouser legs of his grey suit where they rubbed against each other. And now there was a raw, flapping wetness in the air that would be downpour again at any minute. He shivered, holding himself tense against the cold.

This was the view he had been thinking of. Vaguely, without really directing his walk, he had felt he would get the whole thing from this point. For twelve years, whenever he had recalled this scene, he had imagined it as it looked from here. Now the valley lay sunken in front of him, utterly deserted, shallow, bare fields, black and sodden as the bed of an ancient lake after the weeks of rain.

Nothing happened. Not that he had looked forward to any very transfiguring experience. But he had expected something, some pleasure, some meaningful sensation, he didn't quite know what.

So he waited, trying to nudge the right feelings alive with the details – the surprisingly familiar curve of the hedges, the stone gate-pillar and iron gatehook let into it that he had used as a target, the long bank of the rabbit-warren on which he stood and which had been the first thing he ever noticed about the hill when twenty years ago, from the distance of the village, he had said to himself 'That looks like rabbits.'

Twelve years had changed him. This land no longer recognised him, and he looked back at it coldly, as at a finally visited home-country, known only through the stories of a grandfather; felt nothing but the dullness of feeling nothing. Boredom. Then, suddenly, impatience, with a whole exasperated swarm of little anxieties about his shoes and the spitting rain and his new suit and that sky and the two-mile trudge through the mud back to the road.

It would be quicker to go straight forward to the farm a mile away in the valley and behind which the road looped. But the thought of meeting the farmer – to be embarrassingly remembered or shouted at as a trespasser – deterred him. He saw the rain pulling up out of the distance, dragging its grey broken columns, smudging the trees and the farms.

A wave of anger went over him: anger against himself for blundering into this mud-trap and anger against the land that made him feel so outcast, so old and stiff and stupid. He wanted nothing but to get away from it as quickly as possible. But as he turned, something moved in his eye-corner. All his senses startled alert. He stopped.

Over to his right a thin, black horse was running across the ploughland towards the hill, its head down, neck stretched out. It seemed to be running on its toes like a cat, like a dog up to no good.

From the high point on which he stood the hill dipped slightly and rose to another crested point fringed with the tops of trees, three hundred yards to his right. As he watched it, the horse ran up that crest, showed against the sky – for a moment like a nightmarish leopard – and disappeared over the other side.

For several seconds he stared at the skyline, stunned by the unpleasantly strange impression the horse had made on him. Then the plastering beat of icy rain on his bare skull brought him to himself. The distance had vanished in a wall of grey. All around him the fields were jumping and streaming.

Holding his collar close and tucking his chin down into it he ran back over the hilltop towards the town-side, the lee-side, his feet sucking and splashing, at every stride plunging to the ankle.

This hill was shaped like a wave, a gently rounded back lifting out of the valley to a sharply crested, almost concave front hanging over the river meadows towards the town. Down this front, from the crest, hung two small woods separated by a fallow field. The near wood was nothing more than a quarry, circular, full of stones and bracken, with a few thorns and nondescript saplings, foxholes and rabbit holes. The other was rectangular, mainly a planting of scrub oak trees. Beyond the river smouldered the town like a great heap of blue cinders.

He ran along the top of the first wood and finding no shelter but the thin, leafless thorns of the hedge, dipped below the crest out of the wind and jogged along through thick grass to the wood of oaks. In blinding rain he lunged through the barricade of brambles at the wood's edge. The little crippled trees were small choice in the way of shelter, but at a sudden fierce thickening of the rain he took one at random and crouched down under the leaning trunk.

Still panting from his run, drawing his knees up tightly, he watched the bleak lines of rain, grey as hail, slanting through the boughs into the clumps of bracken and bramble. He felt hidden and safe. The sound of the rain as it rushed and lulled in the wood seemed to seal him in. Soon the chilly sheet lead of his suit became a tight, warm mould, and gradually he sank into a state of comfort that was all but trance, though the rain beat steadily on his exposed shoulders and trickled down the oak trunk on to his neck.

All around him the boughs angled down, glistening, black as iron. From their tips and elbows the drops hurried steadily, and the channels of the bark pulsed and gleamed. For a time he amused himself calculating the variation in the rainfall by the variations in a dribble of water from a trembling twig-end two feet in front of his nose. He studied the twig, bringing dwarfs and continents and animals out of its scurfy bark. Beyond the boughs the blue shoal of the town was rising and falling, and darkening and fading again, in the pale, swaying backdrop of rain.

He wanted this rain to go on for ever. Whenever it seemed to be drawing off he listened anxiously until it closed in again. As long as it lasted he was suspended from life and time. He didn't want to return to his sodden shoes and his possibly ruined suit and the walk back over that land of mud.

All at once he shivered. He hugged his knees to squeeze out the cold and found himself thinking of the horse. The hair on the nape of his neck prickled slightly. He remembered how it had run up to the crest and showed against the sky.

He tried to dismiss the thought. Horses wander about the countryside often enough. But the image of the horse as it had appeared against the sky stuck in his mind. It must have come over the crest just above the wood in which he was now sitting. To clear his mind, he twisted around and looked up the wood between the tree stems, to his left.

At the wood top, with the silvered grey light coming in behind it, the black horse was standing under the oaks, its head high and alert, its ears pricked, watching him.

A horse sheltering from the rain generally goes into a sort of stupor, tilts a hind hoof and hangs its head and lets its eyelids droop, and so it stays as long as the rain lasts. This horse was nothing like that. It was watching him intently, standing perfectly still, its soaked neck and flank shining in the hard light.

He turned back. His scalp went icy and he shivered. What was he to do? Ridiculous to try driving it away. And to leave the wood, with the rain still coming down full pelt was out of the question. Meanwhile the idea of being watched became more and more unsettling until at last he had to twist around again, to see if the horse had moved. It stood exactly as before.

This was absurd. He took control of himself and turned back deliberately, determined not to give the horse one more thought. If it wanted to share the wood with him, let it. If it wanted to stare at him, let it. He was nestling firmly into these resolutions when the ground shook and he heard the crash of a heavy body coming down the wood. Like lightning his legs bounded him upright and about face. The horse was almost on top of him, its head stretching forward, ears flattened and lips lifted back from the long yellow teeth. He got one snapshot glimpse of the red-veined eyeball as he flung himself backwards around the tree. Then he was away up the slope, whipped by oak twigs as he leapt the brambles and brushwood, twisting between the close trees till he tripped and sprawled. As he fell the warning flashed through his head that he must at all costs keep his suit out of the leaf-mould, but a more urgent instinct was already rolling him violently sideways. He spun around, sat up and looked back, ready to scramble off in a flash to one side. He was panting from the sudden excitement and effort. The horse had disappeared. The wood was empty except for the drumming, slant grey rain, dancing the bracken and glittering from the branches.

He got up, furious. Knocking the dirt and leaves from his suit as well as he could he looked around for a weapon. The horse was evidently mad, had an abscess on its brain or something of the sort. Or maybe it was just spiteful. Rain sometimes puts creatures into queer states. Whatever it was, he was going to get away from the wood as quickly as possible, rain or no rain.

Since the horse seemed to have gone on down the wood, his way to the farm over the hill was clear. As he went, he broke a yard length of wrist-thick dead branch from one of the oaks, but immediately threw it aside and wiped the slime of rotten wet bark from his hands with his soaked handkerchief. Already he was thinking it incredible that the horse could have meant to attack him. Most likely it was just going down the wood for better shelter and had made a feint at him in passing – as much out of curiosity or playfulness as anything. He recalled the way horses menace each other when they are galloping round in a paddock.

The wood rose to a steep bank topped by the hawthorn hedge that ran along the whole ridge of the hill. He was pulling himself up to a thin place in the hedge by the bare stem of one of the hawthorns when he ducked and shrank down again. The swelling gradient of fields lay in front of him, smoking in the slowly crossing rain. Out in the middle of the first field, tall as a statue, and a ghostly silver in the under-cloud light, stood the horse, watching the wood.

He lowered his head slowly, slithered back down the bank and crouched. An awful feeling of helplessness came over him. He felt certain the horse had been looking straight at him. Waiting for him? Was it clairvoyant? Maybe a mad animal can be clairvoyant. At the same time he was ashamed to find himself acting so inanely, ducking and creeping about in this way just to keep out of sight of a horse. He tried to imagine how anybody in their senses would just walk off home. This cooled him a little, and he retreated farther down the wood. He would go back the way he had come, along under the hill crest, without any more nonsense.

The wood hummed and the rain was a cold weight, but he observed this rather than felt it. The water ran down inside his clothes and squelched in his shoes as he eased his way carefully over the bedded twigs and leaves. At every instant he expected to see the prick-eared black head looking down at him from the hedge above.

At the woodside he paused, close against a tree. The success of this last manoeuvre was restoring his confidence, but he didn't want to venture out into the open field without making sure that the horse was just where he had left it. The perfect move would be to withdraw quietly and leave the horse standing out there in the rain. He crept up again among the trees to the crest and peered through the hedge.

The grey field and the whole slope were empty. He searched the distance. The horse was quite likely to have forgotten him altogether and wandered off. Then he raised himself and leaned out to see if it had come in close to the hedge. Before he was aware of anything the ground shook. He twisted around wildly to see how he had been caught. The black shape was above him, right across the light. Its whinnying snort and the spattering whack of its hooves seemed to be actually inside his head as he fell backwards down the bank, and leapt again like a madman, dodging among the oaks, imagining how the buffet would come and how he would be knocked headlong. Halfway down the wood the oaks gave way to bracken and old roots and stony rabbit diggings. He was well out into the middle of this before he realised that he was running alone.

Gasping for breath now and cursing mechanically, without a thought for his suit he sat down on the ground to rest his shaking legs, letting the rain plaster the hair down over his forehead and watching the dense flashing lines disappear abruptly into the soil all around him as if he were watching through thick plate glass. He took deep breaths in the effort to steady his heart and regain control of himself. His right trouser turn-up was ripped at the seam and his suit jacket was splashed with the yellow mud of the top field.

Obviously the horse had been farther along the hedge above the steep field, waiting for him to come out at the woodside just as he had intended. He must have peeped through the hedge – peeping the wrong way – within yards of it.

However, this last attack had cleared up one thing. He need no longer act like a fool out of mere uncertainty as to whether the horse was simply being playful or not. It was definitely after him. He picked two stones about the size of goose eggs and set off towards the bottom of the wood, striding carelessly.

A loop of the river bordered all this farmland. If he crossed the little level meadow at the bottom of the wood, he could follow the three-mile circuit, back to the road. There were deep hollows in the river-bank, shoaled with pebbles, as he remembered, perfect places to defend himself from if the horse followed him out there.

The hawthorns that choked the bottom of the wood – some of them good-sized trees – knitted into an almost impassable barrier. He had found a place where the growth thinned slightly and had begun to lift aside the long spiny stems, pushing himself forward, when he stopped. Through the bluish veil of bare twigs he saw the familiar shape out in the field below the wood.

But it seemed not to have noticed him yet. It was looking out across the field towards the river. Quietly, he released himself from the thorns and climbed back across the clearing towards the one side of the wood he had not yet tried. If the horse would only stay down there he could follow his first and easiest plan, up the wood and over the hilltop to the farm.

Now he noticed that the sky had grown much darker. The rain was heavier every second, pressing down as if the earth had to be flooded before nightfall. The oaks ahead blurred and the ground drummed. He began to run. And as he ran he heard a deeper sound running with him. He whirled around. The horse was in the middle of the clearing. It might have been running to get out of the terrific rain except that it was coming straight for him, scattering clay and stones, with an immensely supple and powerful motion. He let out a tearing roar and threw the stone in his right hand. The result was instantaneous. Whether at the roar or the stone the horse reared as if against a wall and shied to the left. As it dropped back on to its forefeet he flung his second stone, at ten yards' range, and saw a bright mud blotch suddenly appear on the glistening black flank. The horse surged down the wood, splashing the earth like water, tossing its long tail as it plunged out of sight among the hawthorns.

He looked around for stones. The encounter had set the blood beating in his head and given him a savage energy. He could have killed the horse at that moment. That this brute should pick him and play with him in this malevolent fashion was more than he could bear. Whoever owned it, he thought, deserved to have its neck broken for letting the dangerous thing loose.

He came out at the woodside, in open battle now, still searching for the right stones. There were plenty here, piled and scattered where they had been ploughed out of the field. He selected two, then straightened and saw the horse twenty yards off in the middle of the steep field, watching him calmly. They looked at each other.

'Out of it!' he shouted, brandishing his arm. 'Out of it! Go on!' The horse twitched its pricked ears. With all his force he threw. The stone soared and landed beyond with a soft thud. He re-armed and threw again. For several minutes he kept up his bombardment without a single hit, working himself up into a despair and throwing more and more wildly, till his arm began to ache with the unaccustomed exercise. Throughout the performance the horse watched him fixedly. Finally he had to stop and ease his shoulder muscles. As if the horse had been waiting for just this, it dipped its head twice and came at him.

He snatched up two stones and roaring with all his strength flung the one in his right hand. He was astonished at the crack of the impact. It was as if he had struck a tile – and the horse actually stumbled. With another roar he jumped forward and hurled his other stone. His aim seemed to be under superior guidance. The stone struck and rebounded straight up into the air, spinning fiercely, as the horse swirled away and went careering down towards the far bottom corner of the field, at first with great, swinging leaps, then at a canter, leaving deep churned holes in the soil.

It turned up the far side of the field, climbing till it was level with him. He felt a little surprise of pity to see it shaking its head, and once it paused to lower its head and paw over its ear with its forehoof as a cat does.

'You stay there!' he shouted. 'Keep your distance and you'll not get hurt.'

And indeed the horse did stop at that moment, almost obediently. It watched him as he climbed to the crest.

The rain swept into his face and he realised that he was freezing, as if his very flesh were sodden. The farm seemed miles away over the dreary fields. Without another glance at the horse – he felt too exhausted to care now what it did – he loaded the crook of his left arm with stones and plunged out on to the waste of mud.

He was halfway to the first hedge before the horse appeared, silhouetted against the sky at the corner of the wood, head high and attentive, watching his laborious retreat over the three fields.

The ankle-deep clay dragged at him. Every stride was a separate, deliberate effort, forcing him up and out of the sucking earth, burdened as he was by his sogged clothes and load of stones and limbs that seemed themselves to be turning to mud. He fought to keep his breathing even, two strides in, two strides out, the air ripping his lungs. In the middle of the last field he stopped and looked around. The horse, tiny on the skyline, had not moved.

At the corner of the field he unlocked his clasped arms and dumped the stones by the gatepost, then leaned on the gate. The farm was in front of him. He became conscious of the rain again and suddenly longed to stretch out full-length under it, to take the cooling, healing drops all over his body and forget himself in the last wretchedness of the mud. Making an effort, he heaved his weight over the gate-top. He leaned again, looking up at the hill.

Rain was dissolving land and sky together like a wet watercolour as the afternoon darkened. He concentrated, raising his head, searching the skyline from end to end. The horse had vanished. The hill looked lifeless and desolate, an island lifting out of the sea, awash with every tide.

Under the long shed where the tractors, plough, binders and the rest were drawn up, waiting for their seasons, he sat on a sack thrown over a petrol drum, trembling, his lungs heaving. The mingled smell of paraffin, creosote, fertiliser, dust – all was exactly as he had left it twelve years ago. The ragged swallows' nests were still there tucked in the angles of the rafters. He remembered three dead foxes hanging in a row from one of the beams, their teeth bloody.

The ordeal with the horse had already sunk from reality. It hung under the surface of his mind, an obscure confusion of fright and shame, as after a narrowly escaped street accident. There was a solid pain in his chest, like a spike of bone stabbing, that made him wonder if he had strained his heart on that last stupid burdened run. Piece by piece he began to take off his clothes, wringing the grey water out of them, but soon he stopped that and just sat staring at the ground, as if some important part had been cut out of his brain.

30

Ming's Biggest Prey

(1975)

Patricia Highsmith

Ming was resting comfortably on the foot of his mistress' bunk, when the man picked him up by the back of the neck, stuck him out on the deck and closed the cabin door. Ming's blue eyes widened in shock and brief anger, then nearly closed again because of the brilliant sunlight. It was not the first time Ming had been thrust out of the cabin rudely, and Ming realised that the man did it when his mistress, Elaine, was not looking.

The sailboat now offered no shelter from the sun, but Ming was not yet too warm. He leapt easily to the cabin roof and stepped onto the coil of rope just behind the mast. Ming liked the rope coil as a couch, because he could see everything from the height, the cup shape of the rope protected him from strong breezes, and also minimised the swaying and sudden changes of angle of the *White Lark*, since it was more or less the centre point. But just now the sail had been taken down, because Elaine and the man had eaten lunch, and often they had a siesta afterward, during which time, Ming knew, the man didn't like him in the cabin. Lunchtime was all right. In fact, Ming had just lunched on delicious grilled fish and a bit of lobster. Now, lying in a relaxed curve on the tail of rope, Ming opened his mouth in a great yawn, then with his slant eyes almost closed against the strong sunlight, gazed at the beige hills and the white and pink houses and hotels that circled the bay of Acapulco. Between the *White Lark* and the shore where people plashed inaudibly, the sun twinkled on the water's surface like thousands of tiny electric lights going on and off. A water-skier went by, skimming up white spray behind him. Such activity! Ming half dozed, feeling the heat of the sun sink into his fur. Ming was from New York, and he considered Acapulco a great improvement over his environment in the first weeks of his life. He remembered a sunless box with straw on the bottom, three or four of her kittens in with him, and a window behind which giant forms paused for a few moments, tried to catch his attention by tapping, then passed on. He did not remember his mother at all. One day a young woman who smelled of something pleasant came into the place and took him away – away from the ugly, frightening smell of dogs, of medicine and parrot dung. Then they went on what Ming now knew was an aeroplane. He was quite used to aeroplanes now and rather liked them. On aeroplanes he sat on Elaine's lap, or slept on her lap, and there were always titbits to eat if he was hungry.

Elaine spent much of the day in a shop in Acapulco, where dresses and slacks and bathing suits hung on all the walls. This place smelled clean and fresh, there were flowers in pots and in boxes out front, and the floor was of cool blue and white tile. Ming had perfect freedom to wander out into the patio behind the shop, or to sleep in his basket in a corner. There was more sunlight in front of the shop, but mischievous boys often tried to grab him if he sat in front, and Ming could never relax there.

Ming liked best lying in the sun with his mistress on one of the long canvas chairs on their terrace at home. What Ming did not like were the people she sometimes invited to their house, people who spent the night, people by the score who stayed up very late eating and drinking, playing the gramophone or the piano – people who separated him from Elaine. People who stepped on his toes, people who sometimes picked him up from behind before he could do anything about it, so that he had to squirm and fight to get free, people who stroked him roughly, people who closed a door somewhere, locking him in. *People!* Ming detested people. In all the world, he liked only Elaine. Elaine loved him and understood him.

Especially this man called Teddie Ming detested now. Teddie was around all the time lately. Ming did not like the way Teddie looked at him, when Elaine was not watching. And sometimes Teddie, when Elaine was not near, muttered something which Ming knew was a threat. Or a command to leave the room. Ming took it calmly. Dignity was to be preserved. Besides, wasn't his mistress on his side? The man was the intruder. When Elaine was watching, the man sometimes pretended a fondness for him, but Ming always moved gracefully but unmistakably in another direction.

Ming's nap was interrupted by the sound of the cabin door opening. He heard Elaine and the man laughing and talking. The big red-orange sun was near the horizon.

'Ming!' Elaine came over to him. 'Aren't you getting *cooked*, darling? I thought you were *in*!'

'So did I!' said Teddie.

Ming purred as he always did when he awakened. She picked him up gently, cradled him in her arms, and took him below into the suddenly cool shade of the cabin. She was talking to the man, and not in a gentle tone. She set Ming down in front of his dish of water, and though he was not thirsty, he drank a little to please her. Ming did feel addled by the heat, and he staggered a little.

Elaine took a wet towel and wiped Ming's face, his ears and his four paws. Then she laid him gently on the bunk that smelled of Elaine's perfume but also of the man whom Ming detested.

Now his mistress and the man were quarrelling. Ming could tell from the tone. Elaine was staying with Ming, sitting on the edge of the bunk. Ming at last heard the splash that meant Teddie had dived into the water. Ming hoped he stayed there, hoped he drowned, hoped he never came back. Elaine wet a bathtowel in the aluminium sink, wrung it out, spread it on the bunk, and lifted Ming onto it. She brought water, and now Ming was thirsty, and drank. She left him to sleep again while she washed and put away the dishes. These were comfortable sounds that Ming liked to hear.

But soon there was another *plash* and *plop*, Teddie's wet feet on the deck, and Ming was awake again.

The tone of quarrelling recommenced. Elaine went up the few steps onto the deck. Ming, tense but with his chin still resting on the moist bathtowel, kept his eyes on the cabin door. It was Teddie's feet that he heard descending. Ming lifted his head slightly, aware that there was no exit behind him, that he was trapped in the cabin. The man paused with a towel in his hands, staring at Ming.

Ming relaxed completely, as he might do preparatory to a yawn, and this caused his eyes to cross. Ming then let his tongue slide a little way out of his mouth. The man started to say something, looked as if he wanted to hurl the wadded towel at Ming, but he wavered, whatever he had been going to say never got out of his mouth, and he threw the towel in the sink, then bent to wash his face. It was not the first time Ming had let his tongue slide out at Teddie. Lots of people laughed when Ming did this, if they were people at a party, for instance, and Ming rather enjoyed that. But Ming sensed that Teddie took it as a hostile gesture of some kind, which was why Ming did it deliberately to Teddie, whereas among other people, it was often an accident when Ming's tongue slid out.

The quarrelling continued. Elaine made coffee. Ming began to feel better, and went on deck again, because the sun had now set. Elaine had started the motor, and they were gliding slowly toward the shore. Ming caught the song of birds, the odd screams like shrill phrases of certain birds that cried only at sunset. Ming looked forward to the adobe house on the cliff that was his and his mistress' home. He knew that the reason she did not leave him at home (where he would have been more comfortable) when she went on the boat, was because she was afraid that people might trap him, even kill him. Ming understood. People had tried to grab him from almost under Elaine's eyes. Once he had been all the way in a cloth bag suddenly, and though fighting as hard as he could, he was not sure he would have been able to get out, if Elaine had not hit the boy herself and grabbed the bag from him.

Ming had intended to jump up on the cabin roof again, but after glancing at it, he decided to save his strength, so he crouched on the warm, gently sloping deck with his feet tucked in, and gazed at the approaching shore. Now he could hear guitar music from the beach. The voices of his mistress and the man had come to a halt. For a few moments, the loudest sound was the chug-chug-chug of the boat's motor. Then Ming heard the man's bare feet climbing the cabin steps. Ming did not turn his head to look at him, but his ears twitched back a little, involuntarily. Ming looked at the water just the distance of a short leap in front of him and below him. Strangely, there was no sound from the man behind him. The hair on Ming's neck prickled, and Ming glanced over his right shoulder.

At that instant, the man bent forward and rushed at Ming with his arms outspread.

Ming was on his feet at once, darting straight toward the man which was the only direction of safety on the railless deck, and the man swung his left arm and cuffed Ming in the chest. Ming went flying backward, claws scraping the deck, but his hind legs went over the edge. Ming clung with his front feet to the sleek wood which gave him little hold, while his hind legs worked to heave him up, worked at the side of the boat which sloped to Ming's disadvantage.

The man advanced to shove a foot against Ming's paws, but Elaine came up the cabin steps just then.

'What's happening? *Ming!*'

Ming's strong hind legs were getting him onto the deck little by little. The man had knelt as if to lend a hand. Elaine had fallen onto her knees, also, and had Ming by the back of the neck now.

Ming relaxed, hunched on the deck. His tail was wet.

'He fell overboard!' Teddie said. 'It's true he's groggy. Just lurched over and fell when the boat gave a dip.'

'It's the sun. Poor *Ming*!' Elaine held the cat.

The man came down into the cabin. Elaine had Ming on the bunk and was talking softly to him. Ming's heart was still beating fast. He was alert against the man at the wheel, even though Elaine was with him. Ming was aware that they had entered the little cove where they always went before getting off the boat.

Here were the friends and allies of Teddie, whom Ming detested by association, although these were merely Mexican boys. Two or three boys in shorts called 'Señor Teddie!' and offered a hand to Elaine to climb onto the dock, took the rope attached to the front of the boat, offered to carry 'Ming! – Ming!' Ming leapt onto the dock himself and crouched, waiting for Elaine, ready to dart away from any other hand that might reach for him. And there were several brown hands making a rush for him, so that Ming had to keep jumping aside. There were laughs, yelps, stomps of bare feet on wooden boards. But there was also the reassuring voice of Elaine, warning them off. Ming knew she was busy carrying off the plastic satchels, locking the cabin door. Teddie with the aid of one of the Mexican boys was stretching the canvas over the cabin now. And Elaine's sandalled feet were beside Ming. Ming followed her as she walked away. A boy took the things Elaine was carrying, then she picked Ming up.

They got into the big car without a roof that belonged to Teddie, and drove up the winding road toward Elaine's and Ming's house. One of the boys was driving. Now the tone in which Elaine and Teddie were speaking was calmer, softer. The man laughed. Ming sat tensely on his mistress' lap. He could feel her concern for him in the way she stroked him and touched the back of his neck. The man reached out to put his fingers on Ming's back, and Ming gave a low growl that rose and fell and rumbled deep in his throat.

'Well, well,' said the man, pretending to be amused, and took his hand away.

Elaine's voice had stopped in the middle of something she was saying. Ming was tired, and wanted nothing more than to take a nap on the big bed at home. The bed was covered with a red and white striped blanket of thin wool.

Hardly had Ming thought of this, when he found himself in the cool, fragrant atmosphere of his own home, being lowered gently onto the bed with the soft woollen cover. His mistress kissed his cheek, and said something with the word hungry in it. Ming understood, at any rate. He was to tell her when he was hungry.

Ming dozed, and awakened at the sound of voices on the terrace a couple of yards away, past the open glass doors. Now it was dark. Ming could see one end of the table, and could tell from the quality of the light that there were candles on the table. Concha, the servant who slept in the house, was clearing the table. Ming heard her voice, then the voices of Elaine and the man. Ming smelled cigar smoke. Ming jumped to the floor and sat for a moment looking out the door toward the terrace. He yawned, then arched his back and stretched, and limbered up his muscles by digging his claws into the thick straw carpet. Then he slipped out to the right on the terrace and glided silently down the long stairway of broad stones to the garden below. The garden was like a jungle or a forest. Avocado trees and mango trees grew as high as the terrace itself, there were bougainvilleas against the wall, orchids in the trees, and magnolias and several camellias which Elaine had planted. Ming could hear birds twittering and stirring in their nests. Sometimes he climbed trees to get at their nests, but tonight he was not in the mood, though he was no longer tired. The voices of his mistress and the man disturbed him. His mistress was not a friend of the man's tonight, that was plain.

Concha was probably still in the kitchen, and Ming decided to go in and ask her for something to eat. Concha liked him. One maid who had not liked him had been dismissed by Elaine. Ming thought he fancied barbecued pork. That was what his mistress and the man had eaten tonight. The breeze blew fresh from the occan, ruffling Ming's fur slightly. Ming felt completely recovered from the awful experience of nearly falling into the sea.

Now the terrace was empty of people. Ming went left, back into the bedroom, and was at once aware of the man's presence, though there was no light on and Ming could not see him. The man was standing by the dressing-table, opening a box. Again involuntarily Ming gave a low growl which rose and fell, and Ming remained frozen in the position he had been in when he first became aware of the man, his right front paw extended for the next step. Now his ears were back, he was prepared to spring in any direction, although the man had not seen him.

'*Ssss-st!* Damn you!' the man said in a whisper. He stamped his foot, not very hard, to make the cat go away.

Ming did not move at all. Ming heard the soft rattle of the white necklace which belonged to his mistress. The man put it into his pocket, then moved to Ming's right, out the door that went into the big living-room. Ming now heard the clink of a bottle against glass, heard liquid being poured. Ming went through the same door and turned left toward the kitchen.

Here he miaowed, and was greeted by Elaine and Concha. Concha had her radio turned on to music.

'Fish? – Pork. He likes pork,' Elaine said, speaking the odd form of words which she used with Concha.

Ming, without much difficulty, conveyed his preference for pork, and got it. He fell to with a good appetite. Concha was exclaiming 'Ah-eeeee!' as his mistress spoke with her, spoke at length. Then Concha bent to stroke him, and Ming put up with it, still looking down at his plate, until she left off and he could finish his meal. Then Elaine left the kitchen. Concha gave him some of the tinned milk, which he loved, in his now empty saucer, and Ming lapped this up. Then he rubbed himself against her bare leg by way of thanks, and went out of the kitchen, made his way cautiously into the living-room en route to the bedroom. But now his mistress and the man were out on the terrace. Ming had just entered the bedroom, when he heard Elaine call:

'Ming? Where are you?'

Ming went to the terrace door and stopped, and sat on the threshold.

Elaine was sitting sideways at the end of the table, and the candlelight was bright on her long fair hair, on the white of her trousers. She slapped her thigh, and Ming jumped onto her lap.

The man said something in a low tone, something not nice.

Elaine replied something in the same tone. But she laughed a little.

Then the telephone rang.

Elaine put Ming down, and went into the living-room toward the telephone.

The man finished what was in his glass, muttered something at Ming, then set the glass on the table. He got up and tried to circle Ming, or to get him toward the edge of the terrace, Ming realised, and Ming also realised that the man was drunk – therefore moving slowly and a little clumsily. The terrace had a parapet about as high as the man's hips, but it was broken by grilles in three places, grilles with bars wide enough for Ming to pass through, though Ming never did, merely looked through the grilles sometimes. It was plain to Ming that the man wanted to drive him through one of the grilles, or grab him and toss him over the terrace parapet. There was nothing easier for Ming than to elude him. Then the man picked up a chair and swung it suddenly, catching Ming on the hip. That had been quick, and it hurt. Ming took the nearest exit, which was down the outside steps that led to the garden.

The man started down the steps after him. Without reflecting, Ming dashed back up the few steps he had come, keeping close to the wall which was in shadow. The man hadn't seen him, Ming knew. Ming leapt to the terrace parapet, sat down and licked a paw once to recover and collect himself. His heart beat fast as if he were in the middle of a fight. And hatred ran in his veins. Hatred burned his eyes as he crouched and listened to the man uncertainly climbing the steps below him. The man came into view.

Ming tensed himself for a jump, then jumped as hard as he could, landing with all four feet on the man's right arm near the shoulder. Ming clung to the cloth of the man's white jacket, but they were both falling. The man groaned. Ming hung on. Branches crackled. Ming could not tell up from down. Ming jumped off the man, became aware of direction and of the earth too late and landed on his side. Almost at the same time, he heard the thud of the man hitting the ground, then of his body rolling a little way, then there was silence. Ming had to breathe fast with his mouth open until his chest stopped hurting. From the direction of the man, he could smell drink, cigar, and the sharp odour that meant fear. But the man was not moving.

Ming could now see quite well. There was even a bit of moonlight. Ming headed for the steps again, had to go a long way through the bush, over stones and sand, to where the steps began. Then he glided up and arrived once more upon the terrace.

Elaine was just coming onto the terrace.

'Teddie?' she called. Then she went back into the bedroom where she turned on a lamp. She went into the kitchen. Ming followed her. Concha had left the light on, but Concha was now in her own room, where the radio played.

Elaine opened the front door.

The man's car was still in the driveway, Ming saw. Now Ming's hip had begun to hurt, or now he had begun to notice it. It caused him to limp a little. Elaine noticed this, touched his back, and asked him what was the matter. Ming only purred.

'Teddie? – Where are you?' Elaine called.

She took a torch and shone it down into the garden, down among the great trunks of the avocado trees, among the orchids and the lavender and pink blossoms of the bougainvilleas. Ming, safe beside her on the terrace parapet, followed the beam of the torch with his eyes and purred with content. The man was not below here, but below and to the right. Elaine went to the terrace steps and carefully, because there was no rail here, only broad steps, pointed the beam of the light downward. Ming did not bother looking. He sat on the terrace where the steps began.

'Teddie!' she said. '*Teddie!*' Then she ran down the steps.

Ming still did not follow her. He heard her draw in her breath. Then she cried: '*Concha!*'

Elaine ran back up the steps.

Concha had come out of her room. Elaine spoke to Concha. Then Concha became excited. Elaine went to the telephone, and spoke for a short while, then she and Concha went down the steps together. Ming settled himself with his paws tucked under him on the terrace, which was still faintly warm from the day's sun. A car arrived. Elaine came up the steps, and went and opened the front door. Ming kept out of the way on the terrace, in a shadowy corner, as three or four strange men came out on the terrace and tramped down the steps. There was a great deal of talk below, noises of feet, breaking of bushes, and then the smell of all of them mounted the steps, the smell of tobacco, sweat, and the familiar smell of blood. The man's blood. Ming was pleased, as he was pleased when he killed a bird and created this smell of blood under his own teeth. This was big prey. Ming, unnoticed by any of the others, stood up to his full height as the group passed with the corpse, and inhaled the aroma of his victory with a lifted nose.

Then suddenly the house was empty. Everyone had gone, even Concha. Ming drank a little water from his bowl in the kitchen, then went to his mistress' bed, curled against the slope of the pillows, and fell fast asleep. He was awakened by the rr-rr-r of an unfamiliar car. Then the front door opened, and he recognised the step of Elaine and then Concha. Ming stayed where he was. Elaine and Concha talked softly for a few minutes. Then Elaine came into the bedroom. The lamp was still on. Ming watched her slowly open the box on her dressing-table, and into it she let fall the white necklace that made a little clatter. Then she closed the box. She began to unbutton her shirt, but before she had finished, she flung herself on the bed and stroked Ming's head, lifted his left paw and pressed it gently so that the claws came forth.

'Oh Ming – Ming,' she said.

Ming recognised the tones of love.

31

The Village Saint

(1977)

Bessie Head

People were never fooled by façades. They would look quietly and humorously behind the façade at the real person – cheat, liar, pompous condescending sham, and so on – and nod their heads in a certain way until destiny caught up with the decrepit one. The village could be rocked from end to end by scandal; the society itself seemed to cater for massive public humiliations of some of its unfortunate citizens and during those times all one's fanciful, heretical, or venal tendencies would be thoroughly exposed. Despite this acute insight into human nature, the whole village was aghast the day it lost its patron saint, Mma-Mompati. She had had a long reign of twenty-six years, and a fool-proof façade.

Oh, the story was a long one. It was so long and so austere and holy that it was written into the very stones and earth of village life. And so habitual had her own pose of saintliness become to her that on the day her graven image shattered into a thousand fragments, she salvaged some of the pieces and was still seen at the head of the funeral parade or praying for the sick in hospital.

Mma-Mompati and her husband, Rra-Mompati, belonged to the elite of the village. At the time of their marriage, Rra-Mompati held an important position in tribal affairs. It was so important that he lived in a large, white-washed, colonial-style house with many large rooms. A wide porch, enclosed with mosquito netting, surrounded the whole house. It was to this house that the elders of the tribe retired to discuss top-secret affairs and it was in this house that Mma-Mompati first made her début as the great lady of the town.

Their only son, Mompati, was born a year after marriage into this state of affairs – he was born into the Bamangwato tribe, which, as most people know, was famous or notorious for a history of unexpected explosions and intrigues. The child was welcomed tenderly by his father and named Mompati – my little travelling companion. All three members of the family were spectacular in their own ways, but people tended to forget the former names of the parents – they were simply known as Father of Mompati or Mother of Mompati. The child, Mompati, hardly fulfilled the forecast of his name.

Indeed, he travelled side by side with his father for sixteen years, he travelled side by side with his mother for another ten years but when he eventually emerged as a personality in his own right, he became known rather as the warm-hearted, loud-voiced firm defender of all kinds of causes – marriage, morals, child care, religion, and the rights of the poor.

Mompati started his career early in that great white-washed colonial house. Whenever an explosion occurred, and there were many at one stage, the elders of the tribe did not wish the people to know of their secret deliberations and this left the people in an agony of suspense and tension. Some people, under cover of dark, would try to creep onto the wide porch of the house and hold their ears near the window to try and catch only *one* word of the hush-hush talks. A little patrolman soon appeared on stocky, stubby legs with a set, earnest expression who took turn after turn on duty around the porch to keep all eavesdroppers at bay. Seeing Mompati, the eavesdroppers would back away, laughing and shaking their heads in frustration.

'It was no good,' they would report to the people. 'The little policeman was on duty.'

And so life went on in that great house. The tribal intrigues and explosions came; the intrigues and explosions became irrelevant. The great lady of the town, Mma-Mompati, was seen everywhere, She had the close, guarded eyes of one who knows too much and isn't telling. She presided over teas and luncheons in her home, just like any English lady, with polished etiquette and the professional smile of the highborn who don't really give a damn about people or anything. And as though to off-set all the intrigues and underworld deals that went on in her home behind closed doors, Mma-Mompati assiduously cultivated her 'other image' of the holy woman. No villager could die without being buried by Mma-Mompati: she attended the funerals of rich and poor. No one could fall ill without receiving the prayers of Mma-Mompati. Two days a week she set aside for visits to the hospital and in the afternoon, during visiting hours, she made the rounds of the hospital ward, Bible in hand. She would stop at each bed and enquire solicitously:

'And what may ail you, my daughter? And what may ail you, my son?'

At which, of course, the grateful ailing one would break out with a long list of woes. She had a professional smile and a professional frown of concern for everything, just like the priests. But topping it all was the fluidity and ease with which she could pray.

'Oh,' she would say, stricken with sorrow. 'I shall pray for you,' and bending her head in deep concentration she would pray and pray to either God or Jesus for the suffering of the world. Needless to say these gestures were deeply appreciated.

Then one day, without any warning, Rra-Mompati brought his world crashing down around his ears. He just preferred another woman and walked out of the security and prestige of his job and home to live with her. It was one of those scandals that rocked the village from end to end and for a time Rra-Mompati shuffled around shame-faced at his appalling deed. He averted his face so as not to catch the angry looks of the villagers which clearly said: 'Now Rra-Mompati, how could you leave a good woman like Mma-Mompati? She is matchless in her perfection. There is no other woman like her.'

On this tide of indignation Mma-Mompati swept sedately into the divorce court. The whole village memorised her great court oration because she repeated it so often thereafter. It was to God, the Church, the Bible, the Sick, the Poor, the Suffering, the Honour of an Honourable Woman, the Blessings of Holy Matrimony and so on. The court was very impressed by this noble, wronged woman. They ordered that Rra-Mompati, who was rich, settle her handsomely for life, with many cattle. Life in the village became very difficult for Rra-Mompati. People muttered curses at the very sight of him, and as for his new-found lady-love, she dared not show her face. He was also advised by the elders that a man of his low morals could not be in charge of the affairs of the tribe and he ought to look for another job. Rra-Mompati failed to defend himself, except in odd ways. After a long silence he told a sympathetic friend that he was sick of the nonsense of the village and would retire permanently to his cattle-post and live henceforth the life of a cattle-man. He was highly indignant, in an illogical way, at people, for turning against him.

Rra-Mompati was very indignant with his son, Mompati, for turning against him in support of his mother and he clung to these two indignations with a strange stubbornness. Soon after the father had disappeared from the village, he was pursued by Mompati in a heart-breaking attempt at reconciliation. Mompati returned to the village with a shocking story. On approaching his father's cattle-post, he said, his father had walked out of his hut and pointed his hunting gun at him. Then he'd shouted: 'Get away from here! You can support that woman if you like!'

Oh, the Devil had taken Rra-Mompati's soul for good, people said. He would surely burn eternally in hell-fire. Soon after this Mompati became very ill. He lay down for months. He had a terrible weakness and pain all over his body. He developed a fear of any chill or draught. It would end his life and he enveloped himself with warm clothing and blankets in an effort to save his life. Not once did he relate his nervous breakdown to the actions of his father but when he recovered a little he told people very earnestly that he was suffering from 'poor blood'. He kept this ailment as a kind of chronic condition and winter and summer he wrapped himself up warmly against the elements. In summer, the sweltering desert heat of the village reached temperatures of a hundred degrees in the shade. Mompati was wrapped up in two jerseys and an overcoat on such days. One day a perspiring villager remarked on the heat and looked meaningfully at Mompati's jerseys and coat. Mompati shivered and said: 'I have to protect myself. I must take care of my poor blood.'

Mma-Mompati settled in a little Mother Hubbard house with her son. It was neatly fenced. A water tap appeared in the yard, and vegetables and flower gardens tended by servants sprang up all round the pretty little house. Mompati found a job as a manager of a village store and together they resumed the broken thread of their lives. Mompati was seventeen then and astonishingly like his mother in appearance and behaviour. Mma-Mompati kept to her round of funerals, hospital visits, and church-going and her son built up a public acclaim all his own. Like his mother, he cared about everyone and it was due to this that he managed one of the strangest stores on earth. It was always crowded with people but it often ran completely out of goods. Above the clamour of voices, every now and then rose the deep, booming bass of Mompati, either in a hearty laugh or in stern and forcefully delivered advice to those in conflict or pain. He sat in a corner with piles of accounts and book-work but he could be easily distracted from his work. Every now and then he would look up cheerfully at the approach of a friend but that cheerful smile could, in a split second, turn to a worried frown. He would have one finger on his accounting – it would remain firmly pressed there – and a half an hour might pass in earnest discussion of the friend's latest problem. Suddenly, the bass voice would boom through the shop:

'I say, my friend, if you spare the rod, you spoil the child.'

Shoppers never knew the whole story. It did not matter. It mattered that some living being cared intensely and vividly and gloriously about his fellow men. A slight hush would descend on the shop as the bass swelled out and people would smile to themselves. It swelled out about God who was important and behind all things; it swelled out about the morals of the land which were disintegrating and later, when he married, it swelled out about the virtues of family life. He threw his whole heart into people's affairs and then, at the end of the day took all his book-work and accounting home, sitting up until late at night to make up for the hours lost in conversation during the day. Sometimes shoppers humorously queried:

'Mompati, why is it that there is no flour or soap in this shop? I've hunted for these goods for a whole week here and I cannot find them.'

And Mompati would reply: 'That's just what I was praying to God about this morning: "Oh God," I said, "I've forgotten to order the flour and soap again. I beg of you to help me, God, because my memory is so poor." My prayer has been answered my friend, and I expect the flour and soap to be here next week . . .'

This went on for ten years. Both mother and son lived a busy life and people imagined they were two peas in a pod, they seemed so alike in their interests and behaviour. Then Mompati fell in love with Mary Pule, a thin, wilting, willowy dreamy girl with a plaintive, tremulous voice. She had a façade too that concealed a tenacious will. She was so anxious to secure Mompati permanently as a husband that she played a hard game. All during the time he courted her, and it took months, she led him this way and that, with a charming smile. Oh, maybe she loved him. Maybe she did not. She wasn't sure. Mompati was intense about everything, so he was intensely in love. He shared his depressions and elations with his mother. The girl was invited to teas and showered with flattery and teasing until, in her own time, she accepted his proposal. It had nothing to do with either Mompati or his mother. It was her own plan.

A small flat was built in the yard in preparation for Mompati's future married life, and all proceeded well up to a certain point – the month after the marriage. Then Mma-Mompati began to undo herself. Throughout the ten years she had lived with her son, she had played a little game. Mompati used to bring his pay-packet home intact but she wanted him to buy her just a teeny-weeny something – a pair of stockings, a bottle of scent, a little handkerchief or a new dress. It just pleased her, she said, that her son cared about his mother. So she always extracted a teeny bit for her share and handed him the rest. She soon informed her daughter-in-law of this procedure and like all powerful personalities, she secretly despised the weak, wilting, plaintive little wretch her son had married. She needed to dominate and shove the wretch around. So at the end of that month, she over-stepped the mark. She opened the pay-packet as usual and suddenly needed an enormous amount of things all at once—a pair of shoes, a new dress, and a necklace.

What she handed over to her son could barely keep him and his wife in food for a week. She could not follow them into the privacy of their home, but unconsciously her vampire teeth were bared for battle. She noted that her daughter-in-law often looked gloomy and depressed in the ensuing days; her son was cold and reserved. She attacked the daughter-in-law with brittle smiles:

'Well, what's wrong with you, my child? Can't you greet an old person in a cheerful way?'

'There's nothing wrong, mother,' the girl replied, with a painful smile.

At the end of the next month, Mompati walked straight to his own flat and handed his pay-packet intact to his wife, ate a good supper, and fell into a sound sleep after many nights of worry and anguish. The following morning he left for work without even a glance at his mother's home. Then the storm burst. The pose of God and Jesus were blown to the winds and the demented vampire behind it was too terrible to behold. She descended on her daughter-in-law like a fury.

'You have done this to my son!' she snarled. 'You have turned him against me! His duty is to respect me and honour me and you cannot take it away from me! You see that water tap? You shall not draw any more water from it while you are in this yard! Go and draw water at the village tap in future!'

And so the whole village became involved in the spectacle. They stopped and blinked their eyes as they saw the newly-wed Mary carrying a water bucket a mile away from her own home to the village water taps.

'Mary,' they asked curiously, 'why is it you have to draw water here like everyone else when your mother-in-law has a water tap in her yard?'

Mary talked freely and at great length – a long weepy story of misery and torture. And people said: 'Well, we can't believe that a good woman like Mma-Mompati could be so harsh to her own child,' and they shook their heads in amazement at this thunderbolt. That was the end of Mma-Mompati. No one ever believed in her again or her God or Jesus Christ but she still buried the dead and prayed for the sick.

Her son, Mompati, set up home in a far-off part of the village. He never discussed the abrupt break with his mother to whom he had once been so overwhelmingly devoted, but one day his voice suddenly boomed out through the store in reply to some request by a friend:

'I'm sorry,' he said. 'I never do anything without first consulting my wife . . .'

32

Secrets

(1977)

Bernard MacLaverty

He had been called to be there at the end. His Great Aunt Mary had been dying for some days now and the house was full of relatives. He had just left his girlfriend's home – they had been studying for 'A' levels together – and had come back to the house to find all the lights spilling onto the lawn and a sense of purpose which had been absent from the last few days.

He knelt at the bedroom door to join in the prayers. His knees were on the wooden threshold and he edged them forward onto the carpet. They had tried to wrap her fingers around a crucifix but they kept loosening. She lay low on the pillow and her face seemed to have shrunk by half since he had gone out earlier in the night. Her white hair was damped and pushed back from her forehead. She twisted her head from side to side, her eyes closed. The prayers chorused on, trying to cover the sound she was making deep in her throat. Someone said about her teeth and his mother leaned over her and said, 'That's the pet,' and took her dentures from her mouth. The lower half of her face seemed to collapse. She half opened her eyes but could not raise her eyelids enough and showed only crescents of white.

'Hail Mary full of grace . . .' the prayers went on. He closed his hands over his face so that he would not have to look but smelt the trace of his girlfriend's handcream from his hands. The noise, deep and guttural, that his aunt was making became intolerable to him. It was as if she were drowning. She had lost all the dignity he knew her to have. He got up from the floor and stepped between the others who were kneeling and went into her sitting-room off the same landing.

He was trembling with anger or sorrow, he didn't know which. He sat in the brightness of her big sitting-room at the oval table and waited for something to happen. On the table was a cut-glass vase of irises, dying because she had been in bed for over a week. He sat staring at them. They were withering from the tips inward, scrolling themselves delicately, brown and neat. Clearing up after themselves. He stared at them for a long time until he heard the sounds of women weeping from the next room.

*

His aunt had been small – her head on a level with his when she sat at her table – and she seemed to get smaller each year. Her skin fresh, her hair white and waved and always well washed. She wore no jewellery except a cameo ring on the third finger of her right hand and, around her neck, a gold locket on a chain. The white classical profile on the ring was almost worn through and had become translucent and indistinct. The boy had noticed the ring when she had read to him as a child. In the beginning fairy tales, then as he got older extracts from famous novels, *Lorna Doone*, *Persuasion*, *Wuthering Heights* and her favourite extract, because she read it so often, Pip's meeting with Miss Havisham from *Great Expectations.* She would sit with him on her knee, her arms around him and holding the page flat with her hand. When he was bored he would interrupt her and ask about the ring. He loved hearing her tell of how her grandmother had given it to her as a brooch and she had had a ring made from it. He would try to count back to see how old it was. Had her grandmother got it from *her* grandmother? And if so what had she turned it into? She would nod her head from side to side and say, 'How would I know a thing like that?' keeping her place in the closed book with her finger.

'Don't be so inquisitive,' she'd say. 'Let's see what happens next in the story.'

One day she was sitting copying figures into a long narrow book with a dip pen when he came into her room. She didn't look up but when he asked her a question she just said, 'Mm?' and went on writing. The vase of irises on the oval table vibrated slightly as she wrote.

'What is it?' She wiped the nib on blotting paper and looked up at him over her reading glasses.

'I've started collecting stamps and Mamma says you might have some.'

'Does she now—?'

She got up from the table and went to the tall walnut bureau-bookcase standing in the alcove. From a shelf of the bookcase she took a small wallet of keys and selected one for the lock. There was a harsh metal shearing sound as she pulled the desk flap down. The writing area was covered with green leather which had dog-eared at the corners. The inner part was divided into pigeon holes, all bulging with papers. Some of them, envelopes, were gathered in batches nipped at the waist with elastic bands. There were postcards and bills and cash-books. She pointed to the postcards.

'You may have the stamps on those,' she said. 'But don't tear them. Steam them off.'

She went back to the oval table and continued writing. He sat on the arm of the chair looking through the picture post-cards – torchlight processions at Lourdes, brown photographs of town centres, dull black and whites of beaches backed by faded hotels. Then he turned them over and began to sort the stamps. Spanish, with a bald man, French with a rooster, German with funny jerky print, some Italian with what looked like a chimney-sweep's bundle and a hatchet.

'These are great,' he said. 'I haven't got any of them.'

'Just be careful how you take them off.'

'Can I take them downstairs?'

'Is your mother there?'

'Yes.'

'Then perhaps it's best if you bring the kettle up here.'

He went down to the kitchen. His mother was in the morning room polishing silver. He took the kettle and the flex upstairs. Except for the dipping and scratching of his aunt's pen the room was silent. It was at the back of the house overlooking the orchard and the sound of traffic from the main road was distant and muted. A tiny rattle began as the kettle warmed up, then it bubbled and steam gushed quietly from its spout. The cards began to curl slightly in the jet of steam but she didn't seem to be watching. The stamps peeled moistly off and he put them in a saucer of water to flatten them.

'Who is Brother Benignus?' he asked. She seemed not to hear. He asked again and she looked over her glasses.

'He was a friend.'

His flourishing signature appeared again and again. Sometimes Bro Benignus, sometimes Benignus and once Iggy.

'Is he alive?'

'No, he's dead now. Watch the kettle doesn't run dry.'

When he had all the stamps off he put the postcards together and replaced them in the pigeon-hole. He reached over towards the letters but before his hand touched them his aunt's voice, harsh for once, warned.

'A-A-A,' she moved her pen from side to side. 'Do-not-touch,' she said and smiled. 'Anything else, yes! That section, no!' She resumed her writing.

The boy went through some other papers and found some photographs. One was of a beautiful girl. It was very old-fashioned but he could see that she was beautiful. The picture was a pale brown oval set on a white square of card. The edges of the oval were misty. The girl in the photograph was young and had dark, dark hair scraped severely back and tied like a knotted rope on the top of her head – high arched eyebrows, her nose straight and thin, her mouth slightly smiling, yet not smiling – the way a mouth is after smiling. Her eyes looked out at him dark and knowing and beautiful.

'Who is that?' he asked.

'Why? What do you think of her?'

'She's all right.'

'Do you think she is beautiful?' The boy nodded.

'That's me,' she said. The boy was glad he had pleased her in return for the stamps.

Other photographs were there, not posed ones like Aunt Mary's but Brownie snaps of laughing groups of girls in bucket hats like German helmets and coats to their ankles. They seemed tiny faces covered in clothes. There was a photograph of a young man smoking a cigarette, his hair combed one way by the wind against a background of sea.

'Who is that in the uniform?' the boy asked.

'He's a soldier,' she answered without looking up.

'Oh,' said the boy. 'But who is he?'

'He was a friend of mine before you were born,' she said. Then added, 'Do I smell something cooking? Take your stamps and off you go. That's the boy.'

The boy looked at the back of the picture of the man and saw in black spidery ink 'John, Aug' 15 Ballintoye'.

'I thought maybe it was Brother Benignus,' he said. She looked at him not answering.

'Was your friend killed in the war?'

At first she said no, but then she changed her mind.

'Perhaps he was,' she said, then smiled. 'You are far too inquisitive. Put it to use and go and see what is for tea. Your mother will need the kettle.' She came over to the bureau and helped tidy the photographs away. Then she locked it and put the keys on the shelf.

'Will you bring me up my tray?'

The boy nodded and left.

It was a Sunday evening, bright and summery. He was doing his homework and his mother was sitting on the carpet in one of her periodic fits of tidying out the drawers of the mahogany sideboard. On one side of her was a heap of paper scraps torn in quarters and bits of rubbish, on the other the useful items that had to be kept. The boy heard the bottom stair creak under Aunt Mary's light footstep. She knocked and put her head round the door and said that she was walking to Devotions. She was dressed in her good coat and hat and was just easing her fingers into her second glove. The boy saw her stop and pat her hair into place before the mirror in the hallway. His mother stretched over and slammed the door shut. It vibrated, then he heard the deeper sound of the outside door closing and her first few steps on the gravelled driveway. He sat for a long time wondering if he would have time or not. Devotions could take anything from twenty minutes to three quarters of an hour, depending on who was saying it.

Ten minutes must have passed, then the boy left his homework and went upstairs and into his aunt's sitting room. He stood in front of the bureau wondering, then he reached for the keys. He tried several before he got the right one. The desk flap screeched as he pulled it down. He pretended to look at the postcards again in case there were any stamps he had missed. Then he put them away and reached for the bundle of letters. The elastic band was thick and old, brittle almost and when he took it off its track remained on the wad of letters. He carefully opened one and took out the letter and unfolded it, frail, khaki-coloured.

> My dearest Mary, it began, I am so tired I can hardly write to you. I have spent what seems like all day censoring letters (there is a howitzer about 100 yds away firing every 2 minutes). The letters are heartrending in their attempt to express what they cannot. Some of the men are illiterate, others almost so. I know that they feel as much as we do, yet they do not have the words to express it. That is your job in the schoolroom to give us generations who can read and write well. They have . . .

The boy's eye skipped down the page and over the next. He read the last paragraph.

Mary I love you as much as ever – more so that we cannot be together. I do not know which is worse, the hurt of this war or being separated from you. Give all my love to Brendan and all at home.

It was signed, scribbles with what he took to be John. He folded the paper carefully into its original creases and put it in the envelope. He opened another.

My love, it is thinking of you that keeps me sane. When I get a moment I open my memories of you as if I were reading. Your long dark hair – I always imagine you wearing the blouse with the tiny roses, the white one that opened down the back – your eyes that said so much without words, the way you lowered your head when I said anything that embarrassed you, and the clean nape of your neck.

The day I think about most was the day we climbed the head at Ballycastle. In a hollow, out of the wind, the air full of pollen and the sound of insects, the grass warm and dry and you lying beside me your hair undone, between me and the sun. You remember that that was where I first kissed you and the look of disbelief in your eyes that made me laugh afterwards.

It makes me laugh now to see myself savouring these memories standing alone up to my thighs in muck. It is everywhere, two, three feet deep. To walk ten yards leaves you quite breathless.

I haven't time to write more today so I leave you with my feet in the clay and my head in the clouds.

I love you, John.

He did not bother to put the letter back into the envelope but opened another.

My dearest, I am so cold that I find it difficult to keep my hand steady enough to write. You remember when we swam the last two fingers of your hand went the colour and texture of candles with the cold. Well that is how I am all over. It is almost four days since I had any real sensation in my feet or legs. Everything is frozen. The ground is like steel.

Forgive me telling you this but I feel I have to say it to someone. The worst thing is the dead. They sit or lie frozen in the position they die. You can distinguish them from the living because their faces are the colour of slate. God help us when the thaw comes . . . This war is beginning to have an effect on me. I have lost all sense of feeling. The only emotion I have experienced lately is one of anger. Sheer white trembling anger. I have no pity or sorrow for the dead and injured. I thank God it is not me but I am enraged that it had to be them. If I live through this experience I will be a different person.

The only thing that remains constant is my love for you.

Today a man died beside me. A piece of shrapnel had pierced his neck as we were moving under fire. I pulled him into a crater and stayed with him until he died. I watched him choke and then drown in his blood.

I am full of anger which has no direction.

He sorted through the pile and read half of some, all of others. The sun had fallen low in the sky and shone directly into the room onto the pages he was reading making the paper glare. He selected a letter from the back of the pile and shaded it with his hand as he read.

> Dearest Mary, I am writing this to you from my hospital bed. I hope that you were not too worried about not hearing from me. I have been here, so they tell me, for two weeks and it took another two weeks before I could bring myself to write this letter.
>
> I have been thinking a lot as I lie here about the war and about myself and about you. I do not know how to say this but I feel deeply that I must do something, must sacrifice something to make up for the horror of the past year. In some strange way Christ has spoken to me through the carnage . . .

Suddenly the boy heard the creak of the stair and he frantically tried to slip the letter back into its envelope but it crumpled and would not fit. He bundled them all together. He could hear his aunt's familiar puffing on the short stairs to her room. He spread the elastic band wide with his fingers. It snapped and the letters scattered. He pushed them into their pigeon hole and quickly closed the desk flap. The brass screeched loudly and clicked shut. At that moment his aunt came into the room.

'What are you doing, boy?' she snapped.

'Nothing.' He stood with the keys in his hand. She walked to the bureau and opened it. The letters sprung out in an untidy heap.

'You have been reading my letters,' she said quietly. Her mouth was tight with the words and her eyes blazed. The boy could say nothing. She struck him across the side of the face.

'Get out,' she said. 'Get out of my room.'

The boy, the side of his face stinging and red, put the keys on the table on his way out. When he reached the door she called him. He stopped, his hand on the handle.

'You are dirt,' she hissed, 'and always will be dirt. I shall remember this till the day I die.'

Even though it was a warm evening there was a fire in the large fireplace. His mother had asked him to light it so that she could clear out Aunt Mary's stuff. The room could then be his study, she said. She came in and seeing him at the table said, 'I hope I'm not disturbing you.'

'No.'

She took the keys from her pocket, opened the bureau and began burning papers and cards. She glanced quickly at each one before she flicked it onto the fire.

'Who was Brother Benignus?' he asked.

His mother stopped sorting and said, 'I don't know. Your aunt kept herself very much to herself. She got books from him through the post occasionally. That much I do know.'

She went on burning the cards. They built into strata, glowing red and black. Now and again she broke up the pile with the poker, sending showers of sparks up the chimney. He saw her come to the letters. She took off the elastic band and put it to one side with the useful things and began dealing the envelopes into the fire. She opened one and read quickly through it, then threw it on top of the burning pile.

'Mama,' he said.

'Yes?'

'Did Aunt Mary say anything about me?'

'What do you mean?'

'Before she died – did she say anything?'

'Not that I know of – the poor thing was too far gone to speak, God rest her.' She went on burning, lifting the corners of the letters with the poker to let the flames underneath them.

When he felt a hardness in his throat he put his head down on his books. Tears came into his eyes for the first time since she had died and he cried silently into the crook of his arm for the woman who had been his maiden aunt, his teller of tales, that she might forgive him.

33

The Stoat

(1978)

John McGahern

A long-legged student in a turtleneck was following a two-iron he had struck just short of the green when he heard the crying high in the rough grass above the fairway. The clubs rattled as he climbed towards the crying, but it did not cease, its pitch rising. Light of water from the inlet that ran to Ballisadare and was called the Calm Sea blinded him as he climbed out of the coarse tussocks, and he did not see the rabbit at once, where it sat rigidly still on a bare patch of loose sand, screaming; and at the same time he glimpsed the long grey body of the stoat slithering away like a snake into the long grass.

He took a slow step forward but the rabbit still did not move. Its crying ceased, and he noticed the wet slick of blood behind its ear, and then the blood pumping out on the sand. It did not stir when he stooped to pick it up, but never before did he hold such pure terror in his hands, the body trembling in a rigidity of terror as the heart hammered away its blood through the cut in the jugular vein. Holding it up by the hind legs he killed it with one stroke, but when he turned it over he could find no mark other than where the vein had been cut. He took the rabbit down with him, picking his way more cautiously through the long grass than when he had climbed. He left the rabbit beside the clubs while he chipped and holed out, but as he crossed from the green to the tee he saw the stoat cross the fairway behind him. After watching two simple shots fade away into the rough, he knew he had lost his concentration, and decided to finish for the morning. As he made his way back to the cottage his father rented every August in Strandhill, he twice glimpsed the stoat behind him, following the rabbit still, though it was dead.

All night the rabbit must have raced from warren to warren, he thought, the stoat on its trail. Plumper rabbits had crossed the stoat's path but it would not be deflected; it had marked down this one rabbit to kill. No matter how fast the rabbit raced, the stoat was still on its trail, and at last the rabbit sat down in terror and waited for the stoat to slither up and cut the vein behind the ear. He had heard it crying as the stoat was drinking its blood.

His father was reading *The Independent* on the front lawn of the cottage when he got back, facing Knocknarea, his back to the wind that blew from the ocean. A quick look told the son that he was going through the ads for teachers; he always went through the ads for teachers again after he had exhausted the news and death notices, why he would never know, other than from habit or boredom, since he would never leave now the small school where he was principal and the residence that went with it.

'Another colleague who was in Drumcondra the same year as myself has gone to his reward,' he said when he looked up. 'A great full-back poor Weeshie was, God rest him.'

The son made no answer but held up the rabbit.

'Where did you get that?'

'On the links. I heard it crying. And when I went to look there was this weasel. It had cut the jugular vein, and the rabbit was just sitting there. It never moved when I went to pick it up.'

'It must be a stoat. The weasel is extinct in Ireland.'

'A stoat then. I read something about it, but I never came across it before.'

'It's common. You often hear the squealing in scrubs or bushes. No doubt it'll be another specimen for yourself and your uncle to mull over.'

'Well, it's as good as what you find in *The Independent*.'

'What do you intend to do with it?' Other than to rattle the newspaper loudly the father made no response to the counter thrust.

'I thought I'd skin and cook it.'

'Do you think will it be all right?'

'It couldn't be more perfect,' he laughed as he held it up. 'Maybe if I cooked it Miss McCabe might like to have it with us tonight.'

'You better not tell *her* how you came by it,' he looked up in alarm.

'Of course not. Old Luke had rabbits for sale a few days back as well as suspiciously got sea trout and salmon. He said he bought them off fellows with a ferret.'

'Rabbit – the poor man's chicken. What if she doesn't like rabbit?'

'She can say so, and it needn't change anything. There'll be still plenty of time for both of you to have dinner as usual at the Kincora. By the way, what are you going to do for lunch? Are you going to go down to the Bay View?'

'I'd feel like a pint if I went down. If you take a drink too early in this weather it makes the day very cumbersome to get through.'

'There's cheese and bread and a bit of salad. I could make up sandwiches and have coffee.'

'That'd be far better. Good man. Can I give you a hand?'

'No. Stay where you are. I'll bring them out. And what about this rabbit and Miss McCabe? Is it all right with you?'

'I suppose there's no harm in asking her, is there?'

The young student took the rabbit inside. He had no anxieties regarding Miss McCabe and the dinner; she would come even if a cow's head were in question, since by coming to the cottage to dinner she was drawing closer to the dream of her future life, of what she hoped to become.

*

Miss McCabe's dream was still in the womb of time, he reflected with mock ruefulness, when his father had asked him up to the study the Christmas before. It was not a study in any strict sense, but a small room where he corrected exam papers and kept textbooks and books of his college days, and where he liked to impart decisions in an aura of some solemnity that 'not only affects me, but affects my family as well'. Those occasions that used to arouse fear and foreboding in the growing boy had by this time dwindled to embarrassing and faintly comic charades.

'Would you take it very much to heart if I decided to marry again?' at least that opening had the virtue of surprise.

'Of course not. Why do you ask me?' the young man's face showed his amazement.

'I was afraid you might be affronted by the idea of another woman holding the position your dear mother held,' the voice floated brittlely along on emotion that it could not control. The son hoped the father wouldn't break down and cry, for if he did he was afraid he might idiotically join him. The father started to rotate his thumbs about one another as he waited.

'That's ridiculous. I think you should do exactly what you want to do. It's your life.'

The father looked hurt, as if his life had been brutally severed from the other life by the son's words.

'For years I've been faithful to your mother's memory,' he began painfully. 'Now you're a man. Soon you'll be a fully qualified doctor, while I'll have to eke out my days between this empty house and the school. At my age you don't expect much from marriage, but at least I'd have companionship.'

'There was no need to ask me. In fact, I think it's a good idea.

'You have no objections then?'

'None. As I said, I think it's a good idea.'

'I'm glad you approve. I wouldn't have gone ahead if you'd any objections.'

The son was curious if there was already some woman in mind, but did not ask. When later that day his father showed him the ad he had written he was grateful for the dismay which cancelled laughter.

Teacher fifty-two. Widower. Seeks companionship. View marriage.

'What do you think of it?'

'I think it's fine. It couldn't be better.'

'I'll send it off then so.'

Neither had any idea that so much unfulfilled longing for the woe that is marriage wandered around in the world till the replies began to pour in. Nurses, housekeepers, secretaries, childless widows and widows with small children, house owners, car owners, pensioners, teachers, civil servants, a policewoman, and a woman who had left at twenty years to work at Fords of Dagenham who wanted to come home to marry. The postman enquired slyly if the school was seeking a new assistant, and the woman who ran the post office said in a faraway voice that if we were looking for a housekeeper she had a relative who might be interested.

'I hope they don't steam the damn letters. This country is on fire with curiosity,' the father complained.

The son saw much of him that spring term, as he met many of the women in Dublin, though he had to go to Cork and Limerick and Tullamore as well. In hotel lounges he met them, hiding behind a copy of the *Roscommon Herald*, which was how they were able to identify him.

'You've never in your life seen such a collection of wrecks and battleaxes as I've had to see in the last few months,' he said, a cold night in late March after he had met the lady from Dagenham in the Ormond. 'You'd need to get a government grant to do them up before you could think of taking some of them on.'

'Do you mean in appearance or as people?'

'All ways,' he said despairingly.

Because of these interviews the son was able to spend all that Easter with his uncle, a surgeon in a county town, who had encouraged him against his father in his choice of medicine, the father wishing to see him in a bank. After dinner, on the first night, the uncle suggested a long walk, 'It's one of those clear frosty nights. We can circle and come back through the town. It's about four miles.'

'That's fine with me.'

A car passed on the road as they set out. The headlamps lit the white railing and fleshly boles of the beech avenue down to the ragged thorns of the road below. They did not start to stride out properly till they reached the road. The three-quarter moon and the stars gave light enough for them to see their breaths in the frosty night.

'My father's going to get married, it seems,' he confided, in the ring of the footsteps.

'You're joking,' his uncle paused.

'I'm not. He's had an ad this long while in the papers.'

'An ad. You're surely joking.'

'I'm not. I'm in deadly earnest.'

'An ad,' suddenly the uncle became convulsed with laughter, and was hardly able to get the next words out, 'And did he get . . . replies?'

'Bundles. He's been interviewing them.'

'And have you seen any of the . . . applicants,' he had to pause again on the road.

'No, but he said you'd need a government grant to do some of them that he's seen up before you could think of marrying them.'

'A government grant . . . stop it. This is high farce. The man must finally have gone off his rocker.'

'Apparently he's just found someone. A schoolteacher in her forties. She's no beauty, but a shining light compared with the wrecks and battleaxes he's been interviewing.'

'Have you seen this person?'

'Not yet. I'm supposed to see her next week.'

'My god, if you hang round long enough you see everything,' he combed his fingers through his long greying hair as he walked. 'At least, if he does get married, it'll get him off your back.'

'You don't like my father much?'

'He's a decent enough fellow but I find him dull. Probably not nearly as dull as he finds me.'

They had circled the town. Lighted poles appeared in the thorn hedges, and then a paved sidewalk.

'We might as well have a drink in the Grand Central,' the uncle said as they came into the town. 'The trouble with being a bigwig in a small town is that there's either the Grand Central or nowhere,' and though he nodded to some people sitting in armchairs as they passed through the lounge, he headed straight for a corner of the bar. 'We'll stand. That way we can't be so easily cornered. You know, if your father does succeed in getting himself hitched, you'll be able to spend much more time here. I'd like that.'

He'd like that too. With his uncle everything seemed open: 'Life seems to have no purpose other than to reproduce itself. Life comes out of matter and goes back into matter. We inherit it and pass it on. We might as well take as decent a care of it as we can. You cannot go against love and not be in error.' Nothing was closed. This freedom was gaiety, even though it seemed that it caused him to seem mostly lonely.

'I feel guilty about it but the truth is that my father bores me. I fear and hate the unconscious.'

A few Saturdays later he was to meet Miss McCabe in Dublin. Both his father and she were desperately nervous. It made him feel that he was the parent and they the children anxious for his approval. Miss McCabe wore pale tweeds and serviceable brown shoes. She was somewhere in her forties, rather frail, and excitable. He liked her, but he would have encouraged his father to marry her whether he did or not, as he was anxious for the whole play to be over.

'Well, what was your impression?' his father asked him afterwards. That she was so desperately nervous that she spilled both coffee and a small bowl of cream at the luncheon, that she was anxious for approval to such a point that no person should or ought to be from another . . . these he did not say. Who was he to give or to withhold approval from one who had been wandering round in the world long before he.

'I think Miss McCabe is a fine person,' he said.

'You have . . . no objections then?'

'Of course not.'

'I'm glad,' he said and started to explain their plans.

She would come with them to Strandhill this summer, and stay in one of the hotels close to the usual cottage they took for August. If all went well they would become engaged before they went back to the schools at the end of the holidays.

They had been at Strandhill a week now, the boy golfing or studying, the father spending much of his time with Miss McCabe. Sometimes the son would see them arm in arm on the promenade from the tees close to the shore. The sight disturbed him, as if their defence was too brittle against the only end of life, and made it too disturbingly obvious, and he would try to shut it out with the golf ball.

'Will you be seeing Miss McCabe?' the boy asked as he put the coffee and sandwiches on the table.

'I might drop into the hotel. She's going to the salt baths.'

There was a hot salt bath close to where the old cannon pointed out on the ocean, asbestos covered, the yellow funnel of a ship for chimney from which plumes of steam puffed. She went every afternoon for the hot baths and a massage. She had rheumatism.

'And you? What do you intend? Are you studying?'

'No, I'll get in a round, and come back early to cook that rabbit. But ask Miss McCabe. It's just a folly on my part to want to cook it, and I don't mind at all if you'd both prefer to eat as usual at the Kincora.'

They left the cottage together after lunch, the father with a walking stick, the son with the golf clubs, and parted at the lane that led to the clubhouse.

As he went round the course he climbed in that instinct that draws people to places that have witnessed murder or violence to where he had heard the crying that morning, but the blood had dried from the sand, and the place was uncannily still, the coarse tussocks rustling in the sea wind, the strand covered with the full tide, and a white sailing boat tacking up the inlet from Ballisadare to the mouth of the ocean.

He skinned and dressed the rabbit that evening, clinically teasing out the dried blood where the vein had been cut, and Miss McCabe came at eight. The father was plainly uneasy until she exclaimed that the rabbit was delicious.

'I never knew rabbit could be so good,' he added. 'I suppose it's just prejudice again. It was always known as the poor man's chicken.'

'We must praise the cook too. As well as a future doctor we have also a good cook on our hands,' Miss McCabe was so much in her element that she was careless. 'It's much nicer to eat here than at the Kincora. Luke seems to have very good trout as well. Some of them look as fat as butter. You must allow me to cook them for dinner some evening soon. It's crazy not to have fish when at the ocean.'

'Miss McCabe likes you enormously,' the father sang after he had returned from leaving her back to the hotel. 'She has savings, and she says you'll be welcome to them if you ever need money for post-graduate work or anything like that.'

'That won't be necessary. My uncle said I can have as much as I need on loan for those purposes,' the son said cuttingly, and the reference to the uncle annoyed the father as much as Miss McCabe's offer had the son. Irrationally, he felt soiled by meal and rabbit and whole evening, as if he had taken part in some buffoonery against the day, against any sense of dignity, and he was determining how to avoid the trout dinner and anything more got to do with them.

As it turned out there was no need for avoidance. A uniformed bellhop came from the hotel the next evening to tell that Miss McCabe had suffered a heart attack in the salt baths that afternoon. The doctor had seen her and she was resting in her hotel room. She wished to see the father.

'Will you come?' the father asked.

'It's you she wants to see.'

When he got back from the hotel he was incredibly agitated. He could not sit still.

'She's all right,' he said. 'She just had a mild heart attack in the hot baths, but she still thinks we'll get engaged at the end of the month.'

'But I thought that was the general idea.'

'It was. If everything went well. Who wants to marry a woman who can pop off at any minute?'

It sometimes happened, even in the act, the son had heard, but he said nothing.

'Isn't it enough to have buried one woman?' the father shouted.

'Did you tell her?'

'I tried. I wasn't able. All she thinks of is our future. Her head is full of plans.'

'What are you going to do?'

'Clear out,' he said, to the son's dismay.

'You can't do that.'

'It's the only way to do it. I'll write to her.'

'What . . . if she doesn't take it?'

'There's nothing I can do about that.'

As if all the irons were being suddenly all truly struck and were flowing from all directions to the heart of the green, he saw with terrifying clarity that it was the stoat the father had glimpsed in Miss McCabe's hotel room, and he was running.

'What'll you do about the cottage? It's rented till the end of the month.'

'It doesn't matter about the cottage. The rent is paid.'

'Where'll you go to?'

'Home, of course. Aren't you coming?' he asked as if he assumed it was foregone.

'No,' he saw his chance. 'I'll stay.'

'What if Miss McCabe sees you?' the father asked in alarm.

'There's nothing I can do for her or she for me.'

He was not staying by the sea either. Tomorrow he would leave for his uncle's. They were all running.

'What if she asks about me?'

'Naturally, I'll try to avoid her, but if I meet her I'll say I don't know. That it's not my affair. How soon are you going?'

'As soon as I get the stuff into the boot of the car.'

'I'll give you a hand so.'

'Are you sure you won't change your mind?'

'No. I'll stay.'

'Write then.'

'I'll write.'

Already he could hear his uncle's mordant voice. 'You have to take a test to drive a bloody old car around. But any pair of imbeciles of age can go and take a marriage licence out and set about bringing a child up in the world, which is a much more complicated activity than driving an old car around!' There would be good talk for several days, and there was the story of the stoat and the rabbit.

All night the rabbit must have raced from warren to warren, the stoat on its trail. Plumper rabbits had crossed the stoat's path but it would not be deflected; it had marked down this one rabbit to kill. No matter how fast the rabbit raced, the stoat was still on its trail, and at last the rabbit sat down in terror and waited for the stoat to slither up and cut the vein behind the ear. He had heard it crying as the stoat was drinking its blood.

34

Games at Twilight

(1978)

Anita Desai

It was still too hot to play outdoors. They had had their tea, they had been washed and had their hair brushed, and after the long day of confinement in the house that was not cool but at least a protection from the sun, the children strained to get out. Their faces were red and bloated with the effort, but their mother would not open the door, everything was still curtained and shuttered in a way that stifled the children, made them feel that their lungs were stuffed with cotton wool and their noses with dust and if they didn't burst out into the light and see the sun and feel the air, they would choke.

'Please, ma, please,' they begged. 'We'll play in the veranda and porch – we won't go a step out of the porch.'

'You will, I know you will, and then—'

'No – we won't, we won't,' they wailed so horrendously that she actually let down the bolt of the front door so that they burst out like seeds from a crackling, over-ripe pod into the veranda, with such wild, maniacal yells that she retreated to her bath and the shower of talcum powder and the fresh sari that were to help her face the summer evening.

They faced the afternoon. It was too hot. Too bright. The white walls of the veranda glared stridently in the sun. The bougainvillea hung about it, purple and magenta, in livid balloons. The garden outside was like a tray made of beaten brass, flattened out on the red gravel and the stony soil in all shades of metal – aluminium, tin, copper and brass. No life stirred at this arid time of day – the birds still drooped, like dead fruit, in the papery tents of the trees; some squirrels lay limp on the wet earth under the garden tap. The outdoor dog lay stretched as if dead on the veranda mat, his paws and ears and tail all reaching out like dying travellers in search of water. He rolled his eyes at the children – two white marbles rolling in the purple sockets, begging for sympathy – and attempted to lift his tail in a wag but could not. It only twitched and lay still.

Then, perhaps roused by the shrieks of the children, a band of parrots suddenly fell out of the eucalyptus tree, tumbled frantically in the still, sizzling air, then sorted themselves out into battle formation and streaked away across the white sky.

The children, too, felt released. They too began tumbling, shoving, pushing against each other, frantic to start. Start what? Start their business. The business of the children's day which is – play.

'Let's play hide-and-seek.'

'Who'll be It?'

'You be It.'

'Why should I? You be—'

'You're the eldest—'

'That doesn't mean—'

The shoves became harder. Some kicked out. The motherly Mira intervened. She pulled the boys roughly apart. There was a tearing sound of cloth but it was lost in the heavy panting and angry grumbling and no one paid attention to the small sleeve hanging loosely off a shoulder.

'Make a circle, make a circle!' she shouted, firmly pulling and pushing till a kind of vague circle was formed. 'Now clap!' she roared and, clapping, they all chanted in melancholy unison: 'Dip, dip, dip – my blue ship—' and every now and then one or the other saw he was safe by the way his hands fell at the crucial moment – palm on palm, or back of hand on palm – and dropped out of the circle with a yell and a jump of relief and jubilation.

Raghu was It. He started to protest, to cry 'You cheated – Mira cheated – Anu cheated—' but it was too late, the others had all already streaked away. There was no one to hear when he called out, 'Only in the veranda – the porch – Ma said – Ma *said* to stay in the porch!' No one had stopped to listen, all he saw were their brown legs flashing through the dusty shrubs, scrambling up brick walls, leaping over compost heaps and hedges, and then the porch stood empty in the purple shade of the bougainvillea and the garden was as empty as before; even the limp squirrels had whisked away, leaving everything gleaming, brassy and bare.

Only small Manu suddenly reappeared, as if he had dropped out of an invisible cloud or from a bird's claws, and stood for a moment in the centre of the yellow lawn, chewing his finger and near to tears as he heard Raghu shouting, with his head pressed against the veranda wall, 'Eighty-three, eighty-five, eighty-nine, ninety . . .' and then made off in a panic, half of him wanting to fly north, the other half counselling south. Raghu turned just in time to see the flash of his white shorts and the uncertain skittering of his red sandals, and charged after him with such a blood-curdling yell that Manu stumbled over the hosepipe, fell into its rubber coils and lay there weeping, 'I won't be It – you have to find them all – all – All!'

'I know I have to, idiot,' Raghu said, superciliously kicking him with his toe. 'You're dead,' he said with satisfaction, licking the beads of perspiration off his upper lip, and then stalked off in search of worthier prey, whistling spiritedly so that the hiders should hear and tremble.

Ravi heard the whistling and picked his nose in a panic, trying to find comfort by burrowing the finger deep-deep into that soft tunnel. He felt himself too exposed, sitting on an upturned flower pot behind the garage. Where could he burrow? He could run around the garage if he heard Raghu come – around and around and around – but he hadn't much faith in his short legs when matched against Raghu's long, hefty, hairy footballer legs. Ravi had a frightening glimpse of them as Raghu combed the hedge of crotons and hibiscus, trampling delicate ferns underfoot as he did so. Ravi looked about him desperately, swallowing a small ball of snot in his fear.

The garage was locked with a great heavy lock to which the driver had the key in his room, hanging from a nail on the wall under his work-shirt. Ravi had peeped in and seen him still sprawling on his string-cot in his vest and striped underpants, the hair on his chest and the hair in his nose shaking with the vibrations of his phlegm-obstructed snores. Ravi had wished he were tall enough, big enough to reach the key on the nail, but it was impossible, beyond his reach for years to come. He had sidled away and sat dejectedly on the flower pot. That at least was cut to his own size.

But next to the garage was another shed with a big green door. Also locked. No one even knew who had the key to the lock. That shed wasn't opened more than once a year when Ma turned out all the old broken bits of furniture and rolls of matting and leaking buckets, and the white ant hills were broken and swept away and Flit sprayed into the spider webs and rat holes so that the whole operation was like the looting of a poor, ruined and conquered city. The green leaves of the door sagged. They were nearly off their rusty hinges. The hinges were large and made a small gap between the door and the walls – only just large enough for rats, dogs and, possibly, Ravi to slip through.

Ravi had never cared to enter such a dark and depressing mortuary of defunct household goods seething with such unspeakable and alarming animal life but, as Raghu's whistling grew angrier and sharper and his crashing and storming in the hedge wilder, Ravi suddenly slipped off the flower pot and through the crack and was gone. He chuckled aloud with astonishment at his own temerity so that Raghu came out of the hedge, stood silent with his hands on his hips, listening, and finally shouted 'I heard you! I'm coming! *Got* you—' and came charging round the garage only to find the upturned flower pot, the yellow dust, the crawling of white ants in a mud-hill against the closed shed door – nothing. Snarling, he bent to pick up a stick and went off, whacking it against the garage and shed walls as if to beat out his prey.

Ravi shook, then shivered with delight, with self-congratulation. Also with fear. It was dark, spooky in the shed. It had a muffled smell, as of graves. Ravi had once got locked into the linen cupboard and sat there weeping for half an hour before he was rescued. But at least that had been a familiar place, and even smelt pleasantly of starch, laundry and, reassuringly, of his mother. But the shed smelt of rats, ant hills, dust and spider webs. Also of less definable, less recognisable horrors. And it was dark. Except for the white-hot cracks along the door, there was no light. The roof was very low. Although Ravi was small, he felt as if he could reach up and touch it with his finger tips. But he didn't stretch. He hunched himself into a ball so as not to bump into anything, touch or feel anything. What might there not be to touch him and feel him as he stood there, trying to see in the dark? Something cold, or slimy – like a snake. Snakes! He leapt up as Raghu whacked the wall with his stick – then, quickly realising what it was, felt almost relieved to hear Raghu, hear his stick. It made him feel protected.

But Raghu soon moved away. There wasn't a sound once his footsteps had gone around the garage and disappeared. Ravi stood frozen inside the shed. Then he shivered all over. Something had tickled the back of his neck. It took him a while to pick up the courage to lift his hand and explore. It was an insect – perhaps a spider – exploring *him.* He squashed it and wondered how many more creatures were watching him, waiting to reach out and touch him, the stranger.

There was nothing now. After standing in that position – his hand still on his neck, feeling the wet splodge of the squashed spider gradually dry – for minutes, hours, his legs began to tremble with the effort, the inaction. By now he could see enough in the dark to make out the large solid shapes of old wardrobes, broken buckets and bedsteads piled on top of each other around him. He recognised an old bathtub – patches of enamel glimmered at him and at last he lowered himself onto its edge.

He contemplated slipping out of the shed and into the fray. He wondered if it would not be better to be captured by Raghu and be returned to the milling crowd as long as he could be in the sun, the light, the free spaces of the garden and the familiarity of his brothers, sisters and cousins. It would be evening soon. Their games would become legitimate. The parents would sit out on the lawn on cane basket chairs and watch them as they tore around the garden or gathered in knots to share a loot of mulberries or black, teeth-splitting *jamun* from the garden trees. The gardener would fix the hosepipe to the water tap and water would fall lavishly through the air to the ground, soaking the dry yellow grass and the red gravel and arousing the sweet, the intoxicating scent of water on dry earth – that loveliest scent in the world. Ravi sniffed for a whiff of it. He half-rose from the bathtub, then heard the despairing scream of one of the girls as Raghu bore down upon her. There was the sound of a crash, and of rolling about in the bushes, the shrubs, then screams and accusing sobs of, 'I touched the den—' 'You did not—' 'I did—' 'You liar, you did *not*' and then a fading away and silence again.

Ravi sat back on the harsh edge of the tub, deciding to hold out a bit longer. What fun if they were all found and caught – he alone left unconquered! He had never known that sensation. Nothing more wonderful had ever happened to him than being taken out by an uncle and bought a whole slab of chocolate all to himself, or being flung into the soda-man's pony cart and driven up to the gate by the friendly driver with the red beard and pointed ears. To defeat Raghu – that hirsute, hoarse-voiced football champion – and to be the winner in a circle of older, bigger, luckier children – that would be thrilling beyond imagination. He hugged his knees together and smiled to himself almost shyly at the thought of so much victory, such laurels.

There he sat smiling, knocking his heels against the bathtub, now and then getting up and going to the door to put his ear to the broad crack and listening for sounds of the game, the pursuer and the pursued, and then returning to his seat with the dogged determination of the true winner, a breaker of records, a champion.

It grew darker in the shed as the light at the door grew softer, fuzzier, turned to a kind of crumbling yellow pollen that turned to yellow fur, blue fur, grey fur. Evening.

Twilight. The sound of water gushing, falling. The scent of earth receiving water, slaking its thirst in great gulps and releasing that green scent of freshness, coolness. Through the crack Ravi saw the long purple shadows of the shed and the garage lying still across the yard. Beyond that, the white walls of the house. The bougainvillea had lost its lividity, hung in dark bundles that quaked and twittered and seethed with masses of homing sparrows. The lawn was shut off from his view. Could he hear the children's voices? It seemed to him that he could. It seemed to him that he could hear them chanting, singing, laughing. But what about the game? What had happened? Could it be over? How could it when he was still not found?

It then occurred to him that he could have slipped out long ago, dashed across the yard to the veranda and touched the 'den'. It was necessary to do that to win. He had forgotten. He had only remembered the part of hiding and trying to elude the seeker. He had done that so successfully, his success had occupied him so wholly that he had quite forgotten that success had to be clinched by that final dash to victory and the ringing cry of 'Den!'

With a whimper he burst through the crack, fell on his knees, got up and stumbled on stiff, benumbed legs across the shadowy yard, crying heartily by the time he reached the veranda so that when he flung himself at the white pillar and bawled, 'Den! Den! Den!' his voice broke with rage and pity at the disgrace of it all and he felt himself flooded with tears and misery.

Out on the lawn, the children stopped chanting. They all turned to stare at him in amazement. Their faces were pale and triangular in the dusk. The trees and bushes around them stood inky and sepulchral, spilling long shadows across them. They stared, wondering at his reappearance, his passion, his wild animal howling. Their mother rose from her basket chair and came towards him, worried, annoyed, saying, 'Stop it, stop it, Ravi. Don't be a baby. Have you hurt yourself?' Seeing him attended to, the children went back to clasping their hands and chanting 'The grass is green, the rose is red . . .'

But Ravi would not let them. He tore himself out of his mother's grasp and pounded across the lawn into their midst, charging at them with his head lowered so that they scattered in surprise. 'I won, I won, I won,' he bawled, shaking his head so that the big tears flew. 'Raghu didn't find me. I won, I won—'

It took them a minute to grasp what he was saying, even who he was. They had quite forgotten him. Raghu had found all the others long ago. There had been a fight about who was to be It next. It had been so fierce that their mother had emerged from her bath and made them change to another game. Then they had played another and another. Broken mulberries from the tree and eaten them. Helped the driver wash the car when their father returned from work. Helped the gardener water the beds till he roared at them and swore he would complain to their parents. The parents had come out, taken up their positions on the cane chairs. They had begun to play again, sing and chant. All this time no one had remembered Ravi. Having disappeared from the scene, he had disappeared from their minds. Clean.

'Don't be a fool,' Raghu said roughly, pushing him aside, and even Mira said, 'Stop howling, Ravi. If you want to play, you can stand at the end of the line,' and she put him there very firmly.

The game proceeded. Two pairs of arms reached up and met in an arc. The children trooped under it again and again in a lugubrious circle, ducking their heads and intoning

'The grass is green,
The rose is red;
Remember me
When I am dead, dead, dead, dead . . .'

And the arc of thin arms trembled in the twilight, and the heads were bowed so sadly, and their feet tramped to that melancholy refrain so mournfully, so helplessly, that Ravi could not bear it. He would not follow them, he would not be included in this funereal game. He had wanted victory and triumph – not a funeral. But he had been forgotten, left out and he would not join them now. The ignominy of being forgotten – how could he face it? He felt his heart go heavy and ache inside him unbearably. He lay down full length on the damp grass, crushing his face into it, no longer crying, silenced by a terrible sense of his insignificance.

35

The Taste of Watermelon

(1979)

Borden Deal

When I think of the summer I was sixteen, a lot of things come crowding in to be thought about. We had moved just the year before, and sixteen is still young enough that the bunch makes a difference. I had a bunch, all right, but they weren't sure of me yet. I didn't know why. Maybe because I'd lived in town, and my father still worked there instead of farming, like the other fathers did. The boys I knew, even Freddy Gray and J.D., still kept a small distance between us.

Then there was Willadean Wills. I hadn't been much interested in girls before. But I had to admit to myself that I was interested in Willadean. She was my age, nearly as tall as I, and up till the year before, Freddy Gray told me, she had been good at playing Gully Keeper and Ante-Over. But she didn't play such games this year. She was tall and slender, and Freddy Gray and J.D. and I had several discussions about the way she walked. I maintained she was putting it on, but J.D. claimed she couldn't help it. Freddy Gray remarked that she hadn't walked that way last year. He said she'd walked like any other human being. So then I said, put on or not, I liked the way she walked, and then there was a large silence.

It wasn't a comfortable silence, because of Mr Wills, Willadean's father. We were all afraid of Mr Wills.

Mr Wills was a big man. He had bright, fierce eyes under heavy brows and, when he looked down at you, you just withered. The idea of having him directly and immediately angry at one of us was enough to shrivel the soul. All that summer Willadean walked up and down the high road or sat on their front porch in a rocking chair, her dress flared out around her, and not one of us dared do more than say good morning to her.

Mr Wills was the best farmer in the community. My father said he could drive a stick into the ground and grow a tree out of it. But it wasn't an easy thing with him; Mr Wills fought the earth when he worked it. When he ploughed his fields, you could hear him yelling for a mile. It was as though he dared the earth not to yield him its sustenance.

Above all, Mr Wills could raise watermelons. Now, watermelons are curious things. Some men can send off for the best watermelon seed, they can plant it in the best ground they own, they can hoe it and tend it with the greatest of care, and they can't raise a melon bigger than your two fists. Other men, like Mr Wills, can throw seed on the ground, scuff dirt over it, walk off and leave it and have a crop of the prettiest, biggest melons you ever saw.

Mr Wills always planted the little field directly behind his barn with watermelons. It ran from the barn to the creek, a good piece of land with just the right sandy soil for melon raising. And it seemed as though the melons just bulged up out of the ground for him.

But they were Mr Wills's melons; he didn't have any idea of sharing them with the boys of the neighbourhood. He was fiercer about his melons than anything else; if you just happened to walk close to his melon patch, you'd see Mr Wills standing and watching you with a glower on his face. And likely as not he'd have his gun under his arm.

Everybody expected to lose a certain quantity of their watermelons to terrapins (tortoises) and a certain quantity to boys. It wasn't considered stealing to sneak into a man's melon patch and judiciously borrow a sample of his raising. You might get a load of salt in the seat of your pants, if you were seen, but that was part of the game. You'd be looked down on only if you got malicious and stamped a lot of melons into the ground while you were about it. But Mr Wills didn't think that way.

That summer I was sixteen Mr Wills raised the greatest watermelon ever seen in that country. It grew in the very middle of his patch, three times as big as any melon anybody had ever seen. Men came from miles around to look at it. Mr Wills wouldn't let them go into the melon patch. They had to stand around the edge.

Just like all other daredevil boys in that country, I guess, Freddy Gray and J.D. and I had talked idly about stealing that giant watermelon. But we all knew that it was just talk. Not only were we afraid of Mr Wills and his rages but we knew that Mr Wills sat in the hayloft window of his barn every night with his shotgun, guarding the melon. It was his seed melon. He meant to plant next year's crop out of that great one and maybe raise a whole field of them. Mr Wills was in a frenzy of fear that somebody would steal it. Why, he would rather you stole Willadean than his melon. At least, he didn't guard Willadean with his shotgun.

Every night I could sit on our front porch and see Mr Wills sitting up there in the window of his hayloft, looking fiercely out over his melon patch. I'd sit there by the hour and watch him, the shotgun cradled in his arm, and feel the tremors of fear and excitement chasing up and down my spine.

'Look at him,' my father would say. 'Scared to death somebody will steal his seed melon. Wouldn't anybody steal a man's seed melon.'

'He ought to be in the house taking care of that wife of his,' my mother would say tartly. 'She's been poorly all year.'

You hardly ever saw Mrs Wills. She was a wraith of a woman, pale as a butter bean. Sometimes she would sit for an hour or two on their porch in the cool of the day. They didn't visit back and forth with anybody though.

'There's Willadean,' my father would say mildly.

My mother would make a funny kind of sound that meant disgust. 'He cares more about that seed melon than he does his wife,' she'd say. 'I wish somebody *would* steal it. Maybe then—'

'Helen,' my father would say, chiding, 'you shouldn't even think of such a thing.'

About the time the great watermelon was due to come ripe, there was a night of a full moon. J.D. and Freddy Gray and I had decided we'd go swimming in the creek, so I left the house when the moon rose and went to meet them. The moon floated up into the sky, making everything almost as bright as day, but at the same time softer and gentler than ever daylight could be. It was the kind of night when you feel as though you can do anything in the world, even boldly asking Willadean Wills for a date. On a night like that, you couldn't help but feel that she'd gladly accept.

'Boy, what a moon!' J.D. said when I met them.

'Wouldn't you like to take old Willadean out on a night like this?' Freddy Gray said.

We scoffed at him, but secretly in our hearts we knew how he felt. We were getting old enough to think that that sort of thing might be a lot more fun than going swimming in the moonlight.

As I said before, I was a part of the bunch. J.D. and Freddy Gray were my good friends. But because I was still new, there were certain things and certain feelings where I was left out. This was one of them; they were afraid, because I was more of a stranger to Willadean, that she might like the idea of dating me better than she did either of them. This was all way down under the surface, because none of us had admitted to ourselves that we wanted to be Willadean's boyfriend. But far down though it was, I could feel it, and they could feel it.

'I wish I had a newspaper,' I said then. 'I'll bet you could read it in this moonlight.'

We had reached the swimming hole in the creek and we began shucking off our clothes. We were all excited by the moonlight, yelling at one another and rushing to be first into the water. Freddy Gray made it first, J.D. and I catapulting in right behind him. The water was cold, and the shock of it struck a chill into us. But we got rid of it by a brisk water fight, and then we were all right.

We climbed out finally, to rest, and sat on the bank. The big old moon sailed serenely overhead, climbing higher into the sky, and we lay on our backs to look up at it.

'Old Man Wills won't have to worry about anybody stealing his melon tonight, anyway,' Freddy Gray said. 'Wouldn't anybody dare try it, bright as day like it is.'

'He's not taking any chances,' J.D. said. 'I saw him sitting up in that hayloft when I came by, his shotgun loaded with buckshot. That melon is safe as it would be in the First National Bank.'

'Shucks,' I said in a scoffing voice, 'he ain't got buckshot in that gun. He's just got a load of salt, like anybody else guarding a watermelon patch.'

Freddy Gray sat upright, looking at me. 'Don't kid yourself, son,' he said loftily. 'He told my dad that he had it loaded with double-ought buckshot.'

'Why,' I said, 'that would kill a man.'

'That's what he's got in mind,' Freddy Gray said, 'if anybody goes after that seed melon.'

It disturbed me more than it should have. After all, I'd never had it in mind to try for the melon, had I? 'I don't believe it,' I said flatly. 'He wouldn't kill anybody over a watermelon. Even a seed melon like that one.'

'Old Man Wills would,' J.D. said.

Freddy Gray was still watching me. 'What's got you into such a swivet?' he said. 'You weren't planning on going after that melon yourself?'

'Well, yes,' I said. 'As a matter of fact, I was.'

There was a moment of respectful silence. Even from me. I hadn't known I was going to say those words. To this day I don't know why I said them. It was all mixed up with Willadean and the rumour of Mr Wills having his gun loaded with double-ought buckshot and the boys still thinking of me as an outsider. It surged up out of me – not the idea of making my name for years to come by such a deed, but the feeling that there was a rightness in defying the world and Mr Wills.

Mixed up with it all there came into my mouth the taste of watermelon. I could taste the sweet red juices oozing over my tongue, feel the delicate threaded redness of the heart as I squeezed the juices out of it.

I stood up. 'As a matter of fact,' I said. 'I'm going after it right now.'

'Wait a minute,' J.D. said in alarm. 'You can't do it on a moonlight night like this. It's 200 yards from the creek-bank to that melon. He'll see you for sure.'

'Yeah,' Freddy Gray said, 'wait until a dark night. Wait until—'

'Anybody could steal it on a dark night,' I said scornfully. 'I'm going to take it right out from under his nose. Tonight.'

I began putting on my clothes. My heart was thudding in my chest. I didn't taste watermelon any more. I tasted fear. But it was too late to stop now. Besides, I didn't want to stop.

We dressed silently, and I led the way up the creek-bank. We came opposite the watermelon patch and ducked down the bank. We pushed through the willows on the other side and looked toward the barn. We could see Mr Wills very plainly. The gun was cradled in his arms, glinting from the moonlight.

'You'll never make it,' J.D. said in a quiet, fateful voice. 'He'll see you before you're six steps away from the creek.'

'You don't think I mean to walk, do you?' I said.

I pushed myself out away from them, on my belly in the grass that grew up around the watermelon hills. I was absolutely flat, closer to the earth than I thought it was possible to get. I looked back once, to see their white faces watching me out of the willows.

I went on, stopping once in a while to look cautiously up towards the barn. He was still there, still quiet. I met a terrapin taking a bite out of a small melon. Terrapins love watermelons, better than boys do. I touched him on the shell and whispered, 'Hello, brother,' but he didn't acknowledge my greeting. He just drew into his shell. I went on, wishing I was equipped like a terrapin for the job, outside as well as inside.

It seemed to take for ever to reach the great melon in the middle of the field. With every move, I expected Mr Wills to see me. Fortunately the grass was high enough to cover me. At last the melon loomed up before me, deep green in the moonlight, and I gasped at the size of it. I'd never seen it so close.

I lay still for a moment, panting. I didn't have the faintest idea how to get it out of the field. Even if I'd stood up, I couldn't have lifted it by myself. A melon is the slipperiest, most cumbersome object in the world. And this was the largest I'd ever seen. It was not a long melon, but a fat round one. Besides, I didn't dare stand up.

For five minutes I didn't move. I lay there, my nostrils breathing up the smell of the earth and the musty smell of the watermelon vines, and I wondered why I was out here in the middle of all that moonlight on such a venture. There was more to it than just bravado. I was proving something to myself – and to Mr Wills and Willadean.

I thought of a tempting way out then, I would carve my name into the deep greenness of the melon. Mr Wills would see it the next morning when he inspected the melon, and he would know that I could have stolen it if I had wanted to. But no – crawling to the melon wasn't the same thing as actually taking it.

I reached one hand around the melon and found the stem. I broke the tough stem off close against the smooth roundness, and I was committed. I looked toward the barn again. All quiet. I saw Mr Wills stretch and yawn, and his teeth glistened; the moon was that bright and I was that close.

I struggled around behind the melon and shoved at it. It rolled over sluggishly, and I pushed it again. It was hard work, pushing it down the trough my body had made through the grass. Dust rose up around me, and I wanted to sneeze. My spine was crawling with the expectation of a shot. Surely he'd see that the melon was gone out of its accustomed space.

It took about a hundred years to push that melon out of the field. I say that advisedly, because I felt that much older when I finally reached the edge. With the last of my strength I shoved it into the willows and collapsed. I was still lying in the edge of the field.

'Come on,' Freddy Gray said, his voice pleading. 'He's—'

I couldn't move. I turned my head. He was standing up to stretch and yawn to his content, and then he sat down again. By then I was rested enough to move again. I snaked into the willows and they grabbed me.

'You did it!' they said. 'By golly, you did it!'

There was no time to bask in their admiration and respect. 'Let's get it out of here,' I said. 'We're not safe yet.'

We struggled the melon across the creek and up the bank. We started towards the swimming hole. It took all three of us to carry it, and it was hard to get a grip. J.D. and Freddy Gray carried the ends, while I walked behind the melon, grasping the middle. We stumbled and thrashed in our hurry, and we nearly dropped it three or four times. It was the most difficult object I'd ever tried to carry in my life.

At last we reached the swimming hole and sank down, panting. But not for long; the excitement was too strong in us. Freddy Gray reached out a hand and patted the great melon.

'By golly,' he said, 'there it is. All ours.'

'Let's bust it and eat it before somebody comes,' J.D. said.

'Wait a minute,' I said. 'This isn't just any old melon. This is old man Wills's seed melon, and it deserves more respect than to be busted open with a fist. I'm going to cut it.'

I took out my pocket knife and looked at it dubiously. It was small and the melon was big. We really needed a butcher knife. But when the little knife penetrated the thick green rind, the melon split of itself, perfectly down the middle. There was a ragged, silken, tearing sound, and it lay open before us.

The heart meat, glistening with sweet moisture, was grained with white sugar specks. I tugged at it with two fingers, and a great chunk of the meat came free. I put it into my mouth, closing my eyes. The melon was still warm from the day's sun. Just as in my anticipation, I felt the juice trickle into my throat, sweet and seizing. I had never tasted watermelon so delicious.

The two boys were watching me savour the first bite. I opened my eyes. 'Dive in,' I said graciously. 'Help yourselves.'

We gorged ourselves until we were heavy. Even then, we had still only eaten the heart meat, leaving untouched more than we had consumed. We gazed with sated eyes at the leftover melon, still good meat peopled with a multitude of black seeds.

'What are we going to do with it?' I said.

'There's nothing we can do,' J.D. said. 'I can just see us taking a piece of this melon home for the folks.'

'It's eat it, or leave it,' Freddy Gray said.

We were depressed suddenly. It was such a waste, after all the struggle and danger, that we could not eat every bite. I stood up, not looking at the two boys, not looking at the melon.

'Well,' I said. 'I guess I'd better get home.'

'But what about this?' J.D. said insistently, motioning towards the melon.

I kicked half the melon, splitting it in three parts. I stamped one of the chunks under my foot. Then I set methodically to work, destroying the rest of the melon. The boys watched me silently until I picked up a chunk of rind and threw it at them. Then they swept into the destruction also, and we were laughing again. When we stopped, only the battered rinds were left, the meat muddied on the ground, the seed scattered. We stood silent, looking at one another. 'There was nothing else to do,' I said, and they nodded solemnly.

But the depression went with us toward home and, when we parted, we did so with sober voices and gestures. I did not feel triumph or victory, as I had expected, though I knew that tonight's action had brought me closer to my friends than I had ever been before.

'Where have you been?' my father asked as I stepped up on the porch. He was sitting in his rocker.

'Swimming,' I said.

I looked towards Mr Wills's barn. The moon was still high and bright, but I could not see him. My breath caught in my throat when I saw him in the field, walking towards the middle. I stood stiffly, watching him. He reached the place where the melon should have been, I saw him hesitate, looking around, then he bent, and I knew he was looking at the depression in the earth where the melon had lain. He straightened, a great strangled cry tearing out of his throat. It chilled me deep down and all the way through, like the cry of a wild animal.

My father jerked himself out of the chair, startled by the sound. He turned in time to see Mr Wills lift the shotgun over his head and hurl it from him, his voice crying out again in a terrible, surging yell of pain and anger.

'Lord, what's the matter?' my father said.

Mr Wills was tearing up and down the melon patch, and I was puzzled by his actions. Then I saw; he was destroying every melon in the patch. He was breaking them open with his feet, silent now, concentrating on his frantic destruction. I was horrified by the awful sight, and my stomach moved sickly.

My father stood for a moment, watching him, then he jumped off the porch and ran toward Mr Wills. I followed him. I saw Mrs Wills and Willadean huddled together in the kitchen doorway. My father ran into the melon patch and caught Mr Wills by the arm.

'What's come over you?' he said. 'What's the matter, man?'

Mr Wills struck his grip away. 'They've stolen my seed melon,' he yelled. 'They took it right out from under me.'

My father grabbed him with both arms. He was a brave man, for he was smaller than Mr Wills, and Mr Wills looked insane with anger, his teeth gripped over his lower lip, his eyes gleaming furiously. Mr Wills shoved my father away, striking at him with his fist. My father went down into the dirt. Mr Wills didn't seem to notice. He went back to his task of destruction, raging up and down the field, stamping melons large and small.

My father got up and began to chase him. But he didn't have a chance. Every time he got close, Mr Wills would sweep his great arm and knock him away again. At last Mr Wills stopped of his own accord. He was standing on the place where the great melon had grown. His chest was heaving with great sobs of breath. He gazed about him at the destruction he had wrought, but I don't think he saw it.

'They stole my seed melon,' he said. His voice was quieter now than I had ever heard it. I had not believed such quietness was in him. 'They got it away, and now it's gone.'

I saw that tears stood on his cheeks, and I couldn't look at him any more. I'd never seen a grown man cry, crying in such strength.

'I had two plans for that melon,' he told my father. 'Mrs Wills has been poorly all the spring, and she dearly loves the taste of melon. It was her melon for eating, and my melon for planting. She would eat the meat, and next spring I would plant the seeds for the greatest melon crop in the world. Every day she would ask me if the great seed melon was ready yet.'

I looked toward the house. I saw the two women, the mother and the daughter, standing there. I couldn't bear any more. I fled out of the field towards the sanctuary of my house. I ran past my mother, standing on the porch, and went into my room.

I didn't sleep that night. I heard my father come in, heard the low-voiced conversation with my mother, heard them go to bed. I lay wide-eyed and watched the moon through the window as it slid slowly down the sky and at last brought a welcome darkness into the world.

I don't know all the things I thought that night. Mostly it was about the terrible thing I had committed so lightly, out of pride and out of being sixteen years old and out of wanting to challenge the older man, the man with the beautiful daughter.

That was the worst of all, that I had done it so lightly, with so little thought of its meaning. In that country and in that time, watermelon stealing was not a crime. It was tolerated, laughed about. The men told great tales of their own watermelon-stealing days, how they'd been set on by dogs and peppered with salt-loaded shotgun shells. Watermelon raiding was a game, a ritual of defiance and rebellion by young males. I could remember my own father saying, 'No melon tastes as sweet as a stolen one,' and my mother laughing and agreeing.

But stealing this great seed melon from a man like Mr Wills lay outside the safe magic of the tacit understanding between man and boy. And I knew it was up to me, at whatever risk, to repair as well as I could the damage I had done.

When it was daylight I rose from my bed and went out into the fresh world. It would be hotter later on; but now the air was dew-cool and fragrant. I had found a paper sack in the kitchen, and I carried it in my hand as I walked toward the swimming hole. I stopped there, looking down at the wanton waste we had made of the part of the melon we had not been able to eat. It looked as though Mr Wills had been stamping here too.

I kneeled down on the ground, opened the paper sack and began picking up the black seeds. They were scattered thickly, still stringy with watermelon pulp, and soon my hands were greasy with them. I kept on doggedly, searching out every seed I could find, until at the end I had to crawl over the ground, seeking for the last ones.

They nearly filled the paper sack. I went back to the house. By the time I reached it, the sun and my father had risen. He was standing on the porch.

'What happened to you last night?' he said. 'Did you get so frightened you had to run home? It was frightening to watch him, I'll admit that.'

'Father,' I said, 'I've got to talk to Mr Wills. Right now. I wish you would come with me.'

He stopped, watching me. 'What's the matter?' he said. 'Did you steal that melon of his?'

'Will you come with me?' I said.

His face was dark and thoughtful. 'Why do you want me?'

'Because I'm afraid he'll shoot me,' I said. My voice didn't tremble much, but I couldn't keep it all out.

'Then why are you going?' he said.

'Because I've got to,' I said.

My father watched me for a moment. 'Yes,' he said quietly, 'I guess you do.' He came down the steps and stood beside me. 'I'll go with you,' he said.

We walked the short distance between our house and his. Though it was so near, I had never been in his yard before. I felt my legs trembling as I went up the brick walk and stood at the bottom of the steps, the paper sack in my hand. I knocked on the porch floor, and Willadean came to the screen door.

I did not look at her. 'I want to talk to your father.'

She stared at me for a moment, then she disappeared. In a moment Mr Wills appeared in the doorway. His face was marked by the night, his cheeks sunken, his mouth bitten in. He stared at me absentmindedly, as though I were only a speck in his thinking.

'What do you want, boy?' he said.

I felt my teeth grit against the words I had to say. I held out the paper bag toward him. 'Mr Wills,' I said, 'here's the seeds from your seed melon. That's all I could bring back.'

I could feel my father standing quietly behind me. Willadean was standing in the doorway, watching. I couldn't take my eyes away from Mr Wills's face.

'Did you steal it?' he said.

'Yes, sir,' I said.

He advanced to the edge of the porch. The shotgun was standing near the door, and I expected him to reach for it. Instead he came toward me, a great powerful man, and leaned down to me.

'Why did you steal it?' he said.

'I don't know,' I said.

'Didn't you know it was my seed melon?'

'Yes, sir,' I said, 'I knew it.'

He straightened up again and his eyes were beginning to gleam. I wanted to run, but I couldn't move.

'And my sick wife hungered for the taste of that melon,' he said. 'Not for herself, like I thought. But to invite the whole neighbourhood in for a slice of it. She knew I wouldn't ever think of anything like that myself. She hungered for that.'

I hung my head. 'I'm sorry,' I said.

He stopped still then, watching me. 'So you brought me the seeds,' he said softly. 'That's not much, boy.'

I lifted my head. 'It was all I could think to do,' I said. 'The melon is gone. But the seeds are next year. That's why I brought them to you.'

'But you ruined this year,' he said.

'Yes, sir,' I said. 'I ruined this year.'

I couldn't look at him any more. I looked at Willadean standing behind him. Her eyes were a puzzle, watching me, and I couldn't tell what she was thinking or feeling.

'I'm about as ashamed of myself last night as you are of yourself,' Mr Wills said. He frowned at me with his heavy brows. 'You ruined the half of it, and I ruined the other. We're both to blame, boy. Both to blame.'

It seemed there ought to be something more for me to say.

I searched for it in my mind and discovered only the thought that I had found this morning in the grey light of dawning.

'The seeds are next year,' I said. I looked at him humbly. 'I'll help you plant them, Mr Wills. I'll work very hard.'

Mr Wills looked at my father for the first time. There was a small hard smile on his face, and his eyes didn't look as fierce as they had before.

'A man with a big farm like mine needs a son,' he said. 'But Willadean here was all the good Lord saw fit to give me. Sam, I do wish I had me a boy like that.'

He came close to me then, put his hand on my shoulder. 'We can't do anything about this year,' he said. 'But we'll grow next year, won't we? We'll grow it together.'

'Yes, sir,' I said.

I looked past him at Willadean, and her eyes were smiling too. I felt my heart give a great thump in my chest.

'And you don't have to offer the biggest melon in the world to get folks to come visiting,' I blurted. 'Why, I'll sit on the porch with Willadean any time.'

Mr Wills and my father burst out laughing. Willadean was blushing red in the face. But somehow she didn't look mad. Flustered, I began to beat a retreat toward the gate. Then I stopped, looking back at Mr Wills. I couldn't leave yet.

'Can I ask you one thing, Mr Wills?' I said.

He stopped laughing, and there was no fierceness in his voice. 'Anything you want to, boy,' he said.

'Well, I just wanted to know,' I said, 'Was there double-ought buckshot in that gun?'

He reached around and picked up the gun. He unbreeched it and took out a shell. He broke the shell in his strong fingers and poured the white salt into his palm.

'You see?' he said.

'Yes, sir,' I said, taking a deep breath. 'I see.'

I went on then, and the next year started that very day.

36

Journey

(1980)

Patricia Grace

He was an old man going on a journey. But not really so old, only they made him old buttoning up his coat for him and giving him money. Seventy-one that's all. Not a journey, not what you would really call a journey – he had to go in and see those people about his land. Again. But he liked the word Journey even though you didn't quite say it. It wasn't a word for saying only for saving up in your head, and that way you could enjoy it. Even an old man like him, but not what you would call properly old.

The coat was good and warm. It was second-hand from the jumble and it was good and warm. Could have ghosts in it but who cares, warm that's the main thing. If some old pakeha died in it that's too bad because he wasn't scared of the pakeha kehuas anyway. The pakeha kehuas they couldn't do anything, it was only like having a sheet over your head and going woo-oo at someone in the lavatory . . .

He better go to the lavatory because he didn't trust town lavatories, people spewed there and wrote rude words. Last time he got something stuck on his shoe. Funny people those town people.

Taxi.

It's coming Uncle.

Taxi Uncle. They think he's deaf. And old. Putting more money in his pocket and wishing his coat needed buttoning, telling him it's windy and cold. Never mind, he was off. Off on his journey, he could get round town good on his own, good as gold.

Out early today old man.

Business young fulla.

Early bird catches the early worm.

It'll be a sorry worm young fulla, a sorry worm.

Like that is it?

Like that.

You could sit back and enjoy the old taxi smells of split upholstery and cigarette, and of something else that could have been the young fulla's hair oil or his b.o. It was good. Good. Same old taxi same old stinks. Same old shop over there, but he wouldn't be calling in today, no. And tomorrow they'd want to know why. No, today he was going on a journey, which was a good word. Today he was going further afield, and there was a word no one knew he had. A good wind today but he had a warm coat and didn't need anyone fussing.

Same old butcher and same old fruit shop, doing all right these days not like before. Same old Post Office where you went to get your pension money, but he always sent Minnie down to get his because he couldn't stand these old-age people. These old-age people got on his nerves. Yes, same old place, same old shops and roads, and everything cracking up a bit. Same old taxi. Same old young fulla.

How's the wife?

Still growling old man.

What about the kids?

Costing me money.

Send them out to work that's the story.

I think you're right you might have something there old man. Well here we are, early. Still another half hour to wait for the train.

Best to be early. Business.

Guess you're right.

What's the sting?

Ninety-five it is.

Pull out a fistful and give the young fulla full eyes. Get himself out on to the footpath and shove the door, give it a good hard slam. Pick me up later young fulla, ten past five. Might as well make a day of it, look round town and buy a few things.

Don't forget ten past five.

Right you are old man five ten.

People had been peeing in the subway the dirty dogs. In the old days all you needed to do to get on to the station was to step over the train tracks, there weren't any piss holes like this to go through, it wasn't safe. Coming up the steps on to the platform he could feel the quick huffs of his breathing and that annoyed him, he wanted to swipe at the huffs with his hand. Steam engines went out years ago.

Good sight though seeing the big engines come bellowing through the cutting and pull in squealing, everything was covered in soot for miles those days.

New man in the ticket office, looked as though he still had his pyjamas on under his outfit. Miserable looking fulla and not all impressed by the ten-dollar note handed through to him. A man feels like a screwball yelling through that little hole in the glass and then trying to pick up the change that sourpuss has scattered all over the place. Feels like giving sourpuss the fingers, yes. Yes he knows all about those things, he's not deaf and blind yet, not by a long shot.

Ah warmth. A cold wait on the platform but the carriages had the heaters on, they were warm even though they stank. And he had the front half of the first carriage all to himself. Good idea getting away early. And right up front where you could see everything. Good idea coming on his own, he didn't want anyone fussing round looking after his ticket, seeing if he's warm and saying things twice. Doing his talking for him, made him sick. Made him sick them trying to walk slow so they could keep up with him.

Yes he could see everything. Not many fishing boats gone out this morning and the sea's turning over rough and heavy – Tamatea that's why. That's something they don't know all these young people, not even those fishermen walking about on their decks over there. Tamatea a Ngana, Tamatea Aio, Tamatea Whakapau – when you get the winds – but who'd believe you these days. They'd rather stare at their weather on television and talk about a this and a that coming over because there's nothing else to believe in.

Now this strip here, it's not really land at all, it's where we used to get our pipis, any time or tide. But they pushed a hill down over it and shot the railway line across to make more room for cars. The train driver knows it's not really land and he is speeding up over this strip. So fast you wait for the nose dive over the edge into the sea, especially when you're up front like this looking. Well too bad. Not to worry, he's nearly old anyway and just about done his dash, so why to worry if they nose dive over the edge into the sea. Funny people putting their trains across the sea. Funny people making land and putting pictures and stories about it in the papers as though it's something spectacular, it's a word you can use if you get it just right and he could surprise quite a few people if he wanted to. Yet other times they go on as though land is just a nothing. Trouble is he let them do his talking for him. If he'd gone in on his own last time and left those fusspots at home he'd have got somewhere. Wouldn't need to be going in there today to tell them all what's what.

Lost the sea now and coming into a cold crowd. This is where you get swamped, but he didn't mind, it was good to see them all get in out of the wind glad to be warm. Some of his whanaungas lived here but he couldn't see any of them today. Good job too, he didn't want them hanging round wondering where he was off to on his own. Nosing into his business. Some of the old railway houses still there but apart from that everything new, houses, buildings, roads. You'd never know now where the old roads had been, and they'd filled a piece of the harbour up too to make more ground. A short row of sooty houses that got new paint once in a while, a railway shelter, and a lunatic asylum and that was all. Only you didn't call it that these days, he'd think of the right words in a minute.

There now the train was full and he had a couple of kids sitting by him wearing plastic clothes, they were gog-eyed stretching their necks to see. One of them had a snotty nose and a wheeze.

On further it's the same – houses, houses – but people have to have houses. Two or three farms once, on the cold hills, and a rough road going through. By car along the old road you'd always see a pair of them at the end of the drive waving with their hats jammed over their ears. Fat one and a skinny one. Psychiatric hospital, those were the words to use these days, yes don't sound so bad. People had to have houses and the two or three farmers were dead now probably. Maybe didn't live to see it all. Maybe died rich.

The two kids stood swaying as they entered the first tunnel, their eyes stood out watching for the tunnel's mouth, waiting to pass out through the great mouth of the tunnel. And probably the whole of life was like that, sitting in the dark watching and waiting. Sometimes it happened and you came out into the light, but mostly it only happened in tunnels. Like now.

And between the tunnels they were slicing the hills away with big machines. Great-looking hills too and not an easy job cutting them away, it took pakeha determination to do that. Funny people these pakehas, had to chop up everything. Couldn't talk to a hill or a tree these people, couldn't give the trees or the hills a name and make them special and leave them. Couldn't go round, only through. Couldn't give life, only death. But people had to have houses, and ways of getting from one place to another. And anyway who was right up there helping the pakeha to get rid of things – the Maori of course, riding those big machines. Swooping round and back, up and down all over the place. Great tools the Maori man had for his carving these days, tools for his new whakairo, but there you are, a man had to eat. People had to have houses, had to eat, had to get from here to there – anyone knew that. He wished the two kids would stop crackling, their mothers dressed them in rubbish clothes that's why they had colds.

Then the rain'll come and the cuts will bleed for miles and the valleys will drown in blood, but the pakeha will find a way of mopping it all up no trouble. Could find a few bones amongst that lot too. That's what you get when you dig up the ground, bones.

Now the next tunnel, dark again. Had to make sure the windows were all shut up in the old days or you got a face full of soot.

And then coming out of the second tunnel that's when you really had to hold your breath, that's when you really had to hand it to the pakeha, because there was a sight. Buildings miles high, streets and steel and concrete and asphalt settled all round the great-looking curve that was the harbour. Water with ships on it, and roadways threading up and round the hills to layer on layer of houses, even in the highest and steepest places. He was filled with admiration. Filled with Admiration, which was another word he enjoyed even though it wasn't really a word for saying, but yes he was filled right to the top – it made him tired taking it all in. The kids too, they'd stopped crackling and were quite still, their eyes full to exploding.

The snotty one reminded him of George, he had pop eyes and he sat quiet not talking. The door would open slowly and the eyes would come round and he would say I ran away again Uncle. That's all. That's all for a whole week or more until his mother came to get him and take him back. Never spoke, never wanted anything. Today if he had time he would look out for George.

Railway station much the same as ever, same old platforms and not much cleaner than the soot days. Same old stalls and looked like the same people in them. Underground part is new. Same cafeteria, same food most likely, and the spot where they found the murdered man looked no different from any other spot. Always crowded in the old days especially during the hard times. People came there in the hard times to do their starving. They didn't want to drop dead while they were on their own most probably. Rather all starve together.

Same old statue of Kupe with his woman and his priest, and they've got the name of the canoe spelt wrong his old eyes aren't as blind as all that. Same old floor made of little coloured pieces and blocked into patterns with metal strips, he used to like it but now he can just walk on it. Big pillars round the doorway holding everything in place, no doubt about it you had to hand it to the pakeha.

Their family hadn't starved, their old man had seen to that. Their old man had put all the land down in garden, all of it, and in the weekends they took what they didn't use round by horse and cart. Sometimes got paid, sometimes swapped for something, mostly got nothing but why to worry. Yes great looking veges they had those days, turnips as big as pumpkins, cabbages you could hardly carry, big tomatoes, lettuces, potatoes, everything. Even now the ground gave you good things. They had to stay home from school for the planting and picking, usually for the weeding and hoeing as well. Never went to school much those days but why to worry.

Early, but he could take his time, knows his way round this place as good as gold. Yes he's walked all over these places that used to be under the sea and he's ridden all up and down them in trams too. This bit of sea has been land for a long time now. And he's been in all the pubs and been drunk in all of them, he might go to the pub later and spend some of his money. Or he could go to the continuous pictures but he didn't think they had them any more. Still, he might celebrate a little on his own later, he knew his way round this place without anyone interfering. Didn't need anyone doing his talking, and messing things up with all their letters and what not. Pigeons, he didn't like pigeons, they'd learned to behave like people, eat your feet off if you give them half a chance.

And up there past the cenotaph, that's where they'd bulldozed all the bones and put in the new motorway. Resited, he still remembered the newspaper word, all in together. Your leg bone, my arm bone, someone else's bunch of teeth and fingers, someone else's head, funny people. Glad he didn't have any of his whanaungas underground in that place. And they had put all the headstones in a heap somewhere promising to set them all up again *tastefully* – he remembered – didn't matter who was underneath. Bet there weren't any Maoris driving those bulldozers, well why to worry it's not his concern, none of his whanaungas up there anyway.

Good those old trams but he didn't trust these crazy buses, he'd rather walk. Besides he's nice and early and there's nothing wrong with his legs. Yes, he knows this place like his own big toe, and by Jove he's got a few things to say to those people and he wasn't forgetting. He'd tell them, yes.

The railway station was a place for waiting. People waited there in the old days when times were hard, had a free wash and did their starving there. He waited because it was too early to go home, his right foot was sore. And he could watch out for George, the others had often seen George here waiting about. He and George might go and have a cup of tea and some kai.

He agreed. Of course he agreed. People had to have houses. Not only that, people had to have other things – work, and ways of getting from place to place, and comforts. People needed more now than they did in his young days, he understood completely. Sir. Kept calling him Sir, and the way he said it didn't sound so well, but it was difficult to be sure at first. After a while you knew, you couldn't help knowing. He didn't want any kai, he felt sick. His foot hurt.

Station getting crowded and a voice announcing platforms. After all these years he still didn't know where the voice came from but it was the same voice, and anyway the trains could go without him it was too soon. People.

Queueing for tickets and hurrying towards the platforms, or coming this way and disappearing out through the double doors, or into the subway or the lavatory or the cafeteria. He was too tired to go to the lavatory and anyway he didn't like . . . Some in no hurry at all. Waiting. You'd think it was starvation times. Couldn't see anyone he knew.

I know I know. People have to have houses, I understand and it's what I want.

Well it's not so simple Sir.

It's simple. I can explain. There's only the old place on the land and it needs bringing down now. My brother and sister and I talked about it years back. We wrote letters . . .

Yes yes but it's not as simple as you think.

But now they're both dead and it's all shared – there are my brother's children, my sister's children, and me. It doesn't matter about me because I'm on the way out, but before I go I want it all done.

As I say it's no easy matter, all considered.

Subdivision. It's what we want.

There'll be no more subdivision Sir, in the area.

Subdivision. My brother has four sons and two daughters, my sister has five sons. Eleven sections so they can build their houses. I want it all seen to before . . .

You must understand Sir that it's no easy matter, the area has become what we call a development area, and I've explained all this before, there'll be no more subdivision.

Development means houses, and it means other things too, I understand that. But houses, it's what we have in mind.

And even supposing Sir that subdivision were possible, which it isn't, I wonder if you fully comprehend what would be involved in such an undertaking.

I fully comprehend . . .

Surveying, kerbing and channelling and formation of adequate access, adequate right of ways. The initial outlay . . .

I've got money, my brother and sister left it for the purpose. And my own, my niece won't use any of my money, it's all there. We've got the money.

However that's another matter, I was merely pointing out that it's not always all plain sailing.

All we want is to get it divided up so they can have a small piece each to build on . . .

As I say, the area, the whole area, has been set aside for development. All in the future of course but we must look ahead, it is necessary to be far-sighted in these concerns.

Houses, each on a small section of land, it's what my niece was trying to explain . . .

You see there's more to development than housing. We have to plan for roading and commerce, we have to set aside areas for educational and recreational facilities. We've got to think of industry, transportation . . .

But still people need houses. My nieces and nephews have waited for years.

They'd be given equivalent land or monetary compensation of course.

But where was the sense in that, there was no equal land. If it's your stamping ground and you have your ties there, then there's no land equal, surely that wasn't hard to understand. More and more people coming in to wait and plastic kids had arrived. They pulled away from their mother and went for a small run, crackling. He wished he knew their names and hoped they would come and sit down by him, but no, their mother was striding, turning them towards a platform because they were getting a train home. Nothing to say for a week or more and never wanted anything except sitting squeezed beside him in the armchair after tea until he fell asleep. Carry him to bed, get in beside him later then one day his mother would come. It was too early for him to go home even though he needed a pee.

There's no sense in it don't you see? That's their stamping ground and when you've got your ties there's no equal land. It's what my niece and nephew were trying to explain the last time, and in the letters . . .

Well Sir I shouldn't really do this, but if it will help clarify the position I could show you what has been drawn up. Of course it's all in the future and not really your worry . . .

Yes yes I'll be dead but that's not . . .

I'll get the plans.

And it's true he'll be dead, it's true he's getting old, but not true if anyone thinks his eyes have had it because he can see good enough. His eyes are still good enough to look all over the paper and see his land there, and to see that his land has been shaded in and had 'Off Street Parking' printed on it.

He can see good close up and he can see good far off, and that's George over the other side standing with some mates. He can tell George anywhere no matter what sort of get-up he's wearing. George would turn and see him soon.

But you can't, that's only a piece of paper and it can be changed, you can change it. People have to live and to have things. People need houses and shops but that's only paper, it can be changed.

It's all been very carefully mapped out. By experts. Areas have been selected according to suitability and convenience. And the aesthetic aspects have been carefully considered . . .

Everything grows, turnips the size of pumpkins, cabbages you can hardly carry, potatoes, tomatoes . . . Back here where you've got your houses, it's all rock, land going to waste there . . .

You would all receive equivalent sites . . .

Resited . . .

As I say on equivalent land . . .

There's no land equal . . .

Listen Sir, it's difficult but we've got to have some understanding of things. Don't we?

Yes yes I want you to understand, that's why I came. This here, it's only paper and you can change it. There's room for all the things you've got on your paper, and room for what we want too, we want only what we've got already, it's what we've been trying to say.

Sir we can't always have exactly what we want . . .

All round here where you've marked residential it's all rock, what's wrong with that for shops and cars. And there'll be people and houses. Some of the people can be us, and some of the houses can be ours.

Sure, sure. But not exactly where you want them. And anyway Sir there's no advantage do you think in you people all living in the same area?

It's what we want, we want nothing more than what is ours already.

It does things to your land value.

He was an old man but he wanted very much to lean over the desk and swing a heavy punch.

No sense being scattered everywhere when what we want . . .

It immediately brings down the value of your land . . .

. . . is to stay put on what is left of what has been ours since before we were born. Have a small piece each, a small garden, my brother and sister and I discussed it years ago.

Straight away the value of your land goes right down.

Wanted to swing a heavy punch but he's too old for it. He kicked the desk instead. Hard. And the veneer cracked and splintered. Funny how quiet it had become.

You ought to be run in old man, do you hear.

Cripes look what the old blighter's gone and done. Look at Paul's desk.

He must be whacky.

He can't do that Paul, get the boss along to sort him out.

Get him run in.

Get out old man, do you hear.

Yes he could hear, he wasn't deaf, not by a long shot. A bit of trouble getting his foot back out of the hole, but there, he was going, and not limping either, he'd see about this lot later. Going, not limping, and not going to die either. It looked as though their six eyes might all fall out and roll on the floor.

There's no sense, no sense in anything, but what use telling that to George when George already knew sitting beside him wordless. What use telling George you go empty handed and leave nothing behind, when George had always been empty handed, had never wanted anything except to have nothing.

How are you son?

All right Uncle. Nothing else to say. Only sitting until it was late enough to go.

Going, not limping, and not going to die either.

There you are old man, get your feet in under that heater. Got her all warmed up for you.

Yes young fulla that's the story.

The weather's not so good.

Not the best.

How was your day all told?

All right.

It's all those hard footpaths, and all the walking that gives people sore feet, that's what makes your legs tired.

There's a lot of walking about in that place.

You didn't use the buses?

Never use the buses.

But you got your business done?

All done. Nothing left to do.

That's good then isn't it?

How's your day been young fulla?

A proper circus.

Must be this weather.

It's the weather, always the same in this weather.

This is your last trip for the day is it?

A couple of trains to meet after tea and then I finish.

Home to have a look at the telly.

For a while, but there's an early job in the morning . . .

Drop me off at the bottom young fulla. I'm in no hurry. Get off home to your wife and kids.

No, no, there's a bad wind out there, we'll get you to your door. Right to your door, you've done your walking for the day. Besides I always enjoy the sight of your garden, you must have green fingers old man.

It keeps me bent over but it gives us plenty. When you come for Minnie on Tuesday I'll have a couple of cabbages and a few swedes for you.

Great, really great, I'm no gardener myself.

Almost too dark to see.

Never mind I had a good look this morning, you've got it all laid out neat as a pin. Neat as a pin old man.

And here we are.

One step away from your front door.

You can get off home for tea.

You're all right old man?

Right as rain young fulla, couldn't be better.

I'll get along then.

Tuesday.

Now he could get in and close the door behind him and walk without limping to the lavatory because he badly needs a pee. And when he came out of the bathroom they were watching him, they were stoking up the fire and putting things on the table. They were looking at his face.

Seated at the table they were trying not to look at his face, they were trying to talk about unimportant things, there was a bad wind today and it's going to be a rough night.

Tamatea Whakapau.

It must have been cold in town.

Heaters were on in the train.

And the train, was it on time?

Right on the minute.

What about the one coming home?

Had to wait a while for the one coming home.

At the railway station, you waited at the railway station?

And I saw George.

George, how's George?

George is all right, he's just the same.

Maisie said he's joined up with a gang and he doesn't wash. She said he's got a big war sign on his jacket and won't go to work.

They get themselves into trouble she said and they all go round dirty.

George is no different, he's just the same.

They were quiet then wondering if he would say anything else, then after a while they knew he wouldn't.

But later that evening as though to put an end to some silent discussion that they may have been having he told them it wasn't safe and they weren't to put him in the ground. When I go you're not to put me in the ground, do you hear. He was an old man and his foot was giving him hell, and he was shouting at them while they sat hurting. Burn me up I tell you, it's not safe in the ground, you'll know all about it if you put me in the ground. Do you hear?

Some other time, we'll talk about it.

Some other time is now and it's all said. When I go, burn me up, no one's going to mess about with me when I'm gone.

He turned into his bedroom and shut the door. He sat on the edge of his bed for a long time looking at the palms of his hands.

37

The Bath

(1983)

Janet Frame

On Friday afternoon she bought cut flowers – daffodils, anemones, a few twigs of a red-leaved shrub, wrapped in mauve waxed paper, for Saturday was the seventeenth anniversary of her husband's death and she planned to visit his grave, as she did each year, to weed it and put fresh flowers in the two jam jars standing one on each side of the tombstone. Her visit this year occupied her thoughts more than usual. She had bought the flowers to force herself to make the journey that each year became more hazardous, from the walk to the bus stop, the change of buses at the Octagon, to the bitterness of the winds blowing from the open sea across almost unsheltered rows of tombstones; and the tiredness that overcame her when it was time to return home when she longed to find a place beside the graves, in the soft grass, and fall asleep.

That evening she filled the coal bucket, stoked the fire. Her movements were slow and arduous, her back and shoulder gave her so much pain. She cooked her tea – liver and bacon – set her knife and fork on the teatowel she used as a tablecloth, turned up the volume of the polished red radio to listen to the Weather Report and the News, ate her tea, washed her dishes, then sat drowsing in the rocking chair by the fire, waiting for the water to get hot enough for a bath. Visits to the cemetery, the doctor, and to relatives, to stay, always demanded a bath. When she was sure that the water was hot enough (and her tea had been digested) she ventured from the kitchen through the cold passageway to the colder bathroom. She paused in the doorway to get used to the chill of the air then she walked slowly, feeling with each step the pain in her back, across to the bath, and though she knew that she was gradually losing the power in her hands she managed to wrench on the stiff cold and hot taps and half-fill the bath with warm water. How wasteful, she thought, that with the kitchen fire always burning during the past month of frost, and the water almost always hot, getting in and out of a bath had become such an effort that it was not possible to bath every night nor even every week!

She found a big towel, laid it ready over a chair, arranged the chair so that should difficulty arise as it had last time she bathed she would have some way of rescuing herself; then with her nightclothes warming on a page of newspaper inside the coal oven and her dressing-gown across the chair to be put on the instant she stepped from the bath, she undressed and pausing first to get her breath and clinging tightly to the slippery yellow-stained rim that now seemed more like the edge of a cliff with a deep drop below into the sea, slowly and painfully she climbed into the bath.

—I'll put on my nightie the instant I get out, she thought. The instant she got out indeed! She knew it would be more than a matter of instants yet she tried to think of it calmly, without dread, telling herself that when the time came she would be very careful, taking the process step by step, surprising her bad back and shoulder and her powerless wrists into performing feats they might usually rebel against, but the key to controlling them would be the surprise, the slow stealing up on them. With care, with thought . . .

Sitting upright, not daring to lean back or lie down, she soaped herself, washing away the dirt of the past fortnight, seeing with satisfaction how it drifted about on the water as a sign that she was clean again. Then when her washing was completed she found herself looking for excuses not to try yet to climb out. Those old woman's finger nails, cracked and dry, where germs could lodge, would need to be scrubbed again; the skin of her heels, too, growing so hard that her feet might have been turning to stone; behind her ears where a thread of dirt lay in the rim; after all, she did not often have the luxury of a bath, did she? How warm it was! She drowsed a moment. If only she could fall asleep then wake to find herself in her nightdress in bed for the night! Slowly she rewashed her body, and when she knew she could no longer deceive herself into thinking she was not clean she relutantly replaced the soap, brush and flannel in the groove at the side of the bath, feeling as she loosened her grip on them that all strength and support were ebbing from her. Quickly she seized the nail-brush again, but its magic had been used and was gone; it would not adopt the role she tried to urge upon it. The flannel too, and the soap, were frail flotsam to cling to in the hope of being borne to safety.

She was alone now. For a few moments she sat swilling the water against her skin, perhaps as a means of buoying up her courage. Then resolutely she pulled out the plug, sat feeling the tide swirl and scrape at her skin and flesh, trying to draw her down, down into the earth; then the bathwater was gone in a soapy gurgle and she was naked and shivering and had not yet made the attempt to get out of the bath.

How slippery the surface had become! In future she would not clean it with kerosene, she would use the paste cleaner that, left on overnight, gave the enamel rough patches that could be gripped with the skin.

She leaned forward, feeling the pain in her back and shoulder. She grasped the rim of the bath but her fingers slithered from it almost at once. She would not panic, she told herself; she would try gradually, carefully, to get out. Again she leaned forward; again her grip loosened as if iron hands had deliberately uncurled her stiffened blue fingers from their trembling hold. Her heart began to beat faster, her breath came more quickly, her mouth was dry. She moistened her lips. If I shout for help, she thought, no one will hear me. No one in the world will hear me. No one will know I'm in the bath and can't get out.

She listened. She could hear only the drip-drip of the cold water tap of the wash-basin, and a corresponding whisper and gurgle of her heart, as if it were beating under water. All else was silent. Where were the people, the traffic? Then she had a strange feeling of being under the earth, of a throbbing in her head like wheels going over the earth above her.

Then she told herself sternly that she must have no nonsense, that she had really not tried to get out of the bath. She had forgotten the strong solid chair and the grip she could get on it. If she made the effort quickly she could first take hold of both sides of the bath, pull herself up, then transfer her hold to the chair and thus pull herself out.

She tried to do this; she just failed to make the final effort. Pale now, gasping for breath, she sank back into the bath. She began to call out but as she had predicted there was no answer. No one had heard her, no one in the houses or the street or Dunedin or the world knew that she was imprisoned. Loneliness welled in her. If John were here, she thought, if we were sharing our old age, helping each other, this would never have happened. She made another effort to get out. Again she failed. Faintness overcoming her she closed her eyes, trying to rest, then recovering and trying again and failing, she panicked and began to cry and strike the sides of the bath; it made a hollow sound like a wild drum-beat.

Then she stopped striking with her fists; she struggled again to get out; and for over half an hour she stayed alternately struggling and resting until at last she did succeed in climbing out and making her escape into the kitchen. She thought, I'll never take another bath in this house or anywhere. I never want to see that bath again. This is the end or the beginning of it. In future a district nurse will have to come to attend me. Submitting to that will be the first humiliation. There will be others, and others.

In bed at last she lay exhausted and lonely thinking that perhaps it might be better for her to die at once. The slow progression of difficulties was a kind of torture. There were her shoes that had to be made specially in a special shape or she could not walk. There were the times she had to call in a neighbour to fetch a pot of jam from the top shelf of her cupboard when it had been only a year ago that she herself had made the jam and put it on the shelf. Sometimes a niece came to fill the coal-bucket or mow the lawn. Every week there was the washing to be hung on the line – this required a special technique for she could not raise her arms without at the same time finding some support in the dizziness that overcame her. She remembered with a sense of the world narrowing and growing darker, like a tunnel, the incredulous almost despising look on the face of her niece when in answer to the comment

—How beautiful the clouds are in Dunedin! These big billowing white and grey clouds – don't you think, Auntie?

She had said, her disappointment at the misery of things putting a sharpness in her voice,

—I never look at the clouds!

She wondered how long ago it was since she had been able to look up at the sky without reeling with dizziness. Now she did not dare look up. There was enough to attend to down and around – the cracks and hollows in the footpath, the patches of frost and ice and the potholes in the roads; the approaching cars and motorcycles; and now, after all the outside menaces, the inner menace of her own body. She had to be guardian now over her arms and legs, force them to do as she wanted when how easily and dutifully they had walked, moved and grasped, in the old days! They were the enemy now. It had been her body that showed treachery when she tried to get out of the bath. If she ever wanted to bath again – how strange it seemed! – she would have to ask another human being to help her to guard and control her own body. Was this so fearful? she wondered. Even if it were not, it seemed so.

She thought of the frost slowly hardening outside on the fences, roofs, windows and streets. She thought again of the terror of not being able to escape from the bath. She remembered her dead husband and the flowers she had bought to put on his grave. Then thinking again of the frost, its whiteness, white like a new bath, of the anemones and daffodils and the twigs of the red-leaved shrub, of John dead seventeen years, she fell asleep while outside, within two hours, the frost began to melt with the warmth of a sudden wind blowing from the north, and the night grew warm, like a spring night, and in the morning the light came early, the sky was pale blue, the same warm wind as gentle as a mere breath, was blowing, and a narcissus had burst its bud in the front garden.

In all her years of visiting the cemetery she had never known the wind so mild. On an arm of the peninsula exposed to the winds from two stretches of sea, the cemetery had always been a place to crouch shivering in overcoat and scarf while the flowers were set on the grave and the narrow garden cleared of weeds. Today, everything was different. After all the frosts of the past month there was not a trace of chill in the air. The mildness and warmth were scarcely to be believed. The sea lay, violet-coloured, hush-hushing, turning and heaving, not breaking into foamy waves; it was one sinuous ripple from shore to horizon and its sound was the muted sound of distant forests of peace.

Picking up the rusted garden fork that she knew lay always in the grass of the next grave, long neglected, she set to work to clear away the twitch and other weeds, exposing the first bunch of dark blue primroses with yellow centres, a clump of autumn lilies, and the shoots, six inches high, of daffodils. Then removing the green-slimed jam jars from their grooves on each side of the tombstone she walked slowly, stiff from her crouching, to the ever-dripping tap at the end of the lawn path where, filling the jars with pebbles and water she rattled them up and down to try to clean them of slime. Then she ran the sparkling ice-cold water into the jars and balancing them carefully one in each hand she walked back to the grave where she shook the daffodils, anemones, red leaves from their waxed paper and dividing them put half in one jar, half in the other. The dark blue of the anemones swelled with a sea-colour as their heads rested against the red leaves. The daffodils were short-stemmed with big ragged rather than delicate trumpets – the type for blowing; and their scent was strong.

Finally, remembering the winds that raged from the sea she stuffed small pieces of the screwed-up waxed paper into the top of each jar so the flowers would not be carried away by the wind. Then with a feeling of satisfaction – I look after my husband's grave after seventeen years. The tombstone is not cracked or blown over, the garden has not sunk into a pool of clay. I look after my husband's grave – she began to walk away, between the rows of graves, noting which were and were not cared for. Her father and mother had been buried here. She stood now before their grave. It was a roomy grave made in the days when there was space for the dead and for the dead with money, like her parents, extra space should they need it. Their tombstone was elaborate though the writing was now faded; in death they kept the elaborate station of their life. There were no flowers on the grave, only the feathery sea-grass soft to the touch, lit with gold in the sun. There was no sound but the sound of the sea and the one row of fir trees on the brow of the hill. She felt the peace inside her; the nightmare of the evening before seemed far away, seemed not to have happened; the senseless terrifying struggle to get out of a bath!

She sat on the concrete edge of her parents' grave. She did not want to go home. She felt content to sit here quietly with the warm soft wind flowing around her and the sigh of the sea rising to mingle with the sighing of the firs and the whisper of the thin gold grass. She was grateful for the money, the time and the forethought that had made her parents' grave so much bigger than the others near by. Her husband, cremated, had been allowed only a narrow eighteen inches by two feet, room only for the flecked grey tombstone In Memory of My Husband John Edward Harraway died August 6th 1948, and the narrow garden of spring flowers, whereas her parents' grave was so wide, and its concrete wall was a foot high; it was, in death, the equivalent of a quarter-acre section before there were too many people in the world. Why when the world was wider and wider was there no space left?

Or was the world narrower?

She did not know; she could not think; she knew only that she did not want to go home, she wanted to sit here on the edge of the grave, never catching any more buses, crossing streets, walking on icy footpaths, turning mattresses, trying to reach jam from the top shelf of the cupboard, filling coal buckets, getting in and out of the bath. Only to get in somewhere and stay in; to get out and stay out; to stay now, always, in one place.

Ten minutes later she was waiting at the bus stop; anxiously studying the destination of each bus as it passed, clutching her money since concession tickets were not allowed in the weekend, thinking of the cup of tea she would make when she got home, of her evening meal – the remainder of the liver and bacon – of her nephew in Christchurch who was coming with his wife and children for the school holidays, of her niece in the home expecting her third baby. Cars and buses surged by, horns tooted, a plane droned, near and far, near and far, children cried out, dogs barked; the sea, in competition, made a harsher sound as if its waves were now breaking in foam.

For a moment, confused after the peace of the cemetery, she shut her eyes, trying to recapture the image of her husband's grave, now bright with spring flowers, and her parents' grave, wide, spacious, with room should the dead desire it to turn and sigh and move in dreams as if the two slept together in a big soft grass double-bed.

She waited, trying to capture the image of peace. She saw only her husband's grave, made narrower, the spring garden whittled to a thin strip; then it vanished and she was left with the image of the bathroom, of the narrow confining bath grass-yellow as old baths are, not frost-white, waiting, waiting, for one moment of inattention, weakness, pain, to claim her for ever.

38

My Greatest Ambition

(1984)

Morris Lurie

My greatest ambition was to be a comic-strip artist, but I grew out of it. People were always patting me on the head and saying, 'He'll grow out of it.' They didn't know what they were talking about. Had any of them ever read a comic? Studied one? *Drawn* one? 'Australia is no place for comics,' they said, and I had to lock myself up in the dining room to get some peace. My mother thought I was studying in there.

I was the only person in my class – probably in the whole school – who wanted to be a comic-strip artist. They were all dreamers. There they sat, the astronomer, the nuclear physicist, the business tycoon (on the Stock Exchange), two mathematicians, three farmers, countless chemists, a handful of doctors, all aged thirteen and all with their heads in the clouds. Dreamers! Idle speculators! A generation of hopeless romantics! It was a Friday night, I recall, when I put the finishing touches to my first full length, inked-in, original, six-page comic-strip.

I didn't have the faintest idea what to do with it. Actually, doing anything *with* it hadn't ever entered my mind. *Doing* it was enough. Over the weekend I read it through sixty or seventy times, analysed it, studied it, stared at it, finally pronounced it 'Not too bad,' and then put it up on the top of my wardrobe where my father kept his hats.

And that would have been the end of it, only the next day I happened to mention to Michael Lazarus, who sat next to me at school, that I had drawn a comic-strip, and he happened to mention to me that there was a magazine in Melbourne I could send it to. We were both thrown out of that class for doing too much mentioning out loud, and kept in after school, to write fifty eight-letter words and their meanings in sentences – a common disciplinary action at that time. I remember writing 'ambulate' and saying it was a special way of walking. Do I digress? Then let me say that the first thing I did when I got home was roll my comic up in brown paper, address it, and put it in my schoolbag where I wouldn't forget it in the morning. Some chance of that. Lazarus had introduced an entirely new idea into my head. Publication. I hardly slept all night.

One of the things that kept me tossing and turning was the magazine I was sending my comic to. *Boy Magazine.* I had never bought one in my life, because it had the sneaky policy of printing stories, with only one illustration at the top of the page to get you interested. *Stories?* The school library was full of them, and what a bore they were. Did I want my comic to appear in a magazine which printed stories, where it would be read by the sort of people who were always taking books out of the library and sitting under trees and wearing glasses and squinting and turning pages with licked fingers? An *awful* prospect! At two o'clock in the morning I decided no, I didn't, and at three I did, and at four it was no again, but the last thing I saw before I finally fell asleep was Lazarus's face and he was saying, 'Publication!' and that decided it. Away it went.

Now let me properly introduce my father, a great scoffer. In those pre-television days, he had absolutely nothing to do in the evening but to walk past my room and look in and say, 'Nu? They sent you the money yet?' Fifty times a night, at least. And when the letter came from *Boy Magazine*, did he change his tune? Not one bit.

'I don't see a cheque,' he said.

'Of *course* there's no cheque,' I said. 'How can there be? We haven't even discussed it yet. Maybe I'll decide not to sell it to them. Which I will, if their price isn't right.'

'Show me again the letter,' my father said, 'Ha, listen, listen. "We are very interested in your comic and would like you to phone Miss Gordon to make an appointment to see the editor." An appointment? That means they don't want it. If they wanted it, believe me, there'd be a cheque.'

It serves no purpose to put down the rest of this pointless conversation, which included such lines as 'How many comics have *you* sold in your life?' and, 'Who paid for the paper? The ink?' other than to say that I made the phone call to Miss Gordon from a public phone and not from home. I wasn't going to have my father listening to every word.

My voice, when I was thirteen, and standing on tiptoe and talking into a public phone, was, I must admit, unnecessarily loud, but Miss Gordon didn't say anything about it. 'And what day will be most convenient for you, Mr Lurie?' she asked. 'Oh, any day at all!' I shouted. 'Any day will suit me fine!' 'A week from Thursday then?' she asked. 'Perfect!' I yelled, trying to get a piece of paper and a pencil out of my trouser pocket to write it down, and at the same time listening like mad in case Miss Gordon said something else. And she did. 'Ten o'clock?' 'I'll be there!' I shouted, and hung up with a crash.

It hadn't occurred to me to mention to Miss Gordon that I was thirteen and at school and would have to take a day off to come and see the editor. I didn't think these things were relevant to our business. But my mother did. A day missed from school could never be caught up, that was her attitude. My father's attitude you know. A cheque or not a cheque. Was I rich or was I a fool? (No, that's wrong. Was I a poor fool or a rich fool? Yes, that's better.) But my problem was something else. What to wear?

My school suit was out of the question because I wore it every day and I was sick of it and it just wasn't right for a business appointment. Anyway, it had ink stains round the pocket where my fountain pen leaked (a real fountain, ha ha), and the seat of the trousers shone like a piece of tin. And my Good Suit was a year old and too short in the leg. I tried it on in front of the mirror, just to make sure, and I was right. It was ludicrous. My father offered to lend me one of his suits. He hadn't bought a new suit since 1934. There was enough material in the lapels alone to make three suits and have enough left over for a couple of caps. Not only that, but my father was shorter than me and twice the weight. So I thanked him and said that I had decided to wear my Good Suit after all. I would wear dark socks and the shortness of trousers would hardly be noticed. Also, I would wear my eye-dazzling pure silk corn yellow tie, which, with the proper Windsor knot, would so ruthlessly rivet attention that no one would even look to see if I was wearing shoes.

'A prince,' my father said.

Now, as the day of my appointment drew nearer and nearer, a great question had to be answered, a momentous decision made. For my father had been right. If all they wanted to do was to buy my comic, they would have sent a cheque. So there was something else. A full-time career as a comic-strip artist on the permanent staff of *Boy Magazine*! It had to be that. But that would mean giving up school and was I prepared to do that?

'Yes,' I said with great calmness and great authority to my face in the bathroom mirror. 'Yes.'

There were three days to go.

Then there occurred one of those things that must happen every day in the world of big business, but when you're thirteen it knocks you for a loop. *Boy Magazine* sent me a telegram. It was the first telegram I had ever received in my life, and about the third that had ever come to our house. My mother opened it straight away. She told everyone in our street about it. She phoned uncles, aunts, sisters, brothers, and finally, when I came home from school, she told me.

I was furious. I shouted, 'I told you never under *any* circumstances to open my mail!'

'But a telegram,' my mother said.

'A telegram is mail,' I said. 'And mail is a personal, private thing. Where is it?'

My mother had folded it four times and put it in her purse and her purse in her bag and her bag in her wardrobe which she had locked. She stood by my side and watched me while I read it.

'Nu?' she said.

'It's nothing,' I said.

And it wasn't. Miss Gordon had suddenly discovered that the editor was going to be out of town on my appointment day, and would I kindly phone and make another appointment?

I did, standing on tiptoe and shouting as before.

The offices of *Boy Magazine* were practically in the country, twelve train stations out of town. Trains, when I was thirteen, terrified me, and still do. Wearing my Good Suit and my corn yellow tie and my father's best black socks and a great scoop of oil in my hair, I kept jumping up from my seat and looking out of the window to see if we were getting near a station and then sitting down again and trying to relax. Twelve stations, eleven stations, ten. Nine to go, eight, seven. Or was it six? What was the name of the last one? What if I went too far? What was the time? By the time I arrived at the right station, I was in a fine state of nerves.

The offices of *Boy Magazine* were easy to find. They were part of an enormous building that looked like a factory, and were not at all imposing or impressive, as I had imagined them to be. No neon, no massive areas of plate glass, no exotic plants growing in white gravel. (I had a picture of myself walking to work every morning through a garden of exotic plants growing in white gravel, cacti, ferns, pushing open a massive glass door under a neon sign and smiling at a receptionist with a pipe in my mouth.) I pushed open an ordinary door and stepped into an ordinary foyer and told an ordinary lady sitting at an ordinary desk who I was.

'And?' she said.

'I have an appointment to see the editor of *Boy Magazine*,' I said.

'Oh,' she said.

'At ten o'clock,' I said. 'I think I'm early.' It was half past nine.

'Just one minute,' she said, and picked up a telephone. While she was talking I looked around the foyer, in which there was nothing to look at, but I don't like eavesdropping on people talking on the phone.

Then she put down the phone and said to me, 'Won't be long. Would you like to take a seat?'

For some reason that caught me unawares and I flashed her a blinding smile and kept standing there, wondering what was going to happen next, and then I realised what she had said and I smiled again and turned around and bumped into a chair and sat down and crossed my legs and looked around and then remembered the shortness of my trousers and quickly uncrossed my legs and sat perfectly straight and still, except for looking at my watch ten times in the next thirty seconds.

I don't know how long I sat there. It was either five minutes or an hour, it's hard to say. The lady at the desk didn't seem to have anything to do, and I didn't like looking at her, but from time to time our eyes met, and I would smile – or was that smile stretched across my face from the second I came in? I used to do things like that when I was thirteen.

Finally a door opened and another lady appeared. She seemed, for some reason, quite surprised when she saw me sitting there, as though I had three eyes or was wearing a red suit, but I must say this for her, she had poise, she pulled herself together very quickly, hardly dropped a stitch, as it were, and holding open the door through which she had come, she said, 'Won't you come this way?' and I did.

I was shown into an office that was filled with men in grey suits. Actually, there were only three of them, but they all stood up when I came in, and the effect was overpowering. I think I might even have taken a half-step back. But my blinding smile stayed firm.

The only name I remember is Randell and maybe I have that wrong. There was a lot of handshaking and smiling and saying of names. And when all that was done, no one seemed to know what to do. We just stood there, all uncomfortably smiling.

Finally, the man whose name might have been Randell said, 'Oh, please, please, sit down,' and everyone did.

'Well,' Mr Randell said. 'You're a young man to be drawing comics, I must say.'

'I've been interested in comics all my life.' I said.

'Well, we like your comic very much,' he said. 'And we'd like to make you an offer for it. Ah, fifteen pounds?'

'I accept,' I said.

I don't think Mr Randell was used to receiving quick decisions, for he then said something that seemed to me enormously ridiculous. 'That's, ah, two pounds ten a page,' he said, and looked at me with his eyes wide open and one eyebrow higher than the other.

'Yes, that's right,' I said. 'Six two-and-a-halfs are fifteen. Exactly.'

That made his eyes open even wider, and suddenly he shut them altogether and looked down at the floor. One of the other men coughed. No one seemed to know what to do. I leaned back in my chair and crossed my legs and just generally smiled at everyone. I knew what was coming. A job. And I knew what I was going to say then, too.

And then Mr Randell collected himself, as though he had just thought of something very important (what an actor, I thought) and he said, 'Oh, there is one other thing, though. Jim, do we have Mr Lurie's comic here?'

'Right here,' said Jim, and whipped it out from under a pile of things on a desk.

'Some of the, ah, spelling,' Mr Randell said.

'Oh?' I said.

'Well, yes, there are, ah, certain things,' he said, turning over the pages of my comic, 'not, ah, *big* mistakes, but, here, see? You've spelt it as "jungel" which is not, ah, common usage.'

'You're absolutely right,' I said, flashing out my fountain pen all ready to make the correction.

'Oh, no no no,' Mr Randell said. 'Don't you worry about it. We'll, ah, make the corrections. If you approve, that is.'

'Of course,' I said.

'We'll, ah, post you our cheque for, ah, fifteen pounds,' he said. 'In the mail,' he added, rather lamely, it seemed to me.

'Oh, there's no great hurry about that,' I said. 'Any old time at all will do.'

'Yes,' he said.

Then we fell into another of these silences with which this appointment seemed to be plagued. Mr Randell scratched his neck. A truck just outside the window started with a roar and then began to whine and grind. It's reversing, I thought. My face felt stiff from smiling, but somehow I couldn't let it go.

Then the man whose name was Jim said, 'This is your first comic strip, Mr Lurie?'

'Yes,' I said. My reply snapped across the room like a bullet. I was a little bit embarrassed at its suddenness, but, after all, wasn't this what I had come to talk about?

'It's very professional,' he said. 'Would you like to see one of our comic-strips?'

'Certainly,' I said.

He reached down behind the desk and brought out one page of a comic they were running at the moment (I had seen it in the shop when I'd gone to check up on *Boy Magazine*'s address), *The Adventures of Ned Kelly.*

Now, Ned Kelly is all right, but what I like about comics is that they create a world of their own, like, say, *Dick Tracy*, a totally fictitious environment, which any clear thinking person knows doesn't really exist, and Ned Kelly, well, that was real, it really happened. It wasn't a true comic-strip. It was just history in pictures.

But naturally I didn't say any of this to Jim. All I did was lean forward and pretend to study the linework and the inking in and the lettering, which were just so-so, and when I thought I'd done that long enough, I leaned back in my chair and said, 'It's very good.'

'Jim,' said Mr Randell, who hadn't spoken a word during all this, 'maybe you'd like to take Mr Lurie around and show him the presses. We print *Boy Magazine* right here,' he explained to me. 'Would you like to see how a magazine is produced?'

'Yes,' I said, but the word sounded flat and awful to me. I hated, at thirteen, being shown round things. I still do. How A Great Newspaper Is Produced. How Bottles Are Made. Why Cheese Has Holes And How We Put Them In.

And the rest of it, the job, the core of the matter? But everyone was standing up and Mr Randell's hand was stretched out to shake mine and Jim was saying, 'Follow me,' and it was all over.

Now I'm not going to take you through a tour of this factory, the way I was, eating an ice cream which Jim had sent a boy out to buy for me. It lasted for hours. I climbed up where Jim told me to climb up. I looked where he pointed. I nodded when he explained some involved and highly secret process to me. 'We use glue, not staples,' he explained to me. 'Why? Well, it's an economic consideration. Look here,' and I looked there, and licked my ice cream and wondered how much more there was of it and was it worth going to school in the afternoon or should I take the whole day off?

But like all things it came to an end. We were at a side door, not the one I had come in through. 'Well, nice to meet you,' Jim said, and shook my hand. 'Find your way back to the station okay? You came by train? It's easy, just follow your nose,' and I rode home on the train not caring a damn about how many stations I was going through, not looking out of the window, not even aware of the shortness of the trousers of my ridiculous Good Suit.

Yes, my comic-strip appeared and my friends read it and I was a hero for a day at school. My father held the cheque up to the light and said we'd know in a few days if it was any good. My mother didn't say much to me but I heard her on the phone explaining to all her friends what a clever son she had. Clever? That's one word I've never had any time for.

I didn't tell a soul, not even Michael Lazarus, about that awful tour of the factory. I played it very coolly. And a week after my comic-strip came out in print, I sat down and drew another comic story and wrapped it up and sent it to them, and this time, I determined, I would do all my business over the phone. With that nice Miss Gordon.

Weeks passed, nearly a whole month. No reply. And then, with a sickening crash, the postman dumped my new comic into our letterbox and flew on his merry way down the street, blowing his whistle and riding his bicycle over everyone's lawns.

There was a letter enclosed with my comic. It said that, unfortunately, *Boy Magazine* was discontinuing publication, and although they enjoyed my comic 'enormously', they regretted that they had no option but to return it.

My father had a field day over the whole business but no, no, what's the point of going over all that? Anyhow, I had decided (I told myself) that I didn't want to be a comic-strip artist after all. There was no future in it. It was risky and unsure. It was here today and gone tomorrow. The thing to be was a serious painter, and I set about it at once, spreading new boxes of water colours and tubes of paint all over the dining-room table and using every saucer in the house to mix paint. But somehow, right from the start, I knew it was no good. The only thing that was ever real to me I had 'grown out of'. I had become, like everyone else, a dreamer.

39

To Da-duh, in Memoriam

(1985)

Paule Marshall

'. . . Oh Nana! all of you is not involved in this evil business Death,
Nor all of us in life.'

from 'At My Grandmother's Grave'
by Lebert Bethune

I did not see her at first I remember. For not only was it dark inside the crowded disembarkation shed in spite of the daylight flooding in from outside, but standing there waiting for her with my mother and sister I was still somewhat blinded from the sheen of tropical sunlight on the water of the bay which we had just crossed in the landing boat, leaving behind us the ship that had brought us from New York lying in the offing. Besides, being only nine years of age at the time and knowing nothing of islands I was busy attending to the alien sights and sounds of Barbados, the unfamiliar smells.

I did not see her, but I was alerted to her approach by my mother's hand which suddenly tightened around mine, and looking up I traced her gaze through the gloom in the shed until I finally made out the small, purposeful, painfully erect figure of the old woman headed our way.

Her face was drowned in the shadow of an ugly rolled-brim brown felt hat, but the details of her slight body and of the struggle taking place within it were clear enough – an intense, unrelenting struggle between her back which was beginning to bend ever so slightly under the weight of her eighty-odd years and the rest of her which sought to deny those years and hold that back straight, keep it in line. Moving swiftly toward us (so swiftly it seemed she did not intend stopping when she reached us but would sweep past us out the doorway which opened onto the sea and like Christ walk upon the water!), she was caught between the sunlight at her end of the building and the darkness inside – and for a moment she appeared to contain them both: the light in the long severe old-fashioned white dress she wore which brought the sense of a past that was still alive into our bustling present and in the snatch of white at her eye; the darkness in her black high-top shoes and in her face which was visible now that she was closer.

It was as stark and fleshless as a death mask, that face. The maggots might have already done their work, leaving only the framework of bone beneath the ruined skin and deep wells at the temple and jaw. But her eyes were alive, unnervingly so for one so old, with a sharp light that flicked out of the dim clouded depths like a lizard's tongue to snap up all in her view. Those eyes betrayed a child's curiosity about the world, and I wondered vaguely seeing them, and seeing the way the bodice of her ancient dress had collapsed in on her flat chest (what had happened to her breasts?), whether she might not be some kind of child at the same time that she was a woman, with fourteen children, my mother included, to prove it. Perhaps she was both, both child and woman, darkness and light, past and present, life and death – all the opposites contained and reconciled in her.

'My Da-duh,' my mother said formally and stepped forward. The name sounded like thunder fading softly in the distance.

'Child,' Da-duh said, and her tone, her quick scrutiny of my mother, the brief embrace in which they appeared to shy from each other rather than touch, wiped out the fifteen years my mother had been away and restored the old relationship. My mother, who was such a formidable figure in my eyes, had suddenly with a word been reduced to my status.

'Yes, God is good,' Da-duh said with a nod that was like a tic. 'He has spared me to see my child again.'

We were led forward then, apologetically because not only did Da-duh prefer boys but she also liked her grandchildren to be 'white', that is, fair-skinned; and we had, I was to discover, a number of cousins, the outside children of white estate managers and the like, who qualified. We, though, were as black as she.

My sister being the oldest was presented first. 'This one takes after the father,' my mother said and waited to be reproved.

Frowning, Da-duh tilted my sister's face toward the light. But her frown soon gave way to a grudging smile, for my sister with her large mild eyes and little broad winged nose, with our father's high-cheeked Barbadian cast to her face, was pretty.

'She's goin' be lucky,' Da-duh said and patted her once on the cheek. 'Any girl child that takes after the father does be lucky.'

She turned then to me. But oddly enough she did not touch me. Instead leaning close, she peered hard at me, and then quickly drew back. I thought I saw her hand start up as though to shield her eyes. It was almost as if she saw not only me, a thin truculent child who it was said took after no one but myself, but something in me which for some reason she found disturbing, even threatening. We looked silently at each other for a long time there in the noisy shed, our gaze locked. She was the first to look away.

'But Adry,' she said to my mother and her laugh was cracked, thin, apprehensive. 'Where did you get this one here with this fierce look?'

'We don't know where she came out of, my Da-duh,' my mother said, laughing also. Even I smiled to myself. After all I had won the encounter. Da-duh had recognised my small strength – and this was all I ever asked of the adults in my life then.

'Come, soul,' Da-duh said and took my hand. 'You must be one of those New York terrors you hear so much about.'

She led us, me at her side and my sister and mother behind, out of the shed into the sunlight that was like a bright driving summer rain and over to a group of people clustered beside a decrepit lorry. They were our relatives, most of them from St Andrews although Da-duh herself lived in St Thomas, the women wearing bright print dresses, the colors vivid against their darkness, the men rusty black suits that encased them like straitjackets. Da-duh, holding fast to my hand, became my anchor as they circled round us like a nervous sea, exclaiming, touching us with their callused hands, embracing us shyly. They laughed in awed bursts: 'But look Adry got big-big children!' 'And see the nice things they wearing, wrist watch and all!' 'I tell you, Adry has done all right for sheself in New York . . .'

Da-duh, ashamed at their wonder, embarrassed for them, admonished them the while. 'But oh Christ,' she said, 'why you all got to get on like you never saw people from "Away" before? You would think New York is the only place in the world to hear wunna. That's why I don't like to go anyplace with you St Andrews people, you know. You all ain't been colonised.'

We were in the back of the lorry finally, packed in among the barrels of ham, flour, cornmeal and rice and the trunks of clothes that my mother had brought as gifts. We made our way slowly through Bridgetown's clogged streets, part of a funereal procession of cars and open-sided buses, bicycles, and donkey carts. The dim little limestone shops and offices along the way marched with us, at the same mournful pace, toward the same grave ceremony – as did the people, the women balancing huge baskets on top their heads as if they were no more than hats they wore to shade them from the sun. Looking over the edge of the lorry I watched as their feet slurred the dust. I listened, and their voices, raw and loud and dissonant in the heat, seemed to be grappling with each other high overhead.

Da-duh sat on a trunk in our midst, a monarch amid her court. She still held my hand, but it was different now. I had suddenly become her anchor, for I felt her fear of the lorry with its asthmatic motor (a fear and distrust, I later learned, she held of all machines) beating like a pulse in her rough palm.

As soon as we left Bridgetown behind though, she relaxed, and while the others around us talked she gazed at the canes standing tall on either side of the winding marl road. 'C'dear,' she said softly to herself after a time. 'The canes this side are pretty enough.'

They were too much for me. I thought of them as giant weeds that had overrun the island, leaving scarcely any room for the small tottering houses of sunbleached pine we passed or the people, dark streaks as our lorry hurtled by. I suddenly feared that we were journeying, unaware that we were, toward some dangerous place where the canes, grown as high and thick as a forest, would close in on us and run us through with their stiletto blades. I longed then for the familiar: for the street in Brooklyn where I lived, for my father who had refused to accompany us ('Blowing out good money on foolishness,' he had said of the trip), for a game of tag with my friends under the chestnut tree outside our ageing brownstone house.

'Yes, but wait till you see St Thomas canes,' Da-duh was saying to me. 'They's canes father, bo,' she gave a proud arrogant nod. 'Tomorrow, God willing, I goin' take you out in the ground and show them to you.'

True to her word Da-duh took me with her the following day out into the ground. It was a fairly large plot adjoining her weathered board and shingle house and consisting of a small orchard, a good-sized canepiece and behind the canes, where the land sloped abruptly down, a gully. She had purchased it with Panama money sent her by her eldest son, my uncle Joseph, who had died working on the canal. We entered the ground along a trail no wider than her body and as devious and complex as her reasons for showing me her land. Da-duh strode briskly ahead, her slight form filled out this morning by the layers of sacking petticoats she wore under her working dress to protect her against the damp. A fresh white cloth, elaborately arranged around her head, added to her height, and lent her a vain, almost roguish air.

Her pace slowed once we reached the orchard, and glancing back at me occasionally over her shoulder, she pointed out the various trees.

'This here is a breadfruit,' she said. 'That one yonder is a papaw. Here's a guava. This is a mango. I know you don't have anything like these in New York. Here's a sugar apple.' (The fruit looked more like artichokes than apples to me.) 'This one bears limes . . .' She went on for some time, intoning the names of the trees as though they were those of her gods. Finally, turning to me, she said, 'I know you don't have anything this nice where you come from.' Then, as I hesitated: 'I said I know you don't have anything this nice where you come from . . .'

'No,' I said and my world did seem suddenly lacking.

Da-duh nodded and passed on. The orchard ended and we were on the narrow cart road that led through the canepiece, the canes clashing like swords above my cowering head. Again she turned and her thin muscular arms spread wide, her dim gaze embracing the small field of canes, she said – and her voice almost broke under the weight of her pride, 'Tell me, have you got anything like these in that place where you were born?'

'No.'

'I din' think so. I bet you don't even know that these canes here and the sugar you eat is one and the same thing. That they does throw the canes into some damn machine at the factory and squeeze out all the little life in them to make sugar for you all so in New York to eat. I bet you don't know that.'

'I've got two cavities and I'm not allowed to eat a lot of sugar.'

But Da-duh didn't hear me. She had turned with an inexplicably angry motion and was making her way rapidly out of the canes and down the slope at the edge of the field which led to the gully below. Following her apprehensively down the incline amid a stand of banana plants whose leaves flapped like elephants' ears in the wind, I found myself in the middle of a small tropical wood – a place dense and damp and gloomy and tremulous with the fitful play of light and shadow as the leaves high above moved against the sun that was almost hidden from view. It was a violent place, the tangled foliage fighting each other for a chance at the sunlight, the branches of the trees locked in what seemed an immemorial struggle, one both necessary and inevitable. But despite the violence, it was pleasant, almost peaceful in the gully, and beneath the thick undergrowth the earth smelled like spring.

This time Da-duh didn't even bother to ask her usual question, but simply turned and waited for me to speak.

'No,' I said, my head bowed. 'We don't have anything like this in New York.'

'Ah,' she cried, her triumph complete. 'I din' think so. Why, I've heard that's a place where you can walk till you near drop and never see a tree.'

'We've got a chestnut tree in front of our house,' I said.

'Does it bear?' She waited. 'I ask you, does it bear?'

'Not anymore,' I muttered. 'It used to, but not anymore,'

She gave the nod that was like a nervous twitch. 'You see,' she said. 'Nothing can bear there.' Then, secure behind her scorn, she added, 'But tell me, what's this snow like that you hear so much about?'

Looking up, I studied her closely, sensing my chance, and then I told her, describing at length and with as much drama as I could summon not only what snow in the city was like, but what it would be like here, in her perennial summer kingdom.

'. . . And you see all these trees you got here,' I said. 'Well, they'd be bare. No leaves, no fruit, nothing. They'd be covered in snow. You see your canes. They'd be buried under tons of snow. The snow would be higher than your head, higher than your house, and you wouldn't be able to come down into this here gully because it would be snowed under . . .'

She searched my face for the lie, still scornful but intrigued. 'What a thing, huh?' she said finally, whispering it softly to herself.

'And when it snows you couldn't dress like you are now,' I said. 'Oh no, you'd freeze to death. You'd have to wear a hat and gloves and galoshes and ear muffs so your ears wouldn't freeze and drop off, and a heavy coat. I've got a Shirley Temple coat with fur on the collar. I can dance. You wanna see?'

Before she could answer I began, with a dance called the Truck which was popular back then in the 1930s. My right forefinger waving, I trucked around the nearby trees and around Da-duh's awed and rigid form. After the Truck I did the Suzy-Q, my lean hips swishing, my sneakers sidling zigzag over the ground. 'I can sing,' I said and did so, starting with 'I'm Gonna Sit Right Down and Write Myself a Letter', then without pausing, 'Tea For Two', and ending with 'I Found a Million Dollar Baby in a Five and Ten Cent Store'.

For long moments afterwards Da-duh stared at me as if I were a creature from Mars, an emissary from some world she did not know but which intrigued her and whose power she both felt and feared. Yet something about my performance must have pleased her, because bending down she slowly lifted her long skirt and then, one by one, the layers of petticoats until she came to a drawstring purse dangling at the end of a long strip of cloth tied round her waist. Opening the purse she handed me a penny. 'Here,' she said half-smiling against her will. 'Take this to buy yourself a sweet at the shop up the road. There's nothing to be done with you, soul.'

From then on, whenever I wasn't taken to visit relatives, I accompanied Da-duh out into the ground, and alone with her amid the canes or down in the gully I told her about

New York. It always began with some slighting remark on her part: 'I know they don't have anything this nice where you come from,' or 'Tell me, I hear those foolish people in New York does do such and such . . .' But as I answered, re-creating my towering world of steel and concrete and machines for her, building the city out of words, I would feel her give way. I came to know the signs of her surrender: the total stillness that would come over her little hard dry form, the probing gaze that like a surgeon's knife sought to cut through my skull to get at the images there, to see if I were lying; above all, her fear, a fear nameless and profound, the same one I had felt beating in the palm of her hand that day in the lorry.

Over the weeks I told her about refrigerators, radios, gas stoves, elevators, trolley cars, wringer washing machines, movies, airplanes, the cyclone at Coney Island, subways, toasters, electric lights: 'At night, see, all you have to do is flip this little switch on the wall and all the lights in the house go on. Just like that. Like magic. It's like turning on the sun at night.'

'But tell me,' she said to me once with a faint mocking smile, 'do the white people have all these things too or it's only the people looking like us?'

I laughed. 'What d'ya mean,' I said. 'The white people have even better.' Then: 'I beat up a white girl in my class last term.'

'Beating up white people!' Her tone was incredulous.

'How you mean!' I said, using an expression of hers. 'She called me a name.'

For some reason Da-duh could not quite get over this and repeated in the same hushed, shocked voice, 'Beating up white people now! Oh, the lord, the world's changing up so I can scarce recognise it anymore.'

One morning toward the end of our stay, Da-duh led me into a part of the gully that we had never visited before, an area darker and more thickly overgrown than the rest, almost impenetrable. There in a small clearing amid the dense bush, she stopped before an incredibly tall royal palm which rose cleanly out of the ground, and drawing the eye up with it, soared high above the trees around it into the sky. It appeared to be touching the blue dome of sky, to be flaunting its dark crown of fronds right in the blinding white face of the late morning sun.

Da-duh watched me a long time before she spoke, and then she said very quietly, 'All right, now, tell me if you've got anything this tall in that place you're from.'

I almost wished, seeing her face, that I could have said no. 'Yes,' I said. 'We've got buildings hundreds of times this tall in New York. There's one called the Empire State building that's the tallest in the world. My class visited it last year and I went all the way to the top. It's got over a hundred floors. I can't describe how tall it is. Wait a minute. What's the name of that hill I went to visit the other day, where they have the police station?'

'You mean Bissex?'

'Yes, Bissex. Well, the Empire State Building is way taller than that.'

'You're lying now!' she shouted, trembling with rage. Her hand lifted to strike me.

'No, I'm not,' I said. 'It really is, if you don't believe me I'll send you a picture postcard of it soon as I get back home so you can see for yourself. But it's way taller than Bissex.'

All the fight went out of her at that. The hand poised to strike me fell limp to her side, and as she stared at me, seeing not me but the building that was taller than the highest hill she knew, the small stubborn light in her eyes (it was the same amber as the flame in the kerosene lamp she lit at dusk) began to fail. Finally, with a vague gesture that even in the midst of her defeat still tried to dismiss me and my world, she turned and started back through the gully, walking slowly, her steps groping and uncertain, as if she were suddenly no longer sure of the way, while I followed triumphant yet strangely saddened behind.

The next morning I found her dressed for our morning walk but stretched out on the Berbice chair in the tiny drawing room where she sometimes napped during the afternoon heat, her face turned to the window beside her. She appeared thinner and suddenly indescribably old.

'My Da-duh,' I said.

'Yes, nuh,' she said. Her voice was listless and the face she slowly turned my way was, now that I think back on it, like a Benin mask, the features drawn and almost distorted by an ancient abstract sorrow.

'Don't you feel well?' I asked.

'Girl, I don't know.'

'My Da-duh, I goin' boil you some bush tea,' my aunt, Da-duh's youngest child, who lived with her, called from the shed roof kitchen.

'Who tell you I need bush tea?' she cried, her voice assuming for a moment its old authority. 'You can't even rest nowadays without some malicious person looking for you to be dead. Come girl,' she motioned me to a place beside her on the old-fashioned lounge chair, 'give us a tune.'

I sang for her until breakfast at eleven, all my brash irreverent Tin Pan Alley songs, and then just before noon we went out into the ground. But it was a short, dispirited walk. Da-duh didn't even notice that the mangoes were beginning to ripen and would have to be picked before the village boys got to them. And when she paused occasionally and looked out across the canes or up at her trees it wasn't as if she were seeing them but something else. Some huge, monolithic shape had imposed itself, it seemed, between her and the land, obstructing her vision. Returning to the house she slept the entire afternoon on the Berbice chair.

She remained like this until we left, languishing away the mornings on the chair at the window gazing out at the land as if it were already doomed; then, at noon, taking the brief stroll with me through the ground during which she seldom spoke, and afterwards returning home to sleep till almost dusk sometimes.

On the day of our departure she put on the austere, ankle length white dress, the black shoes and brown felt hat (her town clothes she called them), but she did not go with us to town. She saw us off on the road outside her house and in the midst of my mother's tearful protracted farewell, she leaned down and whispered in my ear, 'Girl, you're not to forget now to send me the picture of that building, you hear.'

By the time I mailed her the large colored picture postcard of the Empire State building she was dead. She died during the famous '37 strike which began shortly after we left. On the day of her death England sent planes flying low over the island in a show of force – so low, according to my aunt's letter, that the downdraft from them shook the ripened mangoes from the trees in Da-duh's orchard. Frightened, everyone in the village fled into the canes. Except Da-duh. She remained in the house at the window so my aunt said, watching as the planes came swooping and screaming like monstrous birds down over the village, over her house, rattling her trees and flattening the young canes in her field. It must have seemed to her lying there that they did not intend pulling out of their dive, but like the hard-back beetles which hurled themselves with suicidal force against the walls of the house at night, those menacing silver shapes would hurl themselves in an ecstasy of self-immolation onto the land, destroying it utterly.

When the planes finally left and the villagers returned they found her dead on the Berbice chair at the window.

She died and I lived, but always, to this day even, within the shadow of her death. For a brief period after I was grown I went to live alone, like one doing penance, in a loft above a noisy factory in downtown New York and there painted seas of sugar cane and huge swirling Van Gogh suns and palm trees striding like brightly plumed Tutsi warriors across a tropical landscape, while the thunderous tread of the machines downstairs jarred the floor beneath my easel, mocking my efforts.

40

Of White Hairs and Cricket

(1987)

Rohinton Mistry

The white hair was trapped in the tweezers. I pulled it taut to see if it was gripped tightly, then plucked it.

'Aaah!' grimaced Daddy. 'Careful, only one at a time.' He continued to read the *Times of India*, spreading it on the table.

'It *is* only one,' I said, holding out the tweezers, but my annoyance did not register. Engrossed in the classifieds, he barely looked my way. The naked bulb overhead glanced off the stainless steel tweezers, making a splotch of light dart across the Murphy Radio calendar. It danced over the cherubic features of the Murphy Baby, in step with the tweezers' progress on Daddy's scalp. He sighed, turned a page, and went on scrutinising the columns.

Each Sunday, the elimination of white hairs took longer than the last time. I'm sure Daddy noticed it too, but joked bravely that laziness was slowing me down. Percy was always excused from this task. And if I pointed it out, the answer was: your brother's college studies are more important.

Daddy relied on my nimble fourteen-year-old fingers to uproot the signposts of mortality sprouting week after week. It was unappetising work, combing through his hair greasy with day-old pomade, isolating the white ones, or the ones just beginning to turn – half black and half white, and somehow more repulsive. It was always difficult to decide whether to remove those or let them go till next Sunday, when the whiteness would have spread upward to their tips.

The Sunday edition of the *Times of India* came with a tabloid of comics: Mandrake the Magician, The Phantom, and Maggie and Jiggs in 'Bringing Up Father'. The drab yellow tablecloth looked festive with the vivid colours of the comics, as though specially decorated for Sunday. The plastic cloth smelled stale and musty. It was impossible to clean perfectly because of the floral design embossed upon its surface. The swirly grooves were ideal for trapping all kinds of dirt.

Daddy reached up to scratch a spot on his scalp. His aaah surprised me. He had taught me to be tough, always. One morning when we had come home after cricket, he told Mummy and *Mamaiji*, 'Today my son did a brave thing, as I would have done. A powerful shot was going to the boundary, like a cannonball, and he blocked it with his bare shin.' Those were his exact words. The ball's shiny red fury, and the audible crack – at least, I think it was audible – had sent pain racing through me that nearly made my eyes overflow. Daddy had clapped and said, 'Well-fielded, sir, well-fielded.' So I waited to rub the agonised bone until attention was no longer upon me. I wish Percy had not lost interest in cricket, and had been there. My best friend, Viraf from A Block, was immensely impressed. But that was all a long time ago, many months ago, now Daddy did not take us for cricket on Sunday mornings.

I paused in my search. Daddy had found something in the classifieds and did not notice. By angling the tweezers I could aim the bulb's light upon various spots on the Murphy Radio calendar: the edges of the picture, worn and turned inward; the threadbare loop of braid sharing the colour of rust with the rusty nail it hung by; a corroded staple clutching twelve thin strips – the perforated residue of months ripped summarily over a decade ago when their days and weeks were played out. The baby's smile, posed with finger to chin, was all that had fully endured the years. Mummy and Daddy called it so innocent and joyous. That baby would now be the same age as me. The ragged perimeter of the patch of crumbled wall it tried to hide strayed outward from behind, forming a kind of dark and jagged halo around the baby. The picture grew less adequate, daily, as the wall kept losing plaster and the edges continued to curl and tatter.

Other calendars in the room performed similar enshroudings: the Cement Corporation skyscraper; the Lifebuoy Soap towel-wrapped woman with long black hair; the Parsi calendar, pictureless but showing the English and Parsi names for the months, and the *roje* in Gujarati beside each date, which Mummy and *Mamaiji* consulted when reciting their prayers. All these hung well past their designated time span in the world of months and years, covering up the broken promises of the Firozsha Baag building management.

'Yes, this is it,' said Daddy, tapping the paper, 'get me the scissors.'

Mamaiji came out and settled in her chair on the veranda. Seated, there was no trace of the infirmity that caused her to walk doubled over. Doctors said it was due to a weak spine that could not erect against the now inordinate weight of her stomach. From photographs of Mummy's childhood, I knew *Mamaiji* had been a big handsome woman, with a majestic countenance. She opened her bag of spinning things, although she had been told to rest her eyes after the recent cataract operation. Then she spied me with the tweezers.

'Sunday dawns and he makes the child do that *duleendar* thing again. It will only bring bad luck.' She spoke under her breath, arranging her spindle and wool; she was not looking for a direct confrontation. 'Plucking out hair as if it was a slaughtered chicken. An ill-omened thing, I'm warning you, Sunday after Sunday. But no one listens. Is this anything to make a child do, he should be out playing, or learning how to do *bajaar*, how to bargain with butcher and *bunya*.' She mumbled softly, to allow Daddy to pretend he hadn't heard a thing.

I resented her speaking against Daddy and calling me a child. She twirled the spindle, drawing fibres into thread from the scrap of wool in her left hand as the spindle descended. I watched, expecting – even wishing – the thread to break. Sometimes it did, and then it seemed to me that *Mamaiji* was overcome with disbelief, shocked and pained that it could have happened, and I would feel sorry and rush to pick it up for her. The spindle spun to the floor this time without mishap, hanging by a fine, brand new thread. She hauled it up, winding the thread around the extended thumb and little finger of her left hand by waggling the wrist in little clockwise and counter-clockwise half-turns, while the index and middle fingers clamped tight the source: the shred of wool resembling a lock of her own hair, snow white and slightly tangled.

Mamaiji spun enough thread to keep us all in *kustis.* Since Grandpa's death, she spent more and more time spinning, so that now we each had a spare *kusti* as well. The *kustis* were woven by a professional, who always praised the fine quality of the thread; and even at the fire-temple, where we untied and tied them during prayers, they earned the covetous glances of other Parsis.

I beheld the spindle and *Mamaiji*'s co-ordinated feats of dexterity with admiration. All spinning things entranced me. The descending spindle was like the bucket spinning down into the sacred Bhikha Behram Well to draw water for the ones like us who went there to pray on certain holy days after visiting the fire-temple I imagined myself clinging to the base of the spindle, sinking into the dark well, confident that *Mamaiji* would pull me up with her waggling hand before I drowned, and praying that the thread would not break. I also liked to stare at records spinning on the old 78-rpm gramophone. There was one I was particularly fond of: its round label was the most ethereal blue I ever saw. The lettering was gold. I played this record over and over, just to watch its wonderfully soothing blue and gold rotation, and the concentric rings of the shiny black shellac, whose grooves created a spiral effect if the light was right. The gramophone cabinet's warm smell of wood and leather seemed to fly right out of this shellacked spiral, while I sat close, my cheek against it, to feel the hum and vibration of the turntable. It was so cosy and comforting. Like missing school because of a slight cold, staying in bed all day with a book, fussed over by Mummy, eating white rice and soup made specially for me.

Daddy finished cutting out and re-reading the classified advertisement. 'Yes, this is a good one. Sounds very promising.' He picked up the newspaper again, then remembered what *Mamaiji* had muttered, and said softly to me, 'If it is so *duleendar* and will bring bad luck, how is it I found this? These old people –' and gave a sigh of mild exasperation. Then briskly: 'Don't stop now, this week is very important.' He continued, slapping the table merrily at each word: 'Every-single-white-hair-out.'

There was no real enmity between Daddy and *Mamaiji*, I think they even liked each other. He was just disinclined towards living with his mother-in-law. They often had disagreements over me, and it was always *Mamaiji* versus Mummy and Daddy. *Mamaiji* firmly believed that I was underfed. Housebound as she was, the only food accessible to her was the stuff sold by door-to-door vendors, which I adored but was strictly forbidden: *samosa*, *bhajia*, *sevganthia*; or the dinners she cooked for herself, separately, because she said that Mummy's cooking was insipidity itself: 'Tasteless as spit, refuses to go down my throat.'

So I, her favourite, enjoyed from time to time, on the sly, hot searing curries and things she purchased at the door when Daddy was at work and Mummy in the kitchen. Percy shared, too, if he was around; actually, his iron-clad stomach was much better suited to those flaming snacks. But the clandestine repasts were invariably uncovered, and the price was paid in harsh and unpleasant words. *Mamaiji* was accused of trying to burn to a crisp my stomach and intestines with her fiery, ungodly curries, or of exposing me to dysentery and diphtheria: the cheap door-to-door foodstuff was allegedly cooked in filthy, rancid oil – even machine oil, unfit for human consumption, as was revealed recently by a government investigation. *Mamaiji* retorted that if they did their duty as parents she would not have to resort to secrecy and *chori-chhoopi*; as it was, she had no choice, she could not stand by and see the child starve.

All this bothered me much more than I let anyone know. When the arguments started I would say that all the shouting was giving me a headache, and stalk out to the steps of the compound. My guilty conscience, squirming uncontrollably, could not witness the quarrels. For though I was an eager partner in the conspiracy with *Mamaiji*, and acquiesced to the necessity for secrecy, very often I spilled the beans – quite literally – with diarrhoea and vomiting, which *Mamaiji* upheld as undeniable proof that lack of proper regular nourishment had enfeebled my bowels. In the throes of these bouts of effluence, I promised Mummy and Daddy never again to eat what *Mamaiji* offered, and confessed all my past sins. In *Mamaiji*'s eyes I was a traitor, but sometimes it was also fun to listen to her scatological reproaches: '*Muà ugheeparoo!* Eating my food, then shitting and tattling all over the place. Next time I'll cork you up with a big *bootch* before feeding you.'

Mummy came in from the kitchen with a plateful of toast fresh off the Criterion: unevenly browned, and charred in spots by the vagaries of its kerosene wick. She cleared the comics to one side and set the plate down.

'Listen to this,' Daddy said to her, 'just found it in the paper: "A Growing Concern Seeks Dynamic Young Account Executive, Self-Motivated. Four-Figure Salary and Provident Fund." I think it's perfect.' He waited for Mummy's reaction. Then: 'If I can get it, all our troubles will be over.'

Mummy listened to such advertisements week after week: harbingers of hope that ended in disappointment and frustration. But she always allowed the initial wave of optimism to lift her, riding it with Daddy and me, higher and higher, making plans and dreaming, until it crashed and left us stranded, awaiting the next advertisement and the next wave. So her silence was surprising.

Daddy reached for a toast and dipped it in the tea, wrinkling his nose. 'Smells of kerosene again. When I get this job, first thing will be a proper toaster. No more making burnt toast on top of the Criterion.'

'I cannot smell kerosene,' said Mummy.

'Smell this then,' he said, thrusting the tea-soaked piece at her nose, 'smell it and tell me,' irritated by her ready contradiction. 'It's these useless wicks. The original Criterion ones from England used to be so good. One trim and you had a fine flame for months.' He bit queasily into the toast. 'Well, when I get the job, a Bombay Gas Company stove and cylinder can replace it.' He laughed. 'Why not? The British left seventeen years ago, time for their stove to go as well.'

He finished chewing and turned to me. 'And one day, you must go, too, to America. No future here.' His eyes fixed mine, urgently. 'Somehow we'll get the money to send you. I'll find a way.'

His face filled with love. I felt suddenly like hugging him, but we never did except on birthdays, and to get rid of the feeling I looked away and pretended to myself that he was saying it just to humour me, because he wanted me to finish pulling his white hairs. Fortunately, his jovial optimism returned.

'Maybe even a fridge is possible, then we will never have to go upstairs to that woman. No more obligations, no more favours. You won't have to kill any more rats for her.' Daddy waited for us to join in. For his sake I hoped that Mummy would. I did not feel like mustering any enthusiasm.

But she said sharply. 'All your *shaik-chullee* thoughts are flying again. Nothing happens when you plan too much. Leave it in the hands of God.'

Daddy was taken aback. He said, summoning bitterness to retaliate, 'You are thinking I will never get a better job? I'll show all of you.' He threw his piece of toast onto the plate and sat back. But he recovered as quickly, and made it into a joke. He picked up the newspaper. 'Well, I'll just have to surprise you one day when I throw out the kerosene stoves.'

I liked the kerosene stoves and the formidable fifteen-gallon storage drum that replenished them. The Criterion had a little round glass window in one corner of its black base, and I would peer into the murky depths, watching the level rise as kerosene poured through the funnel; it was very dark and cool and mysterious in there, then the kerosene floated up and its surface shone under the light bulb. Looking inside was like lying on Chaupatty beach at night and gazing at the stars, in the hot season, while we stayed out after dinner till the breeze could rise and cool off the walls baking all day in the sun. When the stove was lit and the kitchen dark, the soft orange glow through its little mica door reminded me of the glow in the fire-temple *afargaan*, when there wasn't a blazing fire because hardly any sandalwood offerings had been left in the silver *thaali*; most people came only on the holy days. The Primus stove was fun, too, pumped up hot and roaring, the kerosene emerging under pressure and igniting into sharp blue flames. Daddy was the only one who lit it; every year, many women died in their kitchens because of explosions, and Daddy said that though many of them were not accidents, especially the dowry cases, it was still a dangerous stove if handled improperly.

Mummy went back to the kitchen. I did not mind the kerosene smell, and ate some toast, trying to imagine the kitchen without the stoves, with squat red gas cylinders sitting under the table instead. I had seen them in shop windows, and I thought they were ugly. We would get used to them, though, like everything else. At night, I stood on the veranda sometimes to look at the stars. But it was not the same as going to Chaupatty and lying on the sand, quietly, with only the sound of the waves in the dark. On Saturday nights, I would make sure that the stoves were filled, because Mummy made a very early breakfast for Daddy and me next morning. The milk and bread would be arriving in the pre-dawn darkness while the kettle was boiling and we got ready for cricket with the boys of Firozsha Baag.

We always left by seven o'clock. The rest of the building was just starting to wake up: Nariman Hansotia would be aligning, on the parapet of his ground floor veranda, his razor and shaving brush and mirror beside two steaming cups, one of boiling water and the other of tea, and we often wondered if he ever dipped the brush in the wrong cup; and the old spinster Tehmina, still waiting for her cataracts to ripen, would be saying her prayers facing the rising sun, with her duster-coat hoisted up and slung over the left shoulder, her yellowing petticoat revealed, to untie and tie her thick rope-like *kusti* around the waist; and the *kuchrawalli* would be sweeping the compound, making her rounds from door to door with broom and basket, collecting yesterday's garbage. If she happened to cross Tehmina's line of vision, all the boys were sure to have a fine time, because Tehmina, though blurry with cataracts, would recognise the *kuchrawalli* and let loose at her with a stream of curses fouler than any filth in the garbage basket, for committing the unspeakable crime of passing in front of her, thereby polluting her prayers and vitiating their efficacy.

Even Daddy laughed, but he hurried us along as we lingered there to follow the ensuing dialogue. We picked our way through sleeping streets. The pavement dwellers would stretch, and look for a place to relieve themselves. Then they would fold up their cardboard pieces and roll away their plastics before the street sweepers arrived and the traffic got heavy. Sometimes, they would start a small fire if they had something to cook for breakfast, or else try to beg from people who came to the Irani restaurant for their morning *chai* and bun. Occasionally, Mummy would wrap up leftovers from the night before for Daddy and me to distribute to them along the way.

It had been such a long time since we last played cricket. Flying kites had also become a thing of the past. One by one, the things I held dear were leaving my life, I thought gloomily. And Francis. What about poor Francis? Where was he now, I wondered. I wished he was still working in the Baag. That awful thrashing he got in Tar Gully was the fault of Najamai and Tehmina, those stupid old women. And Najamai saying he stole eighty rupees was nonsense, in my opinion; the absent-minded cow must have forgotten where she left the money.

I put down the tweezers and reached for the comics. Daddy looked up. 'Don't stop now, it should be perfect this week. There will be an interview or something.'

Avoiding his eye, I said stolidly, 'I'm going to read the comics,' and walked out to the compound steps. When I turned at the doorway Daddy was still looking at me. His face was like *Mamaiji*'s when the thread broke and slipped through her fingers and the spindle fell to the floor. But I kept walking, it was a matter of pride. You always did what you said you were going to do.

The comics did not take long. It used to be more fun when Daddy and I had a race to the door to grab the *Times*, and pretended to fight over who would read the comics first. I thought of the lines on Daddy's forehead, visible so clearly from my coign of vantage with the tweezers. His thinning hair barely gave off a dull lustre with its day-old pomade, and the Sunday morning stubble on his chin was flecked with grey and white.

Something – remorse, maybe just pity – stirred inside, but I quashed it without finding out. All my friends had fathers whose hair was greying. Surely they did not spend Sunday mornings doing what I did, or they would have said something. They were not like me, there was nothing that was too private and personal for them. They would talk about anything. Especially Pesi. He used to describe for us how his father passed gas, enhancing the narrative with authentic sound effects. Now he was in boarding-school. His father was dead.

From our C Block stone steps I could observe the entire length of the compound, up to A Block at the far end. Dr Sidhwa's black Fiat turned in at the gate and trundled laboriously over the rough-hewn flagstones of Firozsha Baag. He waved as he went past. He looked so much like Pesi's father. He had the same crow's-feet at the corners of his eyes that Dr Mody used to have, and even their old cars seemed identical, except that Dr Mody healed animals and Dr Sidhwa, humans. Most of us had been treated by him at one time or another. His house and dispensary were within walking distance of Firozsha Baag, even a sick person's walking distance; he was a steadfast Parsi, seen often at fire-temples; and he always drove over for his house-calls. What more could we want in a doctor?

The car stopped at the far end of the compound. Dr Sidhwa heaved out, he was a portly man, and reached in for his bag. It must be an emergency in A Block, I decided, for someone to call him on Sunday. He slammed the door, then opened and slammed it again, harder now. The impact rocked the old car a little, but the door shut properly this time. Viraf emerged from the steps of A Block. I waved to him to let him know I was waiting.

Viraf was my best friend. Together we learned bicycling, on a rented contraption of bent spokes and patchwork tyres from Cecil Cycles of Tar Gully: Fifty Paise Per Hour. Daddy used to take us to practise at Chaupatty on the wide pavements by the beach. They were deserted in the early morning – pavement dwellers preferred the narrow side streets – except for pigeons gathering in anticipation of the pigeon-man, who arrived when the streets stirred to life. We took turns, and Daddy ran behind, holding the seat to keep us steady. Daddy also taught the two of us to play cricket. Mummy had been angry when he brought home the bat and ball, asking where the money had come from. His specialty on his own school team had been bowling, and he taught us the leg break and off break, and told us about the legendary Jasu Patel, born with a defective wrist which turned out to be perfect for spin bowling, and how Jasu had mastered the dreaded curl spin which was eventually feared by all the great international batsmen.

Cricket on Sunday mornings became a regular event for the boys in Firozsha Baag. Between us we almost had a complete kit; all that was missing was a pair of bails, and wicket-keeping gloves. Daddy took anyone who wanted to play to the Marine Drive *maidaan*, and organised us into teams, captaining one team himself. We went early, before the sun got too hot and the *maidaan* overcrowded. But then one Sunday, halfway through the game, Daddy said he was going to rest for a while. Sitting on the grass a little distance away, he seemed so much older than he did when he was batting, or bowling leg breaks. He watched us with a faraway expression on his face. Sadly, as if he had just realised something and wished he hadn't.

There was no cricket at the *maidaan* after that day. Since we were not allowed to go alone, our games were now confined to the Firozsha Baag compound. Its flagstoned surface would not accept the points of stumps, and we chalked three white lines on the compound's black stone wall. But the compound was too cramped for cricket. Besides, the uneven ground made the ball bounce and rear erratically. After a few shattered panes of glass and several complaints from neighbours, the games ceased.

I waved again to Viraf and gave our private signal, 'OO ooo OO ooo,' which was like a yodel. He waved back, then took the doctor's bag and accompanied him into A Block. His polite demeanour made me smile. That Viraf. Shrewd fellow, he knew the things to do to make grown-ups approve of him, and was always welcome at all the homes in Firozsha Baag. He would be back soon.

I waited for at least half an hour. I cracked all my fingers and knuckles, even the thumbs. Then I went to the other end of the compound. After sitting on the steps there for a few minutes, I got impatient and climbed upstairs to find out why Viraf was buttering up the doctor.

But Dr Sidhwa was on his way down, carrying his black bag. I said, '*Sahibji*, doctor,' and he smiled at me as I raced up to the third floor. Viraf was standing at the balcony outside his flat. 'What's all the *muskaa-paalis* for the doctor?'

He turned away without answering. He looked upset but I did not ask what the matter was. Words to show concern were always beyond me. I spoke again, in that easygoing debonair style which all of us tried to perfect, right arm akimbo and head tilted ever so slightly, 'Come on *yaar*, what are your plans for today?'

He shrugged his shoulders, and I persisted, 'Half the morning's over, man, don't be such a cry-baby.'

'Fish off,' he said, but his voice shook. His eyes were red, and he rubbed one as if there was something in it. I stood quietly for a while, looking out over the balcony. His third-floor balcony was my favourite spot, you could see the road beyond Firozsha Baag, and sometimes, on a sunny day, even a corner of Chaupatty beach with the sun gleaming on the waves. From my ground floor veranda the compound's black stone wall was all that was visible.

Hushed voices came from the flat, the door was open. I looked into the dining-room where some A Block neighbours had gathered around Viraf's mother. 'How about Ludo or Snakes-and-Ladders?' I tried. If he shrugged again I planned to leave. What else could I do?

'Okay,' he said, 'but stay quiet. If *Mumma* sees us she'll send us out.'

No one saw as we tiptoed inside, they were absorbed in whatever the discussion was about. '*Puppa* is very sick,' whispered Viraf, as we passed the sickroom. I stopped and looked inside. It was dark. The smell of sickness and medicines made it stink like the waiting room of Dr Sidhwa's dispensary. Viraf's father was in bed, lying on his back, with a tube through his nose. There was a long needle stuck into his right arm, and it glinted cruelly in a thin shaft of sunlight that had suddenly slunk inside the darkened room. I shivered. The needle was connected by a tube to a large bottle which hung upside down from a dark metal stand towering over the bed.

Viraf's mother was talking softly to the neighbours in the dining-room. '. . . in his chest got worse when he came home last night. So many times I've told him, three floors to climb is not easy at your age with your big body, climb one, take rest for a few minutes, then climb again. But he won't listen, does not want people to think it is too much for him. Now this is the result, and what I will do I don't know. Poor little Viraf, being so brave when the doctor . . .'

Supine, his rotundity had spread into a flatness denying the huge bulk. I remembered calling Viraf a cry-baby, and my face flushed with shame. I swore I would apologise. Daddy was slim and wiry, although there were the beginnings of a small pot, as Mummy called it. He used to run and field with us at cricket. Viraf's father had sat on the grass the one time he took us. The breath came loud and rasping. His mouth was a bit open. It resembled a person snoring, but was uneven, and the sound suggested pain. I noticed the lines on his brow, like Daddy's, only Daddy's were less deep.

Over the rasp of his breath came the voice of Viraf's mother. '. . . to exchange with someone on the ground floor, but that also is no. Says I won't give up my third-floor paradise for all the smell and noise of a ground-floor flat. Which is true, up here even B.E.S.T. bus rattle and rumble does not come. But what use of paradise if you are not alive in good health to enjoy it? Now doctor says intensive care but Parsi General Hospital has no place. Better to stay here than other hospitals, only . . .'

My eyes fixed on the stone-grey face of Viraf's father, I backed out of the sickroom, unseen. The hallway was empty. Viraf was waiting for me in the back room with the boards for Ludo and Snakes-and-Ladders. But I sneaked through the veranda and down the stairs without a word.

The compound was flooded in sunshine as I returned to the other end. On the way I passed the three white stumps we had once chalked on the compound wall's black stone. The lines were very faint, and could barely be seen, lost amongst more recent scribbles and abandoned games of noughts and crosses.

Mummy was in the kitchen, I could hear the roaring of the Primus stove. *Mamaiji*, sinister in her dark glasses, sat by the veranda window, sunlight reflecting off the thick, black lenses with leather blinders at the sides; after her cataract operation the doctor had told her to wear these for a few months.

Daddy was still reading the *Times* at the dining-table. Through the gloom of the light bulb I saw the Murphy Baby's innocent and joyous smile. I wondered what he looked like now. When I was two years old, there was a Murphy Baby Contest, and according to Mummy and Daddy my photograph, which had been entered, should have won. They said that in those days my smile had been just as, if not more, innocent and joyous.

The tweezers were lying on the table. I picked them up. They glinted pitilessly, like that long needle in Viraf's father. I dropped them with a shudder, and they clattered against the table.

Daddy looked up questioningly. His hair was dishevelled as I had left it, and I waited, hoping he would ask me to continue. To offer to do it was beyond me, but I wanted desperately that he should ask me now. I glanced at his face discreetly, from the corner of my eye. The lines on his forehead stood out all too clearly, and the stubble flecked with white, which by this hour should have disappeared down the drain with the shaving water. I swore to myself that never again would I begrudge him my help; I would get all the white hairs, one by one, if he would only ask me; I would concentrate on the tweezers as never before, I would do it as if all our lives were riding on the efficacy of the tweezers, yes, I would continue to do it Sunday after Sunday, no matter how long it took.

Daddy put down the newspaper and removed his glasses. He rubbed his eyes, then went to the bathroom. How tired he looked, and how his shoulders drooped; his gait lacked confidence, and I'd never noticed that before. He did not speak to me even though I was praying hard that he would. Something inside me grew very heavy, and I tried to swallow, to dissolve that heaviness in saliva, but swallowing wasn't easy either, the heaviness was blocking my throat.

I heard the sound of running water. Daddy was preparing to shave I wanted to go and watch him, talk to him, laugh with him at the funny faces he made to get at all the tricky places with the razor, especially the cleft in his chin.

Instead, I threw myself on the bed. I felt like crying, and buried my face in the pillow. I wanted to cry for the way I had treated Viraf, and for his sick father with the long, cold needle in his arm and his rasping breath; for *Mamaiji* and her tired, darkened eyes spinning thread for our *kustis*, and for Mummy growing old in the dingy kitchen smelling of kerosene, where the Primus roared and her dreams were extinguished; I wanted to weep for myself, for not being able to hug Daddy when I wanted to, and for not ever saying thank you for cricket in the morning, and pigeons and bicycles and dreams; and for all the white hairs that I was powerless to stop.

41

Elephant

(1988)

Raymond Carver

I knew it was a mistake to let my brother have the money. I didn't need anybody else owing me. But when he called and said he couldn't make the payment on his house, what could I do? I'd never been inside his house – he lived a thousand miles away, in California; I'd never even *seen* his house – but I didn't want him to lose it. He cried over the phone and said he was losing everything he'd worked for. He said he'd pay me back. February, he said. Maybe sooner. No later, anyway, than March. He said his income-tax refund was on the way. Plus, he said, he had a little investment that would mature in February. He acted secretive about the investment thing, so I didn't press for details.

'Trust me on this,' he said. 'I won't let you down.'

He'd lost his job last July, when the company he worked for, a fiberglass insulation plant, decided to lay off two hundred employees. He'd been living on his unemployment since then, but now the unemployment was gone, and his savings were gone, too. And he didn't have health insurance any longer. When his job went, the insurance went. His wife, who was ten years older, was diabetic and needed treatment. He'd had to sell the other car – her car, an old station wagon – and a week ago he'd pawned his TV. He told me he'd hurt his back carrying the TV up and down the street where the pawnshops did business. He went from place to place, he said, trying to get the best offer. Somebody finally gave him a hundred dollars for it, this big Sony TV. He told me about the TV, and then about throwing his back out, as if this ought to cinch it with me, unless I had a stone in place of a heart.

'I've gone belly up,' he said. 'But you can help me pull out of it.'

'How much?' I said.

'Five hundred. I could use more, sure, who couldn't?' he said. 'But I want to be realistic. I can pay back five hundred. More than that, I'll tell you the truth, I'm not so sure. Brother, I hate to ask. But you're my last resort. Irma Jean and I are going to be on the street before long. I won't let you down,' he said. That's what he said. Those were his exact words.

We talked a little more – mostly about our mother and her problems – but, to make a long story short, I sent him the money. I had to. I felt I had to, at any rate – which amounts to the same thing. I wrote him a letter when I sent the check and said he should pay the money back to our mother, who lived in the same town he lived in and who was poor and greedy. I'd been mailing checks to her every month, rain or shine, for three years. But I was thinking that if he paid her the money he owed me it might take me off the hook there and let me breathe for a while. I wouldn't have to worry on that score for a couple of months, anyway. Also, and this is the truth, I thought maybe he'd be more likely to pay her, since they lived right there in the same town and he saw her from time to time. All I was doing was trying to cover myself some way. The thing is, he might have the best intentions of paying me back, but things happen sometimes. Things get in the way of best intentions. Out of sight, out of mind, as they say. But he wouldn't stiff his own mother. Nobody would do that.

I spent hours writing letters, trying to make sure everybody knew what could be expected and what was required. I even phoned out there to my mother several times, trying to explain it to her. But she was suspicious over the whole deal. I went through it with her on the phone step by step, but she was still suspicious. I told her the money that was supposed to come from me on the first of March and on the first of April would instead come from Billy, who owed the money to me. She'd get her money, and she didn't have to worry. The only difference was that Billy would pay it to her those two months instead of me. He'd pay her the money I'd normally be sending to her, but instead of him mailing it to me and then me having to turn around and send it to her he'd pay it to her directly. On any account, she didn't have to worry. She'd get her money, but for those two months it'd come from him – from the money he owed me. My God, I don't know how much I spent on phone calls. And I wish I had fifty cents for every letter I wrote, telling him what I'd told her and telling her what to expect from him – that sort of thing.

But my mother didn't trust Billy. 'What if he can't come up with it?' she said to me over the phone. 'What then? He's in bad shape, and I'm sorry for him,' she said. 'But, son, what I want to know is, what if he isn't able to pay me? What if he can't? Then what?'

'Then I'll pay you myself,' I said. 'Just like always. If he doesn't pay you, I'll pay you. But he'll pay you. Don't worry. He says he will, and he will.'

'I don't want to worry,' she said. 'But I worry anyway. I worry about my boys, and after that I worry about myself. I never thought I'd see one of my boys in this shape. I'm just glad your dad isn't alive to see it.'

In three months my brother gave her fifty dollars of what he owed me and was supposed to pay to her. Or maybe it was seventy-five dollars he gave her. There are conflicting stories – two conflicting stories, his and hers. But that's all he paid her of the five hundred – fifty dollars or else seventy-five dollars, according to whose story you want to listen to. I had to make up the rest to her. I had to keep shelling out, same as always. My brother was finished. That's what he told me – that he was finished – when I called to see what was up, after my mother had phoned, looking for her money.

My mother said, 'I made the mailman go back and check inside his truck, to see if your letter might have fallen down behind the seat. Then I went around and asked the neighbors did they get any of my mail by mistake. I'm going crazy with worry about this situation, honey.' Then she said, 'What's a mother supposed to think?' Who was looking out for her best interests in this business? She wanted to know that, and she wanted to know when she could expect her money.

So that's when I got on the phone to my brother to see if this was just a simple delay or a full-fledged collapse. But, according to Billy, he was a goner. He was absolutely done for. He was putting his house on the market immediately. He just hoped he hadn't waited too long to try and move it. And there wasn't anything left inside the house that he could sell. He'd sold off everything except the kitchen table and chairs. 'I wish I could sell my blood,' he said. 'But who'd buy it? With my luck, I probably have an incurable disease.' And, naturally, the investment thing hadn't worked out. When I asked him about it over the phone, all he said was that it hadn't materialised. His tax refund didn't make it, either – the I.R.S. had some kind of lien on his return. 'When it rains it pours,' he said. 'I'm sorry, brother. I didn't mean for this to happen.'

'I understand,' I said. And I did. But it didn't make it any easier. Anyway, one thing and the other, I didn't get my money from him, and neither did my mother. I had to keep on sending her money every month.

I was sore, yes. Who wouldn't be? My heart went out to him, and I wished trouble hadn't knocked on his door. But my own back was against the wall now. At least, though, whatever happens to him from here on, he won't come back to me for more money – seeing as how he still owes me. Nobody would do that to you. That's how I figured, anyway. But that's how little I knew.

I kept my nose to the grindstone. I got up early every morning and went to work and worked hard all day. When I came home I plopped into the big chair and just sat there. I was so tired it took me a while to get around to unlacing my shoes. Then I just went on sitting there. I was too tired to even get up and turn on the TV.

I was sorry about my brother's troubles. But I had troubles of my own. In addition to my mother, I had several other people on my payroll. I had a former wife I was sending money to every month. I had to do that. I didn't want to, but the court said I had to. And I had a daughter with two kids in Bellingham, and I had to send her something every month. Her kids had to eat, didn't they? She was living with a swine who wouldn't even *look* for work, a guy who couldn't hold a job if they handed him one. The time or two he did find something, he overslept, or his car broke down on the way in to work, or else he'd just be let go, no explanation, and that was that.

Once, long ago, when I used to think like a man about these things, I threatened to kill that guy. But that's neither here nor there. Besides, I was drinking in those days. In any case, the bastard is still hanging around.

My daughter would write these letters and say how they were living on oatmeal, she and her kids. (I guess he was starving, too, but she knew better than to mention that guy's name in her letters to me.) She'd tell me that if I could just carry her until summer things would pick up for her. Things would turn around for her, she was sure, in the summer. If nothing else worked out – but she was sure it would; she had several irons in the fire – she could always get a job in the fish cannery that was not far from where she lived. She'd wear rubber boots and rubber clothes and gloves and pack salmon into cans. Or else she might sell root beer from a vending stand beside the road to people who lined up in their cars at the border, waiting to get into Canada. People sitting in their cars in the middle of summer were going to be thirsty, right? They were going to be crying out for cold drinks. Anyway, one thing or the other, whatever line of work she decided on, she'd do fine in the summer. She just had to make it until then, and that's where I came in.

My daughter said she knew she had to change her life. She wanted to stand on her own two feet like everyone else. She wanted to quit looking at herself as a victim. 'I'm not a victim,' she said to me over the phone one night. 'I'm just a young woman with two kids and a son-of-a-bitch bum who lives with me. No different from lots of other women. I'm not afraid of hard work. Just give me a chance. That's all I ask of the world.' She said she could do without for herself. But until her break came, until opportunity knocked, it was the kids she worried about. The kids were always asking her when Grandpop was going to visit, she said. Right this minute they were drawing pictures of the swing sets and swimming pool at the motel I'd stayed in when I'd visited a year ago. But summer was the thing, she said. If she could make it until summer, her troubles would be over. Things would change then – she knew they would. And with a little help from me she could make it. 'I don't know what I'd do without you, Dad.' That's what she said. It nearly broke my heart. Sure I had to help her. I was glad to be even halfway in a position to help her. I had a job, didn't I? Compared to her and everyone else in my family, I had it made. Compared to the rest, I lived on Easy Street.

I sent the money she asked for. I sent money every time she asked. And then I told her I thought it'd be simpler if I just sent a sum of money, not a whole lot, but money even so, on the first of each month. It would be money she could count on, and it would be *her* money, no one else's – hers and the kids'. That's what I hoped for, anyway. I wished there was some way I could be sure the bastard who lived with her couldn't get his hands on so much as an orange or a piece of bread that my money bought. But I couldn't. I just had to go ahead and send the money and stop worrying about whether he'd soon be tucking into a plate of my eggs and biscuits.

My mother and my daughter and my former wife. That's three people on the payroll right there, not counting my brother. But my son needed money, too. After he graduated from high school, he packed his things, left his mother's house, and went to a college back East. A college in New Hampshire, of all places. Who's ever heard of New Hampshire? But he was the first kid in the family, on either side of the family, to even *want* to go to college, so everybody thought it was a good idea. I thought so, too, at first. How'd I know it was going to wind up costing me an arm and a leg? He borrowed left and right from the banks to keep himself going. He didn't want to have to work a job and go to school at the same time. That's what he said. And, sure, I guess I can understand it. In a way, I can even sympathise. Who likes to work? I don't. But after he'd borrowed everything he could, everything in sight, including enough to finance a junior year in Germany, I had to begin sending him money, and a lot of it. When, finally, I said I couldn't send any more, he wrote back and said if that was the case, if that was really the way I felt, he was going to deal drugs or else rob a bank – whatever he had to do to get money to live on. I'd be lucky if he wasn't shot or sent to prison.

I wrote back and said I'd changed my mind and I could send him a little more after all. What else could I do? I didn't want his blood on my hands. I didn't want to think of my kid being packed off to prison, or something even worse. I had plenty on my conscience as it was.

That's four people, right? Not counting my brother, who wasn't a regular yet. I was going crazy with it. I worried night and day. I couldn't sleep over it. I was paying out nearly as much money every month as I was bringing in. You don't have to be a genius, or know anything about economics, to understand that this state of affairs couldn't keep on. I had to get a loan to keep up my end of things. That was another monthly payment.

So I started cutting back. I had to quit eating out, for instance. Since I lived alone, eating out was something I liked to do, but it became a thing of the past. And I had to watch myself when it came to thinking about movies. I couldn't buy clothes or get my teeth fixed. The car was falling apart. I needed new shoes, but forget it.

Once in a while I'd get fed up with it and write letters to all of them, threatening to change my name and telling them I was going to quit my job. I'd tell them I was planning a move to Australia. And the thing was, I was serious when I'd say that about Australia, even though I didn't know the first thing about Australia. I just knew it was on the other side of the world, and that's where I wanted to be.

But when it came right down to it, none of them really believed I'd go to Australia. They had me, and they knew it. They knew I was desperate, and they were sorry and they said so. But they counted on it all blowing over before the first of the month, when I had to sit down and make out the checks.

After one of my letters where I talked about moving to Australia, my mother wrote that she didn't want to be a burden any longer. Just as soon as the swelling went down in her legs, she said, she was going out to look for work. She was seventy-five years old, but maybe she could go back to waitressing, she said. I wrote her back and told her not to be silly. I said I was glad I could help her. And I was. I was glad I could help. I just needed to win the lottery.

My daughter knew Australia was just a way of saying to everybody that I'd had it. She knew I needed a break and something to cheer me up. So she wrote that she was going to leave her kids with somebody and take the cannery job when the season rolled around. She was young and strong, she said. She thought she could work the twelve-to-fourteen-hour-a-day shifts, seven days a week, no problem. She'd just have to tell herself she could do it, get herself psyched up for it, and her body would listen. She just had to line up the right kind of baby-sitter. That'd be the big thing. It was going to require a special kind of sitter, seeing as how the hours would be long and the kids were hyper to begin with, because of all the Popsicles and Tootsie Rolls, M&M's, and the like that they put away every day. It's the stuff kids like to eat, right? Anyway, she thought she could find the right person if she kept looking. But she had to buy the boots and clothes for the work, and that's where I could help.

My son wrote that he was sorry for his part in things and thought he and I would both be better off if he ended it once and for all. For one thing, he'd discovered he was allergic to cocaine. It made his eyes stream and affected his breathing, he said. This meant he couldn't test the drugs in the transactions he'd need to make. So, before it could even begin, his career as a drug dealer was over. No, he said, better a bullet in the temple and end it all right here. Or maybe hanging. That would save him the trouble of borrowing a gun. And save us the price of bullets. That's actually what he said in his letter, if you can believe it. He enclosed a picture of himself that somebody had taken last summer when he was in the study-abroad program in Germany. He was standing under a big tree with thick limbs hanging down a few feet over his head. In the picture, he wasn't smiling.

My former wife didn't have anything to say on the matter. She didn't have to. She knew she'd get her money the first of each month, even if it had to come all the way from Sydney. If she didn't get it, she just had to pick up the phone and call her lawyer.

This is where things stood when my brother called one Sunday afternoon in early May. I had the windows open, and a nice breeze moved through the house. The radio was playing. The hillside behind the house was in bloom. But I began to sweat when I heard his voice on the line. I hadn't heard from him since the dispute over the five hundred, so I couldn't believe he was going to try and touch me for more money now. But I began to sweat anyway. He asked how things stood with me, and I launched into the payroll thing and all. I talked about oatmeal, cocaine, fish canneries, suicide, bank jobs, and how I couldn't go to the movies or eat out. I said I had a hole in my shoe. I talked about the payments that went on and on to my former wife. He knew all about this, of course. He knew everything I was telling him. Still, he said he was sorry to hear it. I kept talking. It was his dime. But as he talked I started thinking, *How are you going to pay for this call, Billy?* Then it came to me that *I* was going to pay for it. It was only a matter of minutes, or seconds, until it was all decided.

I looked out the window. The sky was blue, with a few white clouds in it. Some birds clung to a telephone wire. I wiped my face on my sleeve. I didn't know what else I could say. So I suddenly stopped talking and just stared out the window at the mountains, and waited. And that's when my brother said, 'I hate to ask you this, but—' When he said that, my heart did this sinking thing. And then he went ahead and asked.

This time it was a thousand. A thousand! He was worse off than when he'd called that other time. He let me have some details. The bill collectors were at the door – the door! he said – and the windows rattled, the house shook, when they hammered with their fists. *Blam, blam, blam*, he said. There was no place to hide from them. His house was about to be pulled out from under him. 'Help me, brother,' he said.

Where was I going to raise a thousand dollars? I took a good grip on the receiver, turned away from the window, and said, 'But you didn't pay me back the last time you borrowed money. What about that?'

'I didn't?' he said, acting surprised. 'I guess I thought I had. I wanted to, anyway. I tried to, so help me God.'

'You were supposed to pay that money to Mom,' I said. 'But you didn't. I had to keep giving her money every month, same as always. There's no end to it, Billy. Listen, I take one step forward and I go two steps back. I'm going under. You're all going under, and you're pulling me down with you.'

'I paid her *some* of it,' he said. 'I did pay her a little. Just for the record,' he said, 'I paid her something.'

'She said you gave her fifty dollars and that was all.'

'No,' he said, 'I gave her seventy-five. She forgot about the other twenty-five. I was over there one afternoon, and I gave her two tens and a five. I gave her some cash, and she just forgot about it. Her memory's going. Look,' he said, 'I promise I'll be good for it this time, I swear to God. Add up what I still owe you and add it to this money here I'm trying to borrow, and I'll send you a check. We'll exchange checks. Hold on to my check for two months, that's all I'm asking. I'll be out of the woods in two months' time. Then you'll have your money. July first, I promise, no later, and this time I *can* swear to it. We're in the process of selling this little piece of property that Irma Jean inherited a while back from her uncle. It's as good as sold. The deal has closed. It's just a question now of working out a couple of minor details and signing the papers. Plus, I've got this job lined up. It's definite. I'll have to drive fifty miles round trip every day, but that's no problem – hell, no. I'd drive a hundred and fifty if I had to, and be glad to do it. I'm saying I'll have money in the bank in two months' time. You'll get your money, all of it, by July first, and you can count on it.'

'Billy, I love you,' I said. 'But I've got a load to carry. I'm carrying a very heavy load these days, in case you didn't know.'

'That's why I won't let you down on this,' he said. 'You have my word of honor. You can trust me on this absolutely. I promise you my check will be good in two months, no later. Two months is all I'm asking for. Brother, I don't know where else to turn. You're my last hope.'

I did it, sure. To my surprise, I still had some credit with the bank, so I borrowed the money, and I sent it to him. Our checks crossed in the mail. I stuck a thumbtack through his check and put it up on the kitchen wall next to the calendar and the picture of my son standing under that tree. And then I waited.

I kept waiting. My brother wrote and asked me not to cash the check on the day we'd agreed to. Please wait a while longer is what he said. Some things had come up. The job he'd been promised had fallen through at the last minute. That was one thing that came up. And that little piece of property belonging to his wife hadn't sold after all. At the last minute, she'd had a change of heart about selling it. It had been in her family for generations. What could he do? It was her land, and she wouldn't listen to reason, he said.

My daughter telephoned around this time to say that somebody had broken into her trailer and ripped her off. Everything in the trailer. Every stick of furniture was gone when she came home from work after her first night at the cannery. There wasn't even a chair left for her to sit down on. Her bed had been stolen, too. They were going to have to sleep on the floor like gypsies, she said.

'Where was what's-his-name when this happened?' I said.

She said he'd been out looking for work earlier in the day. She guessed he was with friends. Actually, she didn't know his whereabouts at the time of the crime, or even right now, for that matter. 'I hope he's at the bottom of the river,' she said. The kids had been with the sitter when the ripoff happened. But, anyway, if she could just borrow enough from me to buy some secondhand furniture she'd pay me back, she said, when she got her first check. If she had some money from me before the end of the week – I could wire it, maybe – she could pick up some essentials. 'Somebody's violated my space,' she said. 'I feel like I've been raped.'

My son wrote from New Hampshire that it was essential he go back to Europe. His life hung in the balance, he said. He was graduating at the end of summer session, but he couldn't stand to live in America a day longer after that. This was a materialist society, and he simply couldn't take it anymore. People over here, in the U.S., couldn't hold a conversation unless *money* figured in it some way, and he was sick of it. He wasn't a Yuppie, and didn't want to become a Yuppie. That wasn't his thing. He'd get out of my hair, he said, if he could just borrow enough from me, this one last time, to buy a ticket to Germany.

I didn't hear anything from my former wife. I didn't have to. We both knew how things stood there.

My mother wrote that she was having to do without support hose and wasn't able to have her hair tinted. She'd thought this would be the year she could put some money back for the rainy days ahead, but it wasn't working out that way. She could see it wasn't in the cards. 'How are you?' she wanted to know. 'How's everybody else? I hope you're okay.'

I put more checks in the mail. Then I held my breath and waited.

While I was waiting, I had this dream one night. Two dreams, really. I dreamt them on the same night. In the first dream, my dad was alive once more, and he was giving me a ride on his shoulders. I was this little kid, maybe five or six years old. *Get up here*, he said, and he took me by the hands and swung me onto his shoulders. I was high off the ground, but I wasn't afraid. He was holding on to me. We were holding on to each other. Then he began to move down the sidewalk. I brought my hands up from his shoulders and put them around his forehead. *Don't muss my hair*, he said. *You can let go*, he said, *I've got you. You won't fall.* When he said that, I became aware of the strong grip of his hands around my ankles. Then I did let go. I turned loose and held my arms out on either side of me. I kept them out there like that for balance. My dad went on walking while I rode on his shoulders. I pretended he was an elephant. I don't know where we were going. Maybe we were going to the store, or else to the park so he could push me in the swing.

I woke up then, got out of bed, and used the bathroom. It was starting to get light out, and it was only an hour or so until I had to get up. I thought about making coffee and getting dressed. But then I decided to go back to bed. I didn't plan to sleep, though. I thought I'd just lie there for a while with my hands behind my neck and watch it turn light out and maybe think about my dad a little, since I hadn't thought about him in a long time. He just wasn't a part of my life any longer, waking or sleeping. Anyway, I got back in bed. But it couldn't have been more than a minute before I fell asleep once more, and when I did I got into this other dream. My former wife was in it, though she wasn't my former wife in the dream. She was still my wife. My kids were in it, too. They were little, and they were eating potato chips. In my dream, I thought I could smell the potato chips and hear them being eaten. We were on a blanket, and we were close to some water. There was a sense of satisfaction and well-being in the dream. Then, suddenly, I found myself in the company of some other people – people I didn't know – and the next thing that happened was that I was kicking the window out of my son's car and threatening his life, as I did once, a long time ago. He was inside the car as my shoe smashed through the glass. That's when my eyes flew open, and I woke up. The alarm was going off. I reached over and pushed the switch and lay there for a few minutes more, my heart racing. In the second dream, somebody had offered me some whiskey, and I drank it. Drinking that whiskey was the thing that scared me. That was the worst thing that could have happened. That was rock bottom. Compared to that, everything else was a picnic. I lay there for a minute longer, trying to calm down. Then I got up.

I made coffee and sat at the kitchen table in front of the window. I pushed my cup back and forth in little circles on the table and began to think seriously about Australia again. And then, all of a sudden, I could imagine how it must have sounded to my family when I'd threatened them with a move to Australia. They would have been shocked at first, and even a little scared. Then, because they knew me, they'd probably started laughing. Now, thinking about their laughter, I had to laugh, too. *Ha, ha, ha.* That was exactly the sound I made there at the table – *ha, ha, ha* – as if I'd read somewhere how to laugh.

What was it I planned to do in Australia, anyway? The truth was, I wouldn't be going there any more than I'd be going to Timbuktu, the moon, or the North Pole. Hell, I didn't want to go to Australia. But once I understood this, once I understood I wouldn't be going there – or anywhere else, for that matter – I began to feel better. I lit another cigarette and poured some more coffee. There wasn't any milk for the coffee, but I didn't care. I could skip having milk in my coffee for a day and it wouldn't kill me. Pretty soon I packed the lunch and filled the thermos and put the thermos in the lunch pail. Then I went outside.

It was a fine morning. The sun lay over the mountains behind the town, and a flock of birds was moving from one part of the valley to another. I didn't bother to lock the door. I remembered what had happened to my daughter, but decided I didn't have anything worth stealing anyway. There was nothing in the house I couldn't live without. I had the TV, but I was sick of watching TV. They'd be doing me a favor if they broke in and took it off my hands.

I felt pretty good, all things considered, and I decided to walk to work. It wasn't all that far, and I had time to spare. I'd save a little gas, sure, but that wasn't the main consideration. It was summer, after all, and before long summer would be over. Summer, I couldn't help thinking, had been the time everybody's luck had been going to change.

I started walking alongside the road, and it was then, for some reason, I began to think about my son. I wished him well, wherever he was. If he'd made it back to

Germany by now – and he should have – I hoped he was happy. He hadn't written yet to give me his address, but I was sure I'd hear something before long. And my daughter, God love her and keep her. I hoped she was doing okay. I decided to write her a letter that evening and tell her I was rooting for her. My mother was alive and more or less in good health, and I felt lucky there, too. If all went well, I'd have her for several more years.

Birds were calling, and some cars passed me on the highway. Good luck to you, too, brother, I thought. I hope your ship comes in. Pay me back when you get it. And my former wife, the woman I used to love so much. She was alive, and she was well, too – so far as I knew, anyway. I wished her happiness. When all was said and done, I decided things could be a lot worse. Just now, of course, things were hard for everyone. People's luck had gone south on them was all. But things were bound to change soon. Things would pick up in the fall maybe. There was lots to hope for.

I kept on walking. Then I began to whistle. I felt I had the right to whistle if I wanted to. I let my arms swing as I walked. But the lunch pail kept throwing me off balance. I had sandwiches, an apple, and some cookies in there, not to mention the thermos. I stopped in front of Smitty's, an old café that had gravel in the parking area and boards over the windows. The place had been boarded up for as long as I could remember. I decided to put the lunch pail down for a minute. I did that, and then I raised my arms – raised them up level with my shoulders. I was standing there like that, like a goof, when somebody tooted a car horn and pulled off the highway into the parking area. I picked up my lunch pail and went over to the car. It was a guy I knew from work whose name was George. He reached over and opened the door on the passenger's side. 'Hey, get in, buddy,' he said.

'Hello, George,' I said. I got in and shut the door, and the car sped off, throwing gravel from under the tires.

'I saw you,' George said. 'Yeah, I did, I saw you. You're in training for something, but I don't know what.' He looked at me and then looked at the road again. He was going fast. 'You always walk down the road with your arms out like that?' He laughed – *ha, ha, ha* – and stepped on the gas.

'Sometimes,' I said. 'It depends, I guess. Actually, I was standing,' I said. I lit a cigarette and leaned back in the seat.

'So what's new?' George said. He put a cigar in his mouth, but he didn't light it.

'Nothing's new,' I said. 'What's new with you?'

George shrugged. Then he grinned. He was going very fast now. Wind buffeted the car and whistled by outside the windows. He was driving as if we were late for work. But we weren't late. We had lots of time, and I told him so.

Nevertheless, he cranked it up. We passed the turnoff and kept going. We were moving by then, heading straight toward the mountains. He took the cigar out of his mouth and put it in his shirt pocket. 'I borrowed some money and had this baby overhauled,' he said. Then he said he wanted me to see something. He punched it and gave it everything he could. I fastened my seat belt and held on.

'*Go*,' I said. 'What are you waiting for, George?' And that's when we really flew. Wind howled outside the windows. He had it floored, and we were going flat out. We streaked down that road in his big unpaid-for car.

42

Sandpiper

(1994)

Ahdaf Soueif

Outside, there is a path. A path of beaten white stone bordered by a white wall – low, but not low enough for me to see over it from here. White sands drift across the path. From my window, I used to see patterns in their drift. On my way to the beach, I would try to place my foot, just the ball of my foot, for there never was much room, on those white spaces that glinted flat and free of sand. I had an idea that the patterns on the stone should be made by nature alone; I did not want one grain of sand, blown by a breeze I could not feel, to change its course because of me. What point would there be in trying to decipher a pattern that I had caused? It was not easy. Balancing, the toes of one bare foot on the hot stone, looking for the next clear space to set the other foot down. It took a long time to reach the end of the path. And then the stretch of beach. And then the sea.

I used to sit where the water rolled in, rolled in, its frilled white edge nibbling at the sand, withdrawing to leave great damp half moons of a darker, more brownish-beige. I would sit inside one of these curves, at the very midpoint, fitting my body to its contour, and wait. The sea unceasingly shifts and stirs and sends out fingers, paws, tongues to probe the shore. Each wave coming in is different. It separates itself from the vast, moving blue, rises and surges forward with a low growl, lightening as it approaches to a pale green, then turns over to display the white frill that slides like a thousand snakes down upon itself, breaks and skitters up the sandbank. I used to sit very still. Sometimes the wave would barely touch my feet, sometimes it would swirl around me then pull back, sifting yet another layer of sand from under me, leaving me wet to the waist. My heels rested in twin hollows that filled, emptied and refilled without a break. And subtle as the shadow of a passing cloud, my half moon would slip down the bank – only to be overtaken and swamped by the next leap of foaming white.

I used to sit in the curve and dig my fingers into the grainy, compact sand and feel it grow wetter as my fingers went deeper and deeper till the next rippling, frothing rush of white came and smudged the edges of the little burrow I had made. Its walls collapsed and I removed my hand, covered in wet clay, soon to revert to dry grains that I would easily brush away.

I lean against the wall of my room and count: twelve years ago, I met him. Eight years ago, I married him. Six years ago, I gave birth to his child.

For eight summers we have been coming here; to the beach-house west of Alexandria. The first summer had not been a time of reflection; my occupation then had been to love my husband in this – to me – new and different place. To love him as he walked towards my parasol, shaking the water from his black hair, his feet sinking into the warm, hospitable sand. To love him as he carried his nephew on his shoulders into the sea, threw him in, caught him and hoisted him up again; a colossus bestriding the waves. To love him as he played backgammon with his father in the evening, the slam of counters and the clatter of dice resounding on the patio while, at the dining-room table, his sister showed me how to draw their ornate, circular script. To love this new him, who had been hinted at but never revealed when we lived in my northern land, and who after a long absence, had found his way back into the heart of his country, taking me along with him. We walked in the sunset along the water's edge, kicking at the spray, my sun-hat fallen on my back, my hand, pale bronze in his burnt brown, my face no doubt mirroring his: aglow with health and love; a young couple in a glitzy commercial for life insurance or a two-week break in the sun.

My second summer here was the sixth summer of our love – and the last of our happiness. Carrying my child and loving her father, I sat on the beach, dug holes in the sand and let my thoughts wander. I thought about our life in my country, before we were married: four years in the cosy flat, precarious on top of a roof in a Georgian square, him meeting me at the bus-stop when I came back from work, Sundays when it did not rain and we sat in the park with our newspapers, late nights at the movies. I thought of those things and missed them – but with no great sense of loss. It was as though they were all there, to be called upon, to be lived again whenever we wanted.

I looked out to sea and, now I realise, I was trying to work out my co-ordinates. I thought a lot about the water and the sand as I sat there watching them meet and flirt and touch. I tried to understand that I was on the edge, the very edge of Africa; that the vastness ahead was nothing compared to what lay behind me. But – even though I'd been there and seen for myself its never-ending dusty green interior, its mountains, the big sky, my mind could not grasp a world that was not present to my senses – I could see the beach, the waves, the blue beyond, and cradling them all, my baby.

I sat with my hand on my belly and waited for the tiny eruptions, the small flutterings, that told me how she lay and what she was feeling. Gradually, we came to talk to each other. She would curl into a tight ball in one corner of my body until, lopsided and uncomfortable, I coaxed and prodded her back into a more centred, relaxed position. I slowly rubbed one corner of my belly until *there*, aimed straight at my hand, I felt a gentle punch. I tapped and she punched again. I was twenty-nine. For seventeen years my body had waited to conceive, and now my heart and mind had caught up with it. Nature had worked admirably; I had wanted the child through my love for her father and how I loved her father that summer. My body could not get enough of him. His baby was snug inside me and I wanted him there too.

From where I stand now, all I can see is dry, solid white. The white glare, the white wall, and the white path, narrowing in the distance.

I should have gone. No longer a serrating thought but familiar and dull. I should have gone. On that swirl of amazed and wounded anger when, knowing him as I did, I first sensed that he was pulling away from me, I should have gone. I should have turned, picked up my child and gone.

I turn. The slatted blinds are closed against a glaring sun. They call the wooden blinds *sheesh* and tell me it's the Persian word for glass. So that which sits next to a thing is called by its name. I have had this thought many times and feel as though it should lead me somewhere; as though I should draw some conclusion from it, but so far I haven't.

I draw my finger along a wooden slat. Um Sabir, my husband's old nanny, does everything around the house, both here and in the city. I tried, at first, at least to help, but she would rush up and ease the duster or the vacuum cleaner from my hands. 'Shame, shame. What am I here for? Keep your hands nice and soft. Go and rest. Or why don't you go to the club? What have you to do with these things?' My husband translated all this for me and said things to her which I came to understand meant that tomorrow I would get used to their ways. The meals I planned never worked out. Um Sabir cooked what was best in the market on that day. If I tried to do the shopping the prices trebled. I arranged the flowers, smoothed out the pleats in the curtains and presided over our dinner-parties.

My bed is made. My big bed which a half-asleep Lucy, creeping under the mosquito-net, tumbles into in the middle of every night. She fits herself into my body and I put my arm over her until she shakes it off. In her sleep she makes use of me; my breast is sometimes her pillow, my hip her footstool. I lie content, glad to be of use. I hold her foot in my hand and dread the time – so soon to come – when it will no longer be seemly to kiss the dimpled ankle.

On a black leather sofa in a transit lounge in an airport once, many years ago, I watched a Pakistani woman sleep. Her dress and trousers were a deep, yellow silk and on her dress bloomed luscious flowers in purple and green. Her arms were covered in gold bangles. She had gold in her ears, her left nostril and around her neck. Against her body her small son lay curled. One of his feet was between her knees, her nose was in his hair. All her worldly treasure was on that sofa with her, and so she slept soundly on. That image, too, I saved up for him.

I made my bed this morning. I spread my arms out wide and gathered in the soft, billowing mosquito-net. I twisted it round in a thick coil and tied it into a loose loop that dangles gracefully in mid-air.

Nine years ago, sitting under my first mosquito-net, I had written, 'Now I know how it feels to be a memsahib.' That was in Kano; deep, deep in the heart of the continent I now sit on the edge of. I had been in love with him for three years and being apart then was a variant, merely, of being together. When we were separated there was for each a gnawing lack of the other. We would say that this confirmed our true, essential union. We had parted at Heathrow, and we were to be rejoined in a fortnight, in Cairo, where I would meet his family for the first time.

I had thought to write a story about those two weeks; about my first trip into Africa: about Muhammad al-Senusi explaining courteously to me the inferior status of women, courteously because, being foreign, European, on a business trip, I was an honorary man. A story about travelling the long, straight road to Maiduguri and stopping at roadside shacks to chew on meat that I then swallowed in lumps while Senusi told me how the meat in Europe had no body and melted like rice pudding in his mouth. About the time when I saw the lion in the tall grass. I asked the driver to stop, jumped out of the car, aimed my camera and shot as the lion crouched. Back in the car, unfreezing himself from horror, the driver assured me that the lion had crouched in order to spring at me. I still have the photo: a lion crouching in tall grass – close up. I look at it and cannot make myself believe what could have happened.

I never wrote the story, although I still have the notes. Right here, in this leather portfolio which I take out of a drawer in my cupboard. My Africa story. I told it to him instead – and across the candlelit table of a Cairo restaurant he kissed my hands and said, 'I'm crazy about you.' Under the high windows the Nile flowed by. Eternity was in our lips, our eyes, our brows – I married him, and I was happy.

I leaf through my notes. Each one carries a comment, a description meant for him. All my thoughts were addressed to him. For his part he wrote that after I left him at the airport he turned round to hold me and tell me how desolate he felt. He could not believe I was not there to comfort him. He wrote about the sound of my voice on the telephone and the crease at the top of my arm that he said he loved to kiss.

What story can I write? I sit with my notes at my writing-table and wait for Lucy. I should have been sleeping. That is what they think I am doing. That is what we pretend I do: sleep away the hottest of the midday hours. Out there on the beach, by the pool, Lucy has no need of me. She has her father, her uncle, her two aunts, her five cousins; a wealth of playmates and protectors. And Um Sabir, sitting patient and watchful in her black *jalabiyyah* and *tarha*, the deck-chairs beside her loaded with towels, sun-cream, sun-hats, sandwiches and iced drinks in Thermos flasks.

I look, and watch, and wait for Lucy.

In the market in Kaduna the mottled, red carcasses lay on wooden stalls shaded by grey plastic canopies. At first I saw the meat and the flies swarming and settling. Then, on top of the grey plastic sheets, I saw the vultures. They perched as sparrows would in an English market square, but they were heavy and still and silent. They sat cool and unblinking as the fierce sun beat down on their bald, wrinkled heads. And hand in hand with the fear that swept over me was a realisation that fear was misplaced, that everybody else knew they were there and still went about their business; that in the meat-market in Kaduna, vultures were commonplace.

The heat of the sun saturates the house; it seeps out from every pore. I open the door of my room and walk out into the silent hall. In the bathroom I stand in the shower tray and turn the tap to let the cool water splash over my feet. I tuck my skirt between my thighs and bend to put my hands and wrists under the water. I press wet palms to my face and picture grey slate roofs wet with rain. I picture trees; trees that rustle in the wind and when the rain has stopped, release fresh showers of droplets from their leaves.

I pad out on wet feet that dry by the time I arrive at the kitchen at the end of the long corridor. I open the fridge and see the chunks of lamb marinading in a large metal tray for tonight's barbecue. The mountain of yellow grapes draining in a colander. I pick out a cluster and put it on a white saucer. Um Sabir washes all the fruit and vegetables in red permanganate. This is for my benefit since Lucy crunches cucumbers and carrots straight out of the greengrocer's baskets. But then she was born here. And now she belongs. If I had taken her away then, when she was eight months old, she would have belonged with me. I pour out a tall glass of cold, bottled water and close the fridge.

I walk back through the corridor. Past Um Sabir's room, his room, Lucy's room. Back in my room I stand again at the window, looking out through the chink in the shutters at the white that seems now to be losing the intensity of its glare. If I were to move to the window in the opposite wall I would see the green lawn encircled by the three wings of the house, the sprinkler at its centre ceaselessly twisting, twisting. I stand and press my forehead against the warm glass. I breathe on the window-pane but it does not mist over.

I turn on the fan. It blows my hair across my face and my notes across the bed. I kneel on the bed and gather them. The top one says, 'Ningi, his big teeth stained with Kola, sits grandly at his desk. By his right hand there is a bicycle bell which he rings to summon a gofer –', and then again: 'The three things we stop for on the road should be my title: "Peeing, Praying and Petrol".' Those were light-hearted times, when the jokes I made were not bitter.

I lie down on the bed. These four pillows are my innovation. Here they use one long pillow with two smaller ones on top of it. The bedlinen comes in sets. Consequently my bed always has two pillows in plain cases and two with embroidery to match the sheets. Also, I have one side of a chiffonier which is full of long, embroidered pillowcases. When I take them out and look at them I find their flowers, sheltered for so long in the dark, are unfaded, bright and new.

Lying on the bed, I hold the cluster of grapes above my face, and bite one off as Romans do in films. Oh, to play, to play again, but my only playmate now is Lucy and she is out by the pool with her cousins.

A few weeks ago, back in Cairo, Lucy looked up at the sky and said, 'I can see the place where we're going to be.'

'Where?' I asked, as we drove through Gabalaya Street.

'In heaven.'

'Oh!' I said. 'And what's it like?'

'It's a circle, Mama, and it has a chimney, and it will always be winter there.'

I reached over and patted her knee. 'Thank you, darling,' I said.

Yes, I am sick – but not just for home. I am sick for a time, a time that was and that I can never have again. A lover I had and can never have again.

I watched him vanish – well, not vanish, slip away, recede. He did not want to go. He did not go quietly. He asked me to hold him, but he couldn't tell me how. A fairy godmother, robbed for an instant of our belief in her magic, turns into a sad old woman, her wand into a useless stick. I suppose I should have seen it coming. My foreignness, which had been so charming, began to irritate him. My inability to remember names, to follow the minutiae of politics, my struggles with his language, my need to be protected from the sun, the mosquitoes, the salads, the drinking water. He was back home, and he needed someone he could be at home with, at home. It took perhaps a year. His heart was broken in two, mine was simply broken.

I never see my lover now. Sometimes, as he romps with Lucy on the beach, or bends over her grazed elbow, or sits across our long table from me at a dinner-party, I see a man I could yet fall in love with, and I turn away.

I told him too about my first mirage, the one I saw on that long road to Maiduguri. And on the desert road to Alexandria the first summer, I saw it again. 'It's hard to believe it isn't there when I can see it so clearly,' I complained.

'You only think you see it,' he said.

'Isn't that the same thing?' I asked. 'My brain tells me there's water there. Isn't that enough?'

'Yes,' he said, and shrugged. 'If all you want to do is sit in the car and see it. But if you want to go and put your hands in it and drink, then it isn't enough, surely?' He gave me a sidelong glance and smiled.

Soon, I should hear Lucy's high, clear voice, chattering to her father as they walk hand in hand up the gravel drive to the back door. Behind them will come the heavy tread of Um Sabir. I will go out smiling to meet them and he will deliver a wet, sandy Lucy into my care, and ask if I'm OK with a slightly anxious look. I will take Lucy into my bathroom while he goes into his. Later, when the rest of the family have all drifted back and showered and changed, everyone will sit around the barbecue and eat and drink and talk politics and crack jokes of hopeless, helpless irony and laugh. I should take up embroidery and start on those *Aubusson* tapestries we all, at the moment, imagine will be necessary for Lucy's trousseau.

Yesterday when I had dressed her after the shower she examined herself intently in my mirror and asked for a french plait. I sat behind her at the dressing-table blow-drying her black hair, brushing it and plaiting it. When Lucy was born Um Sabir covered all the mirrors. His sister said, 'They say if a baby looks in the mirror she will see her own grave.' We laughed but we did not remove the covers; they stayed in place till she was one.

I looked at Lucy's serious face in the mirror. I had seen my grave once, or thought I had. That was part of my Africa story. The plane out of Nigeria circled Cairo airport. Three times I heard the landing-gear come down, and three times it was raised again. Sitting next to me were two Finnish businessmen. When the announcement came that we were re-routing to Luxor they shook their heads and ordered another drink. At dawn, above Luxor airport, we were told there was trouble with the undercarriage and that the pilot was going to attempt a crash-landing. I thought, so this is why they've sent us to Luxor, to burn up discreetly and not clog Cairo airport. We were asked to fasten our seat belts, take off our shoes and watches, put the cushions from the backs of our seats on our laps and bend double over them with our arms around our heads. I slung my handbag with my passport, tickets and money around my neck and shoulder before I did these things. My Finnish neighbours formally shook each other's hands. On the plane there was perfect silence as we dropped out of the sky. And then a terrible, agonised, protracted screeching of machinery as we hit the tarmac. And in that moment, not only my head, but all of me, my whole being, seemed to tilt into a blank, an empty radiance, but lucid. Then three giant thoughts. One was of him – his name, over and over again. The other was of the children I would never have. The third was that the pattern was now complete: this is what my life amounted to.

When we did not die, that first thought: his name, his name, his name became a talisman, for in extremity, hadn't all that was not him been wiped out of my life? My life, which once again stretched out before me, shimmering with possibilities, was meant to merge with his.

I finished the french plait and Lucy chose a blue clasp to secure its end. Before I let her run out I smoothed some after-sun on her face. Her skin is nut-brown, except just next to her ears where it fades to a pale cream gleaming with golden down. I put my lips to her neck. 'My Lucy, Lucia, *Lambah*,' I murmured as I kissed her and let her go. Lucy. My treasure, my trap.

Now, when I walk to the sea, to the edge of this continent where I live, where I almost died, where I wait for my daughter to grow away from me, I see different things from those I saw that summer six years ago. The last of the foam is swallowed bubbling into the sand, to sink down and rejoin the sea at an invisible subterranean level. With each ebb of green water the sand loses part of itself to the sea, with each flow another part is flung back to be reclaimed once again by the beach. That narrow stretch of sand knows nothing in the world better than it does the white waves that whip it, caress it, collapse onto it, vanish into it. The white foam knows nothing better than those sands which wait for it, rise to it and suck it in. But what do the waves know of the massed, hot, still sands of the desert just twenty, no, ten feet beyond the scalloped edge? And what does the beach know of the depths, the cold, the currents just there, there – do you see it? – where the water turns a deeper blue.

43

Journey

(1995)

Shirley Geok-Lin Lim

Last night, she had dreamt she was shut away in a subterranean world; she had wandered in labyrinths of a thick brown claustrophobia. So dense was the air that her ears felt clogged with cotton-wool, and her feet trod slippery over ground strewn with skulls. This dense silence was her holding her breath, conscious of malevolent eyes in the darkness, watching. Skulls smiled without friendship, then began moving around her, in slow monotony, circling formally, one after the other, as in a ritual dance. She knew then that if she could not open her eyes she would never find her way back. She would have to stay in that labyrinthine world, separated from that breathing body which was hers, but which lay apart, secure in bed and lost. She tried to cry out. Only her mouth twisted soundlessly. She concentrated on opening her eyes, counting one two three, pitching her muscles for the effort, but it was a long time before she succeeded. Night was blacker than the dream twilight. It walled up and pressed into her eyes, a pleasant sensation recalling her from the trembling sweet terror into which she had tumbled.

Now she sat in the half-empty bus. It jolted to a halt at every stop, but no one got in, nor did anyone get off. She was caught up in its reckless rush as it butted stubbornly against the road curb, swung around corners with a wounded shriek, shaking its whole frame in a frenzy of movement, unthinking, self-absorbed, down the straight roads past the housing estates. On either side, the rows of houses started up, then fell back, enshrouded in the greying evening. Now they put on their lights, dusky yellow, blue and dim, smoky red, futile stabs in the twilight which invaded the interior of the bus with a deeper gloom. Stars and moon had not yet shown themselves, perhaps would not appear tonight. The passengers were as dull as the sky. Each sat shut in by whatever thoughts bred in his mind with the coming night, eyes marshalled inwards, only flickering to the doorway in anticipation at every violent thrust of the brakes. But no one passed through the doorway, either going down or coming up. The one woman appeared as well-worn as her *samfoo*, exhausted and faded by having had too many children, too much labour done, too many years lived. The collars of the men decapitated their heads from their shirts, so that they hung in the dusk, with cropped hair, thickened ears, dancing at every shudder of the engine. Only she defied the drab company in her bright uniform, fidgeting with her bag, gnawing her underlip, constantly peering out of the dusty window into the dustier evening to watch the roads whizz under.

She was glad to climb down from the bus, yet there was a curious uncertainty as to where she was to go, a strong reluctance to move away from the stand. She thought if she stood there long enough, the bus would surely return on its journey back and bring her home. She did not have to go anyway. Or she could take a walk, pretending she was going home to her family. There were numerous lanes branching off the little junction, numerous houses sitting under fat protective trees, hiding behind fences and shut gates. There was the pleasant joy of choosing your own little lane, your own snug house.

Still, she could not imagine herself belonging to any of these houses. Windows framed squares of light, curtains drawn to keep them in. Voices called out in a murmur of music. Sharp chinks of spoon against plate reminded her she had not eaten. In these houses were whole families unaware of her standing hungry, out in the dark. Whole families of mothers, fathers and children, living their daily meals and bedtime together, surrounded by their fenced-in gardens and their walls, unaware of her as much as though they and she were apart in separate worlds. She wondered whether her mother knew she was standing in front of these houses, and if she knew, whether she realised why and for what. It was not the same air she breathed in here, heavy with green smells of unknown shrubbery, delicate, sweet in her nostrils, fragrance of unseen flowers weighing their stems down and entwining their heads together in the night. The unfamiliar air as much as the disguising night made her, though she was uncertain whether it was so, or exactly why, frightened.

Her mother's instructions were clear enough, and from being so often repeated, familiar: Walk down the path to your right. Houses on either side touched up the dark with light and hummed with sound. Dogs within their fenced yards ran up and down, barking abuse. One stepped out of shadow but left her timid legs alone. Seventh house to the left. She did not know what she had expected. It was one with the others around it. The gate opened unhesitatingly at her push; the garden was trim with bougainvillea and smelt of leaves. Now she was here, it seemed she had always known it would look like this. An altar faced the open door, unlighted candles placed before the household god, an inscrutable figure who sat and watched the domestic goings-on, always to be placated, never to be pleased, awful Lord of the destiny of furniture, food and family. A gold dragon paced along the sketch of a wall, snaking sinuously on its red paper, agleam with shining scales. Its predatory jaws yawned in eternal pursuit; its talons fiercely rode the air untiringly. When a man emerged out of a darkened interior room, she was embarrased. There was the suggestion she had not been unexpected, yet he appeared ordinary, wiping his mouth with the back of his hand, the way her father did after a meal. She told him what it was she had come for. He offered her a seat and went back into the room from which he had come. She sat down on a seedy wooden stool, then got up almost immediately, disliking to be discovered sitting down, for it appeared irrevocable, as if she had come and meant to stay for a long time. She was very hungry and anxious about catching the bus home. The gold dragonish contours swirled in their red field, jumped in the light, receded again into the red. She was tired of standing before he returned with the parcel. He took the money she gave him disinterestedly, yet she thought his eyes rifled her clothes and she was glad to leave. The little parcel, wrapped roughly in brown paper and tied with a rubber-band, crackled under the pressure of her fingers. It felt of dry leaves and twigs which crumbled even as she held it gently. As she went home, carefully aware that this time directions were reversed, she amused herself wondering what potent magic the parcel contained.

Her mother had kept food for her. The rice was cold, but she had warmed the salty soup and fish for her so that she fell asleep contented. The baby boy was suffering from wind; eldest sister carried him in her arms, patting his back and crooning to him, '*Aii, aii*, go to sleep, little boy, *aii, aii*, little man, strong man, sleep . . .' She could hear her father in the next room with his friends, squatting on their chairs and throwing dice, now and again spitting out an expletive. On the other side of the room, the four boys lay on their mats, exhausted with their play in the streets, their arms and legs flung carelessly across each other. Next to her, Swee Lin slept, softly hiccuping in her sleep, crying even there; for she was second youngest, hardly three years old, and her mother had slapped her this evening. And their mother, strong big-boned mother who was not well and had taken those leaves and twigs and earth, medicine boiled into a black vile brew, lay scarcely a few feet away. She had joined the children after the last baby, and now even she could not remember when their mother had not slept with them. She was that presence in the night who had covered them with their blankets when rain pounded on the roof and hugged them when they started up from nightmares, whimpering. Her mother was not well, but she was strong and always there.

When she woke up, she lay quiet for a long while, wondering what it was that had wakened her. It was too dark to see. Only the deep breathing of her brothers and sisters told her she was not dreaming again. Even the fretful baby was quiet in his cloth-slung cradle. Her father in the next room snorted in his sleep. She thought of them, each wrapped in his cocoon of dream, while she alone lay awake, conscious of the dark passing night, yet there was something that woke her.

She sat up. It was her mother. She heard her sigh, a muffled sound, a body twisted against the matted floor. Her mother was not well. She did not understand why because she could not remember a time when this had happened. Now she was uncertain what to do.

'*Aiyaaa*,' her mother groaned softly. '*Aiyaaaa*.' The sounds of pain bewildered her. They stretched out for long minutes, hovered in the dark room, only to begin again. She heard her mother getting up slowly, the mat rustling under her feet, footsteps stumbling across the room into the kitchen. Frightened, she got to her feet and followed. The bathroom door stood open, her mother huddled on the floor, a dark shape moaning deeply to itself. She called out, whispered, uncertain whether she should put the lights on and unwilling to share the pain which light would reveal. Her mother only groaned, very softly, yet with such distance and intensity that its disguise in the dark frightened her beyond reluctance and she immediately switched on the lights. Dark messes were splattered on the floor, her mother's clothes were blood-red with a flow from some secret wound, while the woman herself squatted, eyes contracted, body rigid and contorted. She was frightened by what she saw. The blood seemed to gush from some fatal injury to the woman's flesh, this woman now unrecognisable as her mother, who groaned and clutched her side, writhing. She was repulsed by the pain and blood. They lay beyond her experience, yet some instinctive sympathy, a habit of sex, made her arms and legs move. Hot water from the baby's flask, warmed towel, hot thick sweet milk given to that body as it contracted and shuddered and held itself rigid as if to will the cessation of that hidden mysterious gush.

When finally the woman lay asleep, covered with two blankets, asleep in the exhausted peace of past pain and suffering, she still moved about the little kitchen, sluicing the blackened floor, scrubbing the clothes while they stained the icy water with a dark dye. As she squatted in the bathroom, pouring the black water away, scrubbing the cloth furiously, she felt the unexpected inversion. Her mother, that strong protective woman who had hugged her whenever she woke up from a nightmare. Tonight she was gone. She could not comfort her in this frightening thing she was doing, washing away the blackened blood in the black night. She had told her. What did it matter what she had told her? The dragon, the man's eyes, the dark road, what was it that had frightened her last night and all those other nights? As she scrubbed the cloth with soap and scrubbed it in water and poured away the black water she thought of her hands immersed in water; thought of the dye penetrating the pores of her skin and under her fingernails. She shuddered in the cold air, shuddered at the shock of cold water, and, shuddering as she washed, the girl cried.

44

The Third and Final Continent

(1999)

Jhumpa Lahiri

I left India in 1964 with a certificate in commerce and the equivalent, in those days, of ten dollars to my name. For three weeks I sailed on the SS *Roma*, an Italian cargo vessel, in a third-class cabin next to the ship's engine, across the Arabian Sea, the Red Sea, the Mediterranean, and finally to England. I lived in north London, in Finsbury Park, in a house occupied entirely by penniless Bengali bachelors like myself, at least a dozen and sometimes more, all struggling to educate and establish ourselves abroad.

I attended lectures at LSE and worked at the university library to get by. We lived three or four to a room, shared a single, icy toilet, and took turns cooking pots of egg curry, which we ate with our hands on a table covered with newspapers. Apart from our jobs we had few responsibilities. On weekends we lounged barefoot in drawstring pajamas, drinking tea and smoking Rothmans, or set out to watch cricket at Lord's. Some weekends the house was crammed with still more Bengalis, to whom we had introduced ourselves at the greengrocer, or on the Tube, and we made yet more egg curry, and played Mukhesh on a Grundig reel-to-reel, and soaked our dirty dishes in the bathtub. Every now and then someone in the house moved out, to live with a woman whom his family back in Calcutta had determined he was to wed. In 1969, when I was thirty-six years old, my own marriage was arranged. Around the same time I was offered a full-time job in America, in the processing department of a library at MIT. The salary was generous enough to support a wife, and I was honored to be hired by a world-famous university, and so I obtained a sixth-preference green card, and prepared to travel farther still.

By now I had enough money to go by plane. I flew first to Calcutta, to attend my wedding, and a week later I flew to Boston, to begin my new job. During the flight I read *The Student Guide to North America*, a paperback volume that I'd bought before leaving London, for seven shillings six pence on Tottenham Court Road, for although I was no longer a student I was on a budget all the same. I learned that Americans drove on the right side of the road, not the left, and that they called a lift an elevator and an engaged phone busy. 'The pace of life in North America is different from Britain as you will soon discover,' the guidebook informed me. 'Everybody feels he must get to the top. Don't expect an English cup of tea.' As the plane began its descent over Boston Harbor, the pilot announced the weather and time, and that President Nixon had declared a national holiday: two American men had landed on the moon. Several passengers cheered. 'God bless America!' one of them hollered. Across the aisle, I saw a woman praying.

I spent my first night at the YMCA in Central Square, Cambridge, an inexpensive accommodation recommended by my guidebook. It was walking distance from MIT, and steps from the post office and a supermarket called Purity Supreme. The room contained a cot, a desk, and a small wooden cross on one wall. A sign on the door said cooking was strictly forbidden. A bare window overlooked Massachusetts Avenue, a major thoroughfare with traffic in both directions. Car horns, shrill and prolonged, blared one after another. Flashing sirens heralded endless emergencies, and a fleet of buses rumbled past, their doors opening and closing with a powerful hiss, throughout the night. The noise was constantly distracting, at times suffocating. I felt it deep in my ribs, just as I had felt the furious drone of the engine on the SS *Roma.* But there was no ship's deck to escape to, no glittering ocean to thrill my soul, no breeze to cool my face, no one to talk to. I was too tired to pace the gloomy corridors of the YMCA in my drawstring pajamas. Instead I sat at the desk and stared out the window, at the city hall of Cambridge and a row of small shops. In the morning I reported to my job at the Dewey Library, a beige fortlike building by Memorial Drive. I also opened a bank account, rented a post office box, and bought a plastic bowl and a spoon at Woolworth's, a store whose name I recognised from London. I went to Purity Supreme, wandering up and down the aisles, converting ounces to grams and comparing prices to things in England. In the end I bought a small carton of milk and a box of cornflakes. This was my first meal in America. I ate it at my desk. I preferred it to hamburgers or hot dogs, the only alternative I could afford in the coffee shops on Massachusetts Avenue, and, besides, at the time I had yet to consume any beef. Even the simple chore of buying milk was new to me; in London we'd had bottles delivered each morning to our door.

In a week I had adjusted, more or less. I ate cornflakes and milk, morning and night, and bought some bananas for variety, slicing them into the bowl with the edge of my spoon. In addition I bought tea bags and a flask, which the salesman in Woolworth's referred to as a thermos (a flask, he informed me, was used to store whiskey, another thing I had never consumed). For the price of one cup of tea at a coffee shop, I filled the flask with boiling water on my way to work each morning, and brewed the four cups I drank in the course of a day. I bought a larger carton of milk, and learned to leave it on the shaded part of the windowsill, as I had seen another resident at the YMCA do. To pass the time in the evenings I read the *Boston Globe* downstairs, in a spacious room with stained-glass windows. I read every article and advertisement, so that I would grow familiar with things, and when my eyes grew tired I slept. Only I did not sleep well. Each night I had to keep the window wide open; it was the only source of air in the stifling room, and the noise was intolerable. I would lie on the cot with my fingers pressed into my ears, but when I drifted off to sleep my hands fell away, and the noise of the traffic would wake me up again. Pigeon feathers drifted onto the windowsill, and one evening, when I poured milk over my cornflakes, I saw that it had soured. Nevertheless I resolved to stay at the YMCA for six weeks, until my wife's passport and green card were ready. Once she arrived I would have to rent a proper apartment, and from time to time I studied the classified section of the newspaper, or stopped in at the housing office at MIT during my lunch break, to see what was available in my price range. It was in this manner that I discovered a room for immediate occupancy, in a house on a quiet street, the listing said, for eight dollars per week. I copied the number into my guidebook and dialed from a pay telephone, sorting through the coins with which I was still unfamiliar, smaller and lighter than shillings, heavier and brighter than *paisas.*

'Who is speaking?' a woman demanded. Her voice was bold and clamorous.

'Yes, good afternoon, madame. I am calling about the room for rent.'

'Harvard or Tech?'

'I beg your pardon?'

'Are you from Harvard or Tech?'

Gathering that Tech referred to the Massachusetts Institute of Technology, I replied, 'I work at Dewey Library,' adding tentatively, 'at Tech.'

'I only rent rooms to boys from Harvard or Tech!'

'Yes, madame.'

I was given an address and an appointment for seven o'clock that evening. Thirty minutes before the hour I set out, my guidebook in my pocket, my breath fresh with Listerine. I turned down a street shaded with trees, perpendicular to Massachusetts Avenue. Stray blades of grass poked between the cracks of the footpath. In spite of the heat I wore a coat and a tie, regarding the event as I would any other interview; I had never lived in the home of a person who was not Indian. The house, surrounded by a chain-link fence, was off-white with dark brown trim. Unlike the stucco row house I'd lived in in London, this house, fully detached, was covered with wooden shingles, with a tangle of forsythia bushes plastered against the front and sides. When I pressed the calling bell, the woman with whom I had spoken on the phone hollered from what seemed to be just the other side of the door, 'One minute, please!'

Several minutes later the door was opened by a tiny, extremely old woman. A mass of snowy hair was arranged like a small sack on top of her head. As I stepped into the house she sat down on a wooden bench positioned at the bottom of a narrow carpeted staircase. Once she was settled on the bench, in a small pool of light, she peered up at me with undivided attention. She wore a long black skirt that spread like a stiff tent to the floor, and a starched white shirt edged with ruffles at the throat and cuffs. Her hands, folded together in her lap, had long pallid fingers, with swollen knuckles and tough yellow nails. Age had battered her features so that she almost resembled a man, with sharp, shrunken eyes and prominent creases on either side of her nose. Her lips, chapped and faded, had nearly disappeared, and her eyebrows were missing altogether. Nevertheless she looked fierce.

'Lock up!' she commanded. She shouted even though I stood only a few feet away. 'Fasten the chain and firmly press that button on the knob! This is the first thing you shall do when you enter, is that clear?'

I locked the door as directed and examined the house. Next to the bench on which the woman sat was a small round table, its legs fully concealed, much like the woman's, by a skirt of lace. The table held a lamp, a transistor radio, a leather change purse with a silver clasp, and a telephone. A thick wooden cane coated with a layer of dust was propped against one side. There was a parlor to my right, lined with bookcases and filled with shabby claw-footed furniture. In the corner of the parlor I saw a grand piano with its top down, piled with papers. The piano's bench was missing; it seemed to be the one on which the woman was sitting. Somewhere in the house a clock chimed seven times.

'You're punctual!' the woman proclaimed. 'I expect you shall be so with the rent!'

'I have a letter, madame.' In my jacket pocket was a letter confirming my employment from MIT, which I had brought along to prove that I was indeed from Tech.

She stared at the letter, then handed it back to me carefully, gripping it with her fingers as if it were a dinner plate heaped with food instead of a sheet of paper. She did not wear glasses, and I wondered if she'd read a word of it. 'The last boy was always late! Still owes me eight dollars! Harvard boys aren't what they used to be! Only Harvard and Tech in this house! How's Tech, boy?'

'It is very well.'

'You checked the lock?'

'Yes, madame.'

She slapped the space beside her on the bench with one hand, and told me to sit down. For a moment she was silent. Then she intoned, as if she alone possessed this knowledge:

'There is an American flag on the moon!'

'Yes, madame.' Until then I had not thought very much about the moon shot. It was in the newspaper, of course, article upon article. The astronauts had landed on the shores of the Sea of Tranquillity, I had read, traveling farther than anyone in the history of civilisation. For a few hours they explored the moon's surface. They gathered rocks in their pockets, described their surroundings (a magnificent desolation, according to one astronaut), spoke by phone to the president, and planted a flag in lunar soil. The voyage was hailed as man's most awesome achievement. I had seen full-page photographs in the *Globe*, of the astronauts in their inflated costumes, and read about what certain people in Boston had been doing at the exact moment the astronauts landed, on a Sunday afternoon. A man said that he was operating a swan boat with a radio pressed to his ear; a woman had been baking rolls for her grandchildren.

The woman bellowed, 'A flag on the moon, boy! I heard it on the radio! Isn't that splendid?'

'Yes, madame.'

But she was not satisfied with my reply. Instead she commanded, 'Say "splendid"!'

I was both baffled and somewhat insulted by the request. It reminded me of the way I was taught multiplication tables as a child, repeating after the master, sitting cross-legged, without shoes or pencils, on the floor of my one-room Tollygunge school. It also reminded me of my wedding, when I had repeated endless Sanskrit verses after the priest, verses I barely understood, which joined me to my wife. I said nothing.

'Say "splendid"!' the woman bellowed once again.

'Splendid,' I murmured. I had to repeat the word a second time at the top of my lungs, so she could hear. I am soft-spoken by nature and was especially reluctant to raise my voice to an elderly woman whom I had met only moments ago, but she did not appear to be offended. If anything the reply pleased her because her next command was:

'Go see the room!'

I rose from the bench and mounted the narrow carpeted staircase. There were five doors, two on either side of an equally narrow hallway, and one at the opposite end. Only one door was partly open. The room contained a twin bed under a sloping ceiling, a brown oval rug, a basin with an exposed pipe, and a chest of drawers. One door, painted white, led to a closet, another to a toilet and a tub. The walls were covered with gray and ivory striped paper. The window was open; net curtains stirred in the breeze. I lifted them away and inspected the view: a small back yard, with a few fruit trees and an empty clothesline. I was satisfied. From the bottom of the stairs I heard the woman demand, 'What is your decision?'

When I returned to the foyer and told her, she picked up the leather change purse on the table, opened the clasp, fished about with her fingers, and produced a key on a thin wire hoop. She informed me that there was a kitchen at the back of the house, accessible through the parlor. I was welcome to use the stove as long as I left it as I found it. Sheets and towels were provided, but keeping them clean was my own responsibility. The rent was due Friday mornings on the ledge above the piano keys. 'And no lady visitors!'

'I am a married man, madame.' It was the first time I had announced this fact to anyone.

But she had not heard. 'No lady visitors!' she insisted. She introduced herself as Mrs Croft.

My wife's name was Mala. The marriage had been arranged by my older brother and his wife. I regarded the proposition with neither objection nor enthusiasm. It was a duty expected of me, as it was expected of every man. She was the daughter of a schoolteacher in Beleghata. I was told that she could cook, knit, embroider, sketch landscapes, and recite poems by Tagore, but these talents could not make up for the fact that she did not possess a fair complexion, and so a string of men had rejected her to her face. She was twenty-seven, an age when her parents had begun to fear that she would never marry, and so they were willing to ship their only child halfway across the world in order to save her from spinsterhood.

For five nights we shared a bed. Each of those nights, after applying cold cream and braiding her hair, which she tied up at the end with a black cotton string, she turned from me and wept; she missed her parents. Although I would be leaving the country in a few days, custom dictated that she was now a part of my household, and for the next six weeks she was to live with my brother and his wife, cooking, cleaning, serving tea and sweets to guests. I did nothing to console her. I lay on my own side of the bed, reading my guidebook by flashlight and anticipating my journey. At times I thought of the tiny room on the other side of the wall which had belonged to my mother. Now the room was practically empty; the wooden pallet on which she'd once slept was piled with trunks and old bedding. Nearly six years ago, before leaving for London, I had watched her die on that bed, had found her playing with her excrement in her final days. Before we cremated her I had cleaned each of her fingernails with a hairpin, and then, because my brother could not bear it, I had assumed the role of eldest son, and had touched the flame to her temple, to release her tormented soul to heaven.

The next morning I moved into the room in Mrs Croft's house. When I unlocked the door I saw that she was sitting on the piano bench, on the same side as the previous evening. She wore the same black skirt, the same starched white blouse, and had her hands folded together the same way in her lap. She looked so much the same that I wondered if she'd spent the whole night on the bench. I put my suitcase upstairs, filled my flask with boiling water in the kitchen, and headed off to work. That evening when I came home from the university, she was still there.

'Sit down, boy!' She slapped the space beside her.

I perched beside her on the bench. I had a bag of groceries with me – more milk, more cornflakes, and more bananas, for my inspection of the kitchen earlier in the day had revealed no spare pots, pans, or cooking utensils. There were only two saucepans in the refrigerator, both containing some orange broth, and a copper kettle on the stove.

'Good evening, madame.'

She asked me if I had checked the lock. I told her I had.

For a moment she was silent. Then suddenly she declared, with the equal measures of disbelief and delight as the night before, 'There's an American flag on the moon, boy!'

'Yes, madame.'

'A flag on the moon! Isn't that splendid?'

I nodded, dreading what I knew was coming. 'Yes, madame.'

'Say "splendid"!'

This time I paused, looking to either side in case anyone were there to overhear me, though I knew perfectly well that the house was empty. I felt like an idiot. But it was a small enough thing to ask. 'Splendid!' I cried out.

Within days it became our routine. In the mornings when I left for the library Mrs Croft was either hidden away in her bedroom, on the other side of the staircase, or she was sitting on the bench, oblivious to my presence, listening to the news or classical music on the radio. But each evening when I returned the same thing happened: she slapped the bench, ordered me to sit down, declared that there was a flag on the moon, and declared that it was splendid. I said it was splendid, too, and then we sat in silence. As awkward as it was, and as endless as it felt to me then, the nightly encounter lasted only about ten minutes; inevitably she would drift off to sleep, her head falling abruptly toward her chest, leaving me free to retire to my room. By then, of course, there was no flag on the moon. The astronauts, I had read in the paper, had taken it down before flying back to Earth. But I did not have the heart to tell her.

Friday morning, when my first week's rent was due, I went to the piano in the parlor to place my money on the ledge. The piano keys were dull and discolored. When I pressed one, it made no sound at all. I had put eight one-dollar bills in an envelope and written Mrs Croft's name on the front of it. I was not in the habit of leaving money unmarked and unattended. From where I stood I could see the profile of her tent-shaped skirt. She was sitting on the bench, listening to the radio. It seemed unnecessary to make her get up and walk all the way to the piano. I never saw her walking about, and assumed, from the cane always propped against the round table at her side, that she did so with difficulty. When I approached the bench she peered up at me and demanded:

'What is your business?'

'The rent, madame.'

'On the ledge above the piano keys!'

'I have it here.' I extended the envelope toward her, but her fingers, folded together in her lap, did not budge. I bowed slightly and lowered the envelope, so that it hovered just above her hands. After a moment she accepted, and nodded her head.

That night when I came home, she did not slap the bench, but out of habit I sat beside her as usual. She asked me if I had checked the lock, but she mentioned nothing about the flag on the moon. Instead she said:

'It was very kind of you!'

'I beg your pardon, madame?'

'Very kind of you!'

She was still holding the envelope in her hands.

On Sunday there was a knock on my door. An elderly woman introduced herself: she was Mrs Croft's daughter, Helen. She walked into the room and looked at each of the walls as if for signs of change, glancing at the shirts that hung in the closet, the neckties draped over the doorknob, the box of cornflakes on the chest of drawers, the dirty bowl and spoon in the basin. She was short and thick-waisted, with cropped silver hair and bright pink lipstick. She wore a sleeveless summer dress, a row of white plastic beads, and spectacles on a chain that hung like a swing against her chest. The backs of her legs were mapped with dark blue veins, and her upper arms sagged like the flesh of a roasted eggplant. She told me she lived in Arlington, a town farther up Massachusetts Avenue. 'I come once a week to bring Mother groceries. Has she sent you packing yet?'

'It is very well, madame.'

'Some of the boys run screaming. But I think she likes you. You're the first boarder she's ever referred to as a gentleman.'

'Not at all, madame.'

She looked at me, noticing my bare feet (I still felt strange wearing shoes indoors, and always removed them before entering my room). 'Are you new to Boston?'

'New to America, madame.'

'From?' She raised her eyebrows.

'I am from Calcutta, India.'

'Is that right? We had a Brazilian fellow, about a year ago. You'll find Cambridge a very international city.'

I nodded, and began to wonder how long our conversation would last. But at that moment we heard Mrs Croft's electrifying voice rising up the stairs. When we stepped into the hallway we heard her hollering:

'You are to come downstairs immediately!'

'What is it?' Helen hollered back.

'Immediately!'

I put on my shoes at once. Helen sighed.

We walked down the staircase. It was too narrow for us to descend side by side, so I followed Helen, who seemed to be in no hurry, and complained at one point that she had a bad knee. 'Have you been walking without your cane?' Helen called out. 'You know you're not supposed to walk without that cane.' She paused, resting her hand on the banister, and looked back at me. 'She slips sometimes.'

For the first time Mrs Croft seemed vulnerable. I pictured her on the floor in front of the bench, flat on her back, staring at the ceiling, her feet pointing in opposite directions. But when we reached the bottom of the staircase she was sitting there as usual, her hands folded together in her lap. Two grocery bags were at her feet. When we stood before her she did not slap the bench, or ask us to sit down. She glared.

'What is it, Mother?'

'It's improper!'

'What's improper?'

'It is improper for a lady and gentleman who are not married to one another to hold a private conversation without a chaperone!'

Helen said she was sixty-eight years old, old enough to be my mother, but Mrs Croft insisted that Helen and I speak to each other downstairs, in the parlor. She added that it was also improper for a lady of Helen's station to reveal her age, and to wear a dress so high above the ankle.

'For your information, Mother, it's 1969. What would you do if you actually left the house one day and saw a girl in a miniskirt?'

Mrs Croft sniffed. 'I'd have her arrested.'

Helen shook her head and picked up one of the grocery bags. I picked up the other one, and followed her through the parlor and into the kitchen. The bags were filled with cans of soup, which Helen opened up one by one with a few cranks of a can opener. She tossed the old soup in the saucepans into the sink, rinsed the pans under the tap, filled them with soup from the newly opened cans, and put them back in the refrigerator. 'A few years ago she could still open the cans herself,' Helen said. 'She hates that I do it for her now. But the piano killed her hands.' She put on her spectacles, glanced at the cupboards, and spotted my tea bags. 'Shall we have a cup?'

I filled the kettle on the stove. 'I beg your pardon, madame. The piano?'

'She used to give lessons. For forty years. It was how she raised us after my father died.' Helen put her hands on her hips, staring at the open refrigerator. She reached into the back, pulled out a wrapped stick of butter, frowned, and tossed it into the garbage. 'That ought to do it,' she said, and put the unopened cans of soup in the cupboard. I sat at the table and watched as Helen washed the dirty dishes, tied up the garbage bag, watered a spider plant over the sink, and poured boiling water into two cups. She handed one to me without milk, the string of the tea bag trailing over the side, and sat down at the table.

'Excuse me, madame, but is it enough?'

Helen took a sip of her tea. Her lipstick left a smiling pink stain on the inside rim of the cup. 'Is what enough?'

'The soup in the pans. Is it enough food for Mrs Croft?'

'She won't eat anything else. She stopped eating solids after she turned one hundred. That was, let's see, three years ago.'

I was mortified. I had assumed Mrs Croft was in her eighties, perhaps as old as ninety. I had never known a person who had lived for over a century. That this person was a widow who lived alone mortified me further still. It was widowhood that had driven my own mother insane. My father, who worked as a clerk at the General Post Office of Calcutta, died of encephalitis when I was sixteen. My mother refused to adjust to life without him; instead she sank deeper into a world of darkness from which neither I, nor my brother, nor concerned relatives, nor psychiatric clinics on Rashbihari Avenue could save her. What pained me most was to see her so unguarded, to hear her burp after meals or expel gas in front of company without the slightest embarrassment. After my father's death my brother abandoned his schooling and began to work in the jute mill he would eventually manage, in order to keep the household running. And so it was my job to sit by my mother's feet and study for my exams as she counted and recounted the bracelets on her arm as if they were the beads of an abacus. We tried to keep an eye on her. Once she had wandered half naked to the tram depot before we were able to bring her inside again.

'I am happy to warm Mrs Croft's soup in the evenings,' I suggested, removing the tea bag from my cup and squeezing out the liquor. 'It is no trouble.'

Helen looked at her watch, stood up, and poured the rest of her tea into the sink. 'I wouldn't if I were you. That's the sort of thing that would kill her altogether.'

That evening, when Helen had gone back to Arlington and Mrs Croft and I were alone again, I began to worry. Now that I knew how very old she was, I worried that something would happen to her in the middle of the night, or when I was out during the day. As vigorous as her voice was, and imperious as she seemed, I knew that even a scratch or a cough could kill a person that old; each day she lived, I knew, was something of a miracle. Although Helen had seemed friendly enough, a small part of me worried that she might accuse me of negligence if anything were to happen. Helen didn't seem worried. She came and went, bringing soup for Mrs Croft, one Sunday after the next.

In this manner the six weeks of that summer passed. I came home each evening, after my hours at the library, and spent a few minutes on the piano bench with Mrs Croft. I gave her a bit of my company, and assured her that I had checked the lock, and told her that the flag on the moon was splendid. Some evenings I sat beside her long after she had drifted off to sleep, still in awe of how many years she had spent on this earth. At times I tried to picture the world she had been born into, in 1866 – a world, I imagined, filled with women in long black skirts, and chaste conversations in the parlor. Now, when I looked at her hands with their swollen knuckles folded together in her lap, I imagined them smooth and slim, striking the piano keys. At times I came downstairs before going to sleep, to make sure she was sitting upright on the bench, or was safe in her bedroom. On Fridays I made sure to put the rent in her hands. There was nothing I could do for her beyond these simple gestures. I was not her son, and apart from those eight dollars, I owed her nothing.

At the end of August, Mala's passport and green card were ready. I received a telegram with her flight information; my brother's house in Calcutta had no telephone. Around that time I also received a letter from her, written only a few days after we had parted. There was no salutation; addressing me by name would have assumed an intimacy we had not yet discovered. It contained only a few lines. 'I write in English in preparation for the journey. Here I am very much lonely. Is it very cold there. Is there snow. Yours, Mala.'

I was not touched by her words. We had spent only a handful of days in each other's company. And yet we were bound together; for six weeks she had worn an iron bangle on her wrist, and applied vermilion powder to the part in her hair, to signify to the world that she was a bride. In those six weeks I regarded her arrival as I would the arrival of a coming month, or season – something inevitable, but meaningless at the time. So little did I know her that, while details of her face sometimes rose to my memory, I could not conjure up the whole of it.

A few days after receiving the letter, as I was walking to work in the morning, I saw an Indian woman on the other side of Massachusetts Avenue, wearing a sari with its free end nearly dragging on the footpath, and pushing a child in a stroller. An American woman with a small black dog on a leash was walking to one side of her. Suddenly the dog began barking. From the other side of the street I watched as the Indian woman, startled, stopped in her path, at which point the dog leapt up and seized the end of the sari between its teeth. The American woman scolded the dog, appeared to apologise, and walked quickly away, leaving the Indian woman to fix her sari in the middle of the footpath, and quiet her crying child. She did not see me standing there, and eventually she continued on her way. Such a mishap, I realised that morning, would soon be my concern. It was my duty to take care of Mala, to welcome her and protect her. I would have to buy her her first pair of snow boots, her first winter coat. I would have to tell her which streets to avoid, which way the traffic came, tell her to wear her sari so that the free end did not drag on the footpath. A five-mile separation from her parents, I recalled with some irritation, had caused her to weep.

Unlike Mala, I was used to it all by then: used to cornflakes and milk, used to Helen's visits, used to sitting on the bench with Mrs Croft. The only thing I was not used to was Mala. Nevertheless I did what I had to do. I went to the housing office at MIT and found a furnished apartment a few blocks away, with a double bed and a private kitchen and bath, for forty dollars a week. One last Friday I handed Mrs Croft eight one-dollar bills in an envelope, brought my suitcase downstairs, and informed her that I was moving. She put my key into her change purse. The last thing she asked me to do was hand her the cane propped against the table, so that she could walk to the door and lock it behind me. 'Good-bye, then,' she said, and retreated back into the house. I did not expect any display of emotion, but I was disappointed all the same. I was only a boarder, a man who paid her a bit of money and passed in and out of her home for six weeks. Compared to a century, it was no time at all.

At the airport I recognised Mala immediately. The free end of her sari did not drag on the floor, but was draped in a sign of bridal modesty over her head, just as it had draped my mother until the day my father died. Her thin brown arms were stacked with gold bracelets, a small red circle was painted on her forehead, and the edges of her feet were tinted with a decorative red dye. I did not embrace her, or kiss her, or take her hand. Instead I asked her, speaking Bengali for the first time in America, if she was hungry.

She hesitated, then nodded yes.

I told her I had prepared some egg curry at home. 'What did they give you to eat on the plane?'

'I didn't eat.'

'All the way from Calcutta?'

'The menu said oxtail soup.'

'But surely there were other items.'

'The thought of eating an ox's tail made me lose my appetite.'

When we arrived home, Mala opened up one of her suitcases, and presented me with two pullover sweaters, both made with bright blue wool, which she had knitted in the course of our separation, one with a V neck, the other covered with cables. I tried them on; both were tight under the arms. She had also brought me two new pairs of drawstring pajamas, a letter from my brother, and a packet of loose Darjeeling tea. I had no present for her apart from the egg curry. We sat at a bare table, each of us staring at our plates. We ate with our hands, another thing I had not yet done in America.

'The house is nice,' she said. 'Also the egg curry.' With her left hand she held the end of her sari to her chest, so it would not slip off her head.

'I don't know many recipes.'

She nodded, peeling the skin off each of her potatoes before eating them. At one point the sari slipped to her shoulders. She readjusted it at once.

'There is no need to cover your head,' I said. 'I don't mind. It doesn't matter here.'

She kept it covered anyway.

I waited to get used to her, to her presence at my side, at my table and in my bed, but a week later we were still strangers. I still was not used to coming home to an apartment that smelled of steamed rice, and finding that the basin in the bathroom was always wiped clean, our two toothbrushes lying side by side, a cake of Pears soap from India resting in the soap dish. I was not used to the fragrance of the coconut oil she rubbed every other night into her scalp, or the delicate sound her bracelets made as she moved about the apartment. In the mornings she was always awake before I was. The first morning when I came into the kitchen she had heated up the leftovers and set a plate with a spoonful of salt on its edge on the table, assuming I would eat rice for breakfast, as most Bengali husbands did. I told her cereal would do, and the next morning when I came into the kitchen she had already poured the cornflakes into my bowl. One morning she walked with me down Massachusetts Avenue to MIT, where I gave her a short tour of the campus. On the way we stopped at a hardware store and I made a copy of the key, so that she could let herself into the apartment. The next morning before I left for work she asked me for a few dollars. I parted with them reluctantly, but I knew that this, too, was now normal. When I came home from work there was a potato peeler in the kitchen drawer, and a tablecloth on the table, and chicken curry made with fresh garlic and ginger on the stove. We did not have a television in those days. After dinner I read the newspaper, while Mala sat at the kitchen table, working on a cardigan for herself with more of the bright blue wool, or writing letters home.

At the end of our first week, on Friday, I suggested going out. Mala set down her knitting and disappeared into the bathroom. When she emerged I regretted the suggestion; she had put on a clean silk sari and extra bracelets, and coiled her hair with a flattering side part on top of her head. She was prepared as if for a party, or at the very least for the cinema, but I had no such destination in mind. The evening air was balmy. We walked several blocks down Massachusetts Avenue, looking into the windows of restaurants and shops. Then, without thinking, I led her down the quiet street where for so many nights I had walked alone.

'This is where I lived before you came,' I said, stopping at Mrs Croft's chain-link fence.

'In such a big house?'

'I had a small room upstairs. At the back.'

'Who else lives there?'

'A very old woman.'

'With her family?'

'Alone.'

'But who takes care of her?'

I opened the gate. 'For the most part she takes care of herself.'

I wondered if Mrs Croft would remember me; I wondered if she had a new boarder to sit with her on the bench each evening. When I pressed the bell I expected the same long wait as that day of our first meeting, when I did not have a key. But this time the door was opened almost immediately, by Helen. Mrs Croft was not sitting on the bench. The bench was gone.

'Hello there,' Helen said, smiling with her bright pink lips at Mala. 'Mother's in the parlor. Will you be visiting awhile?'

'As you wish, madame.'

'Then I think I'll run to the store, if you don't mind. She had a little accident. We can't leave her alone these days, not even for a minute.'

I locked the door after Helen and walked into the parlor. Mrs Croft was lying flat on her back, her head on a peach-colored cushion, a thin white quilt spread over her body. Her hands were folded together on top of her chest. When she saw me she pointed at the sofa, and told me to sit down. I took my place as directed, but Mala wandered over to the piano and sat on the bench, which was now positioned where it belonged.

'I broke my hip!' Mrs Croft announced, as if no time had passed.

'Oh dear, madame.'

'I fell off the bench!'

'I am so sorry, madame.'

'It was the middle of the night! Do you know what I did, boy?'

I shook my head.

'I called the police!'

She stared up at the ceiling and grinned sedately, exposing a crowded row of long gray teeth. Not one was missing. 'What do you say to that, boy?'

As stunned as I was, I knew what I had to say. With no hesitation at all, I cried out, 'Splendid!'

Mala laughed then. Her voice was full of kindness, her eyes bright with amusement. I had never heard her laugh before, and it was loud enough so that Mrs Croft had heard, too. She turned to Mala and glared.

'Who is she, boy?'

'She is my wife, madame.'

Mrs Croft pressed her head at an angle against the cushion to get a better look. 'Can you play the piano?'

'No, madame,' Mala replied.

'Then stand up!'

Mala rose to her feet, adjusting the end of her sari over her head and holding it to her chest, and, for the first time since her arrival, I felt sympathy. I remembered my first days in London, learning how to take the Tube to Russell Square, riding an escalator for the first time, being unable to understand that when the man cried 'piper' it meant 'paper', being unable to decipher, for a whole year, that the conductor said 'mind the gap' as the train pulled away from each station. Like me, Mala had traveled far from home, not knowing where she was going, or what she would find, for no reason other than to be my wife. As strange as it seemed, I knew in my heart that one day her death would affect me, and stranger still, that mine would affect her. I wanted somehow to explain this to Mrs Croft, who was still scrutinising Mala from top to toe with what seemed to be placid disdain. I wondered if Mrs Croft had ever seen a woman in a sari, with a dot painted on her forehead and bracelets stacked on her wrists. I wondered what she would object to. I wondered if she could see the red dye still vivid on Mala's feet, all but obscured by the bottom edge of her sari. At last Mrs Croft declared, with the equal measures of disbelief and delight I knew well:

'She is a perfect lady!'

Now it was I who laughed. I did so quietly, and Mrs Croft did not hear me. But Mala had heard, and, for the first time, we looked at each other and smiled.

*

I like to think of that moment in Mrs Croft's parlor as the moment when the distance between Mala and me began to lessen. Although we were not yet fully in love, I like to think of the months that followed as a honeymoon of sorts. Together we explored the city and met other Bengalis, some of whom are still friends today. We discovered that a man named Bill sold fresh fish on Prospect Street, and that a shop in Harvard Square called Cardullo's sold bay leaves and cloves. In the evenings we walked to the Charles River to watch sailboats drift across the water, or had ice cream cones in Harvard Yard. We bought an Instamatic camera with which to document our life together, and I took pictures of her posing in front of the Prudential building, so that she could send them to her parents. At night we kissed, shy at first but quickly bold, and discovered pleasure and solace in each other's arms. I told her about my voyage on the SS *Roma*, and about Finsbury Park and the YMCA, and my evenings on the bench with Mrs Croft. When I told her stories about my mother, she wept. It was Mala who consoled me when, reading the *Globe* one evening, I came across Mrs Croft's obituary. I had not thought of her in several months – by then those six weeks of the summer were already a remote interlude in my past – but when I learned of her death I was stricken, so much so that when Mala looked up from her knitting she found me staring at the wall, the newspaper neglected in my lap, unable to speak. Mrs Croft's was the first death I mourned in America, for hers was the first life I had admired; she had left this world at last, ancient and alone, never to return.

As for me, I have not strayed much farther. Mala and I live in a town about twenty miles from Boston, on a tree-lined street much like Mrs Croft's, in a house we own, with a garden that saves us from buying tomatoes in summer, and room for guests. We are American citizens now, so that we can collect social security when it is time. Though we visit Calcutta every few years, and bring back more drawstring pajamas and Darjeeling tea, we have decided to grow old here. I work in a small college library. We have a son who attends Harvard University. Mala no longer drapes the end of her sari over her head, or weeps at night for her parents, but occasionally she weeps for our son. So we drive to Cambridge to visit him, or bring him home for a weekend, so that he can eat rice with us with his hands, and speak in Bengali, things we sometimes worry he will no longer do after we die.

Whenever we make that drive, I always make it a point to take Massachusetts Avenue, in spite of the traffic. I barely recognise the buildings now, but each time I am there I return instantly to those six weeks as if they were only the other day, and I slow down and point to Mrs Croft's street, saying to my son, here was my first home in America, where I lived with a woman who was 103. 'Remember?' Mala says, and smiles, amazed, as I am, that there was ever a time that we were strangers. My son always expresses his astonishment, not at Mrs Croft's age, but at how little I paid in rent, a fact nearly as inconceivable to him as a flag on the moon was to a woman born in 1866. In my son's eyes I see the ambition that had first hurled me across the world. In a few years he will graduate and pave his way, alone and unprotected. But I remind myself that he has a father who is still living, a mother who is happy and strong. Whenever he is discouraged, I tell him that if I can survive on three continents, then there is no obstacle he cannot conquer. While the astronauts, heroes forever, spent mere hours on the moon, I have remained in this new world for nearly thirty years. I know that my achievement is quite ordinary. I am not the only man to seek his fortune far from home, and certainly I am not the first. Still, there are times I am bewildered by each mile I have traveled, each meal I have eaten, each person I have known, each room in which I have slept. As ordinary as it all appears, there are times when it is beyond my imagination.

45

Tyres

(2000)

Adam Thorpe

My father started the business in 1925, the year of my birth. It was a good business: roads were rough and tyres were punished. In those days, there was the inner tube, and the outer casing of hard rubber. I always saw these as the body and the soul. Don't ask me why.

The main road is very straight, and always has been: Roman, they say. In those days there wasn't much traffic, although at the time we thought it was busy. Life would go by us, and now and again stop. We were proud that M. Michelin was a Frenchman: for once we had invented something useful, instead of making a lot of noise about nothing. No, really, I am proud of our business.

I started helping my father as soon as I could stand upright, just as he had helped his father, who was a blacksmith, hammering hot iron tyres to wooden rims. I was at first scared of the hiss of the compressors, of the great blade that took off the rubber, peeling it like an orange. I learnt to see a tyre as sad, when its chin lay flat on the ground, melting away – and when it was fat and full it bounced, it was so happy. My father could roll the tyres like a man I once saw in a circus that came to the village. The worn, sad ones lay leaning each upon the other like old men one side of the yard: my father would roll another so that it fell exactly into place against the end. He called this 'playing his accordion'. Some of the farmers would take these old tyres away, for use on the farms, where they would have a second life under a trailer, bouncing behind a horse or perhaps a donkey over stony fields. In very hard frosts, they would heap up the old, dead tyres at the ends of the fields, so that the evil smoke would scare the frost away from the vine-buds. Not everyone did this: it was my father's idea, I believe, and they didn't like to think he could tell them things, a man who had turned away from the land.

My father would tell me, when I was old enough, how one must never fall short of the highest standards, in this job. The road was getting busier, and the future looked rosy. But, he said, if you fall short of the highest standards, and start 'cutting corners', or grow sloppy, and let a man drive away with a set of tyres unevenly inflated, or with an inner tube that – from the very kindest of intentions – you have pretended to yourself is passable, though frayed in one spot, or with a tread that is smooth as here (he'd smack his furrowed brow), you might be sending that man to his death. Every time we heard of a local accident, our hearts beat faster, and not only because this unfortunate occurrence might have involved someone dear to us; many, if not most, of those running around on the roads at that time were putting their faith in our rigour and honesty and skill. Even I, a pimply young lad handling the bicycle trade (how much more considerable it was in those days!) knew that my hands were capable of bringing injury or even death, if I let my attention wander, or felt too lazy to triple-check a pressure or a repair or a bolt or the depth of a tread.

The blessed Trinity, my father called it: the check, the double-check, and the Holy-Ghost-check. Who was a Protestant through and through.

Even the local *curé* would use us. My father and he drank together, in the little office with its Dunlop tyre-clock, talking about Verdun or other things closed to me, while I dealt with the *curé*'s battered old bicycle – a Raleigh, from his time in Flanders. M. Dunlop and M. Michelin: these were my father's gods. I would like to say that my father was like the Michelin man, but he wasn't: I was always, from maturity, bigger than he ever was, but he was never fat. His face has always had an emaciated look, perpetually sucking on its dead cigarette, glossy with grease and seamed with dirt. Tyres pick up the filth of the world, they are not fussy. In their treads I have found the hair and blood of small, hapless creatures. In the great chasms of a giant truck's treads I once found a shrew, intact but quite lifeless, its tiny paws folded as my mother's were on her death-bed, in the room smelling of camphor and candles.

So the road passed by us in a blur, and now and again would come the tell-tale sounds of tyres turning into our yard, scrunching over the grit and dust, and we would lift our heads to look, squinting in the heat and glare or rubbing our hands in the cold.

André Paulhan et Fils. That sign was painted in 1942, when I was seventeen. I was very proud.

The next day, we saw our first German limousine. We had seen German trucks before, passing through the unoccupied zone, on their way to elsewhere, but never before had we seen a big, black Mercedes, with a little flag fluttering on its bonnet, and motorcycle outriders. It did not stop. There was much less activity on the road, after the country was defeated, but my bicycle hands were kept busier. Our old tyres were soon used up, and new tyres were only fitfully available, until my father came to some agreement with the local powers in the town. We had no family there, except some distant cousin of my mother's: we are all from further up, in the mountains, the Paulhans. There is a tiny village in the chestnut country, about ten kilometres from where we lived at the time (when we weren't sleeping on the job, as happened two or three days in the week), which is mostly bats and ruined walls, and a simple church. That was our village, once. At least, the *mas* was ours, and the *mas* was well nigh a village in itself. I won't go into the reasons for our dispersion, or we shall be here all night. Suffice to say that it was not for wanting to see the world, or the descent of the Holy Spirit one Pentecost! We go at each other hammer and tongs, still, the Paulhan clan, until we are threatened. Then we hold as fast to each other as one of my tyres to its rim. We don't meet much, these days.

One time, in March or April 1943, my father came back from town one day, looking very pleased with himself. He was scrubbed clean and in his best suit. He had left very early, before I had even shaved. He had spent the morning in the *gendarmerie*, he told me. 'There are a few new faces I don't know, but there is Jules, getting along fine, with his own office. He is in charge of regularising.' 'What is he regularising?' I asked. (There were no clients about, I might add.) 'The STO,' he said. My heart came into my mouth. By this he meant the latest bad idea of Laval's, the *Service du Travail Obligatoire*. Jules – an old schoolfriend and card-playing companion of my father's – did no more than type out lists and send out letters, but he had a certain control over things. Jules had shown my father round, 'and I shook a few hands.' Just as well he had scrubbed his own, as best he could. That is why I escaped the fate of certain others of my age, amongst them several friends. When I was twenty, I spent a few not unpleasant months in the Vosges cutting wood and gathering charcoal and getting very cold with some young people from places like Lyon – smart, educated people, who had never cut wood in their lives before. But I never went to Germany.

Whether it was because of this visit, and his odd evening with Jules playing for small money and drinking, I do not know – but the Germans used us. That is to say, they used us when it suited them, for they seemed to have their own mechanics, even their own tyre people, like they had their own newspapers and their own films and their own language. Maybe they would have used us anyway, in that case, but my father saw it as his doing. The odd thing is, he hated the Germans – they had, after all, given him his limp, in '17, and the itch would come back with heat. When the *maquisards* really got going, he didn't turn them away, when they came as clients. He served them and pretended that he didn't know, but somehow those boys never paid, only shook hands. But he said to me, one day, after the famous 'Petit Ours' (tall and elegant) had had a tube repaired on his motorcycle one evening, late: 'Don't get mixed up in all that. These boys, they are free. You are not. When all this is finished with, and those bastards are back in Berlin, that sign will have your name on it, and your son will be *le fils*. I will be the old fellow who stands watching the world go by, and getting in your hair, and proving, at ninety, what a damn good grip I still have at the expense of your clients' knuckles!' He laughed uproariously at this, but I think he was nervous, inside. I suppose he was playing a delicate game. He was a man who could never take risks. It was moulded into him, it was part of his job.

When old Mme Renouvin slid off the road in her little blue Peugeot, in 1938, and was found dead as a log in a wild rose bush, where she'd been thrown, and the report in the local paper blamed it on a 'blow-out', my poor father did not eat for days, like a fast of repentance. The fact is, Mme Renouvin was the worst driver anywhere, and in those days you could smooth out a tread in months if you took corners poorly, the surfaces were that gritty. But she was a client, and the last man to have dealt with her tyres was my father. Surprisingly, there was no decline in custom. That, as I said, came with the war, when the road traffic died away to near silence, and everyone went hungry.

If we hadn't had the chestnuts, in our area, I think we might have starved to death. So my father's visit to the *gendarmerie* certainly put things straight.

I was in love, if there is such a thing. It was a girl who passed by on her silver bicycle every morning and every evening. She was a clerk in the silk-works, further up the road. She would work all day in the roar of the river-race and the typewriter clicking away like a mad nuthatch, and I would work in the hiss of the compressor and the clatter of my tools and the intermittent gossip of our clients, dreaming of Sunday, when I could walk in the woods and mountains, and breathe good air, and forget the war. I noticed her first as a very young girl, just coming into womanhood, when she arrived in the yard with a tyre in ribbons, and caught her ankle on the pedal, walking the bicycle towards me. She was nothing much to look at then, except for a mass of beautiful, glossy black hair, but she spoke in a very sweet, soft voice, and had a winning smile. She hardly looked at me, and (both being shy, I suppose) we exchanged only a few commonplaces. But some dart must have wormed its way in, for when I saw her pass on her way to work (as I surmised, and soon confirmed) I recognised her immediately. This must have been just after the war broke out, in '40. I remember poppies between the vines, and the white asphodels that came up always (and still do) in the good-for-nothing field at the back, and the poplars on the river glittering like fountains in a wind – so it would have been late spring. The dust was on the road; the last of the big rains had passed a few weeks earlier. The whole stretch of the road, either way, was empty (just before all those refugees from the north trudged past, with their wheelbarrows, in June); the poppies thinned into one crimson thread of silk either side, and the plane trees dappled nobody but the birds, alighting while the coast was clear. Rubbing my hands on a rag, taking a moment's break between two jobs, I saw coming up from the west, from the town, a dark-haired figure on a bicycle. I stepped back as she drew nearer: I am naturally shy, as I have said, and in the long time it takes for a bicyclist to pass us from first sighting there is much that can happen in the head, and many possibilities for difficult exchanges of regard. As I recognised her from my slightly retracted vantage point, I have to say that I blushed; she was already hot in the face from the ride – but anyway, her skin was so olive that one never saw her blush. My skin is from my mother's side; my mother had red hair, which everyone claimed was from German mercenaries a thousand years ago. What rubbish people speak!

I nodded as she passed, busily washing my hands over the pail. There was a wealthy client, a local meat-supplier, talking with my father, coming out of the big shed. He showed me a three-inch nail that had just been taken out of his nearside rear tyre. I indicated my admiration and commiseration, as one always has to with these bores, and then looked after the girl, who had now dwindled to a dot. I forgot to say that as she ticked past, just before the bore opened his mouth, she glanced at me and smiled. Her lips fell into an open pout as they automatically described a *bonjour*, but mine stayed frozen. They are like that: the muscles of my face have a will of their own, at times. It is because I am shy, with people, unless they are clients. Also, it was because my voice had only just broken, and still threatened to be all at sixes-and-sevens. It was after this that my father gave me a lecture on treating clients as if they are the most interesting people in the world, with their tedious, repetitive histories of three-inch nails and roads full of sharp stones.

You cannot fail to strike up some relationship with those who pass you at definite times six days a week, but it took two years before I had reached a sufficient maturity to wave at her as she passed, and shout some innocuous greeting (I mean, more than *bonjour* or *bonsoir*). The final 'breakthrough' came after three years when, pedalling towards me at the time I just 'happened' to be wiping my hands on a rag at the edge of the road (which is also, of course, the generous entrance to our yard), she wobbled and wandered a little towards the middle of the road. Seeing, as I could, a large military vehicle bearing up behind her at considerable speed, I waved my hand and shouted at her to keep well in. The military vehicle swirled the dust so much that I was not certain for a few moments of her safety, but she emerged from the cloud, hugging the verge, with a somewhat shocked expression, which did not preclude her look of gratitude as she pedalled past me, thanking me very much. A look which I responded to with a clownish shrug, making her laugh. On her way back that evening, when I just happened to be washing my hands in the pail under the old Michelin sign, with its tyre-man pointing potential clients in, the ticking slowed and stopped before I had time even to look up. 'Thank you', she said. I stood, wiping my hands on my overalls (normally I would shake them dry, on such a fine day, because my overalls were of course greasy, but I could not shake them free of moisture with her so near). 'That's all right,' I said. We couldn't think of anything else to say for the moment, but it didn't matter. I was aware of my father hammering in the shed, and of a sleek black *Milice*-type car shooting past, and of a couple of motorcycles stinking of some home-made fuel – dung, probably – struggling to overtake a horse trotting with a cart full of hay and sun-blackened, nattering kids, but it was not to these that I attended with anything more than unconscious instinct. Yet I recall them all very clearly – along with the loveliness of her form and the sweetness of her face, her legs held either side of the bicycle, very straight (I imagined) under the pale blue dress, propping the rest of her body while she could think of nothing to say. What is there to say to someone you have known as a reliable face and form for three years, but with whom you have never exchanged more than a greeting? Someone you know you will see at a certain precise point twice a day, as one sees a tree or a house or even some discarded piece of metal rubbish in a ditch, too jammed in even for the floodwaters to snatch away? Someone who, if suddenly no longer there, can leave a hole in your heart, and a feeling of doom until the moment he or she reappears?

This is all very well, but it is recounted in the warm (oh so warm!) glow of hindsight. Look at me there, in the yard, still the boy who knows nothing of the world, or keeps mum about it if he does. I was filled, let's be honest about it, with a sense of helplessness and near-panic, for this might be the only opportunity I would ever get. Once I had seen her in the market, when my father had heard of an exceptional delivery of Normandy apples and sent me off in a client's 'borrowed' car to grease the vendor's palm. But it was so odd to see her then, stood like anyone else on the ground, and not on two spinning wheels, ticking past, that I failed to do justice to the occasion by positioning myself next to her with some joke at the ready, as many a lad of my age might have done. A few other times I had reckoned I had seen her, at a distance, in one of the streets or on the main square of the town, but she had never come for repairs, or a new tyre. That's what it was like, during the war: people dealt with their own problems, their own repairs, more than in peacetime. Everyone 'cut corners', from necessity. It was a difficult period.

So I was glad when she pointed at the nearest pot-hole and said, 'I was avoiding one of those.' This gave me an opportunity to open up. 'It's the military vehicles that do it,' I said. 'The roads can't take them. The surface is battered stupid by all the trucks.' (This was about six months after the German invasion of the southern zone, by the way.) 'We are all battered,' she said. She looked sad, then, and I noticed how her face had thinned over the three years I had watched her. If she lived up in one of the villages to the north, she must bicycle a lot of kilometres each day, on a diet of boiled chestnuts or whatever. There was something sinewy about her, though, that one could trust. I nodded. I was conscious of my father in the shed, and how he'd told me to keep my mouth shut. 'Petit Ours,' she said, all of a sudden. I felt renewed panic, inside. I frowned. She looked at me, thoughtfully, as if reading my face. Then, because I didn't say anything more, she set off into the distance. 'Chatting up the skirts, then?' yelled my father, from the shed door. 'Hey, young Raoul's picking the cherries as they pass!' There was no one around, and his joke was lost to the air, after echoing as usual in the shed's cavern behind him. I told him to piss off, under my breath. I was exhilarated and at the same time very upset that the girl (whose name I didn't even know) was involved in some way with the Maquis. It never occurred to me that she might be working for the other side: that possibility might have been suggested by my feigned ignorance, but that was an automatic reflex. You've no idea on how many levels one's mind worked, in those days: isolated compartments of body and soul, with a lot of soft rubber in between.

I was upset not only because her existence might suddenly be perilous, but also because she had not stopped just for me, or for her feelings about me. In the end, I never knew how deeply involved she was, but I reckon it must have been on the simplest level of message-carrying, like a lot of kids and teenagers in those times. My position, on the main road, with the cover of the business, would have served the Resistance well. That was obvious. But I was not the one to make that sort of decision alone. Maybe my father did more than just give the *maquisards* 'God's credit', as he used to call it; but if so, I never knew about it – and trust between father and son would mean nothing, in that case.

The Germans – and, naturally, the *Milice* – started to furnish us with increased custom as the war dragged on and things became more and more difficult. Since many of our clients were paying us in blackmarket goods, the 'honest' cash of the occupiers was very welcome. One day, I was sitting in a café on a Sunday morning (the place in the tiny square this side of town), when a man in a peasant's overalls (but not, somehow, a peasant's bearing), sat down next to me and said, 'Try a nail or two. Otherwise we'll be thinking you are collaborators.' With that, he got up and left. My hands were shaking so much I spilt my drink. I imagined the other, mainly old, men in the café were looking at me. The wine tasted sour (it probably was). This was about a month after the girl had stopped to thank me. I decided to do something clownish, to make her stop again. My heart thumping like a drum all night, I rose early and started work before my father had shaved (we were 'sleeping in', that night, in the little rooms above the office). I had never missed her in the morning, but I wanted to be absolutely certain. The advantage of the morning encounter was that my father always did his paperwork until nine, and the thick net curtain across the office window obscured the view of the yard sufficiently to waylay any casual glance – even that of my father's. At a quarter to seven, with the sun laying broad stripes across the white road, so that vehicles seemed to appear and disappear as they approached, I saw the girl in the distance . . . to my relief, I have to say (*nothing can be relied on except death*, and so forth). There was nobody else on the road. I stepped out into the middle with a bucket full of stones and earth and started to pour it into the pot-hole, the subject of our former exchange. I was so nervous I nearly dropped the bucket, for my arms were very weak all of a sudden, but I was already stamping the stuff down by the time she stopped. 'You've no right to do that,' she said. I paused in my work, and my prepared grin froze into what must have been rather a stupid-looking grimace. 'You'll be arrested for overstepping the mark. *Les Allemands sont corrects*.' With that last familiar phrase, I knew she was 'having me on', and my grin restored itself. 'It's for you,' I said. 'I know,' she replied. She giggled (no, not quite – but there is no other word to describe such a sprinkle of delightful, teasing merriment) and pedalled off. I was left gazing after her, empty bucket in hand, little stones caught in my boots. If a truck had not blared its horn, I fancy it would have run me over.

Of course, all doors were open now. My father wondered at my whistling gaiety that day. His eyes narrowed over lunch – which we'd have, on those summer days, at a little table set under the plane tree in the corner of the yard (the road is too noisy for that, now). He poured himself a generous quantity of wine and eyed me suspiciously over the tumbler. His face (no more nor less emaciated than it was before the war, just a little sharper) gleamed with sweat and grease. I smiled back, innocently. Despite the heat, a bird was singing in the branches above us. Or perhaps I imagined that. There was a noon stillness, otherwise – though the Germans never respected our hours, and would shatter the holy quiet at unpredictable moments. I saw the wine go down his throat as I had seen it go down for as long as I could remember, and the throat always glossy and dark. He wiped his mouth and set the glass down more energetically than usual. 'Wipe that bloody stupid grin off your face,' he said. 'Or I'll think you're up to something.'

There was no doubt that the game he played was a strain on his nerves. I have no doubt that men like my non-peasant in peasant's dress had approached him in recent months, when the bolts were turning tighter on our world. He must have felt cornered, in some way. He wouldn't have liked that.

But if he didn't like what was happening under his very nose, then he never said so. That evening she waved with a merry laugh as she passed, and my father was in the yard, jacking up a big white Delage (the one with the electric gearbox that belonged to M. Coutaud, the footwear fellow). I didn't turn to look at him, but neither did he wolf-whistle, or yell something about cherries. The next morning was a Sunday, and I spent it roaming the hills around my family's village, making myself giddy from too much exercise combined with a lack of proper nourishment. We never talked about the war as such around the table: only the lack of food. Now and again the Germans trundled up the little main street, knocking plaster and even stone off the corners of the old buildings, matching their exaggerated wheelbase against the donkey-cart dimensions of the village turns, but otherwise the war was something that went on either far away, or in the subterranean parts of the mind and the land – places one only entered at one's peril. Certainly – let me assure you of this – the Paulhans were never regarded as one of those *salauds* families who put all their eggs into the enemy basket. Many were the folk around us who looked upon the early days of Vichy as times of redemption for the poor, ground-down countryman, but they tended to be Catholics, who didn't even mind very much when the Jews (including a few of our clients, most of whom I had never even thought of as Jews) were taken away. My father disliked Catholics with a two-hundred-year-old force flowing in his veins. Thus he had no time for Pétain. Apart from anything else, he had put all his eggs into the basket of progress, which he saw as intimately connected with the automobile. Now we were living as people had been in his father's time, or even his grandfather's. To my father, the war was a personal attack on his business. Thus he felt no compunction in screwing what he could out of the enemy.

Do I make myself clear? There is nothing obscure about what followed. I will set it out like a spread of cards, as stained and smeared as my own, but no less honest. I lost, I lost more completely than most men lose . . . but let me go on. The girl and I, we slowly discovered each other; her name was Cécile Viala, she came from a small family that farmed in a simple, modest fashion two valleys west of mine, in a village I had never visited – yet we decided that we must have crossed each other's paths at numerous moments during our lives, if only at fairs and festivals, when we were to each other only another strange face under the trees.

She never again mentioned Petit Ours, or anything in connection with the Resistance, or even the war, very much. Twice a day we would talk, and she would arrive earlier and earlier, so as to talk for longer. She shook hands with my father, and my sisters soon learned of my 'affair'. They teased me about it, but I was happy to be teased. They said I should invite her over, for they had learned how pleasant and pretty she was from someone who worked on the machines in the silk-works – and how clever she was, too, and what a fine hand she had, and what a head for numbers. Far too good for a dolt like me! One morning, I said that I would be walking in her valley. (The idea popped into my head, just like that – really, it was not so far as the crow flies, but then I am not a crow!) She looked down, shyly, and said, 'I can be walking there, too.' So we worked out a place to meet, in very sensible tones, as if we were talking about prices, or bent wheel-spokes – and as she pedalled off I realised that I had made my first secret assignation with the one I adored. I felt giddy, and even a little sick. I spread too much grease on the wheel-rims, and dropped a ring spanner on my toe. I had to sigh, as real lovers do – as if someone had taken a pump to my mouth and overdone the foot on the pedal. Each hiss of the tyres seemed to express my own impatience with the ordinariness of things: no young man could ever have been in love as much as I, I considered. Where my palm had rested on the warm leather of her saddle, lay the cold arc of a jack's brace. I turned it with a ferocity that my father happened not to see, or he would have cuffed me on the ear, as in old times.

We met under a certain, ancient chestnut tree already dropping its life-sustaining fruit, on the path that eventually winds up to her village. We avoided the shepherds and their tinkling goats as best we could, and made our way deeper into the woods. Neither of us said much, I remember. Without the long road, the yard, the trucks and bicycles, cars and horses, the dust or the puddles, the regularity of the moment twice in the day and the knowledge that it would not be extended beyond ten or so minutes, we were a little lost. The world was suddenly like an immense garden in which we could wander at will. Before a fine view of the higher mountains to the north, blue fold upon blue fold, I took her hand. Yes – we had not yet held each other's hand! Hers moved in my light hold, like a little rabbit, and I thought I was going to explode. I sighed as silently as I could, and then I said, 'You make me very happy. I would like to do this every Sunday, even in winter, until I'm so old I can no longer walk.' 'What an odd thing to say!' she cried. I felt very disappointed: I had rehearsed it all the way up the slope. Then she said, very quietly: 'Me, too.'

Oh, let's get on, let's get on to the inevitable horror, after God alone knows what happiness of embrace and gentle kiss up there in those lonely, lovely hills. It will bear only brief telling. First, a big truck – a Latil, huge for those days, six cylinders, a twelve to thirteen tonner diesel – passed us one morning, six-thirtyish, at a hell of a lick, scattering grit and clouding the yard in dust. Moments later, two German armoured cars shot past, clearly in pursuit, and I heard a terrible tearing sound, which I believe was some kind of machine-gun fired by the Germans at the truck. My father and I ran out into the road, only to see the Latil swerve as if to turn – in fact, it slewed to a halt in a great vortex of white dust and the Germans did likewise, if only just in time. A figure leapt from the truck and ran off into the vines, with the Germans following on foot, firing like mad. We saw, over some obscuring trees, black smoke rise up in puffs and heard several loud bangs. These, I assume, were the grenades later reported in the local paper as having been thrown at the driver (who escaped, for he still lives to recount it). The truck was full of dynamite, which any one of the many bullets fired could have set off at any moment – and it was near enough to us to have taken our shed clean away. My father and I kept our heads down, as the Germans by this time (early in '44) were very nervous and shot at anything that moved, if they felt it threatened them. But I wanted to warn Cécile, who was due to pass at any minute. To run up the road would have attracted fire, and even to go the back way, through the vineyards, would have been assumed suspicious by the Germans. So I walked up the road. 'Where the hell are you going?' yelled my father. 'For a walk,' I called back, and then kept going, keeping by the verge, with my hands in my pockets, looking as ordinary as possible but with terror beating in my mouth. I had, I think, a fifty-fifty chance of attracting fire, but none came. When I saw Cécile, I waved, and she stopped. 'You're going to be late for work today,' I said. She held my hand. She was quite startled to see me out of my usual place. She took the long, winding back route and arrived safely. My return was easier: the German guards, looking minuscule against the Latil, hardly seemed to look at me. There is nothing worse than facing danger with your spine.

That evening (by which time everything had been cleared up), Cécile thanked me with an open kiss. My father called me 'a bloody fool' and gripped my hand. He was proud of me, for once.

Then the village, one Sunday, was crossed with the darkest shadow of war – that of blood. We were sitting down to eat when the rumble of a convoy sounded. 'Bloody Boche,' murmured my father, followed by something ruder, in *patois.* A few minutes later there was shouting, and sounds of gunfire from the northern end of the village, near the little crossroads. There was lots of banging on doors, and we were all told to pay a visit to the *Mairie*. In the larger room, on the big table there used for the meetings of the *Conseil Municipal*, were laid three bodies. Their guts were literally looped and dripping almost to the floor, ripped open by that brief burst of gunfire. One of them was a local man, the son of the butcher, a little older than myself. The other two I did not know. They looked surprised in death, and it was said later that, though all three members were of the Maquis, no one knew why they had taken that road slap-bang into the German convoy, and then reversed in such panic. I know why: because, for all their bravery, they were mortals, and felt mortal fear. I was sick in the gutter, immediately afterwards, to my shame. We all – the whole village – filed past the bodies and came out silent and pale. A few of us cried. I had never seen anything like it before, the only dead person I had ever looked at being my poor mother, at peace in her bed. The following week they looped a rope around the long neck of Petit Ours, whom they'd caught in a botched raid on the *gendarmerie*, and pushed him from the town bridge – over which the schoolchildren were forced to walk class by class in the afternoon, while the body swayed in the wind. The Mayor had to give a speech, thanking the Boche for keeping public order and so forth. The atmosphere was terrible. It crept up the road and cast my father and I, and most of our clients, into a deep gloom.

But some of our clients, of course, were Germans. One, in particular, was a large, friendly man – and probably the very chap, as an officer of the Gestapo, keeping an eye on things out here, who had ordered the execution of Petit Ours. His huge, soft-topped Maybach (of which he was very proud, and with good reason) needed a change of tyre about a fortnight later: a sharp stone had finally wormed its way in, on his way to the town. Both spare wheels, carried on each side of the bonnet, had been stolen, but we found the right fit. I remembered the words of the fellow in the café, and the ripped stomachs of the three good men, and the swaying body of Petit Ours, three days after his death, sending foul whiffs of gas up the river. In a shadowy corner of the shed, out of the bright sunlight, I took a brand new inner tube and quietly (though my father was in the office, talking with the fellow) shaved its rubber with a small steel file on a certain spot, until it looked frayed, but still just airtight. I placed this inner tube in the new tyre. The officer's chauffeur and some other armed minion watched me fit it onto the wheel – the nearside front one – but I could scarcely stop my hands from trembling. In those days we tightened the bolts by hand with a box spanner, not a gun, so there was no risk of over-tightening, but I kept dropping the tommy bar with a big clatter. Anyway, I was giving the disk chrome a little polish by the time the big man himself stepped out of the office. I saw him, in the mirror-finish of the chrome, advance towards me, all distorted, looming over my shoulder like a big bat, and I composed my face and stood up. He pumped my hand and boomed at me about the state of the roads, and my father handed him the bill, which startled him. The fellow patted the bonnet and began to discuss the future of the automobile, while the two minions leaned on the sweeping mud-guard and smoked. His black gloves did a little dance while he talked. He must have been some sort of technical engineer before the war, for he was full of this idea that would avoid 'grovelling in the road' with a jack and getting your knees dirty: some sort of crowbar lever that would work a fitting under the bonnet, and put up either set of wheels as desired, and bring the whole car into suspension with a final twist. (A few years later, in about '48, a British couple in sunglasses stopped for a puncture-repair in a 1.25 litre MG, and laughed when I searched for the jack. It had exactly the same system as the Gestapo officer had described, and I all but burst into tears. They did not understand my upset: they said something about the French having 'a different sense of humour' – which really means none at all, perhaps.)

While the man was boring us stupid with his broken French, booming from under his glossy peaked cap, his boots as polished as his coachwork, his jacket and breeches as black, I heard the ticking of a bicycle . . . but it cannot be Cécile's, I thought, for there is a grating sound behind it. I glanced at the road – and there was, indeed, Cécile, coming to a halt at the entrance to the yard. She looked tired and worn, as we all did, after the events of the last few weeks. When she saw the Germans, and the big car, she made to go – but thinking only of how suspicious they were, and unpredictably sensitive and vengeful, I made my apologies and went over to greet her. 'You should be ashamed,' she murmured. 'Don't worry,' I said. 'It's not as you think.' Her face brightened, and then looked intense and questioning, and then spotting something over my shoulder, she as quickly disguised her interest behind a soft laugh. The officer had evidently been staring at her, for he then boomed his own greeting: 'And might a fellow take a lift on the saddle from a pretty damsel, like a stick of bread?' – some such tripe. She shook her head, adding: 'No. My chain is loose.' That explained the grating sound, and I offered immediately to mend it. We were nearly six kilometres from the town, and more again from her village. I noticed how sinewy her calves were, to the point of being wasted by effort and lack of proper food. She shook her head and pedalled away, without so much as a blown kiss or a wave. 'Till Sunday!' I shouted after her, recklessly. 'Till Sunday, Cécile!'

There was a banging of doors, and the Maybach purred like a black, evil cat out of the yard, and turned to drive towards the town. It was at that moment that I saw Cécile, in the distance, apparently shudder to a stop. Her head bent down and I could just make out her hand between the wheels. Clearly, the chain had come off at that moment. I began to run towards her, my father shouting after me. The Maybach got there first. As I ran, an ominous sense of doom came over me: a kind of terrible chill, that made my heart slow, though it was pumping hard to keep my speed up. With a hundred yards to go, I saw the luggage locker opened, and Cécile's bicycle placed in it. She appeared to be in conversation with the officer, for I spotted his black glove waving through the side window, like a little black snake's tongue. The long and the short of it is that she was forced – I can only think that the appropriate word – forced by circumstance (my belief is that she hoped to extract something useful from the enemy in that brief drive into the town) to accept his offer of a lift, gallant gentleman that he pretended to be. (Or perhaps was, in another airtight compartment of his brain.)

I was left coughing in a dust-cloud, for they accelerated away at great speed, as was typical – dwindling to a dot and out of sight in no time. I had not even had time to turn on my heel when there was a distant bang and clatter, as of heavy pots and pans falling off a shelf, and smoke began to drift above the plane trees. I ran as fast as I could, in the silence, but could not finally approach the spot for all the uniforms ringing it already, waving their guns – like excited kids around the blazing effigy of the *Petassou*. For myself, though, it was the beginning of winter, not the end. I leave fresh flowers every year, on the anniversary. The terrible scorch marks on the trunk have been long rubbed away by the rain and the sun and the wind, and the dent has grown out. The tree is well again – for we crop the branches close, here, as a matter of course.

I tried – I still try – to explain her presence in the car, but I am not sure, now, anyone really cares, or even remembers her very much. When my father 'retired', in '69, I did no more than touch up *André Paulhan et Fils*; I could not change it, I could not paint it out. Well, I have had no sons, of course, staying unmarried – and anyway, he still hangs around the yard, getting in my hair (what little I have of it left to me), and showing clients what a firm grip he has, at ninety-odd. The road is very busy, of course – business could not be better. But something went out of the job when it all went tubeless, to my mind. I don't suppose I will miss it. You'll see the flowers on your way in, to the left, tied to the trunk. When they begin to fade and wither, I replace them with the plastic type. To be honest, no one knows the difference – shooting past as they do, these days.

46

At Hiruharama

(2000)

Penelope Fitzgerald

Mr Tanner was anxious to explain how it was that he had a lawyer in the family, so that when they all decided to sell up and quit New Zealand there had been someone they could absolutely trust with the legal business. That meant that he had to say something about his grandfather, who had been an orphan from Stamford in Lincolnshire and was sent out to a well-to-do family north of Auckland, supposedly as an apprentice, but it turned out that he was to be more or less of a servant. He cleaned the knives, saw to the horses, waited at table and chopped the wood. On an errand to a dry goods store in Auckland he met Kitty, Mr Tanner's grandmother. She had come out from England as a governess, and she too found she was really wanted as a servant. She was sixteen, and Tanner asked her to wait for three years while he saved his wages, and then to marry him. All this was at a Methodist social, say a couple of weeks later. 'What family have you got back home?' Kitty asked him. Tanner replied just the one sister. Younger or older? Older. She probably thinks I'm a skilled craftsman by now. She probably reckons I'm made. – Haven't you sent word to her lately? – Not lately. – Best write to her now, anyway, said Kitty, and tell her how it is between us. I should be glad to have a new relation, I haven't many. – I'll think it over, he said. Kitty realised then that he could neither read nor write.

They had to start in a remote country place. The land round Auckland at that time was ten shillings an acre, a third of the price going to build the new churches and schools, but where Tanner and Kitty went, north of Awanui, there weren't any churches and schools, and it was considerably cheaper. They didn't have to buy their place, it had been left deserted, and yet it had something you could give a thousand pounds for and not get, and that was a standpipe giving constant clear water from an underground well. But whoever lived there had given up, because of the loneliness and because it was such poor country. Don't picture a shack, though. There were two rooms, one with a stove and one with a bedstead, and a third one at the back for a vegetable store. Tanner grew root vegetables and went into Awanui twice a week with the horse and dray. Kitty stayed behind, because they'd taken on two hundred chickens and a good few pigs.

Tanner turned over in his mind what he'd say to his wife when she told him she was going to have a child. When she did tell him, which wasn't for another two years or so, by the way, he didn't hear her at first, because a northerly was blowing and neither of them could expect to hear each other. When he did catch what she was saying, he hitched up and drove into Awanui. The doctor was at his midday dinner, which he took at a boarding-house higher up the main street. When he got back and into his consulting-room Tanner asked him what were the life statistics of the North Island.

'Do you mean the death statistics?' the doctor asked.

'They'll do just as well,' said Tanner.

'No one dies here except from drink or drowning. Out of three thousand people in Taranaki Province there hasn't been a single funeral in the last sixteen months and only twenty-four sick and infirm. You may look upon me as a poor man.'

'What about women in childbirth?' asked Tanner.

The doctor didn't have any figures for women dying in childbirth, but he looked sharply at Tanner and asked him when his child was due.

'You don't know, of course. Well, don't ask me if it's going to be twins. Nature didn't intend us to know that.' He began to write in his notebook. 'Where are you living?'

'It's off the road to Houhora, you turn off to the right after twelve miles.'

'What's it called?'

'Hiruharama.'

'Don't know it. That's not a Maori name.'

'I think it means Jerusalem,' said Tanner.

'Are there any other women about the place?'

'No.'

'I mean someone who could come in and look after things while your wife's laid up. Who's your nearest neighbour?' Tanner told him there was no one except a man called Brinkman, who came over sometimes. He was about nine or ten miles off at Stony Loaf.

'And he has a wife?'

'No, he hasn't, that's what he complains about. You couldn't ask a woman to live out there.'

'You can ask a woman to live anywhere,' said the doctor. 'He's a crank, I dare say.'

'He's a dreamer,' Tanner replied. 'I should term Brinkman a dreamer.'

'I was thinking in terms of washing the sheets, that sort of thing. If there's no one else, can you manage about the house yourself for a few days?'

'I can do anything about the house,' said Tanner.

'You don't drink?'

Tanner shook his head, wondering if the doctor did. He asked if he shouldn't bring his wife with him for a consultation next time he drove over to Awanui. The doctor looked out of his window at the bone-shaking old dray with its iron-rimmed wheels. 'Don't.'

He tore the prescription out of his notebook. 'Get this for your wife. It's calcium water. When you want me to come, you'll have to send for me. But don't let that worry you. Often by the time I arrive I'm not needed.'

Other patients had arrived and were sitting on the wooden benches on the verandah. Some had empty medicine bottles for a refill. There was a man with his right arm strapped up, several kids with their mothers, and a woman who looked well enough but seemed to be in tears for some reason or other. – Well, you see life in the townships.

Tanner went over to the post office, where there was free pen and ink if you wanted it, and wrote a letter to his sister. – But wait a minute, surely he couldn't read or write? Evidently by that time he could. Mr Tanner's guess was that although Kitty was a quiet girl, very quiet, she'd refused to marry him until he'd got the hang of it. – Tanner wrote: My darling old sister. Well, it's come to pass and either a girl or a boy will be added unto us. It would be a help if you could send us a book on the subject. We have now a hundred full-grown hens and a further hundred at point of lay, and a good stand of potatoes. – After mailing the letter he bought soap, thread, needles, canned fish, tea and sugar. When he drove out of Awanui he stopped at the last homestead, where he knew a man called Parrish who kept racing-pigeons. Some of them, in fact were just arriving back at their loft. Parrish had cut the entrances to the nests down very small, and every time a bird got home it had to squeeze past a bell on a string so that the tinkling sound gave warning. They were all Blue Chequers, the only kind, Parrish declared, that a sane man would want to keep. Tanner explained his predicament and asked for the loan of two birds. Parrish didn't mind, because Hiruharama, Tanner's place, was on a more or less direct line from Awanui to Te Paki station, and that was the line his pigeons flew.

'If you'd have lived over the other way I couldn't have helped you,' Parrish said.

A Maori boy took the young birds out as soon as they were four months old and tossed them at three miles, ten miles, twenty miles, always in the same direction, north-north-west of Awanui.

'As long as they can do fifteen miles,' said Tanner.

'They can do two hundred and fifty.'

'How long will it take them to do fifteen miles?'

'Twenty minutes in clear weather,' said Parrish.

The Maori boy chose out two birds and packed them into a wicker hamper, which Tanner wedged into the driver's seat of the dray.

'Have you got them numbered in some way?' Tanner asked.

'I don't need to. I know them all,' said Parrish.

He added that they would need rock salt, so Tanner drove back into the town once more to buy the rock salt and a sack of millet. By the time he got to Hiruharama the dark clear night sky was pressing in on every side. I ought to have taken you with me, he told Kitty. She said she had been all right. He hadn't, though, he'd been worried. You mean you've forgotten something at the stores, said Kitty. Tanner went out to the dray and fetched the pigeons, still shifting about and conferring quietly in their wicker basket.

'Here's one thing more than you asked for,' he said. They found room for them in the loft above the vegetable store. The Blue Chequers were the prettiest things about the place.

The sister in England did send a book, although it didn't arrive for almost a year. In any case, it only had one chapter of a practical nature. Otherwise, it was religious in tone. But meanwhile Kitty's calculations couldn't have been far out, because more or less when they expected it the pains came on strong enough for Tanner to send for the doctor.

He had made the pigeons' nests out of packing-cases. They ought to have flown out daily for exercise, but he hadn't been able to manage that. Still, they looked fair enough, a bit dishevelled, but not so that you'd notice. It was four o'clock, breezy, but not windy. He took them out into the bright air which, even that far from the coast, was full of the salt of the ocean. How to toss a pigeon he had no idea. He opened the basket, and before he could think what to do next they were out and up into the blue. He watched in terror as after reaching a certain height they began turning round in tight circles as though puzzled or lost. Then, apparently sighting something on the horizon that they knew, they set off strongly towards Awanui. – Say twenty minutes for them to get to Parrish's loft. Ten minutes for Parrish or the Maori boy to walk up the street to the doctor's. Two and a half hours for the doctor to drive over, even allowing for his losing the way once. Thirty seconds for him to get down from his trap and open his bag. –

At five o'clock Tanner went out to see to the pigs and hens. At six Kitty was no better and no worse. She lay there quietly, sweating from head to foot. 'I can hear someone coming,' she said, not from Awanui, though, it was along the top road. Tanner thought it must be Brinkman. 'Why, yes, it must be six months since he came,' said Kitty, as though she was making conversation. Who else, after all, could it have been on the top road? The track up there had a deep rounded gutter each side which made it awkward to drive along. They could hear the screeching and rattling of his old buggy, two wheels in the gutter, two out. 'He's stopped at the gully now to let his horse drink,' said Kitty. 'He'll have to let it walk the rest of the way.' – 'He'll have to turn round when he gets here and start right back,' said Tanner.

There used to be a photograph of Brinkman somewhere, but Mr Tanner didn't know what had become of it, and he believed it hadn't been a good likeness in any case. – Of course, in the circumstances, as he'd come eight miles over a rough road, he had to be asked to put up his horse for a while, and come in.

Like most people who live on their own Brinkman continued with the course of his thoughts, which were more real to him than the outside world's commotion. Walking straight into the front room he stopped in front of the piece of mirror-glass tacked over the sink and looked fixedly into it.

'I'll tell you something, Tanner, I thought I caught sight of my first grey hairs this morning.'

'I'm sorry to hear that.'

Brinkman looked round. 'I see the table isn't set.'

'I don't want you to feel that you're not welcome,' said Tanner, 'but Kitty's not well. She told me to be sure that you came in and rested a while, but she's not well. Truth is, she's in labour.'

'Then she won't be cooking dinner this evening, then?'

'You mean you were counting on having it here?'

'My half-yearly dinner with you and Mrs Tanner, yis, that's about it.'

'What day is it, then?' asked Tanner, somewhat at random. It was almost too much for him at that moment to realise that Brinkman existed. He seemed like a stranger, perhaps from a foreign country, not understanding how ordinary things were done or said.

Brinkman made no attempt to leave, but said; 'Last time I came here we started with canned toheroas. Your wife set them in front of me. I'm not sure that they had an entirely good effect on the intestines. Then we had fried eggs and excellent jellied beetroot, a choice between tea or Bovo, bread and butter and unlimited quantities of treacle. I have a note of all this in my daily journal. That's not to say, however, that I came over here simply to take dinner with you. It wasn't for the drive, either, although I'm always glad to have the opportunity of a change of scene and to read a little in Nature's book. No, I've come today, as I came formerly, for the sake of hearing a woman's voice.'

Had Tanner noticed, he went on, that there were no native songbirds in the territory? At that moment there was a crying, or a calling, from the next room such as Tanner had never heard before, not in a shipwreck – and he had been in a wreck – not in a slaughterhouse.

'Don't put yourself out on my account,' said Brinkman. 'I'm going to sit here until you come back and have a quiet smoko.'

The doctor drove up bringing with him his wife's widowed sister, who lived with them and was a nurse, or had been a nurse. Tanner came out of the bedroom covered with blood, something like a butcher. He told the doctor he'd managed to deliver the child, a girl, in fact he'd wrapped it in a towel and tucked it up in the washbasket. The doctor took him back into the bedroom and made him sit down. The nurse put down the things she'd brought with her and looked round for the tea-tin. Brinkman sat there, as solid as his chair. 'You may be wondering who I am,' he said. 'I'm a neighbour, come over for dinner. I think of myself as one of the perpetually welcome.' 'Suit yourself,' said the sister-in-law. The doctor emerged, moving rather faster than he usually did. 'Please to go in there and wash the patient. I'm going to take a look at the afterbirth. The father put it out with the waste.'

There Tanner had made his one oversight. It wasn't the afterbirth, it was a second daughter, smaller, but a twin. – But how come, if both of them were girls, that Mr Tanner himself still had the name of Tanner? Well, the Tanners went on to have nine more children, some of them boys, and one of those boys was Mr Tanner's father. That evening, when the doctor came in from the yard with the messy scrap, he squeezed it as though he was wringing it out to dry, and it opened its mouth and the colder air of the kitchen rushed in and she'd got her start in life. After that the Tanners always had one of those tinplate mottoes hung up on the wall – Throw Nothing Away. You could get them then at the hardware store. – And this was the point that Mr Tanner had been wanting to make all along – whereas the first daughter never got to be anything in particular, this second little girl grew up to be a lawyer with a firm in Wellington, and she did very well.

All the time Brinkman continued to sit there by the table and smoke his pipe. Two more women born into the world! It must have seemed to him that if this sort of thing went on there should be a good chance, in the end, for him to acquire one for himself. Meanwhile, they would have to serve dinner sometime.

47

Real Time

(2002)

Amit Chaudhuri

On their way to the house, Mr Mitra said he didn't know if they should buy flowers. They were very near Jogu Bazaar; and Mr Mitra suddenly raised one hand and said:

'Abdul, slowly!'

The driver eased the pressure on the accelerator and brought the Ambassador almost to a standstill. Not looking into the rearview mirror, he studied two boys with baskets playing on the pavement on his left.

'Well, what should we do?' Mr Mitra's face, as he turned to look at his wife, was pained, as if he was annoyed she hadn't immediately come up with the answer.

'Do what you want to do quickly,' she said, dabbing her cheek with her sari. 'We're already late.' She looked at the small dial of her watch. He sighed; his wife never satisfied him when he needed her most; and quite probably it was the same story the other way round. Abdul, who, by sitting on the front seat, claimed to be removed to a sphere too distant for the words at the back to be audible, continued to stare at the children while keeping the engine running.

'But I'm not sure,' said the husband, like a distraught child, 'given the circumstances.'

She spoke then in a voice of sanity she chose to speak in only occasionally.

'Do what you'd do in a normal case of bereavement,' she said. 'This is no different.'

He was relieved at her answer, but regretted that he had to go out of the car into the market. He was wearing a white cotton shirt and terycotton trousers because of the heat, and shoes; he now regretted the shoes. He remembered he hadn't been able to find his sandals in the cupboard. His feet, swathed in socks, were perspiring.

He came back after about ten minutes, holding half a dozen tuberoses against his chest, cradling them with one arm; a boy was running after him. 'Babu, should I wipe the car, should I wipe the car . . .' he was saying, and Mr Mitra looked intent, like a man who has an appointment. He didn't acknowledge the boy; inside the car, Mrs Mitra, who was used to these inescapable periods of waiting, moved a little. He placed the tuberoses in the front, next to Abdul, where they smeared the seat with their moisture. Mr Mitra had wasted some time bargaining, bringing down the price from sixteen to fourteen rupees, after which the vendor had expertly tied a thread round the lower half of the flowers.

'Why did she do it?' he asked in an offhand way, as the car proceeded once more on its way. Going down Ashutosh Mukherjee Road, they turned left into Southern Avenue.

Naturally, they didn't have the answer. They passed an apartment building they knew, Shanti Nivas, its windows open but dark and remote. Probably they'd been a little harsh with her, her parents. Her marriage, sixteen years ago, had been seen to be appropriate. Usually, it's said, Lakshmi, the goddess of wealth, and Saraswati, of learning, two sisters, don't bless the same house; but certainly that wasn't true of the Poddars, who had two bars-at-law in the generation preceding this one, and a social reformer in the lineage, and also a white four-storeyed mansion on a property near Salt Lake where they used to have garden parties. Anjali had married Gautam Poddar very soon after taking her M.A. in history from Calcutta University.

As they passed a petrol pump, Mr Mitra wondered what view traditional theology took of this matter, and how the rites accommodated an event such as this – she had jumped from a third-floor balcony – which couldn't, after all, be altogether uncommon. Perhaps there was no ceremony. In his mind's eye, when he tried to imagine the priest, or the long rows of tables at which people were fed, he saw a blank. But Abdul couldn't identify the lane.

'Bhai, is this Rai Bahadur R.C. Mullick Road?' he asked a loiterer somewhat contemptuously.

The man leaned into a window and looked with interest at the couple in the back, as if unwilling to forgo this opportunity to view Mr and Mrs Mitra. Then, examining the driver's face again, he pointed to a lane before them, going off to the right, next to a sari shop that was closed.

'That one there.'

They went down for about five minutes, past two-storeyed houses with small but spacious courtyards, each quite unlike the others, till they had to stop again and ask an adolescent standing by a gate where Nishant Apartments was. The boy scratched his arm and claimed there was no such place over here. As they looked at him disbelievingly, he said, 'It may be on *that* side,' pointing to the direction they'd just come from.

'That side?' Mr Mitra looked helpless; he'd given up trying to arrive on time. What preoccupied him now was not getting there, but the negotiations involved in how to get there.

It turned out that what the boy was suggesting was simple. The main road, Lansdowne Road, divided the two halves of Rai Bahadur Mullick Road; one half of Mullick Road went left, the other right.

'Don't you know where they live?' asked Mr Mitra as Abdul reversed and turned the car around. The over-sweet, reminiscent smell of the tuberoses rose in the front of the car with a breeze that had come unexpectedly through the window. In front of a house on the left, clothes hung to dry as a child went round and round in circles in the courtyard on a tricycle.

'But I've only been there three or four times – and the last time, two years ago!' she complained. 'I find these lanes so confusing.'

The lanes *were* confusing; there were at least two, one after another, that looked exactly the same, with their clotheslines, grilles, and courtyards.

About ten or eleven days ago, they'd noticed a small item in the newspaper, and were shocked to recognise who it was. Then an obituary appeared, and Mr Mitra had called his daughter in Delhi, who remembered Anjali from visits made in childhood. Last week another insertion had told them that 'Observances will be made in memory of Mrs Anjali Poddar, who passed away on the 23rd of February, at 11 A.M. at 49 Nishant Apartments, Rai Bahadur R.C. Mullick Road. All are welcome.'

They didn't expect it would be a proper shraddh ceremony; they didn't think people would be fed. So Mrs Mitra had told the boy at home, firmly so as to impress her words upon him, 'We'll be back by one o'clock! Cook the rice and keep the daal and fish ready!' Without mentioning it clearly, they'd decided they must go to the club afterwards to get some cookies for tea, and stop at New Market on the way back. So they must leave the place soon after twelve; it was already ten past eleven.

The first to be fed was usually a crow, for whom a small ball of kneaded aata was kept on the balcony for it to pick up; the crow was supposed to be the soul come back – such absurd make-believe! Yet everyone did it, as if it were some sort of nursery game. Mr Mitra, looking out through the windshield, past the steering wheel and Abdul's shoulder, speculated if such practices might be all right in this case. Here the soul had made its own exit, and it was difficult to imagine why it would want to come back to the third-floor balcony of Nishant Apartments.

'Ask him!' said Mrs Mitra, prodding her husband's arm with a finger. She nodded towards a watchman standing in front of what looked like a bungalow. 'Ask him!'

'Nishant?' said the thin, moustached chowkidar, refusing to get up from his stool. Behind him was an incongruously large bungalow, belonging to a businessman, hidden by an imposing white gate and a wall. He barely allowed himself a smile. 'But there it is.' Two houses away, on the left.

It was clear from the size of the cramped compound, with the ceiling overhanging the porch only a few feet away from the adjoining wall, that Nishant had been erected where some older house once was, and which had been sold off to property developers and contractors. It must be twelve or thirteen years old. An Ambassador and two Marutis were parked outside by the pavement. Mr Mitra, holding the tuberoses under his right arm, glanced at his watch as he entered the porch, then got into the lift, which had a collapsible gate, hesitantly. He waited for his wife, looked at himself quickly in the mirror, and pressed a button. Mrs Mitra smoothed her hair and looked at the floors changing through the collapsible gate.

A narrow, tiled, clean corridor, going past forty-six and forty-seven, led to the main door to forty-nine, which was open. Faint music emanated to the corridor, and a few people could be seen moving about in the hall. There was a jumble of slippers and sandals and shoes by the door, promiscuously heaped on one another. Mr Mitra took off his with an impatient movement; Mrs Mitra descended delicately from hers – they had small, two-inch heels.

Mr Talukdar, who was standing in a white shirt and trousers talking to another couple and a man, excused himself from their company and came to the newly arrived couple. 'Come in, come in,' he said to Mrs Mitra. To Mr Mitra he said nothing, but accepted the tuberoses that were now transferred to his arms. 'Nilima's there,' he said, indicating a woman who was sitting at the far side of the sitting room upon a mattress on the floor, an old woman near her. So saying, he went off slowly with the tuberoses in another direction.

A small crystal chandelier hung from the ceiling, gleaming in daylight. Near where Nilima, Anjali's mother, sat, a ceiling fan turned slowly. Some of the furniture had been cleared away for mats to be laid out on the floor, but some, including two armchairs and a divan, had been left where they were. On the sideboard was a Mickey Mouse-shaped pencil box, next to a few photographs and curios. A clock upon one of the shelves said it was eleven twenty-five.

Mr Talukdar was a tallish man, heavy, fair, clean-shaven. Most of his hair was grey, and thinning slightly. He'd held some sort of important position in an old British industrial company that had turned into a large public-sector concern a decade after independence: British Steel, renamed National Steel. He was now standing next to a television set, whose convex screen was dusty, and talking to someone.

Mr Mitra seemed to remember that Mr Talukdar had two sons in America, and that the sons had children. But Anjali had had no children, and that might have made things worse for her. He looked at a man singing a Brahmo sangeet on a harmonium in the middle of the room, attended by only a few listeners, and saw that it was someone he knew, an engineer at Larsen & Toubro.

The song stopped, and the sound of groups of people talking became more audible. The hubbub common to shraddh ceremonies was absent: people welcoming others as they came in, even the sense, and the conciliatory looks, of bereavement. Instead there was a sort of pointlessness, as people refused to acknowledge what did not quite have a definition. Mr Mitra's stomach growled.

He looked at his wife in the distance, the bun of hair prominent at the back of her head; she bent and said something to Nilima, Anjali's mother. Suddenly there was a soft, whining sound that repeated itself, low but audible; it was the cordless phone. Mr Talukdar stooped to pick it up from a chair and, distractedly looking out of the window, said 'Hello' into the receiver, and then more words, nodding his head vigorously once, and gesturing with his hand. He walked a few steps with the cordless against his ear, gravitating towards a different group of people. Mr Mitra realised that the tuberoses he'd brought had been placed on that side of the room, beside three or four other bouquets.

He felt bored; and he noticed a few others, too, some of whom he knew, looking out of place. Shraddh ceremonies weren't right without their mixture of convivial pleasure and grief; and he couldn't feel anything as complete as grief. He'd known Anjali slightly; how well do you know your wife's distant relations, after all? He'd known more about her academic record, one or two charming anecdotes to do with her success at school, her decent first-class degree, and about her husband, Gautam Poddar, diversifying into new areas of business, than about her.

'Saab?'

Thank God! A man was standing before him with a platter of sandesh – he picked up one; it was small and soft; he took a tiny bite. It must be from Banchharam or Nepal Sweets; it had that texture. There was another man a little farther away, with a tray of Fanta and Coca-Cola. Mr Mitra hesitated for a second and then walked towards the man. He groped for a bottle that was less cold than the others; he had a sore throat developing.

'Mr Mitra!'

There was a man smiling widely at him, a half-empty Coke bottle with a straw in one hand.

'I hope you remember me; or do I need to introduce myself?'

'No, I don't remember you; but I spoke to someone at the club just the other day who looks very like you, a Mr Amiya Sarbadhikari,' said Mr Mitra jovially, taking a sip of faintly chilled Fanta. A large painting of a middle-aged woman holding flowers faced them.

They talked equably of recent changes in their companies, catching up from where they'd left it in their last exchange; then to their children, and a brief disagreement about whether civil engineering had a future as a career today.

'Oh, I think so,' said Mr Sarbadhikari, 'certainly in the developing world, in the Middle East, if not in the West.' His Coke bottle was now almost empty; he held it symbolically, putting off finishing the dregs to a moment later. There was an uneasiness in their conversation, though, as if they were avoiding something; it was their being here they were avoiding. Of course, people never remembered the dead at shraddh ceremonies; they talked about other things; but that forgetfulness occurred effortlessly. In this case, the avoidance was strategic and self-conscious; the conversation tripped from subject to subject.

'Mr Mitra, all this Coke has swollen my bladder,' said Sarbadhikari suddenly, 'and, actually, from the moment I stepped in . . .'

From his manner it looked like he was familiar with Talukdar's flat. Gathering the folds of his dhuti in one hand, he turned histrionically and padded off in the direction of a bathroom door. A child, the only one among the people who'd come, ran from one end of the hall to the other. There were a few people on the balcony; Mr Mitra decided to join them.

'I told them,' a woman was saying to a companion, 'this is no way to run a shop; if you don't exchange a purchase, say so, but don't sell damaged goods.'

He quietly put down the bottle of Fanta on the floor. There wasn't much of a view; there was the wall, which ran towards the street you couldn't see, and another five-storeyed building with little, pretty balconies. Below him was the porch to the left, and the driveway, which seemed quite close. A young woman, clearly not a maidservant, was hanging towels from the railing in one of the balconies opposite.

Did it happen here? He looked at the woman attach clips to another towel. Apparently those who always threaten to, don't. Anjali had been living with her parents for a month after leaving her husband. She'd left him before, but this time she'd said her intentions were clear and final. There was a rumour that her parents had not been altogether sympathetic, and had been somewhat obtuse; but it's easy to be lucid with hindsight. He was still hungry, and he looked back into the hall to see if he could spot the man with the sandesh. But he had temporarily disappeared. As he moved about exploratorily, he caught his wife's eye and nodded at her as if to say, Yes, I'm coming, and, Yes, it's been a waste of time.

Cautiously, he tried to trace, from memory, the route that he'd seen Sarbadhikari take about ten minutes ago. He found himself in a bedroom where the double bed had been covered neatly with a pink bedcover; he coughed loudly. He opened a door to what might be the bathroom and, once inside, closed it behind him again. As he urinated into the commode, he studied a box, printed with flowers, of Odomos room freshener kept above it; then he shivered involuntarily, and shrugged his shoulders. He had a vaguely unsatisfying feeling, as if the last half hour had lacked definition.

Once inside the car, he said to his wife, 'I don't know about you, but I'm quite ravenous.'

48

On Her Knees

(2004)

Tim Winton

I was sixteen when the old man shot through. A year later we moved back to the city where my mother cleaned houses to pay off his debts and keep us afloat and get me through university. She wouldn't let me get a part-time job to pay my way. The study, she said, was too important. Cleaning was a come-down from her previous job, eighteen years before, as a receptionist in a doctor's surgery, but it was all she could get. She told me there was more honour in scrubbing other people's floors than in having strangers scrub your own. But I wasn't convinced. The only thing worse than knowing she knelt every day in someone else's grotty shower recess was having to help her do it. Some days, between lectures, I did go with her. I hated it. There were many other times when I could have gone and didn't. I stayed home and stewed with guilt. She never said a word.

My mother had a kind of stiff-necked working class pride. After the old man bolted she became a stickler for order. She believed in hygiene, insisted upon rigour. She was discreet and deadly honest, and those lofty standards, that very rigidity, set her apart. Carol Lang went through a house like a dose of salts. She earned a reputation in the riverside suburbs where, in time, she became the domestic benchmark. She probably cleaned the houses of some of my wealthy classmates without any of us being the wiser.

She was proud of her good name and the way people bragged about her and passed her around like a hot tip, but I resented how quickly they took her for granted. I'd seen their patronising notes on floral paper, their attempts to chip her rate down. The householders who thought most highly of themselves were invariably the worst payers and the biggest slobs. It was as though having someone pick up after them had either encouraged them to be careless or made them increasingly determined to extort more work for their money. Through it all, my mother maintained her dignity *and* her hourly rate. She left jobs, she did not lose them.

In twenty years she was only ever sacked the once, and that was over a pair of missing earrings. She came home with a week's notice and wept under the lemon tree where she thought I wouldn't hear. I tried to convince her never to return but she wouldn't hear a word of it. We argued. It was awful, and it didn't let up all week. Since the old man's disappearance we'd never raised our voices at each other. It was as though we kept the peace at all costs for fear of driving each other away. And now we couldn't stop bickering.

The morning she was to return we were still at it. Then, even while I took a shower, she stood in the bathroom doorway to lecture me on the subject of personal pride. It was as though I was not a twenty-year-old law student but a little boy who needed his neck scrubbed.

I don't care what you say, I yelled. It's outrageous and I'm not coming.

I never asked you, she said. When did I ever ask you to come?

I groaned. There was nothing I could say to that. And I knew it was a four-hour job, two if I helped out. Given what the householder had accused her of, it would be the toughest four hours she'd ever put in. But I was convinced that it was a mistake for her to go back. It was unfair, ludicrous, impossible, and while she packed the Corolla in the driveway I told her so. She came back for the mop and bucket. I stood on the verandah with my arms folded. But she must have known I'd go. She knew before I did, and not even the chassis-bending slam I gave the door could wipe the look of vindication from her face as she reversed us out into the street.

The car reeked of bleach and rubber gloves. I sighed and cranked down the window. She drove with both ravaged hands on the wheel, her chin up at a silly, dignified angle. Her mask of composure belied a fear of driving, and the caution with which she navigated made me crazy, but I resolved to show a bit of grace.

What? she said, seeing something in my face.

Nothing, I said, trying not to sound sullen.

You're good to come with me.

Well. Figure you need the help.

Oh, it's not help, love. It's company.

I could have opened the door and got out there and then.

What? she asked.

I shook my head. I couldn't launch into it all again. She was worth twice what those silvertails paid her. She was more scrupulous, more honest, than any of them. She wouldn't even open a drawer unless it was to put a clean knife or fork into it. For her to be called a thief was beyond imagining.

I know it's not easy, she said.

It's demeaning, Mum! I blurted despite myself. Going back like this. The whole performance. It's demeaning.

To who?

Whom.

Well, excuse me, constable! she said with a tart laugh. To *whom* is it demeaning, then, Victor? You?

I looked out of the window, flushing for shame.

You men, she said brightly.

Actually, this is about a woman, Mum. What kind of person accuses you of thieving, gives you the sack and then asks you back for one week while she looks for somebody to replace you?

Well, it's her loss, said my mother, changing lanes with excruciating precision. She knows she won't find anybody better than me.

Not even as good as you. Not a chance.

Thank you.

Five-hundred-dollar earrings, Mum. She hasn't even gone to the police.

As far as we know.

In that postcode? Believe me, we'd know.

She must know I didn't steal them.

She just wants something, some advantage over you. There'll be a note there, you wait. She'll let it slide – this time – and later on, while you're all guilty and grateful, she'll chip you down on the rate. Back to a fiver an hour.

The Law, she said. It must make you suspicious. She's just made a stupid mistake. She's probably found them by now.

And not called?

These people, they never call. Silence, that's their idea of an apology. It's how they're brought up.

But she looked troubled for a few moments. Then her face cleared.

Oh well, she murmured. There's the waiting list. I can still fill a dance card in this business.

Sure, I said without any enthusiasm.

Anyway, we'll show her.

How's that?

We'll clean that flat within an inch of its life.

Oh yeah, I muttered. That'll put her back in her box. Go, Mum.

We pulled up in the leafy street beneath a block of Art Deco flats. You could smell the river. Even after three years at the university, whose lawns all but ran to the river's grassy banks, that constant, brothy presence stank of old money, of posh schools and yacht clubs. Sometimes it reeked of Law itself, of port and cigars, chesterfields, musty paper and the men who owned this city because of it. That smell kept me alert. It made me wary and determined.

Drive on up, Mum, I said. Use her car space.

I wouldn't give her the satisfaction.

I did not roll my eyes. I got out and hoisted the vacuum cleaner off the back seat. She grabbed a bucket full of rags and squeeze bottles along with the mop.

Don't you use her gear?

Not today.

Don't tell me. The principle, right?

She winked and I felt sick for her.

I followed her up the long garden steps. Veins stood out in her calves. Beneath her loose shorts her thighs were white and dimpled. She seemed so old. I balanced the

Electrolux hose on my shoulder and stared at the tennis shoes that she scrubbed and bleached every week to keep them looking new. As if anyone but her gave a damn.

Up on the porch, she fished the key from her blouse. All the keys hung from a piece of string around her neck. The sound of them jangling onto her dressing table at night signalled the end of her day.

The apartment had a closed-up smell intensified by the pong of housebound cats. While Mum went through to the kitchen I stared a moment at the Klee reproductions, the dreadful cat photos in gold frames, and the Kokoschka poster which appeared to be new. I heard an envelope torn open and I came in as she held up the mauve paper, one hand on her heart.

What does it say?

Nothing, she said too quickly. She stuffed the note into her pocket and patted her hair. The envelope lay on the bench. There was money in it.

I opened the fridge, a huge American thing with two doors and an icemaker.

No snooping, she said. Not even today.

There were two kinds of white wine, tomato juice and jars of condiments. On one shelf was a stack of foil boxes, some kind of packaged food without labels. I closed the fridge and looked at the wine rack, a shoulder-high stack of bottles that, after her second week, my mother was requested to leave undisturbed, unrolled, unwiped and undusted.

Don't be a stickybeak, she murmured, pulling on gloves.

Today I just couldn't help myself. It wasn't only resentment. I was curious. What kind of person would do this? After years of faultless service there was no discussion, just the accusation and the brusque termination in three scrawled lines.

Cat tray, she said.

I went into the airless laundry where the litter tray lay beneath the steel trough. The stink was awful. I got down with a garbage bag and tried to breathe through my mouth but the dust from the grit rose onto my lips and tongue and I started to gag. I grunted a bit, swung the hair out of my eyes and got it done, twisting the bag shut. I was supposed to disinfect the tray and I'd never dared cut corners before, but I just tipped some litter in and left it at that.

From the bathroom came the sound of my mother's off-key singing. I paused at the doorway a moment where a stinging fog of ammonia spilled out into the hall. She stopped warbling as if conscious of my presence. She was bent over the tub, Ajax in hand, veins livid in her legs. As I walked on, the sound of her brush panted against the enamel.

I binned the cat bag and began damp-dusting. With every surface so crowded with *objets*, it was slow work. Every trinket, souvenir, ornament and figurine had to be wiped, lifted, dusted beneath and replaced precisely. Standing orders. Mum would inspect it like a sergeant-major at barracks inspection. We both agreed that nobody who cleaned their own place would bother keeping such junk. A week of doing for herself and this woman'd ditch the lot out with the cat litter.

It was a lonely apartment. We'd had a grim few years, Mum and I, but you wouldn't walk into our place and feel the same melancholy you picked up here. Another person might have found it tranquil, but to me it felt as stale as it smelled. I dusted the Andrew Wyeth reproduction and the steel and leather chairs. I brushed and wiped and waxed the long shelves of books and tried to imagine having strangers in our place looking in our fridge, touching our stuff, ripping hanks of our hair from the plughole. You'd have to imagine they were some kind of sleepwalker, that they were blind, incurious, too stupid to notice intimate things about your life. You'd have to not think about them, to will these intruders away. Or just be confident. Yes, I thought. That's what it takes to be blasé about strangers in your house – a kind of annihilating self-assurance.

The bookshelves in the livingroom were stocked with novels and popular psychology. There were big celebrity hardbacks as well as the usual stuff by Germaine Greer, Erica Jong, Betty Friedan. But I found both volumes of the Kinsey Report and boxed sets of erotica I took some minutes to thumb through, wondering how Mum had missed them.

In the study I flicked the duster across slabs of specialist material, academic stuff, lever-arch files and archive boxes. I found biographies of Paul Robeson, Leadbelly, Dorothy Day, Martin Luther King, each of them bristling with tabs of paper and pencilled notes. On the desk beside the typewriter was a pile of what I instantly recognised as student papers. The title of the topmost was *Throwing Off the Shackles: consciousness-raising and the delivery of change.* I turned the cover page and read a few paragraphs. It was all the safe, right-thinking stuff of the time but clumsily written. The comments in red biro were good-natured and forbearing.

I smoothed the paper back into place and dusted the pin-up board of snapshots above the desk. The photos were of people in heavy coats and hats with earflaps, of fir trees, snow, people with big, pink smiling faces and spectacles. Americans. The lantern-jawed woman who appeared in so many – it was her. She looked decent, happy, loved by friends and family. Even as I clawed through her desk drawers, finding nothing more remarkable than a tiny twist of hash in a bit of tinfoil, I knew I wouldn't find anything that would satisfy me. Now I just wanted to get the job over with.

In the bedroom I worked in a frenzy. Every sill and architrave, each lamp and mirror got a grinding wipe. I Windexed the glass, waxed the girly dressing table. When it was done I went out for the vacuum, cranked it up and ploughed my way through the whole place. At one point, when the old girl glanced up from the kitchen floor, I averted my eyes.

The thought kept returning to me. Why would someone not report the theft of a pair of five-hundred-dollar earrings? Even to claim the insurance you'd have to report it. Perhaps it was my own uneasiness at having overstepped the boundaries, at having gone through somebody's stuff, which made me consider the chance that this woman might know about me, be aware that I'd helped here before. Could she have suspected me rather than Mum? Worse still, did she know who I was, that I was an undergraduate at her own campus? And then could it be possible that her failure to report a theft to the cops was an act of kindness towards my mother, an act of mercy toward me?

I vacuumed and raked feverishly. When I got to the bedroom, the cats who'd thus far evaded us leapt out from behind the curtains. They were sulking great Persians. I threw down the nozzle and chased them out of the room.

My mother was still in the kitchen.

Mum, I said. What did the note say?

Did you leave that machine going?

Was it about me? Does she suspect me?

You? Don't be stupid.

I haven't been here for months.

Turn that thing off.

No, I said feeling ridiculous. It doesn't matter, I'm going back.

Don't forget those curtains!

I gave the bedroom curtains a good going over. I could never understand how so much cat hair could accumulate in a week.

Mum came in while I was on my knees still vacuuming the flounces and folds of the patchwork quilt.

Windex? she said.

I pointed to the dressing table. She lingered. I turned the machine off.

What were you on about before?

Honestly, Mum, why didn't we just give the place a light go through? Or better, just take the dough and split.

Because it would look like an admission of guilt.

Shit.

Language.

But this won't convince her, Mum.

No, probably not.

You should report them missing yourself. Ask them to search our place. Force the issue. There's nothing that can come of it.

Except talk. Imagine the talk. I'd lose the rest of my jobs.

She was shining with sweat. Her hair had tightened into damp poodle curls. She had been so pretty once.

So you're stuffed either way.

Love, we grin and bear it.

I shook my head. I hit the button on the vac and blitzed the carpet beneath the bed. I could sense her still behind me, waiting to say something but I pretended to be absorbed in the work. Up at the head of the bed there was a nest of Red Tulip chocolate wrappers. They made a slurping noise as they were sucked into the machine. I only had half of them up when the ping of something hard racketing along the pipe made me turn my head.

Mum stepped on the button. The machine wound down to silence.

Money, probably, I murmured.

Let's open it up.

I cracked the hatch and felt around in the horrible gullet of the dustbag. From wads of lint and hair and dirt came an earring.

Five hundred dollars? she muttered. That's rich.

I didn't know anything about jewellery. I shrugged, gave it to her.

Look under there. The other one's bound to be close by.

I found it hard up against the skirting board.

She's left them on the pillow, she said. Forgotten about them. She's come in and swept them off as she got into bed. She hasn't even looked. That's all it was, just carelessness.

All this fake outrage. She couldn't be bothered going to the cops because they're cheap? Is that it?

I don't know.

It wasn't important.

It was important to me.

Well, you've cleared your name. That's something.

She shook her head with a furious smile.

Why not? I asked. Show her what we found, what she was too lazy to look for. Show her where they were.

All she has to say is that she made me guilty enough to give them back. That I just wanted to keep the job. To save my good name. Vic, that's all I've *got* – my good name. These people, they can say anything they like. You can't fight back.

I looked away at the floor. I heard her blow her nose. I was powerless to defend her. It was the lowest feeling.

I'll finish the kitchen, she said. Ten minutes.

I vacuumed the rest of the bedroom. The earrings lay on the bed. I looked at them. They were pretty enough but I was no judge. Perhaps their real value was sentimental. I snatched them up from the quilt and took them into the laundry. I chucked them into the cat tray. Let her find them there if she cared to look.

In the kitchen Mum was ready to go. The rags and bottles were in the bucket. She walked a towel across the floor and that was it.

What about the money? I said, looking at the scrubbed bench.

I'm worth more, she said.

You're not taking it?

No.

I smiled and shook my head.

You forgot the vacuum, she said.

Oh, yeah. Right.

I went back to the laundry, knelt at the catbox and picked out the earrings. I dusted them off on my sweaty shirt. In my palm they weighed nothing. I grabbed the Electrolux from the bedroom and made my way out again. In the kitchen I put the earrings beside the unstrung key and the thin envelope of money.

My mother stood silhouetted in the open doorway. It seemed that the very light of day was pouring out through her limbs. I had my breath back. I followed her into the hot afternoon.

49

The Contest

(2005)

Annie Proulx

There comes a time when Elk Tooth residents no longer take an interest in winter. Toward the end of March the count of semis tipped over by the wind fails to amuse and driving the long way around to anywhere – Angle Iron Pass is closed even in a mild winter – has become an odious chore. Elk Tooth residents can take no more of reality. They embrace fads and fancies, and fortunes ride on rash wagers.

A few years ago the idea of a beard-growing contest inflamed the male population. Too late in the season to start then, but the Pee Wee regulars signed an oath (in Guinness, for its ink-like color) to put aside their razors the next winter beginning on the day of the first snowfall. The beards would grow and there would be a prize for the longest, to be presented on the following Fourth of July. A few snowflakes drifted on September 12, and M. J. Speet, the large-animal vet, whose opinions were widely respected, declared the start of the contest.

Amanda Gribb, copying rodeo procedure (the rule of law in Elk Tooth), established a prize purse by collecting ten dollars from each contestant. The only businesses in Elk Tooth were the Elk Tooth bank, the Western Wear & Feed store, and the three bars – Pee Wee's, Muddy's Hole, and the Silvertip. Each put fifty dollars in the pot. The propane gas route man pitched in ten but said he'd forgo the chin grass. The money was stowed in a clean mason jar on the mirror shelf at Pee Wee's.

Twenty-seven contestants, from fourteen-year-old Kevin Cokendall to octogenarian Len DeBock, signed up. Kevin Cokendall's father, Wiregrass Cokendall, told the kid he didn't have the chance of a pancake in a pigsty, but Kevin was determined and bought hair restorer with his allowance to help the nascent whiskers along. The other contestants demanded that Old Man DeBock shave before the contest started, as he showed a two-inch frizz in his normal appearance. He shaved, protesting, but it seemed to the others that within days the two-inch frizz had returned. They were heartened when the whiskers seemed to stall at that length without going on to glory. Darryl Mutsch said it was because the hairs were set deep in the crevices and wrinkles of DeBock's ancient face, great furrows indicating a toothless condition. (The story was that back in the 1950s, at some branding or other, a calf had kicked out DeBock's front teeth. With the blood seeping down his chin he had picked up the teeth, rinsed them with coffee, and jammed them back into the vacant spaces. When they, and their loosened neighbors, failed he had yanked every one, cowboy style, with a pair of pliers, bracing his forehead against a gatepost for leverage. Over the years he had become an expert on culinary variations of cornmeal mush, his favorite recipe beginning 'Take a quart of deer blood . . .')

The beards showed odd color and texture variations. Old Man DeBock's whiskers were short and yellow-white. Deb Sipple's, as crinkled as ramen noodles, came in black with streaks of grey down each side, and Wiregrass Cokendall showed thick and fiery red bristle in contrast to the anemic blond hairs of his son, Kevin. The Game & Fish warden, Creel Zmundzinski, also grew a red beard, no surprise as his hair all over was the orange-red the paint store called 'Mandarin Sunset', a color that clashed unmercifully with his official red shirt. Hard Winter Ulph, who'd been born during the blizzard of 1949 in some shack south of Wamsutter, showed jet black, pencil-straight whiskers that stuck out like the spines on a hatpin cactus. A suet-faced Englishman with the chewy name of Lobett Pulvertoft Thirkill, working on Fiesta Punch's ranch for the winter, joined in and contributed a faceful of tan five-o'clock shadow. He was closely watched by Creel Zmundzinski, who knew that men with criminal pasts often took hired-man jobs on remote ranches, and that their warped inclinations found outlet in poaching and carnal knowledge of anything warm. By January the contestants' facial moss had thickened and lengthened to the point where most could scratch their fingers through the underbrush and delighted to do so. Amanda Gribb complained, for the zinc counter was sprinkled with loose hairs night after night.

'Worse'n havin a cat on the bar,' she said.

Shortly after Valentine's Day it was clear that three or four men had forged ahead: Darryl Mutsch, Wiregrass Cokendall, Willy Huson (color of mashed sweet potato), and to his father's chagrin, Kevin Cokendall, whose few whiskers made up in length what they lacked in profusion.

'It's goin a be terrible a shave all this hay off,' said Mutsch.

Deb Sipple, who did not like to hear references to hay, said it would be easy. 'Just cut er down with scissors first, then take you a good hot shower and put on plenty shave cream and you're home.'

'Best thing is go over to Lander to Thone's barbershop. He'll make it easy. Just lay back and let him get it done.'

'No, best way is to go down to Saratoga or over to Thermop to them hot springs and let the waters come up to your nose, then skedaddle for the barbershop before them whiskers dries up and hardens. The sulfur in the water sort a rots the hair or at least softens it up,' said Quent Stipp. 'Course the best way would be to bring your razor in the hot pool but I don't believe they'd allow that.'

'Rots the hair? You must a been duckin beneath the surface pretty frequent,' said Al Mort, looking at Stipp's retreating hairline. 'Anyhow, I ain't goin a shave nothin off. Got this far I'll go end a the rope.'

*

Although the contest started out with jocularity, it turned cruelly competitive. Questions about beards came up which no one could answer. Amanda Gribb tired of bar arguments that beards were or were not good protection against bronchitis, that vegetarians favored beards more than creophagists, that beards inspired political radicalism. Beard talk made a change from speculation on the whereabouts of Darryl Mutsch's missing dog, Cowboy George, but none of the questions raised could be answered. Amanda, on her day off, sought out Mercedes de Silhouette, widow of Bill de Silhouette, a sheep rancher who had graduated cum laude from Princeton and over the years amassed a tremendous number of books on diverse subjects. Mercedes had inherited the sheep, the ranch, the house, and its contents, including the books.

'Oh yeah, I still got em. Sold the sheep, kept the books. I dunno why, don't hardly go in that part a the house. It's like a liberry in there. Stinks a Bill's old cigars, too. Like a ghost was in there ever night smokin cigars and readin books.'

Mercedes led the way around knotty pine corners, through log-girdered passageways, into rooms of trophy heads and leather chairs, and at last into a large dim room with a northern clerestory. There were thousands of books from floor to ceiling, in shelved stacks running the length of the space. She switched on the overhead track lights to augment the natural light, and book titles sprang forth: *Saddle Galls*, *The Rooster Book*, *Into Surinam with Colonel Mascara*, and the like.

'How do you find a particular thing?' said Amanda. 'Has he got them put up like at a liberry?'

'No, And that's the trouble. *He* known where the books was, but nobody else can find a damn thing. I spent days here once lookin for somethin on cowboy songs. He had the books and I knew he had em, especially the dirty ones, but find em I could not. Part a them he arranged by color. See over there? All them shelves a red ones? There's a blue section and green and after that I think he give up. No, there's mystery stories is yella, and that's the most I know.'

'Well, I'm lookin for books about beards. You wouldn't happen to know if there's some a them, would you?'

'Honey, there's everthing else here.'

'How did he ever get all these books?' The idea that there were shops devoted entirely to books would have astonished the Pee Wee cow crowd except for Erwin Hungate, who was a reader, his big tallow-colored face buried in a book even at the bar. Give Deb Sipple a book, she thought, and he'd probably chew the covers off.

'Well, he bought em at junk stores and on the internet, but mostly he'd get em when he went to sheep conferences in different cities? The other men'd go roosterin around, but not Bill. He'd get right at the yellow pages and find him some secondhand book dealers and then he'd go there and claw through them shelves until he'd picked out fifty or sixty he liked and have em sent up home. While he was in the hospital they kept comin, boxes and boxes a books. Over there in the corner. I never even opened them. So, I'm just goin a leave you to look, and if you find what you want you can keep it.'

Amanda Gribb began with the color-coded books and discovered that most of the blue ones concerned the ocean or exploratory voyages, that green books focused on natural history or forestry. She scanned the titles, alert for the words 'beard', 'hair', and 'mustache'. After several hours she discerned some kind of order in the groupings of dusty books and she was briefly hopeful when she found something titled *Haircults.* But this was an annoying collection of photographs of American and English hairdos from the 1960s and '70s, nothing whatsoever to do with the beard. There seemed to be a conceptual separation between head hair and facial hair. At the end of the afternoon she had nothing but grimy hands.

'It feels like there ought a be somethin. I'll come back and look some more if it's all right,' said Amanda to Mercedes.

'Honey, you come back much as you want. I'm real sorry you didn't find nothin.'

The next afternoon when Amanda Gribb arrived at Pee Wee's to relieve owner Lewis McCusky, he said, 'Mercedes de Silhouette called up. Says you come by after your shift, don't matter how late cause she sits up watchin old movies. She found what you want. I'd say go on ahead any time because I'm goin a be right here tonight watchin the game.'

Mercedes de Silhouette was wearing a pair of her dead husband's pajamas and his claret-colored silk bathrobe. She smelled of bourbon.

'Come on in,' she said. 'I think I found you a good one. But it's hard readin. A lot a foreign language and them sideways leanin words.'

'Italics?'

'Yeah. Here it is. Too bad it don't have pictures.' She handed Amanda an orange book titled simply *Beards.* It was an old book, dated 1950, but she saw, opening to a page entitled 'Culinary Instructions for Christian Cannibals', that it was rich in beard history. Richard the Lion-Hearted, she read, once entertained his warriors with a feast in which the pièce de résistance featured the roasted heads of captive Saracens who had been shaved before going into the oven. Farther along she spotted a passage on beards and vegetarians.

'This is good,' she said. 'How did you find it?'

'It was funny. I was cleanin out that big chest in the hall and I come on some a Bill's notebooks. There was one he'd written on the cover, "Book Key". I looked in it and it was the system he used. Made me mad he didn't tell me about it before he went. Each one a them bookcases has a little number at the top, you seen that.'

'I sure did.'

'Well, in the notebook it tells what kind a books is in which bookcases. I looked for beards but there wasn't nothing. So I tried hair, and there was about seven books and this one. You can keep it.'

Amanda placed the book in a prominent position on the bar and it was soon well-thumbed and stained with various alcohols. No one could quite understand what the author, one Reginald Reynolds, was saying as it was written in an abstruse and sarcastic style freckled with irony and untranslated Latin and French. The author also favored maze-like circumlocutions and assumed his readers possessed profound knowledge of history, literature, seafaring, religion, military strategy, dialectic, nursery rhymes, and philosophy. He was given to mossy jokes such as one about the Egyptologist who discovered a bit of wire in an excavation and declared the Egyptians had invented telegraphy, only to be aced by a rival who said that since no such piece of wire had been found in Assyrian site excavations, the Assyrians must have enjoyed wireless telegraphy. Still, the Pee Wee regulars sifted enough wheat from the chaff to make perusal of *Beards* worthwhile.

Amanda brought in a dictionary to aid Mr Reynolds. Gradually the vocabularies of the Pee Wee's patrons swelled with such splendid words as 'pogonophile', 'finookery', 'gnostic', 'countenance', 'postiche', 'obelisk', 'serendipity', and the stirring phrase *Floreat Barba!* Enlightenment did not emerge but curiosity flowered as they read of ancient bearded horse eaters, of a certain abbot who believed that eating too much was the cause of beards and thus explained why the American Indians, who lived on frugal diets, did not have beards. Adam, they discovered, had no beard in the Garden of Eden, the hairy growth punitively linked to the expulsion.

Wiregrass Cokendall was thrilled to find a footnote referencing a Muslim story that the devil had only one hair on his chin, though of exceeding length, and used this nugget to taunt his son, Kevin. Kevin thumbed through until he found a passage describing a civilisation that killed the red-bearded men among them.

There were many examples of beards as fashion statements – metal threads worked in, dyes and gold dust, the pointed beards of Arabs, the rectilinear faux beards of the Egyptians, the curly extravagances of the Assyrians, the Hittites' square-laced beards, plaited beards, immensely long beards that could be parted and looped around the ears, but tempting as these arrangements sounded, no contestant dared sacrifice length to style. Vic Vase took up the book often and read passages aloud, mangling his way through medieval French, church Latin, and antique English.

'Jesus,' said Erwin Hungate, the reader, 'lay off, will you? Sound like Umberto Eco.'

'Who?' said Vic.

'I know him,' said Old Man DeBock. 'Bert Eckle, used a work for Bob Utley. He's out in Nevada now in a home. Home for old cowboys.'

Erwin Hungate lifted his hand slightly and let it drop to show it was hopeless to explain.

The beard growers combed through the Wal-Mart pharmacy in Sack looking for unguents and lotions that would impart vigor to hair. They urged the druggist to order new improved products. Old Man DeBock, rustling through the boxes under his bed, discovered a 1946 *Real Western Stories* magazine that featured an advertisement for a device that when cranked sent mild charges of electricity through the body and was, the ad claimed, a no-fail encouragement to hair. Pictured were three men whose combined hair could have stuffed a mattress. He dug out an ancient electric blanket from his storeroom and slept with it bunched up under his chin, happy to be absorbing whisker-stimulating electric juice. Darryl Mutsch rinsed his beard in a Viagra solution, immediate results not known.

By late April most of the beards were thick and bristly. Men sat around in Pee Wee's eyeing one another's facial adornments. Darryl Mutsch was in the lead, but he had been in the lead before and then had fallen back as Willy Huson passed him by half an inch. Amanda Gribb was called on six times a day to measure someone's beard. She had a little tape measure Creel Zmundzinski once had given her. He had used it for sizing animal tracks and the trout of out-of-state fishermen. Then, two springs back, he had developed a crush on Amanda and brought her the kinds of presents that Game & Fish employees believed superior to chocolates and flowers – an untenanted hornets' nest, a wolf scat, the pelvic bone of a sharp-tail grouse, the miniature tape measure. The romance faded and died when Amanda took an interest in a fellow from Casper who had invented a lotion he called 'Buckaroo Hand Cream', sparking vulgar witticisms among the ranch hand clientele.

Amanda said her friend was going to be a millionaire by the time he was thirty-five.

'Accordin to my arithmetic that ought to a happened about ten years back,' said Creel meanly. He had taken to spending his afternoons in the Pee Wee, one eye nervously on the front window watching for the Game & Fish vehicles. Because of his unpopular liberal views he was a thorn in the flesh of his superiors, who plotted ways to fire him. Amanda Gribb kept a lookout as well, and when one of the department's trucks idled outside she hissed, 'Go fish,' and Creel ducked into the back room with its cases of empties and smelly mops.

Creel's best friend was another bachelor, Plato Bucklew, his counterpart in the Forest Service, a big, ax-headed blond often mixed up in fights and referred to as 'Plate-Head' by those who found that his advocacy of roadless wilderness areas, wolves, and horse logging veered dangerously from traditional attitudes. Amanda had a warning for him, too. When she said 'Sure wish I had some pistachio ice cream,' she meant that a Forest Service vehicle of that color was in sight. The two troublemakers drank, hunted, fished together, and talked about the possibility of quitting their respective services and setting up a consulting business, though who would consult them and on what subjects was vague. They often spent Saturday afternoons in Creel's kitchen, Creel tying flies, Plato fashioning turkey wing-bone calls. There was another bond: both of their great-grandfathers had done time in the territorial prison at Laramie; Cephas Bucklew, a plasterer from Ohio, had stolen a horse blanket from a Cheyenne livery stable, and C. C. Alkerson, a ship's carpenter from Boston imprisoned for perjury when he tried to claim bounty money on three nonexistent wolf hides, enlivened Creel Zmundzinski's maternal lineage. But Zmundzinski's father, who wrote western love stories for true confessions magazines under his wife's name, fell afoul of a jealous rancher. Most of his story ideas came from ranch wives; one suspicious husband who found the elder Zmundzinski's attentions to his wife proof of infidelity shot him as he was fastening the ranch gate. Creel's mother died two years later of complications from breast cancer, and after a few wretched months with his mother's sister and husband in Encampment, he was sent to a boys' home and raised as an orphan.

The two friends helped each other out of tight spots, such as the time when Plato, driving through a blinding whiteout with no visibility, ran off the road and into an open burial pit for a horse Darryl Mutsch had put down and, except for the horse, which was *in situ*, put off filling the hole. The cavity was precisely the same size as a Forest Service truck. It took the two friends most of one night to get the vehicle out with a heavy-duty tripod and winch.

*

On this April afternoon Creel was, aside from Amanda and Old Man DeBock, the only one in the bar. He was deeply thirsty when he came in, for the state was up to its eyebrows in drought and the small lakes and ponds on the wind-clawed prairie had dried up. The wind lifted fine alkali dust from the bottoms of the dead ponds, streamers of mineral particles blowing east. Creel, his throat stinging, had driven through clouds of the stuff. Rarely had beer soothed a more parched throat.

He could see his beard in the mirror and was not displeased. It had grown in thick and had a tendency to curl under, thereby disguising its true length. He thought that when the tape measure came out on the final day he would be a front runner.

'I'll have me another,' he said to Amanda, who pulled him a fresh beer and slid it skillfully down the bar. He had barely lifted the glass when the throaty guzzle of a motorcycle out front drew his attention. An overweight, elderly man got off a silver bike the size of a short-legged horse. He wore a bandanna on his head and a red silk scarf around his mouth in the classic style of stagecoach robbers. As he came into the bar he unwound the scarf and pulled off the bandanna, and Creel Zmundzinski's mouth fell open. From under the silk emerged a huge white beard that could have filled a bushel basket. It covered the man from upper lip to belt buckle and was of a snowy, radiant white that seemed backlit by a full moon. Flowing into it as twin Missouris into the Mississippi were masses of hair that on a lesser man would have been sideburns. And from crown to shoulder blade cascaded heavy, silvery waves of hair. Creel Zmundzinski slowly grasped that he was looking at a tsunami of a beard.

The stranger, ignoring Amanda Gribb's stare, called for a beer, but before he drank he removed a silver straw from his breast pocket, an accoutrement favored by maté drinkers of the pampas. Amanda Gribb nodded with approval. Too often she had been called on to measure damp beards, whiskers clotted with hardened egg yolk, residues of mustard, individual crumbs clinging to hairs like boys swinging on ropes above a swimming hole. Here was a man who cared about his beard. Its luteous glow, its fluffed fullness, the mild fragrance of rose petals that wafted from it all declared a pogonophile-*meister*, as Reginald Reynolds might have said.

Creel Zmundzinski wanted a look at the stranger's license, and he slipped out expecting it would be a Montana plate. There was a belt of eccentrics and oddballs from Cooke City to Livingston. Or maybe he would be from Nevada, a state which featured heavily bearded men everywhere except Las Vegas. This stranger would be a threat in Las Vegas for he could easily hide a full deck of cards in his facial hair. Creel was nonplussed to find identification from Rhode Island, a state he imagined the size of the Wal-Mart parking lot. The motorcycle got a second look as well – one of the new Harleys, a Softail V-Rod. Creel had been saving up for eleven years to buy a Harley, but not this water-cooled model, which he knew had to have set the bearded one back seventeen big bills. He reentered the Pee Wee shaking his head. Amanda caught his eye, and he mouthed 'Rhode Island.'

'Find what you were looking for?' said the stranger, and Creel realised belatedly that the man had been watching him in the bar mirror.

'Just wanted to see where you were from,' mumbled Creel. He could feel his own beard withering and turned half away from the easterner.

'Since you want to know, I was born in Secaucus, New Jersey, on October 13, 1939. Name is Ralph Kaups. My father, Hayden Kaups, was a successful limnologist, and my mother, Virginia Rusling, studied batik in Borneo before the Second World War, then served as curator of Asian fabrics for the New Jersey Textile Institute. I went to Princeton, graduated summa cum laude, did my graduate work in ergonomics, married, divorced, one daughter, taught for thirty-two years at various eastern ratholes, and last week I retired. I am out here to see Mercedes de Silhouette, whose late husband was my roommate at Princeton in the sweet long ago. I plan to buy the old line camp on their place and fix it up. Moving to Elk Tooth for my retirement. That help you out?'

Creel, his ears burning, said 'See you later' to Amanda and left the bar.

As he got in his truck he saw Plato Bucklew coming out of the Western Wear & Feed store with a hatbox under his arm. His bruised face and black eye showed the results of a weekend fight in a distant parking lot. Plato liked to fight.

Creel beckoned him over.

'You want a have the heart tooken out a you, go in Pee Wee's and see what's settin at the bar. There's no sense in goin along with this damn beard thing another day.' But as he spoke the stranger came out of Pee Wee's and began tying his monstrous beard up in its scarves.

'Jesus,' said Plato, scratching his crotch, a nervous habit he'd picked up in the army.

They stared as the man started up his V-Rod and swept away.

'He's movin a Elk Tooth,' said Creel morosely. 'Buyin the old line camp on the de Silhouette place.' There was a considerable silence.

'You know,' said Plato Bucklew, 'I don't care for them new V-Rods. If I was to get a motorsickle it would be one a the old Buffalos. You ever hear a them?'

'Heard a them but never seen one. Heard they never got it off the drawin board,' said Creel Zmundzinski.

'That might just be the best part of it,' said his friend enigmatically.

'Take a horse, myself.'

As far as they were concerned the beard contest was over.

Glossary

p. 5	*Son coeur est un luth suspendu; Sitôt qu'on le touche il résonne.*	'Her heart is like a sprung lute: no sooner touched than it reverberates.'
p. 5	*De Béranger*	Pierre-Jean de Béranger (1780–1857), French Romantic poet
p. 5	*tarn*	mountain lake
p. 7	*ennuyé*	world-weary
p. 8	*Arabesque*	intricately designed
p. 10	*Von Weber*	Karl Maria von Weber (1786–1826), German Romantic composer
p. 10	*Fuseli*	Henry Fuseli (1741–1825), Swiss-born British painter, famous for his nightmare imagery
p. 29	*Sans-Souci*	(French) 'Without Cares'
p. 37	*it sticketh closer than a brother*	a quotation from the Bible: 'A man that hath friends must show himself friendly: and there is a friend that sticketh closer than a brother' (Proverbs 18, 24)
p. 42	*mopboard*	skirting board
p. 48	*flexuous*	lithe, sinuous, curvy
p. 51	*Covent Garden*	the site (until the 20th century) of London's main fruit and vegetable market
p. 56	*narrow clip*	near-run thing, 'close shave'
p. 56	*oiler*	one who oils machinery
p. 57	*bucking broncho*	untrained horse
p. 58	*canton-flannel*	as if dressed in white linen
p. 59	*Sèvres*	a type of fine porcelain
p. 74	*calcining*	heating a substance to oxidisation
p. 81	*prognostications*	forecasts, predictions, prognosis
p. 82	*bleu poudré*	a type of glaze for pottery
p. 82	*Ganymede*	in Greek myth, a beautiful young man, servant to Zeus
p. 82	*Pygmalion*	in Greek myth, a sculptor who gave life to a sculpture of a beautiful woman, and fell in love with her
p. 92	*hansom*	two-wheeled horsedrawn cab

p. 93	*snatch division*	the sudden call for a vote in the House of Commons
p. 93	*unpaired*	MPs from Government and Opposition benches 'pair' when they agree both to abstain during a vote in the House
p. 96	*Houdan hen*	a species of white, or black-and-white, chicken
p. 97	*the House of Rimmon*	a pagan faith mentioned in the Bible (2 Kings 5, 18)
p. 97	*Anabaptist*	member of a strictly reformist Protestant sect
p. 105	*toque*	soft-brimmed hat
p. 112	*chafer*	chafing-dish, crucible, open kettle
p. 117	*children of Israel . . . manna*	in the Bible, the Israelites were sustained with food from heaven on their journey through the wilderness to the Promised Land (Exodus 16, 10–15)
p. 120	*Theocritan*	pertaining to Theocritus (308–240 BC), Greek pastoral poet
p. 121	*the young princes in the Tower*	the children of King Edward IV, murdered in the Tower of London in 1483, supposedly at the command of Richard III
p. 122	*twa poon'*	(Scottish dialect) two pounds
p. 123	*escutcheon*	coat-of-arms; hereditary reputation
p. 125	*Dr Johnson*	Samuel Johnson (1709–84), English man of letters ('When a man is tired of London, he is tired of life')
p. 129	*Job*	in the Bible's Book of Job (pronounced to rhyme with 'globe'), Job's faith is tested by God with a series of calamities, which he bears with patience
p. 131	*President Roosevelt and the New Deal*	the measures taken by US President Franklin D. Roosevelt in the 1930s to cope with the financial Depression
p. 136	*the Peace Ballot*	a referendum on international affairs conducted in Britain in 1935
p. 136	*the Left Book Club*	a socialist literary society founded in 1936
p. 138	*the mark of Plague in the court of the Decameron*	Boccacccio's *Decameron* (c. 1350) is a collection of stories framed by a narrative in which the story-tellers gather in a remote villa to escape the Black Death
p. 140	*the Abyssinian War*	the Italian dictator Benito Mussolini waged war on Ethiopia ('Abyssinia') for territorial gain in 1935–6
p. 145	*appeasement and peace-in-our-time*	following Hitler's invasion of Czechoslovakia in 1938, the British prime minister Neville Chamberlain

		negotiated terms with Hitler, returning from talks at Munich promising 'peace in our time'
p. 148	*Phoenix phoenixissima formosissima arabiana*	(Latin) 'the most phoenix-like and most beautiful Arabian Phoenix'
p. 149	*Cleopatra . . . the du Barry*	the famously temperamental Queen of Ancient Egypt (69–30 BC) and Madame Du Barry (1743–93), aristocratic mistress of the French King Louis XV
p. 151	*evil Baal*	false god or idol
p. 152	*Sara Teasdale*	American lyric poet, born in 1884, who committed suicide in 1933
p. 155	*punchboards*	lottery cards
p. 156	*butts*	cigarettes
p. 160	*the first blitz*	the first German air-raids on London of the Second World War took place in October 1940
p. 187	*Neo-Malthusians*	proponents of the views of the theorist of population-growth Thomas Malthus (1766–1834)
p. 195	*kaffir*	(Afrikaans: offensive slang) 'black man'
p. 195	*verdomte*	(Afrikaans) 'damned'
p. 195	*hotnot*	(Afrikaans: offensive slang) 'black man'
p. 196	*sjambok*	a South African whip made of animal hide
p. 197	*bliksem*	(Afrikaans) 'wretch'
p. 199	*manuka*	a species of flowering New Zealand shrub
p. 201	*sly-grog shop*	bootleg alcohol store
p. 201	*Gallipoli*	the 1917 campaign by the British Allies in the First World War against mainland Turkey in which many thousands of Australian and New Zealand servicemen died
p. 204	*adze*	axe-like tool
p. 208	*pa*	ancient indigenous New Zealand settlement
p. 221	*Holden*	a make of car
p. 222	*Extreme Unkshun*	i.e., Extreme Unction, the ministration of the 'last rites' by a Roman Catholic priest on a dying believer
p. 233	*N.R.M.A.*	(Australian acronym) National Roads and Motorists' Association
p. 238	*drumstick tree*	moringa tree (with edible pods)
p. 239	*swarga*	in Hindu mythology, a staging-post in the afterlife
p. 241	*dhobi*	laundryman
p. 247	*bearish trend in the market*	one in which an investor is motivated to sell at a low price
p. 247	*puja*	ritual of Hindu devotion
p. 248	*gunny sack*	a densely woven material

p. 280	*adobe*	an unfired brick made of clay and straw
p. 290	*'A' levels*	exams taken at the end of secondary education
p. 291	*Lorna Doone, Persuasion, Wuthering Heights . . . Great Expectations*	classic 19th-century novels by (respectively) Walter Scott, Jane Austen, Emily Brontë, and Charles Dickens
p. 291	*Lourdes*	a place of Catholic pilgrimage in France
p. 292	*Brownie*	the 'Box Brownie' was an early make of camera
p. 293	*'I thought maybe it was Brother Benignus'*	on ordination, Catholic monks renounce their given names and are assigned another
p. 297	*two-iron*	a type of golf-club
p. 312	*buckshot*	larger-size shot (used in game-hunting)
p. 312	*double-ought*	i.e. '00'-shot (a large-size calibre)
p. 320	*pakeha*	(Maori) European New Zealander
p. 320	*kehuas*	(Maori) ghosts
p. 322	*pipis*	(Maori) shellfish
p. 322	*whanaungas*	(Maori) relatives, ancestors
p. 323	*whakairo*	(Maori) ceremonial meeting-place
p. 324	*kai*	(Maori) food
p. 340	*Ned Kelly*	Australian outlaw and folk hero (1855–80)
p. 342	*Lebert Bethune*	African-American poet (born 1937)
p. 344	*brownstone*	a type of sandstone, famously used in New York apartment blocks
p. 346	*Shirley Temple*	American child-star of 1930s Hollywood
p. 348	*Berbice chair*	an easy-chair made of wicker and wood
p. 348	*Benin mask*	a stylised African mask, carved in ebony
p. 348	*Tin Pan Alley*	the name given to New York's centre of commercial songwriting in the early 20th century
p. 352	*kustis*	belts worn by Parsees, woven from 72 threads
p. 356	*maidaan*	open square
p. 362	*lien*	a legal claim against an asset used to secure a loan
p. 375	*Aubusson*	a type of fine needlework tapestry
p. 377	*samfoo*	woman's trouser suit
p. 381	*Mukhesh*	a famous Bollywood singer (1923–76)
p. 381	*Grundig reel-to-reel*	a make of early hi-fi
p. 381	*MIT*	Massachusetts Institute of Technology
p. 383	*paisas*	Indian-denomination coins
p. 384	*swan boat*	a famous tourist pedal-boat in Boston's public gardens
p. 390	*stroller*	(American) push-chair
p. 397	*curé*	(French) priest
p. 397	*mas*	(French) farmhouse
p. 398	*gendarmerie*	(French) police station

p. 398	*Laval*	Pierre Laval (1883–1945), French politician, a collaborator with the Nazi occupiers
p. 398	*Service du Travail Obligatoire*	collaborationist legislation obliging citizens of Occupied France to assist in the Nazi war effort
p. 398	*maquisards*	members of the French Resistance movement (the Maquis)
p. 398	*Petit Ours*	(French) 'Little Bear'
p. 400	*Milice*	(French) police militia (the French equivalent of the Nazi Gestapo)
p. 402	*Les Allemands son corrects*	(French) 'Germans are scrupulous'
p. 403	*salauds*	(French) dirty
p. 403	*Vichy . . . Pétain*	Marshal Philippe Pétain (1856–1951), puppet ruler of the collaborationist government of Occupied France (1940–45), based in the district of Vichy
p. 412	*toheroas*	clams
p. 416	*shraddh*	Hindu mourning ritual
p. 416	*aata*	whole wheat used in making roti bread
p. 416	*chowkidar*	watchman
p. 417	*Brahmo sangeet*	religious song
p. 418	*sandesh*	sweet cake
p. 421	*silvertails*	(Australian slang) posh old folk
p. 422	*Art Deco*	architectural style of the 1920s and 1930s
p. 422	*chesterfields*	sofas, settees
p. 423	*Klee . . . Kokoschka*	The Expressionist painters Paul Klee (1879–1940) and Oskar Kokoschka (1886–1980)
p. 423	*objets*	i.e. *objets d'art* (French) decorative objects
p. 424	*Germaine Greer, Erica Jong, Betty Friedan*	noted feminist authors of the 1960s and 1970s
p. 424	*the Kinsey Report*	controversial anthropological studies of human sexual behaviour by Arthur Kinsey and others published in 1948 and 1953
p. 424	*Paul Robeson*	(1898–1976) African American singer, actor, and human rights campaigner
p. 424	*Leadbelly*	Hudy William Ledbetter (1888–1949), African American blues singer
p. 424	*Dorothy Day*	(1897–1980) American journalist and social activist
p. 424	*Martin Luther King*	(1929–68) African American civil rights leader
p. 427	*semis*	trailers
p. 429	*creophagists*	meat-eaters
p. 429	*cum laude*	(Latin) 'with honour'
p. 429	*clerestory*	upper wall with windows
p. 431	*Floreat Barba!*	(Latin) 'Let the beard flourish!'

p. 431	*Umberto Eco*	(born 1932) Italian writer on semiotics
p. 433	*maté*	type of South American tea
p. 433	*luteous*	deep-yellow
p. 433	*pognophile-meister*	master among beard-lovers
p. 434	*limnologist*	expert in freshwater zoology
p. 434	*summa cum laude*	(Latin) 'with highest honour'
p. 434	*ergonomics*	the study of productive efficiency